Jews in France during World War II

Jews in France during World War II

Renée Poznanski

translated by Nathan Bracher

Brandeis University Press

in Association with the

United States Holocaust Memorial Museum

Published by University Press of New England | Hanover and London

Brandeis University Press
Published by University Press of New England, Hanover, NH 03755
in association with the United States Holocaust Memorial Museum
Originally published in French in 1997 by Hachette under the title *Les Juifs en France pendant la Seconde Guerre mondiale*

Published in Association with the United States Holocaust Memorial Museum, this project has received support from the French Ministry of Culture—Centre national du livre, and was published with the help of the Lucius N. Littauer Foundation, Inc. The support and encouragement of Ben Gurion University is gratefully acknowledged.

Printed in the United States of America

Library of Congress Cataloging-in-Publication Data
Poznanski, Renée.
[Juifs en France pendant la Seconde Guerre mondiale. English]
Jews in France during World War II / Renée Poznanski; translated by Nathan Bracher.
p. cm. — (Tauber Institute for the Study of European Jewry series)
Includes bibliographical references (p.) and index.
ISBN 0–87451–896–2 (cloth : alk. paper)—ISBN 1–58465–144–X (pbk. : alk. paper)
1. Jews—Persecutions—France. 2. Holocaust, Jewish (1939–1945)—France.
3. France—History—German occupation, 1940–1945.
I. Title. II. Series.
DS135.F83 P7913 2001
940.53'18'0944—dc21 2001004982

5 4 3 2 1

THE TAUBER INSTITUTE FOR THE STUDY OF EUROPEAN JEWRY SERIES

The Tauber Institute for the Study of European Jewry, established by a gift to Brandeis University from Dr. Laszlo N. Tauber, is dedicated to the memory of the victims of Nazi persecutions between 1933 and 1945. The Institute seeks to study the history and culture of European Jewry in the modern period. The Institute has a special interest in studying the causes, nature, and consequences of the European Jewish catastrophe within the contexts of modern European diplomatic, intellectual, political, and social history.

GERHARD L. WEINBERG, 1981
World in the Balance: Behind the Scenes of World War II

RICHARD COBB, 1983
French and Germans, Germans and French: A Personal Interpretation of France under Two Occupations, 1914–1918/1940–1944

EBERHARD JÄCKEL, 1984
Hitler in History

FRANCES MALINO and BERNARD WASSERSTEIN, editors, 1985
The Jews in Modern France

JEHUDA REINHARZ and WALTER SCHATZBERG, editors, 1985
The Jewish Response to German Culture: From the Enlightenment to the Second World War

JACOB KATZ, 1986
The Darker Side of Genius: Richard Wagner's Anti-Semitism

JEHUDA REINHARZ, editor, 1987
Living with Antisemitism: Modern Jewish Responses

MICHAEL R. MARRUS, 1987
The Holocaust in History

PAUL MENDES-FLOHR, editor, 1987
The Philosophy of Franz Rosenzweig

JOAN G. ROLAND, 1989
Jews in British India: Identity in a Colonial Era

YISRAEL GUTMAN, EZRA MENDELSOHN, JEHUDA REINHARZ, and CHONE SHMERUK, editors, 1989
The Jews of Poland Between Two World Wars

AVRAHAM BARKAI, 1989
From Boycott to Annihilation: The Economic Struggle of German Jews, 1933–1943

ALEXANDER ALTMANN, 1991
The Meaning of Jewish Existence: Theological Essays 1930–1939

MAGDALENA OPALSKI and ISRAEL BARTAL, 1992
Poles and Jews: A Failed Brotherhood

RICHARD BREITMAN, 1992
The Architect of Genocide: Himmler and the Final Solution

GEORGE L. MOSSE, 1993
Confronting the Nation: Jewish and Western Nationalism

DANIEL CARPI, 1994
Between Mussolini and Hitler: The Jews and the Italian Authorities in France and Tunisia

WALTER LAQUEUR and RICHARD BREITMAN, 1994
Breaking the Silence: The German Who Exposed the Final Solution

ISMAR SCHORSCH, 1994
From Text to Context: The Turn to History in Modern Judaism

JACOB KATZ, 1995
With My Own Eyes: The Autobiography of an Historian

GIDEON SHIMONI, 1995
The Zionist Ideology

MOSHE PRYWES and HAIM CHERTOK, 1996
Prisoner of Hope

JÁNOS NYIRI, 1997
Battlefields and Playgrounds

ALAN MINTZ, editor, 1997
The Boom in Contemporary Israeli Fiction

SAMUEL BAK, paintings

LAWRENCE L. LANGER, essay and commentary, 1997
Landscapes of Jewish Experience

JEFFREY SHANDLER and BETH S. WENGER, editors, 1997
Encounters with the "Holy Land": Place, Past and Future in American Jewish Culture

SIMON RAWIDOWICZ, 1998
State of Israel, Diaspora, and Jewish Continuity: Essays on the "Ever-Dying People"

JACOB KATZ, 1998
A House Divided: Orthodoxy and Schism in Nineteenth-Century Central European Jewry

ELISHEVA CARLEBACH, JOHN M. EFRON, and DAVID N. MYERS, editors, 1998
Jewish History and Jewish Memory: Essays in Honor of Yosef Hayim Yerushalmi

SHMUEL ALMOG, JEHUDA REINHARZ, and ANITA SHAPIRA, editors, 1998
Zionism and Religion

BEN HALPERN and JEHUDA REINHARZ, 2000
Zionism and the Creation of a New Society

WALTER LAQUEUR, 2001
Generation Exodus: The Fate of Young Jewish Refugees from Nazi Germany

YIGAL SCHWARTZ, 2001
Aharon Appelfeld: From Individual Lament to Tribal Eternity

RENÉE POZNANSKI, 2001
Jews in France during World War II

CHAERAN Y. FREEZE, 2002
Jewish Marriage and Divorce in Imperial Russia

Der Tod ist ein Meister aus Deutschland.
(Death is a master from Germany.)
—Paul Celan, "Todesfuge"

Our philosophy has become negative. A gendarme who doesn't hit us is a nice guy. A soup that is not absolutely inedible is excellent. A nurse who realizes that a patient is suffering is admirable. Here, everything is measured on the scale of Nazi infamy.
—Noël (Nissim) Calef at Drancy, December 1941

I committed the horrible crime of being born in Poland and, with unrivaled cynicism, my father chose the religion of Judaism for me. Yes, Mr. Maréchal, I am a nasty Jew, a dirty kike, a representative of the damned and condemned race, the epitome of sleaze. But I am twenty years old and I want to live.
—Léon Kecenelenbogen at Douadic, August 27, 1942

The Jews of France have been placed under safeguard of the French people. When the administration of the State betrays this trust, the common people must step forward.
—André Labarthe over the BBC, August 8, 1942

Contents

Illustrations follow page 320.

Preface

The history of the Jews in France during World War II has been written from several viewpoints. From one perspective, scholars have incorporated a study of Vichy's policies toward the Jews into a global analysis of the regime. This specific historical subject has sometimes even constituted the central focus of a general assessment of Vichy.[1] Little by little, historians studying Jewish policy worked out methods of examining the political strategy adopted by Jews in both their official community organizations and their clandestine activities; such studies tended to focus on relations with French authorities. Because the widely shared perception of the Dark Years implied a dichotomy of collaboration and resistance, scholars of Jewish policy previously had little choice but to use that framework. Moreover, historians had to satisfy another demand connected with the Jewish memory of the Holocaust: integrating into their analyses the dual concepts of resistance and passivity.[2] In all of these approaches, the stress has thus been on the political dimension, be it German policy, the policies of the Vichy government, or the political strategy of Jewish organizations.

In recent years, historians studying the Dark Years have shifted their attention from the political to the social realm,[3] and it is in this context that I have conducted my study. In describing the paths taken by Jews in a world that was changing under their very eyes, I was determined to bring them out from under the legal texts that summarily meted out their fate. In other words, whereas Jews have often been treated only as objects or victims of history, I strive to restore to them their role as subjects. What difference did it make in the life of Jews to have to submit to a census? How did they eke out a living when they had been driven from their jobs? What expedient actions allowed them to hold up? In what ways did the plight of Jews during the Dark Years differ absolutely from that of non-Jews? Did the respective plights of both groups sometimes coincide? How did people decide to take their chances outside of the well-known legal paths and to assume a false identity? What sorts of help could they count on? To what hiding places or to which Jewish organizations could they turn? How did people live in the camps? How did they dodge the risks of getting arrested? What information was available to help them understand what was in the making, and how did they grasp these events and gauge the extent of danger? With these sorts of questions, we return to the concrete dimension of human experience underlying the chains of logic and causality established by historians. These questions are connected to four major lines of inquiry.

The first line deals with the variety of experiences concealed under the generic name of "the Jews." Beneath the abstract, fantasized Jew (invariably victim of one and the same set of laws), we can perceive an extremely diverse set of destinies. Indeed, when we focus on the Jews, we are actually dealing with a whole range of subjects. Among the bourgeois French Israelite who had been well integrated into society for many a generation, the Yiddish-speaking, Parisian Communist activist, the small craftsman holding fast to a scrupulous practice of religious precepts, and the shopkeeper from the Middle East, there are enormous differences. No society is ever completely homogenous, but here we find a quite different combination of influencing factors: social or political in some cases, related to national origins in other cases, and still others linked to the various ways of living out an identity. Each of these components of the Jewish population of France had its own specific modes of social integration. When manhunts and roundups of Jews were added to measures of social exclusion, each group was affected differently. Political strategy thus became yet another influencing factor. Finally, the Southern Zone added its own contribution to the many disparate situations. Cities differed from rural areas, as did Catholic from Protestant regions. The experience of communities whose members had been scattered varied from the experience of the Alsatian community that had fallen back and drawn together as a group. The city of Marseilles overlooked the Mediterranean, while Toulouse was located quite close to the detention camps. Lyon, on the other hand, was where most of the Jewish organizations had retreated. One of my first concerns was to pinpoint the specificity of certain types of experiences within this multitude of situations, while at the same time accounting for the destiny of the Jewish population as a whole.

I have limited the scope of my study to mainland France. Granted, it did not take long for the Vichy authorities of the time to extend the antisemitic laws beyond the shores of the Mediterranean. However, the Jews in North Africa led their life in a context too different for there to be any possibility of examining both sides of the Mediterranean in the same study.

The second line of inquiry analyzes the way in which the Jews interpreted events, either explicitly or implicitly. Returning to the representations of that time[4] lets us understand how various modes of anticipation play out; only then can we explain how people responded in face of the increasing persecution. To conduct this line of inquiry successfully, I found it imperative to use the chronological narrative; given the wide scope of the subject and the fundamental break-off points marked by certain dates, a thematic approach would have skewed the picture. By closely following the chronology of persecution, we can see, for example, the appearance of differences between the two zones. At the same time, we can see when the destinies of Jews in both zones seem to overlap. Furthermore, we can gauge the importance of the times when nothing happened: during those empty months, no new measure was applied, habits became ingrained, and rumors seemed discredited. All these elements shaped people's ideas about the future. We can find precisely which rumors quite often took the place of news reports that could not be confirmed. We can understand the consequences of what might be called differentiated time. The turning point, the one that radically changes a person's life, was not the same for Jews and non-Jews, nor was it the same even for all categories of Jews: the chronologies of events for each group were at times superimposed and at times connected.

Finally, chronological narrative highlights the weakness of the linear representation of history, in which a rational analysis of events attempts to draw a clear line leading from the first census law to Auschwitz. It is useful here for us to follow the judicious advice of Pierre Vidal-Naquet: "to understand historical reality, it is sometimes necessary not to know the ending."[5] To the question of *who* knew what about the "unknown destination" where all the deportees were headed, can be added the question of *when* they knew what.

It was just such assessements of events that dictated the majority of responses: people decided to flee or not to flee into the Unoccupied Zone on the basis of what they could make of things in Paris, and on the basis of what they knew about the situation south of the demarcation line.

At the time of social exclusion and then of the roundups, the lives of Jews in France depended to a large extent on their foothold in the surrounding society, which differed according to their various categories. Thus my third line of inquiry: whereas the political history of the French Jews is concerned with the relations between the state and its Jewish communities, I shall concentrate on the multiplicity of links between Jews and the various components of French society. Anti-Semitism legitimized by political practice remains crucial to understanding these relations, but it does not account for everything in an era when the Nazi variety of antisemitism was superimposed on the indigenous one. What type of reception did Jews get in administrative offices? How were day-to-day relations with their non-Jewish neighbors, colleagues, and friends affected by the new situation? What importance did the persecution of the Jews hold for the life of non-Jews? These questions highlight not only the general context of the daily life of the French under the Occupation, but also the ways in which Jews were integrated into French society.

Persecuted by the German Occupation forces and by the French state, Jews found themselves in a double dependency. They relied on society, but also on the Jewish organizations to which they often had to turn for help, information, or consolation. These organizations were also supposed to represent them, and it is here that we must ask just what correlation existed between the mindset of the various segments of the Jewish population and the positions taken publicly by these organizations. What did Jews expect from Jewish organizations? How did their relations with these institutions change over time? After the upheaval caused by the new set of anti-Jewish laws and the police roundups targeting Jews, how did the new places of social interaction function? Thus my fourth line of inquiry: the link between the Jewish population and its organizations rather than the relations between Jewish organizations and the state.

By raising these questions, I do not intend to eliminate the political aspect or to replace it with an analytical alternative. Rather, I shall return to the political dimension by distinguishing among the various pressures exerted from beneath. To a large degree, people's speculations in response to new situations or changes in public opinion account not only for their behavior, but also for the decisions made by the leaders of Jewish organizations. There will therefore be no risk of relativizing the political, ideological, moral setting of the era (a fear expressed by Saul Friedländer in contemplating the work of German historians engaged in *Alltagsgeschichte* [history of the everyday] during the Nazi period).[6] Within this very context, however, concrete situations were being created and new types of normality were becoming standard: in certain cases persecution was central, in others it was buried under other worries. This study focuses on the connections between the usual and the unusual, on the context of the various individual behaviors of Jews, and on the context of political strategies of Jewish organizations.

In 1891, at the time when he was just beginning to set out on his own path (one that would lead him to distinction), the Jewish historian Simon Meirovitch Dubnov advocated a systematic search for all archival material that could be used to found a scholarly history of Judaism in Russia, a subject that until that time had been largely neglected.[7] "Let Us Search and Do Research" was the title of a later version of this widely distributed text. Similarly, in the hunt for archives dealing with the Jews of France during World War II, there were pioneers: Joseph Billig first of all, as well as Zosa Szajkowski, Adam Rutkowski, Lucien Steinberg, David Diamant, and finally Serge Klarsfeld.[8] The collections of documents that they have published provide an extremely useful first selection to the researcher.

Indeed, these are the old papers from which I have also drawn to a large degree, using and reusing testimonies from that era, trying to reap the greatest benefit from the archival holdings that are only gradually being opened up to researchers. And by making use of them as soon as I was granted that precious authorization, I was able to draw on declassified sources. Such was the case with the archives of the Central Consistory and the Maurice Moch archives, which, at the time I was consulting its rich collections, were divided between the library of the Universal Israelite Alliance and the seat of the Central Consistory. Accordingly, the classification markings cited in this book refer to an arbitrary and temporary arrangement.[9] The same is true of the Diamant collection: while I consulted its holdings in Ivry, it has now been reclassified and deposited in the Resistance Museum in Champigny. Similarly, I consulted the archives retained by Lucien Lublin in his home, but they have now been placed in the Centre de Documentation Juive Contemporaine.

Three sorts of sources turned out to be particularly important. First among these are the Jewish sources, in particular the personal diaries. Even if quite subjective, they reflect daily worries and reveal the moods of the time. There are few such sources; more are probably hidden away in families' chests of drawers. I came across a few unpublished ones, such as the diary of Jacques Biélinky,[10] for example. For Drancy, we have Nissim Calef's diary,[11] and for the Southern Zone, the notebooks of Raymond-Raoul Lambert,[12] among others. Compared to the diaries kept by non-Jews, they are even more enlightening for what they reveal about the conjunctions and divergences between the experiences of each respective group. Some families entrusted me with letters from individuals; other private correspondences were those intercepted at the post office by government agents (in which case they were deposited in the National Archives); and others were those received by Jewish organizations—all of these letters provide a hefty supplement to the first type of sources.

Reports dating from that time are equally valuable, for example, the study on the Jews of Paris written by Léo Hamon in April 1941.[13] The archives of the Centre de Documentation Juive Contemporaine, those of the Central Consistory in Paris, and those of the Joint Archives and YIVO in New York contain a great number of such reports. Because they were generally written for the needs of a Jewish organization, they need to be deciphered in view of the organization's religious, cultural, social, or political objectives. Nonetheless, they contain immense riches, as they were contemporaneous with the events they relate, and guided by a desire to describe, document, interpret, or convey a message. These reports thus avoid the pitfalls that a work based on memory can fall into over time and allow us to see the events as they were originally perceived.

The administrative sources constitute the second category of documents. I refer in particular to the archival sources of the General Commission on Jewish Affairs (Commissariat général aux questions juives) and the reports of the General Bureau of Information (Renseignements généraux) in the prefecture archives of the Paris police. They shed light on Jews' daily relations with government bureaucracy. In addition, the investigations carried out by the inspectors from the Police for Jewish Affairs (Police aux questions juives, [PQJ]) and later from the Bureau of Investigations and Inspections (Section d'enquête et de contrôle [SEC]) expose the rich tapestry of individual destinies, reveal the logic of how certain aryanizations were put into effect, and so on. It is often thanks to these police investigations that certain facts can be quantified (for example, how many Jews complied with the census, how many requested an exemption for one reason or another, how many of these requests were granted). We can thus avoid the major pitfalls of this type of research: stressing the anecdotal, choosing examples that would appeal to the imagination but would quantitatively account only for the peripheral and not the essential. Bear in mind, however, gaps in the available documentation sometimes preclude determining definitive numbers.

The third category of sources is the personal memories and testimonies given and published after the Dark Years, testimonies I have complemented with some thirty interviews. Without entering into the debates over the validity of personal testimonies and the precautions necessary for the use of oral sources,[14] let me state that they provided crucial supplementary input: they guided me down many paths of research, allowed me to verify many hypotheses, led me to reflect on new issues, and evoked an atmosphere that would have otherwise remained inaccessible. Newspapers from the era can only bring us partial understanding of the day-to-day existence of Jews: they cannot, even indirectly, describe for us the life Jews led as outcasts. This limitation only bolstered the antisemitic invective used by their detractors.

When one follows the collective life of a group, it is never possible to account for the destiny of each person supposedly included. I apologize at the outset to all who feel that they have not been adequately represented here. The challenge is considerable: when this book is published, a large number of the protagonists of the events described herein will search these pages for the influence of their experience; the author, on the other hand, was born after the war and is striving to give an account of a reality outside her experience. When I had to go beyond the dimensions of everyday life that my whole generation has taken for granted, it was an immense leap: trading the peace and security of a life troubled only by normal ups and downs for the danger of a life in a time of war, a life dominated by the need to survive and the difficulties of procuring everyday necessities.

For all the survivors, however, we are dealing with the most sensitive time of their lives: when life itself was in danger; when they lost loved ones; when in face of hardship, they pushed themselves to the limit. This was a time that had great impact on the choices they would subsequently make. Whether they be Jewish or non-Jewish French citizens, French or foreign Jews, how these people now perceive their identity is based directly on how they lived out their identity at that time. This book cannot escape the issues of memory that weigh so heavily on the events of the Dark Years. And so I apologize at the beginning for venturing out on a terrain so sensitive for each of my readers. I was driven, in this venture, by the desire to understand.

This book owes much to the competence and diligence of all those who helped me in libraries or archival centers: Sarah Halperyn, Vidar Jacobsen, and Sarah Mimoun at the Centre de Documentation Juive Contemporaine; Jean-Claude Kuperminc and Yvonne Lévyne-Berger at the library of the Universal Israelite Alliance; Philippe Landau at the Consistoire Central; Jean Astruc and Anne-Marie Pathé at the Institut d'Histoire du Temps Présent; Chantal Bonazzi and Jean Poëssel at the Archives Nationales; Bernard Garnier at the prefecture archives of the Paris police; M. Billières at the Musée de la Résistance in Champigny; Bronia Klebanski, Yaacov Lozowick and Robert Rozett at Yad Vashem (in Jerusalem); Adina Eshel at the Zionist Archives (in Jerusalem); Denise Gluck and Regina Shinberg at the Joint Archives (in New York); Fruma Mohrer and Marek Web at the archives of the YIVO Institute for Jewish Research (in New York); and finally Eléonor Nikolaïevna Shtshetshilina at the Russian Center for the Conservation and Study of Documents on Contemporary

History in Moscow. Although it seems too conventional, I can only thank them by mentioning them.

This book also owes much to the trust of all those whom I interviewed at length; their names are listed in the Bibliography. While they may not always recognize the specific influence of their testimony in these pages, I want them to know how valuable their personal account has been to me. Similarly valuable were copies of documents from family archives, such as those entrusted to me by Gabrielle Drigeard, Maurice Felzenswalbe, Henri Minczeles, Pierre Vidal-Naquet, and the entire Rodgold family. I am also indebted to the collected archives of Avraham Polonski, Lucien Lublin, and Claude Urman. I am honored by the trust they put in me, and I hope I have not betrayed it. I express my thanks to them here.

This book owes much to the moral and professional support of my colleagues at the Ben Gurion University of the Negev (Beersheba) and the Institut d'Histoire du Temps Présent (Centre National de Recherche Scientifique, Paris). I hope they will forgive me for not citing all their names, but there simply would not be enough space to do so. Work on this book depended heavily on intensive use of the photocopying machine, the use made possible by a grant from the Sidney and Esther Rabb Center for Research on the Shoah at the Ben Gurion University.

Without Pierre Vidal-Naquet, who came up with the idea for the book and suggested that I write it; without Françoise Cibiel, who put her trust in me; without Véronique Bedin and Marianne Lechapt at the Hachette publishing house, who encouraged me and then carefully monitored the transformation of the manuscript into the finished product, this book would not exist.

Thanks to François Blanchetière's careful reading and to Ada Paldor, who translated the book into Hebrew, many errors have been corrected since the publication of the first edition in French.

The publication of the English version of the book owes greatly to Sylvia Fuks Fried, executive director of the Tauber Institute for the Study of European Jewry at Brandeis University and also Phyllis Deutsch, acquisitions editor at University Press of New England. Financing for the English version was made possible by generous assistance from the United States Holocaust Memorial Museum in Washington and its director of publications, Benton Arnovitz, and from the Lucius N. Littauer Foundation. Above all, I thank Nathan Bracher for his marvelous translation; throughout the long task of proofreading the English manuscript, I had the gratifying sense of being understood. The book also owes much to the financial support granted me by the Centre National des Lettres (Paris), the International Institute for Research on the Shoah at Yad Vashem, the French Cultural Services, and the Ben Gurion University; thanks to those funds, I was able to devote an entire year to writing the manuscript.

The book owes much to Yisrael Gutman, who enlightened me with his advice and encouraged me with his trust and friendship. Indeed, this book owes much and even more to friendship. It owes much to my friends who never let me down when I called for help with desperate faxes (I have already cited many of their names), to Nava Shreiber who help me pick out the illustrations, to my friends in Paris who were always willing to send me the latest publications that I was afraid of missing in my Negev desert, to my friends and colleagues Avner Ben-Amos, Simy Epstein, and Denis Peschanski, who listened to me so patiently and provided encouragement and advice at various stages of my work.

Finally, without my son Dovi, who knows virtually everything about computers, I would never have been able to proceed from words to figures and graphics. Without his understanding and patience and that of my daughter Yael and my youngest son Mikhael, without the loving presence of my companion Daniel Blatman, always willing to support me, no work would have been possible.

Tel-Aviv, Israel R.P.
January 2001

Abbreviations

ACIP	Association consistoriale des israélites de Paris (Paris Israelite Consistoral Association)
AEVE	Fédération d'anciens engagés volontaires étrangers (Federation of Former Foreign Army Volunteers)
AIU	Alliance israélite universelle (Universal Israelite Alliance)
AIU, CC	Archives du Consistoire central pendant la Second Guerre mondiale, fonds Maurice Moch, AIU, Paris (Archives of the Central Consistory during World War II, Maurice Moch Collection, AIU, Paris)
AJ	Armée juive (Jewish Army)
AN	Archives nationales, Paris (National Archives, Paris)
AS	Armée secrète (Secret Army)
BCRA	Bureau central de renseignement et d'action (Central Bureau of Information and Action)
BDIC	Bibliothèque de documentation internationale Nanterre contemporaine (Contemporary International Documentation Library, Nanterre)
CADJJ	Comité d'action et de défense de la jeunesse juive (Jewish Youth Action and Defense Committee)
CAR	Comité d'aide aux réfugiés (Refugee Aid Committee)
CC	Archives du Consistoire central pendant la Seconde Guerre mondiale, rue Saint-Georges, Paris (Archives of the Central Consistory during World War II, Rue Saint-Georges, Paris)
CCOJA	Commission centrale des organizations juives d'assistance (Central Committee for Jewish Aid Organizations)
CDJC	Centre de documentation juive contemporaine (Center for Contemporary Jewish Documentation)
CDV	Centre de documentation et de vigilance (Center for Documentation and Vigilance)
CFMN	Corps franc de la Montagne Noire (Black Mountain Elite Commando)
CGD	Comité général de défense (General Defense Committee)
CGQJ	Commissariat général aux questions Juives (General Commission on Jewish Affairs)
CIMADE	Comité inter-mouvements d'aide aux évacués (Intermovement Committee for Aid to Evacuees)
CNR	Conseil National de la Résistance (National Council of the Resistance)
Codi	Comité directeur de l'Organisation sioniste de France (Steering Committee for the Zionist Organization in France)

COJASOR	Comité juif d'action sociale et de reconstruction (Jewish Committee for Social Action and Professional Reorientation)
COSOR	Comité des oeuvres sociales des organisations de Résistance) Social Aid Committee for Resistance Organizations)
CRCEDHC	Centre russe de conservation et d'étude de documents en histoire contemporaine, Moscou (Russian Center for the Conservation and Study of Documents in Contemporary History, Moscow)
CRIF	Conseil représentatif des Israélites (devenu des institutions juives) de France (Representative Council of the Israelites [now the Jewish Institutions] in France)
CUDJF	Comité d'union et de défense des Juifs (Committee for the Union and Defense of Jews)
CZA	Archives sionistes, Jérusalem (Zionist Archives, Jerusalem)
DCA	Direction des centres d'accueil (Head Office for Shelters)
EFI	Entraide française israélite (French Israelite Mutual Aid)
EIF	Éclaireurs israélites de France (Israelite Scouts of France)
ET	Entraide temporaire (Temporary Mutual Aid)
FFDJF	Fils et filles des déportés juifs de France (Sons and Daughters of Jewish Deportees in France)
FFI	Forces françaises de l'intérieur (French Mainland Forces)
FSJF	Fédération des sociétés juives de France (aussi Fédération) (Federation of Jewish Societies in France [also Federation])
FTP-MOI	Francs-Tireurs et Partisans de la Main-d'oeuvre immigrée (Sharpshooters and Partisans of the Immigrant Labor group)
GMR	Groupes mobiles de réserve (Mobile Reserve Groups)
GTE	Groupement de travailleurs étrangers (Foreign Worker Unit)
IEQJ	Institut d'études des questions juives (Institute for the Study of Jewish Affairs)
IHTP	Institut d'histoire du temps présent (Institute for Contemporary History)
IS	Intelligence Service
JJF	Jeunesse juive de France (Jewish Youth in France)
JO	Journal Officiel (Official Journal [recording official government acts and laws])
JOC	Jeunesse ouvrière chrétienne (Christian Workers' Youth)
Joint	Archives of the American Jewish Joint Distribution Committee in New York
KKL	Keren kayemeth le-Israel
LICA	Ligue internationale contre l'antisémitisme (International League against Anti-Semitism)
LVF	Légion des volontaires française (Legion of French Volunteers)
MAE	Archives du ministère des Relations extérieures, Paris (Archives of the Ministry of Foreign Relations, Paris)
MBF	Militärbefehlshaber in Frankreich (German Military Command in France)
MF	Main forte (Strong Fist)

MJS	Mouvement de la jeunesse sioniste (Zionist Youth Movement)
MLN	Mouvement de libération nationale (National Liberation Movement)
MNCR	Mouvement national contre le racisme (National Movement against Racism)
MOI	Main-d'oeuvre immigrée (Immigrant Labor)
OJC	Organisation juive de combat (Jewish Combat Organization)
OPEJ	Oeuvre de protection de l'enfance juive (Program for the Protection of Jewish Children)
ORT	Organisation-reconstruction-travail (Professional Retraining and Reorientation Organization)
OSE	Oeuvre de secours aux enfants (Children's Relief Agency)
OSF	Organisation sioniste de France (Zionist Organization in France)
PP	Préfecture de Police, Paris (Prefecture of the Police, Paris)
PPF	Parti populaire française (French People's Party)
PQJ	Police aux questions juives (Police for Jewish Affairs)
RG	Renseignements Généraux (General Bureau of Information)
RSHA	*Reichssicherheitshauptamt* (Central Security Office of the Third Reich)
SCAP	Service du contrôle des administrateurs provisoires (Provisional Managers' Inspection Office)
SD	Sicherheitsdienst (Security Division of the SS)
SEC	Section d'enquête et de contrôle (Division of Investigations and Inspections)
SER	Service d'évacuation et de regroupement (Office of Evacuation and Regrouping)
SERE	Service d'évacuation et de regroupement des enfants (Office of Evacuation and Regrouping of Children)
Sipo	Sicherheitspolizei (Security Police)
SOL	Service d'ordre légionnaire (Legion Security Force)
SSAE	Service sociale d'aide aux émigrants (Office of Social Aid for Emigrants)
SSE	Service social des étrangers (Office of Social Service for Foreigners)
STO	Service du travail obligatoire (Forced-Labor Service)
TE	Travailleurs étrangers (Foreign Workers)
UFDR	Union française pour la défense de la race (French Union for the Defense of the Race)
UGIF	Union général des israélites de France (General Union of Israelites in France)
UJJ	Union de la jeunesse juive (Union of Jewish Youth)
UJRE	Union des Juifs pour la résistance et l'entraide (Union of Jews for Resistance and Mutual Aid)
YIVO	Archives of the YIVO Institute for Jewish Research, New York
YMCA	Young Men's Christian Association
YV	Yad Vashem Archives, Jerusalem

Jews in France during World War II

1

1940: Jews and Israelites in France

A COMMUNITY?

In the period immediately preceding the war, the total population of France was about 43 million. Among the 43 millions were somewhere between 300,000 and 330,000 Jews. However, they formed a group infinitely more diverse than their collective designation would suggest, for at the time, the Jewish "community" was nothing but a fiction. In the eyes of the law, there was a primary distinction between French Jews and foreign Jews: the former constituted a religious denomination whose numbers could not, according to normal practices of republican democracy, be established by any special rubric in a census, whereas the latter group was statistically dissolved within the various categories of national origin. For these reasons the figures remain imprecise.

This basic distinction, which was essential in the climate of increasing xenophobia that prevailed in the France of the 1930s, only accounts for one aspect of a split that had many ramifications. The uniformity of the category "French Jews" must in fact be qualified according to the varying degree to which they were rooted in French soil. Some 90,000 French Israelites belonged to families that had long been established in France. These people could be distinguished from other groups of Jews by their high degree of integration into the fabric of society and by their assimilation of the basic values of their social environment. Their own diversity was a reflection of the diversity of French society as a whole. There were also the recently naturalized Jews, who had developed their own relationship to Judaism in other lands and in a different social and cultural context; and yet they were French as well.[1] The Jews still residing in the eastern part of France, on the other hand, had constructed their identity outside of the hard feelings between Catholics and proponents of the Third Republic resulting from the separation of Church and State.[2]

Even more striking is the diversity that characterized the itineraries of the foreign Jews. A first wave of Russian, Romanian, and Polish Jews had moved to France from Eastern Europe in the 1880s. Then, after the signing of the treaties formally ending World War I, a second wave of Jewish immigrants from the newly created states of Poland, the Baltic countries, Hungary, and Romania joined the first group. Finally, in the 1930s, the countries of Central Europe added their contingent to the throng of immigrants. Jews first streamed out of Germany after Hitler came to power and then again after the racist Nuremberg laws were adopted. They poured out of Austria after the *Anschluss* extended the reaches of Nazi rule even farther. Jews once again fled from Germany after *Kristallnacht*, the pogrom foreshadowing the wave of mass violence that would be unleashed against them. Czechoslovakian, Hungarian, and Romanian Jews followed the same path. Just under one hundred thousand came to seek refuge in France. Moreover, a good number of Jews from Germany were actually natives of Poland.

These foreign Jews therefore came from a wide variety of places. For the most part, however, they sent their children to the secular public schools of the French Republic. Less than 2 percent of Jewish schoolchildren in France in 1939 attended a Yiddish school or traditional religious establishment.[3] From one generation to another, such academic integration had been completely transforming the mental universe of Jewish immigrants. The Maccabees found themselves superseded by Vercingétorix and the Gauls: the trade-off carried more than a symbolical meaning.

This complex set of social, political, and national identities thus forms a vast mosaic. If we traced out on a graph where individual destinies were beginning and ending, we would see that all the points representing the possibilities for both French Israelites and foreign Jews would be occupied.

The French Israelites

Let us first take the case of the French Israelites.[4] They had been emancipated by the Constituent Assembly on September 27, 1791. The state had granted them full citizenship: the debate had been heated, but they had not had to fight to obtain their rights. Under Napoleon, the state had provided a form of organization, the consistorial system, modeled on the organization of the Protestant church. The Jews' religion was a private matter: they had been emancipated as individuals.

Moreover, the ideals of the French nation, identified with the ideals of the modern liberal state, were held up as the supreme point of reference for Jews. The French Israelites saw in these ideals a reincarnation of the universalist message of the prophets of the Bible and rallied enthusiastically around the cause that they interpreted as a sort of Franco-Judaic syncretism. Indeed, this syncretism paved the way for the acculturation to which they would consent and for which they would take full responsibility.

Whether they were descendants of the Jews of the papal territory of Avignon (who were well established in the Mediterranean South), or direct descendants of the Jewish community of Bordeaux, or, more probably, descendants of the Alsatian community, French Israelites felt tremendously grateful to the country that had emancipated them and to the society that had opened its doors to let them flourish and prosper.

They lived in big cities; those who had come to the capital in the 1840s, 1850s, and 1860s had first established residency in the triangular section of Paris delineated by the Place de la République, the Place de la Bastille, and the Hôtel de Ville (city hall). That they now most often lived in the western part of Paris and were part of the bourgeoisie (and in some cases, part of the upper class) was an indication of their success. The Rothschild family represented only a minority of their fellow Jews, those who had made their careers in finance. A large number of antique dealers had, like the Rothschilds, also moved to the capital from the Alsace region.[5] They distinguished themselves in business; they practiced medicine and law in increasing numbers, just as they secured positions as government functionaries and began to envision an entry into the political realm. Some Jews devoted themselves to careers of public service in the French Republic as prefects, members of the State Council (Conseil d'Etat) or General Council (Conseil Général), representatives in the National Assembly, senators, or even government ministers.[6] The success of such fellow Jews as Lucien Lévy-Bruhl, Henri Bergson, and Emile Durkheim in academia was pointed to with pride.

These French Israelites considered the antisemitism that would crop up at times to be a German import brought on by a temporary social ailment: its nature was thought to be profoundly different from that of Russian or German antisemitism, which were considered chronic, traditional, and deeply rooted in society. In this respect, their analysis of the problem was consonant with views advanced by their allies in the French intellectual world. After all, had not Anatole Leroy-Beaulieu lashed out against "antisemitism, that troublemaker imported from Teutonic countries," whose "profaning hands had not feared to rip apart the seamless tunic of national unity?"[7] The resolution of the Dreyfus Affair had confirmed the protective role played by French law. The French Israelites had every reason to put their complete trust in the government.

Their loyalty was expressed in a collective political neutrality elevated to a principal of survival. True, they did show a definite preference for the radical-socialists,[8] whose frequent references to the ideals of the French Revolution and its stances on economic and social issues were attractive. Their strong attachment to the ideas of republican democracy had sometimes—particularly in the previous generation—led them to affiliate with the Freemasons. Individually, they could count friends in all currents of political opinion. But they were loath to say that their political choices were Jewish as such. When Léon Blum took office, Raymond-Raoul Lambert, editor of *L'Univers israélite*, wrote, "None of us has the right to engage the responsibility of our fellow Jews by giving a Jewish meaning to a personal attitude."[9]

Thus these French Israelites did not display any particular eagerness to participate in the great rallies organized by the International League against Anti-Semitism (LICA): created in 1928, the organization fought against Fascist gangs and clearly sought to ally itself with forces on the Left. Other French Jews, however, whose parents were immigrants took a different approach and favored militant activism to fight against the growing antisemitism. In the September 11, 1936, issue of *L'Univers israélite*, French Jews would learn that a Center for Documentation and Vigilance (CDV) had been created: with the blessing of the consistory, this center intended to counter antisemitism by using more discreet methods and by respecting strict political neutrality.[10] In the end, the Patriotic Union of French Israelites, created in 1934 with the precise objective of opposing leftist Jewish groups, was relegated to a marginal status, even though it received the approval of some of the most prominent members of the Jewish community. At times the French Israelites were worried that Léon Blum was put in the limelight, for he did not hesitate to take clear and public positions on Jewish issues. (But sometimes they secretly admired him for the same reason.)

When the French Israelites did voice their opinions, it was, as far as they were concerned, always in reference to French ideals and objectives, as determined by France's national interest, and in collaboration with non-Jewish organizations and movements. That had already been the case at the time of the Dreyfus affair: most of the Jews—including the chief rabbi Zadok Kahn—spearheading the movement in favor of Dreyfus had in general justified their cause by defending the fundamental principles of the French Republic. The French Israelites remembered their families' commitment in that affair, and it was indeed in the name of universal defense of the rights of man that their parents had taken a stand.[11] They did not realize to what extent the patriotism that bonded them to the French government was leading them farther and farther from the ethnocultural (that the Germans would call *völkisch*) nationalism that was gaining ground all over Europe.[12]

The degree of religious observance among the French Israelites varied, being greater among those who had recently left the eastern part of France to come and live in the capital. And, although it remained the concrete and symbolic sign of their "Jewishness," the frequency of their synagogue attendance also varied.[13] They were as a rule not affiliated with the Jewish institutions that were supposed to represent them. Thus in Paris no more than one in four were connected with the Central Consistory, which, along with the consistories in the provinces, administered the only school for rabbis, designated the chief rabbis, and—although it was an oligarchy largely made up of secular men—was charged with supervising worship services, religious education (which at its peak involved thirteen hundred students)[14] and philanthropy.

Eminently French, the Central Consistory was the French Israelites' collective voice in public affairs. However, in international conferences, it was the Universal Israelite Alliance that spoke in their name. Since 1860, this organization had defended everywhere the model of emancipation exemplified by France. It worked tirelessly to instill French culture in Jewish children all around the Mediterranean basin, thanks to a network of schools that was particularly well implanted in Egypt, Morocco, the Balkans, and the Near East.

Thus we see that an unswerving, carefully guarded patriotism was typical of French Israelites. They were proud to declare it, and took great pride in the considerable honor earned by their fellow Jews who had fought in France's wars. Their families counted many who had fallen on the battlefield and who had won the whole panoply of military decorations—a perfect integration, sealed with their very blood. World War I had been essential to this integration: even Maurice Barrès had admitted as much.

That patriotism did not prevent the French Israelites from sometimes being sympathetic to the achievements of the Zionist movement in Jewish Palestine, although they maintained a firm distance from the nationalist undercurrent and did not feel personally involved. Nor did they forget the bonds of solidarity tying them to fellow Jews who were less fortunate, and who suffered endless persecutions in other lands. They read *L'Univers israélite,* the official publication of the Central Consistory, more or less regularly, and thus were kept informed about the situation in Palestine—but also about the increasingly ominous threat in Central Europe and about the miserable plight of the Jewish populations in the eastern part of the continent. Organized Judaism would mobilize to come to the aid of those who, in the 1930s, fled from Nazi countries and came to seek refuge in France. Did the French Israelites then display only philanthropy just to keep an uncontrolled stream of foreigners from jeopardizing their own status in French society? Or was this the expression of a heartfelt solidarity, taken on as a personal responsibility? Both of these hypotheses were probably true, and one probably alternated with the other. Such ambiguity reflects the difficulty of resolving conflicting imperatives in times of crisis and of the ambivalence that was inherent in the French Isaelites' dual allegeance to France and to their Jewish heritage. They were French citizens of Jewish confession, and their plight was at times hardly different from that of their compatriots.

French Israelites: A Few Examples

The portrait that Raymond Aron sketches of his French bourgeois Jewish family illustrates the conflict. His grandparents were from Lorraine, while another branch of the family was established in the northern part of France. His father gave up the family business in favor of studying at the university; although he proved to be brilliant academically, he failed to achieve the same success in his professional career. As an adolescent, Aron was little different from the rest of his non-Jewish schoolmates at the Versailles lycée, except perhaps for all that was left unsaid. How could the discussion of the Dreyfus affair otherwise be interpreted? During the course of this debate, which pitted him against one of his history teachers who was close to the Action Française, neither of them saw need to mention the Jewish origins of Dreyfus himself nor of one of the participants of the classroom discussion.[15]

In the wake of all that was left unsaid (and which nevertheless shows up in private correspondance), the historian Marc Bloch thought that "when you are a Jew, you run into more difficulties than someone else in being successful. To reach the same point, more work and talent are required from a Jew than from someone else. One should just be aware of this and act accordingly." Those are his recommendations to his eldest son.[16] Robert Aron acknowledges the same reality in the popular saying: "For a Jew to be considered honest, he has to be twice as honest as the next person."[17] As far as he was concerned, attorney Lucien Vidal-Naquet "understood" that certain professional posts were not open to him. Even for the most completely integrated French Israelite, to be a Jew in France at that time was to be a bit less equal than the rest of the French population. Nevertheless, on September 15, 1942, Lucien Vidal-Naquet would write in his diary: "France could ask everything from us, everything down to the highest sacrifice."[18] "I belong to a bourgeois Jewish family that came from Carpentras via Montpellier and Marseilles," writes his son, historian Pierre Vidal-Naquet, who then describes his family as "French, patriotic, and devoted to democratic institutions" and observes that the "traces of religious practice" were extremely rare.[19]

Such was not the case in that little town in the east of France located near Belfort, Luxeil-les-Bains, where there was no synagogue: for the young Jacques Lazarus, it was the Jewish holy days that paced the activities of daily life there. What was to follow was an academic career that would take him to a Jewish school in Strasbourg at the age of fifteen, before he set his sights on a career in the military, one that would be rudely interrupted by the stipulations of the Jewish Statutes. We can understand something of these Jews in the eastern part of France by their inclination toward Zionism, which was actively cultivated among the Israelite Scouts of France (EIF) in Strasbourg, with whom Lazarus was acquainted. In Strasbourg, they did not hesitate to organize Jewish self-defense groups—there were two of them—to fight against right-wing extremists chanting antisemitic slogans. One famous battle, which took place across from the cathedral, long symbolized this determination not to give a free hand to the fascists.[20]

Elsewhere, if your name was Nathan or Kahn, your only contact with your past or your origins (or, in the final analysis, with an affiliation that was not always clearly spelled out) was perhaps an antisemitic incident in primary school or in the lycée. For Denise Siekerski, whose family had long lived in Marseilles and who had grown up worshiping France, "Jewishness" was conveyed negatively: she wasn't Catholic and she regretted the absence of holidays when other French families celebrated theirs. It was with the unionist Scouts that she learned the values of scouting, and it was thanks to her Protestant friends that she became aware of her ignorance of the Bible. A family tradition nevertheless linked her to Palestine, where her grandfather had administered Baron de Rothschild's colonies. Furthermore, her grandmother was the daughter of the first Jewish doctor in Galilee. But that was a substratum that she was unaware of at the time; only later would these roots surface.

In the fresco she paints in her memoirs, Annie Kriegel, a native of the Alsatian Jewish community, offers a more precise and nuanced portrait. She emphasizes in particular the role of the family: while little different from the bourgeois family, it held a virtual monopoly on social relations, and thus perpetuated the existence of a

"Jewish milieu" among families that were nevertheless quite well integrated into French society.[21]

In the final analysis, these various personal experiences reflected the rich palette of French society of that time. And yet, there was a whole series of residual elements peculiar to the recently immigrated Jews in French society: the family traditions, a kinship that stretched far beyond the borders of mainland France, a greater sensitivity to certain subjects, the faint premonition of the precariousness of their status and the supposed antisemitism of the society confronting them.[22]

The Foreign Jews

The foreign Jews occupied the opposite end of this large field of Jewish experiences taken from the prewar period in France. Their Jewish identity had been grown in the soil of Eastern Europe: in this multinational realm, the interaction between a nation's majority population and the minorities that it engulfed dictated the plight of the Jewish minority that bounced around in between. Some Jews disavowed the religious connection. Many, however, openly affirmed their faith, and the scrupulous observance of Judaism governed the rhythms of their daily life, invading every activity, with no respect for the dividing line that French Jews carefully traced between the public and private realms of their lives. In this case, visibility took the place of discretion. Foreign Jews expressed themselves in Yiddish; far from considering the language to be a throwback to an irretrievable past, they often saw it as the secular expression of the specific Jewish culture to which they were attached. In most cases, their work confined them to a small sphere of family and friends that did not afford them the leisure to learn French. When they did speak French, they spoke with an accent that betrayed their foreign background, and no naturalization procedure could ever neutralize the effects of this accent on their relations with French administrative offices.

Their vision of the nature and role of government was shaped by the school of hard knocks inflicted by the state-incited pogroms and by special laws whose first victims were always Jews. Those who had been militant political activists (which was the case for many who had come to France in the 1920s) had most often been treated to a visit in the jails of their native lands. All of these factors led them to view the government as an eminently hostile entity, or at least as something to be wary of. Granted, when coming to live in France, they had taken advantage of the liberal policies practiced by the country that was taking in more immigrants than any other nation in the 1930s. They had been attracted by the ideas of freedom so closely associated with the image of the French Revolution. They were perhaps part of the approximately fifty thousand Jews who, between 1927 and 1940, had availed themselves of the looser requirements granted by the law of 1927 and had become naturalized French citizens.[23] But times had changed. French legislation, beginning with the law of August 10, 1932, was becoming more and more restrictive toward foreign Jews, and this tendency fostered their mistrust of public authorities. From that time on, there were quotas for foreign workers that were fixed by profession, industry, and region. Foreign lawyers, doctors, and craftsmen were also subjected to a quota system by the law of August 9, 1935.[24] An accompanying policy of turning back and expelling undesirable aliens was being applied. Henceforth, many foreign Jews saw their friends reduced to the status of illegal aliens. Furthermore, foreigners were subjected to tighter and tighter identity checks in the late 1930s.

Society had not shown much clemency toward the foreign Jews, either in their native countries nor even in France, which offered a cold shoulder and xenophobia to those who had come in the 1930s. At the time when the "problem of foreigners" was becoming central in political debate, the foreign Jews seemed to be the very embodiment of the triple threat of economic, political, and cultural instability. Where could they find bases of support in that society, when a steady figure of some 350,000 unemployed won over part of the Left (and in particular some in the labor unions) to the xenophobia overtly expressed by the Right?[25] When one has fled Nazi Germany, how would one respond to the contradictory accusation of having paved the way for a fifth column in case of conflict with Germany and of having pushed France to war against these same Germans? How could Jewish immigrants counter the fantasy that French identity was being threatened by foreign invaders? Prestigious and influential intellectuals, renowned writers such as Pierre Drieu la Rochelle, Robert Brasillach, and Louis-Ferdinand Céline and many others had, by making themselves ardent defenders of French thought, demonstrated the pervasiveness of this xenophobic mindset.[26]

When the time of persecutions would come, these foreign Jews would hesitate to seek support from the public. They also knew from experience that xenophobia translated very quickly into antisemitism. Now, as opposed to other groups of foreigners (such as Spanish nationals) they could not count on any existing political organism to take up their defense.[27] Nor had they had the advantage of the infatuation, albeit passing and superficial, that the "exoticism" of the Russians had aroused in the mid-1920s. The Communist Party offered a means of integration for some. But there again, this support was unreliable and subject to larger strategic imperatives. The Jewish Communists who were organized into groups according to their native tongue within the Immigrant Labor group (MOI) were often in conflict with the party leadership, which was accused both of trying to go too easy on the petit bourgeois sectors of French society and also being too timid in taking up the defense of immigrants.[28] Most often it was the group of French Israelites "deeply rooted in French soil" or French Jews who had arrived in France during one of the preceding waves of immigration who interceded for Jewish immigrants in French society.

As was the case for French Israelites, the foreign Jews most often resided in Paris, where almost two-thirds of the Jewish population were concentrated on the eve of the war. Storeowners and natives of the Near East resided in the La Roquette section, while the other Sephardic Jews, who were natives of North Africa, were more or less spread out "according to the random chance and practicalities" of their occupations.[29] But those who had come from Russia at the beginning of the century lived in Montmartre, and those who were devoutly religious lived in the Saint-Paul section: the square had become the arrival station for all immigrants, as it was the first stop on their Parisian itinerary after the "gare de l'Est" (a Parisian train station for destinations in the east of France).[30]

Those who were leftist political activists had probably chosen Belleville or the twentieth *arrondissement,* while those who dealt in secondhand goods or had outdoor sales booths lodged in the eighteenth in Clignancourt. Fur specialists would have probably set up shop in the tenth, while furniture dealers would have preferred the Faubourg Saint-Antoine. They also might have chosen to reside in one of the suburbs extending from these sections of Paris. Those who had just come from Nazi Germany piled into uncomfortable maids' rooms and little hotels: doctors and lawyers would live in the Latin Quarter, while storeowners would be close to the Place de la République.[31]

Those who, like 60 percent of their fellow Jews, were industrial workers or craftsmen often worked at home or in small workshops, especially in the textile and garment industry.[32] While new laws restricted the pace of immigrant employment, the number of undeclared garment workers was steadily increasing. Some tried their luck at the marketplaces of Saint-Ouen, Aubervilliers, and le Kremlin-Bicêtre in hopes of selling a bit of merchandise that they had struggled to bring with them in a suitcase. Such was the fate of many merchants who, because of the meager wages and precariousness of working at home, occasionally had to take to the open-air markets in the cold and rain.[33]

In general, only the lowest paying positions were open to immigrants; thus social demotion befell Jewish immigrants as it had befallen many refugees. "For technicians with a diploma or people in law, medicine, or business, their credentials were worthless. . . . Landlords [worked as] day laborers, engineers as mechanics, lawyers as door-to-door salesmen, doctors as nurses, chemists as lab assistants, and this was in the best of cases, for all were threatened by the risk of falling down in the masses of untrained workers who were not even paid enough to cover basic living expenses."[34]

For these foreign Jews, rarely did having family in France mean a whole network of uncles, aunts, and cousins spread throughout the many regions of the country. It was more likely a circle that they themselves had created, a relative that had preceded them on the road of immigration, companions in political struggles, the people from other lands that would gather together each time there was a Jewish holy day to celebrate at the synagogue, or the people that they would frequent in the context of associations of foreigners from specific areas.

The *Landsmannschaft* was one such organization of foreign nationals that existed in 1939; with some 170 branches, it provided an institutional nucleus. First created for the purpose of dispensing mutual aid and organizing funeral services, its role had been greatly widened, to such an extent that it had become a veritable substitute synagogue for those who never attended services. Under the umbrella group called the Federation of Jewish Societies in France (FSJF), or, since 1938 affiliated with the Union of Jewish Societies in France (the Farband linked to the Communist party), such associations also provided a means for Jews to express themselves collectively on political matters.

It is true that these Jewish immigrants did experience difficulty in joining a French political party. However, they did not feel themselves confined to the restraint that the French Israelites very deliberately maintained. Thus while the organizations with which they became involved were devoted to the widest variety of ends, most of them were naturally politicized. So it was that in cultural organizations the Communists and Bundists (Jewish socialists) came into conflict before splitting off from each other: on the one side, there was the *Kultur* ligue, completely taken over by the Communists; on the other, the *Medem club* had come under the domination of the Bundists. At 10 Rue de Lancry was a veritable "stock exchange" for newly arrived immigrants; you could spend a first night there, find work as a dressmaker or mechanic in the garment industry, or simply chat and make some new acquaintances. A Jewish choir, a group of stage players, a sports club (five hundred members were affiliated with the "Yasc"),[35] a Yiddish library, political lectures, and cultural gatherings were open to everyone, under the control of the Communist Party.

There were no fewer than six hundred Jews enrolled in the different language groups of the Communist Party in Paris in the mid-1930s: 250 of them were part of the Jewish subsection, so named because the language currently used was Yiddish. We can gauge its importance by the fact that its secretary was, ex officio, one of the five members of the Immigrant Labor group (MOI) "collective," which headed all the various language groups. The section for the twentieth *arrondissement* alone was divided into five or six groups.[36] At that time, there were seven hundred Jewish craftsmen and workers enrolled and active in the CGTU labor union.[37] There were 3,500 readers of the only Jewish Communist newspaper published in Western Europe,[38] the *Naïe presse*, which was cited as an example of vitality to the other language groups of the Immigrant Labor group (MOI). When the Popular Front government was being put together (after a legislative campaign in which Jewish electoral committees had been particularly active among Jewish immigrants in France), including both foreigners and naturalized citizens, this figure was doubled, as was also the number of Jews coming under the control of the Jewish-language group.[39] All of these activities, including the soup kitchens for unemployed Jews, functioned without party subsidy. Most, however, were concentrated in Paris.

Some immigrant Jews were content to make do outside of organized channels, meeting friends in cafés, which for some provided the nexus of an intensely animated Jewish life.[40] Often they leaned toward some form of Zionism, ranging from the variety clearly situated on the Left, to the so-called revisionist brand advocated by Vladimir Jabotinski. Each variety had an organization to lead its followers.

Rather than the *Naïe presse,* such immigrant Jews would read the *Paryser haïnt* or, if their French was good enough, *La Terre retrouvée,* which informed them about all the Jewish cultural activities in France and the progress of Jewish colonization in Palestine.

At any rate, be they Bundists, Communists, Zionists, or (in the case of those from Germany and Austria) militant anti-Fascists, immigrant Jews were closely connected to groups with strong ideological orientations. In that respect, their political sensitivity was markedly different from that of the French Israelites. They did not hesitate to go to city hall or to the arena of La Mutualité when the International League against Anti-Semitism organized a huge rally against racism.

All or almost all came from families in which Yiddish was spoken and in which religious precepts were scrupulously practiced. All who had come to France as adults recalled the antisemitic incidents that had repeatedly occurred in their youth and that had rendered them humiliated and helpless. All had had a mixed education: in addition to the curricula of the Polish, Russian, and German schools, there was also the instruction provided by the Jewish schools, which could be either the most traditional and orthodox or, in the Yiddish context, the more modern form that Jewish schools had adopted in some regions. All were quite familiar with the foreigners' office on the sixth floor of the prefecture of Paris police; many times they had requested a resident visa or working permit that had to be renewed at least once a year. All had unpronounceable family names, in which the last letters of the French alphabet were particularly prominent. But for those who were born in France, their first names oriented them firmly toward the future, a future tied to France, even though they still carried the mark of a very present past. For the youngest, there was a complete dichotomy between the world of their French school and their other world of Yiddish, Jewish holy days, meager financial resources, and great ambitions.

For some who had been in France longer and were better integrated than others, the only sign of their Jewishness was the fast of Yom Kippur, the Day of Atonement, or the little bluish box that collected coins for *Keren kayemeth le-Israel,* the KKL, the organization charged with buying up land in Palestine in order to favor Jewish colonization.

Foreign Jews: A Few Examples

Thus behind the generic term "foreign Jews" appears a multiplicity of individual experiences and itineraries, and it is only by the use of concrete examples that we can sketch a composite portrait. A close look at a few individuals will demonstrate the considerable differences between them. Take the case of Suzanne Pelossof, who had come from Greece as a child, but who, even while still in her native land, had considered herself integrated into French culture: she had attended school at the

Universal Israelite Alliance (AIU) and her family read all the French newspapers with facility. What a contrast between her and someone such as Jacques Biélinky, who had come to France from Russia as an adult at the beginning of the century, armed with solid experience as a militant revolutionary! This journalist and art critic became a naturalized French citizen in 1927 and would serve as an intermediary between the foreign Jews, with whom he was so familiar, and the French Israelites in whose newspapers he regularly published.[41] Or consider the case of someone such as Edgar Morin, who was born in France and whose parents had come to France from Salonika in 1910. Morin chose unbelief as his homeland and concluded after the fact that French schools made it possible for "the dust of the diaspora to be diluted in French society."[42] However, referring to this same secular school of the French Republic, Morin speaks of "a mysterious difference, which was the incomprehensible source of almost imperceptible feelings of shame, humiliation, and sorrow" that his schoolmates made him experience.

What bond could tie either one of them with Léon Poliakov, who was brought up in the social milieu of Russian immigrants? Thanks to family tradition and to the extensive travels that preceded his move to France, Poliakov was versed in Russian, German, and French cultural traditions, but lacked any schooling in Jewish culture. What a tremendous gap there was between the carefree lifestyle that he describes in his memoirs[43] and the political activism characteristic of so many immigrants in the 1930s!

Boris Holban was one of these militant Communists and was well acquainted with the jails of Romania. In July 1938, he came "to the land of the Revolution and of the Declaration of the Rights of Man, the land of the Commune and the Popular Front." He became active in politics within the Romanian language group of the party, which was made up largely of Jews, and shared a maid's room with Albert Youdine, who for his part was active in the Jewish section of the party. The Communist Party took the place of family life for them, as it did from Pierre Grinberg, then pursuing his studies in medical school in Paris.[44]

For Adam Rayski, it was the antisemitism he had had to confront in his native Poland that led directly to his joining the Communist Party—and the political involvement led to his expulsion from Poland. He had been in Paris since 1932, and had found his place in the Jewish division of the Communist Party as a journalist with the daily Yiddish newspaper the *Naïe presse,* founded on January 1, 1934. He became a permanent fixture there, and went on to serve as liaison between that paper and *L'Humanité,* the party's official French-language daily in France. Rayski's integration was thus political, accomplished by means of his militant Communism, but it was complemented by a cultural integration nurtured by regular theatergoing. Louis Gronowski-Brunot, too, who had come to Paris in 1929, used his leisure time to walk through the streets of Paris, section after section, with his female companion.

Others were spurred on to immigrate by the bleak outlook in their native countries.

Such was the case for Fayvel Shrager. Once he had finished his secondary schooling in the Hebraic lycée in Poland, he came to Grenoble in 1927 and then went to Nancy, where he undertook studies to become a sales engineer. He found a somewhat frustrating job with a fish merchant and became politically active with an association of Jewish students on the Left. He later left to go to Paris, where he managed to eke out a living by giving a few private lessons in Hebrew and doing some accounting work. Most of his time, however, was devoted to political activities with the *Kultur ligue*.

If we made a list of all the jobs undertaken by immigrant Jews, especially by political activists and students, it would be endless. They were construction workers, dishwashers in restaurants, garbage collectors, makers of artificial flowers, walk-on actors, sandwich men, waiters—anything was possible.

Some of these immigrant Jews who were also militant Communists followed a very special path. Like Fella and Yacov Insel, they first left for Palestine and then were expelled from that land. Coming to Paris in 1936, they met a group of people at the club on Rue Basfroi who had experienced a similar expulsion. While Fella, like the other women in the group, began training to become a nurse, her husband crossed over illegally into Spain to join the International Brigades. They were reunited at the outset of the war in the southwestern part of France: she had had to flee Paris during the exodus and he had been confined to the internment camp of Le Vernet.

Not all were Communists, however. Yehuda Leib Gorzyczanski (or Gorans) had also come to Paris illegally in 1938 from Lublin. He came from a family of traditionalists, and for a while was a cook's helper in the shelter for Jews on Rue Lamarck. Then he joined one of the rural communes organized by the Israelite Scouts of France (EIF). In Saumur, he met up with other foreign Jews not only from Poland, but also from Germany and Austria. With them he worked the land under the gentle leadership of Robert Gamzon, known as "Castor" (literally, "beaver"), at the same time improving his French by reading *L'Oeuvre*.

Completely different, however, was the political experience of the youth in the leftist *Ha-shomer ha-tsaïr* organization of Zionists, whose approximately one hundred members in Paris were nearly all foreigners. While Henry Bulawko remembers the fights that pitted him against the youth of the fascist leagues, Lea Waintrob, who had come to Paris from Poland in 1929 at the age of eight, speaks of the placards that she waved in the 1930s that said: "No to racism, to xenophobia, to antisemitism," and "Open the door to Palestine, our young people want to live." The fight for free immigration to Palestine was thus directly linked to the struggle against fascist gangs.

Within the same ideological movement, the case of Dolly Steinling takes us to another world. He was a Zionist on the Left belonging to the *Ha-shomer ha-tsaïr* movement in Austria who had illegally left that country after the *Anschluss*. Abandoned by the smuggler to whom he had entrusted his fate, he was captured by the Gestapo and spent three weeks in prison. When he was set free, he set out for France via Switzerland. During the course of his journey, a number of people came to his aid, including the Jewish communities living in Basel and Mulhouse, the rabbi in Dijon, and Jews randomly encountered. They provided the useful addresses, financial means of survival, cigarettes, and train tickets that made it possible for him to continue on his way. Once he made it to Paris, he got a cool reception from his cousin. Armed with the fifty francs from one of the refugee aid committees, he had to be content with odd jobs in the markets of Les Halles, where he worked as a cook and a hat vendor in order to support himself. Like other refugees around him who found themselves completely outside of the regular channels of French and Jewish society, he strove to survive in the face of hardship.[45] His youth enabled him to succeed.

Austria's annexation into the Third Reich had been accompanied by a violent explosion of antisemitic hatred. Emmanuel Schwarz's wife and children had been arrested, and he had spent time in Dachau. When he finally managed to take the train to France, he carried with him the memory of these hellish events. It was once again the community that came to his aid, as he, his wife, and his children worked all day long making artificial flowers and put their trust in God, for he was devoutly religious.[46] But Emmanuel Schwarz was an elderly man. The suffering he had endured at Dachau had worn down his health. The respite he experienced was to be short-lived.

This set of examples gives us only a minimal view of Jewish experiences in prewar France. It cannot account for syncretism brought about by the waves of immigration which, instead of separating different groups according to their time of arrival, put them all side by side in similar situations. It cannot account for chance encounters that sometimes determined an individual's fate, neither for the role played by some provincial town that was the first stop for immigrants on their way to the capital, nor for generational factors that scrambled the codes governing integration into French society.

A *Plural Judaism*

The relationship of such varying historical traditions with Judaism took widely dissimilar forms. According to one of the leaders of the Israelite Scouts of France, a movement known for its dynamism and loyalty to a pluralist vision of Judaism, this diversity stemmed "from the complexity of Israel's heritage, which is that of an entire civilization, which is at the same time a religion, a mode of thought, and a history."[47] He continues:

> Those [Jews] who accept this heritage in its entirety, and who want a renaissance of Jewish life to occur in the land of our ancestors and according to ancestral traditions, constitute—at least in France—a minority and are found mainly among people from the Alsace-Lorraine region.
>
> The others want to distinguish between what is essential and what is secondary in this tradition, but there is disagreement as to the nature of what is essential:

> between, on the one hand, the nonreligious Zionists who see themselves as children of a distinct people and who hope for the return to the historical land of Israel as a people who hope for a return from exile, and, on the other, the French Israelites who see in the diaspora an act of providence and consider themselves French citizens of Israelite religious confession on the same basis as French citizens of Catholic and Protestant persuasion, there are countless nuances of opinion. The Zionists are found mainly among the foreign Jews, while the great majority of French Jews favor assimilation.
>
> But here again, we need to make distinctions: if the orthodox Jews refuse to renounce the slightest act in their practice of religion, it is because they think that each act modifies religious feeling not in quantity but in quality. The liberals, on the other hand, draw even in religious life a distinction between what is essential (which they situate in moral conduct or in the purity of myth), and what is secondary (which is where they put the various forms of religious observance).
>
> Not even the very nature of the French Israelites' attachment to France is free from such divergences of opinion: while the French Israelites are indeed highly reluctant to accept Zionist solutions, it is for some because they are so fond of the land and culture of France, and for others because they are not interested in anything that does not bear the stamp of universality.
>
> And this does not account for the Jews who are only Jews because their grandparents were.

Thus there were a whole series of issues that divided what we call the "Jewish community" into quite distinct groups: the relationship of France to their Jewish identity, their degree of social integration, their religious practices, and the nature of their attachment to their origins or their past.

Bridges between Jews and Israelites

Between these groups that were seemingly so different, there were nonetheless important bridges. Religious observance was one of them. Granted, between those who went to the Brith Chalom temple on Rue Saint-Lazare for Judeo-Spanish services, and the Ashkenazic Jews affiliated with the synagogue on Rue Notre-Dame-de-Nazareth; between the wealthy bourgeois who would on occasion attend celebrations of holy days at the Temple de la Victoire (which since 1874 had been the seat of the chief rabbi of France and the chief rabbi of Paris), and the orthodox Jews who on a daily basis crowded themselves into one of the many places of worship on Rue Pavée (the *shuls* that had proliferated in the Saint-Paul section of Paris), there was a great distance. And yet everywhere they fasted on Yom Kippur, the Day of Atonement, they celebrated the Joy of the Torah in the same way a few days later, they seated themselves at the table for Passover and recounted the departure from Egypt, and for an entire week they replaced ordinary bread with unleavened bread. The same God had ordained that meat and milk products not be mixed and had absolutely forbidden the consumption of any and all pork products. Among the French Israelites as well as the immigrant Jews, there were some that abided by all or some of these rituals of a religion that they shared, even if the settings of the observance were generally different.

The antisemite, however, ignored all this diversity and created the negative stereotype that would set the tone during the war years. Foreign Jews made up less than 0.4 percent of the population of France in 1940. They were, however, the favorite target of xenophobes. Foreign Jews seemed indeed to embody all the faults attributed to the entire group of foreigners. Readers can judge for themselves from the following portrait sketched by Jean Giraudoux:

> hundreds of thousands of Ashkenazi escapees from Polish or Romanian ghettos, who reject the religious rules but not the idiosyncrasies of these ghettos. They have for centuries been conditioned to work in the worst conditions, and this eliminates our fellow Frenchmen while at the same time destroying their professional practices and their traditions in all of the trades in the area of handicrafts: the making of garments, shoes, furs, and leatherworks. Scores of them are packed together in single rooms, where they dodge census, tax, and work inspections. . . . By its abnormal and precarious physical constitution, this horde brings thousands that encumber our hospitals.

Such was the "primitive race" that was corrupting the French race, whose "worth was due to twenty centuries of selection and refinement." Giraudoux hopes to give us a concrete image of this "primitive race" by describing four sons of one of these families, that he compares to leeches in a jar: "You could guess which one would sell transparent postcards, which one would be a messenger, in the Stock Market, then the unlicensed broker, then Staviski; which one would be the abortionist doctor, which one would be first the walk-on actor in *Natacha*, then Monsieur Cerf, then Natan."[48]

Concentrated in certain professional branches, the Jews could be collectively blamed for unemployment. Their influence in the cinema was used as a pretext to denounce the cultural threat they posed. They represented no more than 10 to 15 percent of the profession, but were singled out as having invaded 50 to 80 percent of it by a rumor fueled by film historians, such as Maurice Bardèche and Robert Brasillach.[49] Both lawyers' unions, discreetly, and doctors' unions, publicly, spoke of the "plethora of people in the profession" in order to obtain that access to their professions be limited exclusively to French citizens. Public demonstrations organized to promote that cause spread antisemitic slogans far and wide.[50]

In these times, when the basic values of democracy were undergoing a severe crisis, the "myth of the Jewish Republic"[51] considerably strengthened the virulent criticisms that the right-wing and extreme right-wing press were hurling against the regime of the secular French Republic, which was accused of corrupting the France of Christianity, of usurping its power, and of having allowed Jews to integrate into French society. The old traditional Christian wellspring of antisemitism was still alive and even stronger.

Furthermore, during this time of tension with France's powerful neighbor in

Central Europe, as victims of its antisemitic exactions were flowing into France, the political danger posed by these Jewish refugees prevailed over all concerns. In face of the tide of antisemitism that had been unleashed across the Eastern border, the French press was proving to be rather discreet—at least in comparison with the condemnations filling the columns of the British and American press. There was even a degree of surprise about this at the prefecture of the Paris police.[52] Most newspapers expressed their concern for preserving the "autonomy" of French policy, an "autonomous" policy meaning one that would not let itself be influenced by the hazards and uncertainties of German antisemitism. In their pursuit of a policy of appeasement toward Germany, French authorities were, for their part, quite determined to follow this advice.[53] But while, in the French political realm, the combination of a Right-Left confrontation (which had intensified) with the clash between hawks and doves was on the verge of becoming "explosive"[54] the fantasized Jews almost automatically assumed the appearance of gung-ho warriors. At the same time, however, in the person of Léon Blum, they became a symbol of the Left that was so deeply hated in some quarters.

There were indeed certain scandals and highly visible individuals that were easy to exploit for the purpose of showing the dangers posed by the Jews. Such were the cases of the Stavisky affair in late 1933, of the role of Léon Blum during the time of the Popular Front, and of the assassination of Ernst vom Rath, third secretary of the German embassy in Paris killed on November 7, 1938, by Herschel Feibel Grynszpan, a Polish Jew who had recently immigrated from Germany and was residing illegally in France.[55]

Thus the Jews came to embody the quintessential foreigner, while at the same time the foreign Jew came to reveal the true face of the Israelite who claimed to be French. Léon Blum was therefore accused of facilitating the immigration of the victims of Nazi antisemitism into France. The political innuendo lay just below the surface, as evidenced by Giraudoux's denunciation of "Monsieur Cerf": was this not a common name among Alsatian Jews?

It was thus Jews in general that were the target of inflammatory antisemitic pamphlets, and the fantasy of a unified Jewry weighed heavy on the relations between the French Israelites and Jews having recently immigrated to France. In many cases, the positions taken by the French Israelites were largely determined by the accusations that xenophobic, antisemitic propaganda directed against immigrant Jews. The French Israelites therefore made a point of denouncing the political innuendos that were deliberately confusing them with foreign immigrants. At the same time, the foreign Jews were painfully resentful of both the reservations and the paternalism or condescension they felt was being directed toward them.

However, in spite of all the misunderstandings that could mar relations between Jewish refugees fleeing Germany and the charitable organizations officially created by French Judaism to assist them, these organizations nevertheless constituted one of the bridges as they were the source not just of these virtually unavoidable tensions but also of active solidarity. Organizations intended to aid refugees proliferated: no fewer than seven new institutions were created between May and August 1933,[56] before the official channels of the consistory finally centralized most of these activities. Between 1933 and 1940, some forty-five million francs were reportedly collected in France.[57] In addition to all that was undertaken to cover the cost of Jews' emigrating from France to other countries and of their professional retraining in manual labor or agriculture, people also donated material assistance and discreetly intervened on their behalf before public authorities. Such assistance thus reflects themes recurrently voiced by public opinion and interiorized by the French Israelites: it was presented as being in the national interest. Notwithstanding, however, it was the French Israelites who ended up representing the concerns of immigrant Jews before public authorities.

Finally, on the level of collective imagination, all shared the common attachment to the French Revolution, which served as the founding myth of French Jewish identity. "One hundred and fifty years ago, France gave such a noble example," wrote one chronicler for *L'Univers israélite* just before the outbreak of the war in a special issue devoted to the 150th anniversary of the French Revolution. "France showed all humanity the way of progress guided by intelligence and human dignity." While immigrant Jews did not necessarily espouse *L'Univers israélite*'s notion of the French citizen of Jewish profession that was "so completely integrated into the nation that he cannot imagine any particularity whatsoever," they would nevertheless also celebrate this 150th anniversary in a public rally on either June 14 or June 17—depending on whether they were with the federation that leaned toward Zionism or the *Farband*, which was of the Communist persuasion. As a symbol of freedom, as the mother of all past and future revolutions, or as a model for the emancipation of the Jews, the French Revolution conveyed an abundance of themes with which Jews on all sides could identify. It gave the Jews' attachment to the French nation its very meaning, albeit at a time when French nationalism had strayed far from the ideal of the Revolution and was being expressed in an organic conception of French identity.[58] Soon it would be that France they would have to defend against the enemy on the other side of the Rhine River.

WAR: PATRIOTS OR SPIES?

When war was declared, the mobilization effort concerned all levels of Jewish society. "France is marching at the head of civilization. And the Israelites, who owe so much to her, are ready to give their blood down to the last drop," declared an editorial in the September 15, 1939, edition of *L'Univers israélite*. Another edition hastened to point out that although all the Jews were on the side of the Allies, it did not mean that this was a Jewish war, and that the Jews were not pursuing any specific objective in the war.[59]

The immigrant Jewish newspapers did not remain inactive: they spurred Jewish immigrants to enroll in the French army. Some thirty thousand foreign Jews heeded this call and came to sign up in the recruitment offices run only by each of the organizations of Jewish immigrants, but also by the Refugee Aid Committee (CAR); this latter organization, since 1936 and under the guidance of the Central Consistory, had conrolled most of the aid provided to the Jews who had fled Germany.[60]

In spite of the Nazi-Soviet Pact, Communist Jews did not exempt themselves from this call, and the *Naïe presse*, their newspaper, encouraged its readers to join the platoons of volunteers, until it was banned by the French government one day in late September.[61] One description underscored the commitment of these men standing in front of the Ministry of War in long lines that encumbered the Rue Saint-Dominique for several days: "All are hoping for peace. But since Hitler the barbarian wishes to set the world aflame and since he is threatening the independence of our host country France, the foreigner is ready to go do his duty with the rest of the country." [62] It was with no small pride that the paper pointed out some 35 to 40 percent of those coming to sign up were Jews.

The Ups and Downs of Patriotism in Action

While at the time, nothing distinguished one French soldier from another, we cannot conclude that those who had signed up received a ticket for immediate integration into the French army and, accordingly, into French society.

> I have not forgotten how people stared at me crossly when I would begin to speak in the street or in the metro before the war and especially at the outset of the conflict. "Another foreigner," they seemed to say. "Our husbands and brothers have been called into military service and here you see these young, able-bodied foreigners walking the streets." This was particularly painful, as we had from the very first days gone to volunteer, but had waited for weeks to be enlisted.[63]

Such a waiting period befuddled even the most enthusiastic. "We will never understand what sort of diabolical mindset was at that time inspiring the ministry, which was flooding recruitment offices with contradictory memoranda on a daily basis," wrote one volunteer. The divergences thus cropping up between the civilian authorities and the military brass (the latter obsessed by the fear of enemy infiltration) were not visible to the eyes of volunteers who saw their offer to enlist turned down for the widest variety of reasons: "Too advanced in age, term of residency in France too short, or too long—you have been in France for ten years, you should have been called into military service with the others—identity papers too murky, or lack of instructions."[64]

A committee of the Jewish Legion then strove to gain permission to form a Jewish Legion in France that would bring together in one group the foreign Jews that would otherwise be called up and spread out in the various units of the Foreign Legion. Negotiations with authorities were conducted in particular by the writer Albert Cohen, who would also attempt to rally "non-Zionist French individuals" in support of this plan.[65] He was bluntly turned down by the premier, the minister of national defense and war, on November 13, 1939.

Those foreign Jews who surmounted these difficulties wound up in one of the three marching regiments of foreign volunteers constituted at that time, or in the foreign infantry regiments of the Foreign Legion, "poorly equipped, poorly trained, and (at Barcarès, La Valbonne, or Septfonds) poorly armed," but possessing an invincible morale. Or, they would be placed in one of the units put together by Czechoslovakia's government (in exile in London), or with the ranks of the Polish army lead by General Władysław Sikorski. In the latter case, they also had to deal with the antisemitism of the Polish officers, which was so virulent that General Sikorski took the trouble to issue the following order of the day for August 5, 1940: "I strictly forbid any show of hostility, any remark that might be contemptuous or degrading for human dignity toward soldiers of Jewish profession. All of these offenses will be severely punished."[66] Before being punished (supposing that they were) such offenses had reportedly even caused some to desert, not to escape the hardship of combat, but to join the Foreign Legion and fight for France rather than for Poland.

The exact number of these foreign Jews who volunteered and were finally taken into the army is difficult to establish: they probably numbered more than 16,000 out of the 82,000 combatants grouped together in these various corps of the army.[67] And all took part in the fighting: for some, it was at Narvik, but for most of them, it was on the battlefields between the Somme River and Alsace. More than five hundred of them died there. Others were imprisoned in German stalags, or interned in the camps that France had set up. Some even wound up in the Foreign Worker Units (GTE), where the French authorities chose to put them in lieu of demobilizing them, once the surrender was complete.

The Internment Camps

As for the émigrés from Austria and Germany, they did not have the opportunity to volunteer for military service. Granted, they had been urged to join the Foreign Legion and thus get sent to North Africa, but a memorandum of August 30, 1939, stipulated that "all foreign nationals from territories belonging to the enemy must be brought together in special centers."[68] These special centers already existed. On January 21, 1939, at the place called Rieucros in the district of Mende, was the first center set up for foreigners, considered to be a threat to public order because of "their repeated infractions of the rules of hospitality." In the panic created by the defeat of the Republican forces in Spain, refugees swarmed mainly into the southwestern part of France. The thousands of people who thus streamed into Argelès, Barcarès, Saint-Cyprien, and Gurs found themselves locked up in totally unorganized, makeshift facilities. Among them were veterans of the International Brigades and the Jews who had fought in their ranks. When Franco opened his borders and took back a number of these refugees, a return to Spain was inconceivable for the Jews among them.

"Mr. Minister of the Interior," wrote a group of German Jews confined to the internment camp at Gurs on August 28, 1939, "the undersigned . . . in keeping with their collective oath sworn on July 14, solemnly declare that in case of war, they consider it to be their highest duty to join the ranks of the French nation in its fight against antisemitism and racism. They unconditionally place themselves at France's disposal."[69]

But when war was declared, it was the fear of enemy infiltration that drove government decisions. Within a few days' time, German and Austrian refugees were arrested and hastily brought together in special centers. All had become "undesirable aliens." In the Paris region, the Roland-Garros and Colombes stadiums were thus used to assemble some 8,000 "suspects," including 3,000 Jews. At the time of the debacle (the June 1940 collapse), they were led away to internment camps in the South,[70] either the ones that were already in place, or the ones at Le Vernet and Rieucros, which had been specially planned for taking in "foreigners who were considered to be suspect because of their nationality or a threat to public order." Men were sent to Le Vernet, women to Rieucros.

Then throughout the months of war, one wave of arrests would follow another, keeping pace with increasingly harsh laws, until some 18,000 to 20,000 internees filled these camps and a whole slew of improvised assembly centers, created from abandoned factories or prisons, barns or hangars, schools or vacation camps.[71] Within this composite "scum of the earth," most were enemies of the Third Reich—rather strange, to say the least, for people viewed as "enemy infiltrators." Among these people were those "subhumans" despised and rejected by the Nazis: the Jews were thus put in the same category as their persecutors. When fighting broke out in May 1940, all German nationals were subsequently subject to arrest: women, suddenly considered dangerous, would then also come to swell the ranks of the internees.

Exposure to hunger, cold, and epidemics would become the common plight of all those who had fled from Nazi countries to seek refuge in France. Hanna Schramm describes the shacks with paneless overhead windows at Gurs in which the women landed: "Thirty straw mattresses on the left, thirty straw mattresses on the right, no covers, no tables, no chairs, no benches, no nails, no dishes. . . . The water faucets were located all the way on the other end of the camp. There were eight faucets placed above wooden tubs for this entire block of buildings that housed over a thousand women, and these facilities were out in the open, exposed to the view of everyone, sheltered only by a roof."[72] Arthur Koestler speaks moreover of the "daily, prosaic torture" of forced labor that, in Le Vernet camp, "within a few weeks' time transformed [this] gang [of internees] into listless, tattered men with dreary faces and empty stares."[73] Others underscore the hardship of sudden isolations; internees were forbidden from receiving any visit whatsoever. Any newspaper—sometimes "slipped between the pages of a book" and read in secrecy, circulating discreetly "until there was nothing left but crumpled shreds"—was immediately confiscated. Internees awaited letters with great anxiety even though correspondence was censured and the camp administration held mail for many days before delivering it.[74] And in many cases, internees did not know what had become of their spouses or compagnons.

In addition, there were some who deeply resented the injustice created by money within the confines of the camps. At Les Milles, it was possible for those with money to buy from a more agile internee one of the first places in the latrine line, thus shortening the icy wait. Above all, however, money was exchanged for food.[75]

Screening commissions were established to allow the series of regulated liberations provided for in a memorandum dated December 21, 1939.[76] Even then, in order to take advantage of these measures, you had to be under the age of forty, or enlist for five years of service in the Foreign Legion, or else be able to provide documented proof of having been cited for the Legion of Honor award or of being currently in the process of naturalization. These liberations were handled in a completely arbitrary manner. Often they were only provisory, or else turned out to be the prelude to a game of cat-and-mouse with government bureaucracy: because the war precluded the possibility of expulsion, the administrative offices practiced a system of suspensions, which required former internees to request the renewal of their liberation once every twenty-four hours, forty-eight hours, five days, or once a month, according to the whims and fancies of the administrator in charge of these dossiers at the prefecture.

Within the camps, the absurdity and uncertainty of the entire situation fed a steady stream of rumors. In the camp of Arandon, the rumors (called "windmills") originated in the kitchens before spreading through the rest of the camp. David Vogel describes them for us:

> Rumor had it, for example, that we were going to be transferred elsewhere and that Arandon would become a prisoner of war camp. Or that England had just authorized the entry of Jewish refugees into Palestine, that soon a list of volunteers would be drawn up and that they would be sent over there on a boat. The kitchen was next door to the office, and through the wall, you could hear bits and pieces of conversations and telephone calls. It was from these scraps of information that our cooks cooked up nice little desserts for us: a little sugar, a pinch of cinnamon, and they were ready to be served up in the living room.[77]

Certain measures taken by the camp administration encouraged such speculations; for example, the hundreds of lists that were drawn up, and that had to be done and redone again and again:

> There was the list of Austrians, the list of other foreigners, the list of the professions of each and every detainee, a list of ages, of former exact addresses, of husbands whose wives or children were French, the list of those who had certificates of loyalty and those who did not, a whole monstruous frenzy of inventories. What in the world did they need these lists for and what did they do with them? We had no idea. There was the list of those who had blankets and those who did not; then there was the list of the number of blankets of those who had blankets; there were

> lists of those who needed clothes, shoes, underwear. . . . As to what they were going to do with this information, each gave his own opinion as confidently as if he had been secretly told by the captain. Supposedly, the Austrians would surely be released. The other foreigners too. And the ones whose wives were French. And those who had certificates of loyalty (some had almost thirty of these certificates, issued by their baker, their grocer, their butcher, or their concierge). Supposedly, those who had sources of income would be released, as well as those whose presence in the workplace was essential. In short, we were constantly on the verge of being released. The lists proved it! If not, what use would they have served? We were going to receive blankets, clothes, shoes, underwear. The lists proved it!
>
> No one was released. No blankets were given out.[78]

However, there were card files made on the basis of long interrogations conducted at Arandon by the official in charge of the camp. "He was as tricky as an inquisitor, turning questions around every which way to see if I would contradict myself. Little by little, he drew my life story out of me. With an ugly smile, he made up questions that we did not know how to answer. Was it better to lie or to tell the truth?"[79]

Beginning in February 1940, men under the age of forty had to join the units of "foreigners on duty"; they were thus subject to some civilian service, but under paramilitary conditions. In the spring of 1940, some 9,000 refugees had enlisted in the Foreign Legion, while 5,000 wound up in groups of these "foreigners on duty."[80]

Already on September 6, 1939, Emmanuel Schwarz was interned, as were his Austrian or German compatriots, in the Colombes stadium. Lying on the concrete there, he contracted phlebitis. He was first taken to the hospital, then to the Roland-Garros stadium, then to the Damigny camp, and on to the Athis camp before winding up back at Damigny, where he would remain until February 12, 1940, when, thanks to the decision of a screening commission, he was finally released.[81] His ordeal was just beginning.

The Defeat

The French were "unanimous in their determination to fight until the end against the monstruous German war machine" and "in order to win, had resolved to give every effort and make every sacrifice." These were the words used by a Jewish journalist, writing in the yet unpublished "Lettre de Paris." Expressing his conviction—or perhaps his wish—he added with pride: "Jewish blood flows in the North, mixed fraternally with the blood of all of France's children."[82] The actual course of the events was to be a rude awakening. The path leading from the declaration of war to the rapid collapse left the Jews of France in the state of confusion, hope, and disbelief common to all French people. When the French government left Paris on June 11, 1940, the chief rabbi and the main leaders of the Central Consistory and of the immigrant organizations did the same. The exodus flung about one hundred thousand

Jews onto France's roads. Most of them could not rely on relatives living in the provinces that could put them up: they went to stay in furnished apartments or hotels in the South of France. For farmers in small French villages, this would often be the first discovery of the existence of the Jews.

Synagogues would serve as their rallying point, not by the grace of any new religious fervor but because they were there and were the only source of stability in a world that was fluctuating so wildly, and because they made it possible to hear news and to meet other refugees. Somewhere near fifteen thousand Jews from the Alsace-Lorraine region had come before them, fleeing their homes from the beginning of the war in September 1939. Some forty thousand Jewish refugees from Belgium, Holland, and Luxembourg had traced out the same path from the outset of the German attack in mid-May 1940. Aharon Sigman speaks of the panic that took hold of his entire family, as they fled from Anvers with the family silverware as their only fortune. They slept out in the open under the bombardments in the north of France. Their father went to scout out a trail for them, then simply disappeared. What followed were ten days of madness, during which they shared feed with animals, stole eggs, but refused to touch any soup that had unwelcome bits of meat in it. The Sigmans were very religious, and were uncompromising in their observance of the rules of the *cachrout*, which stipulated that cattle be ritually slaughtered and that meat be treated in a very specific manner before it was suitable for consumption. Aharon Sigman remembers a short respite due to one farmer's kindness. He has not forgotten, however, having been run out of a shelter by another farmer right in the middle of a bombardment. The Jews were responsible for the war, weren't they?

From then on, the Germans were everywhere. Moreover, they were behaving so decently. So the Sigmans chose to go back to Belgium. This was not the choice of all the other refugees who kept on fleeing farther to the south, where they would come together in the départements of the Pyrénées-Orientales, the Haute-Garonne, and the Hautes-Pyrénées.

Once the armistice was signed, France found itself chopped up into various zones. More than half of the Jews from France had gone to the south, especially the French Israelites who had friends or relatives in the region, and especially the more wealthy, who could afford to live in different surroundings.

Some, about a third of those who had fled to the South, came back to Paris.[83] Such was the case for Marcel Abraham, an inspector general for universities, former chief of staff at the Ministry of National Education, who "simply wished to fulfill what he felt to be his duty, in other words, resume work,"[84] and who turned a deaf ear to the advice of the prefect Langeron. For similar reasons, Robert Debré also chose to ignore the warning that the prefect Chiappe had delivered to him by messenger.[85] Likewise, some Russian Jews, reassured by the Nazi-Soviet Pact, even registered for repatriation at the Soviet Consulate. Still others, who had no refuge other than their Paris apartment, were reassured by the ostensibly decent behavior of the Germans. Those who at the time of this rapid and unexpected defeat were in the provinces, but north of the demarcation line that was to divide France in two, were most likely to return to Paris, as were those who came to take their business or commerce back in hand. This was a time when inhabitants were coming back to the capital city in masses. Indeed, between 100,000 and 150,000 residents of Paris and its suburbs were returning to their homes each week.[86]

There was nevertheless widespread anxiety. With Hitler triumphant, the plight of the Jews had become precarious. "My children, France has been defeated," the father of Annie Kriegel announced to his family. "And we are Jewish," he added after a pause.[87] "France, having been defeated or reconciled with the Third Reich or placed under its power, was no longer going to leave any place for Jews,"[88] wrote Raymond Aron to explain the decision he had made to set off for England and continue the fight alongside General de Gaulle. There were a good many who followed the same course, and the first to be surprised by the fact was none other than the general himself. Others simply could not bring themselves to leave their country. "A prominent Jew, especially if he serves in an official capacity, must not under any pretext leave his country. He must bear witness," thought René Blum, the brother of the former premier.[89]

The Germans in Paris

In Paris, most of the rabbis were gone in the summer of 1940. During a special session on June 5, 1940, the consistory had decided to give each rabbi freedom of choice. Only volunteers remained in the capital. The first services would be held in the Synagogue de la Victoire by Edouard Schneeberg, the owner of a large Jewish funeral home located across the street.[90] But then beginning with the month of August, the chief rabbi of Paris, Julien Weill, was back.[91] A worried crowd flocked to the synagogue and conjectures abounded, while the traditional prayer for the Republic got replaced by a prayer for France. It was a sign of the times.

Paris was undergoing transformations that were unsettling, to say the least. Identity checks on foreigners living in the capital and in the surrounding area were suddenly tightened. With the obvious exception of German troops and functionaries, foreigners were the first targeted by a systematic census, which was conducted beginning on August 6, 1940, with the assistance of the owners of apartment buildings, apartment managers, and concierges.

A café on the Rue de Châteaudun was the first to put up a placard that had up until this time been unknown in Paris: "Israelites forbidden on these premises." Beginning in July 1940, newspaper vendors, convinced that they could operate with impunity, came to the Temple square (known as the haven for Jewish secondhand clothes dealers), to sell *Au pilori*, the weekly newspaper leading the fight against Jews and Freemasons. On July 26, about three hundred Jews came together and demonstrated at the Place des Vosges in front of the headquarters of the French Guards, an organization that thrived on antisemitism.[92] This, however, was an isolated case. Most ironic was that German soldiers stepped in at times to put an end to the fights that broke out sporadically.[93] The French gendarmes patrolled the streets to prevent such outbreaks. The first antisemitic propaganda fliers stuck to walls in Paris were reported by Prefect Langeron on July 29.[94] The month of August was marked by an increasing number of incidents on the Boulevard de Ménilmontant, at the Saint-Ouen fleamarket, in front of the Bouchara department store, at the Lévitan furniture store, and outside of the cafés on the Place de la République. These demonstrations rallied no more than from fifty to one hundred participants each time, but they managed to rock the boat in Paris during these summer months of 1940.[95]

The weekly meetings of new antisemitic associations seemed moreover to draw an ever-increasing number of participants.[96] For two whole hours on August 20 and 21, a group of young people systematically shattered the display windows of Jewish stores on the Champs-Elysées.[97] In order to avoid becoming "innocent" victims, some stores would display a stamp of respectability. "This is an authentically French business" read the signs given out to lucky recipients by the Paris Federation of High Commerce.[98] The Lissac Brothers store had gotten a head start on this movement. Already on July 25, 1940—a full month before—a sizable ad in the newspapers "appealed to the spirit of solidarity of [their] compatriots from the Massif Central and the Franche-Comté to reaffirm a truth that was particularly dear [to them]." "LISSAC n'est pas ISAAC," they loudly proclaimed. It was "an old name quite native to our country, a specifically French name that is proudly used as the name for several places in France." They went on to add that "it is the Corrèze area that is the cradle of our family, which has many members in this racially pure département." And to confirm these noble, and above all, "pure," origins, they invoked the word of mayors and priests who would vouch for them.[99] Regular, daily antisemitism was thus setting up summer quarters in occupied Paris. Beginning on August 27, it could be freely expressed in the newspapers, as the French government decided to abrogate the Marchandeau decree which, since April 21, 1939, provided for the punishment of any attack launched in the press "against a group of people who by their origins belong to a specific race or religion, when this attack is intended to stir up hatred among citizens or inhabitants."[100]

Jewish musicians, lyricists, and songwriters were then dismissed; Jewish journalists no longer had anywhere to publish their articles, nor Jewish painters any place to sell or even exhibit their work. They were to be the first of an entire category whose ranks would only swell during the war years: the category of the excluded, the new poor who were already coming on a daily basis to feed themselves in soup kitchens where, for two and a half francs, they could get a soup, a thin slice of meat, and as much bread as they wanted.

In addition, "the victors' first theft in Paris" left no doubt as to the Nazis' objectives: the first concern of the German army was to send a team of movers to plunder the entire stock of books from the Lipschütz (who was "a Jew, of course") bookstore.[101] This was on July 15, 1940.[102] The Kra bookstore was similarly looted.[103] In addition, the libraries of the Universal Israelite Alliance and of the Rabbinical School were confiscated, while the archives of the Central Consistory were placed under seal.[104]

It was also in Paris that Alsatian Jews were seen coming in. Indeed, on July 16, along with French citizens deemed to be Francophile, the last remaining Jews were expelled from Alsace. They would be followed a month later by the Jews from the département of La Moselle. Since the fall of 1939, more than fifteen thousand Jews from the eastern part of France, including ten thousand from Strasbourg, had left their homes and moved to the cities of Vichy, Limoges, and Périgueux in the départements of La Dordogne and La Haute-Vienne. A few groups had also gone to the départements of L'Indre, La Charente, La Vienne, and La Corrèze.[105] The new refugees of the summer of 1940—more than three thousand of them—had been brutally expelled: authorized to carry with them only one suitcase and no more than five thousand francs, they had been rounded up, transported, and then left out in the middle of nowhere, just on the other side of the border, by the Germans. Those who had not joined the preceding wave of refugees had gone on to the département of Le Jura or had come to Paris.

Anxieties in the Southern Zone

There was also considerable anxiety in the new Free Zone (i.e., the one not occupied by the Germans). Jewish refugees were streaming in from everywhere: from Alsace-Lorraine, but also from the Bordeaux region in July 1940, and from the département of La Manche in Normandy. Isaïe Schwarz, the chief rabbi of France who had followed the French government on its long journey, saw his fears confirmed by a rash of incidents that did not bode well. In Bordeaux, he was not permitted to join with the archbishop in broadcasting a consoling message over the radio. For Bastille Day ceremonies on July 14 in Vichy, he was unable to get government and army representatives to participate as had been the custom before the war. Then, a "prominent non-Jewish religious personality informed him that measures aimed against the Jews were in the making."[106] While like many prominent French Israelites, he maintained his trust in Marshal Pétain, considered to be "beyond all suspicion," he was fearful of German pressures and of the presence at Vichy of the main voices of the Action Française, who were experienced instigators of antisemitism. It was there at Vichy that the chief rabbinate established its headquarters. However, the leaders of the Central Consistory, the very people who thought that their place was next to that of France's new government, were soon most officially advised to leave the city. They went on to Lyon, where the new offices of the Federation of Jewish Societies in France (FSJF) were located.[107] The main Jewish social programs, on the other hand, had moved to Marseilles.

Certainly, there was anxiety, but it was moderate: France, after all, "could not tolerate just anything." "It is not of little consequence," wrote Raymond-Raoul Lambert on July 15, 1940, "that for a century, my relatives have been melded into France's soil and that I have fought two wars. Neither for my sons nor for myself could I imagine life under other skies: such an uprooting would be worse than an amputation."[108] As was the case for many others, for him to leave the country would amount to leaving it to its own fate, in a way, to betray it. This was unthinkable for these French Israelites, whose patriotism was indelible. "The idea of deserting, of leaving our fellow citizens and our homeland in dangers . . . kept us from taking the plunge," Joseph Weill was later to write.[109]

How indeed could they imagine that, on its own initiative and without the force of the much-dreaded German pressures, the French state would transform them into pariahs? While different parts of the antisemitic laws were being prepared in the padded hallways of government ministries, some French Israelites still thought that only foreigners, be they Jews or non-Jews, would see a change in their status. In point of fact, the xenophobia that had been stirred up in the immediate prewar era was beginning to take concrete form in these laws. The law of July 22, 1940, established a commission charged with reviewing naturalizations that had been completed since 1927. Other laws dating from the summer of 1940 limited access first to jobs in public administration, then to jobs in legal professions. Then access to the bar was restricted to citizens whose fathers were French citizens. In practice, these different measures were rigorously applied to Jews. At times, they were presented outright as a first step toward a Jewish statute that would settle France's Jewish problem; such was the view articulated in the August 22, 1940, edition of the *Agence de presse inter-France*.[110] Jews made up less than 5 percent of those naturalized between 1927 and 1940. Tuning a keen ear to "certain well-informed commentaries in the press," they quickly understood that they were to be the first ones targeted.[111] As it turned out, they would actually represent almost 40 percent of those denaturalized.[112]

Added to all that were the preemptive measures. Hitler's antisemitism was a secret to nobody. Thus a Jewish singer would be forbidden to perform on the radio, while a Jewish legal expert would be suddenly obliged to recall that he was Jewish before accepting a position. Jews were eliminated from various administrations that had been called on to have increased contact with the Germans. Already on July 31, 1940, brokers of unlisted stocks held a meeting and decided to dissolve their association and to reform it by excluding "Israelite members" from its ranks.[113] The unlisted stock market thus was put at the forefront of the purge. Certain administrations in the private sector took similar action.[114]

The antisemitic press was raging in this so-called Free Zone as well. The traditional voices of anti-Judaism, *Gringoire* and *Candide*, were joined by a "multitude of little periodicals," some of them short-lived, such as *Tord-Boyaux* and *L'Alerte*. Inscriptions on the walls of buildings were being honed to perfection. "Down with the Jews," hastily scribbled in chalk gave way to more elaborate slogans that were painted or sketched over regular billboard advertisements: "The Jews are our curse." "The Jews and the English kill our children at Mers-El-Kebir." At times, display windows were shattered and storefronts smashed in Nice, Marseilles, Lyon, Vichy, and Limoges as well on the Champs-Elysées in Paris.[115]

For the Jews scattered throughout the south, returning to Paris was becoming more and more difficult. The German military authorities were beginning to put their apartments under seal and confiscate their libraries, while, starting on September 10, 1940, the Vichy government provided for the appointment of provisional administrators to oversee any business whose directors were absent "for any reason whatsoever": this was the first effect of the German ordinance from May 20 of that same year.[116] Along with the package of measures designed to take things in hand, an application of German racial policy was set out in a memorandum of August 22, 1940. This document advocated taking isolated steps "which will be particularly frightening to Jews precisely because they are less systematic: in other words, they will seem more arbitrary."[117] In addition, the French authorities were already asserting their authority by starting to take control of Jewish property. After all, who in the world could these people (i.e., the business owners prevented from returning to the occupied zone) be, if not, for the vast majority, Jews? Moreover, such a return, which was already discouraged by posters in Vichy as well as at various crossover points on the demarcation line,[118] was soon to be forbidden. This measure had been demanded by the chief of staff of the German military command in France (the MBF), who spelled out the means to be used to hunt down Jews. "Inasmuch as belonging to the Jewish race is not a matter of identity papers, there will be grounds for turning away at the demarcation line all persons whose name or physical appearance suggests they are Jewish, if they cannot prove that they are not Jews."[119] That was the first step down the long road of the special laws that would wreak havoc on their lives.

2

The Occupation Sets In: From the Fall of 1940 to the Summer of 1941

Long lines of people stretched out in front of grocery stores, pork-butcher shops, and creameries in occupied Paris. Some dime stores had nothing but bouillon cubes, jars of mustard, or sacks of flour to sell. The first of the substitutes for coffee, the "national coffee" (consisting of 50 percent roasted chickpeas) was becoming a familiar item. A general rationing system had just been implemented. In the midst of all of these developments, an increasing anxiety gripped Jews in Paris.

Just when these new restrictions on foodstuffs were taking effect, the national council of Jacques Doriot's Parti Populaire Français (PPF) held a meeting and loudly vilified the English, the Jews, the Freemasons, and the Communists—in other words, all enemies of France. These accusations were echoed by the crude antisemitism that was brazenly expressed in the streets, flooding the tenth arrondissement with a large number of fliers bearing the most evocative handwritten inscriptions: "When you are a Jew, you go to Palestine or you scram"; "The Jews will soon be reduced to dust, so pack your bags, little girl"; "One, two, three, boom, and your shop blows up"; "Well then, my little Yid, you don't understand French"; "You're nothing but a jerk and a two-bit Jewish foreigner"; "In France, a Jewish store is a place of illegal business."[1] In one night, Prefect Langeron counted some twenty different expressions inscribed on the walls of the Saint-Vincent-de-Paul section of Paris.

The small hardline collaborationist parties were paving the way, and the political authorities headed down the path. The end of September ushered in a series of measures that had either been taken by Vichy or been adopted by the German military administration with the assistance of the Gestapo's department of Jewish affairs (which was in contact with Jewish organizations). Jews in the Occupied Zone would first of all suffer the consequences of the German laws during these first few months of the Occupation. French Israelites in both zones would eventually see their social status ruined by French policy. Then Vichy interned foreign Jews in the Southern Zone, before the Germans took the initiative and had Jews in Paris arrested and interned on the basis of Vichy's antisemitic legislation. France and Germany were implementing rival, competitive policies toward the Jews at that time, and sometimes these policies were convergent or complementary. With one side emulating the other, the cumulative effect was to tighten the screws on Jews and Israelites of all categories.

Historical hindsight affords us the perspective to make several important distinctions here. On the one hand, we can distinguish between everything that stemmed from the racial theories of Nazi ideology as put into practice in an occupied country, and things that were attributable to a traditional antisemitism in France and particularly prevalent in the rightist circles holding power at the time. On the other hand, we can discern the difference between the effects of a widespread xenophobia in France and the fruits of Vichy's political priorities, namely, the assertion of French sovereignty in both the Occupied and Unoccupied Zones. At the time, however, both the Jews and the majority of all people in France saw mainly the work of Germans in these policies.

THE FIRST GERMAN ORDINANCES

One reason for this perception of German control is that everything began in the Occupied Zone. That was where the head of the German military administration in France issued the ordinance of September 27, 1940, defining a Jew as a person belonging to the Jewish religion or having more than two Jewish grandparents (in other words, who also belonged to the Jewish religion). The ordinance also summoned all Jews to the subprefecture in the département of their residence to inscribe their names in a special register before October 20. Meanwhile, Jewish storeowners were granted a bit more time—until October 31—to place a special placard in both German and French in their storefront windows: "Judisches Geschäft," "Entreprise juive" (Jewish Business). Furthermore, Jews were henceforth forbidden to return from the Unoccupied Zone.

Submitting to a Census

On October 2, 1940, Jews learned from the newspapers that they would have to submit to a census. The prefecture of police informed them that the respective superintendents for each section of Paris would record their declarations, and from October 3 (which was Rosh Hashana, the Jewish New Year) until October 20, Jews in Paris and in the département of La Seine were required to report to the various police stations in alphabetical order, according to their last name.

During these holy days known as Tishri, which set the pace of Jewish life for almost a month, from the Jewish New Year's Day until the celebration of the Torah, synagogues in Paris were full. On the door of the synagogue on Rue Pavée, the oratory for the Orthodox Jews, a reminder was posted both in Yiddish and in French that it was fordidden to talk about politics in the temple.[2] Peace and order prevailed everywhere. Apparently, only the Neuilly synagogue was targeted by an attack, which broke its windows. In the temple located on Rue de la Victoire, census forms were handed out. The mood was seemingly one of solemnity. In his sermon for Yom Kippur, the Day of Atonement and a time of fasting and contrition, Chief Rabbi Julien Weill spoke of Jewish families who had distinguished themselves in service of France, of those whose names brought honor to French culture, of those who had earned glory on the battlefield, and of those who had died for France.

Those who dodged the required declaration were rare. No Jewish organization had advised them to refuse to meet the census requirement. Led "by their refusal to renounce their origins and by their habit of obeying the law,"[3] Jews compliantly lined up outside of the police station in their respective sections of Paris on the prescribed dates. But on October 13, the day of Yom Kippur fasting, when it was the turn of the N's to stand in line for the census, the German military administration decided that a list of Jews would be more effective if census dodgers could be detected. At the time, however, the "official and unique" French identity card did not yet exist. Instituted a few days later, it was actually some time before this card became the most important administrative document.[4]

The prefect of the Paris police was thus requested "to take all measures necessary in order for the Jews' identity cards to be recognizable by specific markings. To that end, the face of each identity card [had] to bear the word *Juif* or *Juive* [Jew], 1.5 cm by 3.5 cm, stamped in red."[5] On December 10, 1941, an ordinance by the prefect of the Paris police officially confirmed a procedure already in application.[6] Indeed, beginning on October 22 and continuing until November 7, Jews were once again summoned to comply with German instructions, this time individually: they left with their identity cards or visas validated, that is, stamped in bold letters.[7]

Foreign Jews also heeded these summons, even militant Communists, the minority most accustomed to the rigors of clandestineness.[8] After all, they were known as Jews in their section of Paris. "How could we not declare ourselves as Jews, when we were born in Poland, hardly spoke any French, and were garment workers making pants on Rue des Immeubles-Industriels?" one of them later explained.[9]

This was also the case for some French Israelites, who at times complied either out of defiance, because of their fidelity to a legalist tradition, or in order not to break ranks with their fellow Jews. It was doubtless also a way of thumbing their noses at the antisemitic press that denounced the "counterfeit *goyim*," those who would supposedly be tempted to dodge the census requirement.[10] Even though he had been officially informed that he was not required to report for the census, the philosopher Henri Bergson made of point of complying like the others. "We saw [him] . . . in his bathrobe and slippers, frightfully ill, going down to the Passy police station to be registered as a Jew."[11] Colonel Pierre Brisac also made the decision to report to the police station as prescribed by the law; he fulfilled his duty, however, in full military attire.[12]

There was also another group who declared themselves to be Jewish, even though they probably were doubtful about it. These were the *subbotniki*, the Sabbatarians, a sect that was not regarded as Jewish in Russia, although some of their rites were taken from the Jewish religion. They would later deploy numerous efforts to try to escape the fate that loomed on the horizon for the Jews who had registered as such with the police.[13] Apparently, certain local police chiefs advised some Jews, on an individual basis, not to register with the census when their family name or first name "did not betray" them.[14] In Sceaux, on the other hand, the local police chief advised some of those who were not sure about their ancestry to declare themselves as Jews: this was the origin of a number of mistakes that would later be pointed out by the General Commission on Jewish Affairs.[15]

By October 21, 1940, some 149,734 Jews had thus registered with the census. Of these, 86,664 were French Jews, and 65,070 foreigners.[16] The census of the Jews in Paris was nevertheless not over. A whole process had just begun: each week, scores of Jews would report to the Paris police prefecture and declare themselves as Jews. There were 569 of these latecomers in December 1940, and 278 in March 1941. By mid-July 1941, more than three thousand Jews had thus come to comply with the law.[17] Another census had already come on the heels of the first one: this was the census prescribed by the French law of June 2, 1941, which applied to all zones of Occupied and Unoccupied France. The measure resulted in the registration of 3,827 more Jews who, week after week until August 1944, kept reporting to the Paris Police Prefecture in order to comply with the law. Some of these declarations doubtless concerned newborn babies (already Jews!) whose birth could not be concealed by the parents.

At first, late declarations were not sanctioned. They were sometimes made subsequent to verifications conducted on the basis of initial declarations, as "the situation of foreign Israelites" was systemically investigated by the Paris Police Prefecture from the month of December on.[18] Every week, the police painstakingly checked out between 1,500 and 2,500 hotel registration forms filled out by foreigners. Some Jews received questionnaires dealing with their "Israelite status" or their "Jewish kinship."[19] Others were summoned to police headquarters. The dynamic nature of the census, which was an ongoing procedure and not just a state of affairs, was evident.

There were in some instances Jewish refugees who had clandestinely returned to Paris and who decided, once they had arrived, to comply with the law. It must be said that this tiny, but steady stream of new declarations is baffling. The escapade of Rabbi Apeloig provides us an example of such obstinacy. At the time, practicing certain professions was simply inconceivable without a properly stamped identity card, including those who worked under the auspices of the most prominent Jewish organizations. Could one imagine a rabbi whose papers did not bear the required registration number? Yet such was the case of Rabbi Apeloig, who had clandestinely come to Paris on June 11, 1941, traveling twenty-four kilometres on foot in the pouring rain in order to make himself available to the Jewish community in the capital city. His first concern was then to put himself in compliance with the law: his identity papers stated that he was a rabbi, but were not properly stamped. He made every effort to comply, calling upon friends and acquaintances, and even getting the chief rabbi Julien Weill to intervene on his behalf. But it was to no avail. In a last-ditch attempt, he finally went to the Marly-le-Roi police station where, with no small amount of difficulty, he managed to convince the local police chief to inscribe his name in a special register, have his card stamped, and promise to notify the German authorities accordingly.[20]

The Jews did not suspect that on the basis of the detailed questionnaires that they had filled out, the Paris police prefecture would, in the true style of the French administrative mindset, create a system of four subfiles making it possible to classify Jews according to name, address, nationality, and occupation. And to prevent the notecards from getting mixed up, they were skillfully color-coded.[21] While the Jews wondered about the ultimate purpose of the census, they did not foresee the ends of repression to which it would serve. Like the other foreigners in the département of La Seine, foreign Jews had already been required to fill out a census form before August 6, 1940. Before the war, they had regularly come to the police prefecture to have their work permit or resident visa renewed. They did not necessarily understand what could be new and different about this formality. The French Israelites, however, did sense that this was something new: until then they had blended so smoothly into the French national community. The development was particularly troubling, coming, as it did, in the midst of other restrictions: on October 3, 1940 they discovered that Vichy was preparing the Jewish Statutes, and then, on October 8, that the Algerian Jews, who had been granted French nationality by the Crémieux decree of 1870, were collectively stripped of their citizenship. Because Algeria was not occupied by German forces, it was an ominous precedent. Then on October 18 and 19, all newspapers announced it publicly: the Vichy government had indeed adopted Jewish Statutes applicable in both the Occupied and Unoccupied Zones of mainland France. "The Jews have finally been run out of government jobs and their access to other professions has been regulated," proclaimed loudly the front page of *Le Cri du Peuple*, Jacques Doriot's new daily newspaper. *Le Matin* underscored the mood of dignity and serenity prevailing in Vichy's efforts to create an "indispensable security" by putting an end to the "insidious and ultimately deleterious influence" of Jews on French society.[22] On October 26, 1940, *La Vérité d'Eure-et-Loir*, the newspaper published by the diocese of Chartres, displayed the headline: "Toward a healthier France, the Jewish Statutes."[23]

The Yellow Placards

For the time being, however, what caught people's attention in Paris was the proliferation of the yellow placards that pointed out stores owned by Jews, the "Jewish

Table 1. Small Businesses Marked by a Yellow Placard in Paris and in the Department of La Seine

Paris (arrondissement)	Food stores[1]	Restaurants and cafés	Businesses linked to Jewish ritual[2]	Clothing stores[3]	Shoe stores[4]	Hair stylists	Coalmen	Dime–stores	Electri-cians	Total
First	10	3		83	4	2				102
Second	7	3		366	14	6			3	399
Third	50	9	1	622	31	18		4	5	740
Fourth	107	35	3	214	31	27	1	3	3	424
Fifth	13	8		67	13	4		7	2	114
Sixth	1	2		51	8	2		1	1	66
Seventh	2	3		18	1					24
Eighth	6	3		128	4	6		2		149
Ninth	22	20	1	316	23	12		11	6	411
Tenth	41	11	1	538	45	27	1	27	26	717
Eleventh	93	15		476	106	26		15	15	746
Twelfth	12	2		83	18	7			8	130
Thirteenth	6			55	44	6		1	9	121
Fourteenth	3			75	17	6		1	4	106
Fifteenth	16	6		126	28	4		3	9	192
Sixteenth	13	3		40	3	8			2	69
Seventeenth	8	5		123	40	5		4	7	192
Eighteenth	62	7		318	76	38		5	11	517
Nineteenth	34	1		133	80	13		7	6	274
Twentieth	82	6		233	124	28	1	8	14	496
Total for Paris	588	142	6	4065	710	245	3	99	131	5989
Suburbs	54	17	0	314	118	30	0	2	11	545
Total for department of La Seine	642	159	6	4378	828	274	3	101	142	6534

Source: AN, AJ 38, 538

1. Including butcher and pork-butcher shops, bakeries, general food stores, grocery stores, fish shops, milkmen, and seedsmen.
2. Including funeral homes, religious bookstores, and public bathhouses.
3. Including tailors, hosiers, garment stores, and shirtmakers.
4. Including shoemakers.

Businesses." There were few surprises at the appearance of streets "decorated" by the 4,660 placards that by December 2, 1940, had already been posted on Jewish places of commerce.[24] A later inventory was to list 6,534 small businesses (not including furriers, jewelers, antique dealers, and furniture traders): 5,989 of these were in Paris proper.[25] The total number of these businesses, including limited liability companies, was in excess of eleven thousand.[26] Tailors, hosiers, and garment makers figured prominently among them. The furriers, jewelers, and clockmakers on Rue de Provence; the fabric shops located between two big department stores (Le Printemps and Les Galeries Lafayette); the grocery stores on Rue Richer; the furniture stores on Rue du Faubourg-Saint-Antoine; the shops on Rue d'Aboukir, and the entire Rue de Rosiers section were covered with yellow placards.

Interestingly enough, one could find a few shops with no placard, even on the streets that the collaborationist press labeled as a ghetto. Equally curious was that most of the dime stores that had been denounced as Jewish before the war did not have their display windows disfigured by any yellow placard. The journalist Jacques Biélinky toured the streets of Paris during this time in order to gauge the effect of these new measures. He found his systematic survey reassuring. As consistently emphasized in all the personal testimony gathered, customers had not changed any of their habits: they continued to buy goods from Jews without raising an eyebrow and at times even demonstrated friendliness—doubtless because, in Paris, it was the Germans who were clearly and directly responsible for the appearance of these yellow signs. In this very first phase of the antisemitic laws, the Jewish storeowners were marked: if they experienced a decline in their sales, however, it was primarily because merchandise was scarce.[27] Nevertheless, in a few instances the yellow stigma attracted window smashing. And the official press rejoiced, proclaiming: "Israel can pretend all it wants not to understand nor see the truth: France no longer belongs to it. This fiefdom that it had held for hundreds of years is slipping out of its crooked hands: none of the efforts and tricks it is using to try to mask its veritable origins are working any more."[28]

Some Jewish storeowners were not content with just displaying signs that clearly identified them as Jewish, as required by the German ordinance; they put up a multitude of signs. "On Rue du Temple," writes Biélinky, "near the Place de la République, a large hosiery story is adorned with the yellow placard: 'Jewish business.' Below is a large white placard trimmed with cardboard in two colors: 'Establishment founded in 1909 by Maurice Lévy, who gave his life for France at Douaumont in 1916. Establishment taken up again by his son, a veteran of the 1939–1940 campaigns who was awarded the military war medal with citations.'"[29] Elsewhere it was the portrait of the present proprietor's ancestor that was on display in the storefront window: as a veteran of Napoleon's military campaigns, he had received the Sainte-Hélène medal. Thus the shameful little yellow placard was often surrounded by citations, decorations, war honors, and lists of veterans who had lost their lives on the battlefield. But such displays would soon be forbidden.

From Marking to Plundering

Then the colors diversified, as little by little yellow gave way to red and new placards came to take the place the first ones. "Managed by an Aryan steward appointed according to the terms of the German ordinance of October 18, 1940," read the inscription on these new red placards. Although Jewish storeowners had been reassured by the reaction of their clientele, and while on some occasions they had given free rein to their pride by publicly displaying their battlefield achievements, they would quickly lower their profile. This second ordinance issued by the German military administration in France now provided for an inventory of Jewish businesses and the replacement of their owners by provisional managers. All Jewish businesses consisting of establishments with storefront windows had to be placed under the control of such managers on or before December 26, 1940.[30] All businesses said to be Jewish (that is, those that were owned or managed by Jews, or that had 30 percent of their stock held by Jews) had to comply. For the German military command, the purpose of this measure was quite clear. It was a matter of "completely eliminating the Jewish influence within the French economy" and this was to be accomplished either by the willing or unwilling sale of the business placed under the control of an appointed steward, or else simply by liquidating it.[31] The General Delegation of the French Government in the Occupied Territories hastened to lend its support to the application of this ordinance, for fear that Jewish property might fall out of French hands. A new "Supervisory Board for Provisional Managers" (SCAP), headquartered at 5, Rue de Florence in Paris, was quickly created. The Germans proceeded to appoint the first of these managers, and then, in hopes of expediting things, authorized the regional prefects and the prefect of the Paris police to appoint them for establishments with storefront windows.[32] The Paris police prefecture thus appointed 1,141 Aryan managers, who were given control over 7,285 Jewish businesses.[33] Then, beginning on June 20, 1941, the SCAP submitted the lists of these new "bosses" directly to the German military administration. The power of the provisional managers to sell and liquidate Jewish businesses was confirmed by a French law dating from February 2, 1941.

On April 26, 1941, the impact of aryanization was magnified by a third German ordinance, which granted the provisional managers a greater latitude of action while making it henceforth impossible for the true owners to receive "anything more than absolutely indispensable subsidies from the revenues under provisional management." This restriction was intended to prevent funds from being reinvested in other ostensibly Aryan business ventures that might become Jewish endeavors. This same line of reasoning was the basis for the restriction beginning on May 28 that prevented Jews from trading their possessions; otherwise they might have thus protected their property by giving it up to someone before it could be aryanized. From then on, Jewish bank accounts were frozen.

Although this process of aryanization and plundering of the Jews got off to a bumpy start, eventually it was carried out. By the end of 1941, some 2,800 provisional administrators held under their control 15,000 Jewish stores and businesses,[34] or three-fourths of those that had been registered as Jewish. By April 15, 1942, the contingent of provisional managers in the Occupied Zone numbered more than seven thousand.[35] By April 1, 1944, the number of Jewish businesses known and registered—29, 831—was the same as the number of businesses placed under Aryan control.[36] In Paris, almost 50 percent of them wound up being sold or liquidated. Once again, it was a process that was put into application gradually.

For Jewish storeowners in Paris, the situation was uncertain at first. At the outset, people thought it was a matter of financial control, the purpose being to gather funds for Jewish charities.[37] Knowing that their future depended on the provisional manager, they would anxiously await his arrival. Some of these managers "showed up, introduced themselves, demanded the keys to the store, and told the owners to leave."[38] People sometimes managed to put off the fateful moment by leaving a non-Jewish worker in the store and claiming that the owner was ill. It was believed for a time, in January 1941, that this confiscation of Jewish stores would be postponed.[39] A notice published in the newspaper *Paris-Soir* put an end to all such hope: the liquidation of all Jewish businesses was still on the agenda, and the old yellow placards were gradually replaced by the red notices.

Jewish storeowners thus became the target of unscrupulous speculators who were finding a chance to make a fat profit. It was not long before they received visits from individuals representing consulting firms that offered to buy their businesses at a ridiculously low price. Confiscation was difficult to escape: informers seeking to make a good deal were on the watch, suddenly displaying an unrivaled sense of civic duty in hunting down Jewish businesses with no placard and in detecting the slightest attempt to maintain hidden control of a store.[40] "On the street where I am temporarily staying, there are three non-liquidated Jewish businesses. I am interested in these businesses and I would be greatly obliged if you would inform me of what requirements must be fulfilled for one to buy one of these stores," wrote one fine Parisian soul to the local police station.[41]

There were some establishments that, perhaps because they sensed what was coming, took their own initiatives before the official measures were enacted. They urged Jewish members of their board of directors to resign, or else hastened to point out that those who were absent were not fulfilling their duties. But that was not always enough to avoid being considered a "Jewish business." The sale of some businesses was voided by the German Occupation authorities, and the money paid by the buyer was placed into a frozen account. Similarly, there were various attempts to transform businesses into companies in which the former owners (Jews) would continue to participate: these, too, were voided. The case of Raoul Meyer and Max Heilbronn illustrates the foolishness of certain attempts to escape the rigors of a law that could not fail to attract speculators. By a secret agreement with the bank "Crédit

Commercial de France," they had carried out a fictitious sale of their stock in the "Galeries Lafayette" department store. Uncovered by the Germans, their scheme fell through.[42]

What a windfall for all those who knew when to cash in on a good deal! Given the difficulty of stocking their shelves and the increasing severity of the new laws, many Jewish storeowners allowed their businesses to wither away: they sold off their merchandise, leaving nothing but their lease, which they continued to pay in hopes of retaining some future for stores that at present could only be closed down.[43] With Jewish storeowners trying to reap some benefit before being plundered, merchandise was being bought and sold at unbeatable prices. One Jewish proprietor of an art gallery had to sell off his paintings at a fifth of their value, while the "100,000 Chemises" clothing store sold its merchandise at 50 percent of the previously marked prices.

The fate of the storeowner whose shop was aryanized depended a great deal on the personal attitude of the designated administrator. "Some of these provisional managers were extremely hostile: they hampered the owners in every way possible, hastening the dismissal of Jewish employees, granting themselves hefty commissions, and hiring their own darlings as employees. However, others proved to be extremely discreet, particularly when dealing with small businesses: they would say that they would come back after a while, and that we should call if they were needed."[44] The worst did not always happen, but it was legally possible. When a Jewish grocer did not manage to pay the sums demanded from him by the manager, he was summarily ordered to close his store. A photographer and his family were driven out of their apartment adjoining the store that the new administrator had just sold off. A Jewish garment maker had no recourse when the administrator now in charge of what had been his workshop confiscated his three sewing machines.[45] "Near the Avenue des Gobelins, an ill-fated Jewish shoemaker had his 'establishment' confiscated—[it was] a wretched hole so little that his customers, unable to come in, had to stand outside."[46]

Curiously enough (was it because of the dire shortage of goods in general that quickly made the problem of leather and footwear a primary concern for the French?)[47] it was the Jewish shoemakers' shops in particular that drew the attention of the "aryanizers." In early April 1941, the shoe stores run by Jews in the Seine-et-Oise département were abruptly closed.[48] "In a very short time," wrote an inspector from the Paris police prefecture in his weekly report of April 21, 1941,

> Jewish shoe stores and shoemakers' shops whose proprietors have not been replaced by Aryans will have to be closed. When it becomes possible to replace the personnel, these stores and shops may stay open, on the condition that the Israelite proprietors and employees are no longer seen in the store or the workplace. The shoemakers targeted by these measures will for the time being be able to carry on with their work provided that they have no contact with the public and do not remain in the part of the shop open to customers. For the cases in which

> no part of the shop is restricted from the public, the business must be closed down for good, unless some Aryan person can greet customers and handle all dealings with them all alone.

It should be noted that the German ordinance barring Jews from any job that would bring them into contact with the public was only given a few days later. One month later, the same inspector (or was it another?) observed with satisfaction that 85 provisional administrators had been appointed for shoe stores and shoemakers' shops, which brought their number to a total of 167 out of the 750 Jewish establishments that had been inventoried in the Paris region.[49] Knowing that in November 1940 there were some seven thousand shoemakers working in the Paris region, we can only wonder about such a haste.[50] One might suppose that there were no Jews among the hundred or so bootmakers from both the Occupied and Unoccupied Zones participating in the shoe fair contest that took place on the Champs-Elysées in Paris in mid-July 1941.[51] However that may be, in order to overcome "the problems created by the rapid liquidation of Jewish businesses," the leather committee made its contribution to the ongoing process of aryanization by creating a company, The Industrial and Financial Company of the Leather Industry, intended to centralize all operations connected with the leather industry at every level.[52]

At Temple Square in Paris as well, people clamored to buy up the Jewish stores that were being sold off. At ten o'clock on April 24, 1941, several provisional managers showed up, closed down the shops, and immediately proceeded to take inventory of the merchandise on display. At four in the afternoon, each one of the Jewish storeowners got his official red placard posted in the window after paying a fee of two hundred francs.[53] Some 225 stores had just been aryanized. On May 15, the owners were henceforth barred from selling on Temple Square. The provisional managers placed seals on the chests, baskets, and storage bins located in the vicinity of the market.[54] The elimination of the Jewish merchants resulted in paralysis of this entire area of business. Out of a thousand stores, there were soon no more than about fifty shops run by Aryans; a certain number of non-Jewish merchants had also closed down their business on their own initiative.[55] The liquidation of stores run by Jewish dealers in secondhand goods at the Saint Ouen flea market took place on July 1, 1941, when two provisional administrators chosen for the job sold off shops and merchandise while their proprietors stood by helplessly.[56] It seems indeed that there were orchestrated "aryanization hits": aimed at a particular branch of activity or a certain part of town, such hits would swoop down on a certain sector and wreak havoc. It was in just such a sweep that the 118 shops of the Charonne marketplace and the 189 stores of the Grandes-Carrières marketplace were handed over to provisional manager.[57]

By the end of 1941, some twenty wholesalers and wholesaler-retailers on Rue Saint-Martin and Rue de Turbigo had all closed down their businesses, along with some fifty textile goods stores in le Sentier, 109 stores in the Temple Square area, and 186 stores on Rue d'Aboukir and Rue du Caire.[58] Doubtless, for many Jewish storeowners, their very visibility was fatal. Large establishments known to be Jewish, areas of the city where a large number of Jewish stores were located, and sectors in which Jewish presence was appreciably greater than in others were more vulnerable than small, isolated stores (which could always fall victim to denunciation, however).

Some of the Jewish storeowners who had been put out of work wandered about sadly in Paris, where they no longer had the right to go into their own stores. More fortunate ones managed to work out an agreement with the provisional administrator assigned to their business. They continued to work, under conditions that could vary radically from one case to another, depending on the character of the new Aryan administrator. An administrator who sinned by being too soft on the Jews could receive a sanction: the Aryan put in charge of a hosiery store on Rue Lepic, "having given the proprietors a free hand," learned this the hard way.[59] Legitimated by law, the arbitrary ruled and called the shots for Jewish storeowners.

Once the street stores had been aryanized, it was the turn of in-home businesses. In order to be more effective and to proceed more rapidly, each local police chief was given a list of storeowners in his section of the city by the Paris police prefecture: it was then up to him to eliminate those with street entrances.[60]

Moreover, by virtue of the German ordinance of April 26, 1941, Jews could no longer work as "employees in charge of other employees or as employees who meet the public."[61] There were thus a large number of salaried employees who found themselves in the same predicament as the proprietors, who had been put out of work and who could find their bank accounts frozen. It was henceforth out of the question for a Jew to be a concierge, for example. The prefect himself had to issue this ruling.[62] On June 15, 1941, Jewish traveling salesmen, door-to-door salesmen, street peddlers, nomads, fruit and vegetable stand operators, and those selling National Lottery tickets were barred from plying their trades by a new application of the ordinance. At the end of the month, they were summoned by newspaper announcements to the Paris police prefecture, where they had to hand over any authorizations they might hold.[63] Garment sellers and secondhand clothes dealers fared no better at a time when people were not getting rid of their old clothes. The only ones to be exempted from these measures were craftsmen and garment makers working for other businesses and not directly involved in the sale of their products to consumers, and those who could produce a certificate issued by their employer (at times none other than the provisional manager of their own business) declaring that "Mr. So-and-So will not be in contact with the public in his work." This was supposing, of course, that the first priority of the provisional manager had not been to fire all Jewish employees, as was often the case. Economic asphyxiation and the development of widespread unemployment were indisputably items on the political agenda. The rapid increase of poverty hit these jobless people doubly hard: they were highly reluctant to apply for unemployment benefits, for fear of attracting the attention of the authorities. Since September 27, 1940, the prospect of being incorporated into Foreign Worker Units (GTE) had loomed on the horizon for foreigners between the ages of eighteen and fifty-five who were "overabundant in the nation's economy." Being "of the Jewish race," they moreover risked being interned "in special camps" at the discretion of the prefect, according to a French law dating from October 4, 1940. And the threat of internment became more real when Jews began to feel the particularly painful effects of this economic asphyxiation.

THE VICTIMS OF VICHY'S PURGE

By the summer of 1941, according to one estimate made at the time, almost 50 percent of Jews found themselves cut off from all means of earning a living.[64] The total number of Jews excluded from economic activity included many from other sectors of society. In this instance, it was the laws enacted by Vichy that were responsible.

The French law containing the Jewish Statutes was signed on October 3, 1940 by Marshal Pétain, chief of state for the Vichy regime, Pierre Laval, vice-premier, and no less than eight other members of the government. Published on October 18, it made its own original contribution to banning Jews from French society. The Jews were defined by French authorities as those descending from three grandparents of Jewish race or from two grandparents of Jewish race if their spouse was Jewish. Thus designated on the basis of racial origin, the Jews would from then on find themselves excluded from government employment and from professions related to the press or cinema. Their access to the medical, pharmaceutical, and legal professions was in danger. First singled out as Jews by the Germans because of their religion, they were now being identified on the basis of their "race" by the French law—which proved to be more "generous" in the attribution of Jewish identity, as it was mindful to count those who, having only two Jewish grandparents, nevertheless had a Jewish spouse. "The purpose of the German ordinance is to take away from Jews all of their economic influence, while the goal of the French is to remove all of their political influence," wrote the general delegate of the French government for the Occupied Zone, La Laurencie, on October 19, 1940.[65]

Once recognized as such, Jews thus found themselves barred from praticing a long list of professions, and restricted in others. This applied first of all to government employment: not only could Jews no longer aim to occupy the highest offices in the nation, they no longer had any chance of serving in the capacity of general secretary of the prefecture either. The French army would henceforth do without the services of its commissioned and noncommissioned Jewish officers. The Ministry of National Education underwent a drastic purge, as did all police offices. For any government jobs that might have escaped the lawmaker's attention, access to employment was limited to war veterans and to those holding military decorations or the Legion of Honor.

Only the State Council ("le Conseil d'Etat") had the power to grant special exemptions for "outstanding services rendered to the French State in scientific, literary, or artistic domains" on a case-by-case basis. The State Council had itself already been purged of all Jews that had previously held a seat on it: none had been granted the slightest exemption. The council's work on this matter was characterized by a slow, parsimonious, mechanical, and strict application of the law, and its rulings on cases deserving special exemptions were coherent, but restrictive.[66] Marc Bloch and Robert Debré thus managed to escape the rigors of the Jewish Statutes,[67] as did eight of their colleagues, four high government administrators from the offices of the secretary of war and the secretary of the national economy,[68] two people in public schools, and three mining engineers.[69]

However, those who found themselves out of a job, as Georges Ascoli did, were considerably more numerous. Ascoli was a professor at the Sorbonne who had received five military citations during World War I and who had been a batallion commander before being taken prisoner by the Germans in the 1940 campaign: upon returning from captivity, he learned that his position had been revoked.[70] Such was also the plight of Gérard Bloch, who came from a family that had been French for centuries. He was a teacher who held the distinguished title of *agrégé* and taught at the lycée Janson-de-Sailly. He had served as an infantry captain in the war and had lost the use of an arm. When he returned from the hospital, he was kicked out of his teaching position. Or take the case of Antoine Sciama, a student in the distinguished Ecole Polytechnique whose grandfather had participated in the construction of the Suez Canal and whose great-grandfather had lost a foot to the cold of the Berezina River in Napoleon's Russian campaign: upon graduation, he was unable to secure any position. Similary, Madame L.'s husband had been killed during World War I and her son was a prisoner of war in Germany: she was dismissed from her position as assistant librarian at the Guimet museum. Granted, if her son were an officer, the waiting period allowed before his demotion would not begin until such time as he would be set free.[71] Established under the terms of a law dating from April 4, 1941, this waiting period applied to all government employees who were prisoners of war. After this grace period of two months, however, such prisoners of war would find that the stipulations of the Jewish Statutes were being strictly applied to them. And in fact, Madame L. was one of the lucky few: by a ruling of May 9, 1942, she regained her position as an assistant in the national museums.[72] But, as we will see, only a tiny number of those hit by the Jewish Statutes were able to reenter their workplace through this little back door. And even so, they suffered great hardships for almost a year and a half.

The lucky individuals who were granted special exemptions found refuge in the Southern Zone of occupied France. The medievalist Louis Halphen had been kept in Paris by his ongoing research: how could he have carried on his work far from his books and his archives? By the summer of 1941, he found himself having to cross the demarcation line "illegally by night," before finally being assigned to the College of Liberal Arts of the University of Grenoble.[73] Louis Halphen was also one of the lucky few.

The Methods of the Purge

Because of these measures and their immediate application, the categories of the unemployed would only widen much more. In every administrative office and in each sector of economic activity that had been targeted, questionnaires appeared and declarations proliferated. How indeed could one flush out these Jews who henceforth had to be removed?

At the Ministry of National Education, Georges Ripert began by handing this task over to the regional superintendents and inspectors of public schools: they were to point out those whom they "personally knew" to be Jewish or who could be considered Jewish on the basis of "common knowledge." On November 18, 1940, the minister of justice sent a memorandum to the central offices of all government ministries in order to help them identify Jews.[74] Its directives were relayed throughout each ministry. Thus General Huntziger, government minister and secretary of state in the Ministry of War, spelled out the procedure to follow in his own memorandum:

> In most cases, the criterion to be considered is whether the person belongs to the Jewish race: the basis for such a presumption shall be the grandparents' or spouse's adherence to the Jewish religion.
>
> For the cases involving Jews having abandoned the practice of their religion, one can find useful indications in the appearance of certain patronyms, in the choice of first names that are given on birth and marriage certificates, and in the fact that their ancestors may have been buried in an Israelite cemetery. If need be, those in this category should be required to provide all necessary information.
>
> In order to facilitate the identification of employees that are to come under the application of this law, all military personnel and civilians working for the Department of War will be required to submit a declaration.[75]

And so, in order to simplify this task, it quickly became standard administrative practice to require all government employees to fill out an information form in which all had to declare whether or not they were Jewish. The impetus for this procedure had come from the Ministry of Finances and the Ministry of Industrial Production.[76]

This rule prevailed throughout France. Within a few months, almost 3,000 Jewish functionaries, including 750 who were still in the Occupied Zone (and among these were 426 Jews who worked for the Ministry of National Education) would be fired in the public sector alone all over the country.[77]

Beginning in November 1940, all members of the teaching profession had to fill out an information form indicating whether they were affected by the Statutes. The vast majority of government employees complied with this demand, doubtless in the spirit of professional discipline.[78] And on December 18, 1940, when the school year was in full swing, three teachers from the Lycée Charlemagne, four government employees from the Lycée Rollin, and two from the Lycée Victor Hugo had to leave their posts. These are just a few examples among many others, for there were scarcely more than twenty teachers who were granted special exemptions.[79] Not only the secondary and elementary teachers who were so rudely dismissed, but also the students who witnessed this disgrace offer vivid recollections of just what such a separation represented.

"The last class given by Marguerite Glotz, a history teacher at the Lycée Molière, was extraordinary: it was a hymn to our country, its history, and its values, ending with a resounding 'Vive la France' that I am not about to forget," relates one of her students.[80] For a good many of these newly excluded individuals, the "last class" was a moment of great emotion. It must be said that, on the whole, school students were inclined to show their sympathy with those who were being removed. Often these teachers received a gift, in some cases art books, in others, a sum of money collected to help the latest victim of the Jewish Statutes hold out. Both fellow teachers and students took up contributions.[81] Only at the Lycée Henry-IV, however, was this sympathy translated into a public action: first it was sixty-seven teachers, and then the vast majority of students in the upper classes, that sent a petition to the regional superintendent Jerôme Carcopino to protest the firing of a philosophy teacher.[82] Here as elsewhere, the law was put into rigorous application. And shock gave way to bitterness.

In keeping with the State Council's ruling, the types of public employment from which Jews were barred were defined rigorously and extensively. Even for subordinate positions, government ministers and secretaries of state were instructed to be sure that these jobs were in the area of technical service and that they offered no prospects of advancement toward a position that would give the employee any influence or authority. Except for those working in military establishments, just about the only ones to be spared were typists or office messengers in technical service, along with a few manual workers doing outdoor work.[83]

At the Ministry of Justice, 38 commercial court judges, 41 government mediators, 35 lawyers, 13 ministerial officers, 3 bookkeepers, 2 chief court clerks, 1 secretary from the public prosecutor's office, 47 magistrates, 2 justices of the peace, 2 salaried alternate justices of the peace, and 24 nonsalaried alternate justices of the peace were fired according to the stipulations of the Jewish Statute of October 1940.[84]

Thus the storeowners who had been put out of business and the government employees who had been purged from their posts joined ranks in the margins of society with those who had been the first to be excluded by the new order of the Occupation. Jewish artists and intellectuals, along with Jewish writers and journalists, had in fact also been hit by the conjunction of official censorship measures and self-censorship decisions. Jewish painters no longer had any place to exhibit their work: beginning with the fall Salon held in mid-November 1940, Jewish painters had been barred by an administrative inspection. There were at that time about one hundred Jewish painters in Paris. Jewish writers and journalists no longer had any venue for publication. The Jewish press, which had been so vibrant in the prewar years, no longer existed. None of the new publications approved by the Germans wanted—

nor could they accept—the writings of a Jew. Actors were also deprived of their means of making a living. When the German authorities stipulated that the Comédie-Française could be reopened only on the condition that all those of Jewish origin be dismissed, the board of directors discussed the matter, and some members proposed that the theater remain closed. René Alexandre, an actor and full member of the Comédie-Française, urged his colleagues not to follow the advice to close and requested that he be given immediate retirement.[85]

The effects of the Jewish Statutes also had an immediate impact on professionals in the world of cinema. As of October 26, 1940, the authorization to practice one's trade in the cinema would only be granted to those who had first obtained a professional identity card, which was only issued after one had provided "proof that one did not belong to the Jewish race." Jewish cameramen, film editors, architects, set designers, props persons, photographers, wardrobe masters, and makeup artists thus found they were barred from practicing their profession, although the law had only explicitly targeted managers and section heads.[86] Henri Calef, a director's assistant who had come to Paris in November 1940, was curtly informed that his presence at a meeting of technicians was inappropriate, "given his origins." We will later find the "Jewish community of the cinema" in the Southern Zone, on the French Riviera, trying to develop an alternative cinema outside of Parisian settings.

As long as their parents were not foreigners, doctors in Paris continued to practice medicine. Although their Jewish patients were becoming more scarce, as many had either left for the Southern Zone or had been impoverished, the Jewish doctors' precarious status had not reduced their non-Jewish clientele. By May 1941, however, there were about 150 Jewish doctors who had lost their authorization to practice their profession because of the law of August 16, 1940. The October Statute moreover provided for the "elimination of Jews who were overabundant" in the legal, pharmaceutical, and medical professions. Thus the threat of unemployment loomed on the horizon for them also. The situation for lawyers was hardly any brighter. Two hundred of them had been disbarred because they were of foreign descent.[87] The clientele of those who had been spared in these first months of the Occupation was constantly diminishing. By mid-April 1941, out of the some 2,400 lawyers practicing in Paris, there were 410 who were Jewish.[88] The newspapers were constantly announcing the enactment of a quota that threatened to limited their numbers. Because business dealings with lawyers are projected over the long term, prudent people hesitated to entrust their interests to a defender who, according to rumor, would soon be stripped of his professional status.

A Host of Individual Balancing Acts

Paradoxically, however, the morale of the Jews seems to have improved somewhat in the spring of 1941. This was chiefly because the antisemitic exactions of the summer of 1940 had over the fall given way to strains of sympathy in French public opinion. Even if such sympathy did not reflect the sentiment of the majority, it comforted the Jews. It was certainly the case that

> the press, the radio, and billboards were constantly disseminating antisemitic propaganda. Posted on the walls in Paris, one sign showed the unknown soldier rising up out of his tomb to cut the throats of Jews and Freemasons. In the corridors of the métro were posted images of a hooklike, rapacious hand reaching for the scepter and the crown: the hand was that of *Le Juif Süss*, a film screened with tremendous publicity at two of the major cinemas.[89]

While the partisans of an autonomous Brittany had managed to have *Bécassine* withdrawn from the featured films at the Paramount cinema (because the stupidity of the servant girl from Brittany seemed insulting to the people of Brittany in general),[90] no one had bothered to protest the antisemitic film.

At the same time, however, the signs "no Jews admitted," which could be seen in the most prominent cafés and restaurants during the summer, had for the most part disappeared.[91] Anti-Semitism seemed to be confined to the collaborationist circles supported by the Germans, while the French population on the whole was proving to be rather reluctant to follow. At least that is what most Jewish observers of the time noted. After having feared a proliferation of antisemitic disturbances in the streets, Jews interpreted the passivity of the French population as a failure of German propaganda. They saw in the majority's indifference an impermeability to the Germans' racism. They were reassured by the fact that their relations with their non-Jewish colleagues and friends were not fundamentally different from the way they had been before. They were touched by the condemnations of antisemitism, however discreet, that they noticed in "illegal literature." Communist tracts demanded equal political rights for all French citizens; one edition of *Pantagruel* emphasized the absurdity of xenophobia and antisemitism; Socialist tracts paid tribute to Léon Blum, and the labor unions' platform condemned the very principle of antisemitism. And as one witness wrote at the time, "the morale of the Jews depends on the attitude that French public opinion displays toward them."[92]

We see here a fundamental dichotomy between, on the one hand, the personal relations between Jews and non-Jews (which do not appear to have deteriorated), and, on the other, the unrelenting application of a set of exclusionary laws that—in the abstract—met with widespread approval in the Parisian populace, when they came from the French authorities.[93] The expressions of kindness and sympathy that streamed in when Jews were victims of German measures (such as the imposition of a yellow placard in Jewish storefronts) reinforced the Jews' impression that they were not totally isolated in French society.

Furthermore, Jewish worship services continued to be held and were even quietly protected by the French police, with no administrative impediments. Because it was centered on textual study, the religious practice of the time could have easily been neglected by those preoccupied by day-to-day concerns. Yet the synagogues had been full throughout the holy days of the fall of 1940. By attending, Jews could keep up with what was happening and find reassurance.

Though placed under the control of a provisional manager, businesses connected with Jewish religious practice—including Jewish butchers and delis (174 had been identified in Paris), the eight Jewish bookstores, the two ritual bathhouses—had nevertheless not been closed.[94] When Passover drew near, Jews could legally purchase their unleavened bread, matzo, in exchange for their bread tickets, or they could even buy what they needed on the black market.[95] Gatherings to celebrate Seder, the ritual Passover meal, were held at the homeless shelter on Rue Lamarck, which at the time housed a good number of Jewish refugees from other countries, and on Rue Elzévir, where about a hundred participants put aside their daily anxieties for a time.[96] It should be noted that neither the police, nor the antisemitic groups disturbed these celebrations.

Although ultra-collaborationist movements managed to seize buildings belonging to Jews with impunity—as was the case with Eugène Deloncle's Mouvement Social Révolutionnaire, which brutally stormed into five buildings on April 9, 1941[97]—the threat that hovered over the Jews' possessions did not seem to entail measures directed against their persons. Ordinances kept coming in rapid-fire succession: they ended the waiting period, translated the danger into concrete reality, and forced the Jews to act. For the time being, however, the physical security of Jews was seemingly not threatened. And while arrests hit a disproportionate number of Jews, they continued to be made on an individual basis, or else could be attributed to causes other than the simple fact that one was Jewish.

Such was the case, for example, of the Palestinian Jews, who were interned in the Romainville fort along with other British subjects. Similarly, some sixty Zionists were locked up in the barracks of Les Tourelles: rumor had it that their names have been found on a receipt book containing the stubs of the "shekels" (coupons for contributions made to the Zionist Congress) that had been left in the meeting-place of one of their organizations in the haste of the exodus from the German onslaught of May–June 1940. Jews who were militant Communists had been detained for political reasons. Finally, there were the foreign Jews who had been intercepted while attempting to return to Belgium or to the Forbidden Zone established by the Germans in France. Those who felt threatened headed toward the outer suburbs of Paris for a while, and then came back to their homes.[98] The notion that arrests were due to specific reasons other than the simple fact that one was Jewish did not fade away for a long time. Witness the many letters received in 1941 and 1942 by the offices of the General Commission on Jewish Affairs, requesting that some detainee, who "had been arrested in a police round-up and who had never been involved in politics," be set free.[99]

Yet throughout these first few months of the Occupation, there circulated rumor after rumor about far-reaching internment measures or a requirement to wear a special armband. These rumors were never denied in the press, and Prefect Langeron mentions them in his memoires.[100] The rumor of a massive internment came back to frighten the Jewish population periodically during the month of January 1941.[101] Jews were particularly fearful for their young people, and had explored various possibilities for getting them out of the country. Jews from North Africa gathered information about the means of returning to the land where they were born, while Polish Jews from countries occupied by the Soviet Union began taking steps they hoped would lead to repatriation.[102]

The fact that on several occasions these rumors proved to be unfounded also played a important role in lulling Jewish opinion into complacency. That is why Léo Hamon, who in the spring of 1941 had been given the task of writing a report on the daily life of Jews in Paris, concluded that "things turned out to be not as terrible as we might have thought at first."[103] This was before the massive roundups that would sweep through the Jewish communities.

On the level of their day-to-day individual lives, Jews had juggled with a multitude of conflicting forces, and everyone was still managing to hold out. The specific consequences as well as the cumulative effect of the various exclusionary measures were being felt only gradually. Storeowners could still live on their reserves. Some had made good profits during the summer and fall of 1940: at that time everyone was transforming cash holdings into merchandise, and German Occupation forces were for the most part purchasing supplies from stores in Paris. Others had been wise enough to sell off their stock before being dispossessed. Those who had fallen victim to the Jewish Statutes had been able to receive severance benefits. For those dismissed by the Ministry of National Education, for example, there were two possiblities: some were paid two months' salary for each year of service, while those who had completed fifteen years on the job and who were considered to have outstanding credentials were granted a partial retirement.[104] Jewish doctors of foreign extraction had only recently been barred from practicing medicine. Up until then, the deteriorating situation for the Jews still seemed to be manageable.

It is nonetheless true that the Germans seemed to have condemned the Jews of the Occupied Zone to be starved out sooner or later. There remained the possibility of aid from Jewish organizations. And it was to these organizations that a good many of those excluded by Vichy's new social order were to turn in hopes of finding financial support, a job, consolation, or information.

Seeking Aid from Jewish Organizations

The active members of the Federation of Jewish Societies in France (FSJF) who had not left Paris had already met on June 15, 1940 to decide what steps to take. For the most part, they were proven political activists who in the prewar years had demonstrated their talents in left-wing and Zionist (*Poale Zion* [two distinct groups, one Left and one Right] and *Ha-shomer ha-tsaïr* [Left]) and non-Zionist (Bundist) organizations. Such cooperation on the level of social assistance was seen as a continuation of the work carried out by the office of social aid created for Jewish immigrants in September 1939 in the context of a coordinating committee sponsored by the Federation.[105]

From then on, these activists worked for the umbrella organization called the Amelot Committee, named for the street where they had their meetings and ran their clinic. They immediately undertook an enormous social aid project. At their disposal, they had only a check for 200,000 francs that the Jewish association for social aid in America, the Joint (the "American Jewish Joint Distribution Committee"), had left them. This sum would enable them to carry out their work for two months.[106]

And so on Rue Richer, Rue Béranger, Rue Vieille-du-Temple, and Rue Elzévir, they ran four soup kitchens that served on the average 1,500 meals a day. A fifth soup kitchen on Rue de Saintonge was run by the Communists and another by the Consistorial Association of the Israelites in Paris (ACIP). The National Relief agency (Secours national) was supposed to provide their supplies, but the necessity of respecting the strict kosher rules had forced those in charge of these kitchens to purchase goods on the public and sometimes even on the black market.

For three francs, the Jewish elderly, children, and newly impoverished could have a meal with generous servings of two dishes, including as much bread as they wanted. (Bread was later limited to 150 grams per person.) At the same time, the National Relief agency, acting on orders from the German authorities, had barred Jews from the soup kitchens that had been set up by city authorities.[107] More than one-third of these meals were served free of charge, and almost 2,500 persons depended on "this basic form of assistance" from day to day.[108] These soup kitchens moreover provided a place to meet people and visit. They made it possible for those who did not care to attend synagogue services to gather together. They were places to come and assess dangers and exchange predictions about what was to come, and places where rumors spread and where people found out what had happened to one another.

When the initial pool of money was exhausted, a Quaker organization coordinated efforts between the leaders of the Joint in the Southern Zone and the Amelot Committee in order to secure new funds that would prevent the closing of the soup kitchens. This intervention by the Quakers was crucial, because the bank accounts of Jewish organizations in Paris had been frozen.[109] So activists now found themselves having to use extralegal and then illegal means to meet the needs of the Jewish population. They did not, however, refuse to take advantage of all the loopholes they could find in the anti-Jewish laws.

As the categories of jobs open to Jews became fewer and fewer in number, direct assistance to families grew more and more prevalent. For example, in December 1940 a group of some forty artists, writers, and actors (whose numbers would double in a few months) each received a sum of 300 francs a month. In an effort to sell some paintings by Jewish artists, the Amelot Committee organized an exhibit of their work.

At the Colonie Scolaire clinic on Rue Amelot, clothing was provided and medical aid was available in the form of free medicine, free doctor's appointments, and even free home visits. The growing scope and development of all of these efforts bears witness to the dire poverty inflicted on increasing number of Jewish families.

As for Jewish young people, who were rather disoriented, some of them were also taken care of by Jewish organizations. In some cases, sponsorship was provided under the pretenses of religious training. In others, they were given the opportunity to take classes. Sixty of them met at the soup kitchen on Rue Elzévir to learn Hebrew and Jewish history. At the same time, almost three hundred young people were given a professional internship in a school run by the Work and Reconstruction Organization (ORT), which specialized in vocational instruction. Similarly, under the leadership of Henry Bulawko, the forest of Sénart offered still others the opportunity of weekly outings.[110]

The Consistorial Association of Israelites in Paris (ACIP) was a long-standing organization run by French Israelites: under its authority were not only the synagogues, but also a Welfare Committee located on Rue Rodier. The mass exodus from Paris under the German onslaught in May–June 1940 had left the association disorganized, and it was only in the fall of the same year that it had resumed its activities. To keep its finances afloat, however, its leaders had to accept the proposition made in November 1940 by Lieutenant Theodor Dannecker. Dannecker was head of the Gestapo's Office of Jewish Affairs in France: his authority extended over the other German offices in Paris on all matters dealing with the Jews. Under Dannecker's watchful eye, the Welfare Committee on Rue Todier had to collect contributions from Jewish storeowners.[111] On January 17, 1941, the full extent of German control became clear: while the Germans encouraged the development of social aid endeavors, they stipulated that any sum taken from the collection for the purposes of social aid had to be approved by Dannecker.[112] This was only the first step in a strategy of constant pressure that Dannecker would keep exerting on the leaders of the ACIP: his end was to make Jews in Paris group themselves together under one sole organization. He would then use this organization to communicate, justify, and apply his decisions.

The social aid that thousands of Jews needed just to survive thus carried a political price. The Coordinating Committee for Jewish Charities was created amid these circumstances on January 30, 1941. It served as the umbrella group for the Welfare Committe (Comité de Bienfaisance), the School Colony (Colonie scolaire), Children's Relief Organization (OSE), and the Shelters for the homeless (Asiles). The ACIP, represented by its charitable branch, was strictly separated from this organization. Neither was the Amelot Committee listed as such under this new umbrella organization.[113] Nevertheless, what was being organized was a coordination of efforts between the leaders of the immigrant Jews and the representatives of the French Jews. As a result, efforts to assist Jews in need were carried out more coherently. At the same time, however, this new setup conformed with the move toward greater centralization desired by Dannecker.[114]

We now have a clear picture of the general strategy guiding German policy toward the Jews in occupied France. The goal was to impoverish the Jewish population and to make it inevitably dependent on the work of Jewish charitable institutions; Jews, of course, were barred from appealing to the National Relief agency for assistance. The Germans would then strictly control these organizations and thus create a mandatory organization (*Zwangsorganisation*) for the Jews: it was this "hostage organization" that was to be the linchpin of the general preparatory plan that would eventually facilitate the deportation of Jews.[115] "The freezing of Jewish assets," explains one German document, "will force the Jews to authorize the Coordinating Committee to ask for gifts from these frozen assets: and the acceptance of this request will in practical terms bring about a forced union of the Jews."[116]

It was difficult to escape such a trap, which placed Jewish leaders before two totally contradictory imperatives. On the one hand, they had to do something about the dire poverty of an increasing number of Jews. On the other, they did not want to give in to the demands made by those who were directly responsible for causing this misery. The strategy of Jewish leaders was therefore to try to stall. But even though they disputed legal points and haggled over technicalities in an attempt to roll back deadlines, they did not succeed in preventing the creation of the Coordinating Committee. Circumstances dictated that the general secretary of this committe, Marcel Sachs, should become its spokesman to Dannecker. Subsequent attempts to get out from under Dannecker's thumb proved futile when Dannecker had two Jews from Vienna sent to Paris to bring about all that he had not been able to obtain from local leaders.

The pace of events then quickened, and on April 19, 1941, some ten thousand Jewish families in Paris, whose names had been gathered in the census files and obtained through Dannecker's intervention, received the first edition of a newspaper that was being sent to them, *Informations Juives*. This first mailing was greeted with protests, which were echoed in the next edition of the paper. There were protests from converts and denunciations of the anonymity that concealed the identity of the paper's writers. "Your newpaper bears the signature of the Gestapo. . . . It is clear to me and to all unbiased readers that you are nothing but an agent for the forces that are seeking to destroy Judaism with no regard whatsoever for moral values and human suffering," wrote a "French Jew, veteran of the 1939–1940 war, recipient of the Military Cross."[117] But others such as Suzanne Pelossof, who had lost her job teaching the large math and physics classes at the Sainte-Élizabeth school because of the Statutes, found work in the paper's classified ads. Although readers turned a deaf ear to the paper's subsequent call for subscriptions, it continued to be delivered to about four hundred addresses.[118]

This paper was the only Jewish publication authorized. Its columns spelled out the regulations that Jews had to comply with. "All Jews must at every moment have in their possession an identity card stampled 'Jew.' . . . Every violation of this rule will be severely sanctioned," read a boxed announcement in the second edition of the paper dated April 25, 1941. Under the pretense of a call for all Jewish groups to unite their forces, a pretext that had proven effective in the past, the paper instructed Jews to register with the Coordinating Committee, the "only committee approved by authorities." For those who had hoped to find a way out of their predicament, the paper issued a reminder of the harsh reality of the situation: "Our appeal was issued to all our fellow Jews and to all who consider themselves to be Jews. We no longer distinguish between one group of Jews and another: such a distinction could only be damaging to those who keep insisting on it. Even Jews who do not belong to the Israelite religion must request a special identity card at police headquarters. This is proof that there is no longer any valid distinction."[119]

The paper contained a large number of cultural items. There were episodes from the history of the French Jews, in which periods of Jewish decline were explained by internal divisions. There were portraits of Jewish artists intended to sketch a profile of the "Jewish culture." The paper also included information about various Jewish communities throughout the world and biblical commentaries. All of these cultural articles served as packaging for the practical information. The paper published the schedule of services in the various synagogues and listed various social aid programs available to the needy. There were even practical tips on putting together packages for detainees when people were interned.

Jewish leaders felt trapped: stalling tactics would no longer do. Two of them had already found out that a refusal to collaborate with the Germans would result in their being arrested. Even more serious, however, was that such a refusal might jeopardize the entire set of social aid endeavors at the very moment when such assistance was more needed than ever. The representatives of the Amelot Committee, who withdrew from the Coordinating Committee (without, however, breaking ties with the various member organizations) were intransigent. They were opposed to the strategy of compromise that the representatives of the Consistorial Association of the Israelites of Paris (ACIP) were advocating. The ACIP was hoping that the new General Commission on Jewish Affairs (CGQJ) created by Vichy on March 29, 1941, would take the place of German authorities and adopt more flexible policies. The cordial relations that they had always maintained with various offices of the French government had made them confident about this matter. Government administrators had often expressed their sympathy, while explaining that they had no choice but to apply the German ordinances.[120] It seemed preferable to have to deal with some antisemitic French bureaucrat than with someone like Dannecker: not only did Dannecker keep heaping verbal abuse on Jewish leaders, he would also "very conspicuously bring a washbowl into the concierge's lodge so he could wash his hands" when he left the offices of the Consistory.[121] Moreover, Xavier Vallat, the commissioner for Jewish affairs, had refused to see a delegation from *Au Pilori,* the newspaper infamous for its extremely virulent antisemitic tirades. It seemed better to choose the lesser of two evils.

At the time, mutual assistance was also the primary objective of the Communists' efforts, as evidenced by the name they had chosen for their new organization:

Solidarité. It had been formed in September 1940. Three months later, there were 130 street committees, 50 women's groups, 20 labor union sections, and several groups of young people who were collecting funds from the more well-to-do.[122] The soup kitchen on Rue de Saintonge and a medical clinic, however, were legal fronts for a more diversified political enterprise. An underground Yiddish newspaper, *Unser wort*[123] (Our Voice, or literally, Our Word) positioned itself in the traditional line of Communist thinking. We know of the contents of this paper from the analysis of police reports made on some of the editions seized on September 29, 1940, and after. We find Vichy's antisemitism denounced on the same basis as the anti-communist persecutions carried out by those same French authorities. At the same time, the general population of France is reported to be sympathetic toward the persecuted.

The paper also contrasts the horror of French internment camps with the more fortunate plight of Polish Jews "liberated" by the Red Army. In the articles written by one Communist activist, anxiety alternated with hope. "We don't know just how far these laws will go," he wrote on November 9, 1940, referring to the Jewish Statutes.

> There is talk of camps, of being barred from certain jobs, and of having to make a declaration of one's possessions. The worst thing is that these totally arbitrary powers are in the hands of the prefects. There is in reality no longer any legislation in France which might provide protection for a Jew. Racism has taken the place of the Declaration of the Rights of Man. All Jews are anxiously wondering, "What will tomorrow hold in store for us?" We must see that we are not the only ones to suffer blows: in spite of prisons overflowing with detainees, things are happening in this country.[124]

In the Communists' view of things, there was a basis for hope in the destiny shared by Jews and non-Jews. Because the fate of the Jews foreshadowed what was to happen to everyone else, they were all united in one struggle.

In June 1941, the various Parisian sections of the Communist Party widely distributed a tract that encouraged such a viewpoint.[125] It denounced the exactions inflicted on small and midsized Jewish stores as being aimed against the common people and revolutionary values, and as a precursor of attacks against other categories of storeowners and craftsmen that would be made "under all sorts of pretenses."[126] It pointed toward the ones who were really responsible for the hardships that the French were then suffering: it was the "capitalist oligarchies" that should be targeted, and not Jews. These criticisms were thus voiced in complete accordance with Communism's traditional view of class struggle. In this perspective, antisemitism was simply a ploy intended to guarantee the bourgeoisie's domination by creating divisions within the ranks of common people.[127] While the perspective was that of Communist orthodoxy, these denunciations were accompanied with recommendations worded in a manner that could only make many Jewish victims feel they were naturally allied with the Communists.

"Dear Aryan shopowners," states the tract:

do not let your neighbor be plundered on the pretext that he is Jewish. Tomorrow it may be your turn.

You Aryans who have been called upon to do a dirty job as provisional administrators, do not go along with this cruel, tragic little game that is being played by the French bourgeoisie and the German Occupation authorities. Refuse to lend your assistance to these dishonest acts that may turn against you in sometime in the future.

Do not help this regime that is creating so much hardship and suffering bring about something that is unspeakably unjust.

. . . Prospective buyers looking for a shop, as few as you may be, refuse to have any dealings with a transaction involving a Jewish seller who is being forced to sell his "holdings." For in that way, you will give him the chance of continuing to live in his little store.[128]

The price to be paid for maintaining these ties with the Communist Party, printing this newspaper, and distributing these tracts was soon to be apparent. In April 1941 came the first arrest of Jews involved in Communist activism, and all Jewish groups came under close surveillance by the secret police from the General Bureau of Information ("Renseignements généraux"). For the month of April alone, patrols were sent out to nearly two hundred public places looking for the slightest indication of some secret meeting; the activities of some fifty organizations underwent close review; and there were no less than five hundred investigations.[129] The separate arrests of these individuals led their victims either to the guillotine, to the firing squad, or to the death camp. Those arrested did not yet realize that the very fact of being Jewish exposed any and every activity to heightened surveillance and that every arrest resulted almost invariably in death.

In short, for those who, as of April 1941, were not taking the risk of getting involved in political activity, the danger was rather apparent: the Germans sought to have the Jews excluded from French society and reduced to dire poverty. The first concern for people was therefore to make sure, in spite of the hardships, that they could find a job or some way of making a living. In addition, they had to keep themselves from getting demoralized. Every Jewish organization provided some form of support. Synagogues, soup kitchens, study circles, and political activist groups made it possible for Jews to break out of their isolation and gather together. In such groups, people sometimes insisted that previous activities should go on as usual, arguing that such continuity was the best way to defy laws aimed at upsetting the order of everyday life. And so, under the leadership of Fernand Musnik, assisted by Emmanuel Lefshetz, the Israelite Scouts of France (EIF) organized meetings and clubs, even though scouting had been banned in the Northern Zone of Occupied France. As in prewar times, such events reportedly brought together some three hundred children and young people in attendance.[130]

French society constituted the other escape from isolation. Each Jew could measure the extent of the Nazis' grip from one day to another in carrying on social contacts and relations begun before the war. The warmth of some students toward a

Jewish co-ed or the kindness of a shopkeeper toward a Jewish housewife could brighten one's day. Even more important, it could give one a sense of security. After all, we just have to wait for the storm to blow over, people told themselves. But the first mass arrest of Jews was to remind them of the precariousness of their situation, particularly for foreigners.

THE PERIOD OF THE POLICE ROUNDUPS

"Mr. X, accompanied by a member of his family, is requested to report to 2 Rue Japy (the gymnasium) at 7 o'clock in the morning for a review of his status. Please make sure to bring ID documents. Anyone who does not report at the specified time on the day indicated will be subject to the severest sanctions. The police chief."[131]

Behind this supposedly routine check that had been ordered by the French police, there lurked something completely different. But who could suspect it at the time? On the afternoon of May 13, French police officers delivered 6,694 such "green notes." Some 3,710 Jews, the majority of them Polish,[132] responded. Some reported to the gymnasium on Rue Japy, others to the barracks on Rue Napoléon, still others to the Minimes barracks located on 52 Rue Édouard-Pailleron or 33 Rue de la Grange-aux-Belles. At each location, the scenario was the same. The Jews summoned were held in detention, while the person accompanying them was sent to go and bring back their personal effects. They were then taken to the Austerlitz train station. From there, they were led away in four special trains to the camps at Pithiviers and Beaune-la-Rolande in the département of Le Loiret.

On May 15, 1941, the daily newswpaper *Paris-Midi* published the following commentary. "Five thousand Jews are gone. Five thousand Jews have spent their first night in a concentration camp. That makes five thousand fewer of the parasites that had infected greater Paris with a fatal disease. This first bit of surgery has been completed; the rest is to follow."[133] People in the sections of Paris that had been hit particularly hard by this police roundup were in shock. Once more, rumor had turned out to be true. During the three weeks that followed, 501 Jews, doubtless convinced that in order to avoid being arrested it was better to have their papers in order, came to declare their identity at police headquarters. By contrast, there had only been 193 such declarations during the three weeks that had preceded this first mass roundup of Jews.[134]

One of the first reflexes of Jews was to go to the synagogues, whose services were still well attended, to keep up with what was happening to people. At one point, they had planned to form a committee to support the families of those who had been interned in the camps. People tried to convince themselves that these mass arrests would not recur, even though the illusion was to be short-lived.[135] "This action was taken indiscriminately and carried out with unheard-of brutality against thousands of men who had committed no offense, other than that of having been born Jewish.

This was the last straw and has thrown the Jewish population into a state of despair," wrote one witness.[136]

The non-Jewish population was not concerned. No newspaper edited by non-Jews reported the event at the time. It was a matter concerning foreign Jews; the arrests had been made without incident and without being exposed to the view of people passing by in the street. Those who were curious about the affair were content with the official explanation, which was that the Germans had removed those whom they considered to be their declared enemies. There is only one letter of protest to be found in the files of the Commission on Jewish Affairs. Written by a "veteran of World War I" and addressed to Xavier Vallat (head of the commission), it declared:

> We are absolutely disgusted by the crass, cynical propaganda that the newspapers have been spreading about the foreign Jews interned in concentration camps. We are Catholics and veterans of 1914 and we declare that this is a disgrace for France, a land of freedom and hospitality. We observed this pathetic procession of prisoners with our heads bowed in shame and tears in our eyes. And you can be sure that there were many people along the way who shared the same feelings of pity and outrage. If you found these Jews to be undesirable because of your unbridled sectarianism, then you should have expelled them from France. But you do not have the right to lock them up behind barbed wire fences and condemn them to forced labor. . . . You see, Mr. High Commissioner, what we fear first and foremost is that when our children go abroad, they will no longer dare to admit they are French! We are sick at heart. We remain, however, cordially yours . . .[137]

The Camps in the Loiret

Those who had just been interned in the camps found themselves suddenly plunged into the universe of the prison. Within two days, they were duly registered, stripped of their money (albeit in exchange for a receipt), and relieved of their identity papers. They were then taken to shabby wooden buildings in a camp surrounded by barbed wire fences and watched by French gendarmes.[138] The Polish Jews who had previously been locked up in the Les Tourelles barracks soon joined them.[139] In a single day, June 24, one hundred ten Polish Jews would be subjected to this transfer.[140]

From then on, living conditions for those interned would be harsh. They had to sleep on thin straw mats in tight quarters offering no privacy. The mats were only changed once every two months and internees often had no blankets to protect them from the cold. Toilet and lavatory facilities were grossly inadequate and food was limited to bare essentials: 125 grams of bread per day, with rutabaga and turnip soup. There was moreover a serious shortage of clothing and shoes, which would only get worse during winter months.

The camp routine included two roll calls a day, a ritual indicative of the detainees' status as prisoners. Within the camp, there were all sorts of chores that had to be done. Some work, such as peeling vegetables and putting up fences, contributed to the camp's daily operation or infrastructure, while at the same time keeping the detainees busy. The leader of each building divided up the work into specific tasks assigned to individuals. Some, such as the doctors, carpenters, hairdressers, and shoemakers, could practice their trade. War veterans and heads of large households were the most fortunate, as they were sometimes employed outside of the camps, in a sugar refinery near Pithiviers, for example, and on farms near Beaune-la-Rolande. Some of them received a small sum of money for their work, but others did not. Some 275 detainees were sent to work on abandoned farms in the Sologne region: their mission was to drain the marshes. When not locked up in the camp prison, those who did not follow the rules of discipline were sent to do construction work on public roads. Most of the time, however, those detained in the camps were left with nothing to do.

Contact with the outside world, however, was not completely broken off. These Polish Jews, whose French was shaky, were allowed to send and receive one letter a week *in French*, so that it could be carefully examined by camp authorities. Detainees were also allowed to receive two packages per month, which, although meticulously inspected, nevertheless reminded them of life outside. Outside of these official channels of communication, ways of transmitting clandestine correspondence soon developed. During the first few months, the detainees were allowed to have short visits: even though strict regulations made them difficult to arrange, they could momentarily dispel the gloom of camp life. These visits, however, were soon no longer permitted. The detainees' families were barred from staying in the villages adjacent to the camps:[141] often they found that they had made the trip in vain, and left without even having a chance to catch a glimpse of their relative. A few leaves (for three days) were granted under the strictest conditions. Jacques Waintrob was thus given a few hours of liberty so that he could get married.

By October 1941, however, these liberal gestures had come to an end. There had been a rash of escapes: between July and October 1941, some 182 detainees had fled the Pithiviers camp, while some 377 escaped from Beane-la-Rolande. At times, detainees had managed to take advantage of the rare moments outside of the camp confines that had been so parsimoniously granted them to meet spouses or friends and receive false documents and identity papers that would make it possible for them to escape once given the opportunity. The policemen who always accompanied them when they went outside were given a bottle of wine to buy their silence. Other escapes, such as that of Zalman Korenblut, who hid under a pile of garbage in a truck to get out of his camp, were more spectacular.[142] Doubtless many others could have attempted to escape, especially those who worked for private individuals outside the camp. But they were as a general rule reluctant to compromise the people who employed them and who would have been held responsible for their disappearance.[143] They were moreover fearful of putting their relatives in danger.

In any case, escaping was still a matter of individual undertakings: this was not yet the time when entire families would envision slipping away into clandestineness. It was only after the first deportations in the spring of 1942 that Jewish Communists would receive the unambiguous word to escape at all costs.[144] "Our primary task shall be to organize and encourage escapes from the camp," wrote Vilner-Fanstein on June 25, 1942, emphasizing the particular urgency now surrounding this matter.[145] Until then however, Communist detainees had been primarily concerned with questions of politics and organization, and it was those activities that had made it possible for them to form a unified front against the camp administration. They had thus succeeded in obtaining less stringent regulations for packages and mail, and in increasing cultural activities within the camp. Their collective efforts had also managed to produce an underground newspaper in each of the two camps: fourteen editions were "published."[146] This paper was written out by hand on fifty copies and distributed in the shelters. It was used as the basis for discussions dealing with specific problems in the camps as well as the general political situation.

The first few months of detention for these men had been dominated by feelings of depression, disbelief, and worry for their families, who had been left to fend for themselves. Once they had obtained a few improvements in the food served, however, they settled into a routine and developed a variety of cultural activities. There was a library, a choir, a series of lectures in French and in Yiddish, and even a theater group. The men put on an exhibit of paintings and organized regular academic classes in language, sewing, geography, and physical fitness. And just as authorities authorized Jewish worship services to continue outside, in the Occupied Zone, so religious holy days were observed in the camps.

It was difficult to obtain release: between June and September 1941, only 183 men had been released from Pithiviers and 232 from Beaune-la-Rolande. Such releases required the approval of the regional German command, which as a general rule only granted it to those who were seriously ill. Before Hitler invaded the Soviet Union on June 21, 1941, more than two hundred detainees had sent a petition requesting their release to the Soviet embassy. They had thought that they could be "repatriated" to Polish territory that was then under Soviet control.[147]

Social workers, some of whom actually lived onsite, played an important role in improving living conditions for detainees. They saw that packages from friends and loved ones were delivered and secretly carried letters in and out of the camps. They helped organized cultural activities and even managed to obtain the release of a few men.

First carried out on an individual basis before the massive operations that began on May 14, 1941, such arrests of Jews added a whole new dimension to social assistance: for the Rue Amelot group and the Coordinating Committee as well as for Solidarité, aid to prisoners henceforth became an integral part of their work. As police persecution intensified, these groups felt compelled to step up their activities: they accordingly took it upon themselves to relieve as much as possible the misery of those who had been locked up. They put together packages and sent them to the Loiret camps. A social worker, officially appointed by the French Red Cross but in reality sponsored by the Amelot Committee, provided basic necessities. Legal services were also organized, in an attempt to have some of the prisoners released. The Amelot Committee moreover began to help those who wanted to use false documents to leave the Occupied Zone and go to the South of France or to another country: efforts attempted through official channels, however, quickly proved to be hopeless.

While the Communists with Solidarité prepared and sent packages to camp detainees, they also engaged in political action. They distributed tracts denouncing the plight of those held in the camps and organized demonstrations by the detainees' wives in front of camp gates. Toward the end of June 1941, one such protest was organized outside the barbed wire fences of the Pithiviers camp by the Union of Jewish Women (Union des femmes juives), a group of Communist persuasion. Participating in it were dozens of prisoners' wives who had come to demand the right to visit their husbands and to send them packages.[148]

Families had been torn apart by all these arrests, with wives and children being left to fend for themselves, without any source of income. To take one example out of countless others, a good number of women merchants in the Porte de Clignancourt flea market were forced to sell off their goods and close down their businesses before May 20, 1941, at the very moment when their husbands had been sent to the Loiret camps. An entire group of people thus found themselves even more dependent on charity. And then they began undertaking administrative procedures in an effort to secure the release of loved ones. A large number of women crowded daily into the police prefecture and the city hall, invoking health problems, particularly difficult family circumstances, and increasing poverty,[149] but all to no avail. On July 20, 1941, some of them turned their anger and frustration against the Coordinating Committee, which was accused of not acting vigorously enough to obtain the release of their husbands. From July 20 to July 31, there were as many as five hundred women who came to demonstrate almost every day outside of the Coordinating Committee's office on Rue de la Bienfaisance. Increasing numbers of violent altercations led one of the two Viennese Jews, Israelowicz, to call in the police to break up the demonstrators.[150]

Sophie Schwartz, one of the women who demonstrated, remembers having put into action instructions received from Solidarité. Following orders from the clandestine Communist Party, French women had been showing up regularly for several months outside city halls: they would ask for coal, demand that the distribution of basic necessities be improved, inquire about the fate of their loved ones who were prisoners of war, and demand that those who had been interned in the camps be released. In Vitry-sur-Seine, Montreuil, Bagnolet, and elsewhere, there were scores of women who would come to voice these demands.[151] The Paris police prefect concluded that these actions were being orchestrated by the Communists with the aim of involving "non-Communist women in a campaign to stir up public sympathy for children and prisoners."[152] Even when viewed as part of the overall political strategy of the Communist Party, these July 1941 incidents on Rue de la Bienfaisance testify to the ambivalence of several segments of Jewish society toward the social aid organizations: while these organizations came to their assistance, they represented at the same time the Jews' only link with the authorities who were responsible for all their suffering and hardship.

Elsewhere in the Provinces

In the provincial cities of the Occupied Zone, the situation was a bit different. Outside of Paris and its suburbs, there were only about twenty thousand Jews,[153] mainly in the cities of Bordeaux and Nancy, in the Seine River basin, and scattered throughout various départements, especially in the areas in proximity of Alsace and the département of La Moselle, which had been annexed by the Third Reich. There were also some living near the demarcation line separating the Occupied Zone from the Unoccupied Zone. The Jews fleeing Paris were not about to rush into this area occupied by the Germans, unless it was their first stop on the way to the southern, Unoccupied Zone. And there were many Jews who were getting out, as evidenced by the fact that by the end of 1940, one fourth of those who had been counted in the October census had left the département of les Côtes-du-Nord.[154]

The application of the German ordinances was particularly strict in the provinces and several factors made it easier to carry out the measures aimed at excluding and plundering the Jews. For one thing, there were fewer Jews to deal with, and a smaller proportion of refugees. Moreover, application of the ordinances was rigorously monitored by the regional German military command. In some instances, the local German Occupation authorities took their own initiatives before the ordinances were issued. Such was the case in the département of Les Côtes-du-Nord, where a preliminary census of Jews (in this instance, foreign Jews) had already been taken by the prefect in mid-July 1940, upon the request of the local German military command.[155]

As one observer points out, however, the suffering brought about by the policy of plundering the Jews was at times mitigated by the fact that Jewish families were well integrated into the social fabric of the local French population. In these same départments, there were many Jewish families who were quite well assimilated, having lived there for hundreds of years. For example, out of the 1,081 Jews tallied in the lower areas of the Seine River basin, 75 percent were French citizens.[156] In the département of L'Eure-et-Loir, two-thirds of the 125 Jews counted in the census were French citizens.[157]

Here is Pierre-Jacques Lévy's census declaration of October 19, 1940.

> In order to comply with the ordinance decreed by the German Occupation authorities, I declare the following: I am Pierre-Jacques Lévy, an Israelite of French nationality born in Paris on March 24, 1898; my mother, a French citizen who was born French, was born in Paris on April 18, 1872.
>
> My mother and father were themselves born of French parents born in France. The same is true for the parents of their parents going all the way back, I am told, to the creation of birth records in France.

> My wife, whose maiden name is Hirsch, is as I am an Israelite born of a French mother and a French father. I have four children, two boys and two girls, ranging in age from six to twelve years.
>
> As an engineer with a diploma from the Ecole des Arts et manufactures in Paris, I am at the head of an industrial and commercial business whose headquarters are located in Chartres, on 5, Boulevard Chasles.[158]

The declaration submitted by his father is scarcely different, except for the following statement at the end: "Neither of us have attended anything but public, secular schools."

On January 30, 1941, all of the Jews who had made their declaration (which is to say all Jews in that département) received a letter from Police Chief Lautier of the prefecture in Chartres. In keeping with the instructions received from the regional German military command stationed in Chartres, the letter instructed them to declare without delay the value of their personal property, the shares they held in any business establishments, and any real estate they owned. On July 5, 1941, those who were about to lose their property received a letter from the prefect for the Eure-et-Loir département's special police chief. This letter announced that "according to the instructions received from the supervisory office for provisional managers of General Commission on Jewish Affairs (CGQJ), a steward manager had been appointed to sell off their business." They were therefore summoned to report a few days later to the subprefecture at Dreux "to receive instructions" from their new master.

Out of the twenty-three Jewish businesses that had been declared, five had been purchased by a new owner, fourteen had had their goods liquidated, and four were in the process of being taken over by the end of September 1941.[159] There had been no lack of eager buyers coming to see the Police for Jewish Affairs (PQJ) to indicate their interest in acquiring these businesses. One such offer was made by a man who wanted a place to live. There was another from someone who was looking to acquire either a grocery store, a pork-butcher shop, or a dairy store. Still another individual was willing to purchase either a perfume, leather goods, lingerie, or hosiery shop. There was a father who wanted to set up his son in the business of new fashions and garments. Someone else sought to acquire wooded property—"with or without adjoining buildings," he noted—having formerly belonged to Jews and having been seized by the authorities.[160]

Within this same context, two of the nine doctors practicing medicine in this département were born of fathers who were foreign nationals: their status was therefore in jeopardy according to the decree of August 16, 1940. They had the good fortune, however, of receiving the support of the secretary-general of the Federation of Medical Unions of the Eure-et-Loire département, who personally interceded on their behalf.

By November 26, 1940, some fourteen hundred Jews of the département of La Charente-inférieure had been counted by the census and issued an identity card bearing the "special stamp" required by the German authorities.[161] The operation was finished. By contrast, however, identity cards for the small number of Jews residing in the occupied portion of the département of L'Allier had still not been stamped by mid-December 1941.[162]

As soon as they had arrived in Besançon in June 1940, the Germans had set up a surveillance committee to monitor the property of Israelites. The committee was sponsored by the chambre of commerce and housed in its buildings. Jewish businesses were reopened and assigned a manager chosen among former employees. It was this procedure that would later make French authorities fear that most of the seizures in this area had only been fictitious.[163]

In the départements of Brittany, seizures of the slightly fewer than two hundred Jewish businesses was carried out with much ado, often with the assistance of committees from various professional organizations.[164] In the département of L'Yonne, it was practically over by May 1942.[165]

In Bordeaux, some 5,722 Jews had declared their identity.[166] By the beginning of 1941, all Jewish stores—about three hundred of them in the first stage—had either been closed down or sold.[167] However, a good many of these sales had apparently been fictitious, even though the union of doctors and pharmacists seems to have proved to be particularly zealous in applying the quota limiting the number of their Jewish counterparts.[168] Here as elsewhere, Jews working for the government were dismissed, as provided for in Vichy's antisemitic laws: those employed in the offices of the prefecture and in the postal services lost their jobs overnight.

The Germans were indeed there, and Jews were being arrested everywhere, under all sorts of pretexts. Mr. Gomez, age eighty-two, who was president of the Jewish community of Bayonne, was imprisoned for having refused to hand over to these new masters of the region the membership list of the Jewish worship group.[169] In the city of Epernay, a Jewish butcher wound up getting arrested for having declared that if there was a shortage of meat, it was the Germans' fault.[170]

In all these areas, Jews managed to eke out a living by doing odd jobs and occasional work. In Blois, for example, one secondary school teacher gave private lessons.[171] Circumstances sometimes created strange bedfellows, as in Nancy, where a right-wing royalist (a "camelot du roi") reportedly stood up in defense of the Jews out of his love for France and hatred of the Germans.[172] The loyalty displayed by some people at times made it possible for a Jewish proprietor to keep on running his business behind the scenes. Such was the case of Gustave Nordon in Nancy who, by August 3, 1941, had been officially removed from his business and replaced by his former accountant.[173]

As can be seen from these cases, factors specific to certain areas and cities made a crucial difference on an individual basis. On the whole, however, the double stranglehold of German and French authorities on a Jewish population of greatly inferior numbers made it possible to carry out the operations of counting up the Jews, excluding them from the social mainstream, and plundering their property, all with noted efficacity.

There were other camps in the Occupied Zone in addition to the ones at Pithiviers and Beaune-la-Rolande. The one at Troyes, for example, detained the Jews from Boulogne, who had been taken there one morning in December, 1940. They had first been penned up for an entire day behind the fences at the bishopric and then marched through the city streets under armed guard. They had to spend a whole week in a school building in Troyes, where they were poorly fed and treated as common criminals, having their mug shots taken from the front and the side, with a number on the shoulder.[174] The camp was controlled by French guards who were themselves kept under the watchful eye of the Germans. Whenever there were escapes, as was the case in February 1941, camp security was stepped up: as a result, it was strictly forbidden for detainees to go out of the camp confines.[175] By the spring of 1941, there remained only some forty elderly people and children, who could not possible escape by themselves.

There was also the La Lande-des-Monts camp near the city of Tours, where some 470 Jews, including 104 children, were locked up toward the end of March 1941.[176] Most of the people in this camp were foreign Jews from Strasbourg and Metz, who had first been expelled from their hometown by the Germans and sent to Bordeaux. In Bordeaux, they were ordered to report to the train station on Sunday morning. Some were then placed under house arrest, while others were interned in camps: authorities made the choice at random. There they found themselves stuck without an identity card or food rationing papers. They were subjected to daily inspections and were forbidden from going to neighboring villages. Unlike the Spanish or Polish nationals interned in the camp, they were also barred from working.[177]

At the break of day on July 15, 1941, some 70 to 74 French Jews from two neighboring communities near the towns of Arcachon and La Teste-de-Buch were added to the group of about fifteen foreign Jews who had already been interned at the Mérignac-Beau-Désert camp. They had been arrested at their homes by French gendarmes. Behind the barbed wire fences were four generations of a same family. The grandmother was in her eighties and virtually a total invalid. Along with the parents, who were in their sixties, was a young woman whose husband, a French army officer, had been killed on the battlefield in France in June 1940, and her two little girls, ages three and four.[178] Robert Aron was also one of the internees. Eleven days later, forty of them were transferred to the La Lande camp.[179]

And then there was the camp at Poitiers, where several hundred Jews were temporarily interned. Those who had been brought there from the Gironde area were joined by the 339 Jews who had been arrested by the Germans in their villages in the département of La Vienne. This operation, like the one carried out against the Jews in Arcachon and La Teste-de-Buch, had also taken place on July 15, 1941. Nothing had been done to prepare their living quarters. Rain poured through the roofs of dilapidated buildings. There were neither chairs, nor benches, nor tables. Mice and rats scurried around everywhere, eating everything, including the few clothes detainees had to wear. The food was inadequate, and camp authorities were uncooperative in letting internees receive the items that had been collected and sent to them. Jews were barred from working and from going out of the camp, which was under the guard of French gendarmes.[180] The same situation would recur elsewhere, both at Drancy and in the internment camps in the Southern Zone. The first few weeks of detention were sometimes the hardest, as everything had be set up from scratch. Afterwards, with the help of Jewish aid organizations, living conditions were less chaotic.

The Poitiers camp provided the Amelot Committee the opportunity to develop a special type of activity. They sought out homes in the region that could host the hundred Jewish children that they managed to get out of the camp. One such case was in Migne in the département of La Haute Vienne, where one center lodged an entire group.[181] In other cases, Jewish families took in a single child. At any rate, the goal was to spread the children out. That would be the focus for similar undertakings carried out in the Occupied Zone starting in the summer of 1942, when internments would hit large numbers of children. In the southern part of France, this concern was already part of everyday life: getting the children out of the camps had become the top priority for the leaders of social aid organizations.

It was indeed in the Southern Zone, where France was supposedly "sovereign," that one found the majority of foreign Jews who had been confined to camps set up and controlled by French authorities. It was also in the Southern Zone that a good many French Israelites had gone to seek refuge: they fled the areas occupied by the Germans and entrusted the French authorities with their fate.

3
The State, Society, and the French Israelites in the Unoccupied Zone

THE NEW DEAL

A Preliminary Dispersion

"Communities" just as diverse in their composition as the entire Jewish community in France were thus formed or strengthened in the southern half of France. There were in the first place the "natives," the Israelites who were either well rooted there or who had immigrated in the prewar years to pursue their studies. Second, there were the newcomers, French and foreign Jews, in both cases refugees who were forced to stay in the area by the German Occupation. They were not actually settled there: they kept pouring in waves from one département after another, "with the hope of escaping, at least temporarily, the repressive antisemitic policies enacted in some départements but not yet in others."[1] Often they were literally reduced to the status of "Wandering Jews," as Xavier Vallat would later label them.[2] "Yep," said a farmer, as he stood at the counter of the grocery store in Lauzès (which also served alcoholic beverages), "the Jews are a tribe just like the people in the traveling circuses."[3] What else could one make of a group of people roaming from one place to the next, if you had had no prior contact with them and had been told that they were responsible for all of France's hardships and suffering?

In the fall of 1940, it was already possible to differentiate among the various poles of attraction for Jews that were beginning to develop. In Toulouse, there were a large number of Belgians as well as a good many foreign Jews who did not really know where to go. In Vichy, the French Israelites were the dominant group, while in Lyon there were many Alsatians and storeowners who resumed their business. Those who had been lured to the coast by the mirage of departure by boat had rushed down to Marseilles. The more well-to-do took shelter in Nice or in Cannes. Many Jews from the Alsace region, on the other hand, had congregated in the southwest of France in Limoges and Périgueux.[4] But cities were not the only places where Jewish refugees gathered: there were also a good many villages, particularly in the southwestern part of France, that saw a large number of Jews stream in.

Because for most of these Jews it was unthinkable to return to the Occupied Zone, the various Jewish organizations, including the Central Consistory, the rabbi's office, charitable organizations, and associations of all sorts, set up administrative offices in the cities of Lyon, Marseilles, Nice, Montpellier, Toulouse, and Nîmes. The former center of Jewish life in Paris had been broken apart, and the new concentrations of Jews in the provinces were all being polarized. This was the first stage of the scattering of Jews throughout mainland France: two years later, it would result in a veritable fragmentation of the Jewish population.

In synagogues, prayers for France took the place of prayers offered for the republic before being tacitly relegated to an optional part of the service.[5] Indeed, synagogues, where they existed, came to represent the only element of stability in a rapidly changing world. For Jewish newcomers trying to get their bearings and looking for ways to eke out a living, the offices of the various Jewish organizations very quickly came to serve as meeting places. This was only the case, of course, for those who had no friends or relatives to lodge them where they had fortuitously landed.

The local inhabitants of these areas were often irritated by this influx of refugees, who were for the most part foreigners. Prefects for these regions often echoed the xenophobia that began to crop up here and there.[6] Money was sometimes enough to overcome the reticence of those who owned empty buildings but hesitated to house Jews in them. When Ernst Papanek first offered to rent the Montintin chateau in order to put up some 150 Jewish children, in many cases natives of Germany and Austria, that the Children's Relief Organization (OSE) was evacuating toward the south, the owner flatly refused. When he was finally offered a considerable sum of money—in fact, the entire budget Papanek had been given by the OSE[7]—he changed his mind. The most deeply rooted antisemitic stereotype was indeed that of the wealthy Jew. Léon Werth, who had moved to a little village near Saint-Amour in the Jura, relates what he overheard two farmer's wives say to each other. The dialogue occurred at a later time, but is revealing: "Referring to a refugee, the first lady said, 'He's a Jew.' And the other replied, 'No, he's not Jewish!' To which the first replied, 'Then why did he say he was rich?'"[8]

In reality, however, the vast majority of these Jewish refugees suffered from one of the basic consequences of their status as refugees: unemployment. They had to depend almost exclusively on the financial resources that they had managed to gather in their rush to flee, and these funds often dwindled rapidly. Even as early as the summer of 1940, one representative from American Jewish aid organizations estimated that there were some thirty thousand Jews in the Unoccupied Zone that would have to be supported entirely by charitable aid. Another twelve thousand would need to receive a supplement to their income just to get by. And these numbers did not include Jews interned in the camps.[9] Some local authorities seemed willing to come to the assistance of certain refugees, as was the case in Toulouse. In the Alpes-Maritimes region, however, there was absolutely no public aid available. This inconsistency can be attributed to the fact that defeat and the German Occupation had thrown France into a state of extreme disorder. In one case, a refugee had been officially released from a camp and was eligible for government assistance. When he applied for his benefits, however, he was instead once again locked up in a camp in another département. Meanwhile, as the specter of a general shortage of basic necessites loomed in the Southern Zone, measures that would reduce Jews to the status of pariahs were already being prepared.

An Antisemitic State

Because in the Occupied Zone the Germans took more drastic measures than the French authorities and applied them more harshly, Vichy's laws appeared only as a supplementary derivative of the Nazis.' In the Unoccupied Zone, where the French State officially maintained its sovereignty, the antisemitic legislation took on a completely different meaning. The law of October 3, 1940, known as the Jewish Statute, had declared the Jews to be different from other French citizens, and according to the law of October 4, 1940, foreign Jews were subject to internment at the mere discretion of prefects.

Three-fourths of those who had been removed from their jobs by this Statute were in the Southern Zone, as were a large number of doctors and lawyers who had been barred from practice because they were of foreign descent. And Jews who had been forced to sell off their business in anticipation or in application of aryanization measures keep streaming into the Southern Zone from the north.

The avalanche of restrictions and exclusions did not stop there. The next step was for the French state to create a special administrative entity that would be specifically charged with handling everything concerning the Jews. Unlike the preceding measures, however, the initiative came from the Germans. Under the direction of Dannecker, the *Judenreferat* had assumed the leadership role in the formulation and application of German policy toward the Jews in France. Its main purpose was to be effective and efficient. The best means of achieving these ends was by centralization, which would facilitate transmission and application of orders from those in command.

For these reasons, Dannecker thought it indispensable to create one central agency for Jewish affairs. Placed under French direction, it could assume a number of importance responsibilities. It was to keep tabs on Jews, exercise authority over Jewish property, organize internment camps, and inspect and monitor the mandatory Jewish organization that was to be created. It was also expected to oversee the application of the Jewish Statute and keep track of the pernicious effects of Jewish influence. Finally, it was to determine the orientation of anti-Jewish propaganda.[10]

This quite ambitious project would result in the creation of the General Commission on Jewish Affairs (Commissariat Général aux Questions Juives [CGQJ]) by the Vichy authorities on March 29, 1941. Its mission was threefold. First, it was to take the initiative for all laws and regulations concerning the Jews. Second, it was to keep the pace of the liquidation of Jewish property in step with the needs of the national economy. Finally, it was given the responsibility for the provisional Aryan managers of Jewish businesses. In all of these areas, the new agency fulfilled the

Germans' wishes while at the same time maintaining the appearance of a great deal of autonomy. And in point of fact, the text of this new law was not submitted to the Germans for their approval, nor were they consulted about the choice of the first commissioner, Xavier Vallat.[11] Vallat was a dyed-in-the-wool French nationalist whose anti-German tendencies might indeed have irritated the Germans. They could only be reassured, however, by his outspoken antisemitism. After all, on June 6, 1936, in the National Assembly, "the very heart of the state,"[12] had he not marked the arrival of Léon Blum as France's new premier in his own special way, by expressing his regret that France, "this old Gallo-Roman country [should be] governed by a Jew!"

In the Occupied Zone, it was hoped that, since it had been created by the French authorities, the new commission would act as a buffer between the Germans and the Jews, and thus result in a somewhat gentler treatment. This notion was to have a direct influence on the judgment of prominent Jewish leaders who had moved to the Southern Zone. Not everyone shared such an opinion, however. Raymond-Raoul Lambert, for example, pointed out that the "Commissioner for Jewish Affairs was located in Paris but placed under the direction of Berlin" and thus expressed his fear of a new Jewish Statute which would be harsher than the first one.[13] This pessimistic view was borne out by subsequent events: by June 2, 1941, Xavier Vallat had put the finishing touches on the new Jewish Statute that would soon take effect.

From now on, it became more and more difficult to avoid being classified as Jewish, as the criteria of both race and religion would be used more effectively to hunt down those presumed to be Jews. Religion was now considered a basic factor in determining who was Jewish from generation to generation. The criterion of race was used to trace the relationships of those who adhered to another religious confession or who declared themselves to be freethinkers. Race was also used to classify as Jewish a child who had been repudiated or never recognized.

Jews were now barred from working as middlemen, from professions involving financial activity, and from subordinate positions in public administration. From now on, according to the memorandum on the application of the new Jewish Statute that was sent by the Ministry of the Interior to the various prefects, "no Israelite, unless he should benefit from exceptions specifically provided for by the text of the law, could be employed in any way whatsoever in public administration or in any government-controlled public service or concession, nor even in any business receiving a government subsidy."[14] Those holding technical or subordinate jobs, such as "section leader, writer, office employee, and temporary office and service assistants, with no possibility of promotion, could continue working at their posts, provided they had received special honors, particularly in military service. These included the holders of the war veteran's card, those who had been cited for the Military Cross medal for their service in the campaigns of 1939 and 1940, those who had been awarded the Legion of Honor, war orphans and their guardians, and widows and children of soldiers who had died in the line of duty.[15]

Thus in application of the Jewish Statute of June 2, 1941, some 512 additional government employees were dismissed.[16] This brought the total number of government employees who had lost their jobs as a result of Vichy's statutes to thirty-four hundred.

Granted, the General Commission on Jewish Affairs had considered reassigning Jewish veterans of war who had previously held positions of responsibility to technical or subordinate jobs. There had even been an interministerial conference on the subject on November 4, 1941.[17] But the results were singularly meager: most government ministries had no positions to offer those who had fallen victim to the statutes, as they had been specifically told that such reassignments were in no manner a right, but at the very most a possibility for some individuals meeting special requirements. Vallat considered moving such government employees from one ministry to another. A high-ranking lycée teacher might thus have been given a job in the Ministry of Finance as a fee and duties clerk or as a district tax collector, for example. Similarly, a policeman would have been employed as a courtroom caretaker or a janitor at a university.

But Vallat's proposal was judged to be unacceptable by most government ministries. "I want to inform you right now that, in my offices, I intend to oppose the reassignment of Jewish functionaries who have been fired in accordance with article 2 of the laws enacted on October 3, 1940 and June 2, 1941, even if they fulfill the conditions listed under article 3 of the latter. On several occasions, you yourself have called my attention to instances of public commotion, particularly in the département of La Loire, caused by the presence of Israelites in the offices of the Administration of Basic Necessities and Supplies. It is consequently out of the question to assign any other Jews to posts in these areas or anywhere else." So wrote the secretary of state for Basic Necessities and Supplies in a letter to the General Commission on Jewish Affairs on December 9, 1941.[18] It was a typical response, and gives us a good idea of the prevalent attitude in high government administration.

It is true that the second Jewish Statute's article 8, which allowed for certain exemptions, had been expanded. It proved, however, to be a purely hypothetical extension. What was more, the other provisions had been refined and made more rigorous. And now that the French authorities had their own special commission on Jewish affairs, it was clear that they were determined to carry out a policy that would systematically exclude Jews from the mainstream of society. In accordance with governmental decrees on the application of the second Jewish Statute, soon only a small number of Jews would be allowed to practice medicine, pharmacy, and law, have careers in commerce and industry, or to work as craftsmen. The numbers of Jewish lawyers, doctors, architects, midwives, and pharmacists were thus strictly limited by a series of decrees issued between the months of June 1941 and January 1942. Other restrictions would follow. The number of Jewish students admitted to French universities was also limited by decrees dating from June 1941.

And that was not all. The mandatory census of Jews had now been extended to the Southern Zone by a French law that had been enacted along with the second

Jewish Statute. Those who did not comply with this census would face internment in special camps even if they were French citizens. The measure thus affected each and every Jew in the Southern Zone, as they all had to declare themselves to be Jewish. On June 21, 1941, just a couple of weeks after this measure was taken, the commissioner for Jewish affairs ordered that files be kept on Jews. These files were to be similar to the ones already existing in the Occupied Zone, as the latter "had proven their utility."[19]

On July 29, 1941, the prefects of the southern "Free Zone" received a memorandum from the national police. The document provided instructions for using the two series of six file cards that were to be filled out for each Jew registered. Along with the memo, the prefects were also sent a sample set of file cards.[20] An "individual declaration" had to be made by or for each member of the family, following a specified format. The Jews had to provide a considerable amount of information about themselves, their spouses, their offspring, and their ancestors. They had to include not only their family and given names, place of birth, date of entry into France, nationality, record of military servive, level of education, and address, but also their occupation and an inventory of their property.

Finally, in order to standardize aryanization policy in the two zones, the law of July 22, 1941, spelled out procedures for aryanizing all businesses, goods, and holdings belong to Jews. This process would be accomplished by provisional managers, monitored by the General Commission on Jewish Affairs. Their mission was to elimate "Jewish influence in the nation's economy." An ideological motivation thus complemented the French State's political and economic agenda. On the administrative level, the Vichy authorities sought to take over from the occupying forces wherever they could. Economically, they hoped to prevent the Germans from snatching up Jewish property and wanted to favor a greater concentration of French industry. As Henry Rousso put it, "in striving for its political autonomy, Vichy was not going to quibble about the price that the Jews would have to pay."[21] On August 25, 1941, the General Commission on Jewish Affairs issued a memorandum on the circulation of Jewish capital. Once again, this was a measure that took up where the policy of the occupying forces left off, since the German ordinance of May 2, 1941 had, in the Occupied Zone, frozen all Jewish assets and merchandise not yet under the control of an Aryan manager. For the Jews who had fled to the Southern Zone, but had left their financial resources in the northern Occupied Zone, it was now impossible to receive extra money for food, unless they obtained special permission. Such permission, however, was not regularly granted and had to be for a documented need.[22]

After November 2, 1941, it was no longer possible for a Jew to acquire a store without prior permission. On November 17, a new set of regulations restricted the Jews' ability to purchase real estate, as any such property they had could be "aryanized." Other regulations issued on the same day barred Jews from dealing in insurance, shipping, livestock, paintings, and antiques.[23] From month to month, the number of jobs that Jews were authorized to hold kept dwindling down almost to zero. In the fall of 1941, to ensure that all these regulations were enforced as rigorously as possible, the French State created the Police for Jewish Affairs (PQJ) for both the Occupied and Unoccupied Zones. This special force was first placed under the authority of the Ministry of the Interior, and later under the direction of the General Commission on Jewish Affairs.[24]

In June 1941, a new practice was begun: Jews were now getting expelled from one region into another. The first area to be thus purged was Vichy-Cusset-Bellerive, where 1,333 French and foreign Jews had joined some three hundred Jews who had already been living there before September 1, 1939.[25] The warrant for their expulsion was issued on June 3, 1941: it specifically barred them from living or even staying temporarily in the département of L'Allier.[26] In the early morning hours of June 12, 1941, the police served this warrant, swooping down en masse on all hotels, boardinghouses, and furnished apartments that housed people from outside the area. "Are you a Jew?" they were brusquely asked. With their resident visas confiscated, they were summoned on the very same day to a local elementary school. There they were instructed to sign a paper indicating their agreement to leave by a specific deadline and were ordered to leave the Allier département within four days.[27]

Relocation, however, was highly problematical, as the départements along the Mediterranean coastline as well as the départements of La Savoie, La Haute-Savoie, L'Allier, and Le Puy-de-Dôme were off-limits.[28]

A special commission on resident visas was set up in order to examine the cases of those who appealed this decision. Most of the appeals were rejected: the more fortunate were granted a bit more time to comply.[29] A few months later, the prefect for the Limoges region also decided "to purge the city of Limoges of all the foreign Jews living there." To this end, he instructed the Police for Jewish Affairs to "conduct the needed review of the resident status" of the people concerned.[30] A special inspector from the prefect's office was assigned to help in this task. The result was a series of investigations, solemnly labeled "reviews of the resident status of foreign Israelites residing in Limoges in view of eliminating the problem of overpopulation." The conclusion of such investigations was often that A or B did not have any good reason to live in Limoges, that they could afford to find another place to live, and that their departure would free up an apartment for someone else.[31]

In some cities, all foreign Jews were summoned individually to the office of the prefect and ordered to report to a center for house arrest. Such was the case in Aix-les-Bains before March 15, 1942.[32] On June 2, 1942, it was announced by the press in the Clermont-Ferrand region that all "Israelites who were French citizens having come to Clermont-Ferrand and its outskirts after January 1, 1938" were required to gather their identity papers and report to the Special Office of Police Supplies between June 5 and June 10. On the following day, June 3, the "foreign Israelites" received a similar summons ordering them to report to the same place. Once they showed up, they were told in no uncertain terms that Admiral Platon, a secretary of state in the Vichy government, had decided to expel them from the administrative region of Clermont-Ferrand, which included the départements of L'Allier, Le Puy-de-Dôme, Le Cantal, and La Haute-Loire. Some two thousand people were affected by this "removal decision." Only a tiny number of students and government employees allowed by the Jewish Statutes, namely, those who were disabled war veterans or war orphans, were granted exemptions.

A memorandum issued by the Ministry of the Interior on April 18, 1942, rounded out the measures designed to monitor and control Jews. It established a special set of rules about declaring a change of residence. Specifically, it required Jews to come to the city hall or the police office in the place where they arrived in order to declare any change of residence for more than thirty days. Those who did not comply with this order, be they French citizens or foreigners, would face being interned in a camp or placed under house arrest.[33]

Foreign Jews were living under the constant threat of such sanctions. According to the law of October 4, 1940, a simple decision by the prefect for the département in which they resided could send them to the internment camps or place them under house arrest. The Ministry of the Interior assumed responsibility for the Le Vernet camp, which was designated for the detention of individuals who threatened public order. It also took over the semipunitive Gurs camp. It was there that 6,504 Jews who had been expelled by the Germans from Baden and the Palatinate on October 22, 1940, were immediately interned. The Ministry of the Interior also took over the camps at Bram, Argelès, and Saint-Cyprien, which were intended to house Jews, and the camp at Les Milles for foreigners seeking to leave the country.[34]

During the first few months of the war, the French Republic had already put those it considered a threat to its security in such camps. Now, under Vichy's French State, they would hold as many as forty thousand Jews by February 1941.[35] This number did subsequently go down, but only because the means used to monitor foreign Jews were diversified. On the one hand, a number of social assistance centers were created upon the initiative of Jewish aid organizations. On the other, a law dating from September 27, 1940, required all foreign males between the ages of eighteen and fifty-five and "in overabundance in the national economy" to be placed in the Foreign Worker Units (Groupements de travailleurs étrangers [GTE]). These units, which would later be referred to first as "Palestinian" and then later as "homogenous" platoons, were composed of able-bodied men chosen by screening commissions in the camps and of Jews taken at random in police roundups. Altogether, they took in as many as twenty thousand Jews.[36]

Foreign Jews were thus highly vulnerable to arrest and detention. It could be suddenly decided, for example, that a proper celebration of May Day required that foreign Jews supposedly responsible for the black market be arrested. Official publications had long used such manipulative associations. Such was the case in the far-reaching operation carried out between the end of April and July 5, 1941, in the départements of Les Alpes-Maritimes, Le Var, and Les Bouches-du-Rhône: scores of foreign Jews were interned in the camps and several hundred were placed under house arrest.[37] Vichy's laws pushed all Jews to the margins of French society. Those who could not boast of several generations of French citizenship in their families were placed in the most precarious position.

Official Commentary and Propaganda

There was no lack of explanations offered to the general public about this array of laws that was having such a profound impact on lives of Jews in France—the collaborationist press saw to that. In addition, however, the Quai d'Orsay, seconded by the General Commission on Jewish Affairs, provided official commentary that justified the various provisions of the Jewish Statute and loudly proclaimed that they were of French initiative. One government declaration preceding the publication of the first statute explained that the Jews and certain foreigners "had taken advantage of our hospitality and contributed in no small way to our defeat":

> Jewish influence has infiltrated our society little by little and has in the end become deleterious. Observers on all sides agree that their activity over the course of recent years, during which they were largely in control of public affairs, has been highly negative. The facts are there and demand a response from the government, which must take on the painful task of putting France back on its feet. . . . The disaster that we have experienced has placed us before the obligation to consolidate the strengths of the French people whose characteristics have been established by a long hereditary process.[38]

"One of the things that had to be done to get France back on track was to remove Israelites from a certain number of professions that allowed them to exert what all have seen to be a deadly influence on public administration, youth, and public opinion." Such was the explanation provided to France's ambassador in Washington so that he would be able to explain to the United States the rationale for the new legal measures taken against Jews.[39]

Local newspapers took it upon themselves to stress that the Jewish Statute reflected a calm, moderate approach. "This is a dispassionate measure that in no way repudiates the ideal of humanism that has always inspired France," commented *L'Eclaireur de Nice*.[40] One of the most eminent members of the Central Consistory, General Boris, wrote to Marshal Pétain on November 10, 1940. He protested that the "virtually official comments" that had accompanied the statute along with the reports published by the minister of foreign affairs formed a kind of outline of the government's motives and "made the content of the measure even more cruel."[41] Chief Rabbi Isaïe Schwartz remarked that "the commentaries were even more horrible than the Statutes."[42] In any case, these efforts to "explain" the Jewish Statutes to the public did nothing to restrain those who added the insult of "moral humiliation" to the injury of "material damage" that the statutes inflicted on the Jews.[43]

From the perspective of history, one can indeed point out that official propaganda emanating from the French state remained relatively discreet before the summer of 1942. No particular jingle was heard on the radio, no posters were put up by the Vichy government, and not one word against the Jews was pronounced in the speeches delivered by Marshal Pétain. However, when Pétain attacked the Communists or the "trusts," official commentary interpreted it to mean the "international Jews."[44] The standard stereotypes of the Jews depicted them as the antithesis of the "new man" touted by the National Revolution and its attendant propaganda. The new set of laws had confirmed that Jews were "by definition" excluded, and Marshal Pétain had given them his official sanction. Moreover, Jews were the target of an unrestrained barrage of propaganda coming from German-financed fronts. There was no need to add anything: the message was clear.

Finally, there was the crass antisemitism voiced by an institution that was fundamental to the new regime, the Legion of Veterans. Over the waves of Vichy's radio network, the legion devoted a daily program to antisemitic and anti-Communist propaganda.[45] The Jews were blamed for the defeat, as it was Jews such as Léon Blum who had supposedly sabotaged the technical preparation of the armed forces, while others, such as Georges Mandel, were charged with goading France on to war. And had it not been the Jews' individualism and their tendency to exclude others that had undermined "the moral foundations of the French family?" These broadcasts were produced and rebroadcast by regional stations in Lyon, Nîmes, Toulouse, Marseilles, and Antibes.

At a time when basic foodstuffs were in increasingly short supply in the Southern Zone, how was the French public supposed to interpret the notices in the newspapers announcing that, due to the negative effects of the black market, measures designed to remove Jews from large urban centers were under preparation?[46] How could the general public be expected to perceive the heavy-handed association of all Jews with unassimilable foreigners and recently naturalized citizens, which was prevalent in certain local newspapers? Take the Catholic newspapers in the département of L'Aveyron, for example, which increased their number of subscriptions twofold between September 1939 and November 1942. Their articles adamantly denounced Jews as unassimilable parasites and blamed them for the defeat and all the other hardships and suffering that the French had to endure.[47]

In addition to all that was the "information" circulated by the General Commission on Jewish Affairs. General Commissioner Xavier Vallat provided to the press the most fanciful statistical data on the Jews in France. His purpose in releasing all these figures was to prove that "the problem that France faced was that of the concentration of Jews, which was against France's national interest in a number of domains."[48] Vallat made such releases on several other occasions: each time, he aimed to justify laws enacted for the "general interest," laws that were not promulgated in a spirit of hatred, but that constituted "simple defensive measures"[49] seeking only to give Jews "their rightful place in French society."

At the time, "France" was the unoccupied Southern Zone. Certainly, people supposed that those in government were under heavy pressure from the Germans. But the Germans were *not* there, and that explains the discrepancy between the occupied Northern Zone and the South of France. In the Northern Zone, French determination to stand up to the virulent racism of the Germans could be gauged by reactions in society. In the Southern Zone, such determination could be measured by analyzing the laws enacted by Vichy. This set of laws, however, spared not one single Jew and was of strictly French origin. The Jews themselves nevertheless looked for the marks of change in French society to gauge their changing status.

The Contradictory Messages from French Society

"In social life," remarked one observer in the summer of 1941, "Jews are given the same reception as before. At first, their acquaintances offer consolation, telling them not to worry and that everything will work out all right. Soon, nobody even mentions it."[50]

And in fact, it was something that people did not talk about outside their circle of close friends. This is confirmed in the following remarks by Raymond-Raoul Lambert. "On an individual basis," he wrote, "people are still friendly to the Jews, but public opinion remains indifferent to the large-scale problem. . . . At present, France is apathetic. Under this highly authoritarian regime, people no longer enjoy any individual freedom; instead, they think only about the question of supplying their everyday needs, which is becoming more difficult day by day."[51] These observations are borne out by the fact that most diaries kept by people on all sides rarely make mention of the Jewish Statute.

Was this a matter of indifference, apathy, or inertia on the part of a public that had been overwhelmed by a crushing defeat and had blindly latched on to the mythified, savior image of Marshal Pétain? Or was the public acquiescing to measures that largely fulfilled its own wishes? The question remains unresolved.[52]

The key to understanding this confrontation between Jews and French society lies in the very contradictions that seem to characterize it. There was on the one hand a widely shared indifference to the plight of the Jews, which would suggest a total incomprehension of what the situation entailed for the Jews in France and which would also explain the public's silence on the matter. On the other hand, personal relationships remained in general as friendly as they had been before the Occupation, even though the new political context allowed grassroots antisemitism to express itself freely. On the whole, then, there was a total dichotomy between the domains of public and private, collective and individual.

The primary concern for people in France was to make sure they could supply their basic needs and to overcome the trauma of the defeat: Jews were the last of their worries. If they had been questioned, they probably would have condoned the measures that were said to be vital to the reconstruction of France. When face to face with the situation of a Jewish family hit by the statute, however, they were moved to sympathy and, at times, outrage. A large number of them would have doubtless subscribed to the formula that Marie-Thérèse Gadala borrowed, when writing these words in Vichy: "I am anti-some-Semites."[53] The quip was written in a personal diary containing many criticisms of the repressive policy toward the Jews.

Such dualism can be found at every level. It characterized relations between the president of the Central Consistory and Marshal Pétain from the very beginning. On the basis of his many cordial meetings with Pétain, Jacques Helbronner had gotten the impression that he enjoyed considerable support at Vichy and that there were a number of faithful allies their that would speak up when the time would be right. But Pétain carefully refrained from telling Helbronner that he (Pétain) had been personally involved in writing the Jewish Statute. It was he who had insisted on completely eliminating Jews from the Ministry of Justice and from the Ministry of Education.[54] Helbronner had been told that it had been a handful of hotheads (Alibert, Ripert, Peyrouton, who had since been forced to leave the government) who had been the real authors of the Jewish Statute. And as soon as Pétain took things in hand again, he would surely see to having it abrogated.[55] It is this notion of several rival groups formulating Vichy policy that explains how Helbronner could adamantly condemn one part of the regime while at the same time condoning the protagonists.

"Our only hope lies in the fact that Marshal Pétain is the Chief of State. I have had numerous contacts with him, and he has given me the hope that one day we will receive reparations for the injustices that have been imposed on us,"[56] explained Jacques Helbronner to the members of the Central Consistory meeting in Lyon on March 16 and 17, 1941. In a later meeting with Pétain which only strengthened Helbronner's hope, the Marshal gave him his promise that he would not sign any measure before consulting with him.[57] When Helbronner told Pétain in no uncertain terms that the Jewish community in France was intent on having all special laws concerning the Jews revoked because they were "a blight on France," the Marshal acquiesced, saying that he was sorry that he had not been in a position to stand up to pressure from the Germans more than he had. Finally, Pétain gave Helbronner his word that he would be more liberal in granting the exceptions provided for in the special laws. Whether or not these words represented Pétain's true attitude, they nevertheless heavily influenced the course of action taken by the Central Consistory.

And here and there, people noticed a few signs that seemed to confirm Helbronner's interpretation. When, on December 15, 1941, the German Military Command in France announced that one hundred Jewish Communists and anarchists would be shot in reprisal for the terrorist attacks against Germans that had been carried out in the Occupied Zone, had not Pétain seemingly protested?[58] Furthermore, the Marshal's military chief of staff, General Campet, had explained to Helbronner's personal secretary, attorney Robert Kiefe, that Pétain had sent the Germans a written protest that was much stronger that the one published in the press: the Germans had obliged him to publish only a "watered-down version of the press release."[59] Further, "Vichy's quiet disagreement with the Germans is in a certain sense quite revealing, since this is the first time that we have heard such comments, especially when Jews are concerned." Such was the remark made in the diary of a Polish journalist, who, while recording a long series of antisemitic statements, was struck by these words of protest.[60] Those worried by this "pro-Semitic" laxism were doubtless reassured by Xavier Vallat's words on Vichy radio on December 20, 1941. The measures enacted against the Jews were defensive measures, he reiterated: they were aimed at preventing the Jewish race from carrying out its plan to dominate the world.[61] French authorities seemed to be sending highly contradictory messages to the public.

Moreover, the apparently warm and friendly attitude toward the Jews was displayed not only by Marshal Pétain, but also, to take one example, by the prefect of the Rhône region. When Jacques Helbronner came to announce that the Central Consistory planned to install its headquarters in Lyon, he was treated cordially and granted a meeting with Xavier Vallat. Raymond-Raoul Lambert also received a warm expression of friendship from his former superior in the army, Commander Pascot, who was now assigned to the General Commission on Sports.[62] At the time, he was well aware of the limits of such personal gestures, even though this awareness would not last. A few months later, when he was received "with affection" at Vichy, his optimism would be restored.[63]

Examples of such gestures of goodwill and expressions of kindness coming from leaders of the French State abound. Take the case of Joseph Barthélémy, then minister of justice. On the one hand, he gave warm, friendly assurances to William Oualid, a member of the Central Consistory who had been his colleague at law school in Montpellier. In an article dating from April 1, 1941, however, he wrote that although "he was heartbroken when [he] thought of so many tragic individual situations," he remained convinced "that it was truly necessary to take measures, even unwillingly, to give surgical treatment to the French soul which was suffering from a disease that has led us to the situation we now find ourselves in."[64]

Prominent Jewish leaders were not always aware of the huge gap separating the two levels of social relations and were often misled by the warmth and friendliness that was displayed toward them, especially since they rarely were met with a flat refusal. Whenever they tried to intervene with French authorities, it was hard to pin down the responsibility for a decision. They were inevitably referred, albeit with courtesy, to another administrative authority who, they were always told, was the only one in a position to resolve the problem. When on April 21, 1941, the president of the Central Consistory requested that French Israelites be accepted as members of the French Legion of Veterans on the same basis as other French citizens, Xavier Vallat replied that he did not have the power to issue orders to that administrative entity. When on April 29, 1941, the chief rabbi asked that cinemas be banned from showing the film *Le Juif Süss*, Vallat explained that the information offices of the vice premier of the French State were in charge of the matter.[65] The same Xavier Vallat, seemingly shocked by Raymond-Raoul Lambert's description of conditions in the internment camps, protested to the latter that he had no power over the police.[66] And whenever Jacques Helbronner spoke with Pétain, the Marshal would invariably claim that he was not in a position to resist the pressure from the Germans.

What holds true for leaders of the French Jews concerning their relations with Vichy officials is also valid for Jewish organizations in their relations with the new institutional entities of the French State. It also applies to French Israelites in general in their relations with their regular interlocutors in French society. Their deep roots in French society made it possible, on a personal level, for previous relations to continue.

At this time, in 1941, Jewish war veterans were still accepted into the French Legion of Veterans. Supposedly, Xavier Vallat had even encouraged Helbronner to urge Jews to join this institution, one of the pillars of the new French State.[67] Certainly, Jews were hesitant to participate in an organization that put out such blatantly antisemitic propaganda: they would often say as much to the local head of the legion, who sometimes would give them his reassurances. They would enroll, but not without expressing reservations. "French Israelites are accepted into the legion on an equal basis with other French citizens, and that's the way it should be," wrote Louis Lehmann, who held membership card number 280150 in the Rhône legion, to the regional president of the French Legion of Veterans on September 1, 1941. "However, it appears that the legion systematically refrains from having commemorative ceremonies held in synagogues. . . . If I were to die tomorrow on the battlefield, . . . the legion to which I now belong would refuse to remember me." Lehmann thus requested that the regional president give the reassurances to which he and his fellow Jews were entitled.

The reply came without delay. On September 6, the regional president of the French Legion, Emile Roux, explained:

> Almost every day, I receive letters written in about the same terms as the ones you have used. . . . There are matters of general, almost international policy, that go far beyond the context of the legion.
>
> . . . While services are not held in synagogues, please know that in the hearts and minds of good French people, all those who have died for our country are revered equally and that in their sacrifice, there is no distinction among them, whatever their race or religion might be.
>
> As far as the fliers you may have seen posted on city walls are concerned, surely you observed that these notices were not intended for the Jews, but for Jewish powers, in other words the dreadful forces of money that have caused us so much suffering. In matters of general policy, it is inevitable that there are a few victims.[68]

Ambiguity prevailed. As a general rule, Jews who had been provided reassurances and sponsorship by a local president joined the French Legion "to serve France with honor in peacetime just as they had served during war." A few months later, they either withdrew from the organization, or, as was the case in Annemasse and some other cities, were ordered to resign. For a time, however, the fact remained that one of the bastions of the new French state had not excluded all Jews from its ranks, even though it loudly voiced antisemitic slogans. On August 31, 1941, the Israelite Worship Association of Nice even invited the prefect of the Alpes-Maritimes region to attend a religious service held in the temple in observance of the first anniversary of the French Legion.[69]

In Toulouse, it was the charitable works branch of the House for the Soldier, for the Search for the Missing in Action, and for Aid for Prisoners of War from the South of France that took the initiative in contacting the Israelite Worship Association and asked them to hold a religious service to commemorate those missing in action from both wars and to pray for the return of prisoners. When the ceremony was held on October 26, 1941, the synagogue was filled to the rafters with people: the mayor of Toulouse, among other local personalities, was in attendance.[70] The rabbi of Toulouse had in the most official way been invited to participate in ceremonies observed in the Protestant house of worship and in the Catholic church on the same day.

Jewish and non-Jewish organizations also continued their contacts on a local level. Groups of Israelite Scouts often met with non-Jewish youth groups. In Montpellier, for example, Rabbi Schilli, who served as head of the local Scout organization, reported that he had participated in various events, including a reception for Marshal Pétain and Lamirand (minister of youth), Saint George's Day festivities bringing together all Scouts for a dinner and a campfire, and a reception given by the Compagnons de France (Companions of France). He was also invited to attend the annual parties of various groups.[71] In a time when French Scouts were more prominent than ever, the groups of Israelite Scouts continued to play an important role.[72] It is certainly true that some unpleasant incidents occurred. For example, on August 31, 1941, at the legion's commemorative ceremonies, where various youth groups were in attendance, some members of the legion demanded that the Israelite Scouts leave. When the leaders of the other groups of French Scouts voiced their opposition to this demand, however, everyone calmed down and the ceremonies went on.[73]

Up until the middle of September 1941, Jewish youth were still accepted in youth hostels, though they were not allowed to hold any position of responsibility there.[74] They also continued to be incorporated into the new French State's "Building Grounds for Youth" program (les Chantiers de jeunesse). In the spring of 1941, Rabbi Samuel Klein, who was chaplain for youth, wrote a letter to Jewish youth participating in the program. Some four hundred copies of the letter were made and handed out by the leaders of the forty-two existing groups of Jewish youth enrolled in the "Building Grounds for Youth." Rabbi Klein's visits to the "Building Grounds" camps in two regions (in the Var and in Auvergne) made him optimistic: he was particularly pleased by the warmth and friendliness with which local leaders had greeted him.[75] Similarly, the rabbi of Lyon was invited to give a lecture on Jewish religion by the head of the "Building Grounds" camp in the Haute-Savoie region.[76] This invited lecture, which was to be part of a series of lectures on great religions of the world, was proof that Judaism was not uniformly despised.

Administrative authorities could at times also show a willingness to cooperate with Jewish social relief work. When the decree of August 11, 1941, severely restricted the numer of Jews allowed to practice medicine, the upper-level employees' branch of the unemployment bureaus in Lyon and Toulouse sent to the Jewish Children's Relief Organization (OSE) the list of doctors, surgeons, and pharmacists who had applied for unemployment benefits.[77]

And that was just one example. In seeking to carry out its aid programs, the OSE found a number of allies in the administrative offices of the French government. Such was the case in the Dordogne region, where an orphanage and a home for the elderly were established in buildings requisitioned by the prefecture. It was equally in the Dordogne region that the Minister of Public Health not only granted the OSE permission to create a mobile medical team, but also requested that all refugees (there were at the time some forty thousand French people who had been evacuated from the eastern part of the country near the German border) be eligible for its services. In the département of L'Hérault, the offices of the prefect and of the mayors of local villages were instrumental in helping a large number of Jews find jobs working on farms.[78] There was even a case of an inspector for the Police for Jewish Affairs who replied favorably to a request to open a nursery for Jewish infants in Poulouzat, in the département of La Haute-Vienne.[79]

However, the optimistic assessment of the situation that we glean from certain reports written at the time should be mitigated. In the first place, there is no lack of individual testimonies that, unlike the ones we have just cited, relate a very negative experience. Second, we must not lose sight of the fundamental reality of the situation. The Jewish Statutes were rigorously put into effect at every level of government administration, and we find no opposition to their application. The warm, friendly contacts cited were situated in a completely different realm. They occurred on the concrete level of individual human relationships removed from the world of the statutes. That is to say, such cordial relations were possible as long as there was no present or anticipated conflict with one of the explicit stipulations of the law, as long as there was no risk in ignoring the law, and as long as being friendly did not entail condemning antisemitic measures.

There was thus an ambiguity that made it possible for Jews to go on with their lives and even feel comforted by a smile or a friendly gesture—but that also made it impossible for some to perceive the gravity of the situation. Moreover, it should be pointed out that the kind, friendly gestures mentioned were extended mainly to French Jews. Some people felt sorry for them for having been confused with the Jews who had no county: while France should throw the latter category out, their thinking went, these French Israelites were well-integrated people who had simply had the misfortune of being born Jewish. Foreign Jews and naturalized French Jews whose national origins were still quite evident did not experience warm treatment nearly so often.

The Jews sometimes also wondered why such gestures of kindness were surrounded with such obvious discretion. There could be only one answer, they thought: "The French mind has been muzzled."[80] In June 1941, the president of the Central Consistory had acquired "the firm conviction, judging by public gestures made by the clergy and by contacts with the most eminent intellectual circles, that the most prominent groups of people in France are on our side, but cannot express themselves freely: they will speak out for us as soon as it will be possible." And so they latched on to the slightest nuances of language in a speech that might be interpreted as a condemnation of the fundamental ideology behind the Jewish Statutes. The rabbi of Lyon made a point of thanking Cardinal Gerlier for saluting, on the day of Pétain's official visit to the archbishop's church in Lyon, "[t]hese people who constitute the good people of France, whatever their race may be."[81]

Jews thus adopted an understanding attitude that Cardinal Gerlier did not fail to encourage: he hastened to inform the president of the Central Consistory, Jacques Helbronner, of the statement issued by Catholic cardinals and archbishops meeting in Paris on July 25, 1941. In this declaration, Cardinal Suhard voiced his condemnation of "all injustices, all excesses committed against anyone" and stressed the importance of "preaching brotherly love, the love of Christ which must be extended to all men."[82] Moreover, added Gerlier in his message to Helbronner, "We deliberately chose to give this message a discreet wording that would be the least likely to arouse hostile reactions in certain newspapers: we would have suffered as much as you from such a backlash. But we want to let you know what we meant in this sentence. Furthermore, you will agree that it is hardly necessary to spell it out." None of these statements, however, explicitly referred to the Jews or to the circumstances they now confronted.

On March 26, 1941, Pastor Marc Boegner broke with such discretion and wrote the chief rabbi of France, Isaïe Schwartz, to express the Reformed Church of France's friendship with the French Israelites and to condemn the antisemitic laws. In this text, metaphors, generalizations, and what could be understood between the lines were abandoned in favor of a clear denunciation, which was widely publicized in the Southern Zone. It was Jewish leaders, however, and not Pastor Boegner, who circulated the message, before the newspaper *Le Pilori* gave it public attention—and Pastor Boegner was more surprised than anyone about the matter.[83] On the one hand, the pastor's letter emphasized "the values that France has always defended: respect for the human person, fidelity to commitments made by the state, and the demand for justice." On the other hand, just how were foreign or recently naturalized Jews to take a declaration that did not fail to mention the "serious problem for the State caused by the immigration of a large number of foreigners, whether or not they be Jewish, and by a number of hasty and unwarranted naturalizations"?[84]

On April 12, 1941, at 8:25 in the evening, a message specifically addressed to French Israelites was sent over the waves of the BBC in London by René Cassin. "French Israelites," he told them, "you know that the French people are not responsible for the measures that our enemies and their collaborators have used to attack your human dignity even more than your material interests." In the same message, Cassin emphasized the importance of the "unity of France's spiritual families, [which was] its most valuable source of strength," and recalled that the Nazis, these "modern barbarians," were threatening "an entire civilization and every principle that could oppose their totalitarian domination."

French Israelites could take comfort in these words. On the other hand, however, not a word was said about the other Jews in France, those who had not been living in the country for ten centuries. There was only a vague allusion to the "bodies of the Zouaves and of the Jewish volunteers in the Foreign Legion" that "are still standing guard at Verdun and Carency, and shall stand their for centuries to come."[85] But who, outside of a small circle of well-informed people, knew that foreign Jews had had a most illustrious record of service on the battlefields at Verdun and Carency in the First World War?

Discretion also seemed to be the order of the day within the ranks of the budding Resistance movements in mainland France. In underground newspapers, there appeared an article or two protesting against the exclusion of the Jews. But it was only after the second Jewish Statute was promulgated in June 1941 that something more than vague objections were articulated. Within Resistance groups, as in other social circles, there persisted the general notion of the existence of a Jewish problem. In November 1940, Henri Frenay, the founder of the Resistance group Combat, had written a manifesto in hopes of rallying a greater number of militants to his movement. In this document, Frenay rejected the policy of collaboration with Germany and proclaimed his "enthusiastic support for the work of Marshal Pétain." Concerning the Jews, he added: "All who come to serve in our ranks shall be, as are those who are already with us, genuine French people. Jews shall be able to come serve in our ranks, as long as they have actually fought in one of the last two wars."[86] Created by Philippe Viannay and Robert Salmon (who was Jewish), the newspaper *Défense de la France* voiced its vehement opposition to collaboration and condemned the antisemitic measures. At the same time, however, it let itself fall into a sort of personal admiration for Marshal Pétain that at times smacked of antisemitism. And so it was that even in late January 1941, Philippe Viannay, referring to the problem of the presence of foreigners in France, denounced "the invasion of France by Israel or any other group of foreigners."[87]

There were nevertheless a few early signs of resistance to the antisemitic laws. In one city, fliers posted overnight in the streets denounced *Le Juif Süss* as "the Krauts' film."[88] There were also planned demonstrations against the showing of the film in May 1941 at the Scala theater in Lyon and in June of the same year in Bourg-en-Bresse.[89] It should be said, however, that the target of protest in these cases was the crass antisemitism of the Germans, and not the "reasonable" antisemitism of those advocating social and political renewal in France. It should be furthermore pointed out that audiences gave a long round of applause when the same film was shown in Marseille and Toulouse in May 1942.[90]

Grassroots Anti-Semitism

Anti-Semitic propaganda from official sources did indeed have an influence on the French public. One witness to the Dark Years stressed that antisemitic themes explicitly or implicitly bearing the stamp of the Vichy government had great resonance within the public. Small towns and villages seem to have been particularly receptive to such propaganda. In certain rural areas, some places closed their doors to people with names such as Lévy or Weill. In some cases, this meant that the only grocery store in town and even nearby farms were off-limits to Jews. In other places, the game warden reportedly warned Jews in the most public and solemn manner to avoid all contact with the rest of the population.[91] In yet another place, an insurance company suddenly refused to insure Jews.[92] In Aix-les-Bains, a delegation of people went to the mayor's office to request that he expel the Jews, who were blamed for the black market. However, an investigation into the matter established that the persons implicated were actually Catholics. The expulsion measure was canceled.[93]

One observer of the era noted that although people were starting to mutter criticism of the Vichy regime under their breaths, the spirit of protest vanished whenever the subject of the Jews came up; there was always a consensus of opinion against them. Storefront windows of Jewish businesses were in some instances shattered, as was the case in Vichy on October 16, 1940[94] and in Nîmes in late April 1941.[95] As in Paris, however, this sort of incident was more common during the summer of 1940: the situation tended to calm down in 1941. Anti-Semitic fliers, on the other hand, continued to proliferate: Jacques Doriot's militants and members of the Legion of Veterans saw to their distribution. They were posted in Nice, Cannes, and Antibes during the months of April and May 1941.[96] Elsewhere on the French Riviera, the Legion of Veterans' security force, whose antisemitism was particularly virulent, harassed and intimidated Jews. On several occasions, they lashed out at Jewish places of worship, interrupting the service, injuring worshipers, and profaning the sanctuary.

In the spring of 1942, the local section of Youth from France and Abroad undertook its own antisemitic campaign in Millau.[97] Apparently there was no lack of violent incidents in which a Jewish family peaceably sitting at a table in a café or restaurant would be attacked by some passerby who all of a sudden felt like insulting them. Whenever such an incident occurred in Cannes and Toulouse (and probably in other cities as well), the other customers, as a general rule, apparently displayed indifference. Nobody dared to intervene.[98] One morning in January 1942, some Jews in Clermont-Ferrand received a strange typewritten tract in a sealed envelope: "Sir, for the coming year, the French people advise you to leave their LAND. Other wise [*sic*], they will have no other choice but to carry out a vast POGROM. Long live Pétain, long live France, death to the Jews."[99]

The atmosphere was so gloomy for the Jews in the Southern "Free" Zone that a number of them who had fled Paris reportedly remarked that "here we can still go from place to place without having to fear that we will be arrested at any minute. But as far as the attitude of French people is concerned, we feel much more at home in France in the Occupied Zone."[100] The reason for this situation was that in the Unoccupied Zone, signs of antisemitism could not be attributed to the presence of the Germans.

The situation of the Jews in the southern Unoccupied Zone was thus characterized by inconsistencies and paradoxes. The laws of the French state had relegated them to the margins of society. Grassroots antisemitism was expressed openly and freely. On a personal, individual level, however, Jews (and in particular those who were French) often received expressions of understanding and friendship, albeit with great discretion. The crushing defeat and the omnipresent shadow of the Germans seemed to explain everything. People found allies in their own social circles. Finally, Jews in the Southern Zone could consider themselves fortunate when they compared their own situation to the problems facing those who had been interned in the camps or when they heard of what was happening in the Occupied Zone.

THE SHOCK FOR FRENCH ISRAELITES

The Shadow of the Germans and the Sacrifice for France

"I am intent on complying with the laws of my country, even when they have been dictated by the invader," wrote Pierre Masse, senator for the Hérault district and former government minister, to Marshal Pétain on October 20, 1940. In the same letter, he asked ironically if he should tear the stripes off the uniforms of his family members who had given their lives in service of their country.[101] At a later date, Raymond-Raoul Lambert also felt compelled to ponder the situation: he "kept telling [himself] that it was Germany that was calling the shots so that [he] could excuse this insult to a long heritage."[102] This dualistic notion of the Jewish Statute as a law demanded by the Germans but put into application by French law was by far the dominant perception at the time. Even as late as March 1941, the members of the Central Consistory meeting in Lyon on the sixteenth and seventeenth of the month presumed that "these laws bore the marks of pressure from the Germans."[103]

Some were therefore willing to accept the sacrifice that had been imposed on them: after all, they had in the past been prepared to sacrifice their lives on the battlefield. Max Hymans, who represented the département of L'Indre in the National Assembly, wrote the following words to Marshal Pétain:

> When I see that I am subject to the restrictions and exclusions of the law promulgated on October 3, 1940, I think that it has been imposed by the Germans. If these measures represent the means of a foreign policy designed to lighten the burden of sacrifices required of our nation, I am almost proud to offer my moral suffering to my country. If this statute were to remain in effect in the future, however, I would for the sake of France deplore an act that can only be compared to the revocation of the Edict of Nantes, whose consequences are still evident even three centuries after the fact.[104]

Another Jewish member of the National Assembly spoke of the same sacrifice: "I know very well, Mr. Marshal, that the ordinances enacted in the Occupied Zone were issued outside of your government and that the laws promulgated on June 2 were imposed on you." So wrote Alfred Wallach, former representative from the city of Mulhouse on June 24, 1941. And he asked Pétain to use his authority to stand up to German pressures and to remove "this shadow that hides the bright light of the National Revolution that will bring about a renewal in France." Wallach added:

> I declare to you, Mr. Marshal, that the French Israelites and in particular those that I have represented are still confident that better times will come: their patriotism remains intact. . . . I am certain that I speak for all of them today in expressing my fervent hope that the sacrifices required of them and the ordeal that they have to undergo will be compensated by the knowledge that they have alleviated their country's present hardships, and that this ordeal will be made easier to endure by the reconstruction of a new, great and glorious France, one and indivisible.[105]

Although Max Hymans was a socialist, he had, on July 10, 1940, voted in favor of giving Marshal Pétain full constitutional authority. Wallach had been an opponent of the Popular Front. Their letters differ in tone, but both blame the Germans, affirm their steadfast patriotism, and declare their willingness to make the sacrifices that may be required of them.

It was just such a willing sacrifice that Jacques Helbronner, a member of the State Council and then vice president of the Central Consistory,[106] expected from the members of the consistory meeting in Chamalières on December 2, 1940. He indeed asked them "all to accept silently the measures that have hit us, and to refrain from doing anything that might get in the way of the patriotic efforts undertaken by the chief of state to put our country back on track after suffering the worst defeat in France's entire history."[107]

That request is just another example of the general mind-set. Edgar Morin, who was also a French citizen but whose parents where foreign nationals, testifies to the same outlook. At the time, he acknowledges today, he was prepared to accept the notion of "the sacrifice of the Jews if that was what it took to save France, if the logic of History had determined such a fate."[108] The same was true for Léon Werth, who on December 9, 1940 sadly observed in his diary that "in order to build this France that [I hold] so dear, it was necessary for a number of people to be hanged along the roads of Brittany in the time of Madame de Sévigné. The people from Lorraine and the Jews are making the fabric of history as did those who were hung in Brittany."[109]

The sense that they were making a requested or required sacrifice for the general good was therefore widely shared by French Jews, irrespective of their previous political leanings. This sacrifice sometimes appeared as an expression of allegeance to Marshal Pétain, while in other instances, it gave rise to the idea that at this juncture in history, the Jews were being sacrificed for more pressing political and economic priorities. In each case, it was always tied to French patriotism as well as to another idea deeply anchored to the political attitudes traditionally adopted by French Jews: namely, the notion that their identity as Jews should never influence their political stances. "As a Jew, am I going to reduce the world to what will be convenient for Jews in tomorrow's Europe? Is my judgment going to depend on the fact that, for the last few weeks, I have no longer had the right to be marshal of France?"[110] asked Léon Werth, who had sought refuge in his village in the Jura. The same concern was also voiced early on by Roger Stéphane (Worms), who had joined the Resistance at the very beginning, when he learned that the Jewish Statute had been enacted. On October 6, 1940, he stated that he felt "humiliated only by the burden that would weigh heavily on [his] freedom of mind" and was shocked by the thought that, from now on, he would be suspected of "being an opponent because he was a Jew."[111]

As events progressed, such views of the responsibilities incumbent upon the various protagonists would change. Nevertheless, this notion of a painful offering remained in place for many long months. On May 30, 1941, just a few days before new measures were to be taken against the Jews, the leaders of the Consistory, drawing the lessons from the first Jewish Statute and from the various policies and commentaries that accompanied its enactment, focused their attention on the most serious matter: "All French Israelites join in asking the chief of state that, for the sake of truth and for the sake of their human dignity, the measures under preparation not be presented to the public as a governmental policy dictated only by reasons of national interest, but as a ransom demanded by previous pressures made on the government and as a sacrifice that will benefit all French people."

This time the confusion over who is really behind the Jewish Statute is deliberately being maintained. The primary consideration here, however, is the long-term necessity of integrating the Israelites into French society, even if it means making sacrifices. A delegation of war veterans went before the general commissioner for Jewish affairs, Xavier Vallat, to express their indignation. They handed him a text that ended on the following note:

> The fathers and the children of those who have died in battle, along with the survivors and those left wounded or maimed by war, declare through our voices that far from renouncing their allegiance to France, they are intent on adding their silent sacrifice of the present to the sacrifices they made in the past, in spite of all that they are now suffering.
>
> They thus hope to doubly deserve the status of being a French citizen in a future holding more justice and liberty, for they will never in their hearts abandon their French citizenship even if it is snatched away from them by force.[112]

Records of the discussions among the leaders of the French Jewish community in consistory meetings show that, by the summer of 1941, they doubt that the Germans are responsible for adoption of the statutes. They nevertheless continued to use and misuse this argument. In the first place, they wished to give their interlocutors within the French administration the opportunity to soften the anti-Jewish laws without losing face. Second, they hoped to save the future of Jews in France.

When the second Jewish Statute was adopted, and especially when the Jews in the Southern Zone were submitted both to a census and to the aryanization law of July 22, people interpreted these measures as part of the French authorities' efforts to bring their anti-Jewish policies in line with those of the Germans in the Northern Zone. The day after this law was published in the *Journal Officiel*, Jacques Helbronner declared that he was no longer going to try to intervene by talking to Vichy authorities. The declaration marked a turning point in his and others' awareness of the real nature of the situation. It did not, however, bring about a change in political strategy. On March 20, 1941, General Boris wrote to Jacques Helbronner: "Let us at least save our honor—and more if possible—with objections, formal requests, and written observations that will make our persecutors either admit that they are deliberately treating us this way or refer to pressures made by the Germans: this is a valuable argument for the future, if there is to be a future."[113] A dialogue with French authorities indeed ensued, though it was neither smooth nor cordial.

Objections for the Sake of Honor

> We felt . . . that the first duty of the Central Consistory, the only organization able to speak for French Jewry, was not to let any of the measures that have been taken against the Jewish community in France go through without voicing our objections. These objections have varied in tone, but have never been disrespectful. We have been increasingly adamant in insisting that we did not recognize the legitimacy of the laws to which we were being forcibly subjected. We believe that we have thus fulfilled our primary duty. There may be little or no practical outcome in the immediate future. Over the long term, however, these objections may well have a lasting future effect. We have tried to save the honor of French Jewry not for ourselves who as individual persons are transitory and perishable, but for history and for the many generations of our children. We have also tried to control the damage as much as possible. It is on this level that our political strategy has been the least successful, albeit through no fault of our own.[114]

These were the words used by President Helbronner in the fall of 1941, as he assessed the outcome of the strategy used by the Central Consistory and disclosed the objectives pursued through the tireless protestations made to the authorities of the French State. Signed by the most prominent leaders of French Jewry, the letters contested each one of the new legal measures taken against the Jews. They were sent first of all to the head of state, with a copy personally delivered to Cardinal Gerlier for his information.

On October 22, 1940, the chief rabbi of France, Isaïe Schwartz, issued a long protest against the Jewish Statute. He lashed out against the set of racial laws on which it was based and against the accusations of internationalism: "It is in the very nature of all civilized religions to be universal." He demanded equality before the law and endorsed the motto of Vichy's new order of things, "Work, family, country." "No notion could be dearer to our hearts," asserted Schwartz. He recalled the Jews who were heroes in the First World War and those died fighting for their country. Finally, Schwartz concluded, "Our response to this special law shall be one of unswerving devotion to our country. At the same time, we remain faithful to the belief in the one and only God and to the revelation of Mount Sinai."[115] Chief Rabbi Schwartz's letter was not even acknowledged.

On the next day, October 23, 1940, the chief rabbi of Paris, Julien Weill, assured Marshal Pétain that French citizens of the Jewish religion remained faithful to their country, "whatever the rigors of the new law may be."[116] In his response dating from November 12, 1940, Pétain emphasized the importance of obeying the law and spoke of the spirit of sacrifice that he expected from all his fellow citizens "whatever their particular circumstances may be."

The strategy of protest was maintained throughout the following months. On April 21, 1941, the emphasis on equality was at the heart of a new protest, this time sent to Xavier Vallat.[117] It demanded equal treatment for all French citizens, the inclusion of Israelites within the Compagnons de France, and equal treatment of all foreigners, whether or not they be Israelite. In addition, there was a repeated demand that antisemitic propaganda be curbed. On May 30, Jacques Helbronner lodged another protest with Marshal Pétain. On June 10, 1941, a delegation of war veterans went to complain to Xavier Vallat. Finally, on July 1, new objections against the Jewish Statute of June 2, 1941 were solemnly voiced.[118] There was, in the latter set of objections, particular indignation over the legal measures now authorizing the internment of both French and foreign Israelites in the camps.

In each of these protests, we thus see the same main ideas: recalling the great, fundamental principles that had made France what it was; affirming an unswerving patriotism illustrated by the many Jews having given their lives for their country; adopting an attitude of strictly legalistic obeyance and fidelity, but expressing indignation over the enactment of measures denounced as illegitimate. Certain protests were also concerned with finding manual labor jobs for those who had lost their positions because of the Jewish Statutes. Such job placement was also suggested as an alternative to internment in camps for foreign Jews: there was thus a convergence of interests among all French citizens, Jews and non-Jews alike, it was argued.

Responding to Antisemites

At the same time, an entire strategy of argumentation was developed to respond to anti-Semites. The leaders of the consistory presumed that objective information could produce the desired effect. And so to underscore all that Jews had contributed to the French economy, they drew up a list of industrial establishments founded and managed by Jews[119] and submitted it to Marshal Pétain, as he had declared to Jacques Helbronner that "the Jews had amassed a colossal fortune by practicing parasitical trades."[120] A study was immediately undertaken to counter this accusation. Solicited by the Consistory and its regional delegates, Jewish industrial leaders painstakingly described their rich professional activity and their contribution to the nation's economy. They provided a description of a wide variety of industrial activities, ranging from a cannery in Carpentras, a textile factory producing worsted wool in Reims, a cotton-twisting factory in Remiremont, a shoe factory in Benfeld in the Bas-Rhin region, to a honey-producing enterprise in Montfavet-Avignon, in the Vaucluse region. And so Helbronner was in a position to make the following comments when he sent this report to Pétain:

> The textile industrial plants in Normandy and in the East were founded by patriotic Alsatians of Israelite confession who wanted to remain French after the war of 1870. Among the personalities who have given distinguished service to the industries they created and who in some cases still occupy executive positions in their enterprise, we should cite: the Péreires, who began the railroads and the Société Transatlantique; Lazare Weiler, who founded and initiated the copper wire industry in France and who founded the wiremill plants in Le Havre; André Citroën, who became a leader in the automobile industry after having started a weapons-manufacturing industry from scratch in the middle of World War I; Georges Bechmann, chief engineer in the Department of Roads and Bridges who was put in charge of the defense of Paris in 1870, who founded the Nord-Sud company, who equipped Paris with its current water and sewer systems; Léon Ecker, who was at the head of the Thomson company; Henri Cahen, who was vice president of the National Economic Council and who helped develop the electrical industry in France; Raymond Berr, head of the Kuhlmann establishments, who became president of the Society of Civil Engineers; Alexis Aron, head of the company Forges et Aciéries [steel plants] du Nord et de l'Est, and who played a major role in the metal industry and in the councils of the Comité des forges.

This list "will prove to you that, contrary to the accusations made by the antisemites, the French Israelites are not just parasites who live off speculations on stock and commissions on other people's work," added Helbronner.[121] It was a remarkable fresco, but it did not seem to make much of an impression on Pétain.

A study of the number of Jews who had served in World War I was undertaken, followed by a study of Jews having served in campaigns of 1939 and 1940. Inspectors with the Police for Jewish Affairs did not fail to voice their suspicions. Wrote one inspector:

> It can be feared that the census of Jewish war veterans conducted at the request of the chief rabbi may be an attempt to assimilate all Jews to the minority who have been living in France for several generations and to those who have fulfilled all their duties during the most recent wars. In short, while this activity by Jewish organizations may not be anti-national, it should nevertheless be very closely monitored by special units such as the Police for Jewish Affairs.[122]

Finally, in order to "counter the false numbers given by our adversaries with numbers that are accurate, nothing more, nothing less," the Consistory undertook a vast study of the genealogy of old Jewish families.[123] Responding to a form that was used for this survey sent to him in May 1941,[124] the inspector general Jules Isaac, author of several famous history textbooks, sent back on August 13, 1941, a genealogical table going back to 1747.[125] And as would many others, Robert Aron plunged into research about his ancestors and accumulated a stack of documents on the subject. Such efforts to draw up family trees occasioned an intense correspondence between many Jews. Letters—sometimes entirely devoted to this one subject—were first exchanged within families in an attempt to track down a missing ancestor. People sent large number of inquiries to various archival sources to check on a birth date or to substantiate some point of doubt. They exchanged information about such and such genealogist who had proven to be particularly helpful in drawing up the family tree that was expected by itself to refute the allegations made by the antisemites.

Among these genealogical experts, Rabbi Ginsburger, father of Pierre Villon, was doubtless the most often solicited. He put his vast knowledge of the Jews in Alsace to use in serving those who were feverishly tracking down their French ancestry. People constructed wonderful family trees. They were sometimes drawn without much skill, with the names and titles of various collateral relatives rather clumsily aligned on paper. In other cases, there were highly sophisticated trees that must have required many long hours of effort and research.

Pierre Vidal-Naquet describes the search conducted by his father,[126] who looked

> not only into family papers, but also in the homes of his cousins, including the elderly unmarried Vidal-Naquet women, who had been elementary school teachers in Montpellier, and especially into the home of Georges Alphandéry, a beekeeper in Montfavet in the Vaucluse area, who collected documents and autographs. In Bordeaux, in Montpellier, and especially in Carpentras, Lucien Vidal-Naquet sought information from archivists and from the curator of the Inguibertine Library. Copies of certificates of birth, death, and circumcision, along with all sorts of other documents, came pouring in by the hundreds.[127]

Pierre Vidal-Naquet, who is a historian, also lets us in on one of the secrets to the success of this search. Granted, it was conducted in response to an explicit request from the Consistory, and its purpose was certainly to refute official propaganda by proudly displaying a number of French-Jewish dynasties. But in addition, it also made it possible for a large number of French Israelites to find comfort by delving into the roots of their identity. After a trip to Provence, Lucien Vidal-Naquet spoke of "the invigorating bath, since [he] had found roots in a town that [he] had not known but where [his] family had struggled to live and now rested in a modest cemetery." And he added: "'The ashes of the dead are what makes one's homeland,' said Lamartine. I have the assurance—or the bitter knowledge—that these ashes have also been made from the remains of family members."[128] Doubtless there were considerable psychological benefits for each of those who set out to reconstitute the family tree.

In addition to these efforts to prepare a counterpropaganda effort, in-depth studies were conducted, covering all aspects of Jewish history and culture, and including not only the contribution of Jews in all fields but also the attitude of eminent French intellectuals toward the Jews. There was also an analysis of contemporary issues concerning the so-called Jewish question in France and throughout the world. Jules Isaac, Aimé Pallières, Robert Aron, Raymond Lindon, Henri Hertz, Philippe Erlanger, Louis Halphen, Jacques Biélinky, and many, many others lent their talents to this effort and wrote some sixty monographs on these subjects. All of these studies were supposed to serve as the foundation for the strategy of discreet intervention that had been adopted and that was intended to secure the repeal of the antisemitic laws.

Instructions to Obey

It was also by basing their arguments on such indisputable facts that Jews could—as they were compelled to—respond with dignity to antisemitic allegations. Such was the message contained in the pastoral letter read during the festival of Hanukkah in the winter of 1940.[129] Report after report was written in the research office of the Central Consistory in order provide adequate responses to everyone confronted with antisemitism.[130]

Particularly significant, however, are the instructions given to Jews and printed in a memorandum intended for wide distribution among both Jews and non-Jews. These instructions were an attempt to put into practice the basic notions we have already seen: they provided a reading of the events that were unfolding, expressed concern for preserving the future, defended a high sense of dignity and honor, and reaffirmed unswerving patriotism in the face of all government measures:

> You do not have to accept any of the things that have placed you outside of the set of laws that apply to everyone else. But however bitter you may be, summon your love of a France that shall always remain generous and free and comply as usual to the obligations placed on you by the laws, rulings, and regulations of the French government.
>
> Do not hide the fact that you are an Israelite. You would not only expose yourself to severe sanctions in the likelihood that you should be discovered, you would also display a lack of courage and honesty in such an occasion, and this could cause great damage to the reputation of Jews in general, since your behavior would be exploited in hasty generalizations. . . .
>
> Live as modestly as possible. Avoid ostentation. . . . It is incompatible with both the preservation of our dignity and the respect for the suffering of those who are living in the squalid, overcrowded conditions in the work brigades and internment camps.[131]

The consistory thus displayed its concern for the image of Jews as formed in public opinion. The Consistory's literature stressed the violations of the law inherent in the Jewish Statutes, while at the same time appealing to Jews to remain in strict compliance with its various provisions: the goal was to deprive the antisemitic press of one of its main arguments. The Consistory also encouraged its constituents to respond to the stereotype of the Jew as a rich exploiter of others by maintaining a modest lifestyle. Such modesty was part of what was required of the French Israelites' solidarity with foreign Jews.

The general strategy of the Consistory was therefore for Jews to accept their plight with pride and to display the image of a community that maintained its dignity in the midst of great suffering. A long tradition of legalism deeply anchored in the experience of French Israelites contributed to this quixotic stance. The unjust set of laws had originated in a France that had been "battered and constrained." The implication here was that the Germans were behind all the hardships endured by the Jews. The France "that shall always remain generous and free" could in no way be blamed, since, as a "battered" country, it had to deal with its own lot of suffering. The Occupation and the measures imposed by the Germans were also "theoretically and initially" responsible for the antisemitic propaganda spread by the press, over the radio, and in cinema newsreels.

"That is one of the most painful and saddening aspects" of the new situation imposed on the Jews, declared the authors of a report intended to guide community leaders in their action. In their conclusion, they reaffirmed their unshakable love of France:

> We are not in a position to voice accusations and complaints; as long as two-thirds of French territory remains under enemy occupation, French Israelites will submit themselves to these measures that have been unjustly taken against them, however unpleasant they may be. . . .
>
> With a feeling of gratefulness to their country, a feeling that endures in spite of the ordeals that they have had to suffer, they proclaim their love of France and their unreserved confidence in its renewal.

On July 3, 1941, Chief Rabbi Schwartz sent out a pastoral letter reiterating these same "instructions and recommendations inspired by the love of our religion and our country": "In accordance with the council of the true Jewish tradition . . . let us turn more toward vocations involving physical labor and craftmanship . . . in order thus to convert the rigors imposed upon us into blessings. . . . The Jewish life is a constant call to sacrifice." Moreover, "the honor of Judaism commands us to comply with the provisions of the law concerning the census of Jews." Rabbi Schwartz explicitly condemned the abandonment of the Jewish faith and held up honor as the supreme value. Therefore, he continued, "if, in order to ease your conscience, you enclose along with the completed questionnaire a declaration expressing with moderation and dignity all the bitterness that you feel as a French citizen and as an Israelite, who could blame you?"[132]

Thus we can see that the instructions that Jewish leaders sent out to their constituents were completely consistent with the themes they used in their discussions with the authorities of the French State. Incidentally, this determination on the part of rabbis and community leaders to keep their followers cool and level-headed caught the attention of the French government's General Bureau of Information (les Renseignements généraux), which spoke of it in a report dated May 29, 1941.[133]

Jewish Public Opinion

Nowadays, analysts shudder when they see Jewish leaders placing dignity and honor before any reaction to the persecutions that we now know will ultimately lead to the death camps. At the time however, such was the widely shared attitude. Furthermore, the Central Consistory's stance seems to have been in harmony with the various shades of opinion existing within different groups of French Israelites: between the autumn of 1940 and the summer of 1941, their thinking followed a similar evolution. The promulgation of the first Jewish Statute in October 1940 had indeed produced a deep shock. After the initial period of uncertainty produced by the first statute, the census requirement and the aryanization measures had been expanded to include the Southern Zone and widespread plundering had ensued. Jews therefore came to realize that conditions in the southern Unoccupied Zone were generally the same as those that prevailed in the northern Occupied Zone. As a result, their relationship to France and to Judaism was seriously called into question.

At the request of the consistory, a survey of the situation of Jews in the Unoccupied Zone was taken by Israelite Scouts of France. The resulting report was filed on July 18, 1941. The responses gathered by the six delegates in charge of carrying out the survey provide an insight into the mind-set of the Jews and what they were expecting from their leaders. The most striking aspect is without doubt a state of shock, dismay, and confusion: Jews expected their organizations to inform them about what was really going on. They were anxious to get precise information, reliable instructions on how to act, analyses of the changing course of events, and indications on how to interpret each of the new measures coming out. After all, only the official, tendentious publications were available to them as they tried to make sense of the new laws that were totally upsetting their lives. And the situation would get even more confusing in the following months. Each time that a new decree or a new law would come out, their first concern was in many cases to grab a copy of the *Journal Officiel* and try to understand its full repercussions. This practice was so common that there were sometimes shortages of the publication, even in Vichy.[134]

Other responses to the survey give evidence of caution, wariness, and above all a very meticulous legalism: Jews generally stressed that they did not want to take any action without the consent of the government. They also emphasized the importance of avoiding the voluntary creation of a ghetto and displayed a strong interest in everything that related to professional retraining. We can thus see that determination to respect the law and adapt to new circumstances dictated the conduct not only of Jewish leaders, but also of a large portion of the Jewish population in general.[135]

And so the majority of them complied with the census requirement.

The Census

It was with the following words that Léon Werth recorded his trip to the prefecture on July 9, 1941, in his diary:[136]

> Thus Marshal Pétain and Xavier Vallat forced me to declare that I was a citizen of a Jewish homeland to which I really did not feel I had any ties . . . the most basic sense of dignity requires me to identify with that country. . . . And in that way, they think that they can force me to be a citizen of another country and to belong to another group. What an act of cowardice it would be for me to deliberate on the question as to whether or not I considered myself a Jew. If you insult my Jewish name, I am Jewish, passionately Jewish, Jewish down to the roots of my hair, viscerally Jewish. After that, we shall see. . . . I made my declaration at the prefecture, I cried out the word "Jewish!" as if I were going to sing the Marseillaise.

Certainly not everyone had such an invigorating experience of solidarity in declaring their Jewish identity in compliance with the law, but the general tendency was not to attempt to dodge the requirement. And so all went to make their declaration, some at the prefecture and others at their local city hall. A new division had appeared in these administrations: alongside the offices for "Weapons Permits" and "Authorizations for Public Dances," noted Raymond-Raoul Lambert, there was now an office for "Jewish Affairs. [137] Official forms for the Jews' declarations had been prepared and were waiting to be filled out. Some of the spaces on these forms were too small to contain all the information requested. There was not enough room, for example, for the list of university degrees earned by Edgar Fribourg, nor for the record of military service for another individual making his declaration. Still another individual did not find enough room to write down all the information that he thought necessary to provide about the services that he had rendered to France.[138] Information such as details about the French origins of ancestors, lists of military medals and decorations, and notes about the purely religious nature of their Jewish identity therefore had to be written on the back of the form in tiny letters.

In certain areas, such as the département of Le Gard, for example, the printed forms did not arrive in time.[139] As a result, the entire declaration had to be sprawled out over blank sheets of paper and the deadline for making the declaration was postponed. By July 31, however, mayors had received instructions to draw up lists of people known to be Jewish in order to hunt down those who wanted to avoid the declaration and also to give a wider publicity to the census requirement. The secretary-general of the police feared that announcements in the press, over the radio, and on publicly posted notices would not be sufficient, and so recommended that "in small communities, the municipal decree should be publicly proclaimed with the sound of a trumpet and a drum roll."[140] As for Maurice Kahn, who was bedridden, it was impossible to go to the police station. But never mind: he wrote down his declaration on notebook paper and sent it to the prefect. He was thus able to devote an entire page to his family, about which he concluded: "I belong to a French family that has honored France."[141]

This abundance of information nevertheless did not satisfy government administrative offices, who could not have cared less about the honor of the families in question and their affirmations of patriotism. Far from being impressed, one investigator sent by the General Commission on Jewish Affairs to the city of Annecy observed that 25 percent of the addresses given in the declarations were incomplete and that 60 percent of the declarations failed to specify the individual's occupation. Many of those who had put "French by family relationship" aroused the suspicion of government administrators, and most people had not signed their declarations.[142] In the département of Les Hautes-Pyrénées, fifteen hundred Jews responded to the summons ordering them to return and complete their declarations.

There were still a large number of omissions, and in order to locate the Jews who might have escaped their notice, the administrative offices of the prefecture referred to lists used by those monitoring mail.[143] The Police for Jewish Affairs considered taking another census as early as January 1942. They even designed a new declaration form that would make it possible to add political information to the economic data already gathered on Jews. The secretary-general of the police decided not to go ahead with the plan, as he already had in the works a new, unique type of identity card that would label its bearer as Jewish. This was in February 1942: it was in December of the same year that identity cards of Jews in the Southern Zone would be stamped with the word "Jew."[144] In the South as in Paris, an entire process was therefore set into motion. Those who had made their declation on notebook paper because the administrative offices were not adequately prepared were summoned to come back and fill out the official forms. Those "individuals identified as belonging to the Jewish race or presumed to be Jews by mayors and police agents" and who had not taken part in the census had their names sent by regional prefects to the Ministry of the Interior, to the main office of the police responsible for monitoring foreigners and the national territory, and also to the General Commission on Jewish Affairs.[145] These same individuals were then sent a letter that read:

> Monsieur, it has been reported to me that you did not think you needed to comply with the mandatory provisions of article number 1 of the law of June 2, 1941, which ordered that a census of Jews living in France be taken before July 31.
>
> You did not have the right to exempt yourself from such a strict requirement without having proof that you were not included in the definition given by the law of June 2, 1941. Specifically, in order to be exempt, you must establish:
>
> —that three of your grandparents belonged to a religion other than the Jewish religion;

—that if two of your grandparents are Jewish, you adhered to a religious faith other than the Jewish religion before June 25, 1940, and if you are married, that your spouse is not Jewish.

I urge you to send such proof to me before [March 10, May 20, etc.] I consider it my duty to call your attention to the severity with which article 2 sanctions the infractions of the law of June 2, 1941.

Yours cordially . . ."

Investigations were conducted. It only took eight days for the assistant director of the Commission for Jewish Affairs in Montpellier to find out that one of the individuals "presumed to be Jewish" was in fact "a persecuted Catholic": four of the "suspects" had in fact registered with the census in early November, while another woman had been in Switzerland at the time and had registered when she returned on October 20. Another "suspect" turned out to a non-Jewish Belgian national, while yet another had died in April. Others had registered with the census elsewhere, some in the département of L'Hérault and some in the département of L'Aveyron. One individual had gone to America on April 1, 1941. The whereabouts of nine others, who had perhaps left without giving an address, remained unknown, and registered letters remained unanswered.[146]

Accordingly, each regional prefecture drew up a list of "delinquent declarations" and made a point of sending it to the General Commission on Jewish Affairs. On December 31, 1941, the prefect for the département of Les Bouches-du-Rhône sent his seventh list of delinquents, which included sixty-three names. By May 27, 1942, some 402 delinquents had made their declaration at the prefecture for the Rhône region. Not all Prefectures proved to be so efficient. As for the General Commission on Jewish Affairs, it insisted that "there be a distinction between those who have presumably shown their unwillingness to comply with the law—and who must be sanctioned—and those who had a legitimate excuse."[147] The reasons for the delays were thus revealed: sometimes, there had been illness; in many cases, declarations had been made in Paris in the fall of 1940; there were children who had been included in the declaration of their parents; and there were prisoners of war who had just returned home.

While the signature was sometimes found to be missing from the census declaration, the letters addressed to Marshal Pétain and Xavier Vallat were all signed, and they expressed the same ideas: they registered protest against a shamefully unjust measure, recalled those who had sacrificed their lives on the battlefield, reaffirmed unshakable loyalty and unswerving patriotism, expressed pride in Judaism, invoked the ideal of a France that would never die, and, finally, stated their willingness to obey the law. "It is an honor for me to confirm for you two values that shall always remain indestructible for me: my French nationality and my Jewish religion," wrote Marc Haguenau to Xavier Vallat on July 31, 1941.[148] Although they evidenced a willingness to obey the law, these letters represented a strong protest against the very principle of the Jewish Statutes and they were imbued with dignity. But they were also full of sadness. "You said to the people of France: 'do not despair, do not be bitter, for you have not been betrayed or abandoned,'" wrote Madame René Lipmann to Marshal Pétain on June 20, 1941, adding:

> Alas! those of us who are French and who were born in the Jewish faith have indeed been abandoned. And nevertheless . . .
>
> My son was killed on June 5, 1940 in Foudrinoy, near the city of Amiens. He was cited for honor within his division. . . . In one of his last letters, my son wrote: "You must not count on me, my fate is too uncertain; my life belongs to France. I shall never turn back, I will fight until death. . . ."
>
> I have no doubt that this present situation is due to demands made by the Germans. But on the subject of these statutes, France is allowing commentary and propaganda that is hurting too many innocent people. Monsieur le Maréchal, on behalf of my child who has died as a hero for our beloved France, for this France in which I want to take pride, I dare demand justice for all.[149]

What we can sense welling up to the surface in this letter is "the bitterness felt by men who belong to France with every fiber of their being, who are steeped in its culture, and who are proud of its history," to use the words written by Paul David in a letter sent to "his friend" Peyrouton when the first Jewish Statute had just been announced by the press.[150] But it was a bitterness that did not diminish a fierce patriotism, and was sometimes given symbolic expression. Bernard Picard and Albert Weill both had a child after the enactment of the Jewish Statute: one called his daughter Francine and the other named his firstborn François. "Both of us wanted to prove that we were French in spite of the statute and that our national identity could not be taken away from us," wrote Picard.[151] Similarly, Raymond-Raoul Lambert named his daughter, born January 27, 1942, Marie-France, "a first name that symbolizing affirmation and hope."[152] And it was not by coincidence that M. and O.B., French Jews from Strasbourg, chose Francis Bernard as first names for their son, born in February 1940, and Nicole Marlyse, France as first names for their daughter, born in January 1942.[153]

As Bernard Bloc, a young scout from Grenoble, expressed it, such patriotism could even lead to sacrifice:

> With no consideration whatsoever for his Legion of Honor, his Military Cross or his citations, [my father] is going to be fired, his name will be stricken from the list of leaders of the French army, and he will be kicked out on the street, all because of this outrageous decree concerning the Jews. . . . I want to believe that, as much as you hated to do so, you had to offer up the Jews as a burnt offering to the Hitlerian Moloch, in hopes of satisfying his ferocious appetite. If such were indeed the case, Monsieur le Maréchal, French Jews would accept this humiliation with patriotic resignation and would be proud to suffer in service to our distressed country."

On June 20, 1941, a prisoner of war also wrote to Marshal Pétain, not at all to request that the exclusionary laws be abrogated, but to protest the way in which their causes and objectives were being presented. "Instead of all these phony excuses, to my mind it would have seemed more dignified for France if a government spokesman had stepped up to the microphone and, for the sake of truth, had delivered a speech that went as follows:

> My fellow French citizens of the Israelite faith, by decision of the powers that have defeated us and from which we cannot escape, I am sad to announce to you that even though you are all children of France on the same basis as your compatriots, you will all be persecuted. I know that in the past France said: "There are French who are Catholics, there are French who are Protestants, and there are French who are Israelites: all have the same duties and the same rights." I am also aware that immediately after the armistice you were officially told that your personal well-being and your belongings would be safeguarded. And today, with a heavy heart, I must announce to you that France is forced to go back on its world. I also know how much you are suffering in your human dignity to feel that you have been brought down to the level of third-class citizens, and, along with your children, to become veritable pariahs, despised by the masses whose heads are gradually held higher and higher. I am equally aware of the way in which you have been stripped of your property in the Occupied Zone, and of how you will be plundered in the Unoccupied Zone, and of the resentment you must feel toward those among your fellow citizens who shameless run up to take part in the feeding frenzy over your property. For in the end, the whole matter can be summed up by the attitude of "move-over-and-let-me-get-mine" that the Germans are encouraging. Nor am I unaware of the fact that most of you will disapppear as soon as you have exhausted the few possibilities that remain open to you, as you have not only been deprived of the fruits of your labor, but you have also been barred from working and earning a living. The only consolation that I might offer you is the following: imagine that all of you—men, women, and children alike—were soldiers and that you were sacrificed, for example, in a rear-guarding operation in an attempt to save the rest of the army. I suppose, moreover, that it is in this way that History shall judge your fate and exalt you. Take courage and persevere, there is nothing eternal here on earth.[154]

In the instances where such letters receieved a response, those responding remained on a totally different wavelength from those who had initially written. As evidenced by the following exchange of letters between one Jew and the General Commission on Jewish Affairs, administrative offices remained totally impervious to the appeals being made.[155]

This correspondence began in mid-June 1941, when G.H. wrote to the commissioner for Jewish Affairs and recounted the history of his family in the city of Colmar. The story went all the way back to the beginning of the nineteenth century. H. enclosed official documents testifying to the consideration his ancestors enjoyed from public authorities, and listed the prestigious capacities in which they had served. The response from Xavier Vallat was sent back to him on July 2, 1941: "The information that you have given me, in spite of all its interest, does not prove that your grandparents were Aryans." H. was outraged, and sent another letter on July 3, 1941: "I am quite surprised. I never attempted to prove that my grandparents were Aryans." And so, to avoid all confusion, he specified that his father had been a member of the Israelite Central Consistory.

We can similarly refer to the case of the retired artillery colonel E.H., an officer of the Legion of Honor who had been decorated with three citations. On July 31, 1941, he wrote to "Mr. Commissioner for Jewish Affairs":

> I have the honor, on behalf of my wife, whose maiden name was L.F., and myself, of renewing the declaration of religion that we made in October for the German authorities. As for the declaration of personal possessions, I also renew the one that I made previously.
>
> In doing this, however, I am intent on raising the most vehement protest against a measure completely outside of all common law and common justice, and moreover in violation of the constitution that still rules France. "All French citizens have equal rights." Now, my great-great-grandfather on my mother's side was born in 1750 in the Moselle region; his wife was born in Sarrelouis, which was then in France. My great-grandfather on my father's side served as a soldier under Napoleon and his son, my grandfather, was born in 1808 in Puttelange (Moselle region). Since the beginning of the nineteenth century, five members of my family have graduated from the Ecole Polytechnique and one from Saint-Cyr.
>
> I shall leave the conclusion to you and your spirit of justice. Thanking you again for your cordial reception, I send you my respectful greetings.[156]

On August 1, 1941, he received the following response: "I want to specify to you that you did not need to renew your declaration, as it had already been made in October. Only the declaration of your personal property was necessary, as at this time a more general declaration than before is required." And so pride in family origins ran up against the cold stone wall of bureaucracy.

In two months, some 109,244 Jews were thus duly registered under the census taken in the Unoccupied Zone.[157] Six months later, another statistical report stated that some 109,983 Jews had been registered under the census taken in the Unoccupied Zone.[158] The difference between these two figures is probably due to the first group of late declarations that were filed during these first few months.

Once they had completed this formality and placed the receipt for their declaration in their pocket (that is, in places such as Marseilles, where a receipt had been prepared; instructions sent from the governement made no mention of any receipt), the "declared Jews" no longer resembled other people in any way except outward appearance. Robert Aron describes "the long, worried faces whose eyes had the look of someone on the run who felt guilty even though he had done nothing wrong." Aron expresses his despair over an excommunication that had suddenly been made so concrete and palpable. In face of such an implacable fate, he felt shocked and dismayed, and was left dumbfounded and depressed over the abyss that now separated an apparently normal life from the feeling that he was "tied to unfathomable forces, foreign decisions, bound up in all his mental faculties, in his flesh, in his spirit, in his strength, in his feelings."[159] Léon Werth, who, as we have seen, maintained such a dignified composure, nevertheless felt humiliated "not by being a Jew, but by being presumed to be of an inferior nature because [I am] a Jew,"[160] even though he stressed the absurdity of such a feeling. "I should feel rich for having two worlds, but instead I am poor for having them," wrote Clara Malraux after having declared herself as a Jew at the town hall in Ambérieu. She had in fact hesitated before making her declaration, but for her as for others, it was a sense of dignity and the determination "not to deny who she was" that won out over caution.[161]

The number of those that Xavier Vallat termed "recalcitrant" remains difficult to assess. On the eve of the census law, the offices of the General Bureau of Information referred to a "veritable cabal to boycott it" that was being organized through the mail and in private conversations.[162] There was in fact no cabal or boycott, but some 4,000 to 5,000 Jews apparently did avoid the census requirement, according to one report filed at that time. M. Ducret, who was in charge of the office of Jewish files with the Census Bureau under the Ministry of the Interior, estimated that some 15 to 18 percent of Jews had not registered with the census, and criticized the way in which the census was carried out in most prefectures.[163] Wives and husbands of Aryans seemingly represent the largest category of those who had not complied.[164] Nearly 50 percent of Jews in the département of Le Puy-de-Dôme reportedly did not comply with the census requirement,[165] but that is probably a later estimate that took into account all those living on the fringes among the Jewish population—in other words, those who had come clandestinely from the Occupied Zone due to increased persecution or who had chosen to lead a semi-clandestine life at a later date.

Without the overwhelming presence of the Germans, it was easier to hide in the Unoccupied Zone than in Paris. The threat of incurring sanctions did not seem so great, and it was easier to blend in with the rest of the population, at least for those whose refugee status was not too obvious or who were already well integrated into groups of French people hostile to Vichy. Moreover, eight months had gone by since the census had been taken in the Occupied Zone: many people had lost their illusions and seen much more clearly the advantages of concealing their identity. In addition, those who had fled the Occupied Zone after having submitted to the census were much more aware of the pitfalls of making a declaration. Those who did not submit to the census requirement were sometimes denounced to the French authorities, who then prosecuted them in court. In the département of Les Bouches-du-Rhône, the first court convictions of those who had not complied with the census were made public in the press in order to incite other noncompliant Jews to make their declaration.[166] Those convicted had to serve between forty-eight hours and three months in prison. In other cases elsewhere, some were acquitted, some were fined, while others—foreign Jews—were interned in the camps.[167]

A New Relationship with Judaism?

For a large number of Jews who up until that time had not been directly affected by the antisemitic laws, the census requirement for the Unoccupied Zone led to a new awareness of themselves. Such was the case for Claude Lévy, a young lycée student at the time who had become aware of his identity as a Jew during the very first months of the Occupation, when he heard an antisemitic radio program in Limoges. Lévy describes the reaction that was triggered in him when his family, who had recently moved to Lyon, was summarily ordered to register with the census. They had not thought it wise to avoid the summons: after all, they thought, what risk did they run, as they had "French children"! It was at that moment that Lévy began looking for books that could teach him more about this Jewish identity, which had previously meant so little to him; he went to the municipal library and checked out all the works about the Jews that he could find. What he found in these books held a number of surprises for him: on the one hand, he discovered the antisemitic writings of the Tharaud brothers; on the other, he took a momentary interest in Zionism. Similarly, Denise Siekierski had previously been more comfortable with the Unionist Scouts: after the anti-Jewish laws of June 1941 were enacted, she joined the Israelite Scouts.

For some, showing solidarity with Judaism now that it was being persecuted meant joining forces with the Consistory. Raymond Lindon expresses this view better than anyone. On May 27, 1941, just before the second Jewish Statute was to be made public, he wrote a letter to the president of the Central Consistory and requested the president to accept his membership application. Lindon explained that he was not coming back to a religious practice that he had abandoned, but was joining the consistory "in order to defer to the memory of [his family] and to show [his] attachment to the freedom of conscience that had been violated."[168] And Georges Cahen wrote on December 2, 1941, "I am with Bergson, with the persecuted and against the persecutors. I therefore declare myself a member of the worship association from which I had deliberately distanced myself."[169] There were of course others who, hoping to avoid the "intellectual ghetto" in which Vichy's antisemitic laws tended to confine them, went so far as to ban the subject of Jewishness from family conversations.

Some Jews, hoping to escape from the condition of pariah to which the new laws had reduced them, gave in to the temptation of converting to Catholicism. But this strategy was illusory: those who had formulated the laws had taken care to specify a cutoff date, June 25, 1940, after which a conversion would no longer allow a person to be exempt from the rigors of the Jewish Statute. Rabbis became worried about this matter: immediately after the second Jewish Statute was enacted, the chief rabbi of France, Isaïe Schwartz, learned that such conversions were becoming more and more common in Marseilles, where they were being encouraged by people going door to door. The newly converted apparently had thought that they would be like the Marranos, the Spanish Jews who had secretly continued to practice Judaism after having been forced to convert to Catholicism.[170]

As pointed out in a report filed with the General Bureau of Information, "it should be observed that since the publication of the last decree, there have been many conversions to Catholicism, moreover dimly viewed by the majority of Jews."[171] So while the temptation was there, the consensus seemed to be to reject it.

It is obvious, at any rate, that the majority of Jews felt that conversion to Catholicism represented a renunciation and did not approve of using the Marranos as an example to legitimize it. Suzanne Hamon, who refused her husband's proposal to have their children baptized, offered a singular reason for her attitude: such a gesture would be disrespectful toward "our Catholic friends," she told him. "It would be improper to transform what to them is a sacrament into a purely opportunistic administrative expedient."[172]

The most frequent candidates for such conversions were without doubt the children of mixed couples who thus hoped to place their children out of danger. Antedated, fake certificates of baptism were sometimes thought to be safer than a true conversion, which would have come too late to be "effective." Such was the observation made by Clara Malraux, who had her daughter baptized "in order to shelter her" from harm, but who felt more reassured when her husband (from whom she was separated at the time) had a fake certificate of baptism sent to her.[173] The wide range of attitudes toward conversion that we can find among Jews is certainly a reflection of different personalities, but also results from the varying nature of their individual relationship with Judaism.

Jewish public opinion was indeed in a state of shock. "I am a semi-exiled person who has lost her place in society," wrote Andrée Brunschwig. "I am nothing more than a second-class citizen in the land where I was born and where my family is buried," wrote the attorney Lucien Vidal-Naquet.[174]

"From a spiritual point of view, French Judaism has now been paralyzed. . . . From an economic point of view, it is the total asphyxiation [of Judaism]."[175] And so we see the French Israelites facing the threat of being interned in the camps if they did not comply with the provisions of the Jewish Statutes. Nationality, "even French nationality, is thus no longer anything but an accessory without value or consequence." The extension of the aryanization of Jewish property to the so-called Free Zone shattered any illusions Jews may have still had. Neither property nor persons were safe from the antisemitic laws, neither in the Occupied Zone nor in those regions under the direct control of French administrative offices.

The shock was felt far and wide among the Jewish population. As a result of the Jewish Statutes, Jews found themselves and their very existence placed in a state of double dependency: they could only either turn toward both French society and Jewish aid organizations, or alternate between the two in an effort to find support. When it came to finding a job, securing a place to live, receiving assistance in time of need, breaking out of moral isolation, the law of the state was of little or no avail. Different people suffered appreciably different plights, depending largely on their attitudes toward these two basic poles of reference.

4

From Shock and Dismay to Adaptation

"As it is now, my sons could choose between a career as rock breakers, agricultural workers, or door-to-door peddlers. And even then, the latter profession may be closed to them tomorrow, since it involves being in contact with the public.'"[1] This was the bitter observation that the various provisions of the Jewish Statute inspired from Raymond-Raoul Lambert. Léon Werth chose to record his derisive remarks in his diary: "Jews will no longer be able to be stockbrokers' backers. This profession will regain its grandeur and go back to the tradition of Joan of Arc," he wrote on June 14, 1941.[2]

All joking aside, finding employment was indeed the main problem confronting Jewish refugees in the Southern Zone. As was the case for all refugees, they had to find a place to live. In addition, however, they found themselves in a situation where Jews had been officially designated as enemies, and in numerous cases, they had no friends in the area who might facilitate contacts. As was true for the rest of the population, the problem of supplying themselves with basic necessities was a constant concern. The situation was particularly acute for the Jews: they had been city-dwellers who could not avail themselves of family connections with farmers, whose special reserves allowed so many French people to stock their pantries with food not available under the system of rationing and food tickets. To overcome such problems, one had to have money. But the number of those put out of their jobs by the Jewish Statutes was increasing, and the categories included were increasing in number from month to month: there were government employees barred from civil service; journalists and writers barred from expressing themselves in the public arena; all Jews who had formerly held professions in the worlds of finance, publishing, and show business; doctors and lawyers who had been prohibited from continuing their practice because of the quota capping the number of Jews in medicine and law; storekeepers whose stores had been "aryanized," and many others. Some had found themselves without any means of making of living as early as the fall of 1940, while others had not felt the effects of the Jewish Statute or of the decrees for its implementation until several months had passed. Nevertheless, the living conditions for the great majority of Jews in the Unoccupied Zone were defined by two basic facts: first, they were refugees;

second, they had to seek a means of supporting themselves at the very moment when all doors were being closed. The search for work became the first of their priorities.

ECONOMIC EXCLUSION IN ACTION

Government Employees Hit by the Purge

Once dismissed, government employees were left without salary. True, they were granted severance pay (at the rate of two months of salary for every year of service completed) and even retirement benefits if they had fifteen years of seniority and what were considered to be excellent credentials. But how were they to make do while their cases (determining the category in which they would be placed) were pending? An advance in the form of three months' salary sometimes made it possible for them to make ends meet. But it was not always granted, and this amount was quite inadequate to make it through the waiting period during which the appropriate administrative offices finally ruled on their case.

"Monsieur le Ministre," wrote Y.A. from Toulouse to Roger Lehideux, minister of industrial production on December 3, 1941:

> I would like to solicit your indulgence in examining my individual case, which is a special one. I am an Israelite born of French parents in Paris. I had been working as a forwarding agent in the construction shop in Issy-les-Moulineaux since April 1, 1939. In June 1940, I accompanied this establishment to Albi, where it had been ordered to move in wake of the German invasion. When the shop returned to Paris, I requested to be assigned to the construction shop in Toulouse beginning October 14, 1940. I have just been dismissed from this position as a result of the Statute of the Israelites enacted June 2, 1941. I left the construction shop in Toulouse on October 7, 1941; their accounting office paid me for the seven days of work that I had completed with them, and nothing more. I would like to refer you to article 7 of the law of June 2, 1941: employees who have not completed fifteen years of service shall receive an indemnity, to be paid by a ruling of a government administrative office.
>
> However, I have been without work for two months now, and since I left Paris with only the bare necessities, I have had to spend a considerable amount for clothes and housing. I would be most grateful if you could examine my case with indulgence, and, if possible, expedite the ruling from the government administrative office which is to pay me an indemnity, which, I assure you, will be most welcome.
>
> Since I am an Israelite, it is very difficult for me to find work, and since it is impossible for me to return to Paris, I am doomed to remain in the [southern] Free Zone, far from my family and my daughter, and that's why, Monsieur le Ministre, I dare stress the urgency of my request, which, I hope, will receive a favorable response from you. Hoping to receive an affirmative response, I remain, Monsieur le Ministre, respectfully yours.[3]

There was nothing special about this case. The decree from government administrative offices was not issued until February 3, 1942. And once the indemnity had been received, how long did it allow Y.A. to hold out?

Government employees from "what was formerly the Alsace-Lorraine region" were granted an indemnity for a "grace period of three months," which meant that their entire salary for this time plus all the other benefits to which they were entitled were paid out to them over three months. This decision to bring the treatment of the Jews from the Alsace and Moselle regions in line with the treatment applied to non-Jews from the same region was not made until December 1941.[4]

Government employees who had been dismissed also immediately lost the right to receive government subsidies for families. When consulted on the subject, the Ministry of Finance refused to soften this measure, claiming that "such compensations constitute fringe benefits. They therefore cannot be maintained for former employees any longer than the employees receive all or part of their salary."[5] A large number of these government employees thus found themselves suddenly without any source of income: those without any personal fortune to fall back on were utterly destitute.

Should One Ask for Special Exemption?

On an individual basis, Jews could request special exemption, without the rest of their family being able to benefit from it. That was supposing that they had "rendered exceptional service to the French State" and that their "family [had] lived in France for at least five generations," specified article 8 of the law. The latter clause did not facilitate things for many of those seeking special exemptions: if they were from the Alsace or Moselle regions, they could hardly carry out the research necessary to establish their family lineage: the archives were located in a region that had been annexed by the Third Reich.

Moreover, while such an exemption could theoretically remove a particular prohibition specified in the request, it could under no circumstances eliminate the other consequences of the application of the Jewish Statute and its corollaries for the person exempted. Those who received special exemptions were required to register with the census as were other Jews: the General Commission on Jewish Affairs took care to put out a special notice on the matter in the press, so that things would be perfectly clear.[6]

But in order to receive a special exemption, one still had to file a request. In many cases, the initiative for making such a request was taken by administrative superiors on the behalf of Jews who worked under their supervision. The request would then meander through the maze of Vichy's bureaucracy, working its way up through the hierarchy until it reached the appropriate government minister or secretary of state, who would rule on the matter and then transfer the dossier to the General Commission on Jewish Affairs. Based on the government minister's ruling and the legal precedents available from the various government ministries, the commission would then write a report on whether or not the candidate's services had indeed been exceptional and place it in the dossier. The commission would then verify the length of time that the candidate's family had lived in France as well as the record of service. The entire dossier was then sent to the State Council, which issued its ruling and then transferred the dossier back to the appropriate government minister, who would ask Marshal Pétain to make the final decision on the matter.[7] In any case, however, such a request for special exemption could not grant a reprieve: job dismissals took effect immediately.[8] And even when special exemption was granted, many long months would pass by, during which the candidate would remain without work and without income. S.L., a teacher, filed a request for special exemption on July 4, 1941. The decree granting full restitution of her functions was signed on May 12, 1943.[9]

During their meeting of June 16, 1941, the members of the Consistory debated over what their attitude toward article 8 should be. As recorded in the minutes of the meeting, the various stances taken on the subject shed light on the stakes of the impending decision. All agreed that the most dignified attitude was not to seek any benefit from this article. Jacques Helbronner and General Boris personally pledged to abstain from making any such request. President Helbronner nevertheless believed that if a good number of Jews received special exemptions, they would be better equipped to plead the cause of Jews in general. Jacques Meyer was of the opinion that if a large number of solid requests were filed, it would show that the French Israelites had fully done their duty in World War I as well in the battles of 1939 and 1940 and would also establish the fact that the number of "those whose families had been living on French soil for five generations was quite high." That would have been a fine rejoinder to the spurious claims made in official propaganda. As far as the chief rabbi was concerned, he favored an outright rejection of a "procedure from which the vast majority of Jews would not benefit."[10] It was no simple matter to sort out the differences between giving priority to either the viability of future lobbying efforts, or to providing reasoned responses to prevailing antisemitism, or to the firm refusal of any compromise. The leaders of the Consistory finally opted for cooperation with public authorities on the issue.

The issues sparking this debate were also of great concern to France's Jewish population in general. In order to receive special exemptions, some people filled more than four pages with a glorious genealogy going back five generations and listed all their credentials and decorations.[11] The fine genealogies produced at the request of the Consistory sometimes served as a basis for very specific requests. On December 4, 1941, J.L., a writer employed in the offices of the Paris police prefecture who had been dismissed in December 1940 in application of the first Jewish Statute, requested restitution of his position by virtue of article 8 of the second Statute. Along with his request, he provided an unusually complete dossier, including his university degrees and even a record of his primary and secondary schooling. In addition to all the required documents he had taken great care to enclose, he also gave an abundance of details about his lineage, but was unable to say anything about the fourth generation of his ancestors because the information was lacking. In order to fill this gap, the consistory found inscribed on the rolls of the patriotic contribution of the city of Metz in 1789 and 1790, the name of a certain L. Salomon who could be considered as the patriarch of the fifth generation. Two of his uncles had lost their lives in battle. His father, formerly a merchant in Charleville, had been the founder and leader of several philanthropical and charitable programs. His mother was related to the D. family, who had been benefactors of the Université de Paris. "Nothing stands in the way of restoring him to his position in the administration," concluded the office of the vice president of the State Council.[12]

Others, such as Léon Werth, were indignant: "The most disgusting thing are the exceptions provided for in the law. Will the Jews who are thus authorized to practice their trade have to choose between starving to death and accepting the favor granted to them by the likes of Vallat, Darlan, and Pétain in Vichy?"[13] Many would abstain from making such a request, and some took up the pen to explain that they felt it beneath their dignity to have recourse to article 8: "I do not feel that I have rendered exceptional service just because I joined the military in 1916 and happened to get a few pieces of lead in my leg from the explosion of an artillery shell. . . . I do not consider the fact that I have published a certain number of scientific books and textbooks to constitute exceptional service," wrote René Guastalla to the principal of the Lycée Thiers in Marseilles on August 27, 1941.[14] The Minister of National Education Carcopino had urged him to file a request to be restored to his position, and, in spite of the response from Guastalla cited above, reiterated the suggestion two months later. The second reaction of René Guastalla was scarcely different from the first, as he added that "to request to be exempted from the order of dismissal to which [he had] fallen victim" would have been "to recognize the legitimacy of a law with which [he had] indeed complied . . . but whose legality [he denied]."[15]

While a good number of French Israelites did indeed recall their record of service to express their indignation over their plight, they proved, because of their sense of dignity, more reluctant to invoke their record in order to alleviate their hardship. From the middle of May to the end of August 1941, there were all only eighty-five names on the list of requests for special exemptions.[16] By July 24, 1942, the head of the Office of the Status of Persons under the General Commission on Jewish Affairs had registered 201 requests, filed by government employees who had been dismissed in application of the Jewish Statute enacted in June 1941. At that point, ten requests had been granted and eighty-two had been denied after the State Council had issued an unfavorable ruling. One year after the second Jewish Statute had been enacted, 5 percent of such requests had been granted, 40 percent had been denied, while 55 percent were still waiting for an answer.[17] There were in addition 120 Jewish government employees holding subordinate, technical jobs who had referred to article 3 of the statute in asking to retain their positions: they were either war veterans, recipients of the Legion of Honor, or else parents, widows, or orphans of French soldiers who died in service to their country. By the end of July

1942, seventeen of these requests had been granted and sixty-eight refused, this time by the General Commission on Jewish Affairs.

According to this summary, then, some 321 of the 3,400 government employees who had been dismissed (in other words, less than 10 percent) had filed a request to retain their positions. One year after the application of the second Jewish Statute, only twenty-seven of them had won their case. Another report on the special exemptions granted gave different figures: according to this document, twenty exemptions had been granted in reference to article 8, while twenty-two Jews were allowed to retain their jobs by virtue of article 3.[18] These numbers show that only a tiny minority were lucky enough to be exempted. Claude Singer notes that a total of twenty teachers and professors were granted exemptions.[19]

The documents providing these figures contain gaps, and are in many cases incoherent and contradictory. While they confirm that special exemptions were parsimoniously granted, they do not account for the number of Jewish government employees who retained their jobs in the lower echelons of the offices of certain government ministries. There were some 215 such persons in the Occupied Zone, according to a memorandum written on June 3, 1942 by the chief of staff of the General Commission on Jewish Affairs.[20] Letters notifying applicants that their request for exemption had been denied displayed the same bureaucratic insensitivity that we saw previously. "Without a doubt, your record of military service in war is an honorable one," Gaston Hirtz was informed on June 25, 1941, but "this service record is not an exceptional one, since there can be nothing exceptional in the fact that a Frenchman has served his country. All French families have done what your family has done.[21]

The Forbidden Professions

The list of professions from which Jews were barred far surpassed those contained in the various offices of government ministries. Theoretically, it was possible to obtain special exemption for those positions as well. Between May 1942 and October 1943, some 392 individuals tried their luck with the General Commission on Jewish Affairs. The list of those requesting these exemptions includes people from every city and every occupation in the country: one finds a horse trader, a cellist, a theater actor, a dental surgeon, a manager of a food company, an insurance man, a stenographer, a lycée teacher, a primary school teacher, a mailman, a logging company owner, an insurance broker, a gendarme, a wood salesman, an antique dealer, an industrial mechanics engineer, and many, many more.[22]

It is also true that some of the rulings issued by the General Commission on Jewish Affairs would seem funny if they did not in each case involve Jews who had suddenly found themselves without any means of making a living. "A farmer who buys horned animals or horses in view of reselling them after having fed them on land that he works has to be considered to be active in the commerce of livestock or horses which has been forbidden to Jews by article 5 of the law of June 2, 1941. Not concerned by article 5 are farmers content with renting their land for the raising of horned animals or horses owned by the renter and farmers who sell only livestock born and raised on their own farms," decided the Office of the Status of Persons at the General Commission on Jewish Affairs on April 8, 1942.[23]

We could also take the following example: "The job of theater usherette is a subordinate job. Thus if the person checking tickets and showing people to their seats does nothing more than seat various customers, that person holds a subordinate position. If on the other hand this individual manages the entire seating area and if at any time it is in that individual's responsibility, the job is no longer a subordinate one." In this instance, we are dealing with a ruling issued to the General Commission on Jewish Affairs by the chair of the committee on the organization of the cinema industry in the Unoccupied Zone on January 14, 1942.[24]

And then there is this little gem: "A flour mill or semolina processing plant which does not buy merchandise for resale, but is limited to transforming it, and which receives payment for this transformation, is not engaged in the commerce of cereals forbidden to Jews. Accordingly, a Jew may be employed as a sales representative for a business working under these conditions." Monsieur Lunel, who had been forced to quit his previous job in Marseilles upon the insistence of the regional delegation of the General Commission on Jewish Affairs in that same city, could have therefore once again found employment. The restitution had been authorized by this initial ruling, and was seemingly confirmed by a response sent from the offices of the General Commission on Jewish Affairs. The letter containing that response, however, was suppressed: "NO," was handwritten over the letter in red ink, "none of this *pilpoul* [*sic*],[25] Jews have been barred from this profession by article 5." As a result, Jarnieu, the chief of staff at the General Commission on Jewish Affairs, sent out a letter to the director of the commission for the Marseilles region. In it, he specified that the "flour mill [had] to be considered a profession involved in the commerce of cereals. Jews are therefore barred from this profession." Consequently, Monsieur Lunel did not receive his professional identity card.

One could cite any number of such examples, ranging from the prohibition of publishing in a stamp collector's journal (as "collectible postage stamps are involved in commercial operations"), to the rule prohibiting Jews from working as private detectives or salaried artists for an advertising agency. However, Jews could still work as newspaper vendors: that was a subordinate position involving manual labor.[26]

Not all Jews who had been dismissed from their jobs received an indemnity. Journalists were deprived of any such compensation, because their dismissal resulted "not from any initiative taken by the employer but from a legislative measure. . . . The provisions of the law of March 29, 1935, which established a statute for journalists and which provided for a leave period and severance benefits [are therefore] not applicable."[27] This was the sort of situation that often prevailed.

The quota limiting the number of Jewish lawyers and doctors allowed to practice their profession was also gradually taking effect. Jewish practitioners of law and medicine born of foreign parents were forced out of their practices first. They were soon joined by French lawyers and doctors born of native French parents. Those who were war veterans were sometimes allowed to continue their practice, but as for the others, the General Commission on Jewish Affairs carefully monitored the application of the quota in order to keep the number of Jews in law and medicine as low as possible. Whether or not there had been an influx of refugees, under no circumstances was this number to exceed the figure that had prevailed in a given region before June 25, 1940. Moreover, if the complicated calculations involved in applying the quota resulted in a decimal number, it was always rounded to the next lowest figure. "If, for example, one comes up with 0.80, no Jewish doctor will be allowed to practice. If one gets 1.80, only one will be authorized," wrote the general commissioner on Jewish affairs to the secretary of state for family and health on March 3, 1942.[28]

In practice, the various councils of the order of doctors and the appeals courts could adopt policies that were completely different from one another's. But the careful oversight of the commission left few loopholes. While we do not know the exact number of doctors who were put out of practice by this measure, we do know that for the département of La Seine alone, 726 were barred from practicing medicine following the decree of August 11, 1941.[29] We can surmise that a good number of them came to try their luck in the Southern Zone. The Central Consistory reported thirty-six doctors put out of practice the département of Les Bouches-du-Rhône in early 1942.[30] The full significance of this figure can only be understood when we place it next to other numbers: there were, in addition, thirty-six dentists, a few pharmacists, and several dozen teachers that were all put out of work.

The information we have about lawyers outside the Paris region who were excluded from their profession is also fragmentary. In Nice,[31] where there were 195 lawyers at the time,[32] four out of the eight Jewish lawyers practicing were debarred. Along with the lawyers, some 116 Jewish magistrates were also excluded from the legal profession by virtue of the two Jewish Statutes. Out of the sixteen of them who applied for special exemption, five received it on a provisional basis.[33] Here again, some held on to the hope that they could possibly be exempted from the measures of professional exclusion applied to their colleagues. But this was a faint hope: those who did manage to continue practicing law, such as Robert Kiefe and Raymond Lindon, were few in number.

On November 13, 1942, at a time when the situation was getting considerably worse and the danger was of another nature, Attorney Lucien Vidal-Naquet, who had been barred from the legal profession since May 12, 1942, commented on Vichy's recent decision to reject the proposals "approved by the Paris court, according to which thirteen lawyers were to be kept in the ranks of the order, outside of the quota."[34] He wrote:

> It is difficult to imagine how calmly I am taking this development; perhaps I should rather speak of my indifference, or even relief. I had strictly nothing to do with the application for my exemption. I only learned of the proposal and the role that he had played in bringing it forward from the person in charge of my dossier, Thiébaut. . . . It was therefore a good thing that I had not besieged him with requests, and when President Millerand[35] had indicated to me that he intended to write to the president of the bar, I vigorously and sincerely insisted that these plans be dropped: because I had been a lawyer for twenty years and felt that I had certain rights, I firmly rejected all favors. Nevertheless, I was touched by the gesture of my colleagues as well as by the court's approval of their iniative. There remained, however, the question of Vichy. And on that score, I kept telling myself that it would be contrary to my notion of honor to accept anything from Vichy. I was so set on this issue that, with the support of my wife, I was seriously planning to refuse any special exemption that might be granted to me. Now I shall not have to bear the burden of such a refusal. To my great relief, the whole dilemma has gone away.

And just as there had been "last classes" for teachers who had been removed from the profession and were teaching their classes for the last time, there were "last cases" pleaded in court by lawyers. After pleading his final case, Attorney Marcel Bloch decided to address a few words from the witness stand to the first chamber of the court on January 9, 1942:

> Messieurs, I have just pleaded my last case in court. Laws change periodically. The most recent laws have made me a persona non grata. Indeed, my name has not been included in the list of those who have been exempted. So be it.
>
> Twenty-four years ago almost day for day, led by the former president of the bar, the late Henri-Robert, I was sworn in at this same witness stand. I had previously devoted all my energy to lightening the burden of those who had been left blind by the war. My first priority had been to restore the independence that they had lost in noble service to their country.
>
> Since then, I have fought for the idea that a man can escape from darkness and despair. As an attorney, I have pleaded and worked for my clients, and I have succeeded. The last twenty-four years of my work have been full of happiness and exhilarating effort. Now, everything has collapsed.
>
> Now I shall have to close my eyes and fight again, but with peace of mind. I am not afraid. My suffering will without doubt be deep and my life uncertain. But what is that next to all the hardships now suffered by my country, France, which has always been in my thoughts whenever I have pleaded a case, and to which, upon leaving the court, I would like to give the last, fervent salute of a French lawyer.[36]

Systematic Application

At the time, Bloch's France was systematically applying the laws it had enacted. Raymond-Raoul Lambert had commented on France's diligence shortly after the enactment of the first Jewish Statute.[37] A few months later, he added: "My greatest anxiety at present . . . is to open the newspaper every morning and every evening and look for specific directives concerning the application in the Free Zone of the draconian statute that has already taken effect in the Occupied Zone."[38] After three more months had gone by, he referred to the "Germanic tenacity" evident in the flurry of measures.[39]

Report number 28, dealing with the period between August 7 and September 7, 1941, and based on "verifications" (a nice euphemism for investigations carried out by intercepting mail and wiretapping) specified: "Many Jews were overtaken by fear and discouragement upon the publication of the decree setting a September 15 deadline for Jews to have ceased all commercial and industrial activity and to have left all administrative positions."[40] Such discouragement can also be understood in light of some of the information that was filtering down from the Occupied Zone. In addition to the law adding more professions to the list of those barred to Jews and the one requiring them to submit to a census, there was the law of July 22, 1941, which, contrary to all the prior assurances that had been given, hit Jews' personal property: all of these measures were interpreted as an attempt to bring the situation in the Southern Zone in line with what prevailed in the Northern Zone. And then in August, it was learned that mass arrests in Paris had sent thousands of Jews, many of whom were French citizens, to a new camp, Drancy. After the shock of the census and the announcement that Jews were now barred from still more professions, the virtual loss of employment made people worry more and more about the rumors that only added to the menace.

Moreover, each new decree provided further confirmation that Vichy was determined to apply the special anti-Jewish laws meticulously. There was often considerable room for interpretation in applying the law. Some measures taken had not been provided for in the Jewish Statute: certain lower-level employees were fired and certain trade associations refused to let Jews set up shop in the Southern Zone, even though there were not many such businesses in town.[41] In the Dordogne region, not one administrative employee, from the head of the Office of General Commodities and Supplies Administration to the nurses and secretaries at the hospital to the cook's helper and the warehouseman, was spared from dismissal.[42]

It was true that Jews could still be employed in subordinate positions as workers, unskilled employees and technicians in industry, commerce, and agriculture. However, the nature of a subordinate position is not always obvious to everybody. Witness the misfortunes experienced by R.B., the grandson of Fernand Nathan (the Parisian publisher), who was living in Avignon at the time. Having worked as an office employee for a publisher since November 10, 1941, he assigned to do layouts, proofreading, and other technical tasks. Nevertheless, he had to deploy all his talent in trying to convince the General Commission on Jewish Affairs that this job was a subordinate one. Both the consistory and his boss intervened on his behalf, but to no avail. The regional office of the General Commission on Jewish Affairs issued its response on May 9, 1942: "Publishing is a profession from which Jews have been barred." R.B. had to give up his job.[43]

Furthermore, rare were the employers who would risk hiring Israelites, the regulations of the statute governing their employment being so complicated and their future so uncertain.[44] Classified ads testified to the fact and sometimes spelled it out: "No Israelites," stated one ad in the July 5, 1941, edition of *Le Temps*.[45] And for every ad that said as much, an untold number of potential employers made this exclusion their practice without advertising the fact.

Sometimes entire professional branches went far beyond the provisions of the Jewish Statute. On August 23, 1941, edition 1,029 of the Marseilles paper *Cinéma Spectacles* carried a message that it termed very important: theater directors, orchestras, and others involved in show business were asked to make sure that "groups and performers asking to put on a show are Aryans, as employers could be held responsible for any infraction of the law." In truth, no provision or regulation barred Jews from being employed as theater performers, except in government-subsidized theaters and in cinemas.[46]

In light of this incident, it is easy to understand why some potential employers were so cautious, as they had to request clearance from the General Commission on Jewish Affairs before hiring a Jew. In order to be sure that they would not make any embarrassing blunder, the garment manufacturer G.P. requested the authorization of the General Commission on July 25, 1941 before offering to hire as a technician a French Jew who was a war veteran decorated with the Military Cross and other medals and left handicapped from his wounds. But since this was a matter of employing a mere technician, there was no need to obtain authorization, replied the Commission.

That is just one example of the many such cases that can be found in the files of the General Commission on Jewish Affairs.[47] Responses given to such requests were rarely favorable. For example, although the occupation of traveling sales representative remained open to Jews, one provisional manager was strongly discouraged from hiring any Jewish employees as sales representatives or traveling agents, "as there are at present Aryans and returned prisoners of war who are out of work." And the regional head of the commission added:

> I nevertheless would like to inform you that the present legislation concerning the Jews places no restrictions on employing them as traveling agents or sales representatives. However, any business that would use the services of Jewish employees or of former customers or suppliers whose names have been stricken from the register of commerce would be in danger of being placed under a provisional manager, who would be charged with monitoring the nature and the influence of Jewish personnel on the business in question.[48]

The rulings of the General Commission also foreshadowed restrictive measures that "might" be adopted. That is why the prefect for the département of La Corrèze was advised to issue an occupational identity card only to those Jews who could document their record of military service, as the government planned to enact a law severely restricting the access of Jews to the profession of traveling sales representative.[49]

And how many Jews ran into the same problem as Dobrine Nathan, who was just about to be hired as a draftsman by the General Commission on the Building Grounds for Youth (Chantiers de Jeunesse) in Chatel-Guyon? After having given an affirmative answer to the question "Are you an Israelite?" he was firmly rejected.[50] And André Lucien, an office employee awaiting dismissal, wrote in a letter to Marshal Pétain,"Since I am a Jew, all doors will be closed to me just as they have been closed to my fellow Jews. I shall thus be barred from working."[51]

In reality, situations varied from one département to another, following the whims of administrative practices that were often incoherent. A decree dated September 9, 1940 specified that the creation or expansion of any commercial business, industry, or handicraft activity was to be submitted to the prefect for approval, which would be granted after the local chamber of commerce had ruled on the question. The fate of such a request thus hinged on the goodwill of any given prefect and the various special interests of any given chamber of commerce. Strange things could happen. In December 1940, the prefect for the Alpes-Maritimes refused to allow a Polish Jew who had been a tailor in Paris for twenty years to move to the region. At the same time, however, the tailor was authorized to work for a Jew who had lived in Cannes all his life. Even when Jews were allowed to move to an area, they still faced the challenge of finding work there. There was also, in February 1941, the case of a Jew who was "an Israelite from the Near East." He had been a volunteer in the army and had clandestinely left the city of Rennes, where he had worked as a peddler, to come to the département of L'Indre. The prefect authorized him to ply his trade within the département. And then there was the case of the Jewish man—this time a French citizen—who had fled Paris: in May 1941, the prefect for the département of La Haute-Savoie gave the necessary authorization for him to work as a sales representative for a replacement parts industry.[52] Indeed, Jews could still work as sales representatives, except in the déparments of La Creuse and La Haute-Vienne, where local authorities assimilated the job to that of a middleman: as a result of this assumption, they refused to issue a professional identity card to J.L., who was thus forced to find residence in the département of L'Indre.[53]

A prefect's authorization did not always solve the problems. The General Commission on Jewish Affairs could step in and bar someone from practicing medicine, as it barred Dr. Blicher from his practice in the département of L'Aveyron.[54] And as in Marseilles, the order of lawyers could refuse to inscribe on the rolls of the bar Jewish lawyers who had fled Paris, even though all of them were war veterans and even though their number did not exceed the quota of 2 percent that had been fixed by the decree of July 16, 1941.[55]

Aryanization in the Southern Zone

Economic aryanization added its own number of victims to the ranks of the unemployed. From July 22, 1941 on, the elimination of all Jewish influence on the national economy was also part of the official agenda for the Unoccupied Zone. As in the northern part of France, provisional managers were being named, which meant that "persons owning or managing property had to relinquish it" (article 3). The process became a large-scale operation in the fall of 1941. In order to bring aryanization in the Southern Zone in line with what was happening in the Northern Zone, the General Commission on Jewish Affairs was given the task of organizing the operation. The undertaking required the efforts of the 407 specially contracted agents and the 360 temporary helpers who were working for the commission as of October 20, 1941.[56]

As sales and liquidations proliferated during the first six months of 1942, the proceeds were placed in frozen accounts in a special government bank, the Caisse des Dépôts et Consignations. However, because French aryanization agents did not have to give an account to the Germans of the progress of this plundering of Jews in the Southern Zone, the extent of the operation and its various stages are more difficult to gauge.[57] A considerable number of small commercial businesses had been created in the Southern Zone since the fall of 1940, thus increasing the number (which, as we have seen, was not very large) of those owned by Jews in these regions. Still, they were much less numerous than in Paris, and were for the most part concentrated in the big cities. Up until the end of the war, the Southern Zone only accounted for 15 percent of the total number of provisional managers.[58] The 1,954 business owners that were aryanized in the Southern Zone and some three thousand business owners in the same region whose cases were still pending in February 1944[59] were all completely plundered. Some lost their business, some their little store, and others their buildings: all lost 100 percent of their property.

And while the Germans and the French were arguing over who would control a few large businesses, and while the committees of business organizations for the most part sought to take advantage of their former competitors—this was particularly true in the leather, clothing, and furniture industries—the Jews had to devote their energies to dealing with the provisional managers. The regional branches of department stores whose main office was in Paris were the first to be placed under the control of an Aryan provisional manager.[60] Once this new manager was appointed, Jewish employees could be dismissed "without taking into consideration the formalities and conditions required by the laws, decrees, regulations, customary ways, agreements or contract that normally applied."[61] Jewish sales employees would cease to receive pay and the business owner would generally not be granted any subsidies he might request.[62] When, for example, a business such as Le Muguet de Paris in Toulouse was sold by its Jewish owner to a former associate, an investigation would be conducted, as it was in this case in Toulouse, by the Division of Investigations and Inspections (the SEC, which had taken the place of the PQJ).

To preclude any remaining Jewish influence, investigators would make sure that the person acquiring the business was of Aryan descent, that the person's spouse was of good morals, that the funds had come from Aryan sources, and that the former owner had indeed been eliminated from the management.[63] And to prevent any fictitious sales, a ruling issued in January 1942 stipulated that all sales of stores and buildings that had been placed under provisional managers had to take place at a public auction.[64] The *Journal Officiel* published the names of those appointed to be provisional managers, but it was the local newspapers that announced the sales of Jewish property. The only ones supposedly exempted from aryanization were "Jewish craftsmen, having French citizenship . . . provided that they themselves do the work, assisted by their families and one or two workers at most," and on the condition that they had never been convicted "of anti-government propaganda, price gouging, black marketeering, or any other offense."[65]

This general provision, however, did not keep the little store run by M-L. Z. from being aryanized in Limoges. M-L. Z. was a French citizen who had been born in Poland and naturalized in 1929. A tailor by profession, he had fled from Paris in June 1940 and had first established residence in the suburbs of Limoges, where he was able to live off the public assistance funds granted to refugees. Then in October 1940, he had received authorization from the office of the prefect to open a store where, aided by four of his children, he repaired secondhand clothes and did darning and mending. His business prospered. But when the aryanization measures were enacted, an inspector sent by the General Commission on Jewish Affairs was of the opinion that "in spite of the small-scale, family nature of this business, there was an interest in eliminating the Jewish element from this branch of economic activity [which was] almost entirely controled by Jews." M-L. Z.'s store was thus placed under a provisional manager, pending aryanization.

Once the commercial property of Jews was confiscated, it was the turn of private property, including personal possessions and real estate, to be exposed to plunder. One victim, B.R., expressed his surprise in the following terms: "This decision is absolutely unacceptable, as I have never been involved in politics. Moreover, since October 1940, I have resigned from all the boards of directors to which I belonged. Since that time, I have not been involved in any commercial or industrial activity." This case was nevertheless far from isolated.[66]

There was no lack of prospective buyers of Jewish possessions in the year 1942. Thanks to its connections with the General Commission on Jewish Affairs, a certain real estate firm jumped the gun on the official public notices, hoping to offer some particularly good buys to its clients. One of the General Commission's dossiers registers from ten to fifteen requests for acquisition of a commercial business per month beginning in November 1941. And that is for the city of Toulouse alone. Some were not very particular about the kind of store they would so eagerly acquire: either "a perfume shop, an antique store, or a hairstyling salon," wrote one person on July 22, 1942. Others were greedy enough to designate their target with greater precision: "I would like a piece of land producing a variety of crops," wrote another person on August 7 of the same year, eager to get in on a good deal. One woman would have been satisfied with a movie theater. Other inquiries abound with details about the commercial business that was desired: "A wholesale pelt and fur business, preferably in an apartment in your city," specified one applicant on July 22, 1942. For the month of May, potential buyers seem to have set their sights on hosiery stores. On June 10, 1942, a wood dealer went around in the départements of Le Lot, L'Ariège, and La Haute-Garonne to gather information about wooded farms, properties, and pieces of land that would soon be available due to the aryanization measures. Certain hotels would have been happy to take over the property of some hotel owner who had abandoned all he owned in Alsace. And then there were people who were just looking for a bargain and who requested the list of all Jewish stores in need of a buyer. In some cases, these letters specified that the establishment seeking to acquire the Jewish business was French: one buyer even gave a full account of his grandparents' "pedigree."[67]

Except for a few special cases, the delegations from the General Commission would simply refer these prospective buyers to the official announcements published in the local press and let them seek the object of their desire there. The General Commission just did not have the personnel to do otherwise: all its employees were busy hunting down Jews who might have been tempted to dodge commercial and administrative aryanization.

Hunting Down the Noncompliant

The role of the General Commission on Jewish Affairs was not limited just to looking into requests for special exemption and overseeing the corps of provisional managers. A considerable amount of correspondence between the commission, government ministries, and offices of the regional prefects gives evidence of the unceasing efforts to flush out Jews that might still have been employed in one capacity or another. On October 14 and 15, the commission wrote to the prefects of the départements La Corrèze, L'Indre, and La Creuse and asked them to explain why Louise-Andrée Cahen was still working in the office of the prefect of La Corrèze and why André Lévy was still employed by the Bureau of General Commodities and Supplies. How could it be that André Morhange was still a secretary with the Bureau of Small Scale Trades and Handcrafts, that Catherine Grégoire was still working in the state tobacco plant in Châteauroux, and that Georges Dreyfus was still employed in the accounting office of the regional administration in Châteauroux? Similarly, in the départements of La Haute-Vienne and La Dordogne, the commission zeroed in on the cases of Jean Steinberg, who worked for the Unemployment Commission, a nurse, an accountant's assistant, a chauffeur and mechanic, a typist and supplykeeper, some doctors, a chemist, a librarian, and Hélène Hermann, a laundrywoman working for the National Relief agency.[68]

Government ministries and offices of prefects sometimes took the initiative of pointing out "anomalies": for example, the Office of the Secretary-General for Information and Propaganda expressed its concern about the presence of Jewish journalists on the editorial staffs of various newspapers in Lyon, Perpignan, Clermont-Ferrand, and Marseilles.[69] The prefects for the départements of L'Indre, La Haute-Vienne, and La Dordogne checked with the General Commission on Jewish Affairs to see whether Jews living in their area were indeed authorized to engage in such and such professional activity. They also requested that investigations be conducted.[70]

This interaction between government agencies made it possible to carry out a complete purge of Jews from certain sectors of the economy, as can be seen in the case of the employees working for the Office of Commodities and Supplies in the Aix-en-Provence-Marseilles region. A.K., who had been a master printer before the war, had found gainful employment in this office, along with C.A., a former storeowner in Marseilles who, since February 15, 1942, had worked in the same office as an accountant. While the Office of Commodities and Supplies employed a total of some 340 employees, the regional director of the General Commission for Jewish Affairs became concerned about the racial purity of thirty individuals and sent a corresponding number of forms to be filled out by the suspects. There were three columns in which the suspects were to provide information about their grandparents, and three columns dealing with their nationality, their race, and their religion. Suspects were well advised to use only three words to fill in the spaces: French, Aryan, Catholic. And in order to be more convincing and to erase any remaining doubts, some specified "Apostolic Roman Catholic" and "Aryan, non-Jewish."

R.K., however, did not fill in the column devoted to the race of his ancestors, nor did G.K. and her husband. Such was in fact the case for most of those having filled out the forms. A.S., on the other hand, pointed out that his grandparents were white, and stressed the fact with a double underline (as it was, two of his grandparents had been born in Algeria). S.R., who was born in Saigon, had a similar reaction to the form, as she took pains to emphasize that her grandparents were Catholic. Only two of the thirty people who filled out these forms identified themselves as Jewish. One was B.G, a Jew who was born in Rumania and became a naturalized French citizen in 1930. A chemist in Paris before the war, he now worked as a chemist's helper in the regional laboratory of the Office of Commodities and Supplies in Marseilles. The director of the Office of Commodities and Supplies for the département of Les Bouches-du-Rhône carefully sent in the properly completed forms. He specified that two of his Jewish employees had already been dismissed, leaving only three others. A few months later, the inspector charged with monitoring the case expressed his satisfaction: "All the Jews have been dismissed with the exception of one person who has filed a request for special exemption," he wrote in his report. "All Jewish influence has thus been eliminated from this administration."[71]

Given the number and variety of professions from which Jews were barred or to which they had only limited access, monitoring these cases was no simple matter. The list of people who wrote to the General Commission on Jewish Affairs about the regulations governing the employment of Jews is equally diverse and extensive.

They range from the head of the office of the clerk of the court of commerce, who was prepared to provide—verbally, at least—details about Jewish storeowners under the jurisdiction of his court, to the delegate from the Committee of the Organization of Artistic Industries and Professions in the Unoccupied Zone, who offered to inform the commission about Jewish businesses within their ranks.[72] There was also the regional head of the General Bureau of Information for the département of La Dordogne, who was well supplied with detailed reports on foreigners (in fact, Jews) employed, with or without authorization, in various professions in his area.

These reports were based on investigations of several different professional groups.[73] Lécussan, the regional delegate of the General Commission on Jewish Affairs in Toulouse, answered each letter and regularly requested French government authorities to apply the existing laws even more restrictively. In one instance, he complained that if doctors in such and such villages were allowed to continue their practice for a limited time thanks to a special exemption, young Aryan doctors would be discouraged from starting their medical practice in the area.[74]

Moreover, the General Commission and the Police for Jewish Affairs were the favorite partners of informers of every stripe. It must be emphasized here that denunciations were openly encouraged through the press and that every public notice that appeared in the newspapers brought in another series of letters. "I have just read in a weekly newspaper that it is the duty of every French citizen to denounce the Jews' shady dealings," wrote one hotel owner from Hyères on May 26, 1942, as he went on to call the misdeeds of a certain Jew to the attention of the commission. "Although we are reluctant to denounce someone, we have been encouraged to do so by numerous newspaper articles telling us: 'Denounce vigorously and with determination and render powerless all the enemies of Marshal Pétain.' We have also been encouraged to denounce people by a recent speech, in which Marshal Pétain acknowledged that it would take a good deal of time to overcome all the opponents of the new order of things." And so it was in Marseilles that a group of "good French citizens, who were sorry that they could not sign their names," began a long letter to Xavier Vallat on June 21, 1941. In it they denounced a Jew, who had formerly been a watchmaker and jeweler, as a "Jew, a dyed-in-the-wool Communist, a gold smuggler, who was also reported to be involved with concealing bicycles."[75]

Each denunciation led to an investigation. "Having been expelled from Vichy, three hundred Jews have reportedly moved into Saint-Pourcain-sur-Sioule," wrote one person, who turned in the names of some of her neighbors.[76] Jews were often reported to be going to another small town. Another denunciation involved Jews who were supposedly receiving packages. Still others reported a Jewish store still in business and Jews who had supposedly not submitted to the census and were pursuing an occupation forbidden to them. The diversity of cases reported reflects the complexity of the antisemitic laws.

Personal animosities, ideological conflicts, and professional jealousies and rivalries found a natural outlet in such denunciations. But Jews could also find themselves subjected to an investigation simply by coming into contact with a government administrative office. Such was the case for those receiving government benefits: in each département, inspectors from the Police for Jewish Affairs, sometimes working on their own initiative and sometimes responding to a request from the office of the prefect, would go over their situation with a fine-tooth comb. In one such matter, eighty Jews who had fled from the north and had settled in Saint-Géraud-le-Puy in the département of L'Allier were reportedly receiving government assistance benefits for refugees even though they were rich and had taken out insurance policies for considerable sums of money. The ensuing investigation revealed that there were only thirty-seven Jews living in the community and that only seven of them were receiving refugee benefits.[77]

Any Jew having fled the Occupied Zone and who received a postal money order from the north was in for a bad time. The director of the post office would report the individual to the authorities and, again, an investigation would be conducted.[78] When a traveling salesman would request a permit to move about freely in order to carry out his profession (one of the few that remained open to him), his case was submitted to the General Commission on Jewish Affairs, which would hand it over to their inspectors for an investigation. In most cases, these inspectors would advise against issuing such a permit, especially when it involved a foreign Jew. They would invariably argue that such a document could be conducive to all sorts of illegal trafficking. The argument was difficult to refute: as presumption prevailed, the inspectors had no need of backing up their argument with proof.[79]

And so the commission's representative in the city of Limoges asked that the professional identity card held by I.Z., a Polish Jew, be withdrawn and that he be assigned to a Foreign Worker Unit (GTE): "since it is not desirable to have foreign Jews traveling around, . . . this measure would have the advantage of eliminating an activity not appropriate for a foreigner and especially not for a Jew."[80] There were many similar cases.

Any store sold to a third party by a Jew would come under suspicion. Any business that employed Jews could be subject to an investigation. The National Aeronautical Construction Company of the Southwest in the town of Marignane had too many foreign or recently naturalized Jews employed as engineers, draftsmen, and calculators, according to the chief of police for Jewish Affairs in Marseilles.[81] The firm Radioscil in Brive was singled out for being in the same situation. And then there was the case of D.G., a radio engineer from the city of Nancy who risked losing his job. He was granted yet another grace period:

> since it is difficult to replace a technician as valuable as the foreign Jew D.G. on the spur of the moment, and in order to avoid negative repercussions on the production of the firm Radioscil, it is appropriate to grant this firm another grace period so that it can find equally qualified French technicians, who will be called upon to replace the foreign Jews who are truly too numerous in this company. In view of the circumstances, it is not desirable to allow such a large number of foreign and moreover, Jewish, supervisors to remain in French companies.[82]

These "circumstances," which are never spelled out in so many words, come back over and over again in all such recommendations. And every investigation would invariably reach the conclusion that although such and such foreign (in other words, Jewish) technician was indeed perhaps very competent, it would still be advantageous to replace him with a French technician. The firm Radioscil obviously refused to comply; in March 1943, authorities were considering placing it under provisional management in order to see that all foreign Jews would be eliminated from its personnel.[83]

After the La Rochette cardboard factory in the Savoie region was placed under provisional management, the new manager was requested to check very carefully "the situation of capital distribution, the conditions in which stocks were transferred, the new stockholders' ability to pay bills, or in other words, to carry out every verification procedure necessary to ensure that the new stockholders are not just a front for the Jews that have been eliminated." Moreover, all Jews connected with the business were to be dismissed regardless of their position. "Employee military records, as honorable as they may be, may not be taken into consideration because that might allow some Jewish influence to remain in this public limited company." A petition signed by company personnel was unsuccessful in its bid to keep the former owners, Messieurs F., in charge. Only one of them, "as the son of a man who had given his life to the country," managed to obtain a technical job with the company.[84]

There were a great many investigations of this nature, which would involve a broad number of administrative services, government ministries, professional organizations, prefectural police bureaus, and various offices of the General Commission on Jewish Affairs, which had its own police agency. By May 22, 1942, the Police for Jewish Affairs in Marseilles had by itself made 493 reports. Between the middle of November 1941 and the middle of December 1942, the inspectors in Limoges wrote more than five hundred reports.[85] Such reports carried in and of themselves a significant "capacity for harassment,"[86] and although there was occasionally friction between the Police for Jewish Affairs and the regular police (who, beginning in January 1942, had authority over the Police for Jewish Affairs), in most cases the information gathered by one group would help advance the investigation being carried out by the other. Nevertheless, conflicts between rival bureaucracies, inconsistencies of administrators and police in dealing with an extremely complex set of laws, the multiplicity of the agents involved, and a society that remained pluralistic made it possible for a large number of Jews to find loopholes and hold out in spite of everything.

SURVIVING

Finding Work

Success or failure in searching for a job often depended on being in the right place at the right time or on meeting the right person. The record of these desperate job hunts has been preserved in the archives of the Central Consistory. A mutual assistance organization for intellectuals was founded in March 1941 within the Israelite Welfare Committee in Lyon, and was presided by Paul Mantoux, an honorary professor with the National Conservatory of Engineering. Its goal: "To secure new positions of employment for workers who, although perhaps highly specialized, are qualified by their high level of education to take on the widest variety of jobs."[87] In Grenoble, Robert Mossé, who had himself lost his position as a law professor because of the Jewish Statutes, set about collecting all the information on other victims of the statute who were looking for work.

The responses that he gathered were incomplete. Not everybody was willing to have such personal information recorded. Some had already found another job. Others "fear[ed] they would be sent to Russia."[88] However, in addition to providing some rather incomplete statistics, the responses gathered show that Jews were trying to make as complete an inventory as possible of their training and credentials in order to secure new employment. One elementary school teacher who had been removed from her duties on December 18, 1940, mentioned her aptitude for farm work, painting, and working with leather. A jurist stressed his knowledge of German. A lycée professor spoke of his love of the theater and all he had done in that field in the past. "Any intellectual work," wrote down on the form one philosophy professor who had been dismissed and who had been giving private lessons since December 1940. A teacher who specialized in technical training added that he would be willing to do "any job requiring a trustworthy person." Judging from the form he filled out, he really had no further hopes of finding employment. Responding from Marseilles on February 16, 1942, one doctor from Paris pointed out "incidentally" that he knew German and Italian. Gérard Bloch, who prior to the war had been a professor at the Lycée Janson-de-Sailly, was prepared to take on any job, including giving private lessons, correcting papers, or anything else. A clerk who was formerly employed in a bailiff's office in Paris and who had taken refuge in Saint-Etienne "[was] able to work in any legal domain." However, he did not refrain from adding, "Needless to say, I would happily accept another job."[89] A doctor from the département of L'Aveyron inquired about a job with a wood company: "I would be willing to accept anything in order to escape this depressing idleness." And he was far from the only one who would have taken "anything": for the sparse statistics (gathered in some cases thanks to the meticulous work of a prefect or to someone who had been approached by the General Commission or the Police for Jewish Affairs) show that anywhere from 30 to 50 percent of Jews registered in a given region were now "without occupation."

Some solved the problem on an individual basis, through their personal contacts. Those whose spouse was Aryan lived off their household's income. One doctor managed to continue his practice because of his good reputation, but he had to do so unofficially, which meant that he was subject to the whims of his French colleagues who handed him the most onerous tasks such as night calls, emergencies, and care for the dying. Another doctor continued to treat patients by having a cooperative colleague write his prescriptions. In some cases, he gave no prescriptions and limited himself to treating his patients with over-the-counter drugs that no pharmacist could refuse to dispense. In Montpellier, one teacher was happy to be able to make her living checking out customers in a garment shop. Another teacher wound up working as a typist. In Lyon, Camille Haguenauer gave private lessons to students sent to her by her former colleagues.[90] In Toulouse, after first having sold some paintings in order to recover a bit of cash, Clara Malraux gave private lessons in German: fifteen minutes before each lesson, she would herself learn the basic elements of grammar that she was about to teach.[91]

Money from savings and from the sale of a few possessions that they had taken with them made it possible for many Jews to hold out in the beginning. Many who had come from the Occupied Zone relied on the help of friends or of a concierge to whom they would entrust their savings before fleeing into the unknown: once they had settled in somewhere, they would ask that the funds be sent to them. Others used such savings as an investment to make a profit on the black market. Thanks to a leasing agreement negotiated by Joseph Fisher, director of *Keren kayemeth le-Israel*, a few Jews managed to hang on to their property, but without being able to maintain control over its use. These Jews lent him funds that were immediately used by Jewish social aid organizations; the American Jewish Joint Distribution Committee guaranteed that the funds would be reimbursed either after the war was over or upon their arrival in the United States, if they planned to emigrate.[92]

Some teachers managed to make a living by giving private lessons or by teaching in private schools. More and more Jews were also turning to all sorts of trades. One became a machinist in the wood industry, another worked as a milk collector in Argenton, and a third found employment in a dry-cleaning establishment.[93] David Knout, a poet and journalist, took to working as an attendant in an asylum for the mentally ill. A former butcher who had had a shop on the Rue des Rosiers in Paris took up peddling newspapers. Although he was unable to get his newspaper business officially registered, he continued to sell his papers on the street.[94]

Some tried to bend the law in order to hold on to their means of making a living or to find a job. A certain Mademoiselle Lévy kept her job with the Banque de France, but changed her name to Mademoiselle d'Alsace in order to do so.[95] A tailor who unfortunately bore the name Weill attracted customers by placing advertisements signed "A. Well" in local papers. A used furniture dealer used only his first name, Philippe, in order not to reveal to potential customers that he was Jewish.

A few particularly farsighted Jews were able to save a part of their property through "voluntary aryanization." During the first phase of the anti-Jewish laws, good relations with local authorities made it possible to avoid aryanization. Such was the case for Paul Ullman, who had been living in the département of Le Puy-de-Dôme since the latter part of the nineteenth century. However, that only afforded him a temporary reprieve, and he was well advised to entrust his various financial holdings to reliable employee, who hid them for him until the Liberation.[96] A fashion shop was transformed into an outdoor hat stand in order to fulfill the requirements of the law.

In some businesses, former owners managed to stay on after aryanization by taking on a subordinate or technical job in the store that had once been theirs. There were apparently a good number of such cases, and they did not fail to come under the scrutiny of the French administrators in charge of economic aryanization. Take the example of I.S., a French Jew who in January 1941 was authorized to open a stationery shop in Limoges. In May 1941, he sold his store to his Aryan mother-in-law. She immediately drew up a notarized document granting the power to operate the store and manage the business to her daughter, who then continued to employ I.S.[97]

Finally, there were a few (no more than fifteen) Jewish business owners who were so sure of their rights and so trusting in the French State that they appealed to the State Council to overrule the decision to place their business under provisional management. Their requests were based on two arguments. First, although the General Commission on Jewish Affairs could appoint an Aryan manager, there was nothing in the law that required it to do so. Second, the influence of a Jewish business on the French economy had to be seen as negative. When it could be proved that there was no such negative influence, the General Commission was abusing its power in appointing a provisional manager. It always took the State Council a very long time to investigate the specifics of these requests, especially since it depended on detailed explanations provided by the General Commission on Jewish Affairs in order to justify having placed a given business under provisional management. Nothing prevented the General Commission from taking its time. In the ten or so rulings—all dating from 1944—issued by the State Council, the two basic arguments mentioned above obviously failed to convince members of the Council. The only decisions overruled were those involving non-Jewish business owners and businesses in which Jews only held a small fraction of the capital.[98]

In addition to this tiny loophole—which did not provide much help to those naive enough to try to slip through it—there were other, more significant gaps in the anti-Jewish laws. Some students who had not been allowed to pursue their course of study at the university and who had been stricken from the rolls, continued to attend classes as auditors; according to a memorandum from the National Ministry of Education dating from December 15, 1941, this possibility still remained open to them. A few students in Montpellier who were not among the tiny fraction of Jews allowed by the quota thus completed an entire course of study. They even secretly took the exams and had their results validated after the Liberation.[99] A large number of Jews became traveling sales representatives, as did one former master printer in Epinal and one film producer born in Russia who took to working for a soup company. Small crafts also remained open to those who had the necessary skills.

For a certain time, those who had been driven out of the film industry in the Occupied Zone were able to find employment in the Southern Zone, where the professional identity card was not required until September 1941. And so the Jewish cinema community found refuge on the French Riviera.[100] The first film shot in Nice after the armistice—a film dedicated to Marshal Pétain -was financed by two Jewish film producers. Film production in Nice provided work for various professionals until June 1942, when the Vichy government stepped in and brought activities under its rein. A small number of these professionals were even hired clandestinely by Jacques Cohen in Juan-les-Pins in May 1941. Cohen had managed to interest financiers from North Africa in the creation of a unit for making scenarios that would be used at the time of Liberation. By sharing profits, it was possible to pay a regular salary to those who could no longer work in the open. From twenty to thirty scenarios were apparently prepared in that manner, before the invasion of the Southern Zone by the Germans put an end to the experiment.[101]

Foreign Jews also sought to gain acceptance on the basis of their credentials as war veterans. That is why they had registered en masse with the Federated Associations of Foreign Volunteers for Military Service (Fédération des amicales d'anciens engagés volontaires étrangers) that had been created in July 1941. They often made up more than 50 percent of the membership in the various regional associations. In order for their organization to be legally declared and registered, however, General Goudouneix and the president and founder Puaud had to pledge that none of the groups would have a majority of Jews and that non-Aryans would be excluded from leadership positions. Even after the ensuing purge of June 1942, the Federation reportedly continued to include 1,579 Jewish members out of the total of 3,784 members in twenty-one local groups.[102] Granted, these members could not use their status with the federation as a basis for claiming special exemption. For some Jews, however, being a certified war veteran eliminated the threat of internement. And in a context where the symbolism attached to being a war veteran was so heavy, membership in the federation could in some cases open doors to employment that would otherwise have remained closed. It was a way of breaking out of the highly negative stereotypes that French society of the time associated with Jews (and in particular, foreign Jews).

Finally, there were those who decided to go along with the strategy of changing occupations and so recycled themselves in agriculture on an individual basis. Such was the case for Marcel Ruff, a graduate of the prestigious Ecole Normale Supérieure: after being fired from his teaching position at the Lycée Mignet in Aix-en-Provence, he moved in early 1941 to a piece of land in the country nearby and for the next few months devoted himself to farming.[103] We could also take the example of M.E., a Turkish Jew who before the war ran a lingerie factory on the Rue des Immeubles-Industriels in Paris. After having sought refuge in Argenton-sur-Creuse in the département of L'Indre, he acquired a piece of fallow land where an apartment building was to go up in the city limits of Périgueux. After using his life's savings on finishing the necessary construction work, he and his family lived off the produce of the garden and the revenue from the four renters that lodged in his building.[104] A Jewish man and his two sons, who had formerly been cattle dealers in Nancy also decided to buy a piece of fallow land and farm it. But that was in November 1940. A year later, Xavier Vallat rejected many such requests, since "it [was] not possible for [him], under present circumstances, to grant authorization for a Jew to buy French land."[105]

The only exceptions made were when the person requesting authorization was a French Jew decorated with many military medals, when the property sought was small and in poor condition, and when the buyer promised to work the land himself, assisted only by his family.[106] Another exception was made for Emmanuel Berl, who nevertheless experienced many difficulties before being able to acquire "a piece of fenced land within the city limits of Argentat, which included a house with two rooms, a vegetable garden, a pasture, and a thicket, amounting to a total of four hectares [about 10 acres]." "The projected use of this property does not seem to be of the sort that would remove any cultivated or cultivatable land from agricultural use," specified the main office of the government's agricultural bureau, and Emmanuel Berl "would be entirely supportive of the new regime," the prefect for the département of La Corrèze had added. Authorization was first refused, then granted, but even then had to be confirmed, as the notary overseeing the transaction "did not want to put [himself] into the awkward position of having consented to a sale whose authorization seemed dubious [to him]."[107]

For the intellectuals who could afford it, there remained the possibility of taking refuge in intense intellectual activity. Such was the choice of Julien Benda, who—in spite of the rather precarious material conditions of his life in a small town in the provinces—was "infinitely happy to devote himself exclusively to the life of the mind and to concentrate" in a way that he had never been able to previously.[108] When, however, on March 28, 1941, he learned that the Germans had looted his personal library in Paris, taking not only his books, but also "all of his notes, all of his notecards, all of his dossiers, along with everything he had used and acquired over fifty years of work," he was overwhelmed with sadness. Only by taking refuge in his work could he forget moreover that all the books he had written were banned in France, that he was barred from publishing anything whatsoever, and that he had been "completely eliminated and done away with [*sic*] as a writer."

There were in addition special places such as Dieulefit and Le Chambon-sur-Lignon, those Huguenot strongholds where professors who had been revoked by Vichy could still teach.[109] These were exceptional communities that did much more than just provide work to Jews who had been excluded from employment: their role would take on its full significance when job exclusions gave way to manhunts.

In the final analysis, the success of such personal readaptations depended largely on French society and on the extent to which Jews were integrated into that society. In order for Jews to be able to give private lessons, the teachers in a given area had to send them pupils: obviously, it was easier to develop such a network of relations when one had taught in the same location. While French Jews suffered intensely on a moral level, it was easier for them to gain employment than for foreign Jews. Jews who had been living in an area for many years had many more avenues open to them than did those who had fled from the Paris region. Those who had savings could plan for what was coming. The plight of various individuals differed according to the influence of all these factors combined. However, the fact remains that a large number of Jews who had awakened one day only to find themselves "without gainful employment" were living from hand to mouth.

Aid from Jewish Organizations

For those who could not obtain the support they needed from society, the Jewish organizations that had now moved to the southern part of the country often provided an importance source of assistance. Regional delegations from Marseilles, Lyon, Montpellier, and Périgueux streamed into every city that had a significant number of Jews.

A number of those who had fallen victim to the Jewish Statutes found employment with these organizations. The Central Consistory put to the best use possible those talents that had become available because of the anti-Jewish laws, using lawyers and professors for the new administrative positions created by the consistory's reorganization. Most had never worked for any Jewish organization before the war, but there was no lack of talent to handle new situations. The conundrums posed by the new laws could be analyzed by the Legal Commission. Presided over by René Mayer, the commission included a lawyer, Attorney Lubetzki; a member of the State Council, Seligman; a professor, William Oualid; and a president of the bar, Paul David. All of them had been excluded from their professions because of the new anti-Jewish laws.

The idea of creating a parallel system of education for Jews was also put forward, and the former school inspector Jules Isaac was given the task of preparing the project, which never came to fruition. When information about victims of the Jewish Statutes was needed in order to provide assistance, Robert Mossé, as we have seen, devoted his skills to the task. Although not officially formed before April 1942, the Central Consistory's office of studies undertook a long documentation effort. Presided over by Georges Halphen and directed by Léon Algazi, it benefited from the specialized knowledge of some forty intellectuals: men of letters, doctors, engineers, and in particular university professors who had been stripped of their professional titles.[110] When the French Israelite Mutual Aid association (EFI) decided to create a rural center for vocational training, a professor of agricultural science, who had been removed from his position as chief controller with the Office of Cereal Grains, oversaw the project and led it to completion.[111]

The Children's Relief Organization (OSE) took in doctors and employed a number of social workers who were new to the profession to work in its children's homes (of which there were eight in the Unoccupied Zone at the end of July 1941), its five dispensaries, and the internment camps. When the organization was integrated into the General Union of French Israelites (UGIF), there were some 280 official employees of the OSE.[112] In Montpellier, a group of some twenty-five to thirty doctors managed to survive thanks in part to subsidies received from the OSE. They also had to work the grape harvests, or, as in the case of A. Grinberg, make fish croquettes in order to make ends meet. By the fall of 1941, there were about three hundred doctors receiving assistance in one form or another from the OSE. This assistance sometimes took the form of vocational retraining: at the Bron worksite near Lyon, young unmarried doctors learned how to farm.[113]

A number of Jews, including intellectuals, doctors, and legal specialists for the Consistory, found work in simple administrative positions in Jewish aid organizations. Daniel Mayer, for example, became the head of the regional office of the EFI in Marseilles,[114] and his spouse was employed by the Committee on Aid to Refugees (CAR). Nevertheless, he avoided registering with the census, and when, in 1941, he began making trips in connection with his work for the socialist branch of the Résistance, he changed his name from "Mayer" to "Mayet." The eldest daughter of the renowned historian Marc Bloch, Alice, worked in one of the OSE's children's homes.[115] Suzanne Kiefe was employed by the CAR in Lyon. In every Jewish organization, one could find Jews who before the war barely knew that such specifically Jewish institutions existed. The most surpising example is perhaps that of Léon Poliakov, an agnostic if there ever was one; yet he wound up becoming the secretary for the Association of Practicing Israelites, an ultra-orthodox group, led by Rabbi Zalman Chneerson in Marseilles.[116]

In the summer of 1941, the French Israelite Mutual Aid assocation (EFI) was created in order to respond adequately to the unemployment facing many Jews in the Southern Zone. This new organization was aimed more specifically at providing needed assistance to French Israelites, in particular by giving grants for vocational retraining. Indeed, the Central Consistory decided to channel all resources available for education into professional reorientation and training for manual work. They even rejected the idea of establishing a Jewish university. "Whatever hope we may have of seeing the French State do away with these measures, it is nonetheless desirable to ensure a better distribution of professional orientations among French Jewish Youth," wrote Rene Guastalla as president of the consistory.[117] This was a widely shared opinion. In keeping with a program already in place prior to the war, the Israelite Scouts of France (EIF) worked at developing agricultural training for Jewish youth, to which task the OSE contributed greatly.

Finally, the Professional Retraining and Work Organization (ORT) drew its own conclusions from the "exclusion of Jews from the normal cycle of the economy." Because it "acknowledged and understood the imbalance in economic structure of the Jewish community," it adopted the goal of "enabling its members to participate as they desire in all of the functions of the society in peace and equality."[118] This was not a new idea: the economic emancipation of Jews had been part of the agenda of the ORT since its creation. But the repercussions of the Jewish Statute lent a new urgency to the theme. One of the major objectives of the ORT, which was intent on "bringing a new Judaism out of present suffering and hardship," was thus to convince French Jews of the necessity of sending their children to vocational schools, whose classrooms were already full of "the children of our foreign brothers."

By July 31, 1941, the OSE, EIF, and ORT together were sponsoring no fewer than seventeen schools for vocational reorientation and training in crafts and trades. In them were some 1,112 young Jewish schoolchildren learning about electrical appliances, sewing, leather crafts, carpentry, hairstyling, ironworks, and fancy leather work. Their number grew over the months that followed.[119] For Jews who desired professional reorientation for agricultural work, the ORT also had five centers for youth and thirteen training grounds for adults.[120] In addition to these vocational training centers, the EFI in the cities of Marseilles and Périgueux planned to set up supplementary courses by correspondence on so-called secular subjects. These courses were "intended for very gifted young people who have been forced to abandon their studies and devote their time to manual labor."[121]

The creation of these vocational schools and professional retraining centers were part of an attempt to adapt and to adjust to the new demands of society. It only made sense to provide the young and the not-so-young the means of supporting themselves, which meant teaching them "trades that would allow them to live with dignity."[122]

But there were in fact many who did not find gainful employment and had to depend on assistance. The number of Jews having no source of income would only increase over time: by the middle of April 1941, Professor Olmer estimated that out of some 830 "victims of the Jewish Statute," about 250 were in need of immediate assistance. He added that from January 1942 on, some 350 other Jews deprived of all compensation would be added to that figure.[123]

The number of Jews who had to turn to aid associations for assistance during that time rapidly rose. Jews continued to leave the Occupied Zone in waves to go live under supposedly more clement skies. Individual and family financial resources kept dwindling. People were more and more hesitant to seek the government benefits to which they were entitled, for fear of being sent to an internment camp. Such was the case, for example, of many families who in the past had received subsidies from the military and who were entitled to receive similar benefits from the civilian authorities. Those who had come from the Alsace-Lorraine region were in a similar situation. Foreign refugees found themselves in an even more precarious situation, since they were terrified by the threat of internment. For example, while nearly 23 percent of French Jews in Brive (in the département of La Corrèze) were receiving government refugee benefits, only 11.3 percent of foreign Jews were getting similar compensation.[124] For foreign Jews, turning to French authorities for help meant designating themselves as belonging to the category that was "overabundant in the national economy." Any contact with the police or with a government administrative office became a nightmare: a resident visa might expire on such and such day; on another day, foreign Jews were required to obtain an identity card; on yet another, they had to get a special pass. Many refugees declared they were receiving assistance from Jewish organizations just to prove that they expected nothing from public funds.[125]

In September 1940, there were about 4,800 people receiving assistance from the Committee on Aid for Refugees. By December of the same year, there were already more than 9,500; by March 1941, those depending on such aid numbered nearly 14,000, and this figure does not take into account those interned in the camps.[126] Nor did this number include the 5,741 famillies among the general population evacuated from the Alsace-Lorraine region who were being aided by the Israelite Social Aid Program (Oeuvres d'aide sociale israélite).[127] The Federation of Jewish Societies in France (Fédération des sociétés juives de France) strove to provide direct assistance to intellectuals, craftsmen, students, shopkeepers, rabbis, peddlers, foreign cantors (whose communities had been scattered), scholars, journalists, and artists without income. There were some 2,800 of them receiving such aid in January 1941. They numbered nearly 4,000 by August of the same year, and almost 6,000 by December.[128]

The total amount of this aid was far from adequate to meet the need. While the French government allocated a sum of seventeen francs a day for the needy that it assisted in the summer of 1941, Jewish refugees who were living from subsidies provided by the CAR could scarcely count on receiving more than thirty-five to forty francs per week.[129] Moreover, the amount allocated per family receiving assistance from the Federation kept diminishing constantly. At the same time, the organization that, since the fall of 1940, had been striving to establish some basic coordination between all various Jewish aid groups was, by June 1941, receiving an average of six hundred letters a month, most them pleas for assistance.[130]

Those who had the responsibility for distributing aid (and who also sought to improve the living conditions for those detained in the camps) felt that they had been given a vital mission. That is why these social aid activists were thrown into such shock and dismay when Xavier Vallat announced the plan to bring all existing Jewish organizations under one umbrella group to be under his control.

The Logic of Charity: The UGIF

Vallat got the idea of bringing all Jewish organizations together under one group from Theodor Dannecker, who for many months had been trying to apply the concept in the Occupied Zone. With the creation of the Coordinating Committee, he had managed to unify the work of the various Jewish aid organizations in Paris. By bringing to Paris two Viennese Jews under his orders, he had succeeded in launching a Jewish newspaper that published the instructions he wanted Jews to follow in Paris: the paper called upon Jews to become affiliated with the Coordinating Committee if they hoped to have any chance of receiving assistance. In spite of the passive resistance of the various organizations' leaders, Dannecker first sought to recruit members directly from the Jewish population for the "hostage organization" that would play the role he had in mind. He then turned toward the authorities in Vichy to achieve his goals. On August 29, 1941, he ordered Xavier Vallat to institute without any further delay the aforementioned compulsory organization for Jews in the Occupied Zone.[131] Vallat's concerns were twofold: first, he wanted the authority of the French government to take the place of German control; second, he wanted to bring the policy toward the Jews in the Southern Zone in line with existing policy in the Northern Zone.

With those ends in mind, Vallat took up where the Germans left off. Beginning in the fall of 1941, he began negotiations with Jewish leaders from the Northern and Southern Zones on the creation of a single Jewish organization that would span the entire country and would bring all preexisting entities together under its authority. Several factors persuaded Jewish leaders in the Occupied Zone to go along with the idea. It seemed absurd to continue trying to resist pressure from the Germans, especially as massive police roundups of Jews seemed prompted by such refusals to comply. The possibility of seeing French authorities stepping in to mediate between German military command and Jewish organizations also incited them to accept the notion of creating one overarching organization.

In the Southern Zone, the situation was completely different: the entire Jewish community was represented at Vichy by the Central Consistory and its president, Jacques Helbronner. What is more, the main Jewish aid programs had been brought together under one common coordinating structure by Chief Rabbi Isaïe Schwarz on October 31, 1940: this was the Central Committee for Jewish Aid Organizations (CCOJA). Its central office had been located in Marseilles in June 1941. The CAR, under the leadership of Raymond-Raoul Lambert, was its chief operating agency. Immigrant Jews were represented by the Federation (FSJF).

Xavier Vallat first took up the matter of an overarching, mandatory organization for Jews with Jacques Helbronner. When Helbronnner voiced his reservations, he turned to Raymond-Raoul Lambert. Discussions between Jewish leaders and Vallat lasted in fact until January 8, 1942, at which time was issued a decree designating the eighteen members of the board of directors for the new organization that had been created by a law promulgated on November 29, 1941. These discussions can hardly be considered as negotiations: it was clear that although Vallat preferred to win the collaboration of leaders that were recognized by Jewish organizations, he was determined to proceed on his own if he failed to get it. And while all Jewish leaders were theoretically opposed to this new measure, all sorts of specific considerations were present in the debate within the various Jewish groups; opposition was not equally strong in all quarters.

Leaders within the Consistory were vehemently opposed to the very principle of such a mandatory organization, which would have the effect of a ghetto: it would place French and foreign Jews in the same group, implicitly replace the religious definition of a Jew with a racial one, and further widen the gap that each new antisemitic measure was creating between French Jews and their non-Jewish compatriots. They were worried about the moral implications of the possible use of the so-called Solidarity Funds, which came from the sale of plundered Jewish property, for the purposes of social aid.[132] They rejected the idea of an organization charged with any duties involving issues other than religion. And they believed that they could influence the final decision on the matter by working through their political contacts among Pétain's entourage.

The CCOJA's opposition was based on the same arguments, but they considered their priority to be the continuation of their social aid efforts. The CCOJA was thus fearful that the consistory's "political" opposition would jeopardize the social assistance on which foreign Jews were particularly dependent. Raymond-Raoul Lambert, who was the most concerned about Xavier Vallat's impatience, was intent on "saving" Jewish aid efforts. The leaders of the Federation, and in particular its president Marc Jarblum, were opposed to having any contact with the General Commission on Jewish Affairs: they were opposed to bringing all Jewish organizations under the control of an antisemitic government that collaborated with the Germans.

Various strategies were adopted in efforts to prevent Vallat from carrying out his plans for an overarching organization for Jews. Jacques Helbronner presented an alternative plan, even though his action was denounced by the other members of the consistory. An appeal was made to have the State Council arbitrate the issue, but to no avail. The existing Jewish organizations formed a common front and submitted a memorandum detailing the extent of aid activity that would be jeopardized by the planned organization. There were regular consultations between Xavier Vallat and Raymond-Raoul Lambert. Vallat was convinced that he had found a spokesman for the Jews in France, while Lambert felt that he had no choice but to trust Vallat if he wanted to have any future hopes of continuing aid to Jews in need.

What resulted was the creation of the General Union of French Israelites (UGIF), whose "purpose was to ensure that Jews were represented to public authorities, particularly on the issues of aid, planning, and social reorientation." By virtue of article 2 of the law instituting the new overarching organization, all Jews "who have their home or who reside in France [were] required to belong to [it]," and "all [previously] existing Jewish organizations [were] disbanded, with the exception of the legally constituted Israelite worship groups." The Central Consistory, considered a purely religious institution, and the local worship groups thus remained autonomous. Aside from the term "particularly," which allowed interpretations and developments of all sorts to crop up, the Consistory could theoretically keep its role of representing of French Jews to public authorities.

The leaders of the new overarching, mandatory organization for Jews were placed under the direct authority of the General Commission on Jewish Affairs. The organization was indeed financed partially (but not totally) by the Solidarity Fund, and use of those monies was not an imperative. In reality the new law had created two separate organizations, one in the Occupied Zone and another in the Southern Zone, each with its own board of directors.

In the opinion of Raymond-Raoul Lambert, who was to serve as secretary-general of this new organization, the decree creating a "racial grouping" held terrible implications. Lambert was convinced that the French government was under constant pressure from Berlin on Jewish matters. He was determined to "hold up and make it through," and kept telling himself that his acceptance of this "technical job" did "not mean [he accepted] the [anti-Jewish] laws."[133]

Over the course of these months, many sharp differences of opinion had arisen among the various Jewish leaders, who were either sure of having a better strategy or jealous of their prerogatives. It took a long time for tensions to ease. The marked opposition between the Central Consistory and the new UGIF would weigh heavily on events that were to follow. Jewish organizations nevertheless complied, and in early March 1942 were integrated into the new overarching organization. In the southern section, Raymond-Raoul Lambert granted the greatest possible autonomy to the various "sections" of the new organization: under this new administrative term, they simply carried on their activities as they had previously.[134] The OSE became the third "health" section of the UGIF in March 1942, but as far as their leaders were concerned, in practice nothing was changed. It was in these terms that Dr. Joseph Weill spoke to the director of the French Israelite Mutual Aid association (EFI) in Périgueux when all Jewish aid programs were to be integrated under the umbrella of the UGIF: "The publication of the dissolution decree on March 8 does not change the situation. Instead of being director, you have been appointed administrator. Close out your books on March 8 and reopen them on the ninth. Our work continues unchanged."[135] The Israelite Scouts of France, which had now become section 4 of the UGIF "youth," likewise changed none of its activities, except for a few minor details: its stationery had been modified to include the new name; the official printed matter put out by the organization of French Scouts no longer mentioned them; and they made no further public appearences, except when they received a special invitation. Moreover, the Israelite Scouts of France handed over the leadership of religious education to a commission created by the Central Consistory—in other words, to an entity outside of the UGIF.[136] For its part, the Federation (FSJF) quickly put together a parallel structure that would escape the UGIF's control. "Except for that miserable Brith family—the UGIF in coded language—we have the possibility of doing good work," wrote Marc Jarblum to his correspondents in the Zionist organization in Switzerland.[137]

But although it seemed to be business as usual in many areas, creation of the UGIF was really a sign of the continuing marginalization of Jews in French society. Because the needs were so urgent, however, the leaders of Jewish charitable organizations knowingly chose to follow a dangerous path. Others worried about the consequences of this decision. The renowned historian Marc Bloch,[138] who had kept his distance from all specifically Jewish groups, took a singular initiative at the time when the UGIF was being created. He organized a collective letter signed by the most prestigious names of the French Israelite intelligentsia. In it, he exhorted Jewish leaders to "maintain the closest unity possible between us and our French brothers, [to] propose nothing, [to] do nothing, [to]try nothing, even with the intention of relieving the most respectable misfortune, that might end up directly or indirectly isolating us morally from the national community: even though we have been targeted by the law, we want to remain faithful citizens of our country."[139] Pointing to the "moving expression of solidarity" he had received from "fellow non-Jewish citizens of France," Marc Bloch took exception to "shrinking back from the social mainstream into a posture of mutual aid." For Marc Bloch and his friends, there were "no concerns that took precedence over their attachment to France."

As can be seen in these words, Marc Bloch was not condemning the UGIF at that time for symbolizing collaboration rather than resistance. Rather, he criticized its existence for jeopardizing what he conceived to be Jewish identity in France and for representing one more step down the road toward a "ghettoization" that, as a Jew, he feared more than anything. He also refused to cooperate with the documentation enterprise undertaken by the study office of the Central Consistory in Lyon. "We shall one day have to ask to recover our place in the French community that, morally, we have never left. . . . Let us avoid giving any arguments to those who would confine us to a ghetto of any sorts," he wrote to Jean Ullmo in a letter dated April 2, 1941.[140]

It was elsewhere in French society that Marc Bloch was to find the support that many other Jews received from the UGIF and the consistory. Once they were sure of being able to put bread on the table, Jews also sought—and found—alternative microsocieties in which they were able to strengthen their defenses against an environment largely hostile to them.

5

Seeking Refuge in Social Interaction

Instability was now a regular part of everyday life and there was great worry among the Jewish population. The frequent appearance of new laws and the changing events of the war kept people in a state of uncertainty: they made adjustments, but it was only a short while before new strategies became necessary. And those who found themselves in a new social or geographical setting had to be constantly adapting to a new situation. People concentrated all their energies on preparing for a long period of waiting. The precariousness of their social and economic situation was heightened by the fact that they were now widely scattered throughout the country: as of June 1941, the Central Committee on Jewish Assistance Organizations (CCOJA) was in touch with fifteen thousand families spread out over 295 different locations.[1] And Jews were not the only refugees in this part of France who were looking for loved ones "lost" in the panic of the mass exodus of civilians fleeing the German onslaught in May and June 1940. However, they generally chose not to place a classified ad in the major newspapers that devoted an entire rubric to "reuniting refugees," as that would have required them to have their ad approved at the police station or the city hall. And they rarely availed themselves of the radio, which broadcast a daily program for refugees looking for family members. More and more they preferred to use the "search office" set up by the CCOJA in February 1941.[2] The call for aid was only one factor contributing to the creation of new social groups forming around Jewish organizations. Social groups were crystallizing everywhere, and their diversity reflected their various ways of living out their Jewish identity. Some were formed in response to the new situation that had been imposed on Jews in France. Others formed in the margins, creating a sort of parallel society. Still others placed themselves in direct opposition to the dominant society. In some cases, continuity played a major role and prewar ties predominated. In other cases, lives that had seemingly been all laid out ahead of time changed radically due to chance encounters or to the awakening of individual consciences. The action taken by a particular Jewish organization was decisive in some instances, but not always. And while the formation of some of these new groups was a sign of withdrawal back into a Jewish world, others were completely turned toward society.

FALLING BACK AND TURNING INWARD

Jewish Youth and the "Back to the Earth" Movement

In the context of Vichy's "National Revolution" that placed so much renewed emphasis on rural values, professional "reorientation" and going "back to the earth" offered some Jewish youth a way out of an increasingly difficult situation. The Israelite Scouts of France chose this path without hesitating. Within a year, more than two thousand young Jews were grouped together under the auspices of twenty-six Scout units in the Unoccupied Zone, thus providing support for young French Israelites who were bewildered and distressed as well as for young foreign Jews who had lost their ties with society. The ranks of scout leaders had swollen with the large numbers of officers, government employees, and professors who had fallen victim to the Jewish Statute and been forced out of their jobs: they now planned to lead Jewish youth.[3] Training camps for these new leaders were organized in September and December 1940, then in April and May 1941, and then again during the summer of 1941: their purpose was to ensure that the spiritual leadership of Jewish youth be in keeping with the ideals of scouting and that the foundations of Jewish culture be blended harmoniously with the imperatives of unswerving fidelity to France. The National School of Leaders in Uriage was explicitly cited as an example.[4] Although in 1930 the Scouts of France had refused to admit the Jewish scouts into their national organization and directed them to become affiliated with freethinkers, in September 1940 the Israelite Scouts of France were formally accepted as members of French Scouting.[5] In July 1941, the Israelite Scouts of France received the official approval of the secretary of state in the Ministry of Youth and National Education.

Some of the directives issued by the Israelite Scouts could indeed be easily integrated into the objectives of the French State. Such was the case with the planned "back to the earth" movement, an idea first conceived in the summer of 1940. While leaders of the Israelite Scouts had been convinced that such a shift was necessary well before Vichy had begun to glorify rural values, the notion seemed to echo the main ideas of the new regime. Before the war, there had been a lot of talk about occupational reorientation that would make it possible to transform the social structure of the Jewish population: the idea was to "normalize" this social structure and level it out. An increase in the number of specialized craftsmen, it was thought, would compensate for what was considered to be an excessive number of intellectuals, lawyers, and doctors.

The transformation began smoothly. Removed from their previous positions by new French laws, a number of doctors, high-level government administrators, teachers, professors and engineers devoted themselves to the task. As for the youth demoralized by their image in society, they often found a warm welcome as well as a concrete answer to their worries withing the structures created by the Scouts. And so it was that at a rural worksite created on November 1940, there were some forty "land clearers" between the ages of sixteen and twenty-five. Included among them were a graduate from the prestigious Ecole Normale Supérieure, a doctor, a mathematics student, a law student, a student from the Ecole des Chartes, as well as fifteen lycée graduates. In addition to doing agricultural work in the fields and receiving training in carpentry, masonry, and electrical workshops, they took theoretical classes and engaged in sports. They also took part in study circles devoted to intellectual and spiritual enrichment: it was here that Jewish subjects were given great emphasis.

In the summer of 1941, there were some twenty young Jewish men in Taluyers in the département of Le Rhône clearing land, plowing fields, hoeing, trimming, harvesting crops, raising chickens and cattle, while at the same time taking part in a rich program of cultural activities. Beginning in March 1941, the Viarose group in the département of Le Tarn-et-Garonne set out to convert the Charry estate for agricultural production. Their numbers grew in August 1941 with the arrival of new members coming from the Rivesaltes internment camp.[6]

Life in these groups was considerably different from the prewar dreams envisioned at weekly meetings of the Scouts or Zionist youth groups. The spiritual leader of the Charry estate, Isaac Pougatch, echoed this disillusionment:

> The existence of the rural worksite, the kibbutz, is not very much like the meetings we used to have that were filled with song, dance, exciting readings, mystical services, long, passionate speechs followed by a few beers on the counter in a bistro, and ended by long hikes through Paris, because of course we had missed the last métro. . . . We have really changed our tune! Is that what collective living is like? Moving around twenty-four hours a day in the same house, under the same leaky roof, in the same cold drafts? Working from sunup to sunset, and in a regular, proper manner? We would like to sing and dance in the evening, but we are too tired and are always in hurry to go to bed in our frigid sleeping quarters.

"It is no fun to live on a farm in this harsh and rugged country in the département of Le Tarn,"[7] observed Robert Gamzon, secretary-general of the Scouts, and known as Castor ("beaver").

Added to all that was that young people from the widest variety of backgrounds had come together at these sites. There were "Zionists and anti-Zionists, atheists and believers. . . . There [were] natives of Germany, Poland, Rumania, Hungary, Austria, Russia, and even French youth who had come from a regiment, from the Building Grounds for Youth [Chantiers de Jeunesse], from the Foreign Legion, from the university, from carpentry shops, [and] from training farms. [The] student [would] become a farmer, workers would at times be students. Now, when all these people come together and begin bumping into each other, you get quite a row!"[8]

Over the winter of 1941–42, while they tried to till the soil for the first time in their life, the land-clearers on the Charry estate managed to complete three full basic courses: universal history beginning with antiquity, Jewish history from its beginnings to the contemporary times, and fundamentals of agriculture. Occasional courses in French and Hebrew rounded out this phase of training. There were also lectures on the meaning and origins of all the Jewish holy days throughout the year, the way they were celebrated in Palestine, and biblical subjects. Finally, there were sessions devoted to Hebraic literature, Zionism, and Zionist youth movements.[9] When the fifty-odd books that they possessed in the fall of 1941 no longer sufficed, they read and commented on the Zionist press of the prewar years. A documentation center was later created in Moissac, with a library that soon had about a thousand books available for circulation.[10]

What we have in the case of the Charry estate is a sort of protected enclave. At a time when the pressures of persecution were increasing, these youth led a life structured by the combined rhythms of nature and Jewish holy days. The Sabbath was observed with the traditional singing: for each holy day marked on the Jewish calendar, the use of this liturgy was a way of showing that Judaism was still alive. This was a time when France was focusing on notion of national reconstruction: the leaders of the Jewish Scouts participated in their own way in this undertaking and gave it their own distinct interpretation. Wrote Isaac Pougatch,

> The time seems to have come to bring new life back to Judaism in order for youth to practice it immediately. For strictly observant Jews, we must show that the universal worldview is a truly biblical one. To atheistic nationalists and champions of Yiddish culture, we must teach respect for our faith and a wider interpretation of the notion of God. For practicing Jews, we must stress the practical application of morality, without which religious observances are worthless.[11]

For these Israelite Scouts, belonging to the Jewish people became a source of pride at the very time when the state was pushing them to the margins of society. They indeed constituted a protected enclave, in spite of their constant hunger, in spite of hard, thankless work, and in spite of the cold they suffered in living quarters that were, to say the least, uncomfortable. They even felt so protected that Robert Gamzon had his wife and two children, who had taken refuge in Portugal, come back to join him in France for Passover in 1941. Although times remained troubled, it seemed possible to adapt while waiting to reach the light at the end of the tunnel.

The ambition of the Israelite Scouts encompassed all of the Jewish youth in France. And because their basic principles did not conflict with the French State's official ideology, the Scouts were the only official Jewish youth movement to receive Vichy's recognition. They were "the only organized movement . . . the only Jewish youth movement that has been maintained," Gamzon liked to say.[12] Accordingly, their action was not limited to the creation of rural training sites: the various units spread throughout the Southern Zone engaged in traditional scouting activities, supplemented by a particularly intensive program of Jewish cultural events. Moreover, the Jewish Youth of France (JJF), which was intended to bring together all of the other Jewish youth groups disbanded by the war, was founded with the encouragement of the Israelite Scouts and modeled on their example. The JJF was only created in June 1941, and actually only operated pending its official recognition by the secretary-general for youth in Vichy. Because the creation of the UGIF made such recognition moot, the JJF was never more than an unofficial entity: nevertheless, as did the Israelite Scouts, the JJF focused on opening workshops and rural training camps where youth could "not only learn a trade, but also live a life of camaraderie in a Jewish context."[13]

The aim was thus to provide an alternate social structure. The essentially religious nature of Jewish identity would be preserved, supported by the study of the cultural and historical foundations of Judaism. At the same time, however, this alternate social structure found itself in the margins of French society. In the first place, it was there that social integration largely compensated for the negative image of Jewish identity fostered by the French State. Furthermore, the very nature of cultural activities emphasizing the specificity of Jewish identity and solidarity among Jews tended to impose a national conception of Judaism. In addition, the spiritual leaders of the Scouting movement, Edmond Fleg in particular, were staunch Zionists. Finally, aiding young foreign Jews soon became the movement's main concern.

Even before the war, the Israelite Scouts had emerged from within the assimilated community, and, with the blessing of Jewish institutions, formed a bridge between the various components of Jewish identity in France. Scouting provided a context for the expression of a pluralistic vision of Judaism, and particularly of Zionist leanings.[14] The movement was able to develop and become institutionalized thanks to the particular circumstances prevailing in the early stages of the Occupation. But as the situation got progressively worse for Jews in France and as public opinion changed with new events, Israelite Scouting would evolve. From an organization situated at the margins of French society, it would later join the ranks of the organized opposition to the Vichy regime.

Refuge in Social Assistance: The OSE and Children's Homes

The development of the Children's Relief Organization (Organisation de Secours aux Enfants, [OSE]) followed a path similar to that of the Israelite Scouts, but its basic principles and traditions gave it a rather different orientation. Ever since its founding in 1912 by a group of doctors in Saint Petersburg, the OSE had focused on aiding children and providing medical care to Jewish populations suffering persecution. Its headquarters had been located in Paris since 1933. Under the Occupation, however, its main offices had been transferred to Montpellier.[15] Spanning out from Montpellier, it set up medical and social aid centers for impoverished Jews and refugees in various cities of the Southern Zone, including Marseilles, Toulouse, Lyon, Grenoble, and Limoges. These centers strove to reach the largest possible number of Jewish families that had been scattered throughout the region. At the same time, a mobile dispensary circulated in the département of La Dordogne to provide care for the thousands of refugees from the Alsace and Moselle areas. Over the months of July and August 1941, the medical team visited twenty-six different sites, giving some 346 medical examinations, making 482 home visits (during which food and dietary supplements were distributed), and filling 100 prescriptions.[16] During the first six months of 1942, more than 3,400 families availed themselves of the assistance provided by these various centers.[17]

Generally speaking, aid was not limited to a one-time basis. Each family was assigned a social worker who would monitor its needs, procure medicine, arrange doctor visits, and occasionally send weaker children for a cure in the mountains or a vacation near the sea. The centers established links to hospitals, prevention centers, and convalescent homes; when necessary, they obtained prescribed prostheses. It was through these activities that they truly became places for socialization, creating ongoing relationships between families in need and the personnel of the OSE's dispensaries.

The organization's facilities were used for many other kinds of activities. The offices of the OSE in Limoges, for example, were used to prepare correspondence course materials for those participating in the program directed by Jacques Cohn. The OSE center in Marseilles, which had been established on June 1, 1941, was used as a regular meeting place for more than sixty Jewish doctors who had been barred from medical practice. It was there that they could consult books in the library created especially for them and attend the lectures scheduled every week.[18] OSE facilities also housed the headquarters of youth organizations—Marseilles in particular. The creation of a school for Jewish social workers was even planned for April 1941, but the prefect put an end to the project after the first few courses, as "the social workers that the OSE would send swarming all over France could easily be tempted to engage in activities hostile to our country."[19]

"Some Jews establish their residence at the OSE: they have their mail sent there; they gather there to do business, especially the business of exchanging products of limited availability that they procure on the black market. The OSE functions pretty much like a 'club' for a large number of Jews who have come down here from the north." Such was the conclusion of an inspector for the Police for Jewish Affairs in the Montpellier region at the end of March 1942.[20] Obviously, we might question the reliability of any analysis given by the Police for Jewish Affairs. But for many Jews who had taken refuge in the Montpellier area, most Jewish organizations in the Unoccupied Zone, and among them, the OSE, probably represented first and foremost a "club."

For Jewish doctors and social workers, the OSE provided living quarters and sometimes a mission; for families in contact with one of its dispensaries, it offered support in face illness; for many others, it served as a meeting place. Most important, however, the OSE created a network of children's homes: for children in particular, it established a safe haven in a world that had been turned upside down.

Originally, the children's homes had been created to take in refugee children from Central Europe and Poland and to care for children whose impoverished families could no longer support. During the Occupation years, they proliferated. The rapid increase in their number began with the evacuation of children from the Paris region undertaken in September 1939 in collaboration with the Israelite Scouts of France. By November 1 of the same year, 988 cases of children who urgently needed to be evacuated had been recorded. There was, for example, an eleven-year-old boy whose mother had remained in Czechoslovakia and whose father had been incorporated into the Czech army. There was also a seven-year-old boy whose Polish parents did not have a work permit. And there were two little girls, ten and eleven years old, whose father was in Palestine and whose mother had been left in Paris without any source of income. And then there was the little nine-year-old boy who had come to France from Germany in 1938 with his family: his father had been locked up in an internment camp and his mother was unemployed.[21] In order to take in all these children, the OSE began by preparing three chateaus located in the département of La Creuse. By the spring of 1941, there were seven homes housing 647 children in the Southern Zone.[22] By November 1, 1941, the OSE had assumed the responsibility of taking care of twelve hundred children. These children were spread throughout nine homes run by the OSE, four others that it subsidized and for which it provided medical care, and one other children's home under its partial control.[23] In addition, there had been five hundred other children who had come to stay temporarily in these homes during the summer in order to take a much-needed respite from their new life as refugees. The number of children staying in the OSE's homes would continue to increase until the summer of 1942.[24]

The makeup of these groups of children changed also. The first group of children was from Central Europe: their parents had not been able to follow them on the paths of immigration. They were joined by children—often of foreign parents—who had fled from the Occupied Zone, children whose parents had been interned, and by children who had themselves been released from French internment camps. Later, there would be children whose parents had been deported. For the summer of 1941, some 22.5 percent of these youngsters were refugees from Central Europe who had lost all contact with their parents; 23.5 percent had spent varying amounts of time in one of the internment camps; 27 percent were Polish children whose parents had disappeared or were still in the Occupied Zone; 11 percent were orphans or semiorphans; and 16 percent of them had parents in the Southern Zone who were so impoverished that they could not meet their children's needs.[25] These percentages varied over time, in response to changing events. Some left to emigrate while others came after being released from internment camps. The enactment of even harsher measures against the Jews in the Occupied Zone brought still more children to the OSE's homes. For an ever-increasing number of children, these homes were not just a resting point but the only place of refuge.

The decision to care for these children through a collective organization became imperative for a number of reasons. The OSE's experience in Russia had illustrated the effectiveness of such an organization in the struggle against persecution. There were also ideological considerations. The OSE had given itself the mission of raising these children, who were often orphans. If they wished to keep control of the training of these children and ensure that the chldren would preserve the meaning of Jewish values, the OSE could accept no substitute for its own children's homes. As for children whose parents were only temporarily unable to provide for their needs, the OSE's homes offered security without putting another set of parents in place of the children's own, which might have caused lasting emotional problems that would be hard to overcome.[26] Finally, there were practical reasons. With xenophobia as prevalent as it was in France in 1940 and 1941, there was certainly no flood of volunteers to take in and take care of foreign (often German or Polish) Jewish children.

The heterogeneity of the children in the OSE's homes (in terms of their family situation, national origin, and age) and the problems periodically posed by shortages of various commodities throughout France were a constant reality. Although such factors made it difficult to organize daily life and make ends meet, the homes focused on education.[27] There were some older children whose only dream was to emigrate to the United States: this was the case for more than one-third of the 698 children lodged in the OSE's homes in October 1941.[28] There were also the very small children who arrived mainly during the first few months of 1942: their daily routine did not mesh very well with the older children's. Some children were still in contact with their parents, while others did not know what had become of their immediate family. Some spoke French flawlessly; others, in spite of their efforts, had to put up with schoolmates who constantly made fun of their accent. Indeed, for the most part, these children went to local schools in neighboring villages, which at times meant they had to walk two or three kilometers with frightfully worn shoes. In homes housing the children of practicing Jews, religious instruction was provided on the spot. Wherever possible, vocational training played an important role in the children's schooling: many workshops for carpentry, leatherworking, and sewing were set up. Small vegetable gardens were sometimes planted on the grounds of children's homes. These gardens not only demonstrated the desire to introduce the children to agriculture, they also made it possible to improve a food supply whose quality and quantity fluctuated.

The fact remains that these children were taken in, cared for, and educated: the main concern of those in charge of these homes was to see that the children had as "normal" a life as possible. And the little societies of children that were established in this way took a burden off the shoulders of many parents, who were thus able to find means of providing for themselves before trying to secure a place to live.

Religious Renaissance or Cultural Renewal?

The Jewish religion and its practices were not affected by the provisions of the Jewish Statutes. Synagogues were not closed, and the pursuit of religious worship was relatively undisturbed during this time, at least in the Unoccupied Zone. "Religion, the worship service, the religious community, and the worship association remain today for us French Israelites the only firm and free ground," declared the chief rabbi of France in the pastoral letter written on December 11, 1941, for the occasion of Hanukkah, which had been decreed the celebration of worship.[29]

A few violent attacks, however, did sporadically disturb the relative peace and quite of Jewish places of worship. Such was the case on May 18, 1941, when a bomb shook the walls of the synagogue in Marseilles. On August 6 of the same year, a similar attack took place at the synagogue in Vichy. But the perpetrators of these attacks were disavowed by French authorities and were even convicted by the criminal court in Cusset: the court recognized the Central Consistory's right to press charges and awarded it the symbolic franc that it had sought in payment for damages.[30] The authorities of the Catholic Church expressed their indignation over these attacks on the freedom of worship. Bishop Delay in Marseilles wrote to the chief rabbi on May 18, 1941, to express his outrage over the attack on the Marseilles synagogue.[31] The bombing of seven synagogues in Paris inspired the same compassion from the primate of the Gaules, Cardinal Gerlier,[32] and letters of sympathy from the bishop of Belley, the bishop of Périgueux, the archbishop of Avignon, the bishop of Montauban, and others.

In September 1942, at the height of the massive roundups and deportations of Jews, Chief Rabbi Kaplan received the following information about Laval's intentions: "He does not desire collaboration in the realms of mind and spirit, because he wants France to remain attached entirely to its own traditions. Therefore, no restrictions will be made on the observance of religious pratices."[33]

And while the chief rabbi was flatly denied permission to publish a weekly newsletter, he was allowed to put out a Jewish calendar. This calendar was a most valuable reference work that enabled practicing Jews to celebrate holy days at the appropriate time; the Hebraic lunar calendar would make the date of any particular celebration vary from year to year on the French calendar. Duly inspected by the censor, it was the only Jewish publication to be approved since the Armistice. It was in the fall of 1940; a year later, after the censor's cuts had affected more than half the texts inserted into the calendar, the rabbi's office discontinued its publication.[34] For the observance of Passover in 1941, the worship associations generally managed to come up with the necessary ration tickets and took care of making the unleavened bread that for a period of eight days takes the place of regular bread for practicing Jews. Those interested in learning modern Hebrew could get a grammar book or a text from the Grünewald bookstore in Limoges or the Bloch bookstore in Lyon. Religious items could also be found on Avenue de la Gare in Luchon and at Axelrad's in Toulouse. One printer in Marseilles, S. Langer, was able to print a Haggadah so that religious Jews could commemorate the flight from Egypt with a Passover seder, in keeping with tradition.

In a few instances, the instructions of the rabbi concerning the observance of this holy day were published. They were intended to ensure that the holy day be observed according to the rules; at the same time, they allowed for the special circumstances imposed by the Occupation. And so in spite of the usual restrictions, some foods were authorized: for lack of certain fresh vegetables and other products, for example, some dry foodstuffs, normally prohibited during this week, were allowed even if they had been tapped before the Passover period. Rules governing the treatment of cooking utensiles were softened. Alternatives were suggested for the ceremonial order of the seder: a double portion of lettuce could take the place of the bitter herbs; a second egg could be used instead of the shoulder bone; and an ersatz was allowed to replace kosher wine.[35] For the 1942 Passover, these instructions were reissued in almost the same terms.

For the holy days occuring in the fall of 1941, Orthodox Jewish leaders in the Friends of the Jewish Tradition put out a special tract on the subject of miracles; namely, the miracle that, in all times and in the midst of the worst wars, had made it possible for "ideas in all their frailty" ultimately to prevail over "robust matter." This was the miracle that was, in New York, behind the creation of a "grand center for philanthropy which [was] accomplishing its good works throughout a suffering Europe [and] making it possible for our unfortunate brothers to survive the disaster, and drawing men, women, and above all traumatized children to this land of hospitality." Finally, it was also a miracle that had made it possible to protect the life and health of the majority of Jews. Behind these and many other miracles—sometimes wrongly attributed to random chance—was the hand of the Eternal.[36]

For the celebration of Hanukkah two months later, the emphasis was on the "spirit of sacrifice." Sacrifice was presented as a virtue and an obligation ingrained in "Israel's national character" and written "in blood on each page of [its] history." It was thanks to this spirit of sacrifice that Israel had always managed "to rise up again out of misery." The illusion of being safe from all persecution had led to decadence, and now it was necessary to pay the price. "Those who might be tempted to betray the common cause in order to preserve their material wealth or the future of their children such as they see it" were sternly reminded of the sacrifice of Isaac (*aqedat Itzhak*; actually, the tying up of Isaac). "Let there be no disgraceful cowardice" was the exhortation for devout Jews and those who were expected to become devout. What followed were instructions for celebrating Hanukkah in keeping with tradition even in this time of restrictions and shortages. Candles, for example, were to be used sparingly or shared with a less fortunate neighbor. And the prayer (the *kiddush*) intended for the wine could be said over the bread or over another beverage if there was no wine to be had.[37]

There were even ritual baths (a *mikvah*), a creation of Rabbi Deutsch, which were set up on the banks of the Vienne river at a well-known bathing spot, Chez Vitrat. Devout Jews could go there and purify themselves twice a week until the facility was largely destroyed by an act of vandalism in early 1943.[38] The ritual baths in Vichy had already been pillaged the previous year.[39] The scarcity of ritual baths, however, made it possible for Rabbi Chneerson, the leader of the Association of Practicing Israelites, to obtain travel permits for foreign Jewish women, as, he argued, it was only in Lyon that their religious requirement of ritual bathing could be fulfilled according to the strict rules of orthodoxy.[40]

Jews could find kosher butcher shops in Nice, Limoges, Nîmes, Lyon, Périgueux, Marseilles, and doubtless elsewhere. And where there were larger numbers of Jews, there were restaurants serving kosher menus.[41] Not all Jewish butcher shops had survived the turmoil of war: in certain places their number had declined appreciably. In Marseilles, for example, there remained only one of the seven kosher butcher shops that had existed in the late 1930s. And, of course, some had been placed under the control of a provisional manager. Such was the case with a certain kosher butcher shop in Montpellier, where the provisional manager never failed to confiscate the money taken in each day. The owner had been forced out of business by the local representative of the General Commission on Jewish Affairs. When he was replaced by his helper, however, customers threatened to boycott, and he was called back to his shop.[42]

At any rate, ritual slaughter was still authorized, and authorizations were as a general rule renewed when necessary, even though certain newspapers sometimes led a campaign against the practice.[43] Although the Society for the Protection of Animals in Lyon and the General Commission on Jewish Affairs tried to intervene and put an end to ritual slaughter, they were thwarted by a ruling of the State Council dating from March 27, 1936. The council had indeed ruled that the decree issued by a certain mayor and forbidding this kind of slaughter was illegal; it was not necessary to ban ritual slaughter in order to preserve the public order. It was later necessary to refer back to this legal precedent.[44] And so, officially, Jews were allowed to continue the practice of ritual slaughter. In some places, however, there was so much red tape surrounding the ruling that it lost all substance.

Because of the difficulty of obtaining many basic foodstuffs, rabbis loosened somewhat the very strict dietary requirements. And so even when they were not "in keeping with ritual," butter, milk, and cheese were allowed, especially for growing children and the undernourished, even by the most orthodox rabbis.[45] When rabbis gave their authorization for a family to eat an impure meat, however, they sometimes had tears in their eyes. Candles for the *Shabbos* were often obtained from a church. It was not always a simple matter to observe ritual in this time of restriction, and when a family celebration was held, ritual requirements narrowed even more the range of products available for the woman of the house in charge of preparing culinary treats. And so fish heads were the centerpiece of Aharon Sigman's *bar mitzvah* meal, which turned out to be a merry occasion nevertheless.[46] But although for devoutly observant Jews, life was full of material difficulties and surrounded by general hostility, they nevertheless did not have to go underground in order to practice their religion. History had proven religion's value as a refuge, and present circumstances confirmed the need for such a spiritual haven.

Local situations varied from city to city according to the mood of local authorities. It was in Nice more than anywhere else that synagogues came under attack. On

June 3, 1942, around six-thirty in the evening, some twenty-five to thirty young men armed with clubs, iron bars, and rocks charged into the group of twenty worshipers gathering in the temple on Rue Dubouchage. They smashed the tables and silver candelabras, drove an iron bar into the armoire holding the sacred scrolls, profaned the scrolls, and ripped down the curtains. At the same time, a second group lashed out against the worshipers while a third committed similar acts of vandalism in an adjoining annex. Two of the worshipers were hospitalized with broken legs and bruises on the head and all over the body as a result of the attack. Five other people were treated in their homes for injuries they had sustained. Three of their assaillants had been arrested, but immediately released by the police who had arrived on the scene. The other attackers had run away, carrying with them articles used for worship. This incident had been preceded by numerous others. In May 1942, for example, the doors of another synagogue (on Rue Deloye) had been pried open, and the intruders had tried to set the place on fire. And rocks had been thrown at the windows during the *Shabbos* worship service.[47]

In Cannes, where the number of Jews was judged to be excessive, local authorities refused authorization for the opening of an oratory. However, they did make accommodations for Sabbath-day services that were attended by some four hundred families. These services were tolerated, or at least apparently tolerated until one Saturday morning in August 1941, when police burst into the apartment where services were being held and chased out the worshipers. It was only thanks to the goodwill of Pastor Monod that the Jewish holy days occurring in the fall of 1941 were able to be observed in the celebration hall of a Protestant school. Similarly, it took the intervention of the bishop of Nice to convince the prefect to reconsider his decision to prohibit the opening of an oratory in early 1942, although he renewed this prohibition a few months later.[48] It was also in the Protestant parish hall that the holy days of Hanukkah were observed in December 1941 in Thonon-les-Bains.[49] In Millau, services were held in the homes of the thirty-seven members enrolled in the local worship association, who took turns hosting.

In Annecy, a new synagogue was opened on October 28, 1940: over the course of 1941, two mariages, four burials, three births, and three bar mitzvahs were celebrated in the facility. Services, however, were only held during the weekend. In Lyon, on the other hand, worshipers gathered for services in the synagogue every day. The Jewish population in the city had tripled, and eight hundred families were registered on the synagogue's membership rolls. Over the same year 1941, some 19 mariages, 123 burials, 35 births, and 92 bar mitzvahs had been celebrated there. In Marseilles, 300 families were affiliated with the worship association, while in Vichy there were 225.[50] By May 1, 1942, there were 265 contributing members of the worship association in Clermont-Ferrand, out of a total population of around seven thousand Jews in the area. In Nice, there were some five hundred to six hundred. In Brive, the 220 registered members in the worship association attended services held twice a day in a facility that had been rented since November 15, 1940: over the course of 1941, four mariages, seventeen burials, nine circumcisions, and eight bar mitzvahs were celebrated.[51] Finally, out of the 3,500 Jews who had registered with the census in Montpellier, some 750 were affiliated with the worship assocation: Henri Schilli, the first rabbi present in the city since medieval times, came to serve them.[52]

What was happening was that communities were breaking up and spreading out. As a result, there was a renewal of religious life in all these places where there had been no such fervor before the war. When French rabbis gathered for their general assembly in Chamalières on September 10 and 11, 1941, they expressed their satisfaction with this "return of disoriented and assimilated Jews to Judaism."[53] When in late April 1942, the rabbis' central office did a survey of religious activity in Vichy France for the year 1941, respondants all echoed the same observation: "Recently, worship services have been attended better than for as long as anyone can remember"; "Courses giving religious instruction have met with much greater success than expected."[54] In Toulouse, where the temple had previously been almost empty, there was now a crowd of worshipers in attendance at the weekly service. In Pau, the 150 seats in the synagogue were no longer sufficient for the two hundred refugee families interested in regularly attending services. In Béziers, La Châtre, Agen, Grenoble, and Aix-en-Provence, it was necessary either to rent a facility or to make use of property kindly made available to the community for worship services. In Montpellier, Rabbi Schilli held three services one after the other in the synagogue on Saturday mornings in order to meet the demand.

Granted, those who started returning to the synagogue remained a minority, and we would doubtless do well to distinguish a true religious renewal bringing former agnostics back to the fold from all that could be attributed to the arrival of observant Jews from the Paris region in the Southern Zone. Furthermore, worshipers coming to the synagogue displayed no eagerness to register officially with the local worship association. But the number of Jews coming to temples kept on increasing throughout the year 1941, to such an extent that the consistory undertook projects that would put this increase to good use. One such project by Georges Wormser, "New methods for new times," proposed the addition of prayer in French to the worship service and the scheduling of a series of talks devoted to the problems of the day. Wormser's intent was "to take advantage of the fact that worried Jews are turning to us, so that they might not only be protected and guided but also led back to religion."[55]

Around the same time, Léon Algazi also pointed out that a good many Jews "seem[ed] to be becoming more aware of their Judaism and that places of worship were filling with a larger and larger crowds of fervent people." Algazi accordingly proposed to simplify and shorten the worship service, to provide extensive explanations by the rabbi, and to encourage more active participation from worshipers.[56] Although none of these projects ever saw the light of day, they testify to a sort of "divine surprise" for those worried by the decline of religious practice among a community of Jews that was more and more assimilated on the eve of World War II.

As was the case for worship services, there was also a proliferation of courses providing instruction not only in religion but also in Jewish history and even in Hebrew. In Nice, which seems to have always led the way in surmounting obstacles and organizing some semblance of Jewish life, religious classes were forbidden. To get around the ban, children were divided into groups of two, three, or four, or were given private lessons.[57] Elsewhere, however, such obstacles did not exist. And so, in Affreville some 70 percent of Jewish children took courses in religion, as did 50 percent of the Jewish children in Le Puy, a few in Agen, a hundred-odd in Brive, thirty in Béziers, thirty also in La Châtre, and thirty-five in Grenoble. Here again, this sketchy list only provides a fragmentary account of a phenomenon that was becoming more and more widespread, and that was being handled more and more effectively by the consistory during these first two years of the Dark Years.

Most often, it was a nucleus of Jewish refugees from Alsace who were the most dynamic catalysts of this evolution. In contrast with other categories of Jewish refugees scattered throughout many towns and cities in southern France by the German onslaught and the ensuing occupation of the Northern Zone, the Alsatian community withdrew and fell back into specific départements as a group and under the guidance of its leaders. Once these groups came together as communities, they formed poles of attraction not only for Parisians who still had family ties with Alsatians, but also for those who were looking for a place of refuge where some forms of solidarity would be likely to appear in these troubled times. The département of La Dordogne played a key role in this new dispersion of Jews, and the new Jewish community in Périgueux constitutes a particularly interesting case.

Before the Jewish community from Strasbourg took shelter in the area, there were only five or six Jewish families living in the département of La Dordogne. After the arrival of these newcomers, there were more than six thousand Jews[58] scattered throughout 122 towns and villages. A good many of them were from the département of Le Bas-Rhin, but there was also a large contingent of Polish Jews. Daily worship services bringing Alsatian and Polish Jews together were held in Périgueux in a building made available to the community by the Office of Low-Cost Housing. There were scarcely more than three hundred members officially registered with the worship association, but there were 152 pupils taking courses in religious instruction (studying the *Talmud Torah*), while eighteen young people were learning Hebrew and eighty-four other youths were enrolled in various study circles focusing on the Bible, great figures of Jewish history, and the social aspect of Judaism. At twelve other locations in the Dordogne area, 133 children were attending courses given by the rabbi.[59]

Along with the flurry of religious activity, however, often came friction between communities. Polish and Alsatian Jews were not always on good terms in the Dordogne area, particularly in Terrasson and Brantôme. Similar problems could also be found elsewhere, in Montluçon, Néris-les-Bains, and Roanne, for example. In Nîmes, there were disagreements between refugees and Jews native to the area. It was certainly true that the sixty Jewish households that had been living there before the war felt overwhelmed by the sudden arrival of nearly three hundred new families, for many of these newcomers were strictly observant Jews who remained wary of the worship association controlled by the families from Nîmes. In order to ward off animosity between the two groups, a special room was set aside for the newcomers to hold their service with all the desired "rigor of worship." And in spite of the misgivings expressed by a minority, the board of directors of the worship association decided on November 22, 1941, to allow the refugees to become registered members, although the results for better cooperation obtained were less successful than had been hoped.[60]

In Toulouse, the conflict took on more serious proportions. Bringing the local upper-class Jews together with the numerous immigrant Jews often from Belgium and of Polish descent never went without problems. The ones who had been in Toulouse the longest were fearful that the foreigners were going to take over all religious activity. Conflict between the two groups came to a head over the appointment of the rabbi; that is to say, the question of replacing Rabbi Moïse Cassorla (who was not French) by another to be named by the Consistory. "The young people in Toulouse all back their rabbi," declared a petition sent to the chief rabbi of France. "They would be heartbroken if the one they rightly consider to be their spiritual leader were taken away from them. They would not understand the meaning of such an action which could only be justified by arbitrary discrimination determined by such secondary issues as nationality, which, at the present time, should no longer be raised among Jews who share the same plight and who are undergoing the same ordeal."[61] It should be noted that those who signed the petition, including David Knout, Pinhas Roïtman, and others, were young Zionists committed to political activism: that is what explains the particular style and tone of their language, one that was becoming more and more common among young people, but was rarely used by adults.

Their petition nevertheless clearly shows that, in Toulouse as well as in other places, the synagogue served as a place that drew together a community seeking out its path. It was at the temple that the young Israelite scouts held their activities, just as the various groups of young Zionists who were coming back together used the temple to meet and recruit new followers. As was the case in Nîmes, it was often at the synagogue that the Jewish aid organizations, especially the local delegations of the Committee for Aid to Refugees (CAR), had their headquarters. The Federation of Jewish Societies in France (FSJF) also took great interest in the social and cultural activities that were being organized in connection with the synagogue.

Such was the case in Toulouse, where the Federation stressed the synagogue's importance as a gathering place for young people and children: "Children gladly spend their free time here on Thursday afternoons and Sunday mornings. They come not only to learn about the Bible and Hebrew, but also to study the history of the people of Israel, to sing, and to perform various little skits on themes related to national holidays."[62] "On the evening of the celebration of *Simhat Thora* in 1940, I had been attracted to the old synagogue on Rue Palaprat [in Toulouse]," wrote Claude Vigée, who described himself as "an assimilated Jew from an Israelite family that [had] been living in France for many long years."[63] "In spite of the large crowd," added Vigée, "I was seeking entrance in order to come into contact with Jewish fugitives who were, like me, persecuted and miserable." Thus although the renewal of Judaism quite often took on a religious appearance, it occurred in response to social needs and was expressed more in terms of cultural activity than religion.

It was therefore the needs of certain sectors of the Jewish population that gave rise to this renewal of Judaism involving all sorts of activists. The older ones felt that they had been given responsiblity, while the younger ones were thus able to avoid the indignity of idly standing by. Working together, they created a social and cultural network that sometimes overlaid French society, sometimes duplicated it, and sometimes offered an alternative. Working as members of the Central Consistory's Commission on Confessional Information, delegates traveled from city to city informing Jews about the consistory's position on various issues of the time and giving lectures (which was the official justification for their visit). While they were there, they inquired into the nature of Jewish opinion on various matters.[64] The organizing of this network linking synagogues with the Central Consistory had just about been completed by July 1942: it provided a structure that was parallel to the UGIF and flexible enough to adapt to all sorts of changes.

The entire development of social aid programs had created a vast web reaching an even larger portion of the Jewish population far beyond prominent leaders and observant Jews. There were many more than two networks, and their lines often interwined, but the Central Consistory and the UGIF were both used as moral reference points and safe havens for almost all Jewish organizations. Their existence made it possible for groups of Jews who either could not or would not blend in with French society to avoid atomization. Initially, they did not offer any way around the imperatives dictated by the choice of respecting legality. Spurred on by their own internal dynamics, however, they often carried out their activities at the very fringes of the law: it was for that very reason that their potential to pose a challenge to the law aroused suspicion among Vichy authorities.

A Suspicious Activity

"It is imperative to disband Jews who are using every means possible to gather together."[65] Voiced by the head of the Division of Investigations and Inspections (SEC) in Limoges, this opinion in fact reflected the attitude of the Vichy regime's police forces. To them it was obvious that, considering the persecutions suffered, the Jews were far from enthusiastic supporters of the Pétain government. Vichy authorities looked quite favorably on Jewish relief efforts, as such undertakings spared them from the consequences of the situation created by the French State's own actions.

At the same time, however, any spillover into another area immediately became suspect, even when it had occurred in absolutely legal circumstances. On the list of suspects singled out by the General Commission on Jewish Affairs and the Police for Jewish Affairs, one finds such individuals as Albert Manuel, secretary-general of the Consistory; Robert Gamzon; Raymond Lindon; and Marc Jarblum, president of the Federation. All were figures who held leadership positions in legally constituted organizations and who had been recognized by the state. And this was in 1941, when none of them had yet had the chance to become involved with any illegal practices.[66] In early 1942, searches were conducted in the homes of four rabbis. These raids "resulted in the seizure of a certain number of documents that turned out to be of interest to the bureau of secret assocations and that proved that these rabbis were tied to the independent and universal order of B'nai B'rith." Such was the reply given to the chief rabbi of France when he registered his protest against the raids with the police in Vichy.[67]

Any course of instruction given by a Jewish group came under suspicion. The little Israelite seminary in Limoges, where a group of about twenty youths ranging in age from fourteen to nineteen were taking classes to prepare them either to assume leadership roles in the Jewish world or to continue training to be rabbis,[68] did not escape the watchful eye of the inspectors charged with monitoring Jewish society. "It would be desirable to have the establishment closed, as it is probably maintaing seeds of national hatred," concluded the report on the seminary.[69] Chief Rabbi Maurice Liber (who would eventually become the director of the little seminary, but who was at the moment only the head of the rabbinical school in Chamalières, where five future rabbis were studying) was thus found suspect by the police: "given his highly elitist, parochial attitude, we have every reason to believe that his professional activity allows him to influence the minds of pupils and worshipers in a way that is clearly against the government."[70]

Study circles also worried authorities. On January 8, 1942, the head of the General Bureau of Information for the département of La Dordogne, troubled by the rising number of study groups in his area, noted: "To this day, no authorization to meet has been requested and the censor has not been consulted. However, I think it of prime importance that any lectures about Jewish history and literature in particular be first submitted to review by the censor."[71] The correspondence courses offered in Limoges by Jacques Cohn (called "Bo"), a French citizen of German descent, came under investigation. The inspector in charge of the matter noted indeed that Cohn had a university degree in philosophy, that he had received a scholarship from the University of Strasbourg, that he had been mobilized on September 16, 1939, and had served as served as a medical orderly at the rank of sergeant. After being demobilized on August 9, 1940, he first took refuge in Paris, then in Clermont-Ferrand, then in Vichy, where he worked as a teacher of religion. Given official notice that he was to leave Vichy by November 13, 1941, he left before the specified date and arrived in Limoges on November 3. It was an itinerary that should not have given much cause for concern.

"Bo" had been appointed to his present position by the French Israelite Mutual Aid association (EFI) in Périgueux, which had been in contact with Rabbi Samuel Klein in Lyon and Rabbi Deutsch in Limoges. He received his directives for the Israelite Scouts of France from the center in Moissac. His courses, given at the boarding school run by the OSE in Limoges, were attended by some sixty pupils.

Around January 15, 1942, according to the inspector for the General Bureau of Information, a center for spiritual and religious training of young people was established, and Jacques Cohn was charged with coordinating its activities. Courses were typed at the OSE's boarding school and sent through the mail to subscribers. Course number 9, on Palestinography (the geography of Palestine), had been printed on the stencil from the center in Moissac. There were about thirty subscribers to each course. "Everything has now been put in place to bring together and guide Jewish youth," concluded the inspector. "The reasons given for this activity (social assistance, professional reorientation, religious instruction, scouting) can be accepted as valid, but one must fear that under the cover of these programs, leaders and directors might spread propaganda against the government among these young people." The distribution of Israelite publications of a strictly confessional or scholarly nature was not illegal, he recalled, but should be very closely monitored. He also pointed out that the center in Moissac had duplicating machines forbidden by the law.[72]

This report was quite reliable: most of the information contained in it is accurate and true. As of April 15, 1942, there were ten different courses being sent to 357 subscribers. Course number 9 had indeed been typed in Moissac, while, with the exception of two courses prepared in Marseilles, the others had been put together in Limoges.[73] More important, however, this case provides us a fine example of how these various organizations, be they of a social, religious, or cultural bent, not only combined forces to take interest in young people, but also linked themselves either to the consistory or to what was to become the UGIF.

Because they were so suspicious, authorities also pored over every text put out by Jewish organizations. One circular printed by the French Israelite Mutual Aid association urged Jews to join the Israelite Scouts of France: the circular was barred by the censor. "This is a tragic time for the Israelites of France," stated the circular. "The number of victims keeps rising . . . it is clear that we must count first and foremost on ourselves in order to be saved from an irremediable catastrophe." Vichy's censors were doubtless shocked to see such tendentious arguments in what they termed a "tract."[74] In February 1942, the General Commission on Jewish Affairs issued an unfavorable ruling on the publication of "brochures" put together by the Friends of the Jewish Tradition. Its call for solidarity was perhaps legitimate, but "it was indecent for this call to be accompanied by criticism of internment measures," and "indecent for it to be loaded with fervent praise for the Jews who had been interned." As for the text devoted to charity, it was "interspersed with comments that do more than allude to the internment measures taken against certain Jews."[75]

Even the social aid programs managed to arouse a certain amount of suspicion, precisely because organizations collaborated with each other so much in carrying out their work. Did not the activity of the EFI, under the leadership of Fanny Schwob in Périgueux, transgress the usual limits of social welfare? She seemed to have endless resources, and she went to great lengths to further the cause of the Jewish religion. This leads us back to the center in Moissac. There was a network of social workers spread throughout the entire country: one was supposedly on the lookout near the demarcation line; another was thought to be taking care of the secret delivery of certain types of correspondence; still another was allegedly in contact with London, attempting to get children out of the country.[76] A few months earlier, the regional head of economic aryanization in Limoges had called on the regional prefect to curb the OSE's burgeoning activity: "This association sends out a massive number of circulars to everyone who owns a house of some size in the country: under the guise of a charitable organization, it seeks to rent a place and turn it into a home for Jewish children, almost all of whom are foreigners."[77] In the eyes of authorities, such "Jewish methods" were simply unacceptable.

Authorities frowned on such efforts because this entire set of cultural, spiritual, and social activities tended to involve a group of people that was otherwise being pushed to the margins of society. Under a more political label, the activity of Zionist groups played a similar role.

Zionism: Education in Service of a Political Strategy

Two of the most important Zionist leaders were in Lyon.[78] Marc Jarblum had been a Socialist and Zionist from the inception of the movement, while Joseph Fisher was the leader of the *Keren Kayemeth le-Israel* (the KKL), the organization that bought up land in Palestine in order to develop Jewish colonies there. At the time, however, reorganization was proving to be difficult, as former activists were now scattered all over the country. A new issue of the KKL's newspaper, *La Terre retrouvée*, had been banned by the censor, on the pretense that it was not the proper time for such a publication.[79] A Zionist conference had been held earlier at the synagogue in Marseilles in December 1940, although attendance had been rather low. The conference was primarily devoted to the most pressing concerns of the moment, such as organization and social aid. The major goals of the Zionist movement were nevertheless not neglected; there were also discussions of the situation in Palestine and of the form that Zionist literature should take in the future.[80]

Two other conferences were later held in November and December 1941 in Lyon. Their purpose was to lay the ground for the creation of a Zionist Organization of France (OSF), which became a reality on January 23, 1942. The steering committee first set up its operations in Lyon, and then was moved to Nice: it gave rise to regional committees in Limoges, Toulouse, Nice, Grenoble, and Roanne.[81] The Zionist infrastructure, put together by the federation (FSJF), played an essential role throughout the entire Occupation, as it was initially organized on a legal basis and provided the nucleus of social aid efforts. It immediatedly thrived and later moved toward clandestine activity.

Contact with the now-scattered Jewish population was achieved through the use of circulars sent out as personal letters, so as not to appear to violate the ban on such mailings. A text written by Justin Godart, titled "Take Courage! Act!" and initially intended for the censored issue of *La Terre retrouvée*, provided the content of the first such letter: "In the tempest that is now raging, Zionism remains the beacon whose light must provide bring hope to many an eye filled with tears."[82] David Knout, who was himself a Russian Jewish poet involved in the Jewish Zionist Resistance, later wrote, "Jewish literature was above all seeking not to abandon Jews in their horrible solitude."[83] Probably compelled by the same conviction, Joseph Fisher sent from four to five hundred letters twice a month to spread news from Palestine.[84] The information contained in these letters came from Dr. Shmuel Scheps, the director of the *Keren kayemeth* in Geneva whom Fisher saw regularly in Annemasse.

These regular mailings created ties among Zionist activists and established a link with the outside world; they also set up a structure that made it possible to coordinate social aid activities. A system for collecting money was established whereby the American Jewish Joint Distribution Committee pledged to reimburse after the war and in the United States all funds given directly to aid organizations in France. This system made it possible to keep collecting money indirectly for the colonization of Palestine; for each dollar thus transferred, the Joint Distribution Committee gave ten French francs to the *Keren kayemeth* in New York.[85] Officially, it was Fisher who obtained the authorization to transfer to Jewish aid organizations in France funds belonging to immigrants coming to the United States, funds that they received from the *Keren kayemeth* upon their arrival in New York.[86]

The Zionist Organization of France (OSF) encouraged and financed the so-called *hakhshara* (agricultural preparation) work, which meant setting up agricultural worksites, but in view of preparing future emigrants to Palestine. Two farms were under the direct leadership of the Zionists: Fretteserpes, near Toulouse, and Blémont, near Limoges. They functioned in a way similar to that of the farms run by the Scouts.

The structure created and maintained by Fisher's newsletters also made it possible to coordinate the cultural initiatives of various Zionist organizations and their followers who organized informational meetings and conferences all over the country in order to spread their message. This message was also communicated in conjunction with a more traditionally cultural program: courses in Hebrew, Jewish history, and Jewish culture were offered, and two thousand copies of a secretly reprinted Hebrew textbook were distributed.

Young people constituted the chief audience for this material. "Youth are seeking new paths to a solution of the Jewish question, and people from the most assimilated social milieus have never been closer to the Zionist outlook than they are at the present time," wrote Joseph Fisher in April 1942, as he reported on Zionist activity in France.[87] This was just after all Jewish organizations had been dissolved into the UGIF. The Zionist organization thus strove to place its cultural activities within the framework of the Consistory while keeping the actual political work a secret.[88] Elsewhere, Fisher was concerned with "stirring up Jewish awareness, which appears first of all as the fervent desire to become morally and intellectually associated with the great heritage of Jewish culture, to learn the Hebrew language along with Jewish history and culture, and to study the history and geography of Palestine."[89] Zionist activists most often held their meetings at the synagogue, and it was also in the synagogue that they organized study groups.

Aside from these organizational efforts initiated by the Zionist "establishment" of the prewar years, there developed in Toulouse a movement that not only brought together Zionists of various tendencies, but also had a strong contingent of revisionists among its promoters: in 1941, it gave rise to the Jewish Army (AJ). The founders' objectives were to maintain the Zionist stance, defend it in face of the enemy,[90] advocate the idea of a Jewish State, win over (thanks to the context of the war) a growing number of Zionist partisans, and create a Jewish armed force in order to defend these ideas.[91] At the inception of the movement, there were two couples: the Jewish writer David Knout and his wife Ariane Scriabine-Knout (called "Sarah" following her conversion to Judaism, she became known as "Régine" in the Resistance), and Avraham Polonski (known as "Pol" or "Maurice Ferrer") and his wife Eugénie ("Génia," who told peole to call her "Bat Mattitiahu" or "Mattathias' daughter," thus linking herself to the tradition of the Macchabees). And there was the secret organization these two couples created: Strong Fist (Main forte, [MF]). That was in the fall of 1940.

In Toulouse there was a Mutual Aid and Assistance Committee. Placed under the authority of the president of the Jewish community there, the committee dealt with the thousands of Jewish refugees who had gathered in the city. The committee was formed in order to send money and packages to Jews who had been interned, as most of the internment camps were in the Toulouse region. It thus was able to give a significant impetus to the recruitment of new Zionists, especially as its local secretary, Isaac Friedman (known as "Perrin"), gave daily reports on potential members to the leaders of the Zionist Organization of France.[92] Other followers were recruited within the internment camps themselves.

David Knout and Paul (Pinhas) Roïtman also led a group that met to study Judaism in the facilities provided by the synagogue. In addition to courses in modern Hebrew, there were "discreet colloquiums," whose topics included such diverse subjects as the work of Maimonides (the author of *Guide for the Perplexed*), Central European synagogues and sacred artifacts, and of course the history of the Zionist movement. Claude Vigée relates one of these evening sessions that was held in the fall of 1941, when participants reopened the trial of the historian Flavius Josephus, the author of *The War of the Jews* who had participated in the Jewish revolt against the Romans before finally joining sides with them.[93] At the end of the discussion, "Flavius Josephus was unanimously condemned to death for being a traitor to the cause of Israel."[94] The gathering of Jewish young people at such activities led to the creation of the B'nai David (the sons of David) over the winter of 1941: this was the National Movement for Jewish Action, which was eventually incorporated into the Jewish Army.

And then there was Lucien Lublin, a socialist Zionist who had been involved with the prewar Zionist organizations and who by the force of circumstance was led to join forces with Polonski. It was Polonski along with David Knout who led MF, which had been constituted as a clandestine organization: the most ideologically "reliable" individuals were taken into the MF,[95] which supposedly had control over the Jewish Army's action. Along with Lucien Lublin, Polonski also commanded the clandestine Jewish Army, which developed ties with all of the other Zionist organizations, including both those representing the official "establishment" and those made up mainly of young people.

A manifest drawn up in January 1942 by David Knout expressed the new movement's ideology: "Jews will become aware of the meaning of their collective experience by preparing themselves to become a nation once more and putting an end to their dispersion. They will either come back to life collectively or perish individually." The text sharply contrasted the Jews of the era of assimilation who "had abdicated their spiritual heritage and given up their nationality because they believed they could thus obtain peace and security" with the Palestinian Jews who "could never be penned up in concentration camps where they would die of hunger in abject conditions." The Palestinians "live as Jews" and "will prove themselves capable of dying like men, if necessary." The organization B'nai David, a "national, revolutionary movement of the generation of young Jews," was created with two major goals in mind. The first was to participate in the discussions that would find a solution to the Jewish crisis at the end of the war ("the adversaries of the Axis will be victorious"), and the second was to obtain a "legally recognized national independence" in Jewish Palestine. This nation was to be an "intact citadel," a country that "is all ours in spirit and in flesh."[96]

Of all the undertakings (including efforts on the international level) described in this manifesto, the most rapid to develop were social aid programs and cultural activities. "Support of those who are the hardest hit by current events is not carried out by virtue of charitable emotions or any so-called confessional solidarity," but through the action of a sort of "Jewish self-government." Some very specific sorts of organizational work were also considered to be essential.

Anyone who wanted to join Strong Fist (and later the Jewish Army) was led blindfolded into a dark room. There, after having given one's family name, first name, and date of birth, one had to take the following oath, repeating sentence after sentence of the text pledging allegeance to the Jewish people, to the ideal of a Jewish State in *Eretz Israël* (in the Land of Israel), and to the organization that was working toward those ends:

> Placing my right hand on the blue and white flag,
> I swear fidelity to the Jewish army
> And obedience to its leaders.
> May my people live again,
> May *Eretz-Israël* be reborn.
> Liberty or death.

Then the recruit learned the movement's motto: "Be everywhere present to face adversity." Finally, the new recruit was reminded of the laws governing the movement's action: "Trust, Obedience, Silence." The new "soldier" was then given a roll number and incorporated into a unit of seven such soldiers, which was in turn divided into two subgroups of three, with one leader.[97]

Some were a bit taken aback by this oath, while others did not attach any particular importance to it. Many, however, like Rabbi Kapel, were "impressed by this ceremony that opened the door to a clandestine Jewish organization, amid an atmosphere of mystery and adventure."[98] Finally, there were others who refused to submit to this ceremonial ritual, and who were exempted from the requirement in order not to hamper the spread of the movement. The urgent necessity of taking action subsequently lowered the number of those who lent themselves to the exercise, but those who joined the ranks of the Jewish Army kept its symbolism present in their minds.

Whether they were followers of new Jewish study groups or "soldiers" in the Jewish Army, all of these Zionist activists and those who took part in their activities were recruited among youth. It was young people who gave rise to an original, integrative structure, that of the Zionist Youth Movement (MJS). The idea for the movement was conceived during the Zionist conference held in Lyon in December 1941,[99] and finally became a reality with the movement's first convention, which brought together twenty-two young Zionists of all tendancies on May 10, 1942, in Montpellier.[100] Diverging political opinions and religious outlooks were put aside for the sake of the unity that was fostered in particular by Simon Lévitte and Jules Jefroykin. The strong alliance of this new movement with the Israelite Scouts of France was symbolized by Simon Lévitte's prominence in both organizations. Jules Jefroykin, on the other hand, was a member of the steering committee of the Jewish Army. Close collaboration with the Zionist Organization of France was assured not only by the influence of Joseph Fisher and the appointment of Léonce Bernheim to the position of honorary president, but also by the participation of Jules Jefroykin in the Zionist Organization's leadership council.[101]

The leaders' emphasis on education came in response to young people's pressure on them to address the need. It was after all these very youth who were turning toward an affirmation of the very Jewish identity that had been imposed upon them, but about whose historical and cultural foundations they still knew little. This tendency would only strengthen, and a few months later, the movement would define itself as an "educational movement." The imperative of education was to prevail over all other needs connected to political or social struggle, and the "current pressures and necessities of the hour" let no one waver from its pursuit.[102]

On the eve of the massive roundups of the summer of 1942, intensive training sessions were being organized for both the future leaders of a self-conscious community and those who were going into farming.[103] "Interior Judaism is our only refuge," stated Edmond Fleg on July 27, 1942, stressing the primacy of educating Jewish youth.[104] Upon the initiative of the Zionist Organization of France, a conference on Jewish education was held at the synagogue in Lyon on June 28, 1942. The groups present—including the OSE, the Scouts, the Professional Retraining and Reorientation Organization (ORT), the Federation, the Central Consistory, the Zionist Organization, and the Zionist Youth Movement—all agreed to coordinate their efforts in this domain by forming a new committee on Jewish education. We thus see a tendency toward unification in two areas, the distribution of social aid and the propagation of ideology and culture. For under the guise of culture, what they really were striving to achieve was a stronger sense of Jewish identity.

There was also a subtle shift from legality toward increasingly marked forms of dissimulation. Certainly, the founders of the Jewish Army had immediately chosen to follow the paths of clandestine activity. There were some who occasionally had recourse to extralegal means to achieve their ends, whenever the law became an obstacle. And there were those who set about building an alternative organization once the UGIF was imposed upon all: such was the case of the Federation. Others accepted incorporation into the UGIF, but only on the condition that they be able to preserve their ideological autonomy: this was the stance initially adopted by the Zionist Youth Movement. And as we have seen, some sought to place themselves under the legal umbrella of the consistory, which was not subject to the control of the General Commission on Jewish Affairs. Although proceeding at a different pace in each domain, all of these activities were gradually moving toward the margins of legality, while at the same time moving toward the goal of Jewish national integration.

THE APPEAL TO SOCIETY

Jews Speak to the French People

By definition, Zionist efforts both to strengthen the Jews' sense of their identity and to focus their eyes on Palestine amounted to a sort of propaganda campaign aimed at Jewish integration. The campaign was mounted at the very moment when Jews had to confront an even harsher set of antisemitic laws, yet noted signs that public opinion was becoming more sympathetic to their plight. It was in this context that Marc

Jarblum, along with Henri Hertz, a Jewish French writer who had long been involved with Zionism, decided to appeal directly to public opinion. They called on the consciences of those who were "responsible for upholding civic principles in France, of those who must maintain France's honor and prestige in the arts and sciences, in public education, and in Protestant and Catholic places of worship."[105] The first tract was prepared under the direction of Hertz and Jarblum. Although it enjoyed only a limited distribution, it was inspired from a dialogue they had had with Cardinal Gerlier at the cathedral in la Fourvière in December 1941.

According to the testimony of Henri Hertz, the creation of the UGIF was key; it spurred their decision to "draw up an anonymous, irrefutable indictment to show to the French people." It was indeed on the very day when the federation, meeting in Marseilles, decided to disband officially in order to "secretly become the secret federation," that Henri Hertz made his first draft of a long tract "Silence is Crime's Accomplice."[106] In order to carry out this work, Hertz moved into a tiny cubicle in a small river-going yacht that was moored in Marseilles. The yacht belonged to the nephew of the bookseller located on the Place de l'Odéon, Lipschütz, whose bookstore had been looted by the Germans a week after they had entered Paris. Hertz's text was proofread by Léo Glaeser, a lawyer born in Riga who had been an activist for the federation. Indeed, it was in Glaeser's apartment that those who were to form the Amelot Committee (in which he served as treasurer)[107] met on June 16, 1940. Glaeser also assisted in editing the final version of the tract, while Marc Jarblum chose an excerpt from a text by Anatole Leroy-Beaulieu to be used as an epigraph. The tract was finally printed on green paper, which is why it was known then and now as the "green document." In two printings spaced three months apart, five thousand copies were made and distributed by a team of eight volunteers that included both Jews and non-Jews, led by Marcel Livian, who was directly tied to Socialists operating clandestinely.[108]

The main objectives of this "green document" were to fight ignorance, to inform public opinion about the persecutions being inflicted on the Jews, and, above all, to incite the public to break the silence, to take a stand, and to protest. "From 1940 up until the present day, more than two hundred laws, decrees, rulings, and memoranda have been issued against the Jews. Gradually and implacably, this legislation has demonstrated a fierce determination to tear the Jews away from France, deprive them of the ability to make a living, and to deny them the very right to love their country," read the tract, which laid out and described in detail the plethora of antisemitic laws that had been accumulating. The tract unequivocally denounced French responsibility for this situation: it was only defeat that had allowed a group of "partisans" to take command of the state and to seek revenge by taking hostage those "fervent supporters of the Republic," the Jews.[109] The tract also unsparingly denounced the UGIF, which made Jews into "pitiful signatories of their own demise and degradation." Absolutely no concession was made to the values of the new regime. On the contrary, the tract stressed the importance of a secular, religiously neutral state and the absurdity of capping the number of Jews admitted into the university according to a quota based on past military service. The tract spoke in one unified voice for all Jews, French Israelites and immigrants alike.

Nevertheless, the "green document's" main concern was to make an impression on public opinion:

> Is there no possible recourse [for the Jews?]; is there no channel open for them to appeal their case? . . . On the contrary, there remains one sovereign authority. That authority is public opinion, you: you, in what you can say and cry out to the chief of state, to his government ministers, to prefects, and to the government employees under their authority, to your friends and relatives. You, by the protest that you can endlessly convey to everyone all around you. You, by refusing to add the shame of turning a deaf ear to your conscience and of renouncing the principle of equity to the suffering of a defeat inflicted by outside enemies!

This appeal to public opinion was not isolated. There were on the contrary a number of such appeals that emanated from a wide variety of Jewish milieus. They were made precisely at this time, just before the massive roundups of the summer of 1942, and their convergence is striking.

Take for example the anonymous tract printed in Marseilles by "a group [that had been] French Israelites for several centuries along with a number of recently immigrated Jews who had immediately enrolled in the armed forces to fight alongside the French." On March 13, 1942, they spoke to the French people:

> Your silence is no longer sufficient for us. . . . Who will stand up to protest the insult inflicted on us? . . . Will it be someone in the army, someone at the university, or someone in some sort of collective body who will be brave enough to disavow [this persecution] and thus refuse either to take part in the injustice or to take advantage of the openings it has created? . . .
>
> Is it possible that there is no longer anything in France but silence? Is this possible in France, where protestations in favor of all peoples have always originated? In France, the home of the pampheleteers and the country of the Fronde? When History shall recount the events that we are now experiencing, will it have no one to glorify, will there be no name to cite? . . .
>
> Is it true that writers, intellectuals, and French public opinion have consented to keep bowing down for so long? Is it true that no one is saying or writing anything, nor will say nor will write anything?
>
> We do not yet want to respond, we do not dare say to ourselves: no one. It is also from you, sir, as well as from others that we are hoping for and expecting the answer.[110]

Variations on such texts can moreover be found in the archives of a number of Jewish associations: while their origin is not clear, they all responded to the same urgent situation. "We are asking you to protest along with us," states one such text. "In this France that is silent, but still alive, where all injustice is put to shame, we are asking you to say and to write that anything that is unjust or cowardly or degrading, and that any antisemitic policy beginning with calumny and ending in theft is not a French policy."[111]

It was possible to appeal to the opinion of an enlightened public at this time because relations between French society and the Vichy government were undergoing major changes. Vichy could no longer take advantage of the honeymoon with public opinion that it had enjoyed in the months that followed the signing of the armistice. According to mail intercepted and read during this period, the public tended to reject fiercely the presence of German occupying forces.[112] Henri Hertz confirms that the authors of the "green document" had been encouraged by the underground newspapers that were proliferating at the time.[113]

It was also over the months of April and May 1942 that the authors of the *Cahiers du Témoignage Chrétien* put together *Antisémites:* twenty thousand copies of this underground publication went into circulation in the Southern Zone beginning in June 1942.[114] Father Chaillet would moreover speak of the "shame of silent complicity,"[115] thus echoing the title of the "green document." The following issue, devoted to the "Rights of Man and of the Christian," provided a chronicle of "antisemitic achievements" in the Unoccupied Zone in a piece called "Silence and Complicity."

Underground publications emanating directly from the Communist Party and from some of its special units had already protested the antisemitic laws as they were being applied in the Occupied Zone. In the months of May and June 1942, a special issue of the newspaper *J'accuse* was put out specifically to fight against racism and anti-Semitism.[116] *Fraternité* was the underground newspaper put out by the "French Forces Against Racist Barbarianism." In an undated issue published prior to the summer of 1942, one of its editors wrote: "There is no French citizen mindful of the future of France who does not feel the urgent need to safeguard the values that constitute the genius and glory of France and to contribute to the work that will determine its destiny. . . . The campaign to poison public opinion that has done the most damage (because it has put our spiritual values and the very existence of France as an independent state in mortal danger) is the antisemitic campaign."[117]

A few months later, the papers *J'accuse* in Paris and *Fraternité* in the Southern Zone were to become the voice of the National Movement Against Racism (MNCR), which emanated from Jewish Communist organizations. Its objective would be to appeal to all levels of French society in order to fight racism and antisemitism, not only by protesting, but also by providing material assistance to Jews now threatened by deportation.

The Jewish Communists

Jews who had been involved in one way or another in a Communist organization before the war and had come down from Paris and the Occupied Zone were also scattered out in the south of France. The first ones had come mainly to the Toulouse region: soon a large number of them had been locked up in internment camps. As an increasing number of repressive measures were enacted, clamping down more and more on the Jewish immigrant population in Paris, they kept on streaming out of the capital toward the Southern Zone. Their favorite meeting places were cafés in large cities, such as those on the Place des Terreaux in Lyon, around the Capitole in Toulouse, or on the quays of the Canebière in Marseilles: there they were still congregating openly to play cards but, more important, to keep up with what was happening and to find out about other friends that had arrived. Both the Union of Jewish Students and the synagogues, where they sometimes came in search of aid, played a similar social role.[118]

Such gatherings led to the creation of people's aid committees, which in the Southern Zone were the equivalent of the solidarity committees in Paris. There were nevertheless problems and restrictions: they were prohibited from engaging in any overtly political activity, plagued by repression, and lacked the necessary financial means to develop large-scale aid activity. By the spring of 1941, leaders in Paris had decided to organize and centralize their activities in the Southern Zone. Because of the precarious conditions facing the refugees, however, they had to turn to the Jewish organizations that were already well established in the region. With the goods they collected from storeowners, members of people's aid committees put together packages for those interned in the camps.

The first ones to benefit from this assistance were veterans of the International Brigades who had been interned in the camps at Gurs and Le Vernet. They also made up the majority of political activists who had some experience in the Southern Zone. At that time, most of the Communist activity was developing in Paris. Efforts to create an underground infrastructure for political activity for the moment only involved a minority of Jews scattered throughout towns and villages in the South of France. At the very moment the Communists were getting organized, however, groups of Jews were coming back together. As was the case with other resistance movements, it was these groups that provided the structures for taking in a large number of Jews.

Individual Adjustments

In reality, however, whether they were French Israelites, young immigrants, or immigrants who had come to France many years ago, most Jews found enough support among neighbors, colleagues, and friends to blend into the anonymity of society and make themselves as inconspicuous as possible. And that is precisely why it is hard to trace a collective profile of Jews in this era: in addition to their attempt to be discreet, each of the paths they followed was highly individual. What they shared was a greater vulnerability and an awareness of a threat.

They also shared a greater responsiveness to the fledgling resistance movement. Following a tradition firmly anchored in the history of French Jewry, they joined on an individual basis. Given that they had been the first victims of the German Occupation of France and that they had also been rejected by Vichy, whose increasingly restrictive laws often made it impossible for them to work, it is hardly suprising to find so many Jews involved in the earliest stages of the Resistance.[119] Furthermore, this involvement made it possible for a minority of French Jews to be part of a countersociety that fully integrated them while at the same time explicitly rejecting the presence of the German occupying forces and Nazi ideology. At this point we should note that the proportion of Jews in the Resistance was greater than that for the French population as a whole. The Resistance was not, however, free of its own ambiguities: some tendencies within it were tainted with strains of xenophobia that seemed to echo the dominant themes of official publications. It nevertheless remained an alternative society that had taken in Jews on an equal basis and offered them a chance to act without changing any part of their identity.

This Jewish counter-society thus reflected the same plurality that existed in prewar Jewish society. A Communist brotherhood was developing, as was a brotherhood of résistants. Individual alliances remained possible in society. The changes occurring were visible in the swelling of Jewish organizations, which were now compelled to play a role not only in bringing Jews back together and providing material assistance, but also in responding to new cultural and spiritual needs.

Jews in France were thus torn between integrating themselves into a French society now turning back to values of another time, and falling back on the proud tradition of Jewish values based on solidarity and the rich cultural heritage that they were once again learning. Their dilemma found a particularly eloquent expression in the French composition written in April 1942 by a fourteen-year-old girl who had been given the following topic: "Among all the illustrious heroes in history and literature, including those created by both modern and ancient writers, which one would you put forward as a model? Explain your choice by sketching a portrait of the person you have picked out in your essay."[120]

Her composition is worth quoting in its entirety:

> At one time or another, each of us has wished to become an illustrious hero or a great heroine, just as we have all ardently desired to save our country and our loved ones.
>
> I would like both to come to the aid of the poor, as did Saint Vincent de Paul, and to save France, as did Joan of Arc. I would like to follow the example of Pasteur, who served the cause of science while at the same time serving humanity. But as it is difficult to choose among people of such great soul, such great devotion, and such great wisdom . . . I feel like a child who only has a few pennies, mulling over a wide selection of candies; if I take these, I will have to give up those other ones. . . . After having thought it over thoroughly, however, my preference falls on Esther. Indeed, I cannot help drawing a parallel between her era and the one in which we live. How I would like to save my people as she did! Already in those times, innocent people were going to be massacred. All Jews were to die, according to the order issued by an unbeliever. And what was the reason for such barbarity? Because all bowed before Aman, all flattered him even though they knew him to be a vile, cowardly man. All except for Mordecai . . . and what a

> great number people had to suffer for it! This was always the way things were when a people was unsatisfied: something has to be found to serve up to them.
>
> When Nero set Rome afire, did he not accuse the Christians in order to turn the wrath of the Romans on them? Throughout the long course of history, however, tyrants most of the time preferred to prey upon the Israelite minority.
>
> Today, in the twentieth century, called the century of civilization, in which equality is favored, can anyone deserving to be called human admit infamies worthy of the Middle Ages? Are religious wars thus not yet over?
>
> But this is not a religious war that is being waged, it is instead a war against the Jewish people and a war on the Jewish race. And yet I remember having learned in class that there are only four races on earth: the white race, the black race, the yellow race, and the red race.
>
> Could it be possible that a fifth race has recently been born around me? When I observe my schoolmates, I find no physical dissimilarity between us. As for psychological traits, we have shared a considerable number of impressions, and we have suffered the same pain in hearing news of the war, the defeat, the departure of our brothers.
>
> But when France, my own country, called its children to take up arms and defend their country, citizens of all denominations without exception heeded her call. And the unknown soldier, the glorious unknown soldier who lies in the sacred tomb at the foot of the Arc de Triomphe, is he a Catholic, a Protestant, a Muslim, or a Jew? Nobody poses this question: for all, he is a Frenchman.
>
> As for me, I have not yet been persecuted or threatened, but a great number of innocent people are suffering in concentration camps, simply because they are Jewish. And yet I am certain that each one of them has done their duty to their country with all their heart.
>
> If, moreover, another minority found itself in the same situation as the Israelites, if others were unjustly oppressed, I would unhesitatingly take their side; I would shout over the face of the earth the right of all to live.
>
> Esther, Esther, inspire me. What must I do to save the Jews who are once again threatened. There is no Xerxes seeking a wife, but it is nevertheless a crime to be Jewish. And although I wish so much for France to be saved, I would say: I am guilty.
>
> But will I have to follow your example, Esther? France is the country from which came the noblest, most beautiful, the most generous, and above all the most just of all ideas. France's glorious past was raised to new heights by the great Revolution of 1789 and by the influence of its philosophers. With its Declaration of the Rights of Man and Citizens, France has always given to the world the example of totally unselfish devotion, of an admirable altruism that takes the side of the weak. France will not abandon its children.

Present-day readers of this composition can only be moved by this young girl's fervent patriotism, her attachment to a noble idea of France, her fidelity to universal values, and the sense of solidarity with others that she exhibits. Her choice of Esther as a heroine in April 1942 can perhaps be explained by the proximity of the Jewish holy day of Purim, which fell on March that year: every year, it is on the day of Purim that Jews celebrate the defeat of Haman, King Xerxes' diabolical minister who had plotted to have the Jewish people massacred. We should note that the Friends of the Jewish Tradition as well as orthodox Jews had chosen to emphasize values connected with solidarity in the messages delivered during religious ceremonies for Purim in 1942.[121]

It was a message of hope for the future that this Jewish child educated in the secular schools of the French Republic sought to draw from this episode of Jewish history. We might suppose—since we know nothing about her—that her response to the question as well as her analysis of the social causes that have always been at the root of antisemitism came from what she had learned in one of the special classes or study groups for Jewish youth that, as we have seen, proliferated at that time. And yet, she drew her conclusion from the Declaration of the Rights of Man and of the Citizen.

Not everyone shared her admirable confidence, however, as many Jews in France sought safety beyond its borders.

THE CHOICE OF EMIGRATION

Deciding to leave the country was no simple matter. There was something shameful connected with fleeing: for many French Israelites, who feared that in doing so they would only further widen the gap between themselves and the rest of France, it was almost a sign of treason. Indeed, the press did not fail to depict those who had thus chosen to put their family in a safe haven as "deserters of civic duty"[122] and as vile cowards abandoning France at the very moment when the country was drawing on all its forces in a tremendous effort to get back on its feet.

But Jews hesitated to flee, even when their entourage largely approved of such a choice. "The only ones whose flight from the country is condoned are the Israelites," wrote Marie-Thérèse Gadala in Vichy. "As was the case for the aristocracy in 1789, they knew that the guillotine was ready for them. However, such is not the opinion of Jacques Nam, himself a Jew, who finds there is more elegance in remaining here. When, he tells me, you have received work, well-being, and a good way of life from a country, you do not abandon it in its time of misery and ill fortune."[123]

When exclusion from French society became unavoidable and when at the same time it became obvious that France was modeling its society in the shadow of Nazi Germany (a society in which there would be no place for Jews), the decision to leave the country often placed Jews in a painful dilemma. A "privileged" individual such as Marc Bloch, who had secured special visas for himself, his wife, and four of his children to emigrate to the United States, nevertheless gave up on his plans because he would have had to leave his mother (who was eighty-two) and two of his children behind him.[124]

Different groups of people sought to leave the country at different times, depending on the various measures excluding Jews from public life and employment. In late October 1941, the General Bureau of Information observed that the number of Israelite doctors and lawyers applying for entry visas to Cuba had sharply increased:

the quota capping the number of Jews allowed to practice law and medicine had just taken effect.[125]

The outcome of efforts to emigrate was moreover uncertain. By the end of May 1941, more than thirty-five thousand requests to leave the country had been recorded in the Marseilles office of the HICEM, the Jewish emigration organization.[126] Only a small fraction succeeded: there were to be exact 1,568 lucky ones that the HICEM managed to send to another country between January 1 and June 30, 1941.[127] About the same number emigrated during the second half of the year and almost three thousand over the first six months of 1942.[128] Between the signing of armistice in late June 1940 and the end of the year 1942, a total of 6,449 Jews had left France thanks to the HICEM.[129]

French nationals as well as citizens from belligerent countries who by their age were theoretically eligible for military service in their native countries, were not permitted to leave the country. And those individuals who, according to article 19 of the armistice agreement, were to be handed over to the Germans, were also retained in France. And to leave the Occupied Zone, one either had to have an *Ausweis* issued by the German authorities or cross the demarcation line illegally. Now in order to leave France to emigrate to another country, one had to carry an exit visa. Obtaining a transit visa or a permanent visa presented an even more complicated set of problems. Spain and Portugal were constantly changing their regulations. Spain would sometimes open its borders for a few days or even just a few hours before closing them again.[130] But most ships heading for the United States, Mexico, Cuba, or some country in South America would leave from Portugal. At the time, America was taking in about 85 percent of the immigrants from Europe: it looked long and hard at each individual case before granting the precious visa authorizing entry into the United States. Mexico changed its visa requirements in April 1942, and canceled overnight an entire series of visas that had already been issued. At the same time, Cuba, which in the past had for the most part opened its doors to anyone having a certain fortune, suddenly stopped granting visas and canceled those already issued.[131] Such visas, moreover, were never valid beyond a certain time. In addition, the rules for exiting France over land were different from the rules for leaving the country from one of its seaports.

Exit visas thus only opened one way out, a way that could turn out impractical due to changing regulations. One visa might expire before the second one was finally granted or before the proper means of transportation—which was becoming harder and harder to find—could be secured. And only the HICEM would take the risk of chartering a boat. Private companies were no longer willing to take the chance: the risk of having passengers held back at the last minute, unable to exit France, was too great. Furthermore, there was little profit to be made from passengers who could barely scrape together enough money to pay for third-class sleeping berths. Finding the funds to pay for such transportation was indeed no small matter: prices had risen sevenfold over the course of a few months and had to be paid in foreign currency, which was not easy to come by either. All of these things had to be obtained at the same time, or within a very short time frame: otherwise one of the vital papers might expire, and the whole process would have to be started over.

The misadventures befalling Madame Rosenfeld and her husband in their efforts to emigrate from France were not unusual. Marie Rosenfeld had come from Belgium to join her husband, who had first been interned at the time of the German offensive in May 1940 before being transferred to the camp at Gurs, and then to the camp at Les Milles. Their daughter, who was living in the United States, had obtained a tourist visa valid for one year for them, and had booked passage for her parents on one of the American Export Line's freighters, scheduled to leave Lisbon in early July 1941. But a new route to the United States through La Martinique was suddenly opened. Rushed by the French government administrative offices, which were anxious to see them leave as quickly as possible, the internees detained at Les Milles canceled their reservations on ships leaving from Lisbon in order to depart from Marseilles heading for the French Antilles at an earlier date. But none of the expected freighters arrived in La Martinique: the first had been stopped by the British navy, while two others had been blocked in Casablanca by the French Admiralty. The boat on which Madame and Monsieur Rosenfeld had booked passage did not even leave port. The HICEM then made a desperate effort to arrange the couple's departure, as Madame Rosenfeld had fallen seriously ill. The assistance of the French Red Cross, the French national rail company, the administrative office of a clinic in Marseilles, the authorities of the camp at Les Milles, and the cooperation of still other administrative offices had to be solicited in order for the couple to be able finally to emigrate. However, the HICEM simply did not have the means to take all such problems in hand and follow up step-by-step for each case.[132]

Marseilles was full of such "Jewish nomads who went from one hotel to another or stayed with friends"[133] and

> these miserable people seeking to leave who run around checking at every consulate, collecting the most exotic visas in order to be considered as individuals on the verge of departure. The awful situation in which many of them found themselves was simply unimaginable. More rumors about such and such possibility for leaving the country were being spread every morning, and every evening these mirages would vanish. Some people were spending their very last resources and awaiting the future with anxiety.[134]

To help them leave France, legally or illegally, meant also helping them to survive while waiting for departure. Those seeking to leave included "these writers who could no longer receive their royalties or even send in their latest manuscript to their publisher, these painters who now had nowhere to sell their paintings, these professors who had had to abandon their positions in the French university system and who no longer were receiving any salary, and these scientists who had been driven out of their laboratories by the Nazi invaders. All of them were hungry."[135] And yet those specifically targeted by the second paragraph of article 19 of the Armistice agreement (which required the French authorities to hand over to the Germans all German citizens wanted by the Third Reich) could count on the assistance of the American Relief Committee set up by Varian Fry. Before its activities ended on June 2, 1942, this committee succeeded in clandestinely sending out of France hundreds of scientists, artists, writers, and political opponents who were under threat from the Nazis.[136]

But what about all those Jews who remained anonymous and whose plight was made even more precarious by their very anonymity? There were foreigners who risked being systematically kicked out of the département of Les Bouches-du-Rhône by the Marseilles police involved in efforts to clear them out of the area. There were also those who were in danger of being interned in a camp or being placed into one of the Foreign Worker Units (GTE) before they could get together all of the precious documents that would allow them to leave: once they had been interned, there would be no way of obtaining these papers. We can only wonder just how many cases there were like those at the Gurs camp in June 1941. These were thirty-three urgent, complete, and detailed dossiers of persons who had in hand their summons to the American consulate in Marseilles, passage booked on a specific boat, and, in some cases, sufficient funds to be able to go and live at their own expense in Marseilles: the camp administration kept on refusing to let them go.[137] Ten of them had already lost their place on the boat and their turn to leave.

And once refugees finally did manage to leave, they sometimes found themselves on a strange trip. If they managed to board a ship for Cuba, they could wind up stuck for weeks on end in La Martinique, penned up in a camp at Lazarète or Balato without running water or toilet facilities, underfed and threatened with "repatriation" back to France because they carried with them only French francs and not the American dollars that were demanded to pay their travel via Santo Domingo.[138]

The long, complicated journey experienced by the Sigman family illustrates some of these difficulties. Once they had finally obtained a transit visa, the Sigmans were held back at the Spanish border: Spain had just closed its borders, so they had to return to France. After having gone to considerable effort and expense, Mr. Sigman managed to book passage on a boat heading for Oran. They were in danger of being interned when they arrived in Casablanca, but once again the Sigmans were lucky: they managed to board a ship for the United States, one of the very last to use this particular route.

In April 1941, the OSE set up a collective program to favor the emigration of children. However, in spite of the very active assistance of the Quakers, it did not achieve its expected goals. Requests nevertheless kept pouring in: by November 15, 1941, the organization had recorded 1,408 of them.[139] Three convoys were successfully organized in June, August, and September 1941, and then in May and June 1942: about three hundred children were thus brought to the United States.[140] This was a tremendously complex undertaking: among other things, entry and exit visas had to be secured, children had to be sorted out, berths had to be reserved on ships, and the trip had to be funded (at a cost of 440 dollars per child over the age of ten: the cost for younger children was half that amount).[141] Children over the age of sixteen were considered as adults and automatically stricken from the list of those scheduled to leave.

For some of these older ones, however, the only family that remained was the younger brother who was eligible to emigrate. If they were natives of Germany or Austria, children over the age of twelve were, beginning in December 1941, considered as "enemy aliens" by American authorities and thus barred from obtaining a visa. Richard H., age ten, whose parents had stayed in Germany, had refused to leave on his ship because he did not want to be separated from his brother Kurt, who had been kept from leaving with the rest of his convoy because he was sixteen. Now Richard's chances of being able to emigrate out of France were seriously compromised.[142] And the administrative obstructions on the part of French authorities were not the least of the obstacles standing in the way of such efforts to organize the emigration of children.

By July 18, 1942, there was no more hope of legally emigrating. Required to hand over its contingent of Jews to be deported, Vichy now stood in the way of all such departures. Even those who after countless efforts had finally obtained the precious exit visas were barred from using them.[143] A few who had not yet been placed in the categories of Jews to be deported still managed to slip out of the ever-tightening noose. A case in point is that of Claude Vigée, who, after experiencing all sorts of ups and downs in his efforts to secure the life-saving visas, finally managed to cross the Spanish border through the Pyrenees. The OSE and the YMCA made desperate attempts to get the children who had escaped deportation out of France. Five hundred such children (who were to form a first contingent) were chosen for immediate departure, and one hundred of them were brought together in Marseilles, where they were provided a group visa for the United Sates and prepared for the journey. But no argument could make Laval change his position: Vichy refused to grant the children exit visas.[144] And after the Allies landed in North Africa on November 8, 1942, the Germans rushed down to occupy the Southern Zone a few days later. The last glimmer of hope flickered out.

6

Living in a Camp, in a Foreign Worker Unit

After the Armistice had been signed and the army had been demobilized, neither the foreign nationals from countries formerly at war with France, nor those who had enrolled in the Foreign Legion or been incorporated into the Foreign Worker Units were free to resume their normal lives. There were a few fortunate exceptions in the latter group: in July 1940, they included those who could prove they resided in the Unoccupied Zone and had sufficient financial resources to support themselves; in August, it was those whose wives and children were French citizens; and in September, it was the turn of those who had served in the French Foreign Legion, along with a handful of others.[1] Some of the women at Gurs feared that if they left the camp, they would never see their husbands again. And so, although they could have gotten out, they stayed and waited for word from their husbands, at times to no avail. Some of the men who had been interned in the camps were sent to North Africa: there, under dreadful conditions, they were employed in the construction of a trans-Saharan railway.[2]

"The army was demobilized. . . . But as for us, we still remained in the camp, devoured by fleas and bedbugs, constantly worrying about our families and our somber prospects for the future," wrote one man who had voluntarily enrolled in the army and who found himself reduced to the idleness and boredom of life in the Septfonds camp, as he waited for a ruling on his case. He watched with terror as a German commission visited the camp to seek out its prey.[3] Only a hunger strike followed by 60 percent of the foreign volunteers in the Septfonds camp succeeded in obtaining the demobilization, and thus the liberation of those who had enough money to support themselves and who could not be incorporated into the Foreign Worker Units.

The new French regime had pledged to hand over all those that Germany would demand and had moreover initiated its own policy of bringing foreigners together: in practice, this meant surveillance and repression for all foreigners, especially Jews. While the camps were in part a legacy of the Third Republic, the ones in the Southern Zone took on a new character: they now became, under Vichy, the most tangible expression of a policy of ever-widening exclusion.

FOREIGN JEWS UNDER HEAVY SURVEILLANCE

Considered as "foreigners who were in overabundance in the national economy," Jews who had been conscripted into labor were thus incorporated into a new formation, the Foreign Worker Units (Groupements de travailleurs étrangers [GTE]). Over the fall and winter of 1940–41, camps were once again filled, this time taking in foreign Jews sent there by the prefects in the south of France who were applying the law of October 4, 1940, giving prefects the power to intern all foreign Jews. The first targeted were those having already been interned at the outset of the war and those having received government benefits. After a memorandum from the prefect notifying mayors in the département of La Haute-Garonne that all government welfare benefits had been eliminated for refugees who were not French citizens, a census of foreigners was begun in Toulouse.[4] In Marseilles, all foreign refugees living in the city and receiving government benefits were summoned by newspaper announcements to report to the prefecture for the département of Les Bouches-du-Rhône between October 15 and October 17.[5]

In addition, some 1,400 German Jews in the Bordeaux area[6] were expelled from the Occupied Zone into the Unoccupied Zone by the Germans. Then on October 22, 1940, the Germans drove some 6,504 Jews out of the Baden and Palatinate regions into France. While Vichy protested this violation of the Armistice agreement, it interned the first group in the Saint-Cyprien camp and the second contingent at Gurs. The camps were then transferred out of military control and placed under the authority of the Ministry of the Interior.

On February 19, 1941, the Office of Social Services for Foreigners was created within the framework of the Commission on the Fight Against Unemployment. The leadership of this new agency was entrusted to Gilbert Lesage, who had established it. Lesage had been involved with the Quakers since the age of nineteen[7] and had previously been active in offering social assistance to refugees, most notably while working with the Compagnons de France. Lesage went to the Commission on Unemployment, which was responsible for the Foreign Worker Units, and offered to organize aid for the families of foreign workers.[8] On July 4, 1941, prefects in the Southern Zone were notified of the existence of this new agency that was just emerging from the limbo of preparations. On January 1, 1942, it became the Office of Social Services for Foreigners (Service Social des Etrangers [SSE]). More important, it was now given an expanded role, as the idea of bringing together families of foreign workers and removing women and children from the camps was gaining ground.

A general inspection agency for the camps was created by decree on September 18, 1941, and placed under the authority of the prefect André Jean-Faure within the ministry of the interior.[9] This new administrative service was charged with coordinating the administration of the camps and maintaining a coherent and consistent internment policy. Improving the conditions of detainment rapidly became another one of the agency's objectives: this new priority resulted both from the shock experienced by the inspectors who had come to take stock of conditions existing in each of the camps and—perhaps most important—from the rather embarrassing reports that American newspapers had published about the inhumane living conditions prevalent in French camps.[10]

The impetus for improving conditions in the camps came from the Coordinating Committee on the distribution of aid in the camps, which united under its umbrella the representatives of various charitable organizations and strove to alleviate the hardships suffered by detainees. After a meeting at the ministry of the interior, the delegates of these organizations declared that they were ready to work with the government to improve camp living conditions. However, they also expressed their desire to see a "person appointed by the ministry of the interior to have complete authority in all matters of camp policy" and to be the official spokesman with whom they could negotiate.[11] That was on February 11, 1941. Shortly after, a memorandum from the head office of the Police in charge of territorial security and foreigners formally recognized the necessity of designating an inspector general for the camps.[12] Although the application of such a measure was to be delayed for a few more months, the decision to create such a post was made in April.[13]

The Camp System

In the fall of 1940, there were seven main camps: Le Vernet and Rieucros (which was reserved for women)[14] were punitive camps, while Gurs was semipunitive. Bram, Argelès, and Saint-Cyprien were called lodging camps, and Les Milles, used for people in transit, was assigned to take in foreigners trying to leave France. In addition to the camps, there was an entire array of measures aimed at "bringing Jews together" and keeping close tabs on them, including a regimen of constant surveillance for people placed under house arrest in a village or shelter.[15] Living conditions in these various places could be completely different, and there was a certain amount of mobility between them, at least up until the summer of 1942, when the deportation trains gradually emptied them out and sent all detainees toward one destination. In some places, camps were closed only to be reopened shortly afterward. In others, new camps were opened and existing camps gave rise to annexes. Similarly, some detainees were set free only to be interned again or transferred from one camp to another. Other detainees were sent out of a camp and placed in a Foreign Worker Unit, in a shelter, or under house arrest. What mobility there was could thus work both ways, taking detainees from the worst conditions to better ones, and from difficult conditions to the very worst.

Swamped by a flood of Jewish refugees in dire need, the Jewish community of Toulouse had created a Relief and Mutual Assistance Committee: acting on their own initiative, they turned to the prefect of the département of La Haute-Garonne

Table 2. Approximate Number of People Interned in the Camps, February 1941–July 1942[1]

Camps	Feb. 1941	March 1941	April 1941	May 1941[2]	June 1941	July 1941	Sept. 1941	Oct. 1941	Nov. 1941	Dec. 1941	Feb. 1942	July 1942
Argelès	15,600	14,000	6,000	5,000 (3,000)	400*	200*	120					10*
Gurs	12,250	11,200	7,000	7,000 (6,200)	6,500*	6,200*	4,000	4,600	4,600	4,600	4,000	2,300*
Rivesaltes	2,100	4,000	8,000	4,500 (8,000)	2,500*	2,000*	6,800	5,000	5,400	5,400	4,000	1,150*
Le Vernet	3,200	3,000	3,000	3,000 (2,000)	1,200*	800*	1,900	1,900	1,900	1,900	1,900	350*
Noé		1,700	1,700	1,700 (1,550)	1,000*	1,000*	1,300	1,300	1,300	1,300	1,450	950*
Récébédou	60	200	1,800	1,800 (1,800)	1,000*	1,200*	1,450	1,450	1,450	1,450	1,500	1,050*
Les Milles	1,000	1,100	1,100	1,300 (1,500)	1,000* 1,000*	1,200	1,300 1,300	1,300	1,350	800*		
Total	34,210	35,200	28,600	24,300 (24,050)	13,800*	12,600*	16,770	15,550	15,950	16,150	14,425	6,6 10*[3]
Total A.G.[4]	47,000 40,000*		22,000 16,000						15,000 11, 150*		15,000 10,500*	9,800
Total Bauer[5]	33,910 Jan. 41		34,100							25,610 14,850*		12,000* 13,000*

*Specific numbers of Jews. For the other numbers given, the proportions of Jews and non-Jews are not clear.

1. According to a handwritten document, AIU, CC-25, and the general report, Jefroykin, Marseille, August 31, 1941, Joint, General, France, 595. The data for July 1942, AIU, CC-29 come from statistics given by the general chaplain's office.

2. Figures in parentheses are those given by Joseph Weill in *Contribution à l'histoire des camps d'internement dans l'Anti-France* (Paris: Éditions du Centre, 1946), pp. 52–53. By adding to them the camps at Rieucros, Septfonds, other smaller camps, and the camps in North Africa, Weill arrives at a total of 41,500 persons interned at the time.

3. The document from the camp chaplain's office providing the figures for July 1942 arrives at a total of 7,660 because it includes not only two centers for the mentally ill (in Lannemezan in the département of la Haute-Garonne and in Lizous in the département of l'Aude) but also the Jews staying in the Bompard, the Terminus Nord, and the Hôtel du Levant in Marseilles. The same document puts the total number of those in the camps at 11,577. Jews supposedly made up 66 percent of those interned.

4. Anne Grynberg, *Les Camps de la honte*, p. 12.

5. Yehuda Bauer, *American Jewry and the Holocaust. The American Jewish Joint Distribution Committee, 1939–1945* (Detroit: Wayne State University Press, 1981), p. 164.

and requested permission to create a shelter for refugees in Brens, a little community near Gaillac.[16] But what at first had been a relief for the refugees as well as for the aid organizations that had taken them in wound up being a trap, as authorities began to send newly arrested foreign Jews to the shelter as a matter of course. Then, in mid-January 1941, those who had been housed in the shelter had to give up their identity papers: it now became impossible for them to leave what had thus been transformed into an internment camp. The process was carried a step farther when the refugees were transferred by entire groups to the camps: some were sent to Noé, others to Rivesaltes, and the remaining ones to Gurs. On March 4, 1941, the Brens shelter was able to close its doors for the time being: more than thirteen hundred foreign Jews had come to this "refugee center" before ending up in an internment camp.

Three new camps were created in early 1941. Rivesaltes, destined to become a "center for family regrouping," received its first internees in early January: they had been evacuated from the camp at Agde. Noé and Récébédou were established in February 1941 to take in invalids and couples over the age of sixty. The camps at Saint-Cyprien and Argelès were devastated by a severe storm that had torn through the coastal area of the Roussillon, and had to be closed.[17] Agde was also eliminated from the list of camps. The result in each of these camp closings was a massive transfer of detainees.

Up until the spring of 1941, those who could prove that they had a sufficient amount of income managed to secure their own release. But by the summer of 1941, such releases had become more and more difficult to obtain. A memorandum from Admiral Darlan dated June 25, 1941, ordered prefects "not to release foreigners of the Israelite race who had not resided in France before May 10, 1940."[18]

Not only does this fluctuating situation complicate the task of the historian attempting to use hard facts and lay out the history of a population under heavy surveillance, it illustrates the precariousness that was part and parcel of the daily lives of those either interned in the camps or under the risk of internment.

Not surprisingly, this precariousness can be seen in the fluctuating number of detainees. According to a report from the Office of the Secretary General of the Police, there were in November 1940 about twenty-six thousand foreigners being held in camps in the south of France. A selection commission set up in October by the National Security had allowed about one thousand of these internees to be released. Some two thousand foreigners had been sent to join the ranks of Foreign Worker Units. But then some eleven thousand new internees who had fled into the Unoccupied Zone from the Northern (Occupied) Zone were put in the camps.[19] However, the commission on camp statistics for the Coordinating Committee of the organizations providing relief to foreign internees and refugees in France reported that there were at least 53,610 people in the camps in November 1940.[20] The ministry of the interior anticipated that by mid-March 1941, there would be 42,000 people interned.

After a preliminary peak reached in November and December 1940, the highest number of detainees apparently did occur by March 1941. According to a statistical report emanating from the office of the camp chaplains, there were at the time 35,200 foreigners interned in the main camps in the south of France. This figure subsequently went down, as new ways were found to monitor and persecute the foreign Jews, who made up an ever-increasing proportion of the detainees. By the summer of 1941, Jews constituted 90 percent of those interned at Gurs, 80 percent at Les Milles, but only 40 percent of those detained at Rivesaltes, and 20 percent of those at Le Vernet.[21] From March 1941 to July 1942, the number of Jews detained in the camps gradually decreased to reach the figure of slightly under 8,000 out of a total of 11,577 internees.[22] These figures, however, do not take into account internees who had been spread out among the "little" camps, and only more thorough research would make it possible to arrive at a more accurate numerical assessment.

What was actually taking place beneath the surface appearance of these decreasing figures was that other people were being newly interned. Between November 1940 and June 1942, nearly half of the 2,320 people having arrived at Gurs were foreign Jews who had been arrested, while the other half consisted of people transferred from one camp to another.[23] Nevertheless, the decreasing numbers themselves need to be interpreted. Releases of internees only account for a tiny portion of the decrease. Let us take the example of Gurs: only 840 of the 16,165 internees who left the camp between the months of October 1940 and June 1942 were set free.[24] What is more, only half of those released were Jews, even though Jews made up more than 90 percent of the camp's population. There were many who could not endure the harsh conditions of their incarceration and fell victim to epidemics, cold, and the "hunger sickness." Some managed to emigrate to North or South America. Others were spread throughout various shelters (in particular, those set up by the Office of Social Services for Foreigners) and lodgings where they remained under house arrest. Children were released and transferred to centers run by the OSE. Adolescents went to various vocational schools. Finally, many of the men were incorporated into the Foreign Worker Units, as was the case between November 1940 and June 1942 for some twenty-four hundred male internees at Gurs.

"Palestinian" Foreign Workers

The first Foreign Worker Units, made up of groups of volunteers, had been composed of foreigners: there was no special designation for Jews. The idea of requiring Israelites to be placed in special groups under certain conditions was first mentioned during an interministerial conference held on June 13, 1941: it involved the ministry of the interior, the General Commission on Jewish Affairs, and the Commission on Unemployment. On December 8, 1941, the plan was put into execution, as the vice premier issued the order for the first measures of the special conscription of Jews. A press release published on December 10[25] included these measures that appeared between two others: the one preceding it concerned "foreigners caught in the act of inciting someone to commit a crime," while the one following targeted Communists for mass arrests. Taken all together, these were "exceptional repressive measures . . . targeting not only those directly responsible for assassinations [of the officers and soldiers of the German Occupation forces], but also those who, directly or indirectly, are responsible for the fever leading to such murders."[26] By order no. 654, the press was instructed that this communiqué had to be printed on the front page.[27] On January 2, 1942, prefects in the Unoccupied Zone received precise instructions for the concrete application of these measures.

The measures were specifically aimed at Jews who had entered France since January 1, 1936, become destitute, and were between the ages of eighteen and fifty-five, even if they had subsequently acquired French citizenship.[28] Their incorporation into the Foreign Worker Units was to take priority over the incorporation of the other foreigners considered to be "overabundant in the national economy," and was to be completed before March 1, 1942. It was up to those subject to these measures to report to the various offices of the police, of the General Commission on Jewish Affairs, or of the prefect by February 22, 1942, and a placard urging them to do just that was posted in various public places.[29] Those holding a job deemed useful to the national economy could keep on working in their current capacity, but nevertheless had to comply with the requirement by having themselves incorporated into a Foreign Worker Unit and receiving the special designation of "monitored workers."[30] Jewish males between the ages of fifteen and twenty-five had to be placed in special professional training centers established by the Office of Social Services for Foreigners. That is, they went to training centers, provided they could prove a sufficient level of financial resources: if not, they were incorporated into the Foreign Worker Units as soon as they were eighteen. The placard also carried a reminder that those who had the financial resources were required by a memorandum dating from November 3, 1941, to be placed within a group under house arrest. Those who were already participating in a vocational retraining program were exempted from that requirement, but were still placed under the control of the Foreign Worker Units. No foreigner was allowed to leave any of these centers without receiving authorization from the office of the prefect.[31]

Within the Foreign Worker Units, Jews had to be put into homogenous groups—that is, made up solely of Jews—curiously termed "Palestinians" in administrative jargon. The segregation of Israelites who had already been incorporated into such units had been stipulated by memoranda from various government ministries: "Supervised groups of Palestinians must be made up only of Palestinians, and if they are integrated into a larger unit, they must administratively be placed all together in a Palestinian section."[32]

Even before this measure had been taken, some fifteen thousand Jews had been incorporated into the Foreign Worker Units. Moreover, the measures were applied inconsistently. Some men who had up until then been interned in camps were transferred into Foreign Worker Units even though their weak physical condition brought on by the harsh conditions of their confinement should have exempted them from labor: "Here we have the result of all our work with these men debilitated by hunger," wrote one employee with a charitable organization in Rivesaltes on April 9, 1942. "We saved them only to see them led away to forced labor. They stop in front of every hut and, without really choosing, take about anybody who can stand on his own two feet."[33] Such incidents took place even when the men were about to leave camps: some two hundred were suddenly incorporated into Foreign Worker Units in January 1942, when they were at Les Milles preparing to emigrate from France to North or South America.[34] Some foreign Jews who were still free got caught in the trap. On February 18, 1942, the police came to the Committee on Aid to Refugees (CAR) in Montauban to investigate the organization's clients: all the men found on the committee's lists were taken to the Septfonds camp and placed into Foreign Worker Units.[35] The total number of men who were thus conscripted into forced labor, as well as the precise number of Jews among them, has still not been determined with certainty. As of mid-May 1942, the chaplains' office for the camps knew of some thirty-one such units of "Palestinians," but gave no indication as to the total number of workers involved.[36]

PENNED UP BEHIND BARBED WIRE FENCES

Assortments of Disparate Groups of People

"Assortments of disparate groups of people" populated both the internment camps and the Foreign Worker Units.[37] "In the punitive camps," wrote Dr. Joseph Weill in May 1941, in a report that was later given to Marshal Pétain by Cardinal Gerlier:

> one finds common-law criminals placed side by side with political suspects and totally harmless people who have come under suspicion simply because of an anonymous letter or some concierge's idle gossip. One also finds people who, even though their papers were in order, had the misfortune of finding themselves in the middle of a police roundup; one can also discern former members of the French Foreign Legion and volunteers for marching regiments, some of whom had rushed to get here from faraway lands in order to serve in the armed forces and repay their debt of gratitude to the country that offered hospitality.[38]

Such were the terms used by Weill to describe the population of the camp at Le Vernet. Elsewhere, one could find side by side veterans from the International Brigades, refugees from Holland and Belgium, the entire Jewish community of Baden, "with their religious and community leaders, their renowned scholars, . . . their poets and their painters, their artists, their sick and mentally ill, their wives, their elderly, expectant mothers and thousands of children, ranging from frail infants to sickly adolescents."[39]

Weill was thinking of Gurs when he penned these lines: out of the some 12,000 peopled interned there in February 1941, there were 4,300 women, 350 children under the age of fourteen, and 2,500 internees over the age of sixty.[40] Indeed, after having been brutally driven out of their homes on October 22, 1940, and then subjected to an exhausting journey, some 6,054 Jews—most of whom considered themselves well assimilated into German culture—were transferred to the Gurs camp. Upon their arrival, those already interned (Germans having fled Hitler's regime for ideological reasons) suddenly became aware of a reality that up till then had been an abstraction to them: deportation. "We knew that Hitler had driven people out of their homes and had transferred them somewhere else," wrote one such woman. "We had considered it scandalous and inhumane, but we had not seen it with our own eyes. In a way, this sort of event went unheeded, as is the case with everything that one reads about in the newspaper. We were horrified, but indirectly so. . . . At present, we were witnesses. Now we could feel the tremblings of fear with our own hands, and we could see with our own eyes the tears of sorrow and fatigue. At present, we could hear the crying out and weeping of those who had been beaten."[41]

In the Gurs camp as elsewhere, all sorts of people were thrown together without any privacy: there were the young and the not so young, deeply religious Jews and Jews imbued with the culture of Communism, intellectuals and shopkeepers, those who had nothing and those who were well-to-do, people suffering from chronic illnesses or from a serious infirmity, others who became seriously ill, natives of Poland and natives of Germany, Jews who had neither friends nor family, families that had been torn apart, and countless, countless others who spoke Yiddish, German, Polish, Russian, and even broken French. Yet everyone did their best to preserve a minimum of personal life, "in order to feel [that they were] not all stuck together and dissolved into one solid lump of mud" by the situation thus imposed on them.[42]

They had had to abandon their former life of freedom to go and live behind barbed wire fences. There were at Gurs some thirteen or fourteen housing units, each containing an average of 1,400 people. Each unit was "totally surrounded by at least one double row of barbed wire fencing and watched by a guard armed with a revolver, who was always posted at the entry, right in the central alley; . . . the people who are in the camp may not leave unless they have been summoned by the administration or received a ticket from the unit leader." Such was the description given in June 1941 by Jean Pochard, head of the investigative team from the Office of Social Services for Groups of Foreigners.[43] Pochard continues, "The first thing that can be observed in almost all internees is an obsessive fear of barbed wire. It is true that barbed wire can be found everywhere, even in places where you might think it was unnecessary."

One could go out of a unit only with great difficulty, because of the ticket system that was used: each unit leader had tickets that were lent one at a time to those requesting them. Most of the internees could leave the unit no more than once every two days at the very most: this was true even for married couples confined separately in different units. Even at that, the system was relatively liberal compared to the one prior. Internees came up with gems of ingenuity in finding ways to get around such obstacles. For example, the crowds that soon congregated at each burial provided the occasion to converse with a spouse or a loved one. On the occasion of Passover in 1941, those interned at Gurs were allowed to circulate freely between units for three days. At the very same time in the Rivesaltes camp, however, all Jews (who numbered 3,500 at that date) were transferred in the pouring rain to the most dilapidated unit in the camp—which was also isolated from the others.

Inside these barbed wire fences, the picture was not very bright. In all the camps, the buildings used to house internees were poorly constructed. Ranging from 50 to 60 meters long, they slept up to ninety-six people, whose beds were stacked two high, even though there was only one meter of space on the sides of the building. For bedding, there was straw that was never changed. Filth and vermin were everywhere present. At Argelès, the men had to sleep on the sand, while at Gurs there was a wooden floor, and at Rivesaltes, there was concrete. In some camps there was no ventilation and lighting was poor. In others, in winter, icy winds blew in through all sorts of openings, creating clouds of sand in Argelès and eddies of fine red dust in Les Milles, which had formerly been a tile factory. Rain transformed Gurs into a giant bog, while Rivesaltes would become "a city on water."[44] Along with hot weather, there would be a proliferation of rats, followed by roaches, mosquitoes,[45] and all the parasites brought on by the highly unsanitary conditions that prevailed in the camps. And each camp had its own stubborn, overwhelming odor: at Gurs, for example, it was the smell of clay mixed with the stench of urine.

As a general rule, internees had only one set of clothes and underwear that they wore all the time, and the situation in the camps did not make it possible to keep clothing in good condition. There were few washing faucets and the water supply was not dependable. Showers were too infrequent, and access to latrines was surrounded by mud and never cleaned. Such was the unhealthy environment in which thousands of men, women, children, and elderly people spent many long months.[46] Added to all that, the camp administration kept constantly asking for all sorts of lists. These lists would group people according to nationality, age, and religion. They sought to determine whether Madame X had children or relatives in another city and for how long Monsieur Y had been in France. Other lists would ask what had been the profession of Monsieur Z. And then, from December 1940 on, specific details were required on a question of prime importance: the racial group to which one belonged.[47] These lists created an atmosphere of confusion and fueled all sorts of rumors.

Cold, Hunger, and Isolation

"The men are crowded together in cramped quarters, unshaven, and wear tattered clothes: many do not even have shoes. They complain of hunger and cold. And there are many intellectuals here, who moreover suffer from having nothing to do."

So concluded on January 6, 1941, Colonel Alex Cramer, a doctor who had been sent by the Red Cross to take stock of the internees' situation at Argelès.[48]

We will never know whether they suffered more from hunger or from cold. In any case, hunger was still considered the chief hardship in May 1942.[49] The administration of the camps had at its disposal 11.5 francs per day to feed each internee, but on the average, only spent four francs. For one day, internees would each receive a barely sweetened serving of ersatz coffee, less than 200 grams of bread, two servings of soup with turnips or rutabagas, but without any fat. Twice a week, they would get about 60 grams of meat. Given such a regimen, the entire camp population would have been reduced to famine without the constant aid efforts provided by various relief organizations that had quickly come to work onsite in the camps.

Such aid was absolutely indispensable, even though it provided just enough to maintain some semblance of physical equilibrium for the internees. Nevertheless, it was only available to a minority and was not sufficient to prevent the edema brought on by hunger or the rash of symptoms linked to malnutrition, and the increasing number of deaths among the weaker detainees. Gurs seems to have set the record on that score. From October 1940 until June 1942, it registered 1,005 deaths.[50] The winter of 1940–41 was the most deadly; the hardest hit were the Jews expelled from Baden, as on the whole they constituted an older group. In the winter of the following year, hunger ailments affected all the camps, "threatening a population of more than 10,000 people, including men, women, and adolescents."[51] That was a medical observation: it was the mesurable counterpart of the internees' constant obsession and permanent source of torment: finding something to eat. It was the objective aspect of an experience not easily translated by words: the experience of relentless pangs of hunger. The verbal formula nevertheless makes it possible for us both to imagine the anxious expressions on internees' faces when bread was distributed and to hear the arguments that might break out over an unequal portioning of food.

All through these two winters, the cold penetrated into every corner of these dilapidated buildings that let the winds through and as a rule were not heated. At the same time, socks, shoes, stockings, clothes, and undergarments became in increasingly short supply. And so the lack of privacy coupled with tight quarters became even harder to bear, as everyone had to crowd inside in the stale air and stay closed up in the stench for days on end.

Over the winter of 1941–42 at Rivesaltes, some of the children, who had neither socks or shoes, "just stayed wrapped in their blankets and went about their activities."[52] There were indeed many children in the camps: in December 1940, their number was estimated at four thousand.[53] In May 1941, there were 350 Jewish children at Rivesaltes, which was called a family reunification camp. Elsewhere, households were separated. The food given them differed little from what was served to the adults: for children over the age of six, breakfast was reduced to black "coffee," while the younger ones were served "coffee" with milk. This meant that from six o'clock in the evening until eleven in the morning of the next day, they put nothing in their little stomachs. Rations of milk were distributed in the afternoon, but at a distance of one kilometer from where they were lodged: they had to cover this distance while fighting against the mud and wind. Often they gave up.[54] "For the distribution of rice provided every day by the Swiss relief agency for all the children in the camp, they sometimes came with bloody knees, because they had been knocked down by the wind."[55]

It would be impossible to list all the different ailments that afflicted the majority of the internees, children and adults alike. And it would be difficult to write and unbearable to read about all the complications that resulted from there being no medicines nor any infirmary, all the suffering that could not be relieved, and the demoralizing impotence of those who witnessed it. And how could we adequately describe the unbearable disheartenment that came with the darkness of the evening and its accompanying isolation? "It would take a master poet like Rimbaud to render all the nuances of misery afflicting thousands upon thousands of people, men and women of all ages," wrote Professor A. Reich about Gurs, in a letter smuggled out of the camp.[56] "When you have spent a few days and a few nights inside one of these centers," adds Joseph Weill in May 1942, "you can get an idea of the countless individual tragedies that, taken altogether, compose the gripping story of human breakdown."[57]

To get out of this depressing state, people found ways to become active. Hanna Schramm describes the psychological benefits of the feverish activity internees deployed to fight the epidemic of dysentery that had broken out in the Gurs camp in the fall of 1940.[58] Schramm also points out the great variety of jobs taken on by all sorts of internees to earn a little money; having money helped ease their plight by enabling them to buy vital supplements of food.

The internees' feelings of isolation weighed all the more heavily upon them because their suffering and depression were hidden from the view of the outside world. A buffer zone had been established around Gurs, prohibiting the families of internees from coming to stay within a radius of thirty kilometers around the camp.[59] As a result, visits became impractical, as they were limited to meetings in the camp visitors' room, which were restricted to certain hours. Even then, visits were only possible after having gone through endless red tape. There remained the possibility of mail, but it was also limited (to three letters per week at Gurs), subjected to camp censorship, and restricted to what could be written on a stamped correspondence card that was already half-written. It is hardly surprising, in those circumstances, that the number of letters sent out of Rivesaltes was much lower than the number that arrived there, even though the mailboxes in the neighboring village kept the region's mailmen quite busy!

In January, the situation visible from the areas around the camps was straightened out, especially as American newspapers had published some of the letters describing the conditions in the French camps. Mail sent out from the areas surrounding the camps was henceforth submitted to regular inspections, and for a good while, every letter sent from a camp was first routed through the commission for monitoring prisoner of war mail in Lyon.[60] "Our only glimmer of light is the mail," wrote Professor Reich, "and the hope of receiving a little package, or at least a little note from a friend or relative; but when the mailman has come without bringing any relief whatsoever, we are plunged into an even deeper despair than before; we feel like survivors of a shipwreck who have seen a boat, but who have not themselves been seen by those who are in safety and who could rescue them."

When a package did come, it was meticulously inspected by guards, who confiscated a good deal of its contents. Such was the fate of all products whose sale and distribution had come under governmental restrictions and that in many cases had been acquired only with great sacrifice by the sender.

In this domain as in others, each camp had its own rules. The organization of everyday life depended to a large extent on the head of the camp and on the degree of severity with which he controlled both the actions of the camp personnel and the activities of the internees. Conditions in each camp varied, depending on the internal rules determined by the head—in Gurs, for example, there was much freer circulation between units when a new head took control of the camp—and the latitude granted to the charitable organizations working inside camp confines.

At Les Milles, internees' quarters were heated and the rules were a bit more relaxed than elsewhere: it was easier to get permission to leave the camp to go to Marseilles and pursue the steps necessary to obtain a visa.[61] That was the activity that dominated the thoughts of internees at Les Milles: the hope of departure guided their each and every act.[62] In the meantime, however, the food was no different from food in the other camps. The Rivesaltes camp had been created with the intention of bringing families together. But this reunification did not occur before all Jewish families had been transferred to the block in the unit that was the most unsanitary: it was a veritable "exodus of women, children, and elderly people through the wind and rain."[63] Noé and Récébédou were supposed to take in households whose members were over the age of sixty, the disabled, and the seriously ill. There was no barbed wire at Noé, only a wooden fence, and the living quarters were made of concrete and building blocks. There were real beds, with straw-filled mattresses and sleeping bags. There were shelves over every bed. "This was real luxury, compared with Gurs."[64] Yet even though the internees were just as undernourished at Noé as in any other camp and were tourmented by constant pangs of hunger, camp discipline was made harsher in order to squelch any display of discontent. Yet the most frequently used punishment consisted of depriving recalcitrant detainees of food.[65] The same scenario developed at Récébédou. In these two "hospital camps," where internees suffered from tuberculosis and from an epidemic of cachexia (the "hunger malady"), medical care often turned out to be nothing but a facade.

There were at times improvements in living conditions for the internees. The most unsanitary camps were shut down. The improvisation marking the early phases of the camps gave way to an internal type of organization that became more and more efficient. Some repair work improved the condition of camp buildings. Some housing units were repaired at Gurs, and heating was added to some buildings at Rivesaltes. Kosher cooking was authorized, and religious instruction was also permitted.[66] But all that simply amounted to a more effective management of human misery. Whatever improvements there were resulted mainly from the work of the relief organizations: it was their work that not only improved the conditions in the camps, but also opened a window to the outside world.

We should perhaps dwell on the latter point in order to begin to understand the role of the aid organizations in the camps. The representatives of these groups "were probably not aware of the consolation and benefits that they brought to us," wrote Hanna Schramm. "For us, they were messengers from the outside world, whose absence had weighed so heavily on us for such a long time. Now we were no longer stranded and forgotten on an island. We took heart, for now we felt that people were concerned about us and that people were trying to come to our assistance. No longer were our cries of suffering lost in a vacuum: our plight was known to the outside world."[67] Whether they were Jewish or non-Jewish, the social workers, doctors, nurses, and educators who came to stay in the camps while working for the OSE, the Swiss Relief agency, or any other assistance organization, doubtless represented a sort of counter-authority[68] in face of the camp administration every time a seemingly unsurmountable problem arose. "They were a protection against the silly restrictions from administrators eager to exercise power."[69] But they also embodied hope, "a door opened to whatever [remained] of the civilized world beyond the barbed wire fences."[70]

Organizing Daily Life

The intervention of these relief organizations was requested and encouraged by collective initiatives from within the camps. In most camps, the priority was to organize things in a way that would at least make living conditions bearable. Internees created camp committees on their own. In the Gurs camp, for example, a voluntary taxation system had been set up in four of the units housing women: it was based on a certain amount that would be collected for every money order or package received by an internee. This social fund, which would later be augmented by shows put on by the committee, made it possible to buy supplements of food prepared by the internees themselves. And in turn, this food service, which was devoted first of all those who had the very least, sometimes produced a profit.

It was this committee that went to see Rabbi Léo Ansbacher, who was the chaplain for the Jewish internees, as well as the organizer of a central aid committee among the men at Gurs: the women invited the rabbi to visit them in order "to milk him for everything he was worth."[71] And it was the leaders of this same committee of women who secured from Rabbi Kapel, another chaplain for the camps, the promise that he would visit the camp regularly and bring supplies for the internees. In cases where such committees were not formed spontaneously, social workers and rabbi-chaplains encouraged their creation. At Rivesaltes, on the other hand, it seems that Doctor Isa Malkin, a volunteer with the OSE who had come to live and work in the camp, was unhappy with the internal conflicts paralyzing the internees' committee: he therefore set up an alternative structure to coordinate the social aid programs.[72]

On the whole, however, there were a number of factors that spurred on the development of these aid programs. First, living conditions in the camps were unbearable, particularly for the poorest internees. Second, by taking charge of their situation in this manner, the strongest personalities in the camp found a way to relieve their own suffering. Third, the arrangement enabled camp administrations to hand over responsibility for the most obvious problems to someone else. Finally, there were those organizations whose very vocation was charitable activity. All of these elements contributed to the growth of aid activity both within and without the camps.

Beginning in the winter of 1940, some twenty-five charitable organizations, including the OSE, the Professional Retraining and Reorientation Organization (ORT), the Quakers (American Friends Service Committee), the Joint, the CIMADE (a Protestant relief agency for refugees), the YMCA, the Swiss Relief agency, and others united their efforts under the umbrella of the Coordinating Committee for Camp Aid or the (interfaith) Nîmes Committee in order to improve daily living conditions for internees.[73] For its part, the Central Committee for Jewish Aid Organizaions (CCOJA) created a commission on the camps that established an office in Toulouse in March 1941. Finally, the rabbis that had served as chaplains for the military—and Shmuel René Kapel was the first among them—had been able to gain entrance into the camps because of their official status. In order to coordinate the action of these committees and overcome the opposition of some of the heads of the camps that restricted their access to them, a chaplains' office was established and placed under the leadership of Chief Rabbi René Hirschler in March 1942.

In reality, these various efforts to coordinate aid work had to deal with a multifaceted situation. Some were so outraged by the horror of living conditions that internees were forced to suffer that they felt like revolting against authority. Others were more inclined to cooperate in various ways with Vichy's bureaucracy. As a general rule, however, the relief efforts taken on by all these organizations prevailed over doubts, at least before the summer of 1942. The chief supplier of money was the Joint, which regularly increased its contribution during this first phase.[74] As for the internees, they mainly dealt with the delegates who had come to live and work in the camps and the social visitors who came there on a regular basis.

While it seemed to be the top priority for Jewish leaders, the problem of aiding the internees proved to be a dilemma from the very outset. This observation was made by the Joint Distribution Committee's representative in France as early as July 1940, after he had met the leaders of the various Jewish aid organizations of the prewar years. If the Jewish organizations took the responsibility for supplying food and providing clothing for the camps, French authorities might be tempted to rely entirely on them to keep the camps in good order. Even worse than that, they might be tempted to open new detention sites in order to intern more foreign Jews. Herbert Katzki thus concluded that it would perhaps be good to send funds to the Quakers: since they already had access to the camps, they could distribute the necessary aid without granting any legitimacy to the isolation of Jews.[75]

The various charitable organizations nevertheless committed themselves to the task of aiding the internees and did not hesitate to express their disapproval in the most official manner. For example, when the minister of the interior, Peyrouton, by means of a communiqué published by newspapers in the Unoccupied Zone, announced that he was henceforth authorizing the administration of the prefectures to accept support from the aid organizations in order to improve the food supply and living conditions in the camps (now euphemistically called shelters), the Nîmes Committee reacted by sending a memorandum to several government ministries and by forming a delegation that went to see the minister of the interior. While they declared that they were willing to work with the government to bring about a series of improvements in camp life, the various organizations represented by the committee "specif[ied] that they [would] never accept the notion that the camps were normal and desirable. They [were] convinced that the camps should disappear in favor of more humane means of housing and monitoring refugees whose only offense is to be refugees. [The organizations were] ready to work to that end."[76] Accordingly, all future proposals to improve camp life were preceded by specific requests for the release of certain detainees, with the aid organizations offering to take reponsibility for the welfare of those set free, whether they be children, elderly, or of other categories.

Nevertheless, a major part of the relief organizations' efforts were from the outset devoted to improving conditions of detention, simply because the needs were so urgent and manifest. And so they set about dividing up the work among the various groups. The Unitarian Service took charge of schooling, while the Quakers and the Swiss Relief agency looked after matters of food supply, and the OSE took responsibility for problems of hygiene and sanitary needs. They also divided up the task of distributing the various foodstuffs: the Quakers provided rice and dried vegetables; the Swiss Relief agency gave out milk, and the OSE supplied the camps with flour, fruits, jams, and fresh vegetables by the truckload.[77] A full three-fifths of the budget of the Committee for Camps was devoted to food aid.[78]

Thanks to these efforts, all of the internees benefited at one time or another from a supplement of food. The creation of additional kitchens, which were organized by the camps' social committees and stocked by the relief organizations, helped first those in the most dire need. "Outside, at the far end of the camp, a dozen pots spread out over makeshift fires are part of an effort to provide at least once a day a more or less decent meal to the most indigent internees, who, since they have no personal resources, would otherwise have nothing more than the food officially provided by the camp administration," reported Rabbi Langer, after visiting the camp at Les Milles. As of fall 1941, about one hundred internees were benefiting from this kitchen organized by the social committee of the camp.[79]

The main emphasis was placed on fighting cachexia, which broke out in the camps toward the end of winter in 1941 and kept gaining ground. The OSE along with the Quakers and the Swiss Relief agency set up a large-scale medical program and devoted themselves wholeheartedly to solving the problem.[80]

They established a system for identifying those at risk, and distributed thousands of supplementary meals, with a special menu for those suffering from cachexia. In order to carry out this action, they first had to receive authorization from the camps' administration (namely, from Inspector André Jean-Faure); after a few preliminary difficulties, permission was granted. However, Jean-Faure's acceptance of the plan turned out to be less of an authorization than of a transfer of responsibility. In fact, the French administration was going to rely completely on charitable aid programs to save those that it had itself reduced to a state of famine.[81] Not only was this evidence of a singular cynicism on behalf of French authorities, it also constituted a trap for the relief organizations. For who could remain insensitive to the urgency of bringing back to life an internee who had been weakened to the point of despondency by hunger and was only waiting to die?

Providing food supplements for children in the camps was also a priority. Preschool nurseries were organized, and additional coal was even supplied for the buildings housing them. Indeed, in every camp there were makeshift social groups coming together, with the aid and encouragement of the relief organizations. In this "caricature of a life,"[82] apathy gave way to the darkest despair. It amounted to a sort of escapism based on fictions that nobody really believed but that probably were needed to keep on living.

Divided into three groups, the 350 children of the Rivesaltes camp had been going to school since May 16, 1941. Although they had no school supplies and had to sit on the ground, they followed their instruction with great interest. There were no textbooks nor any instructional materials or supplies at Gurs, but in a specially arranged building, in "the only school in the world where the sole method of punishment was to deprive the child of a day of class," there was "a team of highly talented educators, able to stimulate children's minds and intent on seeing that they did not forget all they had learned."[83] One of Stefan Zweig's relatives even organized a little theater group of children that performed for the internees.

In order to avoid remaining idle, internees developed various occupations that also made it possible for some to earn a little money. They made all sorts of different objects, and at Gurs, they even organized an exhibit. Some tended little gardens within the camp confines. The Professional Retraining and Reorientation Organization (ORT) made it possible to set up workshops within some camps that would at the same time provide vocational training for young people. In January 1942, there were 147 pupils taking classes in carpentry, leatherwork, sewing, and basket-weaving at Rivesaltes.[84] At the Récébédou camp, there were at the same time 144 pupils who, in addition to studying languages and drawing, were also learning to make neckties. Needless to say, all this work was being done in unheated workshops. In the sewing rooms, internees mended clothes that were completely in tatters. Again in the Gurs camp in June 1941, some 373 of the internees had formed a unit of workers within the camp: they took care of landscaping jobs.

There was also a small library that would make the rounds between the housing units. At Gurs, there were some four thousand volumes in the library in April 1942.[85] The development of cultural and artistic activity over the course of the year 1941 was unprecedented. "The darkness, cold, and hunger made artistic activity spring up all over as if in powerful protest: it was as if human beings in their suffering were mounting all their strength to affirm their existence."[86]

In every housing unit at Gurs, there was one building that had been arranged to serve as cultural center for giving plays, concerts, and lectures. There was certainly no lack of singers, pianists, violinists, composers, and writers. Completely original cabaret shows composed by professionals were presented on a makeshift stage. Stage settings, posters, and invitation cards were designed by painters in the camp, and concerts were also given: the organist of the Strasbourg cathedral (Hans Ebbecke), a highly talented composer and pianist (Hans Mayerowitz), and the first violin of the Vienna philharmonic (Frizt Brunner) made sure that a rich repertory was offered. Experienced singers performed operatic arias and Hebraic tunes, while musical instruments and sheet music was provided by the YMCA. Professional actors put on various plays for the internees. Performers were paid with food items, and any profits that were made went to the camp's social assistance fund.

One song composed by the internee Heini Walfisch probably conveys the content of these shows better than any description.

> We have put on plays at Gurs,
> Do you know what that means?
> The world was fading out of sight behind the barbed wire fences.
> There were eight thousand of us poor men and women who have
> been uprooted and torn away from our homes.
>
> We were living in the deepest poverty and despair,
> forgotten, orphaned,
> penned up in sinister, ramshackle buildings.
> The winds of war had raged over our heads.
> Do you know what that means?
>
> We performed to stay alive,
> Nobody really knows what that means.
> For Ibsen, a sixteenth of a loaf of bread,
> for *A Midsummer Night's Dream*, an egg
> and maybe a handful of semolina, given with disdain.

We rehearsed through icy nights,
famished, almost ready to faint,
we sang and danced, laughed and cried,
and brought joy and light, life,
to thousands of spectators.
You do not know what that means.

We revived the desperate,
we gave them courage, hope, and faith again.
All the suffering of humanity
we have ourselves experienced,
but we put on plays. . . .
Ponder what that means.[87]

Others sought refuge and comfort in practicing their religion. "I have attended religious services celebrated in the camps at Gurs, Noé, Récébédou," wrote Rabbi Kapel in January 1942, "and I can say that never in our French synagogues have I observed as much piety and religious fervor as in these cold, humble, ramshackle buildings used as makeshift places of worship." According to his estimate, there were at that time some thirteen hundred practicing Jews detained in the camps who asked to eat kosher food.[88] In the same report, Rabbi Kapel stresses that a good number of internees came to attend classes in Jewish history, the Bible, and the Talmud that were given within camp confines. Camp chaplains did all they could to satisfy the internees' needs, especially in the organization of Jewish holy days, when even the least religious of the internees would come to see them.

For these holy days in the fall of 1941, some three hundred copies of the main prayers to be used for the major observances were run off and distributed at Les Milles: each copy included five pages printed front and back. Seven hundred of the internees observed a complete fast, even though there were only about one hundred regularly practicing Jews in the camp. The social committee at Les Milles prepared an additional dish for the meal marking the end of the fast. A large *sukka*[89] had been set up in a sort of shed whose tile roof had been replaced with leaves and branches that internees—still under surveillance—had gone to gather at a distance of five kilometers from the camp.[90]

"I got back late from a festival celebration with the Jews in unit B," wrote the resident social worker with the Swiss Relief agency on December 19, 1941, at one-thirty in the morning. "They are celebrating Hanukkah to commemorate the victory of the Maccabees over the pagans two thousand years ago: according to the tradition, God miraculously contributed to this victory. How strange: they are living here, persecuted, without a homeland, still hoping to go back to their ancient homeland, Palestine, and still hoping for their Messiah to come."[91]

For the Passover of 1942, some 516 of the internees at Les Milles requested unleavened bread. Almost 250 internees had declared that they wished to eat ritual food during Passover week.[92] Not all of these requests were granted.

In fact, the only thing getting in the way of aid programs in every domain was the camps' administration. "Once the facilities have been set up, with cafeterias opened, infirmaries functioning, and schools in session, relief workers did their utmost to fine-tune and consolidate the progress already achieved: from that point on, the fact that the camps would be fatal to these detainees and that only freedom could save these persons from their death sentences, was only a vague, distant reality."[93] Such is the sad assessment of the social relief work in the camps made by one of its main founders, Doctor Joseph Weill. He had been the very first to sense the limits of the relief programs, and he was crucial in getting leaders to use underground means to thwart French policy instead of helping authorities handle the problem that they themselves had created.

For her part, Nina Gourfinkel expressed her outrage over the relief groups' strategy of "normalizing a nightmare." In her memoirs, she vehemently attacks the "polite assistance of well-meaning people" who did not have the "courage to shake off the sedative effect of abstractions," to "pound their fist on the table," and to "shout out as loudly as when one is attacked by thugs on the highway."[94] That may well be. But such is the ambivalence that by definition characterizes humanitarian intervention, *all* humanitarian intervention. And the humanitarian invention in the French camps was accompanied by an active strategy for getting people out: hundreds of Jewish children owed their lives to it.

Getting Out of the Camps

Getting the children out of the camps was indeed the priority in the strategy first implemented systematically in September 1941. At first, the Quakers expressed some reservations, but the leaders of the OSE, who were being encouraged to head in this direction by their own American branch, finally prevailed.[95] Beginning in early 1942, the OSE also took charge of the release of adolescents.[96] The leaders of the organization secured permission from the French authorities, who first gave such authorizations on a case-by-case basis, then collectively.[97] OSE leaders also gained the cooperation of the government employees working at the prefectorate in the département of L'Hérault; in order to be released, the children had to have a certificate proving that they would be housed and fed, and this certificate had to be issued by the prefect for the département in which they would be living.[98] And so the children who were released first had to spend time in one of the OSE's houses in Palavas-les-Flots before going on to one of its other children's homes. On May 21, 1942, there was a celebration for the departure of the last convoy of children to leave Rivesaltes.[99] As for the 227 Jewish adolescents who were still in the Gurs and Rivesaltes camps in May 1942, their departure had also been scheduled.[100] In July 1942, only 540 children under the age of fifteen remained in the camps: most were non-Jews whose parents had refused to be separated from them.[101]

Aided by the other relief organizations, and in particular by the Polish Red Cross, the Swiss Relief agency, the Quakers, and the Czechoslovakian Center for Aid, the OSE had managed to get hundreds of children out of the camps before June 1942. Among them were 623 Jewish children, mainly from Gurs and Rivesaltes.[102]

"Hey, look! There isn't any barbed wire!" That was the first remark made by a five-year-old girl who had been freed along with the earliest group of children, when she saw chickens running around in the street.[103] Obviously, the "barbed wire complex" did not just affect adults. Once they had gotten out from behind the barbed wire fences, the children were given close attention and special care in the OSE's homes in order to restore them to good health. Some were given lessons in French; others received vocational schooling. It required an infinite amount of patience to overcome their "hunger phobia," which pushed them to devour enormous quantities of food and stuff their pockets so as to prepare for the future while at the same time remembering their parents who were still in the camps.

Before they had reached that stage, however, they had had to undergo the ordeal of separation. The parents consented, but it was a wrenching decision; it meant that they had to be willing to send their children into the unknown without being able to hear from them. But they nevertheless consented: they could no longer bear to remain powerless while their little ones kept saying "I'm hungry." They had given up all hope for their own future, but they had not lost hope for their children. They would often insist that their children be sent to the United States to be saved, even though that made for an even more heartbreaking separation. When the first group of children was sent off in May 1941, a social worker with the OSE, Vivette Samuel, obtained a three-day "furlough" for ten mothers, who were thus able to see once again for a short while their children (released a few months earlier in some cases) and watch them board ship.

Vivette Samuel describes one of these separations that occurred on Friday, January 16, 1942:

> The parents had been granted the favor of accompanying their children to the trucks. . . . Parents and children were then separated. No one cried, as the last recommendations were given and bags were checked. After the last call, the camp gates opened. It was still dark, and cold. The wind, that fierce north wind that blows over the south of France, whipped across the open bed of the truck, but, holding their heads high toward the sky, the children sang heartily in the wind and the cold and the dark to show the joy of being free again. And the parents' tears began to flow. Would they ever see their children again?[104]

Once they had managed to achieve this moment of self-control, some parents suffered a breakdown from which they never recovered.

In addition to this special effort to secure the release of children, there were two plans aimed at getting some of the adult victims out. One of these plans emanated from part of Vichy's administration, the Office of Social Services for Foreigners (SSE). The idea was that of Gilbert Lesage, who contacted the Central Consistory in mid-December 1941. He proposed to broaden the mission that he had been given by law (which consisted of placing young foreign Jews in vocational training centers under his authority) by creating shelters that would take in all who seemed to be forgotten by the new measures and who, as a result, risked being interned in the camps. These individuals included men unfit to work in a Foreign Worker Unit, women, children, and elderly people. Well-to-do foreign Jews would be brought together in residential centers: these would be small towns or villages, "sometimes hotels that would be reserved for well-to-do foreigners in seaside resorts now idle, sometimes tenement buildings for refugees, where those concerned would pool all their resources and organize themselves into a managed cooperative system."

Essentially designed for professional reorientation and training, such centers, promised Lesage, would prepare their clients for future emigration out of France. They would be monitored by a non-Jewish overseer, who would only be "authorized to use funds that [were] designated under his name." All the other leaders, however, were to be Israelites, who were to be appointed by the authorities after having been chosen by the Consistory. Family reunification would be the guiding principle. Such centers had already been established for Polish nationals after the Polish Red Cross had been disbanded. Because the sixteen francs allotted by the administration were insufficient to cover the cost of renting housing facilities, paying employees, and covering other expenses, the Central Consistory would make up the difference. "Even though [we do] not look favorably on collaborating in the implementation of measures that seriously restrict the liberty of people whose only crime is that of belonging to the Israelite faith, " the Consistory accepted, on the condition that the General Commission on Jewish Affairs would officially agree to the arrangement. The Consistory's chief aim here was to "relieve considerably the suffering of those hit by the exclusionary measures."

Its decision was doubtless also influenced by rumors from the Occupied Zone: in particular, the news that the Germans had arrested several hundred prominent French Jews and interned them at Compiègne and that the German policy of taking hostages in reprisal for acts of resistance was hitting Jews harder than others. Rivalry with the budding UGIF, which Lesage had deliberately kept out of his plans, was probably also a factor. In the new scheme of things that was developing, the UGIF came under the control of the General Commission on Jewish Affairs: this amounted to a political dependence, while the consistory appeared like a moral authority that was lending its aid to providing social services. Jean Lévy, director of France's national train system (SNCF), was appointed general director of these shelters for foreign Jews and was given the task of choosing the directors of the centers that were to be created. Jacques Helbronner officially contacted the Joint to requested its financial support.[105] The consistory thought that the plan might concern from 5,000 to 6,000 people and that it would take a budget of 300 francs per person per month to cover the expenses to which they had already committed.[106]

It seems that this plan was in the end never carried out.[107] Nevertheless, the Office of Social Services for Foreigners' action made it possible to bring families back together and to secure the release of some of the Jews in the camps. Taken within the system, it was one of the initiatives that attempted to alleviate the effect of the exclusionary measures by taking advantage of loophooles in the law.

Abbot Alexandre Glasberg, vicar of Notre-Dame-de-Saint-Alban in Lyon, was the author of another initiative aimed at freeing at least some of the internees. Here again, an official cover was secured. Over the course of the first few months of 1941, Abbot Glasberg, Nina Gourfinkel,[108] and Doctor Joseph Weill created a Main Office for the Shelters (DCA) which were to take in foreign Jews released from the camps. They obtained the support of Cardinal Gerlier,[109] and then, on June 13, 1941, received an authorization from the ministry of the interior,[110] which specified clearly that this was a transfer—not to be confused with a release—and that those internees involved could not stray more than five kilometers from their shelter. Even then, in order to get people out of the camps, it was still necessary to receive permission from several administrative offices, ranging from local authorities to the prefect's offices and finally, to Vichy's central authority for the camps.

On November 25, 1941, the first group of internees was allowed out of the Gurs camp. In order to cut down on administrative procedures, it had been decided that all the candidates for such a "release" would be designated from those detained there at Gurs, where Ninon Haït, David Donoff, and Théo Bernheim represented their interests. This time, it was a group of men and women between the ages of twenty and forty-five that was been set free: they could resume a normal existence, with no need of going to nursing homes where "the only thing people could do was to wait for death."[111] The means used to finance this project were particularly original: since one-third of those released paid for everyone in the group, the shelters thus maintained financial self-sufficiency. The people who would pay were chosen from among the older ones, according to the criterion of family reunification, while the central commission on camps granted a one-time subsidy to initiate the program.

In March 1942, the General Commission on Jewish Affairs raised an objection: "the archbishop of Lyon's gesture risked appearing a sly way to protest the anti-Jewish laws of which apparently he did not approve." This objection, however, did not hinder the project. Three houses were opened, two of them before the summer of 1942. Fifty-seven persons from Gurs were transferred to the La Roche d'Ajoux shelter in Chansaye (in the département of Le Rhône) in November 1941, with twenty more arriving in May 1942. And fifty-two other internees from Gurs were released to the le Pont-de-Manne shelter in the département of La Drôme in May 1942. Contrary to the expectations of the project's initiators, however, those released from the camps did not instantly form a harmonious, self-administrating community. Certainly, they were now living in decent, if modest, conditions: in place of barbed-wire fences, there were trees. But this "fortuitously assembled group of men and women who had suffered heavily in the harsh conditions of the camps"[112] did not have a community spirit. Moreover, they continued to be part of the population that was placed under strict control.

In addition, the Lastic shelter in Rosans in the département of Les Hautes-Alpes took in forty-five young people between the ages of thirteen and twenty, as well as eleven supervisors under the age of thirty in May 1942: all had been released from Gurs. In Vic-sur-Cère, in the département of Le Cantal, there were forty girls between the ages of fifteen and twenty: they had been freed from Gurs and Rivesaltes. Both of these shelters were run with the aid of the OSE.

According to Nina Gourfinkel, about a thousand people, two-thirds of whom were Jewish, stayed in these shelters at one time or another. Because Abbot Glasberg was working outside of official Vichy channels with the support of the most prominent figure of the Catholic hierarchy, he had had better success than Gilbert Lesage, who tried to win over the Jewish hierarchy to the idea of reaching a working agreement with the system. But even that assessment must be qualified a bit; the number of Jews who benefited from these shelters was relatively small, and those released to live there remained under police control. When the time of police roundups would come, both Lesage and Glasberg would use their influence to limit the application of the new measures hitting Jews; to various degrees, they resorted to illegal channels.

Unless they were sponsored by some organization, it was difficult for foreign Jews to gain release from the internment camps, especially when they had no money. Prefects were not very generous with their housing certificates. The subprefect for the département of Le Puy-de-Dôme, for example, refused to grant Kohn Felsenberg permission to spend two or three months with his father-in-law's family in a small village; such an authorization would have let him leave the Rivesaltes camp where he was interned with the rest of his family. He was turned down even though he had an immigration visa to the United States in his possession. One hundred foreign Jews in this same département met with the same refusal over the course of the summer of 1941.[113]

Chief Rabbi Schwarz also tried to intervene to obtain a collective release of internees: accompanied by representatives of the Joint, he went to see the minister of the interior in January 1941. In exchange for the Joint's pledge of 1,200 francs for every camp internee set free, the Vichy government seemed willing to consider a wider range of releases. But to secure the release of a thousand internees would have cost the Joint more than 40 percent of its entire budget for France in 1941. In August of the same year, it decided that the cost was too great and abandoned the project.[114]

Four shelters had been set up by the CIMADE, a Protestant group to take in former internees in Le Chambon-sur-Lignon (in the département of La Haute Loire), Pomeyrol (near Tarascon in the département of Les Bouches-du-Rhône), Vabre (in the département of Le Tarn), and in Marseilles.[115]

As for the Communists, they had, after a period of confusion, opted in the fall of 1940 for the strategy of escaping from the camps and returning former political activists to their native countries by using several channels.[116] But while they were in the camps, they played a key role in camp committees: such was the case of Maurice Margulies at Saint-Cyprien. When they managed to escape, Jews often returned to Paris, where they were some of the most experienced activists. But whether in Paris or in Toulouse, they again devoted their time to the task of political organization.

The decrease in the number of camp internees over the winter of 1940–41 actually stemmed mainly from all the various initiatives for getting people out. Those behind such initiatives sometimes concerted their efforts, in spite of the reticence of certain individuals. The summary of activities from the secretary of the social office of the camp at Rivesaltes reports that there were 224 releases (or transfers) between June 15 and June 30, 1942. Twenty-three percent of those set free went to live in one of the Office of Social Services for Foreigners' shelters, 8 percent went to one of Abbot Glasberg's homes, 12 percent went to a shelter run by the OSE or the Israelite Scouts of France, 6 percent were incorporated into a Foreign Worker Unit, and slightly more than 50 percent were released under the policy of reunifying families of Foreign Workers.[117]

And so people sometimes did get out of the camps. In the worst of cases, it was only to be incorporated into a Foreign Worker Unit. Those who had a bit of "luck" or money wound up in a situation of house arrest.

ON THE EDGES OF THE CAMPS

Forced Labor

To speak of the incorporation of foreign Jews into a Foreign Worker Unit (GTE) as a persecutory measure is not to speak rhetorically. One seller of fine leather goods in Belleville found himself suddenly working as a logger in Saint-Priest-Taurion (in the département of La Haute-Vienne), while a dealer in secondhand clothing suddenly found himself doing road work in Saint-Georges-d'Aurac (in the département of La Haute-Loire). Intellectuals (doctors, lawyers, journalists, professors), storeowners, industrial leaders, and men in small crafts who often came to spend many months in camps were assigned to do work making canals in Mont-Louis-sur-Tet (in the département of les Pyrénées-Orientales) or drying up marshes in Barsanges (in the département of La Corrèze). Some were even sent to work in an arsenic factory in Auzon (département of La Haute-Loire).[118]

Once onsite, they generally found themselves subjected to a regimen of forced labor. There was a daily roll call followed by a salute to the flag. Correspondence was kept under strict control, with letters written in Yiddish often held for weeks on end. In some cases, there was a rather "liberal" use of sending workers to solitary jail cells for disciplinary purposes. Packages sent by families would be systematically confiscated. In some cases, it was forbidden to leave the camp; in others, workers were prohibited from buying goods in the stores of a neighboring village. Leaves were rarely granted, and some workers could not use them because they had no housing certificate. Others were not able to use leaves to visit their families: they were too far away, and travel was too difficult. In practice, family reunification was not working.

But amid these infernal conditions, miracles sometimes happened, as was the case one Sunday in Egletons, when the owners of the patisserie shop gave chocolate milk and cookies to workers in Palestinian group no. 665 of the Foreign Worker Units (from Soudeille, in the département of La Corrèze).

The most important determinant of living conditions for those in the Foreign Worker Units was the head of the camp. In the Mauriac camp, a virtual reign of terror had been instituted by a virulently antisemitic converted Jew. At Saint-Cyr in the département of La Haute Vienne, on the other hand, the camp commander proved to be humane. But housing conditions were poor everywhere. Foreign workers were lodged in wooden huts that let in rain, as was the case in the camp at Neuvic-d'Ussel (département of La Corrèze). They were also put in barns, as at Saint-Georges-d'Aurac; the straw was not changed. In some cases, such as at the Lafavède camp (département of Le Gard), they were housed in stone buildings. In situations where they worked at a prohibitive distance from a camp, they were put up in temporary barracks.

Every written account of these camps reports similar conditions: nonexistent hygiene, tattered clothing, torn and worn-out shoes. Even more serious was that the food provided was totally insufficient to sustain these forced laborers: at the Ruffieux camp (département of La Savoie), workers received 210 grams of bread, colza and turnip soup, and a supplement of meat or fish once a week. At Saint-Georges-d'Aurac, there was coffee in the morning, rutabagas and carrots at noon, and lentil soup in the evening. For more than one thousand Jews, the situation was particularly serious, as they refused to eat anything but kosher food.

Jews in these Foreign Worker Units had to work eight or nine hours a day, and in many cases, even longer, yet their salary was only half that given to other civilian workers. At times, it was linked to their output, which could hardly be astronomical, given their physical condition and their past experience. Many an intellectual and storeowner lost a finger cutting wood in the stands of pine at Saint-Cyr-sur-Mer (département of Le Var). In spite of all that, authorities had no qualms about deducting from the workers' meager salaries the cost of their room and board, which was fixed at a high level: workers at Ruffieux , for example, only received about fifteen percent of their total pay after all deductions had been made.

In short, those in the Foreign Worker Units were in a pitiful state. The most dramatic case seems to have been unit no. 664 from Saint-Georges-d'Aurac. There some two hundred Polish and German Jews (some of whom had been in France for twenty years) from the Mauriac camp were subjected to the harsh rule of Colonel Lévy. There was a proliferation of strict rules, and those who broke them were sent to a disciplinary camp: such was the fate of twenty-two men over the course of twelve days. Eighty percent of the workers were sick, and those who were assigned to the arsenic plant had their faces and bodies covered with rashes. In other places such as Tombedouc and Casseneuil (département of Le Lot-et-Garonne), the regimen was more tolerable. There and at Soudeilles (département of La Corrèze),[119] they were sometimes assigned directly to farmers, with the least fit among them doing work in gardens. Some were fortunate enough to work in sewing or leather-goods shops. Others, however, because they had complained, wound up in one of the disciplinary units, at Aubagne (département of Les Bouches-du-Rhône), at Le Fort-de-Chapoly (département of Le Rhône), or in Auchères (département of La Corrèze): these were veritable penitentiaries in which detainees were placed under the guard of former members of the French Foreign Legion and often hit.[120]

As was the case in the camps, internal committees were sometimes created within Foreign Worker Units. They collected relief funds to aid the neediest workers and organized cultural activities that provided a bit of relief from the daily routine of harassment: having gone to great lengths to put together a library, they struck up songs in the evening and managed as if by magic to revive the past.

There was one rather peculiar group of performers put together by Foreign Worker Unit no, 653 at Egletons that gained some degree of renown from its productions. Over the winter of 1941–42, it gave shows in various towns in the départements of La Corrèze, La Dordogne, and La Haute-Vienne: benefits sometimes went to the National Relief agency, the Red Cross, and the French Legion of War Veterans. Between December 1941 and mid-August 1942, they gave twenty-seven concerts in twenty different places. The total amount taken in exceeded 30,000 francs.

The group was led by Rudi Aufer, an Austrian Jew: he, along with a cellist and two pianists (all three also Austrian Jews) were the core. But the group also included a singer who was a Russian Jew, a Polish Jew, and six Spaniards (a guitarist, two singers, and three dancers). Two other dancers—one Spanish, one Austrian—also participated. The four Austrian Jews moreover would give a concert every Sunday in Brive, at the Café de l'Etoile et du Parc. The group was disbanded, however, by the police roundups of August 1942: three of the Austrian Jews were deported, while the fourth fled.[121]

Under House Arrest

If they were legally registered with authorities at the prefecture, those having escaped internment were placed under house arrest. Beginning in November 1941, such was the plight of Jews fortunate enough to be self-sufficient: by July 1942, they reportedly numbered almost ten thousand.[122] Among them were those who had fled the onslaught of the German blitzkrieg in May and June 1940, those who had subsequently slipped across the demarcation line, and a considerable number of Jews who had begun their long, difficult journey in one of the internment camps. Such was the case of a Jewish married couple from Strasbourg who were doctors. The husband was from Russia, the wife from Poland: both arrived in Périgueux on July 16, 1940. Shortly after, he was interned in Barcarès, then in the camp at Argelès. Released on November 19, 1941, he was placed under house arrest in a small town in the département of La Dordogne, where his wife came to join him before long. Since then, observed an inspector with the Police for Jewish Affairs in March 1942, they had been living modestly, and without receiving any refugee benefits from the government—a vital deprivation, to avoid being sent back to a camp.[123]

The places where Jews were placed under house arrest

> were almost always obscure, remote little dumps, without proper facilities for communication and daily living. . . . In one tiny village without a bakery in the Pyrenees, the gendarmes prohibited Jews from going to a neighboring town to get bread. . . . The poor, who constituted the majority, found themselves having to pretend as if they were well-to-do. . . . Because many of them lived off aid from Jewish organizations, any such financial assistance should have been provided to them with the greatest discretion. Unfortunately, however, many people were summoned to the police station or the gendarmerie and instructed to prove on the spot that they had sufficient financial resources."[124]

An oft-used method of meeting such a requirement was to borrow a few bills from somebody and then pass them back and forth. In some villages, such as Saint-Pons in the département of L'Hérault, there were only about thirty people placed under house arrest, while in others, such as Lacaune in the département of Le Tarn or Aulus-les-Bains in the département of L'Ariège, there were some four hundred to five hundred.

It was there in Aulus-les-Bains, a small agricultural village of no more than four hundred nestled against the base of the Pyrenees and isolated from everything, that this large group of Jews mainly from Poland and the Netherlands, was placed under house arrest in late May 1942.[125] They had first stayed in Toulouse, and then were placed in house arrest in Luchon, in the département of La Haute-Garonne, before finally being transferred to Aulus-les-Bains.[126] In July 1942, they were joined by 150 refugees from the département of Le Tarn.[127] All were lodged in village farms, in wooden huts, and in old abandoned buildings, where the lack of privacy and heating imposed severe hardship in winter months. Most lived from funds provided by the UGIF, and the poorest could eat at the soup kitchen that had been set up by a local Jewish committee, which provided a hundred meals a day. Among those placed in house arrest in Aulus-les-Bains were a group of strictly observant Jews from Anvers, who turned an old ramshackle building into a synagogue. As for the young people, Rabbi Kapel managed to put them in touch with the Scouts in Moissac. The Scouts saw to it that they received their education, and gave religious instruction and Hebrew classes on the spot.

And so, as was the case elsewhere, these foreign Jews placed under house arrest in this little village organized their daily life as best they could. The atmosphere was one of uncertainty mixed with vague fears about the future: at times, people managed to forget these worries, but more often their anxieties were overwhelming.

On the Margins

French newspapers did not report what happened on the other side of the barbed-wire fences. Although there was a world of difference separating the Jews who lived in a camp and those who were in town, the camps were nevertheless present in the lives of a growing number of Jews. In the first place, the camps constituted a threat: people knew that arrest and internment were constant risks. Even more important, however, was that soon every family counted one of their friends, relatives, or neighbors among those who had been interned in the camps. Many families were constantly busy with the preparation of food packages for the internees, even though in this time of shortages it often meant that they themselves would have to forgo basic necessities. A great deal of energy and time was spent trying to gain the release of loved onea. Such efforts had to be discreet, and often relied on relations with well-placed individuals. In other cases such efforts followed administrative channels and were based on the most rational of arguments. Many families also tried to move as close as possible to the camp where their relative was interned.

But nothing could alter the fact that the internment of a loved one meant separation with no foreseeable end. A head of a household incorporated into a Foreign Worker Unit was supposedly to be reunited with his family, but that rarely happened in practice: the Worker Units changed worksites too often and lodging was generally unavailable in the area. In many cases, families were able to be together only during the ten days of regular leave granted after one year of work.[128]

For families in such a situation, worries for loved ones detained in camps overshadowed all else. One can well imagine the nightmares of the children who had been released while their parents were left there to waste away in the camps. And think of the anxiety of the wives of the Foreign Workers employed in the arsenic plant: they had heard rumors about the conditions there.[129]

Moreover, these families quite often lived in poverty. A ministerial memorandum dating from June 23, 1941, explicitly included the families of interned Jews among those who were to receive government benefits.[130] Many, however, fearing that they themselves might be interned themselves as people "without any financial resources," were discouraged from applying for them. While some of the women whose husbands had been incorporated into the Foreign Worker Units received a subsidy of 7.5 francs, plus 4.5 francs for every child,[131] many preferred to forgo the aid.

Employees and volunteers working for the various relief programs, along with the young people who found in these groups the social interaction denied to them in French society, spent a great deal of their time trying to improve the daily living conditions of those interned in the camps. For Scouts, the basic tasks consisted of preparing packages of supplies for Gurs or Rivesaltes, visiting one of the camps and bringing them food, and adopting one of the children or families in the camps: such is the description in the notes of a Cub Scout in January 1942.[132] Every month, the Wolf Scouts in the Bar Cochba pack (the first in Toulouse) would organize a collection of food and clothing. The food was taken directly to the camps by the young people themselves, and the clothing was handed over to the aid committee in Toulouse.

In participating in such activities, however, the children were put in touch with dire poverty.[133] And so were the youth in the Jewish Army. On June 15, 1941, Claude Vigée noted in his diary: "Went this afternoon to the concentation camp (so-called hospital camp) at Récébédou. It surpasses our conception of the horrible. They have people—thousands of Jews from Baden, Poland, and Austria who have done nothing wrong but are simple accused of belonging to the same people I belong—dying of hunger, exposure, and despair." And for June 19–24, 1941, he notes: "Returned Sunday to the Récébédou camp, along with Paul Roïtman and Doctor Epstein, loaded with food that was confiscated at the camp entrance by these Messieurs with the State Police, who will sell it off among the prisoners on the black market and make an enormous profit. Depressed and tired. When will this agony ever come to an end?"[134] Those who witnessed the spectacle of such human indigence would be forever marked by what they had seen.

For those seeing to the well-being of the internees, the gradual shift toward clandestine activity occurred almost imperceptibly: one first step would facilitate later transitions. Paul Roïtman smuggled loaves of dark bread, and, during Passover, unleavened bread, into the camps. Vivette Samuel, who was working to get the children out of Rivesaltes, had at first been fooled by Joseph, an adolescent who had without her knowledge lowered his age by a year in order to remain officially under the age of sixteen; at that time an identity card was mandatory and release from the camp impossible. By the time Vivette Samuel discovered the hoax, the prefecture in Montpellier had, contrary to all expectations, issued an identity card. It was this success that incited her to use a similar scheme, this time on her own initiative, to secure the release of other adolescents.[135]

Robert Gamzon got the idea of how to fabricate a false identity during his efforts to take in a young man who had escaped from a Foreign Worker Unit.[136] At that time, in November 1941, all he had to do was to transform a German Jew into a French Israelite. The changes of identity that would proliferate a few months later would be much more radical. In the case of both Gamzon and Samuel, the gradual shift toward illegal action resulted from the urgency of the situation. The few preliminary hesitations vanished quickly in view of the objectives, and, a successful first attempt led to other operations of a similar nature.

On June 27, 1942, the secretary-general of the police wrote to the General Commissioner for Jewish Affairs: "The Gurs camp in the département of Les Basses-Pyrénées still holds a large number of Israelites expelled from Germany," he said. "However, given the poor state of the buildings there, whatever we do, it is not possible to foresee any improvement that would make it possible for the camp's detainees to spend the winter there in suitable conditions." Accordingly, the secretary-general planned to have the detainees transferred from Gurs to various centers, and perhaps to station them in three towns in the département of Le Gers (in L'Isle-Jourdain, Nogaro, and Gimont). These were people, he recalled, who presented no danger to the public order, and who could in effect remain under the control and surveillance by police from the internment camps.

The General Commissioner for Jewish Affairs responded on July 10, 1942: "I must remind you that the operation currently under way, which you and I discussed recently in Paris, makes any transfer absolutely pointless at present, as the Jews concerned fit into the category targeted by the aforementioned operation."[137] The operation in question here was deportation. Improving conditions in the internment camps was no longer on the agenda; although the internees did not yet know it, another phase of life in the camps, infinitely more ominous, was beginning.

7

From Drancy to the Yellow Star: The Situation in Paris from the Summer of 1941 to the Summer of 1942

The arrests made in mid-May 1941 had ushered in a new phase in the life of Jews in Paris. The bonds of repression were being tightened and the threat of being placed in an internment camp, which at that point had not reached the same proportions as in the Unoccupied Zone, loomed closer on the horizon. It was obvious that Polish Jews were being targeted in particular, but both French and foreign Jews were still subjected to one census after another, and their exclusion from a growing number of professions was having an increasingly palpable impact. One decree after another kept spelling out the specific applications of the anti-Jewish laws, and the lists of professions from which Jews were barred regularly appeared in press communiqués. The liquidation of Jewish stores continued implacably, and the adoption of a second Jewish Statute had shattered the illusion nourished by certain Jews that the creation of the General Commission on Jewish Questions would ease their condition. With one set of laws slapped on top of another, it quickly became clear that the measures taken by French authorities were not alleviating the plight of those who had been hit by the rigors of the German ordinances.

FROM POLICE CHECKS TO MASS ARRESTS

From One Census to the Next

The fact that the second Jewish Statute took effect on the same day a census was to be taken illustrated the gravity of the situation. The General Commission on Jewish Affairs had itself observed that "when in the Occupied Zone, French laws and German ordinances both apply, French law is sometimes stricter, especially when it comes to the very definition of Jewish identity, the question of employment, and so on."[1] The commission decided, however, that the law should be applied. And yet, many letters written at the time give evidence of widespread illusions on the matter. Some Jews wrote to the General Commissioner on Jewish Affairs and, at times pointing to their distinguished record of military service, asked if they could resume their business activities in their furniture store or in an open-air market. In response to such requests, they were invariably told: "The ordinances that bar you from continuing your business have been issued by German authorities: they apply to all Jews without exception."[2]

By the fall of 1941, however, such requests stopped pouring in: people's illusions were vanishing. From then on, it was clear that the exemptions provided for in the French law were inapplicable in the Occupied Zone. It was always the harshest version of the law that took precedence. The General Commission on Jewish Affairs hastened to put out a press release that specified "since the law of June 2, 1941 gave a more precise definition of who was Jewish, all persons residing in the Occupied Zone who were Jews according to article 1 of the aforementioned law and who had not yet made their declaration in October 1940 were required to do so by July 1941." Moreover, they had to "declare the *totality* of their possessions, and not just certain types of property, as had been the case in October."[3]

This notice only led to a small number of new declarations, fewer than five hundred in all. But the prefecture of the Paris police nonetheless kept busy; before mid-August, 1941 they had to process more than 20,500 declarations of possessions filed by Jews.[4] "So, Mr. High Commissioner, it turns out that it is one of our own French laws that prevents me from obtaining justice," complained R. M. in his letter to Xavier Vallat. R.M. was a person who had made his declaration as a Jew in October 1940. In May 1941, he learned from newly issued German measures that as far as the German authorities were concerned, he was not considered to be a Jew, as only two of his grandparents were Jewish and he had (in a civil ceremony) married a Catholic woman. But he had been surprised to learn at the prefecture of the Paris police that, as far as French authorities were concerned, he remained Jewish, as he could not prove that he belonged to any other religious faith. "You must indeed be considered

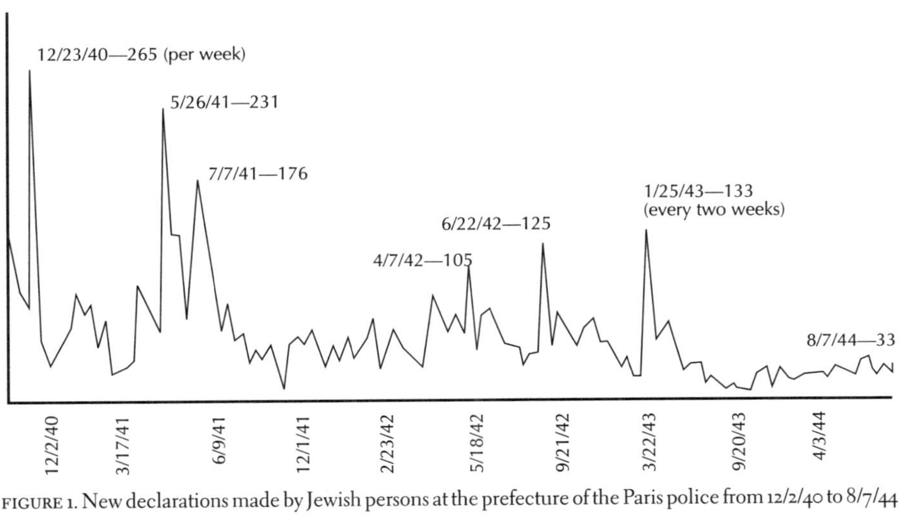

FIGURE 1. New declarations made by Jewish persons at the prefecture of the Paris police from 12/2/40 to 8/7/44

to be Jewish under the French law," he was told in the typically bureaucratic response from the General Commission on September 19, 1941.[5]

Cases such as R.M.'s constituted a real problem for the prefecture of the Paris police, and also for the division of the Status of Persons within the General Commission. Every day, they had to issue a ruling on the doubtful cases concerning people who had declared their Jewish identity in the fall of 1940 without giving it much thought but who were now using the definition of Jewish identity resulting from the French law of June 2, 1941 as a basis for contesting their classification as "Jews."[6] One of the most peculiar cases concerned the Jews from the region of Georgia. In order to figure out what their status was to be, it took a lengthy exchange of letters between the General Commission, the prefecture of the Paris police, and the German military command that extended over several years, lasting all the way until June 1944. The Georgians had made the required declaration, but then the German authorities decided that they were not Jews. As a result, the prefecture of the Paris police found itself in the position of having to strike their names from the lists of Jews and issue them an identity card that did not have the word "Jew" stamped in red. In the eyes of French authorities, however, they remained Jews, and their businesses were consequently subject to aryanization. And in December 1942, after the Vichy regime had decided to require that identity papers for Jews carry a special stamp, the problem arose again.[7]

As freedom of movement was increasingly curtailed for Jews and as threats to their existence loomed ever closer, the General Commission had to branch out into another activity: issuing papers that certified that a person was *not* a Jew. These papers were for certain French citizens who, for reasons that they themselves had to explain, wished to distinguish themselves from the accursed race. The first such certificates were issued in June 1941.[8] In order to avoid the risk of mistakenly issuing such a certificate to Jews trying to escape their plight, the commission soon had to call on the services of a specialist. In mid-December 1941, Professor Georges Montandon was brought on to work for the General Commission as an ethnologist. In cases where there was a doubt as to people's racial identity, it was his job to examine them (at their own cost, obviously) and make the final ruling.[9] The "eminent professor," who had written a book entitled *Comment reconnaître le Juif?* (How to recognize Jews), was a proven antisemite who specialized in theories of race. The people at the General Commission could be sure that he would be able to detect the slightest subterfuge and find the Jews who were hiding behind an Aryan identity.[10] In order to ward off any attempt at concealment, the Vichy government barred Jews from changing their names and using pseudonyms as of February 10, 1942.[11]

Meanwhile, R.M. and others who found themselves in a similar situation were actually rather reassured by another census to which they had to submit. This time it concerned Jewish war veterans. "I don't have any worries on that score, but while we are waiting for everything to fall back into place, time keeps going by and we are suffering from the restrictions." For everything to fall into place, indeed. Jean-Jacques

Bernard was another person who had nourished illusions at the time. The census "had given [him] reassurances, perhaps fragile reassurances, but reassurances nonetheless."[12] Jacques Biélinky stressed instead the cumulative effect: "Yet another census of the Jews," he wrote. "They have not counted them enough. This time, it is the turn of the war veterans to have to go register with the police chiefs and prove their brilliant record of service along with the wounds they suffered, the decorations they earned and all the rest."[13] Dannecker showed interest in the results of this census, but not one single war veteran received any benefit as a result.[14]

The following month provided the occasion for still another census. This one ushered in a "verification" procedure on all French and foreign Jews over the age of fifteen."[15] Summoned by notices in the newspapers, all Jews were required to report to the annex of the prefecture of the Paris police on the date indicated, in an order determined by the first letter of their last name. The operation had originally been scheduled to start on October 1, but was then postponed for one day in response to the appeal from the chief rabbi of Paris, Julien Weill, who had objected that Yom Kippur fell on precisely the same day. The operation was rigorously executed: an army of young women worked together in one large room, filling out questionnaires that Jews signed without reviewing their responses.[16] According to Serge Klarsfeld's assessment, the discrepancies between the first census and the verification procedures carried out in October 1941 included a "deficit" of some seventeen thousand Jews.[17] Clearly, these were Jews who had sometime over the course of the preceding twelve months either sought refuge in the southern Unoccupied Zone or taken up the clandestine life with all its discomforts: it was impossible for them to have disappeared in any other way, as they had duly registered with the first census.

The figure of 17,000 Jews who were unaccounted for probably also included some of the 2,900 who had not responded to the summons issued by the "green document" and who been living on a makeshift basis ever since. Such was the case of Israël Belchatovski, who, in order to keep from being turned in to the police by his concierge, had no other alternative but to spend many long days in the Père-Lachaise cemetery.[18] The "verification" procedure was carried out in an atmosphere more charged than ever: new arrests had torn families apart; Drancy was now part of the daily life of Parisian Jews; antisemitic propaganda had become more insistent; finally, rumors about the possible imposition of an armband for Jews were once again being spread in Jewish sections of the city. Some of those who thought it best to comply with the summons and register with the census later made arrangements to flee.

A few months later, the prefecture of the Paris police rounded out the data already collected by taking a census of Jewish children under the age of fifteen.[19] Lucienne Rodgold, who was fourteen at the time, comments on this measure in a letter to her father interned at Beaune-la-Rolande: "As you probably know, children under the age of fifteen must now register with the census. It's hilarious, everything has to be declared: gold, silver, metals, children."[20]

Because at that time Lucienne's father had already been interned for some ten months, she was in a good position to know that authorities were not just interested in taking a count. Every day the most concrete measures were restricting Jews' freedom of action more and more. On August 13, 1941, Jews were deprived of their radios. They were expected to turn them in to the local police authority—in Paris, it was the police station for each arrondissement—in exchange for a receipt before September 1. As a result of this measure, neighbors with a more modest set sometimes benefited from an exchange: they came and picked up their Jewish neighbor's more sophisticated set and gave their cheaper one to be taken down to the police station (from where it would be sent to Germany).[21]

Jews had scarcely gotten through with the verification procedure in October 1941 when they found out that they would have to become affiliated with new organization, the General Union of French Jews (the UGIF). This requirement was just one of the exclusionary measures affecting the daily lives of Jews. Now Jews were being held collectively responsible for assassination attempts on German soldiers: they were threatened with forced labor, a hundred Jews were to be shot, and they had to pay a fine of one billion francs. Indeed, collecting funds to pay the fine was the first mission given to the UGIF. Traveling was henceforth out of the question. "It is forbidden for Jews to change their present place of residence," announced the sixth German ordinance on February 7, 1942. The prefecture of the Paris police had already studied the question. As of December 10, 1941, even changing one's place of residence within the département of La Seine required a fully completed declaration at the "police stations nearest both the original residence and the new location." To move out of the département required a special authorization that was only granted in "rare and exceptional cases."[22]

Any Jews who might have avoided the previous October's verification procedure were now warned that they risked suffering the consequences whenever they had to show their identity papers. Violators were regularly arrested, and with the proliferation of rules and restrictions, their numbers increased steadily. Going out to see a show in the evening was now also out of the question, thanks to the application of a curfew for Jews only that had been instituted by this same ordinance of February 7, 1942. "Too bad for those who go to the movies or plays," remarked Jacques Biélinky. It is interesting to note that in this same year 1942, theaters and cinemas drew record numbers of spectators, surpassing even the attendance rates of 1938.[23] But Jews missed out on the fun. Some Jews who were caught leaving a theater had to pay a fine, but most were interned at Drancy, by order of the German commander for the greater Paris region. (Young people under the age of eighteen, however, were released after being detained for forty-eight hours.)[24]

Following the bombing of Renault's car factories at Billancourt by the English, Biélinky notes another consequence of the curfew: "In case of an air raid, Jews will not be able to take refuge in the bomb shelters and will have to endure the risk of dying in their homes."[25] The bombing claimed 623 lives on March 23, 1942:[26] the newspapers reported that there had been 500 deaths and 1,500 people injured. The Germans displayed generosity toward the victims of the bombing, "but made the Jews pay the bill. One hundred million francs were deducted from the "Jews' fortunes" (and this sum was taken out of the billion-franc fine) and handed over to the Workers' Relief Committee (Comité ouvrier de secours). It was the latter group that had come up with the idea, as "it is an act of justice to shift the burden for a major part of the indispensable reparations over on those who, by openly approving British aggression, bear the moral responsibility for it."[27]

In order to aid the storeowners, craftsmen, and small industries that had suffered from the bombing, the General Commission on Jewish Affairs was given the job of quickly locating 120 empty boutiques and 30 empty workshops in the bombed area that belonged to Jews: these facilities were to be either requisitioned or given over. André Baur, who was then president of the UGIF in the Northern Zone, was present at this meeting. He pointed out that this was a section of the city that did not have many Jewish residents. "Our fellow Jews have already suffered calamity, even though they were not hit by English bombs. If we can be of assistance to others who have suffered, we will be more than happy to do so," he dutifully added.[28] Actually, the forty-odd Jewish stores in the Boulogne section of Paris[29] that had been registered by the census had already been placed under the control of a provisional manager, if they had not already been sold off. Baur's offer was therefore irrelevant.

Jews had indeed already suffered calamity. Even their bicycles had been confiscated.[30] But now authorities were no longer content with systematic plunder. The dreadful summons of May 14, 1941, was only the precursor of a whole wave of arrests. The time of massive roundups of Jews had come.

From One Police Roundup to the Next

The entry of the Soviet Union into the war and the ensuing anti-communist repression provided the pretext for the first massive roundup of Jews. The same event had already been the basis for the arrest of 622 people: while most were Communists, the group also included "110 undesirable Jewish aliens,"[31] probably those who were carrying a Soviet passport.[32] This time, it was the "Communist agitation" that was blamed, and the German authorities who had initiated the operation proved to be more eager than ever to make a clean sweep. They planned to arrest about 6,000 Jews and "decapitate the leadership of the Jewish masses."[33]

For the first time, hundreds of French Jews also fell victim to the operation. "This measure was most timely, occurring at the very moment when the Jews were gloating over Russian resistance and again lifted their heads in hopes of German defeat and a British victory." Such was the assessment offered by the General Commission on Jewish Affairs.[34] Within the ranks of the Vichy government, officials were surprised that they had not been notified in advance and did not appreciate that orders had been issued directly from German authorities to the prefecture of the Paris police. Vichy timidly requested that war veterans be released, but was a bit more insistent on the subject of three prominent personalities. One of them was Edmond Bloch, former president of the Patriotic Union of French Israelites, and another was Pierre Masse, former government minister and former senator from the département of L'Hérault.[35] But the prefecture of the Paris police had carried out German orders, and in the opinion of the General Bureau of Information, had at times been a bit too eager to do so.[36]

Beginning at 5:30 in the morning on August 20, 1941, the Eleventh arrondissement was completely surrounded. The French police had been ordered to arrest all "male Israelites between the ages of 18 and 50," except for those who were American citizens.[37] The police also came prepared to conduct searches of private residences, armed with lists put together from the card file at the prefecture of the Paris police. "In cases where the Jew being hunted was absent, they took another member of the family. Police agents went from house to house, street by street. Metro stations had been closed in the entire arrondissement. . . . Police barricades had been set up at all the streets leading out of the arrondissement, and were as a general rule backed up by the German army."[38] And so it was that on the first day of the operation, some three thousand Jews were brutally torn away from their homes.[39] They were first led to local police stations, then taken by bus to the internment camp at Drancy. Arrests continued on the following two days in other sections of Paris. Some Jews were apprehended at their homes, others in a café, in a restaurant, and in all sorts of public places. Often the victims had nothing but the clothes on their back (summer clothes or workclothes, in most cases) when they were arrested. A total of 4,232 Jews were rounded up over three days. By September 1, some 4,279 Jews had been interned at Drancy.[40] Among them were forty-four lawyers.[41]

Sporadic arrests continued in the weeks that followed. Jews living in sections of Paris with a high percentage of Jews now hesitated to risk going out into the streets. The festival days of *Tishri* drew smaller crowds to the synagogue than in the preceding year, even though a notice posted at the entrance announced that Jews would not be disturbed during these holy days. And all those who came to attend—either to remain faithful to tradition or to glean some information on what was happening—bore long, sad faces.[42]

Everyday life for Jews in Paris at that time was carried out in a number of highly contrasting contexts. As did all other Parisians, Jews held their breath when they learned of Germany's invasion of the Soviet Union. Like everybody else, they had heard that the German naval cadet Moser had been killed at the Barbès-Rochechouart métro station by Pierre Georges ("Colonel Fabien") and that in reprisal the Germans planned to send hostages before a firing squad. And like all other Parisians, they constantly had to struggle with finding food and basic commodities. The arrests, however, created a panic. "People are saying that sixty Jewish lawyers that still practice the legal profession have been arrested," wrote Jacques Biélinky on

August 22, 1941. "I do not know whether that is true," he added. And then he gave the following notation: "A new white placard posted on walls is announcing the hostage system (following the murder of a German soldier). It is difficult to procure basic commodities: there will be no meat at my local butcher's shop until next Thursday. There are few vegetables and no potatoes, even though there is no shortage of rationing tickets for them."[43]

Biélinky quickly learned by observation that Jews always figured prominently on the lists of hostages shot. During the following months, moreover, the horror of conditions for detainees at Drancy fueled many a conversation. Still, people took comfort somewhat in the fact that 750 Jews were released from the Drancy camp in November 1941. Sixteen of them gave testimony to the Amelot Committee as soon as they were set free. The written account[44] of their experience underscores the awful living conditions in the camp: the worst part, however, seems to have resulted from the total disorganization in the early phases of life in Drancy. Each time the report describes these frightful conditions, it notes slight improvement, particularly concerning sleeping arrangements, heating, food, and so on. "At first, it was total chaos, . . . buildings started getting heat in early November. . . . A few improvements were made in daily servings of food: the soup is now thicker. . . . Detainees were allowed to receive packages of food; the Red Cross was permitted to visit the camp; and the gendarmes are not so vicious now that they have realized that they are not guarding dangerous criminals." These lines have been taken directly from the written account of the testimony provided by those that had been interned at Drancy. The number of persons released and the improvements made in the living conditions indicates that sending the Jews to die was not on the agenda. This was meager consolation, however, as those detained were not that far from death: in the space of two and one-half months, the ones lucky enough to be released had lost between fifteen and twenty kilos and had become "sacks of skin and bones who could hardly stand up."[45]

And then on December 12, 1941, there came a new wave of arrests. This time, the Germans took things into their own hands and struck "at the head." Some 743 Jews, for the most part French citizens and all from the upper echelons of society, were arrested at their homes in the early morning hours. Some were given a few minutes to gather food and blankets, but others were not granted this privilege. Brought together at l'Ecole Militaire where they were held under the threat of machine guns, they were brutally transferred to the camp at Compiègne-Royallieu that very evening, and there joined by three hundred internees from Drancy.[46] All were destined for deportation, but the action was postponed due to an insufficient number of trains.[47]

The end of 1941 was to be marked by the Germans' execution of hostages. Of the ninety-five victims sent before a firing squad at the Mont Valérien on December 15, 1941, fifty-one were Jews. Various numbers circulated through the streets of the Jewish sections of Paris, with all sorts of hypotheses and the beginning of rumors about deportations. With each new day, people learned that a number of Jews had been taken from Drancy by Dannecker. At the same time, newspapers were publishing reports of more executions of Communist hostages. More than one thousand hostages were to be shot in this manner by the Germans, and Jews made up a heavy proportion of them.[48]

Moreover, the winter cold was getting more and more biting while coal was becoming ever scarcer. The number of people lining up in front of food stores was dwindling, since supplies were not arriving. In addition to all that, there was a resurgence of antisemitic propaganda in Paris.

Antisemitism in Paris

It is important to note that each one of the anti-Jewish laws was called for, announced, and supported by a virulently antisemitic propaganda campaign led by various collaborationist groups. Tracts handed out in the street warned Parisians of the menace posed by the Jews: "Do we want to live as French people or die as Jews?" asked one such tract, of which ten thousand copies were distributed through the efforts of the Ligue Française in October 1941.[49] At the very same moment, the newspaper *Le Pilori* was demanding the creation of one central Israelite committee.[50] Toward the end of December 1941, the paper *Les Nouveaux Temps* voiced indignation over the fact that Jews were being allowed to change their names and get baptized.[51]

Each collaborationist movement led its own propaganda campaign. Doriot's Parti Populaire Français undertook this task in early December. On December 7, it drew fifteen hundred people to the Magic City hall to denounce the collusion between Jews and Bolsheviks and to discuss the "seizure of Jewish possessions." The event was presented under a cloak of respectability by the announcement that proceeds would be used for French prisoners of war.[52] Such a propaganda theme was sure to satisfy Doriot's friends among the Germans, who had given de facto tolerance to his party since April 1941 and who indeed had just granted their official authorization in this same month of December 1941.[53] In early January 1942, the Parti Populaire Français put out tracts and placards with the heading: "The Jews have stolen 500 billion francs from French labor."[54] Then it handed out fliers with the slogan "Down with the Jews," along with others calling for "Doriot at the head of the government" and "Stalin on the scaffold." Two months later, this same Parti Populaire Français called upon its North African sympathizers to come to the rescue: at the Magic City hall, representatives of the Muslims were able to proclaim to an audience of six hundred people that "the greatest enemy of Islam is the Jew."[55] Just before the Germans issued their ordinance that required Jews to wear the yellow star, this propaganda campaign intensified: the film *Le Juif Süss* was screened at the facilities of several organizations.[56]

Most of the antisemitic agitation at that time, however, was focused on creating an institute specifically designed to lead an effective anti-Jewish propaganda campaign in Paris. The plan for the Institute for the Study of Jewish Affairs (IEQJ) had been formulated by Theodor Dannecker, who wished to place antisemitic propaganda under a French banner.[57] The institution was funded entirely by the Germans and, although ostensibly placed under the direction of captain Paul Sézille, in fact remained under the authority of the Gestapo. The inauguration of the institute on May 11, 1941, along with the speech delivered at this occasion by Serpeille de Gobineau were shown to the public in Paris by cinema newsreels screened in movie theaters throughout the capital.[58] Beginning in the month of June, there were large antisemitic posters all over the walls of the métro and on billboards in Paris streets. The *Propaganda-Staeffel* in Paris had overseen the production and distribution of these posters, but it was the Institute for the Study of Jewish Affairs that was listed as the publisher.[59] "Frenchmen, help!" read the first poster, which pictured an enormous bird of prey carrying a Star of David around its neck getting ready to tear apart a body stretched out on the ground.[60]

This poster was soon to be accompanied by huge placards announcing what was to be the centerpiece of the Institute's activity during its existence: an exhibit at the Palais Berlitz, "Le Juif et la France" (The Jew and France).[61] Visitors to the exhibit were greeted by "a large allegorical composition representing a sort of vampire with a long beard, fat lips, and a hooked hose, whose emaciated fingers, similar to the claws of a bird of prey, clutched a terrestial globe in its grip."[62] So wrote Robert de Beauplan in the September 20, 1941, edition of *L'Illustration*. Visitors had been lured to the exhibit by a noisy propaganda campaign in the form of posters, numerous press articles, and radio programs. And they had perhaps been enticed by its inauguration as presented in cinema newsreels (right after the inauguration of the annual Paris fair)[63] or attracted by the arguments developed by Paul Sézille three weeks earlier (once again, in the context of newsreels shown in Paris movie theaters).[64] Under the obelisk at the Place de la Concorde, an arrow attached to a street lamp pointed the way to the exhibit. Loudspeakers placed on the boulevards between the Opéra and Place de la République incited passersby to go to the exhibit. And at the entrance, a leaflet explained to visitors that they were about to be made aware of "the whole extent of the peril posed by Jews for [their] country and for the world." If the catalogue visitors bought bore a number, they were in luck: it meant that they had won a bread card.

The exhibit was inaugurated on September 5, 1941: by the time it closed its doors on January 11, 1942, there had been some 200,000 visitors who had paid the three-franc entry ticket. In addition, a good many had been admitted free. All had the chance to study the highly expressive material on display on two floors; the Italians had gotten the first chance to take it in at the exhibit "The Eternal Jew" in Rome. The German embassy in Paris took charge of elaborating the main thrust of the rhetorical arguments. The public that crowded into the halls of the exhibit included a certain number of Jews, who doubtless came to try to get a better understanding of an antisemitism that was becoming increasingly virulent. It is also likely that Jews were trying to gauge the reactions of the "other" visitors as they looked at the billboards that spelled out the racial characteristics of Jewry and told the story of the Jews and of the crimes for which they were everywhere responsible: indeed, the exhibit denounced their stranglehold on the world, tracing their ties to Bolshevism and internationalism. It even announced that Jews were starting to be driven out of Europe.

At the meeting that closed the exhibit, Paul Chack, president of the Committee for Anti-Bolshevik Action, announced before an audience of five hundred people that a new exhibit focusing on Bolshevism and Europe would continue the work of the one that had just ended, as "Bolshevism and Judaism are identical."[65] In order to make this connection clear, the newspapers *Paris Soir* and *Notre Combat* sponsored a lecture by André Chaumet in the exhibit's theater on "the Communist, a Jewish product." The speaker, who was one of the two directors of the Institute for the Study of Jewish Affairs' journal *Cahier jaune*, strove to demonstrate to the four hundred people in attendance how Jews had made use of the political theories of their coreligionist Karl Marx.[66]

Indeed, everything fit together: on the one hand, Parisians could visit this new exhibit and inform themselves about the diabolical links between Jewish influence and the Bolshevik menace; on the other, violent events featured on newsreels showed that the hostages shot by the Germans were being taken from Communist ranks among which Jews figured prominently. A few months earlier, when "The Jews and France" was being advertised all over Paris and just when Jews were ending the Yom Kippur fast with a traditional meal (albeit simplified due to general shortages of many food items) the French capital city was rocked with loud explosions. No fewer than seven bombs went off during the night of October 2 to October 3, 1941, causing various amounts of damage in the seven synagogues that had been hit. There were pillars and doors blown off, windows shattered everywhere, candelabras damaged, peristyles riddled with shrapnel, and interiors demolished. On Rue de la Victoire, Rue des Tournelles, and Rue Pavée, there was deep sorrow.[67] In Neuilly, the windows of the synagogue were shattered by handthrown rocks. In Champigny, uniformed members of the People's National Legion (Légion nationale populaire) tried to force their way into the synagogue.[68]

Among Jewish circles, these bombings were attributed to France's extreme right working with the complicity of German technicians.[69] And in fact, it had indeed been Eugène Deloncle's group, directed and aided by the Gestapo, that tried to give a new twist to antisemitism in Paris.[70] On that level, it turned out to be a failure. "Although they do not like the Jews, the French are displeased when they see Jews massacred and when their places of worship are blown up," observed the *Propaganda-Abteilung*, which was under the authority of the German military command.[71] A report made at the prefecture of the Paris police stated "The announcement of the bombings perpetrated against synagogues in Paris did not create any public outcry. The widespread opinion is that those responsible for these bombings must be foreigners or people working for foreigners: as a result, the public does not give any more importance to this incident than to any other violent crime."[72] As evidenced by this police report, antisemitic propaganda cannot be discounted, since it did make an impact. However, such propaganda ran up against many obstacles.

In the Occupied Zone in general, and especially in Paris, the racial laws were seen as merely a by-product of the Occupation: as such, they were thought to be part and parcel of the overall situation, and not something that deserved any special attention. At the same time, there existed a widespread dislike of the Germans, a sentiment fueled by the problems in procuring basic commodities that preoccupied everyone. In the Southern Zone, it was the farmers and their supposed greediness that were blamed as the main cause for the growing number of shortages. In Paris, however, it was above all storeowners who were singled out as responsible, as they were thought to engage in a sort of barter that protected them from shortages but made products unavailable to the general public.

The Germans were also blamed for causing shortages because of all the commodities that they creamed off from the overall supply.[73] After the Soviet Union entered the war, reports from the Russian front became a regular part of everyday life: hope for a defeat of the Germans was widely shared, and the Soviets' resistance to the German attack was beginning to suggest that this was a real possibility. The roundup of more than four thousand Jews in the month of August was seen in just such a perspective: it was clear that the most dedicated enemies of the Germans in this war were the Communists and the Jews. It only stood to reason that Jews be targeted in such police operations. Moreover, the chief victims had been foreigners. In addition, newspapers presented Drancy as "a sort of working-class section of town that was quite extensive, with stands of trees at various places around the perimeter": in such a place, "the plight of the Jews that had been interned there [was] no more tragic than that of our dear prisoners of war."[74]

Some Parisians nevertheless condemned the operation, particularly when they had personally witnessed an arrest and when they saw that French Jews had been taken.[75] In such cases, they became aware of the concrete effects of an antisemitic act that until then had been buried under a whole series of measures that did not affect them. A fifteen-year-old lycee student who lived near the Champs-Elysées mentioned for the first time in her diary the arrests of Jews made during the December roundup: that operation had targeted known Israelites, including some people who probably lived in the same section of town as she did.[76] And since it was the Germans who were behind the roundup, anti-German sentiment was given an outlet at the very moment when hostages were being executed and the menace seemed closer to home than ever. Whenever a German soldier fell victim to an assassination, there was nevertheless a feeling of relief when the Germans' reprisal struck only at Jews and Communists.[77] There were thus various contradictory strains of public opinion: at any rate, people were first and foremost concerned about their own situation. When all was said and done, current thinking in Paris pictured Jews as victims of a situation that was also claiming victims among the general population.

However, there was in reality a huge difference between the plight of the Jews and the lot of other Parisians. The only ones who seemed to be aware of it (or at least the only ones who clearly expressed their awareness) were the Communist intellectuals. "The Communists have used the racial policies—and especially the anti-Jewish measures—put into place by the French government and the German Occupation authorities as the basis for causing agitation among intellectuals," observed an inspector for the prefecture of the Paris police on February 2, 1941.[78] Indeed, *L'Université libre* seems to have been the only paper to combine the struggle against racism and antisemitism with its fight against Nazism on a regular and permanent basis.[79] For the rest of the underground newspapers, which were in various stages of formation at the time, the subject is either absent or incorporated into the rhetoric of class struggle, as was the case in *L'Humanité*. The only exception was *La France continue*, which devoted an article to the Jews in each of the first thirteen editions it published: it was in particular the only paper to speak out against the exhibit at the Palais Berlitz. In October 1941, an article in *Pantagruel* denounced the "horrors of antisemitism."[80] Occasionally, there were a few lines on the situation of Jews in Poland, and *Libération* (in the Northern Zone) made reference to the arrest of thousands of Jews in the Twentieth arrondissement. *Liberté* devoted a paragraph to the death of Henri Bergson and emphasized that since the greatest of French thinkers had been Jewish, he would not even have been granted admission to the university under the Jewish Statute.

But that is as far as the underground newspapers went in their treatment of the Jewish question.[81] A change occurred in May 1942 in *Libération*: for the first time, it now specifically denounced the "odious antisemitism," even though it did not fail to mention the "problem of the naturalization and the more or less rapid assimilation of foreigners, be they Jews or non-Jews."[82] The voice of René Cassin had made itself heard from London in April 1941, but since then the French had to wait for a year before hearing Georges Boris's warning on April 28, 1942: large-scale requisitions of workers were about to occur in France, and since the fate of Jewish workers in Lettonia was not very promising, all French people faced the threat of becoming "pariahs of the New Order."[83] The imposition of the yellow star seems to have turned the situation around. However, the twelve-minute broadcast on the subject on June 12, 1942, was devoted almost entirely to the visit paid to Xavier Vallat on August 11, 1941, by eighteen war veterans who had come to protest not only against the measures of the Jewish Statute, but also more vehemently the official commentaries that had accompanied and justified them.[84]

Jews in Paris understood all of these things to mean that ultimately everybody was largely indifferent to their plight and that their suffering was peripheral to the concerns of French society on the whole. Even when Jews were subjected to infernal conditions at Drancy, they were not sure they could count on the general public's support. "France was downtrodden, and shuddered under the grip of the Nazis," explained one such internee. "Tremendous suffering was overwhelming 40 million inhabitants. With all their human misery, the 4,600 poor wretches in Drancy were lost and drowned in an ocean of calamity. There were too many hardships and sorrows for anyone in particular to stand out. . . . Without consciously realizing it, the internees knew all that and pondered it over."[85] Still, the threats were becoming clearer and clearer, and the virtually normal relations that Jews enjoyed with neighbors and storeowners were not protecting them against these dangers.

Nor did it prevent them from falling victim to a new type of swindlers who specialized in systematically exploiting their vulnerability as outcasts. Evidence of these swindlers' activities can be found in the weekly reports made at the prefecture of the Paris police. But for every such case that caused a stir, we can easily imagine that there were many others that were never reported. After all, what could Jews expect from a government that was after them? The most widespread scam consisted of a man disguised as a policeman who would come to conduct a search in a Jewish home and confiscate everything that had any value.[86] Other unscrupulous individuals found a convenient occasion for blackmail. Jews approached by such shady characters had to pay large sums of money to avoid a possible internment.[87] Such crooks had a solid future, for this was only the beginning of the internments, and Jews were increasingly aware of just how serious a matter it was to be interned in a camp.

From One Camp to the Next

In addition to the camps in the département of Le Loiret, two more internment camps, Drancy and Royallieu at Compiègne, became ingrained in the lives and minds of Parisian Jews between the summer of 1941 and the summer of 1942. First, there was the camp for the Jews: Drancy. Drancy would be dreaded throughout the occupation: it was first a synonym of terror, and later became an almost obligatory stop on the way to a sinister unknown destination.

Before being used as an internment camp for Jews, Drancy had housed British prisoners of war. When emptied to make room for the more than four thousand Jews placed in detention there on August 21, 1941, the facility was minimally prepared and grossly inadequate: everything was makeshift. The building was a long, crude, horseshoe-shaped, visibly incomplete construction five stories high made of reinforced concrete. It was surrounded by a double row of barbed-wire fences separated by a path for the guards. The interior courtyard was covered by cinders and guarded at each of the four corners by lookout towers. Toilets were housed in a building made of red, flat bricks that closed the horseshoe: it was called the "red castle" by the internees.[88] A few days after the first group arrived, they were joined by other Jews who had previously been held at Les Tourelles camp. Les Tourelles's population had already dropped appreciably with the opening of camps in the département of Le Loiret: now, its numbers fell dramatically.[89]

Drancy was placed under the authority of the prefect of the Paris police, who was in charge of the gendarmes as well as the offices overseeing the questions of commodities and supplies for the prefecture of the département of La Seine, and a police chief became director of the camp.[90] The first few weeks were the most trying. The prefect for the département of La Seine, who was responsible for working out the material conditions of the facilities and for supplying food and basic needs, was only informed of the police roundup two days in advance. When the internees arrived, he had only received twelve hundred wooden bunkbed frames:[91] as a result, they had to sleep on boards or even bare concrete, with no straw mat and no blanket. After first having been stripped of their identity papers, food ration cards, and any sum of money over fifty francs, they were penned up together in groups of fifty to sixty internees per room.[92] They were given 250 grams of bread and three servings of soup without vegetables to eat per day, which they had to drink in makeshift receptacles shared by several people. On September 10, 1941, the prefect for the département of La Seine pointed out that no pasta or dry vegetables had been distributed for the month, that the quantity of potatoes was unknown, and that only one meat ticket per week could be honored. Moreover, internees were barred from receiving mailings, and a large number of packages sent to the Jews interned at Drancy were returned to their senders.[93] Famine was part of the camp agenda, and

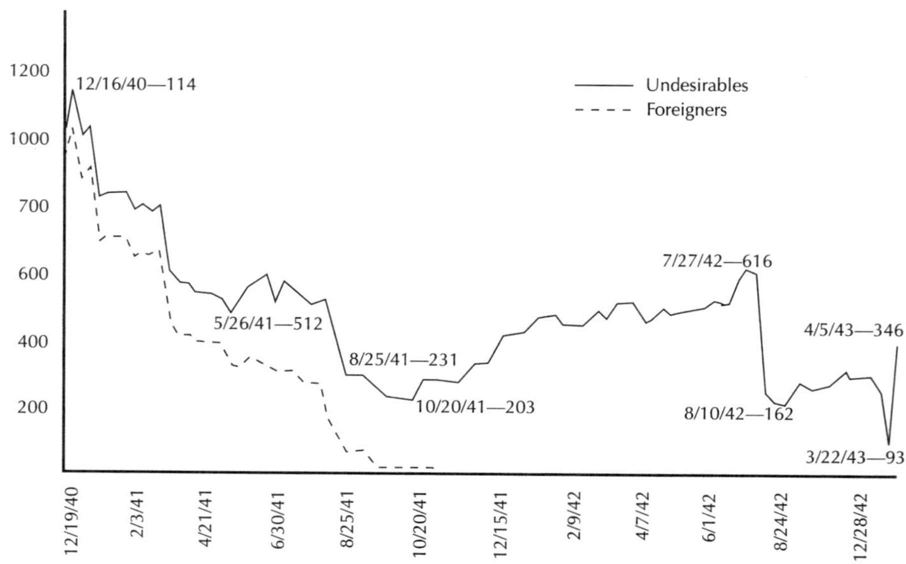

FIGURE 2. The Camp at Les Tourelles

at Drancy as in the other camps, the most important time of the day was the dividing up of the bread: "How can one cut up one large two kilo loaf of bread while trying to remember that fifty men are entitled to seven loaves! . . . Our entire life has been concentrated in this animal-like expectation, accompanied by the loud music of hunger droning up and down in the background. . . . The portions were of course unequal."[94]

Except for the work required for camp maintenance, internees were generally forced to remain idle and allowed to go out of their rooms for only one hour a day, stairwell by stairwell: they were not supposed to mingle with others, but this rule was generally ignored. Soon some internees would no longer be strong enough to get out of their "bed" except—since they did not have the choice—to drag themselves painfully out for the roll call. Indeed, just as in the most punitive camps, the daily routine was paced by first one, then two roll calls in the courtyard. The most coveted of chores was to peel vegetables, as internees could thus secretly take a few vegetables (at the risk of increasing their chances of suffering dysentery after a long period of general constipation). Soon the "red castle," which provided 60 toilet holes for 4,500 internees, was no longer adequate, and a stench slowly invaded the whole camp. A horrible form of diarrhea became the internees' constant daily fear. "They have locked us up in a frightful enclosure, leaving our mind free to do nothing but think about either the shithouse or the grub," raged Noël Calef in his diary.[95] Such was the lot of the first wave of Jews interned at Drancy. All were men: 72 percent of them were foreigners, 175 held the veteran's card for fighting in both wars, 26 were doctors, and 44 were lawyers.[96]

There was one bar of soap for ten people, one comb for twenty, one toothbrush for five, and one razor for ten. In each room, there was "one faucet that opened seven little curved pipes through which water ran down into a sort of long wooden trough covered with zinc plates"[97] (when there was water, that is). As the days went by, vermin proliferated. "Everybody [was getting thin], everybody [was] disgustingly dirty."[98] Lice and scabies became regular part of everyday life.

After being interned for three weeks in a "reserved" room, the lawyers were first photographed in the camp courtyard for an illustration to accompany an article in the newspaper *Le Petit Parisien* and then, upon Dannecker's orders, were scattered throughout the camp and forbidden to meet with each other.[99] That was only one form of deliberate humiliation. Many others were invented: for example, the prohibition against going from one stairwell to another. In order to comfort themselves a bit, internees looked through the windows to see their wives on the other side of the barbed-wire fences: this was the only contact possible. As a result, the windows were closed and the windowpanes painted blue to put an end to these violations of camp discipline.[100] The most common punishment given for each breach of discipline—such as the one that occurred when the internees shouted out their distress during a "hunger protest"—was a shaved head and a few days of solitary confinement in a dark, cold cell.

Internees were subjected to an internal hierarchy: there were five block leaders, twenty-two stairwell leaders, and one leader for every room, with each leader having clearly defined responsibilities. Every day a different stairwell was charged with doing chores. Leaders enjoyed certain advantages: for example, they ate in a separate dining hall and got larger servings of soup than regular internees, even though it did not stave off the ever-present hunger. The social composition of the internees had been wide-ranging from the beginning, and the conditions existing at Drancy did nothing to smooth over differences stemming from social status and national origins: French Jews were pitted against foreign Jews, Jews from the Middle East against Ashkenazim from either the Romanian or Hungarian clan. None of these groups mingled much with the others.

The state of total unpreparedness that prevailed in the beginning gave way to organization and improvement of the situation: more bunk beds began to arrive, as well as straw mats and blankets, although there were never enough. Various services were put into place and performed by the internees themselves, including bookkeeping, mail service, and workforces. Showers at last became functional.[101] Roll calls took place in the rooms. After the first two weeks, packages of clothing were accepted. On September 20, 1941, the Red Cross was authorized to establish a permanent presence in the camp: it provided food (given by the Amelot Committee) for all detainees. Five weeks after the internment of the Jews, straw mats arrived. On November 4, the heating was turned on. Once the internees had been registered and assigned numbers by the judicial police, they were allowed to have mail service. Outgoing correspondence was limited to one postcard every two weeks, and it was strictly forbidden to mention the current problems encountered by internees: food, tobacco, and medical care were taboo.

Internees could only seek out the kindness or venality of a gendarme who might agree to transmit a note, an object, or a piece of information. At first, the cost for this "service" was ten francs, but prices in the Drancy camp quickly rose to one hundred francs for a letter, and five hundred francs for a family visit in the fall of 1941.[102] These letters written in Russian, French, Yiddish, German, and Polish contain messages of both reassurance and alarm, but invariably bear witness to the internees' chief concerns. The main themes are constant: the contents of food packages, the wrapping necessary to prevent food from spoiling, and worries for loved ones from whom they have not heard. They also give directions for securing their release: for example, looking up a consul or obtaining the spouse's certificate of baptism. The handwriting is always very fine, designed to fit the most possible into the space provided.[103]

A black market was developing within the camp. One ration of bread initially cost three hundred francs, but then the price fell after food packages were authorized. One cigarette brought 125 francs (this was the benchmark value). To indulge in the pleasure of the small creamy cheese called "petit suisse" cost seventy times more at Drancy than outside the camp.[104] The gendarmes on duty at Drancy fueled this commerce, thus reaping a hefty share of the profit.

And then there was the phenomenon typical of all the camps in which relations with the outside world were limited to smuggled letters or newspapers: the rumor mill, known at Drancy as "Outhouse Radio." Examples included: "The Russians are at the gates of Warsaw"; "the Germans are evacuating Paris"; or the notion that detention was limited to forty days. The latter notion was so deeply rooted that it even spread to the families. And then there was, among many others, the illusion that the camp would close on November 25.[105] Internees hung on to these illusions without really believing in them: it allowed them to forget for an instant that they were hungry. After his release, one Jewish doctor related that he had willfully spread one such rumor in order to prevent the detainees from falling into a general state of demoralization.[106]

And as was the case for camps in the Southern Zone, illusions were also nourished by the incessant composition of new lists: lists of amputees, of invalids, of naturalized French citizens, of French citizens by descendance, of foreign nationals from neutral countries, of elderly and young people, of war veterans, and of those who had no bedframe. None of these groups, however, were ever released, nor was their condition ever alleviated.[107]

It was probably also to keep up their morale that internees at Drancy celebrated the holy days of *Tishri* and Rosh Hashanna, which fell on September 22 in that year 1941, after one full month of detention. Activities were organized by Edouard Schneeberg, who owned a funeral home on Rue de la Victoire and who had already organized the first worship services under the Occupation at the synagogue on the same street.[108] The makeshift temple hardly had room for more than three hundred people, but more than a thousand internees wanted to attend: diversion from the daily rigors was hard to come by at Drancy. The cantor *(hazan)* thus provided a moment of grace for all who managed to squeeze inside. The *Kol nidre* prayer, always offered on the occasion of Yom Kippur, and the long recitative that followed, "chanting for all the misery of the ages," brought tears to the internees' eyes and for a moment calmed their intense suffering.[109]

Even as early as September 7, 1941, a doctor from the prefecture of the département of La Seine, Dr. Tisné, reported that there were 300 internees at Drancy suffering from serious chronic illnesses. It was the internees themselves who had to force their way into the infirmary, which had been transformed into a storage shed. Although the Germans did nothing to oppose this action, they had taken the trouble to remove all the medicine stored there.[110] In view of the widespread physical misery of the internees, Dr. Tisné was afraid of seeing an increasing number of illnesses and deaths if the ban on food packages were maintained.[111] However, it was not until the number of deaths began to rise after October 20, 1941, that this warning was heeded.

Even then, it took a death toll of thirty between October 20 and November 5 and the absence of Theodor Dannecker from Paris before the doctors from the prefecture could obtain authorization from a German military commission for the release of several hundred internees. Before that time, the rules imposed by the Germans had indeed been perfectly clear: no internee was to be released without a written order issued by the German military authority housed in the Palais Bourbon and bearing the seal of German headquarters.[112] Moreover, this liberal gesture was reserved solely for amputees, the blind, and the deaf and dumb. A short while later, on December 23, 1941, there were a few more fortunate souls, such as the Italian nationals released thanks to the efforts of the Italian government.[113] In early November 1941 a concerted effort was begun to seek out those internees suffering from cachexia and oedema in hopes of gaining leverage from the scandalous number of walking cadavers that could be seen among the Jews detained at Drancy. As a result, some 750 Jews were released in the space of several days.[114] On November 12, however, these releases were suddenly ended. From that time one, the only way to get out was to escape. But how many were able to face the risks involved? Only thirty-odd internees succeeded in escaping from Drancy before the end of March 1942.[115]

Furthermore, not all the sick had been set free. When the fifteen beds installed in the camp infirmary were no longer sufficient, some of the seriously ill were first transferred to a room in the Tenon hospital, where they were monitored by police inspectors. It turned out, however, that the task of monitoring patients was too difficult: after seven patients had escaped,[116] the prefecture of the Paris police and the prefecture for the département of La Seine had to make use of two separate buildings of the Rothschild hospital in early December. The prefect of La Seine paid the entire cost of hospitalization, while the prefecture of the Paris police took care of guarding the patients termed detainees. On December 8, 1941, the two medical branches involved with treating the internees, Dr. Worms's office and Dr. Hertz's surgical service, opened 150 beds, which in two weeks grew to 240. The prefecture of La Seine repeatedly asked that the detainees be returned to Drancy in order to cut costs. Police officers were stationed in the yard outside the building and guarded the entrance. Teams of two or three armed inspectors were posted inside the building. "Guards made frequent nocturnal rounds, brusquely shaking the patients out of sleep in the most painful way and reminding some of the designation of hostages that they had witnessed in the camp."

After four escape attempts (three of which were successful), new measures, including in particular the locking of windows at night, were put into place. Patients were forbidden from having any communication with the exterior, except for the most seriously ill, who were allowed to receive a visit. Once a week, the doctor, assisted by a social worker, would accept a visit from the detainees' families in the hospital parlor. Once Dannecker came to visit the hospital himself: he ordered one-sixth of the patients to be sent back to Drancy and had the director arrested. At six o'clock in the morning on July 3, 1942, French police forces cordoned off the area, and in less than an hour, all the patients were led away. That was the end of the medical service for the internees at Drancy.[117]

After November 1, 1941, internees were finally allowed to receive mailings of food: as announced by a notice posted in the camp courtyard, each internee was limited to one package weighing no more than three kilos every week. The first packages arrived on November 5, but before being turned over to their rightful recipients, they were ripped open and searched. "The guards split the bread from one end to the other, letting the crumbs go to waste. They plunged knives into jam and rummaged around, and did the same with the butter. They unwrapped pieces of candy to make sure that nothing suspect was hidden under the wrappers. They tore the paper covering off creamed Gruyère cheese, and broke the bars of chocolate."[118] They were looking in particular for cigarettes and tobacco, which were forbidden, and did not fail to confiscate everything they could, either to treat their own family to the spoils or to sell it on the black market.

A poet who has remained anonymous expressed in Yiddish what the arrival of a food package evoked for him:

My beloved! Your first package has come,
Bread, butter, and an egg,
And in my heart a hidden tear,
A tear of your sorrow kept here.

I see the table set for the meal
Still with silver for two . . .
Your hope stops at the window and looks out
To see if I am coming about.

And I did not come . . .

My beloved! Your first package has come,
Bread, butter, and an egg,
In my heart I have hidden my revenge
Revenge for your tortured soul.[119]

All packages sent either by families or by the Amelot Committee were first channeled through the Red Cross, which delivered them to the Jews interned at Drancy.[120] After the creation of the UGIF, families were instructed by its newsletter, *Bulletin de l'UGIF* (the new name for *Informations juives*), to bring packages for internees to one of its facilities on Rue de Belleville.[121]

Putting together such packages, in which food, soap, clothing, shoes, and all sorts of little articles so valuable for everyday life were heaped together, required great sacrifices. Following the series of arrests of Jews in August 1941, municipal offices in Paris had received six hundred applications for government aid to families. According to a memorandum from the secretary of state for the ministry of the interior, needy families of interned Israelites could apply for benefits designated for indigent families of the "undesirable aliens"—in other words the "individuals who posed a threat to national defense or public security"—who had been interned pusuant to the executive order of November 18, 1939. The families of Drancy's internees thus suffered a plight similar to that of families of the internees in the camps in the département of Le Loiret (who had been the original beneficiaries of this liberality).[122] Their distress, however, was not confined to everyday material conditions. Their efforts to gain the release of loved ones were only the first step down a long road of suffering. They sent letters to Marshal Pétain: families typically underscored the innocence of the person interned, the hardships brought on by the sudden absence of their breadwinner, and the internee's loyalty to France as proved by his military service in one or more of the country's recent wars.[123] Finally, they would appeal to the prefecture of the Paris police or to the offices of the UGIF. In the vast majority of cases, all of these efforts were to no avail.

Visits were not allowed at Drancy. But for those spouses, sisters, and mothers of internees who wished to deliver a package directly to the camp in hopes of catching a glimpse of their loved one's silhouette from afar, there were two solutions. They could either weave in and out of the endless lines of women trying to take the bus at the Jaurès métro station, knowing that only two Jewish women were allowed in each vehicle, or they could take the train at the Gare du Nord station, which would leave them a twenty- or thirty-minute walk before arriving at the camp limits. And then, they often arrived at an hour when packages were no longer accepted: the Germans set a different time for receiving them every day and only made their decision at the last minute.[124] There was no line for the return, but the rule limiting each bus to carrying a maximum of only two Jewish women was applied just as strictly, even if the bus returned three-quarters empty. But the families worries' soon took a dramatic change in nature.

On December 12, 1941, the sudden arrival of Dannecker in the Drancy camp created both surprise and terror. He chose three hundred men to be taken away in buses under the threat of the machine guns. Two days later, forty-three others were also removed from Drancy, and then only a few hours later, eight prominent Jewish personalities followed. Thanks to the rumors aired over "Outhouse Radio," internees knew that the Germans had announced that one thousand men were to be deported to the East and that one hundred hostages were to be shot. It was quickly discovered that the group of three hundred internees had been transferred to the camp at Compiègne. The 43 others were indeed among the 95 men shot by a firing squad at Mont Valérien on December 15, 1941. The group of three hundred was supposed to be deported, but difficulties with the means of transportation had delayed the operation.

A new phase had begun for the Jews interned at Drancy: while living conditions had certainly improved, the camp had been transformed into a hostage reserve. On January 27, 1942, fifty men who had volunteered to try agricultural work left the camp, followed by forty-eight others on February 6. Then thirteen more detainees were taken from the camp on February 20. The first two groups had in fact been transferred to Compiègne, while the thirteen Jews in the third group were led by the Germans before a firing squad two days after they had left Drancy.[125]

Such removals of internees from Drancy continued, and this was just the beginning: as the era of deportations was drawing near. On March 27, 1942, some 565 detainees from Drancy were joined by 547 men held in the Royallieu camp at

Compiègne: escorted by French gendarmes, they left France forever in the only deportation train made up of third-class passenger wagons. The term "destination unknown" made its official entry into Drancy.

That same day in Paris, a religious service in memory of two French volunteers killed in Russia while fighting for the Germans was held at the Sainte-Marie-des-Batignolles church in Paris. The economic situation surrounding the retail sale of drinks had created consternation among establishments that sold wine by the drink, as it was planned to close cafés two or three days out of the week. The day after the first deportation of Jews from France, the scrap-metal market opened its gates on the Boulevard Richard-Lenoir. The tubers of a certain variety of sunflowers called "topinambours" were being used as a substitute for more and more vegetables. There were continuing reports that Paris was receiving insufficient quantities of fish, butter, meat, poultry, and other food products. Department stores nevertheless carried on their business: an increased volume of activity was observed at Le Printemps, and although crowds of customers were more sparse at La Samaritaine, there were more people flocking to the woolwear and bedding departments at Les Galeries Lafayette. Elsewhere in the capital, activities had generally slacked off, although a particularly large crowd had participated in the weekly free-market session at the stock market.

Cinema newsreels had shown the French aeronautical industry at work, French movie stars (Albert Préjean, Danielle Darrieux, Viviane Romance) invited to Germany, the booths at the exhibit "Boshevism and Europe" at the Salle Wagram, the soccer match between France and Switzerland in Marseilles, and the bicycle race in Paris on the slope at Ménilmontant. Some attention was also paid to events on the Russian and Finnish fronts, and Parisians learned that General Rommel had received the highest distinction in the order of the Iron Cross from the hands of Hitler himself. There were three new films for moviegoers in the capital: *La femme que j'ai le plus aimée* by Yves Mirande, *La Duchesse de Langeais* by Jacques Baroncelli, and *Boléro* by Jean Boyer. People could also entertain themselves by going to see one of the new revues in a music hall or by attending a formal soirée put on for or by a charity: there were, for example, functions to benefit victims of the March 3 bombardment, the National Relief agency, and prisoners of war. For the "Night of the Cinema" (put on by the Organization Committee of the Film Industry in the Gaumont Palace at Place Clichy), there were 3,500 Parisians in attendance; the event benefited the National Relief agency and the Mutual Aid Committee for prisoners of war and included performances by Tino Rossi, Raimu, and Mistinguett. The three equestrian competitions that took place at Auteuil were also a success with the public, drawing large crowds of spectators.[126] Life went on in Paris.

While the families of those interned at Drancy were totally preoccupied by concern for the well-being of their loved ones, other Jewish families strove to meet their own daily needs. They made their preparations for Passover and tried not to think too much about the threat of being deported "to do forced labor" in Germany or Poland.

The first deportation train carried away internees from two camps: the camp for Jews (soon promoted to the rank of transit camp for those deported to the East) and the punitive Royallieu camp in Compiègne (where the 743 Jews arrested at daybreak on December 12, 1941 were led). These were for the most part French Jews who were joined in the deportation train by the three hundred foreign Jews taken out of the Drancy camp on that same December day.

The *Frontstalag* 122 came entirely under the authority of German military administration and was guarded by soldiers of the Wehrmacht: it held both hostages and political prisoners. Out of the some 54,000 internees that passed through the Compiègne camp between June 1941 and August 28, 1944, about 50,000 were deported.[127] There were two rows of dense barbed wire 2.5 meters high, a watchguard's path around the perimeter, roving patrols of armed soldiers, watchtowers, and high-powered spotlights beamed incessantly from one corner of the camp to another.

There were in fact four camps situated side by side. The camp for Americans was filled shortly after the entry of the United States into the war, which also occurred in December 1941.[128] The first camp used to detain civilians was the one for the Russians, which held both white Russians and Soviets (including 180 Russian Jews) who had been arrested by the Germans after June 22, 1941 (the date of the German invasion of the Soviet Union).[129] The camp for political prisoners had been filled in early August 1941 with opponents to the regime, including many Communists. But it was in the camp for the Jews, which was inaugurated during the night of December 12 to December 13 and liquidated—for the first time—on July 6, 1942, that detainees were subjected to harshest conditions.[130] From the very moment of their arrival and up until February–March 1942, the Jewish detainees (called "Decembrists" by the others) were kept there under total secrecy. Neither correspondence, nor packages, nor visits were allowed: their families were supposed to know nothing about them, not even where they were being held. The Red Cross complied with these rules while at the same time appealing to the Germans to remove these restrictions.[131]

Contrary to what had happened in Drancy, where the situation had improved after the terrible first few weeks, the situation in the camp at Compiègne only got worse. At the beginning, then, there were 1,043 men who wound up in the Royallieu camp in the middle of the night, after a "hallucinating march [through the town of Compiègne] amid the barking voices of the soldiers of the Wehrmacht."[132] Three-fourths of the detainees were French Jews, including five hundred veterans of war, 227 of whom had even been decorated for bravery. More than two hundred of the detainees were over the age of fifty-five, while a group of about twenty were not yet twenty years old. About one-third of the group were doctors, lawyers, pharmacists, and architects; another third were storeowners or store employees; a final third of these men were craftsmen or workers.[133] Those who had been taken from Drancy were in the foremost railroad cars and had settled into one of the blocks. The "prominent personalities" occupied another. There were no small number of conflicts and disputes between these French detainees, who were more French than ever in this

German camp, and the Jews, who were acutely aware of being detained simply because they were Jews. Finally, the situation became so acrimonious that the subject of Judaism was banned from conversations among detainees by the prisoners themselves.[134] This was a case in which the demographic composition of the camp deepened a type of antagonism that, although still present, did not manifest itself so harshly in the Drancy camp.

The Jewish internees slept on straw, shivered from the cold, and, as they were under the same regimen as the "camp for the Communists" and "the camp for the Russians," were served a slightly thicker soup during the first few days. Soon, however, the Jews were served separately, and from that time on, they were given smaller portions of a diluted soup. As long as contact could be maintained with the other camps, the Jews were able to get surpluses of some items that certain "sponsors" from these camps obtained for them. But the Germans began to isolate the Jews from the other internees as much as possible. Then, beginning in January 1942, they limited the number and the weight of packages allowed for the political detainees and the Russians: the surpluses immediately disappeared. As the cold became more and more bitter, frostbite (especially on the feet) became the common lot of all. "I began my New Year of 1942 crying from hunger," wrote Henri Jacob in his Compiègne diary.[135] There were a few collective mailings from the French Red Cross, which for the internees meant that from time to time a day was brightened by the distribution of a date, a cookie, half an orange, or two sugar cubes.

Such occasional small treats, however, could not stave off hunger. Detainees found more and more unbearable the two long roll calls that were conducted outside regardless of the weather. During the first few weeks of their internment, they had organized lectures that were given in the rooms. Whether the subject be agriculture, tobacco manufacturing, Blaise Pascal, the theater, petroleum, economic liberalism, history, or advertising—each racked his memory in order to liven up an evening. And while providing diversion for a few fellow detainees, the lecturers made it possible to preserve their moral and intellectual composure. By mid-February, however, these evening events came to an end: the cold, hunger, and exhaustion had sapped the strength of the lecturers and their audience.[136]

It was impossible for detainees to correspond with their families. Postcards had nevertheless been handed out on January 28. A prescribed message announced that it was possible to send correspondence and three packages weighing up to five kilos every month. These cards were never posted. One month later, there were postcards announcing that mailings of packages—but only those containing clothing—had been authorized: the cards were actually sent this time. The first packages arrived on March 2, stripped of all food and medicine. The internees were moved by the sight of these sleeping bags, mufflers, heavy sweaters, mittens, and balaclavas that they found in these packages.[137] But anxiety followed immediately after. "What frightens me is this abundance of clothing and woolen wear that you have sent to me," wrote

Henri Jacob secretly to his wife on March 12, 1942. "One can only conclude that you have been given very bad news about the possibility of my release."[138]

The only communication by letter with the outside world was by using channels organized clandestinely by the Russians or the political detainees, or by buying off a certain German noncommissioned officer. But that channel was closed when the German soldier's game was discovered in later February 1942. The only consolation came from certain internees' spouses who passed back and forth on the other side of the barbed-wire fences, or in view of windows, thus letting their husbands catch a glimpse of them: this offered a bit of balm to the men's hearts.[139] Henri Jacob wrote to his wife on January 24, 1942, the "44th day of sorrow": "Finally, the second time you passed by, I was able to watch you with joy, but also with unfathomable torment and sadness to see you for so short a time." On February 27, he asked her to come at set times, as he could no longer bear waiting indefinitely in an icy, soaked hallway, and as he could hardly stand with the frostbite on his toe that had gotten worse. He was losing strength.

Add to all that the wretched conditions that favored the development of vermin and infections, and it is easy to understand that this regimen proved fatal to ninety-two Jewish internees who died from hunger, cold, and sickness between December 12, 1941 and April 2, 1942.[140] Compiègne remained the private domain of the German military authorities, who forbade any improvement in camp conditions. A few rays of light nevertheless sometimes brightened the life of internees: a letter, a package, the silhouette of a loved one seen from afar. All these glimmers of hope, however, depended on the complicity either of one of the political detainees, of one of the "Russians," of the woman whose café was used as a mailbox, or of one of the area residents whose home was next to the camp and who lodged a spouse of one of the internees.

Some were released in small, sporadic waves: 35 internees, including 20 over the age of 65, were set free on December 18, 1941; two days later, it was the turn of 38 men who were seriously ill; about 100 Italian, Hungarian, and Romanian nationals were allowed to leave the camp on March 10, 1942; finally, 58 others were released on March 13, 1942.[141] After being subjected to a brutal and meticulous body search, the "final ordeal of [their] captivity,"[142] they experienced the joy of being reunited with their loved ones. However, as had been the case for those released from Drancy in early November 1941, it was also the beginning of a long period of convalescence from which some would never fully recover. Furthermore, the men released on March 13, 1942, did not return to their homes and families in the days that followed: they were instead transferred to Drancy. There they were allowed to send a standardized postcard to their families once every two weeks and to receive food packages. There was a new set of conditions in force: detainees were allowed to exchange a bag of dirty clothing for a bag of clean clothes once every two weeks; they could take showers; and roll calls were now conducted in rooms. All of these things seemed almost miraculous.[143] There were clearly several levels in the hell of camp detention.

But for a large number of these men, this was just another step down the road that was leading to deportation.

It was at Compiègne that Kadmi Cohen, a Parisian lawyer who in the 1930s had been a consultant for the Zionist World Organization (Organisation sioniste mondiale) and a partisan of the revisionist line led by Vladimir Zeev Jabotinsky, created the Masada movement on December 28, 1941. The name was taken, stated the movement's platform, "from the name of the last fortress on the shore of the Dead Sea where Jewish national independence finally succumbed [to the Romans] after the fall of Jerusalem. The name that [formerly] signified an end must [now] signify a beginning."[144] Kadmi Cohen was convinced that Jews should not take sides for any of the parties engaged in the worldwide conflict, but should instead use the situation to create a national state in Palestine. He only succeeded in rallying a tiny minority to his cause, which none of the Jewish organizations espoused.

Mutual Assistance and/or Political Action

The Sephardic Worship Association of Paris was, in a nutshell, just as small, marginal, and ineffective in its efforts as Masada. On September 24, 1941, it attempted to avoid the antisemitic persecutions of the moment by sending a paper titled "The Aryano-Latin Sephardites of the Israelite Faith" to Xavier Vallat. The document was accompanied by a letter signed by its author, Sam Lévy, as well as by Léon Rousseau, the association's president. "In view of the unusually serious and delicate circumstances experienced by Israel at this time," they wrote, "the group in which we are active declares its solidarity, on the religious level, with all of our coreligionists regardless of their particular denomination or allegiance. We therefore do not have the slightest intention of placing ourselves above any racial or ethnic group." Nevertheless, the document stressed their "mentality specific to Latin peoples" and their facility of assimilation and acknowledged that "the events that have been taking place in the West over the last few years have posed the problem of race and nationality with unmistakable acuity." Declaring themselves to be "respectful of the right of peoples to promulgate the laws that seems appropriate for their situation," they informed the General Commissioner of Jewish Affairs that they had "undertaken official procedures with the government of General Don Francisco Franco in order to request the reintegration of the Sephardi into the fold of the Spanish fatherland." While waiting for the worldwide conflict to come to an end, they beseeched the commissioner "to suspend the application, for the Sephardi, of the measures that [he] had seen fit to take with respect to the Jews."[145]

In reality, each group sought to protect itself: Sephardic Jews were appealing to Franco, Turkish Jews had the Turkish consul intervene on their behalf, furriers argued that they were useful in equipping the German army, and Jewish men with Aryan wives went to get certificates attesting that they did not belong to the Jewish race. During the time of deportations, this "every man for himself" attitude was only accentuated.

For the Jewish organizations working to provide aid to their fellow Jews, however, this entire series of persecutions, including the arrests and the poor living conditions in the camps at Drancy, at Compiègne, and in the département of Le Loiret, meant first and foremost that they would face even more dire poverty. In December 1941, one of the leaders of the Federation of Jewish Societies in France (FSJF) spoke of the "thousands of people who, [without their aid], would starve to death."[146] Up until the creation of the UGIF, the Coordinating Committee and the Amelot Committee tried to cope with the situation. But while the Coordinating Committee let itself become ensnared in a "dialogue" with the Germans, the Amelot Committee began to set up an underground organization. Although there were differences over what strategy should be used in providing assistance, the two organizations constantly consulted each other: certain forms of cooperation were thus established. On the eve of the year 1942, an average of fifty thousand meals per month were being served in the various soup kitchens.[147]

The Coordinating Committee, whose leadership had been reorganized, continued to come under pressures exerted by Dannecker and the strategy of stalling for time rarely had the effect hoped for. Following a suggestion by Yakov Tuvel (a follower of Kadmi Cohen's ideas[148] and a newcomer to "Jewish policy") and seconded by Israelowicz, the leader of the *Judenreferat* demanded that the Coordinating Committee supply to him six thousand Jews to do agricultural work in the Ardennes for a German company, Ostland. He accompanied his "proposal" with the promise that there would be no more internments, and even hinted that there would be a general release of those already interned. The Jewish leaders refused to comply, however, pointing out the weakness of their organizational means. This was on August 18, 1941. Two days later came the police roundup in the Eleventh *arrondissement* that reminded the Jewish leaders who really had the power. They accordingly interpreted the roundup as response to their refusal.[149] And so the Coordinating Committee agreed to publish an announcement in *Les Informations Juives* urging Jews to volunteer for work in the Ardennes. At the same time, however, Marcel Stora, secretary-general for the Coordinating Committee, worked behind the scenes to discourage Jews from volunteering.[150] A series of 20 some-odd convoys thus headed for the forbidden zone: rather than risking internment and then deportation, about five hundred men and women had let themselves be tempted by the prospects of working on farms, even though they were under German command,.[151] While the leaders of the Amelot Committee had immediately voiced their opposition to the plan, there were mixed views within the Coordinating Committee.

As we have seen, the notions of returning to the land and vocational retraining were widely shared in Jewish circles. The Israelite Scouts strove to put these ideas into practice, even in the Occupied Zone, as they had reorganized and even enjoyed the legal cover of the Comité de bienfaisance, the Welfare Committee of the Parisian consistory. By the fall of 1941, they were running twelve postsecondary-school vocational training centers. Over the summer of that year, they had, with the approval of the Germans and under the auspices of the Christian Workers' Youth (JOC) organized a camp and a summer program for children in the woods at Santilly, near Neuilly.[152] But the Israelite Scouts were also negotiating with German authorities over the possibility of opening a farm to serve as a training center. Everything had been made ready for September: the farm, the equipment, the technical staff, and the basic agreement with the Germans. "Circumstances," however, prevented the project from coming to fruition. But these projects for farming and vocational training were not foremost in the minds of the Jews. The overriding worry was the threat of being detained in inhumane conditions and the risk of deportation. In that light, working on a farm seemed to be a lesser evil.

It was under these extremely difficult conditions prevailing in the northern Occupied Zone that the saga first of the Coordinating Committee, then of the UGIF, continued to unfold, as Jewish leaders tried first to find and then take advantage of the cracks in the system in order to alleviate the tremendous human suffering, all while ignoring the root causes. But money was needed to carry out their work, and the Germans were regularly brandishing the threat of a mandatory tax that might be levied against the Jews. In order to prevent this from happening, the Coordinating Committee appealed to the Jewish population of Paris, first in July, then in August 1941. "Whether you are believers or unbelievers, French citizens or foreigners, you have been affected by the same measures. At present, you are united in a common plight," read this appeal. In order to keep the contribution voluntary, Jews were urged to display solidarity and to trust the Coordinating Committee, the "only entity recognized as having the authority to regulate welfare programs" for Jews.[153]

The Coordinating Committee also sent a call for aid to the Jewish leaders who had fled to the Southern Zone. In response to this request, Albert Manuel, secretary-general of the Central Consistory, mailed out a circular on September 15, 1941:

> Israelites of the Free [Southern] Zone, I am appealing to you!
>
> We have heard cries of anguish from Paris. Through press communiqués, we have learned that Israelite hostages have been arrested, and we are told that thousands of our fellow Jews, friends and relatives, are being held in camps at Drancy, Pithiviers, and Beaune-la-Rolande. Many a household has been devastated by consternation, worry, dire poverty, and the death of a loved one.
>
> The aid requested from the Free Zone in order to meet the most urgent needs has been set at 200,000 francs for each of the first few months. This is a matter that concerns the well-being of all. Send your contribution to the Central Consistory without delay. As we approach our great religious celebrations, let us repeat these words: duty, honor, trust, charity.
>
> Do not wait to be forced to contribute by some strict regulation.[154]

Manuel's call was heeded: more than 430,000 francs were collected by October 20, 1941. Some 150 contributors gave money during the first phase of this fundraising effort, which brought in 35 anonymous gifts ranging from 100 to 5,000 francs apiece.

Guy de Rothschild had contributed 200,000 francs to the cause.[155] For the entire year of 1941, André Baur received 1,160,000 francs collected from Parisian Jews having fled to the Southern Zone.[156] Soon, however, these sums proved to be insufficient.

The financial situation of the Amelot Committee was not very bright either. Subsequent to December 1941, many of its contributors were interned at Compiègne. "The line of people who come seeking aid from us gets longer and longer every day, and we are terribly afraid that soon we will have to send them away when our accounts are empty," wrote one of the Amelot Committee's leaders. He added, "We know how the authorities want us to find money. That would be to ask Fifteen [XV, in other words Xavier Vallat] to transfer a part of his plunder to us. In addition to the fact that we find such a procurement repugnant, it would be a poor political choice, as Vallat would use it as an excuse to accelerate the liquidation of Jewish property."[157]

The law promulgated on July 22, 1941, had provided for the deduction of 10 percent of the sums gathered from the liquidation of Jewish property: these moneys were to be used for the creation of a so-called Solidarity Fund. Once the costs of provisional management had been paid, the General Commissioner for Jewish Affairs was authorized to allocate part of this fund to the UGIF, which had just been created. The Germans had levied a one billion–franc tax on the Jews, and the leaders of the UGIF were faced with the German demand that the first payment, in the amount of 250 million francs, be made before January 15, 1942. They therefore turned to French authorities and asked to be granted a loan on the basis of the funds derived from the liquidation of Jewish property and from frozen Jewish bank assets.[158] In order to prevent the Germans from snatching up Jewish property, Vichy approved the bank loan. A consortium of twenty-nine banks along with the Banque de France lent the UGIF the billion francs that had been demanded by the Germans, and reimbursed themselves from the most sizable Jewish bank accounts.

The leaders of the UGIF used their own personal funds to provide advances to their organization in order to meet daily needs and keep its services functioning.[159] Then from February 1942 on, the UGIF began to receive regular sums of money deposited by the General Commissioner for Jewish Affairs and derived from the plunder of Jewish possessions. Out of the some 50 million francs thus collected by the commissioner in the Occupied Zone over the course of 1942, the UGIF received 41 million.[160] The UGIF's own receipts for the same period barely exceeded 1.5 million francs. The only alternative to this way of funding was to cease all social aid programs.

In mid-March 1942, André Baur received an order from Dannecker to provide large quantities of shoes, blankets, and food items. Baur strove to stall for time by seeking the support of Xavier Vallat, but Vallat was losing his influence at the time and the UGIF had to comply with Dannecker's order only a few days after the deadline.[161] Other such demands would follow. From then on, Baur knew for certain that these supplies were to be sent along with the deportation trains. The UGIF nevertheless complied: the alternative was to let the deportees leave without anything at all. In every such instance the UGIF was following the strategy of choosing the lesser evil, and a similar feeling of powerlessness in face of circumstances is evident in the protests continually issued by the leaders of French Jewry who had fled to the Southern Zone. In order to register their objections to the December 1941 arrests of Jews in Paris, Chief Rabbi Schwarz and the President of the Central Consistory Helbronner requested an audience with Marshal Pétain on December 19, 1941. In a letter addressed to General Campet, head of the marshal's cabinet, Helbronner explains the meaning of this gesture: "In face of the considerable emotion caused by the news we have received from Paris, our coreligionists would not understand if we did not try to intervene on behalf of those whose life and liberty are threatened. Therefore I ask that you not bear a grudge against me for having requested an audience that I knew to be useless: it was a step that I was forced to take."[162] Everybody knew that it was useless to ask for an audience in appealing for the release of prominent, highly respected French Israelites: to expect any better response to an appeal made on the behalf of Jewish immigrants, craftsmen, and workers was obviously pointless.

The creation of a General Commission on Jewish Affairs had nourished the illusion that the plight of the Jews in Paris could be alleviated by the presence of a French intermediary; although this illusion was being dispelled, it had not entirely disappeared. Led on by Xavier Vallat's xenophobia, André Baur even concluded that Vallat had muted his antisemitism.[163] But there was no defense from the pressures exerted by the Germans.

There were nevertheless several important missions to carry out in Paris: providing the necessary material aid, keeping up the practice of worship in the synagogues, developing vocational training programs in the schools of the Professional Retraining and Reorientation Organization (ORT), welcoming children to activities of the Israelite Scouts of France, and creating a center for Jewish intellectuals on Rue Copernic in February 1942. When public libraries were declared off-limits for Jews, a large number of Jewish intellectuals (mainly from Russia) came to the center. In all of these instances, the UGIF tried to relieve suffering and offer alternatives when society closed its doors to Jews.

For its part, the Amelot Committee refused to be associated with the decisions either of the Coordinating Committee or of the UGIF, and took refuge in semi-clandestine activity. But the appeals sent by the Amelot Committee to the Southern Zone were nonetheless marked by anxiety; its leaders were encountering insurmountable financial difficulties at the very moment when the most destitute immigrant Jews were turning to them for assistance. Those who had just been released from camps were in no condition to resume work, and it became more urgent than ever to come to their assistance. And now that food packages were being accepted at Drancy, it was also imperative to send food to those internees whose families were too poor to help them. Under the auspices of the Amelot Committee, a committee formed of internees' wives was organized and assigned the goal of buying food for the internees at Drancy.[164]

Relations between the two committees at that time were marked by a pragmatism born of the needs of the Jewish population. After a meeting on January 28, 1942, during which the two groups explained their respective positions,[165] the UGIF, as the Germans' interlocutor, continued on a regular basis to inform the leader of the Amelot Committee of what was in the works and refrained from intruding into the latter's work. The Amelot Committee decided to consider the new organization (i.e., the UGIF) to be a "protective structure [allowing] existing organizations to carry on their work" as in the past. They also decided to provide the UGIF all the information it need to play this role, but refused to participate in any way in the groups in charge of the UGIF and declined all responsibility for the UGIF's activities.[166]

The necessity of coordinating the actions of the UGIF and the Amelot Committee was obvious. The UGIF had both the approval of and access to the financial resources of the authorities (at Drancy, for example, the UGIF took the place of the Red Cross). The Amelot Committee, on the other hand, had the social infrastructure and links with the immigrant population (the "clientele of choice" of aid programs). A modus vivendi was thus established: the Amelot Committee and the UGIF exchanged information, referred clients to each other's programs, collaborated in the sending of packages to Drancy, and so on. Yet the leaders of the Amelot Committee jealously preserved the principle of autonomy and, in all subsequent arrangements, took care to avoid being placed in a situation of dependency vis-à-vis the UGIF.

The Jewish Communists, on the other hand, opted for clandestine activity; when required to join the UGIF, they preferred to close the soup kitchen on Rue de Saintonge. Within Jewish circles, they fought relentlessly against the Coordinating Committee, and then against the UGIF. The demonstration put on by women had constituted one of the episodes in this struggle. When the Coordinating Committee had sent out its call for money in the summer of 1941, Solidarity had retorted with a tract entitled "Jews, be wary!"[167] The Communists had at times lashed out with virulent attacks against the organization, characterized as a collaboration enterprise, an agency of the Gestapo, and as a Jewish Nazi *kehilla* (community).[168] Such invective, however, is characteristic of the writings published in Yiddish, which could be read only by immigrant Jews, and is best understood within the context of internal political and ideological rivalries; it was a response to the equally extreme anticommunism of UGIF leaders.

Be that as it may, the emphasis was shifting: the supposed solidarity of the French public, described as impermeable to the racist propaganda typical of totalitarian regimes, was replacing the theme of mutual aid. Strengthened by a "fraternity of blood shed in common that Xavier Vallat's propaganda [will never be able] to destroy," the Jewish masses, strongly "attached to the French people," "victims of the same oppressor," were called to join in the demonstrations of November 11 in order to "denounce the antisemitic laws" and "support the patriots in the fight for freedom."[169] The hostages executed "died for France and freedom as victims of Nazi barbarity," stated other Communist tracts, which exhorted Jews to "fight alongside the French patriots to liberate the country and defeat fascism."[170]

To present an even stronger argument, the political leader of the trio of leaders of the group MOI (Main d'oeuvre immigrée [Immigrant labor]), Louis Gronowski-Brunot,[171] put together a booklet, *L'Antisémitisme, le racisme et la question juive*. Printed clandestinely by the Communist Party, it was distributed by the thousands.[172] This theoretical study of the historical roots and role of antisemitism was complemented a few months later by a text of 117 pages, "Deux ans de persécutions antisémites," (Two years of Anti-Semitic persecutions) which explored the development of antisemitic policies in France since the beginning of the Occupation.[173] This text sought to prove that "the antisemitic propaganda [was nothing] but a smokescreen [concealing] the age-old intention of the Prussians, the destruction of France," and called for "common action on the part of all patriots." This piece was never published, however, because the underground printing press that was to be used had been seized.[174]

There was at the same moment an echo of the alliance strategies prevalent in resistance circles, as unity with Jewish immigrant organizations on the Left was for a time encouraged. This effort was supported by an intensive propaganda campaign centered on an appeal to Jews throughout the world made by the Soviet Jewish poet David Bergelson: it was first broadcast over Radio Moscow on August 24, 1941, and then reproduced on a large scale in the form of locally distributed tracts. "Jewish brothers throughout the entire world . . . the question of the very existence of the Jewish people has been posed with its most far-reaching ramifications," declared Bergelson, who described the plan for the complete extermination of the Jewish people that was being enacted by Hitler. "Help the USSR in its sacred fight against the fascist beast," he implored, "Throughout all our history, we have survived many persecutions. We shall not die, we shall live!"[175]

A Committee for the Union of the Workers' Parties was thus formed:[176] it even published the one and only issue of a joint newspaper in Yiddish, *Unser Shtime* (Our Voice),[177] which spoke for the Jewish National Union. The respective strategies were too dissimilar, however. While some saw the first imperative as assisting and rescuing Jews, others gave priority to the armed struggle in the Resistance: the unified strategies thus disappeared as quickly as they had come onto the scene.

The class struggle within the Jewish population, however, was still part of the political universe of these activists. Among those Jews who had managed to carve out a place for themselves in occupied Paris, we find makers of gloves, knit shirts, and fur goods who had been issued an *Ausweis* by German authorities eager to get this sort of merchandise. There were as many as three thousand immigrant workers who were able to subsist thanks to such valuable documents.[178] And it was against them that the Jewish Communists turned in the fall of 1941, as they urged them first to boycott, then to sabotage a production of goods that profited the Germans. "It is shameful to work for Hitler's war machine," proclaimed issue 36 of the Yiddish paper *Unser wort:*

> "Jewish business owners and workers are successfully carrying out a boycott of production for Hitler's war machine. A wide effort of solidarity must be undertaken in order to support the workers who have chosen to go hungry rather than to work for bands of Nazis. And yet there are certain business owners who, either because they are greedy or because they are under the illusion of escaping the threat of the camps, are refusing to refuse this work. Today, there is nothing more shameful for Jews than to work for the very machine that is destroying them. The Jewish masses will remember such individuals and will not fail to settle their accounts along with those of the riff-raff and traitors."[179]

This was not an empty threat: in May 1942, the workshop of a maker of fur clothes and gloves on Rue Taylor was burned by a group of Communist militants led by Léon Pakin.[180] Before things reached that stage, however, teams of Jewish Communists would systematically visit Jewish workshops to spread the word, demand a tribute of money for helping internees' families, or sabotage machines.[181] In the Etablissements Grundel, for example, whose activity consisted of making equipment, gloves, and coats for the German army and whose personnel was 90 percent Jewish, the Jewish foreman made his rounds among the employees on payday and demanded a tithe of 2 percent for Jews interned in the camps.[182] The watchword to boycott was not heeded by Jewish immigrants who had no other means of providing for themselves and for their families. Instructions to sabotage and go on strike first appeared in the glovemaking business and then in knit goods: they met with greater success and had an effect on the German army's effort to supply itself. Nevertheless, such movements were of limited duration.[183]

Social aid efforts continued on a wide scale: by March 1942, nearly thirty-five hundred people had received financial support through Solidarity.[184] The emphasis, however, was shifting more and more toward another form of activity: armed struggle against the Germans. Young Jews were quick to assume an active role in the efforts of the Special Organization of the clandestine Communist Party that took shape during the second half of the year 1941 (before the creation of the immigrant resistant movement FTP-MOI in the spring of 1942).[185] The Jewish militants who committed themselves to this cause were in many cases former members of the International Brigades who had learned their trade in Spain. At the time, however, they constituted only a small minority of the Jewish-Communist militants and had some difficulty in following the Party directives requiring all such organizations to send 10 percent of their members into the FTP ("Franc-Tireurs Partisans") resistance movement. Still, Jewish militants made up 90 percent of the members of the first detachment of Romanians and Hungarians, and constituted by themselves the second (called the "Jewish detachment") out of a total of the four detachments created. Moreover, it was a team made up entirely of Jewish women answering to a central technical division that carried the weapons sent to the various units.[186] Jews were the first among the FTP-MOI groups of résistants that charged into action, even though things got off to a rather bad start. At 8:25 in the evening of April 25, 1942, in an apartment at 49 Rue Geoffroy-Saint-Hilaire, an explosion rocked the street. Salek Bot and Hersch Zimerman, who had been preparing a bomb to be used against a barracks full of German soldiers, were killed instantly. In the wake of this incident, the former editor-in-chief of the newspaper *Naïe Presse* (from the prewar era), Munie Nadler, along with Joseph Bursztyn and other militants were arrested.[187]

It should also be noted that political activity found friendly terrain among the Jewish population. The sections of Paris that represented the heart of the Jewish population in the capital city, including Les Enfants rouges, Les Archives, La Roquette, La Folie-Méricourt, La Villette, Belleville, and Père-Lachaise, were hotbeds of Communist propaganda: police reports regularly singled them out for having their walls covered with political fliers.[188]

During the spring of 1942, the Communists were heavily emphasizing three themes: the situation of the internees' families, the plight of internees' wives, and the necessity of coming to the assistance of militants having gone underground and their families. Women were urged to flood members of the Vichy government and its representatives in the Occupied Zone with letters of protest and requests for the release of internees.[189] Jewish women were also put to work: they were expected not only to keep on sending packages to those interned but, above all, to alert public opinion. "All children should write letters to their schoolteachers, to their professors, to their doctors and dentists. All families should write to the prefectorate, to the Red Cross, to the German officer Dannecker, to various prominent figures in France, and in general to all the French people. The scandal of Drancy must be known by everyone," wrote Solidarité in the material it distributed in the winter of 1941.[190]

A flood of letters was indeed sent in response to this directive. One such letter was sent to the General Commissioner for Jewish Affairs on February 20, 1942, by the "wives of those detained in the camp at Drancy":

> Six months have gone by since the dreadful day when our husbands and sons were led away to the camp at Drancy simply because they were born Jewish. There were thousands of them, taken from different age groups, from different social milieus, rich men and poor men, healthy and sick, young and old, all equally deprived of food just as they were denied medical care and basic hygiene. And among all these prisoners, there were hundreds of war veterans, including wounded veterans and amputees, hundreds of men who, during the war, had fought for France with the same zeal and the love as the French. . . .
>
> We are not asking for very much; we know it would be to no avail. But we also know that our husbands and our sons are in a miserable state, exposed to danger. We don't know when we will see them again, if ever. While waiting for better times, if they could just see us and even speak to us, they would regain their taste for life, the strength to hold up, courage, and hope. We ourselves, along with our little children who miss their Daddies so much, would feel such great joy and happiness if we could just see our loved ones even for a few short moments.

> Mr. General Commissioner, please grant us such visits. You will put smiles on our poor children's faces, and you will make thousands of people happy. And it's really something to be able to bring a little happiness into people's lives. Our children will bless you, and we mothers will never forget what you will have done.[191]

The use of internees from the camps as hostages modified the nature of such requests:

> We wives and mothers of the men interned at Drancy and Compiègne and in other concentration camps are sending you this letter in order to apprise you of the situation in which we and our husbands find ourselves.
>
> Our husbands and our sons were only going about their everyday business, but now they are being held in horrible conditions. In addition to their severe hunger and unsanitary environment, they live in constant anxiety, not knowing if they will live to see another day or whether they will be shot, as was the case on December 15, 1941, for 43 of them who were sent before a firing squad. Among the victims that day were fathers of large families (including a father of ten children) as well as young men (including one nineteen-year-old), war veterans, wounded veterans and amputees, intellectuals, lawyers, and doctors.
>
> On this past February 23, fourteen other men met the same fate: as was true in the case of those previously shot, their only crime was that they had been born Jewish.
>
> At Compiègne there have already been 36 cases of men known to have died from the lack of food and the horrible conditions of hygiene.
>
> We wives of the interned men have been separated from our only base of support: we live our daily lives in misery and in fear for the lives of our loved ones who have been brutally snatched away from their families.
>
> Monsieur, we come to you to request your aid, which is the only thing that can save our sons and husbands from death. There are already too many children crying for their Daddies who have been shot. Inform the people in your entourage about the cruel danger of death that is ominously threatening innocent lives. Send letters of protest to men of state, to Marshal Pétain, to Ambassador de Brinon, to Monsieur Xavier Vallat, the General Commissioner for Jewish Affairs, and to others, in order to stop this slaughter of innocent human beings.
>
> Hoping that you will take our anxiety into consideration and come to our aid, we give you our warmest thanks, Monsieur.[192]

The letter was handwritten and signed by "a group of wives and mothers of the men interned at Drancy and Compiègne," and copies were circulated throughout Paris.

Other letters were brought directly to the General Commissioner on Jewish Affairs' office. Some should be read aloud in order for the Yiddish accent visible in the spelling errors to be heard. The following letter, dating from March 19, 1942, provides the finest example: it was also written by hand with beautiful, round, neat, childlike letters, and signed by a group of women from the Clichy section of Paris:

> Dear Sir:
>
> For ten months now our men have been locked up en the concentration canp. They never busied themselves with politics. All this—good, honest workers. For only one cause they make him suffer for they were born Israelites. The biggest part of our husbands they have fulfilled their duty for France. In the Drancy

> camp, there are already many men that have been shot. And men are still being shot. Numerous are already the widows and orphans. We the wives of the men that are locked up are experiencing terrible times. Each woman of us wonders, what woud I do if tomorrow the tragedy it goes to happen, and they are going to shot my dearest in the world? So innocent? Our children often ask us questions, that can tear through the hearts without differences: "Momma, what will I becomes if they are going to shot my poor Daddy?" You can easily imagine the painful moments of suffering that we are experiencing. We therefore ask you Sir: There is there no way to stop the shooting of these innocent men?
>
> Please accept our respectful greeting."[193]

All of these handwritten letters, sometimes recopied by a child whose writing was round and careful, express the "constant terror of receiving the short but infinitely painful note" announcing the execution of a son or a husband: they accordingly ask the General Commissioner for Jewish Affairs to intervene. One woman received an "announcement," another got a letter telling her to come get her son's personal effects, and yet another got the package that she had sent, as the loved one to whom she had mailed it was dead. "Every night is a night of anxiety, both for them and for us: we tremble when we hear a knock on the door and our hearts are pounding each time we open a letter," wrote a group of "deeply sorrowful Jewish mothers and wives." These letters are always written in a collective name: for example, one anonymous woman would write on behalf of all the wives of internees, or one child on behalf of the internees' children. They also contain many questions about the reasons for the persistence of their persecutors. These letter writers did not expect an answer, nor they did receive any. Were they really hoping to alleviate the internees' suffering? Probably not. Such letters were quite different from individual pleas: their objective was political. They allowed those who wrote them to become involved in the struggle, and to do so by acting on the issue that concerned them in the most personal way.

And then the threat took on another new form. The first deportation train left Compiègne on March 27, 1942. At that time in Paris, everything, including food and coal, was being rationed, alerts were frequent, and people lived in the fear of bombardments: the full signification of this departure was therefore not immediately evident for the Jews. The noose was nevertheless being tightened. The imposition of the yellow star marking them as Jews was the most significant sign of this newly intensified persecution in France.

THE YELLOW STAR

It was the Germans who decided to impose the yellow star on Jews in the Occupied Zone, just as they had done previously not only in occupied and annexed Poland, but also in Germany, Holland, and elsewhere.[194] The decision was an integral part of their policy of segregating Jews in order to ultimately eliminate them: it was in other words a first step in the application of the Final Solution in France. In this month of June 1942, however, Jews in Paris saw in this measure above all as an attempt to put their relations with French society in general to the test. They no longer nourished any illusions about the French State, whose laws tended to push them farther and farther to the margins of society. And they came under constant attacks in the newspapers, which they read with the closest attention. Nevertheless, the violence of such attacks remained on the verbal level and so maintained a dimension of abstraction, at least for French Jews. True, there were very concrete, material measures that had shaken their lives: loss of employment, internment in camps, and confiscations of stores. But for those who had not been interned, it was possible to go on living once they had made myriad adjustments. In many cases, everyday relations with one's circle of acquaintances had not basically changed. But as the yellow star was to remind each and everyone that Jews were to be considered pariahs, did it not risk destroying their last remaining links with society?

Decorated Jews

The measure was not a total surprise among Jews in Paris; there had been rumors of such an eventuality for a long time, as noted by Prefect Langeron on January 2, 1941.[195] Near the end of April 1941, Léo Hamon had described the recurrent fear that Jews would be forced to wear an armband.[196] In September 1941, fears had been raised by news that the imposition of the yellow star was to be extended to all territories under the control of the Third Reich.[197] Then in mid-May 1942, there were new, more insistant rumors, and the employees of the UGIF found out that the insignia would be distributed to police stations around May 20.[198]

These rumors were not unfounded. The Germans had in fact postponed the imposition of the yellow star: they were hoping that the new general commissioner for Jewish Affairs, Darquier de Pellepoix, would have the French authorities require Jews to wear the yellow star throughout France.[199] Ordinance no. eight from the German military command in France was signed on May 29, 1942, and announced on June 1. It ordered all Jews over the age of six to have a Jewish star sewn solidly to their clothing: this was to be a six-pointed star as big as the palm of a hand and outlined in black. It was to be made of yellow fabric and bear the inscription "Juif" (Jew) in black letters, and it had to be worn in a clearly visible position on the left side of the chest beginning on June 7, 1942.[200] Those targeted by this measure included the French Jews, Jews without any homeland, and foreign Jews from countries that were applying similar measures. Hungarian Jews were soon added to the latter group on July 16, 1942, as were Bulgarian Jews on September 4, and finally all Jews in the Occupied Zone.

And so some 400,000 such insignia were hastily made, and 83,000 people (out of the 100,455 projected by the offices of the Paris police prefecture exchanged a textile point for three yellow stars at their local police station, to which they reported according to the day designated by their place in the alphabet. Only a minority chose to ignore the new obligation placed on Jews: they were in general either young people who did not agree with their parents on the subject or certain very astute militants who had already chosen to lead a clandestine or semi-clandestine existence. "Nobody will get out of this requirement," predicted Jacques Biélinky. "Those (very rare) individuals who are in favor of not reporting [to the police station] and not wearing the insignia are stigmatized as cowards."[202]

For all who had never hidden their national origins and their Jewish identity, it was moreover risky to try to escape the imposition of the yellow star: one single informer weighed heavier than the complicit silence of an entire neighborhood. Unless one was able to suddenly blend in with the crowd, the decision not to comply with the verification procedure usually made it necessary to flee to the Unoccupied Zone. This had already been true in the fall of 1941, and it was still the case in the summer of 1942. It was difficult to make such a leap, for doing so was predicated on having a support network, something that was not available to everyone. It was at this point that many people sought a way to secretly cross the demarcation line separating the Occupied and Unoccupied Zones. It took a long time, however, for the first contacts to be made.

And so at least at first, all or almost all Jews wore the yellow star. Dr. Eugène Minkowski wore it, even when he at the same time was hiding Jewish children illegally.[203] There were young Jews who did not hesitate to violate the curfew in order to go out and have a good time, all while hiding their yellow star as best they could. There were also a few, a tiny number, who requested exemption from the requirement. Such was the case of R.H.: "I must inform you," he wrote to the general commissioner for Jewish Affairs on June 18, 1942, "that I simply cannot resign myself to having to go about in public with the star of Zion on my chest. I regard it to be a stigma unworthy of someone who has been a French war veteran for fifteen generations. I would rather stay at home or obtain an exemption, which I believe I deserve, given my credentials as a French citizen that I shall list below."[204] We can well imagine what was made of this request; even out of the exemptions solicited by Marshal Pétain, countersigned by Laval, and transmitted to the Germans by Fernand de Brinon, only a tiny handful were granted. The authority to grant such exemptions lay with the Germans and with them only.[205]

It was also after the imposition of the yellow star that there was an increase in the number of those asking to be removed from the Paris police prefecture's lists of Jews.[206] Those making such a request were often French citizens, husbands and wives of Aryans, and half-Jews who had never observed any of the rites of the Jewish religion.

The leaders of the UGIF had led a campaign urging Jews to "wear the insignia in a clearly visible manner, and with dignity."[207] The general tendency seems indeed to have been to display with dignity what certain Jews called their "decoration." The first time that they bore this "decoration" in public even seems to have at times provided an occasion to dress up. Moreover, taking a family walk with the yellow star clearly displayed was a means of reassuring the children.[208] Some went so far as to attach their yellow star with an emblem bearing the colors of the French flag. Others pinned their many military medals all around the star. The Germans, however, then forbade this practice. M. Bloch, a surgeon in Paris hospitals, learned it the hard way: for having displayed his decorations along with this yellow star, he was sent to Drancy and then deported a few days later.[209] A studied elegance and a dignified manner of wearing the star were supposedly going to demonstrate the failure of the Germans in this undertaking intended to humiliate the Jews. While on the one hand calming the apprehensions of her father interned at Beaune-la-Rolande, Lucienne Rodgold wanted him to be proud of her attitude about the star, "With our insignia, we were proud and held our heads high when we walked about," she wrote to her father on June 9, 1942, "and when we met a "monsieur" [a German], we held our head even higher and smiled as we walked by, looking them right in the eyes, while they would lower their heads."

On that sunny Sunday, June 7, 1942 (the day when Jews were required to begin wearing the insignia), there were a large number of Jews who strolled up and down between the Opéra and the Place de la République to show that they were not going to be intimidated by the imposition of the yellow star.[210] There were doubtless an even larger number who preferred to wait before appearing in public in these new circumstances.

The majority of Jews did indeed personally feel and interpret the imposition of the yellow star as an attempt to humiliate them. They also saw it as an effort to isolate them from the rest of the population and stir up a wave of hostility against them.

"The result of this measure was exactly the opposite of the one sought by the one who imposed it,"[211] wrote one woman who had volunteered to work for the UGIF, as she noticed the absence of antisemitic incidents in the street. Even Communist militants saw the yellow star from that angle at first. A June 1942 issue of the newspaper *J'accuse*, the voice of what in a few weeks would take on the name of National Movement Against Racism (MNCR) made the following observations on the subject: "In their [the Germans'] minds, [the star] is intended to humiliate the Jews, to separate them from non-Jews, and to provoke incidents that might degenerate into pogroms. But such calculations are doomed to failure. Jews will wear the insignia imposed on them without shame."[212] The article bore the title: "The Invitation to a Pogrom." The reactions of the Jewish population and its leaders in Belgium during the same period were scarcely different.[213]

Jews in the Southern Zone also interpreted the imposition of the yellow star as an attempt to humiliate the Jews and set them apart. "The leper's rattle was only a sanitary measure, not a means of humiliation," wrote Léon Werth in his *Diary* for June 10, 1942. "They were not intending to impose an official humiliation on the leper. If I were forced to accept such a humiliation, I would doubtless deny this fact.

But would I really overcome the anger and the shame?"[214] The measure took on its most ridiculous aspect in the camp at Drancy, where Jews (in other words, all of those interned there) were required to wear a yellow star solidly attached to their clothing. Even there, they wondered how their families were enduring this humiliation, and how it would affect their relations with the public, which was being bombarded with antisemitic propaganda.[215]

Non-Jews understood the purpose of the imposition of the yellow star in the same way. Jean Guéhenno confirms this observation in his *Journal des années noires:* "For eight days now," he wrote, "Jews have had to wear the yellow star and draw public scorn upon themselves. People have never been so kind. That is doubtless because there is nothing more disgusting than to force a man to be ashamed of himself at every instant, and the people of Paris know it."[216] The only person who had no illusions about the matter (and for good reason) was the German writer and soldier Ernst Jünger, who wrote the following words about the non-Jewish students who had been arrested for wearing yellow stars: "These good souls did not yet know that the time for discussion has past. They supposed that their adversary had a sense of humor. They were like children who go swimming, waving their little flippers in waters where there are sharks. They were making it easier to recognize them."[217]

As time passed and the real consequences of the imposition of the yellow star became apparent, others would come to realize what Jünger knew already. The number of those who attempted to hide their yellow star increased steadily: people would fold the lapel of their coat over it, put a sweater over it, carry a stack of books or dossiers on their left side, or use a large bag, which was a convenient solution for those who had one of the large women's handbags then in style. There were also more and more who began to wear the star sporadically. In October 1942, the General Commission on Jewish Affairs even became worried about the situation, and contacted the prefecture of the Paris police to request that an investigation be conducted in the various sections of Paris and in its suburbs in view of arresting those who were not complying.[218]

In any case, it does not seem that the Jews' attitude toward the yellow star can be considered as either submission or revolt, and it would be futile to look for complete coherency in their behavior: the yellow star caused a tremendous shock and the Jews were frightfully apprehensive. Because this star provided a constant visual reminder that they had become pariahs, it very quickly acquired the force of a symbol. The first step down the path of nonsubmission was often the act of going out in public without the star. And all those who wore the star until the Liberation of Paris remember the moment when they ripped it off their chest: it was a gesture that concretely symbolized the end of their ordeal.

The imposition of the yellow star, however, was also a turning point: Jews tried to gauge its impact on the non-Jewish portion of French society. They went out for a walk "decorated in a dignified way" or simply waited with the same objective in mind: to test their relations with French society in order to see how they had changed. Even the most insignificant contact with the public took on a heavy meaning, as the "decorated" Jews anxiously awaited the reaction of the people they crossed in the street. In the gaze of others, Jews sought proof that the German operation aimed at humiliating them had been a decided failure, and that the attempt to plant antisemitism in French society had not succeeded in establishing any roots.

The Parisians' Reaction

In the period just before they had to start wearing the yellow star on June 7, 1942, Jews were voicing several concerns. In the first place, they were afraid of being hassled in the métro or in the lines that would form in front of food stores; these locations were essential for their survival, and it was there that they would have to deal with "anonymous" members of French society instead of the people they saw on a regular basis. They moreover had apprehensions about the first day of school for their children, who they feared would be constantly taunted and bullied by their classmates.[219] We know that when, on January 21, 1942, Admiral Darlan expressed his disapproval of the Germans' proposal to extend the imposition of the yellow star to Jews in the Unoccupied Zone, he argued that such a measure would deeply shock French public opinion.[220] As for the prefecture of the Paris police, it was worried about the possibility of demonstrations against the imposition of the yellow star. A memorandum was sent out that listed various types of possible infractions and indicated the repressive measures to be taken in response to infractions: it was illegal for Jews to wear several types of insignia and to move about in groups, just as it was forbidden for Aryans to wear the insignia improperly, to wear some sort of whimsical insignia bearing, say, the name of a province, or to greet those who wore the yellow star.[221]

As for the Germans, they had learned from their experience in the Netherlands, where the yellow star had been imposed six weeks before it was required in France. They planned to intern those they termed the "friends of the Jews" in Drancy,[222] and to give a large amount of publicity to these arrests aimed at eliminating any desire to identify with the fate of the Jews. (The prefecture of the Paris police had at first urged the Germans to hand such sympathizers over to the judicial police, but then agreed to the "Drancy solution.")

But what actually happened? Although some deplore the fact while others gloat, three different sources all stress that the public was on the whole indignant over the imposition of the yellow star. Vichy agents' analysis of this reaction, based on the letters they had opened and read, emphasized that the yellow star had only made the rest of the population more friendly toward the Jews. This interpretation was correct: the public's negative reception of the imposition of the yellow star stemmed from the general resentment of German domination in the Occupied Zone.[223] Granted, the inspectors with the General Bureau of Information were less categorical in their reports covering the same period, which stress the public's indifference.[224] But this indifference was only superficial, wrote one of the inspectors: "The application of the ordinance requiring Israelites to wear the yellow star . . . was nevertheless offensive to a good number of Parisians who see no necessity dictated by national interest for this measure."[225]

The people in Catholic circles also criticized the measure, "judging [it] uncharitable," point out the police inspectors, who also reported a few reactions among students. Communist propaganda latched onto the theme, and fliers proliferated on the walls of the Ninth, Tenth, and Eleventh arrondissements: "Support the Jews" was written right beside "The USSR will vanquish." One also saw the following messages. "French citizens, for the honor of France, demand the immediate removal of the yellow star that has been imposed on the Jews. Join the National Front." "Let us show solidarity with the Jews in order to irritate Hitler." "Let us put on the yellow insignia, as the Belgians did. Down with antisemitism."[226]

The Germans expressed their disappointment. In his little book on the yellow star *(L'Etoile jaune)*, Léon Poliakov cites reports emanating from the intelligence office of the *Sicherheitsdienst* (SD) reporting that the imposition of the yellow star had displeased public opinion and stirred feelings of pity toward the Jews.[227] "I know a lot of people who detest the Jews and now find them quite likeable because they are being 'martyred,'" wrote a young lycée student in her diary on June 1, 1942.[228] For her part, this girl concludes that the Germans are stupid; at the same time she observes that while French Jews had been forced to wear the star, some foreign Jews were exempted. That Turkish, Italian, English, and American Jews were spared while French Jews were targeted by this measure could not be ignored by a public that had so harmoniously associated foreigners and Jews (the quintessential aliens) in its prewar fantasies. The "discrimination" was not without impact on public opinion in Paris.

Finally, the testimony provided by those who had to wear the yellow star is generally convergent with the observations that we have already noted. André Baur reassured the Jewish leaders in the Southern Zone. "I am sure that you are anxiously awaiting news about the jaundice that I myself had contracted just a few days earlier," he wrote to Albert Manuel.

> I have therefore been able to observe people's reactions. The current incubation period is far from painful. The unexpected effect is that the malady is creating a strong current of kindness never before seen, especially among children. It is causing an obvious embarassment among my acquaintances, and this embarassment is causing symptoms of this same illness to develop spontaneously. The doctors in charge had not foreseen this development, and the temperature that had been so high has fallen back down: still, sudden fever spells are to be expected, because of this initial error in the diagnosis.[229]

André Baur was therefore fearful of reprisals from the Germans, who were angry and resentful for failing to create a wave of antisemitism among the population. In his diary, Jacques Biélinky provides a minute description of the first few times he went out in public "decorated" with the yellow star. He notes the friendly gestures and the understanding smiles, but he observes first and foremost that wearing the yellow star had not isolated Jews from the rest of the population. He even relates the case of a storeowner who made a point of serving Jews before other customers.[230] Outside of the handshakes with strangers and the discreet tips of the hat from certain people in the street, the most common reaction of the public seems to have been not to notice anything different, to act as if nothing had happened. Jews had been fearful of becoming the objects of morbid curiosity, and were apparently gratified to see such an attitude: for them, such indifference to the yellow star was loaded with meaning, as was the gaze that looked them in the eyes before slipping a quick glance at the left side of their chest.

Let us turn to what one of the victims of the yellow star had to say about June 7, 1942:

> I would like to dwell for a moment on an episode that is characteristic, one that depicts the sensitivity and refinement of the French character at its best. Most of the French people take the following tack, which consists of "not seeing," "not noticing," a Jew bearing the insignia. For the vigilant Jewish population feared precisely that: they feared they would become the object of morbid curiosity on the part of the general public; they feared they would be stared at by thousands of eyes, as if they were strange beasts, wherever they would go, wherever they should be, even if this stare were from a friendly face and even if it were accompanied with a sympathetic smile: that would have been a real ordeal for us. We would have had to express the following plea: "Do not overwhelm us, but rather kill us." On this score, the behavior of the general public exceeded all our expectations. Most of the people that we pass in the street do not "notice" us."[231]

However, children's memories sometimes clash with these harmonious testimonies. Lazare, for example, has spoken of the insults he received every time he came out of class and about demeaning treatment from schoolteachers.[232] Annette Müller remembers that, in spite of her schoolteacher's efforts to intervene, a barrier immediately arose between her and her former friends. In his diary, Romain Rolland also records in mid-June 1942 that "in an elementary school in Paris, some kids taunt and bully [their classmates] bearing the yellow star."[233]

While there was more active sympathy for the Jews, a more outspoken hostility to the imposition of the yellow star also appeared. In the streets of Paris one saw whimsical yellow stars sported by non-Jews and bearing such inscriptions as: "Babe from Montmartre," "Auguste from Ménilmontant," "Native of Auvergne," and even "zulu," "goy," "swing," and "papou," among others.[234] Some would pay a heavy price for such audacity; they wound up getting interned at Drancy. There such "friends of the Jews" were greeted emotionally by the Jews in the camp who, in order to express their gratitude, exempted them from all the chores.[235] During June 7, 1942, alone, the French police arrested some fifteen such "Aryans" bearing an insignia.[236] Ten days later, there had been some forty such arrests, most of which involved minors.[237]

Léon Poliakov reports that about twenty such individuals were still locked up as of August 20, 1942.[238] They were released on August 31.[239] However, as the Germans observed with obvious satisfaction, "the displays of sympathy, processions, and demonstrations that were initially expected never happened."[240]

Certain incidents had nevertheless disturbed the peace and quiet in the streets of the capital city. On that same Sunday, June 7, 1942, a dozen members of the Rassemblement National Populaire had gone into various cafés and brasseries along the Boulevard de la Madeleine and the Rue Royale to see to it that employees refused to serve customers bearing the yellow star. Elsewhere, they had hooted and yelled insults at Jews, and forced those who were having a drink at sidewalk tables to go back inside. Later that same afternoon, similar incidents occurred first along the Avenue des Champs Elysées, then on Avenue de Wagram and Avenue des Ternes. This time it had been a group of thirty youths led by two uniformed members of the Legion of French Volunteers (LVF) who were responsible. In the report of the police inspector who relates these incidents, they were termed "minor," and remained isolated.[241] What the Jewish population in Paris feared, however, was that there would be a proliferation of such public harassment.

We must indeed not forget that it was in the context of an unbridled outburst of antisemitism in Parisian newspapers that Jews wearing the yellow star were cheered up by a smile, a helpful gesture or some sort of personal contact.

The Collaborationist Press

Another such antisemitic offensive had been launched in the press on May 21, 1942. "Quick! Put the yellow flowers, the mark, the sign, on the dungheap of Judas. That way we won't step in it, in the manure, any more," wrote Tony Guedel in the newspaper *Le Pilori*, loudly demanding that all Jews in France should be made to wear an armband or an insignia.[242] This was eight days before the Germans adopted the ordinance imposing the yellow star. On that same date, Jean Coutoux, writing for *L'Appel*, advocated "the radical and definitive exclusion of the Jews from social life," and envisaged pogroms in order to "eliminate them if they become too numerous, and therefore, too dangerous." Meanwhile, in *Je suis partout*, P. A. Cousteau put forth a plan on May 23 for resolving the Jewish problem that was "full of humanity and moderation": "[Put] [a]ll Jewish adults, without exception, without any free passes to get out, with no possible protection, behind barbed-wire fences and under military guard."

Le Pilori, obviously well informed and always one step ahead of the German ordinance, came back to the subject a week later. "Watch out! Kikes are full of schemes, excuses, and camouflaging operations," wrote Jean Méricourt on May 28.

> "Not only does it have to be compulsory to wear the insignia, it is also necessary to specify the colors, the dimensions, and the form of the insignia, and indicate the

> place (on the arm or chest) where this sign of disgrace and shame must be attached. It should also be stated that the armband or badge shall always be worn visibly, whatever type of clothing the Jew may be wearing. And of course this decree must be enforced with serious sanctions, fines, and immediate prison terms. . . . In the future we shall take the liberty of suggesting other prophylactic and sanitary measures of primordial and practical interest.

After the imposition of the yellow star was announced, each writer expressed his own sort of satisfaction. In the June 4, 1942, edition of *Le Pilori*, Jean Méricourt was glad to see that his advice had been heeded. "As all public dangers are pointed out to people in the street, why had not the Jewry worn any sign up until now? The filthy Jewish beast must be felled, and this victory should be the first revolutionary act of the new France." On the same date, Jean Coutoux in *L'Appel* was happy that "the Jews are beginning to pay." In the June 16, 1942, edition of *Les Nouveaux Temps*, Guy Crouzat affirmed that "the day when [the yellow star] was made compulsory has taken on the importance of a historical date." Finally, in the June 6, 1942 edition of *Je suis partout*, Lucien Rebatet asserted:

> We are now at the decisive moment in the fight between Aryans and Jews. Aryans cannot permit such an enemy conceal himself. . . .
>
> I stated last winter in this paper my joy at having seen Jews in Germany marked with their yellow seal for the first time. It will be a much greater joy to see this star in our streets here in Paris where not even three years ago this execrable race was walking all over us. Still, we have one deep regret: we regret that the yellow star has not been imposed by a French law.

After voicing their satisfaction over the imposition of the yellow star, each journalist then laid out the measures that should be subsequently taken. "The yellow star is revealing a few Jews. What needs to be done now is to list their number, to denounce them all, and then to chase them out of Europe, for it is urgent to put them out of commission. Meanwhile, they should be put in a work camp: I say a work camp indeed, and not a concentration camp. The French people want to see the Jews bending over French soil, holding a pick in their hands." Such was the opinion of Pierre Constantini, writing in the paper *L'Appel* on June 11, 1942. Editorialists in other papers advocated first and foremost the extension of the yellow star to the Unoccupied Zone: it was a demand that would often be reiterated in their columns. As if all that were not enough, the July 9, 1942, edition of *Le Pilori* suggested that deportation be adopted as a policy in France: it was the "only effective way of neutralizing" the Jews, one that had been used in Slovakia to rid the country of all its Jews.

Even when the German ordinances were not announced and prepared by such propaganda campaigns, each was greeted with enthusiasm by the collaborationist press. When Jews were relegated to the last car on the métro trains, the July 16, 1942 edition of *L'Appel* recommended that authorities "see to it that this car not be invaded by those incurable Aryan imbeciles showing their philo-Semitic sentiments." It would be best, suggested the editorialist, that "only Jews be allowed" in the last car of the métro. Similarly, both the July 7, 1942, edition of *Le Matin* and the July 9,

1942, edition of *Le Pilori* demand that Jews no longer be allowed to use the telephone, which for them is a "means of propaganda, espionage, spreading rumors, trafficking in the black market, [and] sending out watchwords and directives for their deadly action."

In accordance with the ninth ordinance, issued by the Germans on July 8, 1942, Jews were barred from frequenting all public establishments and from attending all public events. The July 15, 1942, edition of *Le Matin* provided commentary in an article titled poetically "Stars that Die Out." This new measure, explained the newspaper, had come in response "to the growing irritation that was surfacing in places infested with yellow stars," and would have "the most positive effects on the moral health of life in Paris."

The cinema also participated in this festival. During the summer of 1942, the movie theater Le Balzac screened a film suggestively titled *Le Péril juif* (The Jewish peril). Granted, this was not the only new film of the week: it was announced at the same time as *L'Ange gardien, Tourbillon express, Le Lit à colonnes,* and *La Nuit fantastique.*[243] But, as we learn in the July 9, 1942, edition of *Le Pilori,* it provided a "unique documentary that shows us the Jew in his physical and moral filth, in his sly, sordid, and rapacious life." The film moreover offered "animated geographical maps showing us how the entire world is being invaded by the Jewish race."[244]

It is more or less impossible to gauge the actual potency of this propaganda as an influence on public opinion in Paris. It should nevertheless be noticed that these articles were becoming more and more virulent whenever new measures were being prepared, when a new ordinance had been issued, or when a massive police roundup was underway. It is as if both the Germans and their allies in the collaborationist press in Paris assumed that an extra amount of propaganda was needed in order to convince people that the new measures were justified. These efforts were not totally in vain: waves of denunciations would pour in not only with each new antisemitic measure, but even more so in response to each new antisemitic offensive in the press. The June 1942 harvest of such denunciations was hardly negligible.[245]

Considering all these various factors, we cannot easily make a precise assessment of the attitude of Parisian society: the very notion is in itself problematical. We can nevertheless offer a few observations. Jews were anxious to see the slightest signs of public sympathy, and they were indisputably ready to read the nonchalance of people in the street as proof that the Germans had failed in their efforts to make them objects of public scorn. They had feared pogroms, and so felt reassured by the general indifference, and encouraged by individual gestures of compassion.

What is also striking in these descriptions of people's reactions to the yellow star is how Jews and gentiles understood the insignia, as it immediately preceeded the massive police roundup of Jews at the Vel d'hiv. Everyone saw it first and foremost as a measure intended to humiliate the Jews, and it was precisely to this attempted humiliation that they first reacted. The real consequences of the law would become apparent to them only later, after other measures were enacted that were harder and harder to escape, precisely because of the yellow star. Once again, we see the recurrent use of a mechanism that had worked in exactly the same way when Jewish stores had been required to display a yellow placard in the fall of 1940. Jews had done so with pride, displaying their achievements on the battlefield by placing their military medals alongside the yellow sign. The public had either shown sympathy or indifference, both of which were observed with relief by Jews. They had feared violent attacks and, all in all, the indifference was reassuring to them. But that was before the aryanization measures had revealed not only the true intentions of the Germans, who had much more in mind than merely humiliating the Jews, but also the intention of many French people to take advantage of the situation. Other factors reinforce this comparison of the public's reaction to the yellow star with its reaction to the yellow placards. First, by contrast with laws that targeted the fantasized Jew, the yellow star was a highly visible measure that now marked in the most conspicuous way concrete individuals, including the Jewish storekeepers that no one had ever complained about before and the Jewish neighbors who suddenly stood out now that they bore the yellow insignia. Moreover, both were measures that had not been extended to the Southern Zone and were therefore clearly the doing of the Germans.[246]

The tension and anxiety of the first few days quickly gave over to the routine of habit. Even while heaping scorn on the "swing kids whose social habits have been totally contaminated by Jews, who are friendly to the Israelites, and who also have been wearing a yellow star,"[247] the collaborationist press itself had to observe that, all in all, "the yellow star ha[d] smoothly become a matter of routine."[248] And the conclusions implicitly reached by the inspectors with the prefecture of the Paris police corroborate that observation. The necessities of everyday life totally dominated people's cares and worries. For the Jews, however, a new series of measures began to throw another light on the Germans' motives for imposing the yellow star.

The Consequences of the Yellow Star

Indeed, it was not long before the true meaning of the yellow star was clearly revealed to the Jews. In the first place, it provided a new reason to arrest them, as those who did not comply were sought out and prosecuted. From the very beginning of the new measure on June 7, 1942, the French police apprehended fourteen Jews without the insignia along with two others who had expressed their opposition to wearing the yellow star.[249] Others fell directly into the hands of the *Feldgendarmerie*. The following week, sixty-six Jews caught without the yellow star were turned over to the *Feldgendarmerie* and taken to Drancy.[250] Twenty-five more were similarly apprehended and taken away the week after; subsequently, there would be another group of Jews apprehended without the star and sent to Drancy. Most of the victims of these arrests were, in the first few days at least, women who had apparently forgotten, when changing from one day to the next, to unsew their stars from one piece of clothing and resew it on the next day's garment.[251] They would first be incarcerated in the camp at Les Tourelles,[252] but that would no longer be necessary once the "camp for the Jews" began to take in both men and women.

One of the women thus arrested was Esther Zimmerman: on June 8, 1942, the police apprehended her in the company of Jews, carrying a suspicious identity card (at least according to the police report on her case). Because she looked Jewish and had a Jewish first name, she was suspected of not complying with the requirement to wear the yellow star. Also arrested for noncompliance was Joseph Zaoui, who had only attached the yellow star to his shirt, while draping his coat over his shoulders in a way that could hide the insignia at any given moment.[253] And then there was Marguerite Gleidmann, who had only attached her yellow star with pins: this was taken as proof that she did not wear it regularly.[254] Finally, there was Tamara Isserlis, who had pinned a French flag under her yellow star.[255]

There were even cases of people who were arrested in their homes after someone had reported to the police that they had not worn the yellow star.[256] In the street, the hunt for individuals with "specifically Judaic facial features" was tenaciously pursued by inspectors with the special "Division of Investigations and Inspections" (SEC) up until the end of the war. Arresting Jews for not wearing the yellow star made it possible to add to the number of internees. One can find evidence of this search for such violators up until July 27, 1944 in some sections of Paris.[257]

More important, the imposition of the yellow star was just one measure that ushered in a whole series of others. The news was first spread by rumor: Jews would no longer be allowed in any but the last car of the métro. It was a rumor, as "no notice ha[d] been posted, no communiqué ha[d] been made public." It was the Métro Company, acting on instructions given by the German authorities, that "circulated in train stations and métro stops a directive instructing agents not to sell first-class tickets to Jews, ordering conductors to inform those wearing the insignia that they are not allowed to use any car other than the last in the second class, and directing guards and inspectors to politely request those Jews they may find in other cars to go to the last car at the next stop."[258] All this was done. It was not before July 8, 1942, however, that newspapers finally published what was presented as a decision of the Métro Company. Following the initial rumor, and then a more or less rigorous application of the directive cited, the measure became a concrete reality: from then on, some Jews would call this last car to which they were relegated the "synagogue."[259] André Baur, as well as the leaders of the Consistory in the Southern Zone (who patterned their response after him), could not even conceive of the possibility that the adoption of the various anti-Jewish measures stemmed from an autonomous logic: they therefore thought that the decision to restrict Jews to the last car in the métro had been prompted by the general wave of sympathy among the French public following imposition of the yellow star.[260]

Two days later, the newspapers published the ninth German ordinance containing new measures. Jews had already been restricted to going to stores only between three and four o'clock in the afternoon; now they found themselves banned from places of entertainment and other public establishments open to the public. On July 15, the newspapers spelled out the details: restaurants, cafés, cinemas, theaters, concerts, music halls, swimming pools, beaches, museums, libraries, exhibits, castles, historical monuments, sports events, racetracks, parks, campgrounds, and even telephone booths were all off-limits for Jews. At the very same time, the post office, telephone, and telegraph service received the order to disconnect all telephones belonging to Jewish subscribers.[261] To keep themselves supplied with basic commodities, Jews could now do their shopping only at an hour when most food stores were closed.

In mid-July 1942, this acceleration of exclusionary measures suddenly took an even more dramatic turn. After the first deportation on March 27, 1942, four more trains filled with internees (including many from the camps in the département of Le Loiret) had left for the east during the month of June. In the camps at Pithiviers and Beaune-la-Rolande, the committees of Communists, who were well organized, received a directive from Paris on May 12: the deportation was to be resisted, for deportation meant death. The tract put out by the Communist committee at Pithiviers on May 14, 1942 (the first anniversary of the creation of the two camps) records those instructions: "Each one of us must understand that our lives are in danger. We must not wait passively. Any and all efforts of resistance will shorten our ordeal and we must strive to tear ourselves away from this trap. Any and all means of escape are good."[262] And yet, the reply that they sent back to their leaders in Paris was more skeptical: "Of course nobody wants to be taken away. But if we were to tell the internees to stay on their bed mats and be taken away only by force, they would not listen to us, and we would be isolated from the others. When we discussed the question, we came to the following conclusion: when they come to get us for the deportation, we will sing the Marseillaise, and that may have a big effect on detainees in the camp."[263]

Deportation meant death: who could really believe it? Now more isolated and more vulnerable than ever, the Jews nevertheless knew that getting arrested could henceforth land them in the salt mines in Poland or Germany or in forced labor camps. The destination was not clear, but the menace was nonetheless terrifying.

8
The Massive Police Roundups

THE POLITICAL PREMISES

The imposition of the yellow star was the most visible sign of a series of new developments whose full impact would be revealed over the course of the summer of 1942. The changes would not only radically transform the status of Jews in both the Occupied and Unoccupied Zones; they would also have a profound impact on the political negotiations between Vichy and the German Occupation forces over the Jewish question.

The return of Pierre Laval on April 16, 1942 was not the first major modification of the power structure at Vichy. In previous personnel changes (for example, when Pierre-Étienne Flandin had replaced Laval as premier and when Admiral Darlan had succeeded Flandin) Jews had been neither hopeful nor disillusioned. Irrespective of personnel shifts made in the governing team during the first part of the Occupation, it was actually the summer of 1941 that had marked the major turning point in both zones: in the northern, Occupied Zone, the new era had been ushered in by the internments at Drancy, while in the southern, Unoccupied Zone, the new phase was marked by the appearance of the census requirement and the aryanization law.

The German invasion of the Soviet Union had marked both zones. In any case, thanks to German ambassador Otto Abetz's maneuvering in Paris, Laval had returned to power for the remainder of the Vichy regime's reign. Having thus received the necessary institutional guarantees, he was now in the position to carry out his political objectives, the first of which was to give a new impetus to the policy of state collaboration.[1] He stated publicly on June 22, 1942 his hope for a German victory over the Soviet Union, a declaration that we know to have been carefully thought out.[2] As Vichy's new premier, and also minister of the interior, of information, and of foreign affairs, Laval wanted to secure a full-fledged, bona fide peace treaty from the Germans and guarantee France's place in the new Europe.[3] For the immediate future, he sought assurances over France's future borders, took up the problem of the colonies, worked to gain the return of one and one-half million prisoners of war and the elimination of the demarcation line, and aimed at restoring the French government's administrative autonomy in the Occupied Zone.

To accomplish these objectives, however, Laval needed a sympathetic ear in Germany. He could not have chosen a poorer time: Hitler had just decided to step up pressure on the Occupied countries. Backed by the German ordinance of May 7, 1942, authorizing the use of force in recruiting manual laborers in the Occupied countries, Gauleiter Fritz Sauckel arrived in France on June 15, 1942, and demanded 250,000 French workers for German industry. Earlier, in May 1942, it was Reinhard Heydrich, second-in-command under Himmler at the head of the SS and chief of the German police (the Reichssicherheitshauptamt [RSHA]) who came to Paris and insisted that there be a parallel police force made up of ideologically committed militants.[4] Finally, Adolf Eichmann, head of the Jewish section of the RSHA, came to Paris on June 30, 1942, and demanded that all Jews in France be deported. From then on, the status of the Jewish question in the negotiations between the French and the Germans would depend directly on the overall haggling begun at that time.

At the same time, both the German and the French authorities made changes in the personnel in charge of Jewish affairs in France.[5] For the Germans, the police operations previously left in the hands of the military command (taken over since February 1942 by Karl-Heinrich von Stülpnagel, the cousin of his predecessor) were now placed under the control of the SS and their new chief in France, Carl Albrecht Oberg, who assumed his position on June 1, 1942. Moreover, the SS team in France was reinforced by the addition of Herbert Hagen. Finally, Theodor Dannecker, chief of the Judenreferat in France, was replaced in July 1942 by the SS-Obersturmführer Heinz Röthke. All in all, these personnel moves meant that the power of the SS in France was being strengthened.

The personnel changes also affected French officials. In addition to the return of Pierre Laval as premier, René Bousquet, the young and ambitious prefect of the département of La Marne, was named to the position of secretary general for the police in the Ministry of the Interior in early May 1942.[6] Jean Leguay became Bousquet's representative for the Occupied Zone. And finally, the head of the General Commission on Jewish Affairs, Xavier Vallat, was replaced by Darquier de Pellepoix on May 6, 1942.

The process of Darquier's appointment revealed much about the mechanisms that would later come into play in all of the haggling between the French and the Germans. Relations between Vallat and Dannecker had greatly deteriorated after the stormy February 17, 1942, meeting between these two antisemites who were so different from one another.[7] Vallat's strong dislike of the Germans, his unchanged determination to apply a specifically French antisemitic policy, and his opposition to an unconditional alignment with German policy in this matter were no longer acceptable to the German Occupation authorities, especially as their objectives had changed and they were not willing to put up with such contrariness. On March 19, 1942, Vallat was dismissed by Darlan, who now faced the problem of finding a replacement. Louis Darquier, who had draped himself under the pseudo-aristocratic name "de Pellepoix," was the Germans' choice for the position. Darquier was a rather shady character, a "failure as a businessman and a peripheral journalist,"[8] and a fanatical antisemite. In the period immediately preceding the war, he had (thanks to German funding) founded propaganda organizations known under the suggestive names of National Club Against Mixed Bloods and Anti-Jewish Assembly, as well as the weekly publication *La France enchaînée* (France Chained Up). As an elected member of the Paris city council, he had been convicted of stirring up racial hatred and spreading racist propaganda. From 1940 to 1942, he had been active in antisemitic propaganda campaigns in Paris, working with the German-controlled Institute for the Study of Jewish Questions. Since September 15, 1941, he had also been in charge of a special task force for the General Commission on Jewish Affairs.[9] Once back in power, Laval decided to appoint Darquier to Vallat's position. By consenting to this gesture for the Germans, Laval was accomodating them on a matter he considered secondary, thus hoping to win their good graces on matters he deemed much more important.

German priorities, however, were to prevail over Laval's, and the settlement of the "Jewish question" was now one of their primary concerns. The Final Solution was under way.

The decision had doubtless been made between the summer and fall of 1941, in the wake of the German army's advances—or failures to advance—on the Soviet front. Although preceded by large-scale massacres of Jews, the bureaucratic means for carrying out the Final Solution were determined at the meeting of high-ranking Nazi officials during the Wannsee Conference on January 20, 1942.[10] The time for preparatory measures and alternatives such as emigration, then expulsions, segregation, and internment, was over. The plan to deport Jews to a faraway land was replaced by the enterprise of extermination. Moreover, this project was no longer relegated to the postwar period, but scheduled for immediate application.

The application of the Final Solution to the Jews in France must be understood in the context of several perspectives. German authorities in France—and in particular Theodor Dannecker and Karl-Theo Zeitschel, the expert on Jewish questions at the embassy, along with the German ambassador in Paris, Otto Abetz—were urging Berlin to include Jews interned in the Occupied Zone in the scheduled transfer of the Jews to the "territories recently conquered in the East."[11] For their part, French authorities viewed rather favorably the possibility of getting rid of the foreign Jews interned in the Southern Zone by sending them back to the East.

At the same time, however, the Vichy government was hoping to spare French Jews from being deported and displayed no enthusiasm for seeing the French police carry out the massive roundups that would be required in the Occupied Zone in order to fill the deportation trains. The young, dynamic minister of the police, Bousquet, was striving to gain the autonomy of a police force that would be reunified under his command, and that was well worth a few concessions. As for the Germans, they only had a limited number of police agents on French territory, and they were aware of the limits of the aid that might be furnished by the French Police for Jewish Affairs (PQJ), which was ideologically docile to their ends but weak in men and materiel. The infrastructure of the French police was therefore indispensable to the Germans, and this advantage was well worth the concession of taking only foreign Jews for the time being and putting off the deportation of French Jews to a later date. At the talks conducted during Heydrich's visit to Paris, Heydrich and Bousquet clearly found common ground on those points.

At the very moment when a second trainload of interned Jews was leaving the Northern Zone on June 5, 1942, Dannecker was in Berlin with Eichmann, discussing the specific technical means of deporting the Jews from France.[12] A vast plan for deportation spanning France, Belgium, and the Netherlands had just been set into motion. In the context of this ambitious project, Dannecker had been charged with delivering 100,000 Jews from France, and expected Laval to supply half of this contingent. That figure, however, soon appeared unrealistic to Dannecker, and he abandoned his initial plan to deport from France 100,000 Jews between the ages of sixteen and forty, beginning on July 13, 1942, at the rate of three trainloads per week. He instead adopted a more modest plan to deport 40,000 Jews within three months: it was this enterprise that provided the basis for discussions with French officials.

During a preliminary stage, Bousquet proved himself willing on June 16, 1942, to deliver ten thousand foreign Jews from the Unoccupied Zone. Dannecker, while continuing to push for his overall objective, kept on sending previously interned Jews off to the East. Three trains filled with Jewish internees from Drancy and the camps in the département of Le Loiret left for Auschwitz on June 22, 25, and 28. In order to fill them, the age limit was lifted from forty to fifty-five years, and Jewish women incarcerated in the barracks at Les Tourelles were added to the group of deportees. "All Jewish women between the ages of eighteen and forty-two in one line!" Then, a moment later, "Turn your backs, face the courtyard! You others, go back inside!"[13] With these words, tersely belted out one day in late June 1942 as three German officers stood by, the Jewish women detained in the barracks at Les Tourelles were separated from the "Aryan" women. When buses took them off to Drancy, some of them struck up "La Marseillaise." And then, more arrests were carried out.[14] The decisions concerning a vast plan of massive police roundups and deportations, however, were being made at another level. And now a belated assertiveness on the part of Laval was apparently calling into question what had appeared to have been already fixed.

Ultimately, everything was worked out between the German and French police chiefs: discussions between the Germans Oberg, Knochen, and Hagen, on one side, and France's Police Chief René Bousquet on the other were held on July 2, 1942. While reiterating Vichy's agreement to deliver to the Germans ten thousand Jews from the Unoccupied Zone, Bousquet at first refused to have French police aid in the arrest of twenty thousand Jews in the Occupied Zone. But then he suddenly yielded to the Germans on this point, doubtless in order to make headway toward the only goal that was really important to him: unifying the French police forces in both the Occupied and Unoccupied Zones under his command.[15] On the following day, he had Laval and Pétain approve the agreement. The coordination of French and German police forces was well under way; equally under way were the logistical preparations for the Vel d'hiv roundup and then the mass arrests of Jews in the Southern Zone.

But Vichy's participation in this vast enterprise of transferring large segments of the Jewish population to Auschwitz did not stop there. Vichy made available to the Germans the files of information on Jews in the Northern Zone that it had meticulously put together: This act of collaboration resulted from the conditions of the Occupation, taking heightened consequence from the systematic census of the Jews mandated by both Vichy and the Germans, and proceeding with a momentum that attends bureaucratic processes. One may make similar observations about the use of the French railway system and the use of French gendarmes to accompany deportation trains. Employing French police in the organization and execution of the massive roundups in the Occupied Zone was the price that Vichy was willing to pay (all in all, rather painlessly) in its attempt to gain certain political advantages.

The decision to hand over to the Germans the foreign Jews from the areas in which France claimed to be "sovereign," however, also stemmed from Vichy's own xenophobic and antisemitic policies, which it had autonomously applied in the Southern Zone. The combination of this ideological outlook with specific political practices also provides a partial explanation for what was probably the most shameful initiative in this sad sequence of negotiations between the French and the Germans. The Germans had not planned to include Jewish children in the first deportation trains.[16] On July 6, 1942, however, Dannecker reported to his superiors the following results of his negotiations with the French government: "All of the stateless Jews in the Occupied Zone and in the Unoccupied Zone will be turned over to us for evacuation," he wrote, "President Laval proposed that when Jewish families would be evacuated from the Unoccupied Zone, children under the age of sixteen be taken away also. As for the Jewish children that might remain in the Occupied Zone, the matter does not interest him."[17]

And so Dannecker still had to wait for approval from his superiors to deport the Jewish children that the French authorities did not know what to do with. It took a long time for the answer to come: it was only on July 20, after several reminders from Dannecker, that Eichmann gave his consent over the phone, and then confirmed with a telex on August 7, specifying that "the children of stateless Jews [should be] deported in the appropriate numbers."[18] This delay was to have grave consequences for the specific means used to deport Jewish children. But the very initiative of ridding French soil of these children, entirely due to Laval, was obviously much graver. In order to make it possible for French diplomats on post in various foreign countries to respond to "malicious commentaries and calumnious phony stories" that the spectacle of the massive police roundups all over France had stirred up in foreign newspapers, Laval wrote to them and explained that the program of "repatriating the stateless Jews," who were "obviously a dangerous element" in French society, "was being done by families, which is to say that children who were minors go with their parents, unless the parents prefer to go alone. . . . This measure was taken out of concern for national health and hygiene and is free of any doctrinal consideration: it is merely intended to free our soil of the presence of immigrants who have slipped into our country in excessive numbers over the last few years."[19]

The terminology and the line of argumentation used here need no commentary. However, as we shall see, the parts of this telegram that deal with the children are deceitful. On September 9, 1942, Laval spelled out his thoughts on the subject to Pastor Boegner, who had come to intercede for the Jews and who had raised the question of the children: "Not one of them must remain in France, " Laval told Boegner.[20] The reasons for Laval's initiative and determination are doubtless to be found in his purely bureaucratic preference for the easiest solution to a problem that he was probably anticipating: what to do with the children whose parents had been deported? The dehumanization of the victims in Laval's mind, as attested by the terms "national health and hygiene," had made such a choice possible for him. And Laval stood by this decision; it provided a convenient answer to the recurring accusation in objections to the mass arrests and deportations: tearing the children out of their mothers' arms.[21]

In mid-June 1942, Dannecker set priorities in the order of the deportations, which in turn determined the pace of the massive police roundups. The provinces of the Occupied Zone were placed at the very top of the list, "not only in order to eliminate the presence of any and all Jews from the coastal area but also because of the basic centralization of the problem in Paris."[22] Next in line for deportation was the concentration of Jews in the greater Paris region, and finally, the Jews in the Unoccupied Zone.

EVERYTHING SUDDENLY CAVES IN

The Provinces Are First on the List

It had been possible to monitor Jews in the départements of the Occupied Zone more rigorously than in Paris, and the Jewish populations in these regions kept on decreasing. In Brittany, for example, the June 1941 census showed a decrease of more than 70 percent from the figure recorded nine months earlier.[23]

A third census was taken in early March 1942. It added even more information to all the data patiently gathered both by the prefects, who conscientiously carried out the monthly verifications requested by the local Feldkommandanturen, and by delegations from the Police for Jewish Affairs (PQJ). The figures obtained from the census widely reflected the decrease in the Jewish population. Most of the Jews still living in these areas had been there for a long time. Out of the 49 declared Jews in the département of Les Côtes-du-Nord in the spring of 1942, for example, 47 were French citizens.[24] Moreover, the restriction barring Jews from living along the coast and their subsequent expulsion from the area had accentuated this tendency. To take once again the example of Les Côtes-du-Nord, there was no need to organize any police roundup in the summer of 1942, as there were no more Jews to deport (only about twenty still remained in this département in July).

In all the regions of the Occupied Zone outside of Paris, one can observe a similar trend. Subjected to heightened surveillance (since it was so easy to check on the local "state of the Jewish population" with unannounced inspections), Jews not only fled in increasing numbers but were also expelled from coastal regions. As a result, there was an ever-greater proportion of French Jews among those who remained. Jews in these départements lived in the constant fear of being arrested and used as hostages: this danger only added to the exodus of Jews from the provinces. On January 14, 1942, ten Jews were arrested in Les Côtes-du-Nord, and twenty-five more in the département of L'Ille-et-Vilaine.[25] On February 26, 1942, twenty-five Jews were arrested in Dijon. In just a few days, only half of the Jews who had been living in the city up until that time still remained.[26] In the Poitiers region, Jews were rounded up and brought to hotels and boardinghouses every night from April 24 to May 3, 1942, on the order of the chief of German police Bruckle: in addition to the Jews, who were sent to the camp at Pithiviers, all those who had come from Paris without a valid reason were arrested.[27] In the Seine-inférieure area, German police arrested seventy-seven Jews during the night of May 6–7.[28]

One month later, those who had not been taken wound up having to trade textile ration points for a yellow star, as in Paris: 974 such insignia were distributed in Nancy.[29] Our information about such distributions as well as the reactions of local people and the ensuing police roundups remains incomplete. In some cases, we must rely on an often partisan monograph: in others we must consult a thesis written by a university student or perhaps some isolated document lost in some more general archival holding. We do know, however, that 206 Jews had to wear the yellow star in Dijon,[30] 84 in Sens, and 89 in Auxerre,[31] just as we know that 36 Jews in the département of L'Eure-et-Loire signed a form confirming that they had received the yellow star: some 102 textile points were thus recovered and sent to the prefect four months later. Only three families in the Eure-et-Loire proved to be recalcitrant, refusing to trade textile points for the required insignia. Among them we find Pierre-Jacques Lévy and his parents, whose case we have already noted in the context of the two censuses of Jews: once again, they protested this new imposition.[32] To no avail: Fernand de Brinon had clearly specified that "in the case of a Jew without any textile points, the yellow star must nevertheless be issued, with the lack of points duly noted on the receipt."[33] Brinon's instructions were carried out.

And finally, we know that Rabbi Hagenauer expressed his satisfaction over the attitude of the general French public in Nancy after the appearance of the yellow star.

People had little taste for the Germans here in this city of the Lorraine region: it was only patriotic to look askance at every measure emanating from their authority. Rabbi Hagenauer's outlook on the imposition of the yellow star scarcely differed from that of his counterparts in Paris: "We are all unanimous in our resolution," he wrote after the measure took effect on June 7, 1942. "We shall wear this insignia not as a material proof of disgrace, but as an act of courage and faith with respect to our religion and our country."[34]

Although somewhat disparate in nature, these anecdotal pieces of information confirm our assessment of the situation in the Paris region. This leads us back to Dannecker's project and the massive roundups scheduled for mid-July 1942: the Hauptsturmführer's ambitions were upset a bit by the agreements reached with Bousquet, as the planned arrests of French Jews were actually suspended. Furthermore, the mass arrests that the Germans had scheduled for the first two weeks in July in the Seine-inférieure area, where they hoped to snare 277 Jews in greater Rouen, were ultimately delayed. It was only on October 9, 1942, that they arrested only some forty people and transferred them to Drancy. In areas where the operation was aggressively carried out, however, the Germans did not always make subtle distinctions of national origin. The commander of the Sipo SD in Angers, for example, totally disregarded the question and included 201 French Jews in the roundup carried out on July 15. He thus succeeded in filling the only deportation train scheduled to leave directly from the départements of the Occupied Zone outside of the Paris region, sending 824 Jews out of Angers on July 20, 1942:[35] they had been picked up in eighty-five different communities scattered throughout nine different départements.[36]

There were thus no more Jews in the département of Les Côtes-du-Nord, nor in the occupied part of L'Allier (or at least not enough to be worth the trouble of a roundup) and the operation was postponed for a few months. Elsewhere, however, mass arrests did indeed take place, often several days before the massive Vel d'hiv roundup. They had not required the same meticulous preparation.

In L' Eure-et-Loire, Jews were arrested and transferred to Pithiviers on July 11 and 12, 1942.[37] On July 12, it was the turn of a small number of foreign Jews in Auxerre.[38] On July 13, twenty out of the twenty-eight potential victims listed were arrested in Dijon.[39] On the same day, thirty Jews living in the département of La Nièvre suffered the same fate,[40] as did ten foreign Jews in the département of Le Calvados on the following day.[41] On July 15, the "pickings" were even more sizable, as two hundred Jews were apprehended in Tours.[42] In the département of La Loire-inférieure, a police roundup was organized. Efforts concentrated on the Saint-Nazaire section netted sixty-six Jews (including fifty-one French citizens); and in all, a group of one hundred Jews from this area was delivered to Drancy. The Loire-inférieure was completely cleared of its last known remaining Jews by a roundup organized by German security police on October 9, 1942.[43] Indeed, October 9 and 10 marked the beginning of the next phase in the long series of mass arrests and police roundups that shaped the history of Jews in this period.

In Bordeaux, the roundup scheduled for July 6 was put off until July 16: the 172 Jews arrested on that day left the city for Drancy on July 18, and on the following day were sent from Drancy to Auschwitz.[44] Three days later, it was the city of Nancy that was the scene of a roundup of Jews. However, only 32 out of the some 350 people slated for arrest were apprehended: the others had been forewarned by French policemen.[45]

When he came back from summer vacation in the Vosges on the following day, the young Henri Kriesher was informed at the train station by two policemen that his mother had gone into hiding and that he should warn other Jews threatened with arrest and deportation. It was these same police inspectors who gave him the false identity papers that he subsequently traded for "authentic" documents at the office of the prefecture in Périgueux and then used throughout the remainder of the Occupation.

As had been the case during the period immediately preceding the roundups, every infraction of the anti-Jewish laws that occurred during the following weeks invariably resulted in arrest and internment. This was true both in Paris and in the provinces for both French and foreign Jews—and the latter also faced deportation. All Madame M.A. had to do to get arrested by the Germans in Les Sables-d'Olonne, for example, was to buy milk from a creamery at ten in the morning on August 7, 1942, thus disregarding the hours when Jews were prohibited from shopping: she was sent via Poitiers to Drancy, and then deported to Auschwitz one month later.[46]

From everywhere there came reports of children who suddenly found themselves without home or family. A few—eight children in Dijon, seven in the département of La Nièvre, six in Chartres,[47] among others—were sent to a variety of locations, some with relatives, others with neighbors, and still others with a social aid organization. Local authorities were in some cases worried about the potential burden these children presented. One can easily imagine the crisis created, for example, by the five children between the ages of eight and fourteen that had been placed in the care of a nanny in the town of Logron on March 27, 1942. On July 1, they had set out to return to Paris, but then found that their mother, a widow, had just been arrested and interned: they returned to Logron on their own initiative. "I am writing to you, Sir," wrote the mayor of Logron to the subprefect, "to request your instructions." Knowing that these children had enough money to cover their room and board for two months, he added: "As far as I am concerned, under no circumstances do I want to see these children who have no ties to Logron to become this community's financial responsibility: when their finances are exhausted, we cannot provide for either their food or their housing, nor can we give them free medical aid."[48]

In Nancy, the UGIF took in a group of some twenty children and put them up in a retirement center.[49] In some cases, children were rapidly sent to the UGIF in Paris from the cities of Dijon, Bordeaux, Belfort, and Montceau-les-Mines under the surveillance of the Police for Jewish Affairs; the costs were paid by the UGIF.[50] Whenever there was just a small number of children, they were spared simply by the fact that they had been scattered out. Otherwise, they had been doomed by the agreements between French and German authorities, the very accords intended to facilitate the massive police roundup in Paris and its suburbs.

The Vel d'Hiv Roundup

While the series of arrests conducted at various locations throughout the provinces of the Occupied Zone drove an increasing number of refugees to the Southern Zone, a rumor was spreading through the Jewish sections of Paris: massive police roundups were in the making. The information leaked out in various ways. As early as July 5, 1942, *L'Université libre* had urged the people of Paris to alert the Jews: "The files on 30,000 Jews have been handed over to the Krauts by the French Police," warned the clandestine newspaper.[51] Some police chiefs let information leak out, and activists with the Communists and the Amelot Committee did everything they could to forewarn as many Jews as they could. Some UGIF employees went door to door.

UGIF leaders, who on July 1 had already been called upon to prepare clothing and blankets for seven thousand people,[52] knew very well that massive deportations were in the works. However, fearing that they might create a panic among the Jewish population, they refrained from spreading this information, and instead tried to learn more while offering protection to the leaders of the Amelot Committee on July 13.[53] The Jewish Communists even put out a tract in Yiddish for "the masses of Jewish people." "According to information that we have received from a reliable source, the Germans are going to carry out a massive roundup of Jews in view of their deportation," they announced, and gave specific instructions to each Jew.

> 1. Do not wait for these bandits in your home. Take all necessary measures to hide, and hide first of all your children with the aid of sympathetic French people.
> 2. After you have ensured your own liberty, join an organization involved in the patriotic fight to defeat the bloodthirsty enemy and avenge his crimes.
> 3. If you fall into the hands of these bandits, resist in any way you can. Barricade the doors, call for help, fight the police. You have nothing to lose. You can only save your life. Seek to flee at every moment.
>
> Not one Jew should fall victim to the bloodthirsty Nazi beast. Every Jew that remains alive and free constitutes a victory over our enemy: we must not, we may not, we will not allow ourselves to be exterminated.[54]

This tract, which probably came out at the very last minute, doubtless had a very limited distribution: otherwise, how could we explain the fact that Communist militants themselves did not always place their wives and children in safety?[55]

Nevertheless, the rumor had spread widely thoughout Jewish households. It was easy to foresee that immigrant Jews would be targeted, but past experience led people to believe that it would be the men who would be singled out, especially as it was only logical to assume that the deportations supposedly aimed at benefiting the Germans would concern those able to do considerable physical labor. In any case, such was the most widely accepted interpretation. "The word is that Jewish men and women between the ages of 18 and 45 are to be arrested and sent to do forced labor in Germany," wrote Jacques Biélinky in his diary on July 15. For his part, he had already taken refuge at the home of a Protestant friend at Le Plessis-Robinson on July 12.[56]

At 4:00 A.M. on July 16, 1942, a massive manhunt began in the streets of Paris. Some 4,500 French policemen[57] had been charged with arresting and then keeping watch over 27,361 stateless Jews in Paris and its suburbs. These were Jews of German, Austrian, Polish, Czechoslovakian, Russian, or undetermined national origin. They included females between the ages of two and fifty-five, and males between two and sixty years of age. Paris's public transportation system, the Compagnie du Métropolitain, had reserved fifty buses for the roundup. Four hours after it began, the prefect of the Paris police was informed that many men had left their homes the previous day and that many policemen had found only women and young children at the address listed:[58] he therefore knew that the victims were for the most part women and children. As of 5:00 P.M. on the following day (July 17), the mass arrest had netted 3,031 men, 5,802 women, and 4,051 children.[59] The final tally of arrests established a few days later put the total number at 13,152 Jews.[60]

In addition to the ones previously mentioned, several categories had been slated for exemption: these included people carrying the authorization card from the UGIF (which had been given out on July 6;[61]); the bearers of an *Ausweis* (which had been provided to furriers working for the Germans); spouses, widows, and widowers of non-Jews; women on the verge of giving birth; women with children under two, the wives of prisoners of war, and Jews married to a person of a nationality other than those listed above. In practice, however, these categories were not really respected.

The heartrending situations surrounding these arrests have been described at length by eyewitnesses and many books on the subject.[62] Certain scenes stand out: pictures would probably better capture the heart of the drama suggested by images of Parisian buses, the cap of a French policeman assigned to this sad chore, the panic visible on a mother's face, a neighbor's helpful complicity with the victims and a concierge's denunciation (or the opposite), the goodwill or the brutality of a gendarme, the sympathy, the indignation, or the indifference on the part of bystanders.

For the victims of the roundup, such scenes were just the beginning of a long ordeal. Their first stops on this trail of tears were at the primary assembly centers: in some cases, it was at a police station, while in others a garage or a school. From there, single adults and couples without children were taken to Drancy; families went to the Vélodrome d'hiver (a covered sports arena).

The utter destitution of the 8,160 men, women, and children penned up for days in the Vélodrome d'hiver before being transferred to the camps in the département of Le Loiret sometime between July 19 and July 22 is beyond description: indeed, absolutely nothing had been done to prepare for their stay in this covered stadium.

And so they had to wait twenty-four hours before the National Relief agency provided some semblance of nourishment in the form of soup ladled out into the cupped hands of those detained—who had thought to bring any sort of receptacle? There were only two Jewish doctors and another from the Red Cross to take care of all the cases of diphtheria, scarlet fever, and measles, as well as all the other diseases that broke out. The only water outlet was a nozzle hooked up by firemen in a small courtyard. There were no toilet facilities and it was impossible to maintain any personal hygiene. A horrible stench intensifying with every hour, the loud murmur of voices incessantly drowned out by screams or names blaring out over the loudspeaker system, and the obligation for the detainees to stay on the bleachers made the stay in the Vélodrome d'hiver a living hell.[63] For some, the nightmare was to last for three days; for others, six. On July 22, the Vélodrome d'hiver was emptied of its last occupants and restored to its original purpose. In less than two months, Parisian cinemagoers were taking in scenes of famous matadors confronting raging bulls in the bullfights that had been put on in the stadium.[64]

"Not One Child Must Remain in France"

"The arrests of foreign Jews carried out on July 16 and 17 have been the subject of numerous commentaries in the public, most of which thought that these operations targeted French as well as foreign Jews," observed one report at the prefecture of the Paris police. "In general, these measures would have been fairly well accepted if they had only concerned adult foreigners. Many people, however, were shocked by the plight of the children, as word quickly got out that they had been separated from their parents."[65] Another report from the same source pointed out that the people of Paris had been troubled by scenes of families being torn apart, and added: "This separation of children from their parents is what has moved French masses the most and stirred up reactions triggering stern criticisms of the government and German Occupation forces."[66]

That indeed was the scene that had struck people's imaginations the most. Describing these "unbearable scenes," Jacques Biélinky had already noted on July 17 that "children had been separated from their parents, that suicides had taken place."[67] For the time being, some children had been taken in by the UGIF, which spread them out among existing or newly improvised children's homes, such as the shelter on Rue Lamarck. The UGIF also tried to find other children who had gotten lost: it even contacted the Amelot Committee and requested that the latter "immediately report children known to the Committee that may have been taken in by a private organization or by families."[68] And then there were some children that the employees of the UGIF had managed to get back during the mass arrests by arguing that they were French by declaration (as they had been born in France), an argument that rarely produced the desired effect. Finally, thanks to random chance or to the foresight of parents who had urged them to flee or to the complicity of a neighbor, there were some children that were now staying with a non-Jewish family with whom they had not previously been acquainted.

Some of these children had thus been saved, while others merely enjoyed a temporary reprieve from their ultimate fate. But because they had been separated from their parents, they were the ones that weighed the most heavily on the consciences of bystanders. Meanwhile, however, some four thousand Jewish children were sent to the camps in the département of Le Loiret, which had been for the most part emptied by the deportations that had occurred regularly throughout the month of June and up until July 17: most were still in the company of their parents at this point.[69] The National Relief agency was worried about what would become of them: it was already stated in a confidential memorandum dated July 24 that

> when [these] Jews have been taken to Drancy, they will be sorted out so that the parents can be sent to the East in sealed boxcars by groups of 50 after [having] been separated from their children. The issue of these children left behind in France will thus be raised in a very short time. These children, of whom there are probably 4,000, absolutely cannot be taken care of effectively by the Public Welfare Office.

At the same time, the report assured the latter office of the National Relief agency's assistance.[70] Jean Leguay, Bousquet's representative in the Occupied Zone, had already taken care of this "problem" on July 17, even without having been alerted by the National Relief agency: he had told the Germans that they should deport the children who had been arrested.

As had been the case at Drancy, at the Vélodrome d'hiver, and in the camps in the Southern Zone, the scene at Beaune-la-Rolande and Pithiviers was first of all one of total improvisation, and of an unpreparedness that provides a starkly painful contrast with the bureaucratic efficiency that had characterized the preparation of the various stages of the massive "Black Thursday" roundup. On July 19, 1942, the police intendant at Beaune-la-Rolande reported a whole host of problems to his superior, the regional prefect: checking in the internees had taken hours; boards were missing from some beds, while straw was lacking from others; food supplies were totally inadequate for feeding the internees, and there were neither plates nor cups. Nothing had been provided for the sick.[71] "Oh, mother!" wrote student social worker Marie-Louise Blondeau on July 29, 1942, as one who had taken care of the children housed in the infirmary of the camp at Pithiviers:

> The arrival took place amid unspeakable chaos. Such a heartrending scene, so many babies on the straw, totally alone and helpless! It was all we could do just to go into these ramshackle buildings. Totally devastated, the women tried to make a place for themselves amid all the confusion of children yelling and crying. Some women argued and pushed their way through, trying to grab everything they could get their hands on; others wept silently. . . . There were very small children only two and a half or three years old, who tragically kept stumbling and falling over the large limestone rocks in the surrounding field, with their tense, grim

> faces: as there was no one to help them up and comfort them, they merely went about their way. Some were alone, while others clung desperately to their mothers for fear of losing them. These were well-dressed little girls and boys from the 20th arrondissement of Paris, little sixteen-month-old angels and eight-year-old boys. They had come from the Vélodrome d'hiver, with panic-stricken eyes and drawn faces made to look older by the ordeal.[72]

The initial bedlam then gave way to the routine of camp life and its usual features: with an almost complete lack of activity, days were marked only by skimpy meals, painful isolation, and all the other details that scarcely differed from conditions in the other French camps.

This situation, however, did not last; the summit of horror had not yet been reached. The French had promised to supply a certain number of Jews to fill the deportation trains. Laval had stated his indifference to the plight of the children of those deported from the Occupied Zone. Their arrest and transfer to the camps in Le Loiret had paved the way for their deportation, and it was the representatives of the French police (Leguay, François, and Tulard) who proposed, during a joint meeting with the Germans on July 17, that they should be deported.[73] Never mind that both the authorization from Berlin as well as the arrest of Jews in the Unoccupied Zone were taking longer than expected; French officials were above all keen on respecting their commitments. On July 31 as on August 3, 5, and 7, mothers were brutally separated from their children and deported. The Vichy police chief's representative for the Occupied Zone, Jean Leguay, had spelled out his instructions to the regional prefect in Orléans in the clearest of terms:

> The children must not leave in the same trains as the parents; they are to be kept in a camp. . . . While awaiting the departure that will reunite them with their parents, they are to be left in the care of women among the mothers, nurses, and schoolteachers who are also to be deported. . . . According to information provided by the German authorities, trains for children have been scheduled to run beginning in the second part of August.[74]

Jean Leguay had thus set the stage for the wrenching scenes of separation that were to follow. Once the names of those to be deported on the next train were known, those detained first had to spend hours outside, then inside barbed-wire fences. They were subjected to a search carried out in three phases, first by camp authorities, then by the Police for Jewish Affairs, and finally by the German authorities. Down blankets were ripped open in hopes of discovering any money or jewels that might have been concealed in them. Afterward came the cries and screams of a separation that was to be forever.

On August 8, some 1,800 Jewish children remained at Pithiviers and about 1,500 at Beaune-la-Rolande.[75] Their parents had for the most part already been sent to Auschwitz, sometimes accompanied by their older siblings. Is there really any need to describe the utter destitution of these little ones, left almost completely on their own, undernourished, with little or no medical care, desperate, going from fits of crying to complete listlessness, and who were forgotten by everyone?

Totally forgotten? Not quite. Approval from Berlin had finally come through, and France could now arrange for their departure and thus take care of an embarrassing problem. Berlin's approval, however, carried with it a stipulation. "Under no circumstances [must] trains exclusively full of children be sent."[76] The Jewish children would therefore first be shipped from Pithiviers and Beaune-la-Rolande to Drancy in order to make it possible to put together deportation trains carrying both children and adults together. A first lot of children left Pithiviers on August 15. On August 19, it was the turn of a second group to leave from Beaune-la-Rolande. "The identification of very small children who had been separated from their parents was made possible by a metal identity tag, similar to French soldiers' dog tags, which was sewn to their clothing on the level of their chest,"[77] noted the register of "internee departures" kept by camp authorities. It was a ridiculously inadequate method of identification; the youngest children no longer even knew who they were. Other children were sent off on August 22 and 25.[78] By that time, the prefect of the département of Le Loiret was in a position to observe that there only remained "a few sick or untransportable children" in the two camps. All of them had been sent to Drancy, before heading down the road to Auschwitz.

Three Trains Per Week

The children had been preceded on their way by 4,992 unmarried individuals over the age of sixteen and childless married couples, who had been transferred directly to Drancy after a brief passage in one of the "primary assembly centers." Among them were 3,003 women.[79] Drancy had already undergone several phases of transition in its short history: the disorganization of the first few weeks, the releases occurring in November 1941, the period when it was used as a hostage reserve, and the beginning of the deportations. A new era was now under way, as the arrival of women and the acceleration of the deportations transformed the camp for Jews into a transit camp for those deported to the East.

Up until late March 1942, the sorting out of internees into different categories sustained a glimmer of hope for possible release. After that point, however, internees could only view any such numerical assessment with deep anxiety. When ninety internees from Compiègne arrived on April 3, the detainees at Drancy heard for the first time an expression that was to save a few of them: the "spouses of Aryan women."[80] A few days later, "those under the age of 25, those over the age of 55, those who were war veterans, fathers of four or more children, and foreign nationals from countries allied with Germany were all separated out,"[81] wrote Georges Kohn (who was to become the Jewish leader of the camp) in his log. On April 29, some 784 internees left Drancy, and those within the camp thought that this was the second deportation train headed for the East. This was indeed the case, but there was first a stop at Compiègne, where the deportees spent a few weeks before continuing on.[82] Another group left on June 22: this departure included all young men between the ages of eighteen and twenty-five as well as a few personalities selected by Dannecker during his visit to the camp.

In each room, the stairwell leader would read the names of those slated to leave from the list that had been prepared the day before by the office that kept track of the numbers of internees entering and leaving the camp. On the following day "would begin the familiar ritual": all persons to be deported would first go to the hairdresser to have their heads shaved, and then they would go to the search building, where they were subjected to a merciless, brutal, absurd, and humiliating search, after which they left the building "with their overcoat and sports jacket unbuttoned, pockets inside out, a shoe untied, clutching against their chest a bundle of clothes and underwear with an open tube of toothpaste leaking its contents out over the wax running out of its open tin."[83] They were then isolated from the rest of the internees in the departure stairwells ("dirtier and stinkier" than the other stairwells) and served slightly more generous meals. Each person to be deported was given something to eat for the trip and, finally, one last postcard on which to jot down a few words—their last—to be sent to loved ones. Then in the early morning hours, they departed for the unknown.

But the real revolution at Drancy began on July 2, 1942, when the internees were notified that they were going to have to move to the west wing of the camp in order to free up half the stairwells. From that point on, there were arrivals and departures of a different sort. Patients from the Rothschild hospital came to occupy one of the stairwells on July 3. On July 16, the first busloads of new internees began arriving at seven in the morning. The new detainees were put in the first eight stairwells, while four others were reserved for women. And it was in the women's quarters that the lack of privacy posed the most serious problems; there were in some instances ninety-five women per room.[84] At the same time, preparations for the departure of deportation trains were under way. The first train for Auschwitz left on July 19, and from then on until the end of September, such departures continued at the rate of three trains, each carrying a thousand people, every week.[85]

On August 7 arrived the first loads of Jewish detainees from the Southern Zone. These were from Gurs; other groups would follow. Then in mid-August came a large group of women who had been incarcerated at Les Tourelles. Even more striking was the arrival of the first group of children from the camps in Le Loiret on August 15:[86] they were filthy, covered with sores, cuts, and bruises, in most cases suffering from dysentery (which was only aggravated by Drancy's cabbage soup) and uniformly sad, so very sad. Some women who themselves were about to be deported the next day organized teams to take care of them, using whatever means they could find. Georges Kohn only recorded one single word in his notebook for August 16: "Pity." The children left a few days later as planned, after having their heads shaved and after having been subjected to a brutal, meticulous search. Mixed in with adults, they too left for an "unknown destination."

The concern for meeting basic everyday needs, though still overriding, was no longer the most important thing at Drancy. It was now the departure stairwells that haunted the minds of the internees; once the list of the next trainload had been prepared, it was there that those condemned to be deported were penned up. The categories of people to be deported were defined in meticulous detail. They were indeed so complicated that it was sometimes necessary to lay out the orders that had been given in the concrete visual form of a table.

Take for example the table used on September 9, 1942, bearing the signature of the chief inspector from the prefecture of the Paris police, Thibaudat: it tells us that women more than eight months pregnant were to be kept in the camp. However, if they were breastfeeding an infant or had a child under the age of two, they were to be deported. The legitimate spouses of non-Jews were not to be deported, but once they had become widows or widowers, they moved into a different category and were to be deported. Children under the age of sixteen whose parents were free were to be kept in the camp, but not those whose parents had been deported, even if only one parent had been deported while the other remained free. Children under the age of sixteen who were French citizens and whose parents were either deported or slated for deportation were to be deported, as were the elderly over the age of seventy, invalids belonging to so-called deportable categories, and blind persons who were accompanied. Even Turks, Romanians, and Hungarians whose cases were considered doubtful were to be deported.[87]

The slightest infraction of the rules exposed violators to the risk of being placed in another category. "Any internee found within camp confines without the insignia properly worn shall be punished by imprisonment and automatically included in the next group preparing for departure," the internees were informed on August 14, 1942.[88] And then there were the "reserves," made up of a group of Jews who were theoretically not to be deported, but were taken and put in deportation trains at the last minute if the trains were not "full."[89]

In addition to loads of Jews that had come from all over France, deportation trains were also filled by people who had been arrested on an individual basis: every evening, between fifteen and thirty people picked up in the greater Paris region were sent to Drancy.

Paris after the Vel d'Hiv Roundup

For those who wore the yellow star, nothing was the same in Paris. Granted, Denise Bloch did learn that she had passed her baccalaureate exam at the lycée Lakanal in Sceaux;[90] Henri Minczeles, then hospitalized for tuberculosis at Bichat, was informed by his friends that he had earned his diploma. But violent acts against the Jews had escalated in Paris. Young members of the French People's Party (PPF) were now participating in anti-Jewish action marked by a renewed activism. On

June 20, some of them had lashed out at a Jew sitting at a sidewalk table of the café Tout Va Bien on the Boulevard Saint-Denis. Thirty of these young PPF members had come to demonstrate on the corner of the Rue Saint-Séverin and the Boulevard Saint-Michel on the same evening, shouting: "Doriot for Premier" and "Send the Jews to the scaffolds."[91] They had fun extorting money from Jews and did not hesitate to use their fists against isolated Jews. At about 11:15 P.M. on July 20, several young men wearing the PPF uniform broke into the synagogue on Rue de la Victoire, where they spent the night vandalizing the sanctuary and profaning articles used for worship until 5:00 A.M. They took the caretaker of the synagogue to PPF headquarters, where, threatening him with a club, they forced him to give several addresses, including that of the chief rabbi. They also demanded that he return the next day with 100,000 francs.[92]

The PPF had set up shop in several former Jewish boutiques and held numerous meetings. It also sponsored screenings of *Le Juif Süss* on numerous occasions. In preparation for the PPF convention scheduled for October 1942, forays against the "Swing Kids" and Jews were planned as part of a whole series of provocations that even included unbolting the statues of the republic, removing plaques indicating the streets bearing English or American names, making inscriptions in Doriot's name, and organizing demonstrations in favor of the leader of their party.[93]

Except for a short time in the summer of 1940, antisemitic violence had until then been marginal, largely confined to the columns of newspapers. And while the violence that broke out during those October nights in 1941 occurred in a context of hatred concentrated against Jews, it nevertheless had seemed to be a foreign import. From May 1942 on, however, antisemitic articles proliferated in the press and grew increasingly virulent. Such writings were now accompanied by attacks on Jews in the streets of Paris.

There was a large disparity between the number of Jews that were supposed to be arrested and the number actually taken during the massive Vel d'hiv roundup. Accordingly, the police had received the order to "save the files on the people who had been momentarily absent during the first attempt to arrest them, in order that the arrest may be carried out at a later time."[94] But even this was not enough, and so the range of people to be deported was widened: Jews from Baltic countries along with Bulgarian, Dutch, and Yugoslavian Jews joined stateless Jews in this category on September 14, 1942. Romanian Jews followed on September 23; then on September 28, it was the turn of Jews from Belgium, Danzig, and Luxemburg; finally, on November 4 and 5, came the turn of Jews from Greece.[95] The object at this point was to fill the deportation trains as much as possible.

This excerpt from a report written in August 1942 gives an idea of the situation of the Jews who had managed to escape the mass arrests:

> Several thousand Jews are hiding in Paris at the present moment, in conditions that recall the situation of hunted animals. They cannot stay with the people who

> had given them asylum, because they do not want to expose them to the danger of reprisals. They cannot go home; their houses and apartments have been placed under police seals. They no longer have any way of making a living, and soon will have no way of getting food, for their ration tickets have been voided. Among all these cases of human misery, there are mothers with several children who wander about without ever sleeping in the same place twice; there are young girls who do not know where to go and who will soon have no choice but either to starve or to fall into the hands of the underworld.[96]

Apartments that remained unoccupied after entire families had been arrested had indeed been placed under police seal.[97] There were also cases in which one of the former occupants was on the run. For them, there was no coming back. But where could anyone find refuge, given the ordinance from the prefect of the Paris police dating from December 10, 1941 and requiring "any Jewish or non-Jewish persons putting up Jews in their homes" to declare so officially at the local police station within twenty-four hours?[98]

Throngs of people were pouring in at the Amelot Committee's headquarters and the offices of the UGIF: there were women who had lost their children, children who had lost their parents, people who came to find out what was happening, and others who offered to lodge people in their homes. Thanks to its vigorous intervention, the division of the UGIF handling relations with the German authorities managed to obtain the release of 817 people between the months of June and December 1942:[99] these were war widows, wives of prisoners of war, and persons working for the Germans, along with their families and 192 children who were French by birth. However, not all of the latter category were spared. And it was sometimes already too late when a release was secured. Such was the case of Schulman, the man who managed a cafeteria on Rue Richer: when his release was finally granted, he had already been deported.[100]

Jews were stricken with a new type of fear that, in the words of one witness, had driven "an uninterrupted stream of women, children, and sick people" over the demarcation line: many had walked from 25 to 75 kilometers.[101] They were seen pouring in the Lyon offices of the Federation of Jewish Societies (FSJF) already on July 19, "exhausted, utterly destitute, without word from loved ones that they had abandoned either in Paris or at the demarcation line."[102]

Fleeing across the Demarcation Line

The exodus had begun well before. It had in fact been a continuous movement that had stepped up considerably in the summer of 1941, after the mass arrests of August and the opening of the camp at Drancy. The fall 1941 census, the attacks on synagogues,[103] and a wave of rumors announcing even then that Jews in France would have to wear a distinctive sign had accelerated the flight of Jews from the Occupied

Zone. French authorities at Vichy had become concerned. The number of infractions recorded by gendarmes in villages along the demarcation line rose dramatically. Those fleeing the Occupied Zone all stated that they had sufficient funds, and they could as a general rule give the address of someone who was expecting them (which in many cases was that of a family member who had gone ahead). All had fled "because of German persecution."[104] On November 27, 1941, a notice published by newspapers in the Southern Zone informed the public that "prefects had been given the strictest of instructions to tighten the surveillance of the demarcation line" and to proceed with the "administrative internment" of foreign Israelites who risked crossing over clandestinely.[105]

The secretary-general for the police reminded prefects in the Occupied Zone in mid-December 1941 that it was their duty to keep foreign Jews from crossing over the demarcation line into the Unoccupied Zone.[106] A "secret" memorandum dated January 26, 1942 spelled out the instructions that had been given in the Unoccupied Zone. Stateless Jews remained subject to either internment in a camp or enrollment in a Foreign Worker Unit (GTE): whatever exceptions might be made could under no circumstances apply to Israelites having entered France after 1936. Only those who had sufficient funds and a current visa could be sent to the center in La Bourboule.[107] On August 6, 1942, another memorandum stipulated that all foreign Jews targeted by the measures being applied in the Unoccupied Zone were to be interned.[108] For many, this signaled the beginning of a clandestine life. But there were many French Jews who complied with the regulations prevailing in the Southern Zone as soon as they arrived there: although it is not possible to provide any statistical data, belated census declarations reported by various prefects sometimes make it possible to follow such legalistic behavior.[109]

There was another flurry of departures after the imposition of the yellow star.[110] The massive police roundups carried out in mid-July changed the nature of the movement, as the departures that had formerly been rather orderly and well prepared suddenly turned into a mad scramble to flee. A synthesis of the letters intercepted and read speaks of a "more or less clandestine exodus."[111]

One such flight began right in Paris. Madeleine, then a child, remembers that her mother had—in the middle of the summer—dressed her in a heavy coat, two jackets, two dresses, and a skirt, and instructed her to keep her coat tightly closed and covered with a shawl in order to conceal the star. She was thus to walk ahead and most important of all, not turn around under any circumstances, regardless of what may happen to her mother behind her.[112]

As a general rule, Jewish organizations were working to facilitate these departures. The leaders of the Amelot Committee in Paris spared no effort to make such crossovers possible. At the UGIF, individuals were encouraged by word of mouth to leave. With the help of resources from the Southern Zone, a secret fund had been created in March 1942 in order to help people get over the demarcation line (among other things).[113] When the yellow star loomed on the horizon of the Occupied Zone, the Central Consistory requested the Vichy government to authorize Jews who were being hunted down to take refuge in the Southern Zone. Helbronner's personal secretary, Robert Kiefe, officially presented this request to Jean Jardin, Laval's cabinet head, on June 3, 1942.[114] Indeed, Jardin had proven to be "very kind, very confidential, very friendly, not at all self-important" and had himself suggested this possibility.[115] On June 22, the Central Consistory deliberated on the matter and submitted its written request two days later.[116]

But on that very same day of June 24, Kiefe learned that although not opposed to the idea, Laval preferred that Jacques Benoist-Meschin take care of the matter. When the Central Consistory met again on July 27, 1942, the issue of the yellow star had been largely superseded by more urgent matters. Discussions were now dominated by the plight of the children whose mothers had been deported,[117] and Helbronner informed the other members of the Consistory that he had asked Laval to reunite the children under the age of fifteen with their mothers. But he had also reiterated his proposal to arrange "the transferal of French Israelites who so [desired] into the Unoccupied Zone." Helbronner had requested that "a certain time be allowed for this transferal in order to gain the assistance of the prefects and to avoid a rush of refugees that might create an increase of antisemitism." He expected that between 20,000 and 25,000 Jews would be involved. President Helbronner obviously thought that he could do nothing for foreign Jews, and came back to a distinction that Kiefe had not mentioned. His proposals and the figures he cites show, however, to what extent he was misleading himself in his assessment of the situation of the French Israelites. On August 14, Robert Kiefe was told in no uncertain terms that transferring Jews threatened in the Northern Zone to the Southern Zone was now out of the question. Kiefe nevertheless continued to propose this idea, and in November 1942, Jardin once more flatly refused.[118]

People at the Federation (FSJF) also strove to intervene at the highest level of the French government, and did obtain certain guarantees. One of Marc Jarblum's envoys was told by a certain Monsieur X: "We will look the other way when Jewish fugitives cross over the demarcation line, but the various decrees and ordinances of the law concerning foreign Jews (concentration camps, work camps, and house arrest) will be applied."[119]

Meanwhile, arrangements were being made to take in those who crossed over into the Unoccupied Zone. The OSE took charge of the children, the Scouts persuaded the local authorities in Moissac to spare the refugees from being interned in a camp, and the Christian Friendship (Amitié chrétienne) organization lodged those who arrived in Lyon. After having provided refugees arriving in Limoges with a small sum of money and an address where they would be welcome, activists with the Federation tried to scatter them throughout less frequented départements such as La Creuse or L'Aveyron.[120] The Federation had also appointed a lawyer to represent those prosecuted for various infractions of the anti-Jewish laws. Everyone strove to convince the authorities that Jewish organizations would take care of these poor fugitives.[121] One month after the Vel d'hiv roundup, just over one thousand Jews, having crossed the demarcation line, had registered for some form of aid in the offices of the UGIF in the Southern Zone.[122] Such was the case of one secondary school teacher who had been dismissed in December 1940 by virtue of the Jewish Statute and who had been giving private lessons in Blois in order to get by: the imposition of the yellow star incited him to cross over clandestinely into the Unoccupied Zone. In August 1942, he appealed to the UGIF to help him find work.[123]

Smugglers were having a field day: the price of a crossover had suddenly increased from twelve- to twentyfold. Those who could not afford the price were out of luck, especially as the rare lodgings available along the demarcation line were being rented at prohibitive prices. A thousand refugees were thus stopped in the "border" villages of Montbron, Marton, Confolans, Chassneuil, and Chabanais. At the Vierzon guard post, the Germans called for more personnel to handle the thousands of Jews trying to sneak over the line.[124] On August 6, some 440 Jews who had been arrested while trying to flee were sent from Poitiers to Drancy.[125] One month later, just over four hundred Jews, having tried to flee the Northern Zone, were placed in the transit camp at La Lande before winding up at Drancy.[126] Some families were torn apart, finding themselves on opposite sides of the demarcation line. And those who had made it to the Southern Zone were just at the beginning of a long trek, for no authorization to allow them to take up residence there had been issued.[127] For those who were French, however, the problem could be taken care of simply by filling out a census form at the gendarmerie.[128]

But such was not the case for foreigners. Some of the men between the ages of eighteen and fifty-five would be sent first to the regrouping camp at Saillat and then on to a Foreign Worker Unit. Others would transit at Egletons before being deported. Another group was sent to the Rivesaltes camp on July 28, after having been stripped of their papers and food ration tickets.[129] They did not stay there very long, and neither did those who followed a similar path to Rivesaltes or Gurs, as unoccupied France was also preparing to deliver its own lot of Jews to be deported. On July 29, prefects for regions along the demarcation line were instructed to have "deportable" foreign Israelites either turned away or interned at Gurs.[130]

When Jews fled toward the south, they thought that French sovereignty over that part of the country would protect them from being interned or deported. They hardly imagined that "such things could happen in the Unoccupied Zone."[131] However, when Raymond-Raoul Lambert and Raphaël Spanien went to Vichy to protest the sudden cancellation of all the emigration visas that had been obtained with such great effort on July 28, they learned from a highly reliable source that the French government was getting ready to hand over to the Germans some 10,000 foreign Jews living in the Southern Zone: these deportees were to be sent to Silesia or perhaps even farther east.[132]

ROUNDUPS AND DEPORTATIONS IN THE "FREE ZONE"

From One Zone to the Other

In fact, there had been nothing but rumors of deportation in the "Free [Unoccupied] Zone" since mid-July. While visiting Vichy on July 23 and 24, Chief Rabbi Hirschler understood that "something was under way," but what exactly? In any case, Jews in the Southern Zone lent a close ear to rumors coming from the Occupied Zone. At times, they had been reassured. Some people had known about Admiral Darlan's letter of January 21, 1942, in which he voiced his disapproval of the proposed imposition of the yellow star for Jews in the Southern Zone and his feeling that the measures taken against the Jews up until this time had been rigorous enough. Raymond-Raoul Lambert quotes the entire document in the February 11 entry in his *Journal* and calls it a "formidable document that proves that Pétain is now resisting the Kraut's demands concerning the Jews."[133] A letter intercepted and read by Vichy's central commission on postal control spoke of "Admiral Darlan's personal assurance that no new anti-Jewish measures were being planned and that there would certainly be a modification of the new legislation imposed by the Germans in the future."[134]

Moreover, the leaders of the Consistory had noticed rising tension between Xavier Vallat and Theodor Dannecker, and even urged André Baur to appeal to Vichy for the general commissioner for Jewish affairs to be maintained in his position. And, although he chose his own means to do so, Baur complied with the request. Jewish leaders in Paris feared at the time that, if the General Commission on Jewish Affairs were eliminated and the Southern Zone placed under the same set of laws as the Northern Zone, things would get even worse for Jews in the Occupied Zone. Marcel Stora thought that he had succeeded in barring Darquier from taking over from Vallat as general commissioner.[135]

But even before antisemitic policy took a new turn in the summer, Laval returned to power, Darquier was appointed to replace Vallat, and a whole new source of trouble began to worry the leaders of the Consistory. They learned that the French government had just adopted specific rules for applying the law of October 1940, which made the French identification card unique and mandatory: it was planned that the "files and identity cards [of the Jews should] in addition bear the word "Jew" marked diagonally by a red ink stamp with one centimeter-high letters."[136] From then on, this subject was regularly broached by Robert Kiefe in his discussions with various Vichy officials. The concern was well founded, but still premature; for the stamping of Jewish identity papers was linked to the large issue of requiring all French citizens to carry one unique identity document, and the implementation of such a measure was proving problematical. The "problem" would finally be resolved by a law dating from December 1942 concerning specifically Jews, both French and foreign.

There was a world of difference between the two zones. On one side deportations were beginning, while on the other officials were working out specific means of segregation. The difference in the pace and severity of the persecution had two opposite effects on people's assessment of things to come in the Unoccupied Zone. On the one hand, one development seemed to prefigure another: rumors were fueled by bits of information from the Northern Zone making their way across the demarcation line and giving evidence of what might happen in the South. On the other hand, the disparity between people's immediate experience and the horrors described in occupied Paris made these same rumors seem less believable. Finally, a large number of measures coming in rapid succession required constant attention.

While Jews in the north were preoccupied by the yellow star, those in Clermont-Ferrand were being told in no uncertain terms that they were to be expelled from the four départements in the region. This was mainly the initiative of the prefect of Le Puy-de-Dôme, who had been trying to have such a measure imposed since August 1941.[137] "This is the first time that one category of French people finds itself collectively targeted by an administrative measure that restricts their right to stay in the country just because of their religion,"[138] wrote Consistory president Helbronner to Admiral Platon in a letter of protest sent on June 10, 1942. But neither the letter nor a direct appeal to Laval managed to accomplish anything more than to postpone the application of the decision from June 15 to June 20 and to exempt Jews from the Alsace-Lorraine region.

Just when those who had escaped the Vel d'hiv roundup began arriving at the demarcation line, the *Journal officiel* announced a new law that was adopted on July 15, 1942: the measure excluded Jews from the Chantiers de Jeunesse training camps, which were compulsory for all other French young people.[139] This exclusion was due to the initiative of the general commissioner of the Chantiers de Jeunesse, General de La Porte du Theil, and of the secretary of state for national education and youth, Jérôme Carcopino. "Israelites are unresponsive to the moral education actively pursued in the camps," asserted de La Porte du Theil; dispensing them from such training "will put one more barrier between them and government offices," Carcopino suggested. "The problem," they added, "is particularly acute in North Africa, where Jews had to be brought together in homogenous groups because of widespread antisemitism" and "the opposition of the races." The General Commission on Jewish Affairs thus prepared the project, which had received the unanimous approval of all the government ministers consulted.[140] The Central Consistory once again lodged its protest. However, this protest proved to be just as ineffective as its previous ones, including the one they had already voiced "against persecutions whose magnitude and cruelty have reached a degree of barbarity rarely seen before in the history of mankind," after hearing what had transpired in Paris in mid-July.[141]

Nevertheless, Consistory leaders refused to believe growing rumors that foreign Jews in the Southern Zone were about to be handed over to the Germans. On July 10, 1942, Jardin did indeed confirm that the Germans had called for ten thousand

German and stateless Jews to be delivered to them from the Unoccupied Zone, but, he indicated to Robert Kiefe, the French government had not complied.[142] On the same day, Kiefe had encountered the indignant reaction of General Campet: "How could you believe for one instant that the French government could hand over people from the Unoccupied Zone?"

But everything had long been decided since July 4, 1942. On the very day when Jardin and Campet were expressing their outrage over rumors about Vichy's intentions, Laval was putting the number of Jews that he was quite willing to send back to the Germans as high as fifty thousand.[143] On July 17, all visas previously granted to Jews now deportable were canceled. Between July 11 and July 23, several officials inspected the camps in the Southern Zone: first Dannecker, accompanied by his assistant and the chief of police for Jewish affairs, and then one of the assistants of the director of national police. On August 4, regional prefects for the Unoccupied Zone received strictly confidential instructions: the secretary-general for the police informed them that "Russian refugees and Israelites from Germany, Austria, Czechoslovakia, Poland, Estonia, Lithuania, Latvia, Danzig, the Saar Basin, and the Soviet Union having entered France after January 1, 1936" were to be transferred to the Occupied Zone.[144]

Since the end of July, when Jewish leaders found out what was being concocted (Raymond-Raoul Lambert had given the alert), they had repeatedly contacted Vichy officials in attempts to exempt as many categories of Jews as possible from deportation. Delegations from several social aid organizations combined, from individual groups (the YMCA and the Quakers), and from the UGIF all tried to appeal to Laval or Pétain or one of their close associates. But soon this diplomatic "activity" gave way to concrete efforts to aid future victims, as activists with the aid organizations abandoned the halls of Pétain's residence in Vichy to go work onsite in the internment camps, with the Foreign Worker Units, and in the train stations used for the transit of deportees.

Interned Jews Are Handed Over

Police operations were carried out in four phases between August 6 and September 15. The first passengers on the four wretched deportation trains headed for Drancy were 3,456 internees from other camps.[145] On August 24, another train left for the Occupied Zone carrying 913 foreign Jewish workers taken from eighteen different Foreign Worker Units and 360 internees from Gurs, Récébédou, and Noé.[146] Then came the turn for 5,885 Jews who had been arrested during the massive police roundups conducted all over the Southern Zone beginning on August 26:[147] they were sent to Drancy beginning on August 29. Finally, those who had managed to escape the mass arrests up until then but were finally taken either in their homes, at the demarcation line, or at the Spanish and Swiss borders were taken to their sinister destination after September 4.[148] It only took a few weeks for the Vichy government to fulfill its commitments to the Germans: it had in fact even exceeded the number of ten thousand Jews that had been fixed for the Unoccupied Zone.[149]

Surveillance was stepped up in all camps, and visits were eliminated beginning on August 1.[150] Rabbi Kapel suddenly found himself barred from entering the camps in the Toulouse region. Regroupings began in the Marseilles region: already on August 3, women and children who had previously been in one of the three hotels adjacent to the camp or one of the hotels in town were brought to the camp at Les Milles along with workers who had been assigned to one of the neighboring communities.[151]

Internees in the Rivesaltes camp were subjected to incessant roll calls after August 3. "I see nothing but enormous, desperate eyes," noted one nurse with the Swiss Relief in her diary for August 8, 1942.[152] The separate buildings housing those to be deported was surrounded by a triple row of barbed wire. The same nurse then described the departure:

> The cries and moans of those tormented people are still ringing in the air. I can see them coming out of their housing units in long lines, panting under the weight of their personal effects. The guards are right beside them. They have to line up for roll call and wait for hours out in a field under the full sun. Then trucks arrive and take them away to the railroad tracks. They climb out of the trucks between two rows of guards and climb into cattlecars, some of them hesitant, others listless, a few defiant, with their heads high. This lasts for hours, until finally they have all been packed into the train cars that are stifling. . . . Two guards have been placed in front of each opening. I observe the faces. Now not even despair can be seen on these aged, worn down, dreary faces.[153]

The first train left Gurs for Chalon-sur-Saône on August 6. There was no problem, the prefect for the Basses-Pyrénées was pleased to say in his report to the secretary-general for the police. The internees thought they were being transferred to another camp in the Unoccupied Zone, he added.[154] That is how he described the fate of 1,003 men and women between the ages of eighteen and eighty-six, loaded into thirty-three freight cars with straw spread out over the floor and with some thirty people per car.[155] Two days later, the situation had become more tense. People destined to leave on the second train on August 8 had gotten wind of certain reports from foreign radio stations. Out of the 600 internees slated for deportation, there were 42 defections: among them, twenty-seven had hidden in various camp buildings, while six had tried to commit suicide. But other internees were substituted both for them and for those whom the Quakers and the rabbis had managed to remove from the list of deportees.[156] The law of compensations came into play; the numbers had to be made good.

The UGIF, the chaplains' office, the Christian and other aid organizations had all adopted one common strategy: "organizing as quickly as possible the defense of poor, miserable people against easily occurring errors and possible excesses on the part of certain authorities."[157] Their first concern was thus to remain present in the camps and improve the deportees' conditions of departure as much as possible by providing them with food (fresh fruit and vegetables, or raisins, cookies, and fruit pastes) and a little money. But they soon learned that the Germans were confiscating everything at the demarcation line, and tended to discontinue the money. They also placed jugs of water and buckets for toilet needs in the freight cars, and came up with as many pretexts as they could to remove the maximum number of people from the deportation lists.

But in this first phase of the transfer operation, when things were done on a makeshift basis, those who were attempting to provide aid often had to remain outside and watch the departure of the poor souls who had just spent so many long months in the hell of the camps. They thus saw "a wretched herd of people being packed into cattle cars that were sometimes locked and sealed."[158] For security reasons, they had been forced to stay outside of the camp confines. This was not the case at Les Milles, however. Nevertheless, even if "it was agreed that the chaplain could accompany his people to the end, should not the aid organizations withdraw from the scene when these measures begin to be really put into execution, in order not to give the appearance of being associated with them in some way?" wondered Rabbi Salzer as he described the deportations at Les Milles. But in spite of their decision to withdraw, the aid organizations stayed until the very last moment, for that is what the deportees had said they wanted. How could aid activists stop handing out the care packages that had been hastily put together or refuse to relay the messages that had been feverishly written by people both inside and outside the camps?[159]

During the first round of deportations from the Southern Zone from August 5 to August 10, 1942, it was possible to entrust the children to the aid organizations, in keeping with ministerial rulings.[160] At Les Milles, the entire day of August 8 was spent persuading families that they should let their children be separated from them. On August 10, seventy children between the ages of five and eighteen left for the Hôtel Bompart: they would be placed in the care of the OSE.[161] One can imagine the heartbreak of the mothers who decided to let their children go. "What a scene under the burning sun! The fathers and mothers must be restrained when the buses [full of children] leave the courtyard. Such cries and tears, such gestures by the poor fathers who caress the face of their son or daughter as if to conserve its imprint in their fingertips before they are finally deported."[162] One can imagine the gems of disingenuousness aid workers had to resort to in order to convince parents of the necessity of this separation without reducing them to despair. Sometimes they made the absurd promise that ties would be maintained between parents who were deported and children who stayed in France. Nevertheless, the results were telling: in the first four deportation trains leaving for Drancy, there were only eleven children.[163]

On August 9, Rabbi Hirschler learned from Gilbert Lesage that camp internees were not the only ones targeted, and that a much larger operation was under way. Hirschler thus found out about the ministerial memorandum calling for the internment and deportation of fugitives in the Occupied Zone. Lesage suggested appointing a representative to the selection commissions at each of the regrouping centers: this would make it possible to apply the exemptions authorized by the law. Lesage also suggested preparing counterlists of deportees to put forward in place of those drawn up by the prefectorates. Hirschler accepted the first idea, but rejected the second, and his position was confirmed at the chaplains' meeting on August 17.

He did not yet know what the various steps of these planned regroupings and mass arrests would be, and where it would be necessary to have a representative present. Each of his inquiries about these subjects with public officials was met with vague replies. The time for the second phase of deportations from the Southern Zone had come. Now it was the turn of those placed in the Foreign Worker Units. At the same time, in his haste to meet the quotas, René Bousquet expanded the categories of those to be deported by adding "a new contingent belonging to the same nationalities [which would] include all those having entered France after January 1, 1933."[164] This time men made up the majority of those deported, men who often left without having said goodbye to their wives and children from whom they had already been separated for many long months. Certain camp commanders, such as those at Miramas and Salin-de-Giraud, gave warning to the internees, who immediately scattered themselves in all directions. Some camp barracks, such as those at Casseneuil, had barely been emptied of their residents when they were used to lodge entire families: these people had just recently been living under house arrest in neighboring villages, and now they were victims of a vast roundup being carried out all over the Unoccupied Zone.[165]

Picking Up and Grouping

The organization of the "operations of picking up and grouping [foreign] Israelites together in large concentrations" planned for August 26 was indeed under way, as authorities were looking all over the Unoccupied Zone for places where Jews could be grouped together and detained between the time of their arrest and their transfer to the Occupied Zone. Special attention was given to the questions of security and the proximity of rail lines. The necessity of bringing large groups of women and children together in these places where nothing had been planned for their stay was indeed cause for concern, but the most important thing was to keep them under close guard. On August 6, André-Jean Faure had given instructions for the Rivesaltes camp to prepare to take in from six thousand to seven thousand internees. Faure had learned from a survey that there were insufficient beds: many detainees would therefore have to sleep on straw spread out over the floor. They would be grouped into two housing units ringed by guards. Another group of sentinels was to be placed between the barracks and the walkways. A group of 120 young people from the Chantiers de Jeunesse had been requisitioned to put up a barbed-wire fence around the two housing units as quickly as possible, in any case before August 20. Finally, a watchtower brought in from Barcarès was to be put in the next few days.[166]

Handling the huge influx of detainees to be transferred and deported was no problem for the Marseilles region: the camp at Les Milles was "putting up" 860 people at the time and could take in two thousand more internees, according to the report sent in by the local police intendant on August 2, 1942.[167] The intendant nevertheless pointed out that it would be a good thing for the transfer of internees to be carried out early in the day in order to comply with the administrative formalities connected with their arrival, as the maximum number of people that could be checked in each day was from 100 to 120 men or 80 to 100 women. Some six hundred German Israelites from the Clermont-Ferrand region could be housed in the camp at Montluçon from August 25 to September 10.[168] As for the département of La Dordogne, "the site selected was a convent in Terrasson that could contain a large number of Israelites and that was easy to keep under guard."[169] And in order to "concentrate" eight hundred Jews together in the Limoges region, the camp at Nexon was promptly emptied of its 215 internees, who were transferred elsewhere.[170]

Finding places to group together such large numbers of Jews in the Lyon region, however, was no simple matter. The authorization to use an abandoned military facility, the Fort-du-Paillet, along with the guarded residential facility at Fort-Barraux finally came down from the prefectoral office of police administration in Lyon on August 18. However, it was necessary to lodge women and children together, even though fort rules prohibited the practice.[171] It was planned to use other sites as well, including the Auvare barracks in Nice and space for one thousand more internees at Gurs. But even that was inadequate and the number of trains carrying Jews to the Occupied Zone had to be increased in order to avoid a bottleneck.

Throughout the evening and night of August 25, and at the crack of dawn on August 26, French policemen came knocking on the doors of Jewish families in the south. The policemen bore lists of people to be arrested. It was the repetition of a scenario already sadly familiar to Jews in the Occupied Zone. On January 2, 1942, Vichy had ordered a census of foreign Jews who had entered France after January 1, 1936: data collected from that census was used to draw up the lists of people to be taken away. The same scene repeated itself in both towns and villages, but with variations that sometimes made all the difference. In Rennes-les-Bains, in the département of L'Aude, the police displayed marked brutality, and in certain locations in the département of L'Aveyron, victims of the mass arrest were not even given enough time to gather a few personal effects before being taken away. And in Pouzolles in the département of L'Hérault, some homes were plundered.[172] In Grenoble, police followed up on residential raids with arrests carried out in the city's tramway.[173] In Nice, arrests continued relentlessly until August 30. Some Jews were apprehended on the beach in their swimming suits.[174] In Marseilles, police carried out identity checks on buses, on tramways, in train stations, and at entrances to all neighboring communities. "Police asked to see papers. Foreigners were also asked what their religion was."[175] The train from Pau to Spain came under particularly heavy surveillance. Abbot Glasberg's Le Lastic center in Rosans (in the département of Les Hautes-Alpes) fell victim to the zeal of a government employee in Gap and was emptied of its residents.[176] In the Clermont-Ferrand area, Jews were picked up mainly in surrounding communities, as they had already been driven out of the city itself.[177] In Montauban, the vast majority of Jews targeted by the roundup had been forewarned, and authorities were more lenient than elsewhere.[178]

The Screening Commissions

The chaplains and activists with the aid programs (including the Jewish groups incorporated into the UGIF and the non-Jewish aid groups) were onsite in the various regrouping centers right after the roundups, at least in those places where they were allowed. In the Pré-la-Reine camp near Clermont-Ferrand, in Nice, and elsewhere, they were forbidden to have any contact with the victims of the roundups. They were sometimes successful in pressuring authorities to remove this restriction, but not always. Where they were allowed to be present, they sat on screening commissions and tried to remove a maximum number of Jews from the lists of those to be deported, using the possibilities afforded by the various exemptions to their greatest possible advantage. They prepared individual case files, and assisted camp internees first and then victims of the mass roundups in bringing together the documents that might save detainees from deportation.

The chaplains and aid workers put forth proposals, argued insistently, and pleaded. But it was the police intendant representing the prefect who had the final word. Granted, more than 1,400 people arrested during the August 26 roundups were spared thanks to these screening efforts.[179] But, when all else had failed, the aid organizations also devoted much effort to alleviating the suffering of those to be deported by taking charge of communications with the outside world, providing the moral support requested, and especially by improving the material conditions first of their wait and then of their long, sad journey.

While these latter activities were strictly limited to handling victims' distress, those who participated in the screening commissions often went beyond relief work and ventured out beyond the boundaries of strict legality. The administration's own contradictions made this possible. One government memorandum followed on the heels of another, rectifying the errors of previous memoranda and widening the category of those to be deported: Jews having immigrated to France after 1936 were thus joined by those who had been in France since 1933. A first list of eleven exemptions sent to regional prefects on August 4 was amended on August 18 by a telegram from René Bousquet: only six exemptions subsequently remained,[180] and they were much more narrowly defined. The exemption for parents of children under the age of five became the exemption for parents of children under the age of two. It was no longer enough to be pregnant, it was now necessary for the pregnancy to be visible to escape being put in the deportation train, and it was now the police intendant who decided, not the doctor. War veterans and army volunteers had (at least on paper) been protected for a time, but now this status lost all its value. There were 782 such individuals—in other words, too many—and Vichy did not have "people on hand" to deliver to the Germans.[181] To escape deportation, it was henceforth necessary to have been wounded, decorated, or cited for bravery. Such distinguished military service could even lead to one's release, that is, at least until Vichy's order suspending all such releases. Those who were "merely" war veterans were thus kept in camp, and then deported.[182]

The fate reserved for children changed completely. They had at first been spared if they were unaccompanied and under the age of eighteen, but they were later included among the deportees loaded into trains. Moreover, during the first phase of the roundup and deportation process in the Southern Zone, the parents had had the possibility of leaving their children with an aid organization in order to keep them from being deported. Bousquet's infamous telegram on August 18, however, eliminated that option.

In the rush and confusion of bringing such large numbers of Jews together, and because of all the contradictory directives being issued, the categories of Jews to be exempted from deportation were sometimes blurred, creating loopholes that aid organizations were able to use to their advantage. There were two possible strategies: the first consisted of using strictly legal technicalities to save people from deportation, while the second involved going beyond the legal loopholes to work outside the law in some cases. Many aid workers tried to bend the rules in desperate attempts to save someone from being put in the cattle cars. They tried anything that might work: they would fudge the age of an adolescent, make false documents that could allow some individuals to be exempted, disguise a girl as a nurse or a boy as a Scout in order to get them out of a camp, hide Jews slated for departure in some corner and then in an "official" vehicle, or supply some drug that would allow someone to fake illness. Aid workers also tried to appeal to various officials, some of whom had special concern for war veterans, while other officials would look into the cases of those carrying an emigration visa. And although they were not spared, the "baptized" received special attention from priests and pastors.

In addition, every aid organization did what it could to shelter its own workers, including assistant chaplains and UGIF employees, from deportation. There had nevertheless been a unanimous agreement not to accept the Office of Social Services for Foreigners' (SSE) proposal to prepare counterlists whose "purpose would be to remove a certain number of Jews that 'might appear worthy' from the lists drawn up by authorities at the prefectorate, except in cases where such lists were used to avoid the deportation of a surplus."[183] Throughout this month of August 1942, however, French authorities were not dealing with any "surplus." They were instead seeking to increase the number of deportable Jews in order to meet the quotas demanded by the Germans. And when some Jews were removed from the lot to be deported, others usually took their place.

Beginning on August 29, the deportation trains leaving the Unoccupied Zone were different from previous ones. The people sent to Drancy came from all over: from Limoges or Montpellier, Lyon or Marseilles, Grenoble or Nice, Montauban or from one of the towns where they had been placed under house arrest. All, however, had been suddenly deprived of their freedom. That is probably one reason why there were so many escapes and suicides, many more than had occurred among the camp internees and the groups of Foreign Workers that had gone before. And it was for similar reasons that, out of all the camps, Les Milles had registered the highest number of escapes and suicides; Les Milles had not been completely sealed off from the outside world. It was at Les Milles during the single day of August 12, 1942, that there were ten attempted suicides[184] and about eighty escapes during the first round of deportations.[185] There were moreover more than five hundred children in these deportation trains.[186]

Saving the Children from Deportation

All the leaders of the aid organizations had agreed to do everything they could to keep children from being deported.[187] Since the Vichy government had decided that the children should go with their parents, the matter was urgent. "So that it could not be said that children were separated from their mothers (an inhumane measure that had stirred public emotion in the Occupied Zone), all those who had been taken out of the camps and placed in the care of either private families or aid organizations [and whose parents had either been deported or slated for deportation] were sought out and picked up."[188] Seventy children were thus snatched from the OSE's homes in the département of La Haute-Vienne.[189]

The only exception was for the thirty-eight children who had already been placed in the hands of the Swiss Red Cross and who were preparing to leave for the summer camp at Montaigu-Plantaurel.[190] There was a certain amount of tolerance in Nice, where twenty-one children were saved from deportation.[191] Thirty other children whose parents had either been slated for deportation or had disappeared were provisionally allowed to leave for summer camps.[192] Chief Rabbi Schilli reported that some fifty people, mainly children, had been released by order of the prefect for the Pyrénées-Orientales region; these children were turned over to the OSE.[193] But those were exceptions. Using legal channels and trying to fudge the rules in a few cases were now totally inadequate to deal with the situation. The signal to change strategy came from the greater Lyon area.

It was in some abandoned military barracks in Vénissieux, where Jews from the region were waiting to be deported, that a crucial event in the saga of efforts to save the children occurred. Working on the screening commissions[194] were, among others,

Gilbert Lesage for the Office of Social Services for Foreigners (SSE), but also Joseph Weill, Hélène Lévy and Charles Ledermann for the OSE, Georges Garel and Claude Gutman for the Israelite Scouts of France (EIF), and Abbot Glasberg[195] and Jean-Marie Soutou representing the Christian Friendship organization. Under the official sponsorship of Cardinal Gerlier and Pastor Boegner, the latter group had specialized in aiding refugees. As was done at Les Milles on August 8, the members of the screening commission referred to the first set of ministerial directives and used every means of persuasion they could to get parents slated for deportation to sign papers relinquishing their parental rights in order that their children might remain in France. The members of the screening commission had to promise them that their children would not be left in the hands of the police to be deported separately (the parents knew about the children from Paris who had been deported), but placed solely in private centers for children or put in the care of families, and in any case, out of the state's reach. They also promised that there would be no attempt to proselytize them.

While all this work was going on, new instructions mandating the deportation of children had arrived at the selection center. However, these orders had been spirited away by Jean-Marie Soutou and Abbot Glasberg. The children released thanks to all these efforts were first taken to an Israelite Scouts of France facility in three police trucks that the Vénissieux camp authorities had made available to the Christian Friendship organization. From there they were promptly taken to a variety of scattered locations. One witness puts the number of these children as 85, another as 90, and other sources cite 108.[196]

When Prefect Angeli became aware of the hoax, it was too late. Two days after the deportation train had left, the police intendant came and demanded that the children be quickly grouped together and loaded into a train coming from Nice and destined for the Occupied Zone. He found, however, that they were no longer at the Scouts' facility: activists with the Christian Fellowship organization who, in cooperation with the Children's Relief Organization and the Israelite Scouts of France, had sent the children to a variety of different places scattered all over, refused to turn them back over to him. Had it agreed to do so, "Christian Friendship's efforts with the parents would only have resulted in allowing children to be deported separately, and its leaders would have been responsible."[197] Efforts to intimidate Cardinal Gerlier were to no avail, thanks to the appeals made to him by Abbot Glasberg and Father Pierre Chaillet. The children had been saved, and Father Chaillet paid the price of his disobedience by being placed under house arrest for three months.

From Instructions to Their Application

As of August 30, Bousquet was not satisfied with the results of the roundup. Depending on the region, the number of Jews apprehended and then transferred to the Occupied Zone only represented from 25 to 60 percent of Jews who had registered with the census.[198] Bousquet thus sent a telegram out to the regional prefects: "I call your attention to the significant disparity between the number of foreign Israelites identified by the census and the number arrested. Pursue and intensify police operations now under way using all available police and gendarmes. Resort to mass arrests, identity checks, home visits, and searches in order to arrest individuals who cannot claim any of the exemptions outlined in the telegram of August 18 and in the subsequent telephone conversations concerning war veterans."[199]

What had happened was that people throughout the Unoccupied Zone had gotten wind of what was going on. A report from the General Bureau of Information had already indicated on August 18 that the Jews, fearing measures "identical to the ones in the Occupied Zone" were leaving big cities to go to small towns.[200] In some cases, they had been forewarned by the social aid workers. In Périgueux, a non-Jewish Scout stopped Jews in the street to inform them of the threat hanging over their heads.[201] As in Paris, some policemen had notified the very Jews that they had been ordered to arrest. Others were in no hurry to force their way in if doors were not opened when they first rang. The opposite was also true in some cases, of course. But throughout the Unoccupied Zone, the number of those "rounded up" was much lower than the number of "deportable" Jews registered by the census.

The massive roundup was over, but individual arrests continued, and those who had escaped the clutches of the police a first time "lived like hunted animals, often not knowing were to sleep and seeking refuge in the forest; not knowing how to find something to eat, as they could not have their food ration card renewed."[202] They sometimes tried to reach the border, where they were easy prey for numerous crooks.

From August 31 on, those who fell victim to individual arrests made in accord with Bousquet's instructions to intensify the search were grouped together and brought to the Rivesaltes camp, the screening point for the entire Southern Zone.[203] There, Jews slated for deportation were isolated in unit K, where they were poorly fed and made to sleep on bare ground in ramshackle buildings infested with bedbugs, rodents, and mosquitoes right up until their departure. Some tried to escape from being put on the deportation trains: those that did were replaced indiscriminately by other detainees. One such departure took place during the holy days of *Tishri*. Some deportees climbed into the cattle cars without having broken the Yom Kippur fast (which in 1942 fell on September 21).

Government employees of all sorts and every rank who were charged with carrying out this wretched task faced two constraints. The first was hierarchical: orders from above imposed strict application of guidelines, and as it was becoming ever harder to fill the deportation trains, directives became even more strict all the time. The second constraint was bureaucratic: once the trains were ready, the schedule had to be followed in order not to disturb commercial rail traffic. These constraints weighed heavily on the course of events when there were not enough "deportable"

Jews on hand. They sometimes resulted in harsher selections, bringing about the nullification of previously granted exemptions: Jews over the age of sixty were thus slated for deportation, even though they were officially "exempt." The constraints also resulted in unscreened deportations, such as the ones that were carried out at the Nexon camp on August 29[204] and at Vénissieux on September 2. At times the number stipulated by the quota took precedence over all else: such was the case at Les Milles, where some sixty people were hoisted into the train cars at the last minute, some half-shaven, without baggage and without even having had a chance to get dressed.[205]

But there was another logic, the logic of humanity, that opposed these two constraints. Confronted with the spectacle of people trying to flee across the demarcation line, the sight of children, and the display of so much human misery, government employees—who were also constantly pressured by activists—were at times moved to compassion. When such was the case, they could take advantage of the confusion created by all the different orders and counterorders, in situations where no one knew any more who was to be exempted. It was always the political people who were intransigent. René Bousquet sent out more and more insistent memoranda; Pierre Laval had the exemptions intended for aid organization assistants limited solely to UGIF employees, for that was the rule applied in Occupied Paris. If some children were indeed spared from the deportation trains, it was because a certain police intendant had given in or a certain prefect had had pity. Those chaplains' assistants—there were about forty such foreign associates, who were as a general rule themselves internees employed by the Chaplains' Office—who were saved could thank a certain government employee who had been satisfied with seeing a phony certificate without seeking any confirmation from Vichy. The Polish government in exile's representative to France noted the "flurry of tough, brutal directives" emanating from Laval and the hesitation that sometimes characterized their execution; he chose to make his appeals only to prefects.[206]

For each victim or potential victim, it was thus random chance that determined whether or not humanitarian concern prevailed over the imperatives of government constraints. Indeed, chance was henceforth omnipresent in the everyday life of Jews. Nevertheless, we should not forget the basic reality: on the whole, the rules spelled out by authorities were rigorously applied. As for the work of the aid associations, André Baur had already given his rather grim assessment in a telegram concerning Paris, and Nina Gourfinkel came to the same conclusion for the Unoccupied Zone: their action could only "limit the damage."[207]

And so it was that up until September 15, 1942, thirteen deportation trains filled with foreign Jews, who had thought to have found refuge in Vichy France, left the Southern Zone for Drancy. The trains headed for Chalon-sur-Saône and Vierzon, where Jews were turned over directly to the Germans. The deportees had left only after long roll calls, entire nights most often spent in boxcars (or in third-class passenger cars into which the women and children were sometimes hoisted). They were under constant surveillance, and even the mobile guard units had been put into action. In most cases, train cars were sealed shut and no contact with the outside was permitted during this first part of the long journey awaiting the deportees. When Chief Rabbi Kaplan learned that one of these deportation trains was passing through the Perrache station in Lyon, he tried to force his way past the barriers to establish contact with the deportees, but had to be content with climbing in a train that was parked alongside theirs. He wrote:

> It was an unbearably painful spectacle. In these cattle cars kept under the surveillance of a mobile guard, there were people of all ages, even some elderly persons, penned up together in a pitifully weakened physical condition. They were barely clothed, and one of them was as thin as a skeleton. All appeared to be physically exhausted. One elderly man in his eighties was, according to his travel companions, stretched out in a train car. Police cordoned off the area between the train full of deportees and the passenger train next to it. . . . If, as one must surmise to be the case, the trip lasts several days, there is every reason to fear a large number of deaths.

So reads the last sentence of his report.[208]

THE DEPORTATION TRAINS

From Drancy to Auschwitz

After the ordeal of the train transfer out of the Southern Zone, the deportees arrived at Drancy. In most cases, they stayed there two or three days, and sometimes five or six. Some were sent off again the very day of their arrival or the day after. It all depended on the availability of trains. On the day before their departure, deportees were subjected to a brutal search by the Police for Jewish Affairs. "Deportees are literally stripped of everything they possess."[209] They were then isolated all night in the departure stairwells and prohibited from going out, even to the outhouse. At the break of day the following morning, the deportees were piled into buses that took them to the Bourget train station, where they were taken out of the buses and put into cattle cars, under the threat of machine guns. In the first deportation trains, men and women were loaded together in the same cars. Then, one fine morning, as the deportees were about to climb into the train, the Germans separated the two sexes, without even leaving them any time to divide up food and blankets.[210]

Beginning on August 25, 1942, a police service made up of internees was constituted, probably to make it easier for the authorities to organize all the coming and going. In any case, it made security procedures less harsh for the internees. Georges Kohn described one deportation scene on September 2, 1942: "The cattle cars have no straw and have not even been cleaned. Some contain remnants of plaster, others fertilizer, and others animal-black [a pigment]. Right on the bare floor of these dirty cattle cars, they put bread for three days, a bucket to be used as a toilet, and fifty internees per car. A man with only one leg is put down on the floor of one car: he probably will not be able to get up before the train arrives at its final destination."[211] Cattle cars had been chosen because it took fewer guards to escort them and keep them under surveillance.[212] As was the case for the number of deportation trains leaving during a given time, only concerns of a practical or bureaucratic nature were taken into account in the application of a political decision once it had been made.

In order to free up space on trains from the Unoccupied Zone, authorities began sending French Jews—who were not "deportable" as long as trains could be filled with other Jews—to Pithiviers. The first transfer took place on September 1, 1942,[213] "following the usual schedule for such moves: internees were awakened at three in the morning, served coffee at four, grouped together with their baggage downstairs, then counted, classified, and called by roll until seven. They were brutally loaded into buses, and then had to climb into cattle cars: fifty internees were locked in each car for the duration of the trip."[214] By the time they arrived at their destination, fleas were all over them.[215]

Those internees who had escaped deportation due to one exemption or another would sometimes become deeply anxious at seeing the camp being emptied. They knew that the necessity of filling the trains took precedence over everything else, and that they would be in danger if there were not enough "deportable" internees on hand. Life for those interned at Drancy was henceforth paced by the waves of arrests in the Paris region and the Occupied Zone, the arrival of trains from the Unoccupied Zone, transfers to Pithiviers, sudden changes in the categories of Jews to be deported, and the constant verification of the situation of those still in the camp. On September 30, 1942, the reserves of "deportable" internees seemed to have been depleted for a time, and the deportations slacked off.

Between March 27 and September 30, 1942, some 38,206 Jews were deported from France in trains destined for Auschwitz.[216] The seventh deportation train, which left Drancy on July 19, was the first whose passengers were gassed as soon as they arrived.[217] Up until early August 1942, some 87.8 percent of those deported from France (7,904 deportees) had been registered and selected to work, while the other 1,096 Jews had been gassed.[218] The extermination complex at Auschwitz-Birkenau had been ready to operate at full capacity for some time, but the makeup of the trains of Jews from France changed following Vichy's initiative relative to the deportation of children. As a result, the ratio of deportees gassed upon arrival versus those selected to work was immediately inverted.[219] Out of these 38,206 Jews who were sent directly from the deportation trains either to work or to the gas chambers, there remained no more than 779 survivors in 1945.[220] There was not a single child among them.

These terrible statistics meant that from July 17 until the end of September, a trainload of one thosand Jews left for Auschwitz every two or three days. For those transported by these trains, as well as for those left behind, the uncertainty was terrible. Where were they being sent? Why had the children, almost four thousand of them, been separated from their parents? Why were they also deported from ten days to three weeks later, after having been allowed to remain in squalid conditions at Pithiviers and Beaune-la-Rolande? How would they find their parents? What kind of work might be in store for them? Why were the personal effects of deportees returned to certain Jewish organizations (the Rue Lamarck shelter, for instance)? Why deport the elderly and the sick? Why was each question met with silence? What was being hidden by the "unknown destination"? Similarly, why had Parisian newspapers (in compliance with orders from the German censorship authority to remain silent) not published anything about the mass arrests that had occurred between July 16 and July 31?[221] *Le Pilori* had indeed spoken of "the definitive elimination of the Jews," albeit in a semicoded manner,[222] and it was hardly a newspaper that Jews would have consulted for answers.

An Unknown Destination?

"There will be grounds for not revealing the true destination to those concerned: they are to be told that they are headed for another camp which is currently being prepared."[223] This type of instruction could be applicable only to internees held in camps in the Southern Zone, and was only valid for a short while. For those who up until very recently had lived in liberty, the official version was modified somewhat: "When they arrive in the camp, the Israelites are to be told that they will be sent to Central Europe, namely to Galicia, where the German authorities are planning to build a large Jewish colony. It should be stressed that the Reich has given its assurances that the Israelites will be treated well, and suggested that they will probably have the opportunity at a later time to have the furniture left in France sent to them."[224]

From the point of view of French authorities, the important thing was to make sure that the arrests and transfers from one zone to the other would cause no commotion. The fate of the deportees was not worthy of attention. Foreign diplomats inquired about this matter, however, and Laval was obliged to pose the question to the Germans. He nevertheless did not worry about what had become of the Jews that he had sent to the east. He asked to be instructed "how to answer in order to avoid any discrepancy with information being given out by [the Germans]."[225] All that mattered for Laval was to keep his answer consistent with what the Germans were saying. The issue, then, is not really what the leaders of the French State did or did not know, for they did not want to know.[226]

In reality, on several occasions before the summer of 1942 Hitler had stated very clearly the fate he had in store for the Jews. On February 26, 1942, the headlines of *Paris-Soir* read: "A message from Adolf Hitler to the members of the National Socialist party. This war will not annihilate Aryan humanity, but only its Jewish components. Preparations are under way for a definitive settling of scores." This was the third time since the beginning of the year that the Führer had publicly announced the extermination of the Jews. He would do so two more times in the fall of 1942.[227] All of these speeches were reprinted by newspapers in the Occupied Zone. Once the plan to exterminate the Jews was put into action, the Germans accompanied these thunderous declarations with a systematic use of euphemisms designed to put a smokescreen around the concrete application of the Final Solution.[228]

These euphemisms made it possible to conceal the truth and to spread confusion, a practice conducive not only to carrying out the murderous project but also to providing convenient answers for those who preferred not to know. The German military command in France had thus ordered that the terms "deportation to the East" be abandoned in favor of "sending into forced labor."[229] And then the term "population transfer" was imposed in order to make the terminology consistent with the deportation of children.[230]

The Vichy government did not want to know, and yet it knew no less than did the Allied governments at the time. It knew of the large-scale massacres perpetrated against Jews in Eastern Europe. And while radio broadcasts from Moscow that alluded to a systematic plan to exterminate the Jewish people might appear suspect, it could have heard a detailed report about the plan's concrete application over the BBC on July 2, 1942: the report stressed that all those who had been sent off to an "unknown destination" had disappeared.[231] Speaking in French over the BBC on July 1, 1942, at 9:30 in the evening, Jean Marin cited an official Polish government report and explained that 700,000 men, women, and children had been murdered because they were Jews. He also mentioned the use of gas chambers mounted on wheels.[232] And although they did not always understand just what all the various pieces of information meant when put together, people both in the United States and in England were at least asking questions about the subject.

In France, meanwhile, the government kept on helping the Germans send the Jews to their "unknown destination." That was henceforth the term used, and the one that the police, acting on Röthke's advice, officially adopted.[233] The transfers of Jews were carried out in full view of the French authorities, who knew perfectly well what conditions deportees had to suffer during their journey. The types of people loaded on to the deportation trains allowed them to question seriously the forced labor story. Even if they persisted in looking the other way, appeals made on behalf of the deportees did not fail to call these "discrepancies" to their attention. As Robert Kiefe had pointed out on July 10 first to Jean Jardin, then to General Campet, once the Jews had been deported from France, one never heard from them again.[234]

Beginning in early August, Donald Lowrie, who chaired the Nîmes Committee at the time, met with one Vichy official after another. When he asked himself why the Germans would want to take back the Jews, he could only come up with one explanation: "The overall German plan for a new Europe calls for all undesirable elements to be purged. While other aspects of the plan were falling short of the original goals (the Russian campaign, for example), this part was in the hands of the fanatics and was being mercilessly conducted according to the initial plans."[235] Robert Kiefe was sent to Vichy by Jacques Helbronner: on August 14 and then again on August 20, he circulated a dossier on the Nazis' extermination plan and their atrocities against the Jews.[236] On August 17, the French representative in Bucarest pointed out to Laval that, in view of the conditions in which deportations were carried out, "few could survive."[237] And then again on August 20 in a letter to Marshal Pétain, Pastor Boegner spoke of the inhumane conditions that prevailed during the transfer of the foreign Jews and also mentioned the "terrible fate" awaiting them.[238] Broadcasting in French on August 23, the BBC announced that Czerniakow, the president of the *Judenrat* in the Warsaw ghetto who had been ordered by the Germans to draw up a list of 100,000 Jews to be deported from the ghetto to an "unknown destination in the East," had committed suicide. "That unknown destination was death, massacre. . . . No! He was not going to take upon himself the responsibility of designating 100,000 victims for the Nazi executioners."[239]

On August 25, the day before the massive roundup in the Southern Zone, the Central Consistory sent a letter of protest to the head of the Vichy government: its message reminded Vichy that the Nazis had massacred hundreds of thousands of Israelites in Eastern Europe and announced their plan to exterminate the Jews. The letter added: "The fact that those turned over to the Germans by the French government were massed together indiscriminately, irrespective of their physical aptitude, and that among them were sick people, elderly people, women, and children, confirms that the German government did not demand these deportees in order to use them for work, but with the firm intention of mercilessly and methodically exterminating them."[240]

On August 28, Kiefe received confirmation that Pétain had indeed studied the dossier sent in.[241] There was no other response, and the same was true for all the other appeals that had been made. Once again on October 6, General Campet was reminded of reports of the massacre of Jews in Eastern Europe. On October 22 and 23, Robert Kiefe informed Jean Jardin that Jews were being gassed in Poland. Jardin demanded some manner of corroborating this information, but Vichy authorities kept on refusing to grant the exit visas requested for children having obtained the right to enter the United States.[242]

Despite the clarity of their protests, however, the leaders of the Central Consistory and the UGIF were at the time probably not fully aware of the existence of a systematic plan to exterminate the Jews. "Our fellow Jews [are being] sent to a penal colony if not to their deaths," they remarked while discussing the terms of this protest.[243] They kept on trying to gather information about the fate of those deported, both from the international Red Cross in Geneva and from another committee headquartered there that was to come to the assistance of the Jewish population hit by the war. But to no avail; the Germans refused to respond.[244] The only official bit of information provided dated from July 6, 1942: "the internees that were transferred out of the camps of Compiègne and Drancy in late March are supposedly in

Auchvitz [sic] in Upper Silesia, where they supposedly are working on farms. They are reported to be fed a normal ration."[245]

Given the silence surrounding the plight of the Jews deported from France, Jewish leaders paid close attention to the news broadcast over the BBC on July 1, 1942: citing a Jewish member of the Polish Diet and members of De Gaulle's Free France resistance, the BBC spoke of mass executions in Polish ghettoes, the annihilation of the Polish Jews, and "systematic extermination."[246] And those who sought to understand just what the term "unknown destination" really meant could only be troubled by the brutality of the arrests carried out in Paris. To hand over Jews to the Germans was to expose them to such brutality and to make them suffer the same plight as the Jews in the capital city. Deportation was indeed associated with death in peoples' minds. That is why there were such vigorous efforts to snatch as many children as possible away from this terrible danger, even if it mean breaking families apart.

It is also the reason why, on August 25, 1942, for the first time, the Consistory gave wide publicity to its protest: previous protests had indeed been made known only to officials with whom it was registered as well as to the regional delegates of the Consistory.[247] Consistory leaders continued to seek an answer to this burning question. The information sent to Jardin on October 22, 1942, was probably taken from the number 2 issue of *J'accuse* dating from October 20. This clandestine newspaper published by Jewish Communists reported that, on an experimental basis, eleven Jews from Poland had been asphyxiated by gas. In the months that followed, as in the summer of 1942, increasing information from a variety of sources would give an ever-greater number of Jews a clearer sense of what was happening.

Among those deported from the Southern Zone, "one version going around would have it that they are being sent to Silesia, perhaps to the region of Sanok, in Ukraine or in Bessarabia. There is total uncertainty as to their subsequent plight. It is said that they are to be used for the construction of fortifications in the East. The fact is, however, that in all the German demands concerning Jews from France, nothing was ever said about handing them over to do work: they just demanded that they be delivered into German hands."[248] The Polish government in exile's representative to France who had reported these rumors also mentioned another: "The conviction generally prevailing among the Jews that are being deported is that they will be gassed after their arrival in German territory."[249]

This is a surprising remark for early September 1942. Still, as was the case for the Jewish leaders, the idea of death was quite present in people's minds: "In our minds, deportation was doubtless associated with death, but with a sort of natural death that would occur somewhere in the forest and in the cold, due to exhaustion, the harsh climate, or insufficient food," writes Nina Gourfinkel.[250] This deep anxiety was experienced in varying degrees: some mothers did not hesitate to let themselves be separated from their children; but some wives demanded that they leave with their husbands; and there were some adolescents whose parents refused to let them go.

The internees at Drancy were also haunted by doubts, anxiety, and images of death, as they did not really know what deportation really meant either. Would they be sent to some unknown place in Silesia or Ukraine? Having managed to prove in time that he was married to an Aryan, Christian Lazard escaped one of these deportations in the fall of 1942. And he rejoiced in "this marvelous coincidence that spared [him] if not from death, then at least from the horrible exhaustion of a deportation from which many will not return."[251] When he saw French Jews from the Pithiviers camp being deported a few weeks later, he could

> find only one explanation for these endless transfers to which sick and elderly men as well as women and children were subjected. . . . That is to bring about the death of the largest number possible, but without murdering them in the usual sense of the word. The pogrom is being carried out calmly, but the result is roughly the same."[252]

Such was the observation of one who remained in the camp. When they managed to send a note just before their departure, those who were deported sought first and foremost to reassure themselves and their loved ones. Writing to his wife on July 16, 1942, Henri Minczelès' father suggested: "Perhaps we shall see each other again in Poland. Do not fear, Dear, they will not kill so many people."[253]

"They will not kill so many people." It was inconceivable: the very idea surpassed the limits of human understanding. But the dark cloud of a massacre was indeed hanging over their heads. There was no need to understand all the technical details of the Nazis' diabolical plan. It was enough to observe the hell of the camps, the brutality of the arrests, the violence of the Germans, and the horror of the transfers. These images also struck French public opinion.

THE PUBLIC IS JOLTED OUT OF ITS LETHARGY

The general population of France had been preoccupied by a thousand other worries. The problem of finding basic foodstuffs and supplies was still constantly in the back of Parisians' minds. Some had observed over the summer vacation period that farmers were better off, which only added to the rancor of people in the capital. In the cities of the Southern Zone, where most people's minds were also haunted by the problems of food and supplies, a similar rancor had existed for some time already. The crisis in textiles attained a new peak, and shoes were virtually unattainable. Terrorist attacks on German soldiers and the ensuing reprisals created a climate of tension that the long stream of German motorized units crossing Paris on July 29 did nothing to calm.[254] The failed attempt by British and Canadian troops to land at Dieppe on August 19, 1942 indicated that a second front would be opened sooner or later, and people lived with this expectation.

In both the north and south of France, the public had followed with curiosity and interest—and a bit of hope—the ceremony that had taken place at Compiègne on

August 11: President Laval had been on hand to see a train carrying recently released prisoners of war meet a train carrying workers to Germany in the context of "La Relève."[255] And in Paris, people still went to listen to the public concerts given by the Germans: there were two or three per week, drawing an audience of anywhere from two hundred to three thousand. The most popular were those given in the Luxemburg gardens and in the Paris garden (on the Champs-Elysées). There was a record crowd of four thousand in attendance for the religious concert given on the evening of August 21 in the Notre-Dame cathedral by the orchestra of the German commander for the Greater Paris region, the German army choir, and the ensemble of the high command of the Luftwaffe.[256]

In Paris as well as in the Unoccupied Zone, it was as if events took place in separate worlds with no connection between them. Keeping silent on many subjects, the official press contributed largely to maintaining this separation: nothing was said about the massive roundups that had taken place in Paris in mid-July, not even in the collaborationist newspapers. And there was not a single word in *Le Petit Marseillais,* to take just one example, about the internment camps in the South, nor was there the slightest mention of the transfers of Jews into the Occupied Zone or anything on the mass arrests of August 26. This blackout was nevertheless contradicted by the concrete events that had taken place under the very eyes of a large number of people.

The wrenching scenes that had marked the Vel d'hiv roundup in Paris had made an impact on people's consciences. A Polish journalist wrote in his daily notes that it had caused great emotion among the French.[257] At the same time, there had indeed been a rapidly spreading rumor among the non-Jewish Poles that their deportation had now been scheduled, which caused a number of people to flee to the rural areas. For her part, Marie-Thérèse Gadala said that there was "universal disgust and outrage over the treatment inflicted on the Jews."[258] And all of the descriptions of the Vel d'hiv roundup written by Jewish activists mention the Parisians' indignation. "We are hearing from many sources that there are an increasing number of friendly gestures toward Jews on the part of Parisians," observed Jacques Biélinky.[259] Reports from the prefectorate spoke rather of compassion. Jewish leaders in the Southern Zone had gotten word of what happened almost immediately and quickly notified the various Jewish circles. The news took longer to reach the French population and the Jews scattered out individually within it. It was only on August 17, 1942 that Léon Werth wrote in his diary: "Vel d'hiv, children penned up, torn away from their parents."[260]

When similar events occurred in the Southern Zone, however, the widely known descriptions of the horrors in Paris prepared the way for a sudden awakening of consciences. Anti-Semitism had grown more in the Southern Zone under the shadow of Vichy, as the French were not confronted every day with the same enemy as the Jews. Nevertheless, observed the Polish government's representative in France, "while antisemitism has gained some ground in France, the attitude of French society in face of the unjust pursuit and persecution of one Jew has formed a monolithic block."[261] While support for republican democracy was accompanied by opposition to the Germans, as illustrated by the demonstrations of July 14, 1942,[262] the public opinion in Paris continued to emphasize the Germans' responsibility for the persecutions now occurring so visibly.

People judged the measures taken against the Jews to be inhumane and were shocked by the brutality of their application. "The persecuted Jew was becoming likable," and the public, particularly shocked by the tearing apart of families, was revolted by "German intrusion into purely French matters." Such is the picture we get from the monthly synopses of wiretaps and the interception of letters and telegrams prepared for Vichy.[263] Jews were suddenly categorized in a new way: they were removed from the heading of "information on anti-national activities of all sorts" and placed in the rubric of "information on the state of public opinion." This new classification indicated that their status had been modified.

Reports from many prefects substantiate this observation: they speak of "compassionate friendliness" toward Jews, of blame being put on the German authorities, and of "a very clear stirring" of public opinion.[264] Twenty-four prefects from the Unoccupied Zone indicated in their reports that public opinion had been jolted. Only two, the prefects for the départements of Le Gers and L'Indre, stressed that people in their areas were satisfied at seeing the Jews leave; these were areas located on the demarcation line that had not appreciated the massive influx of Jews occasioned by the imposition of the yellow star. In five other départements with large tourist centers or rural communities used as sites for placing Jews under house arrest, reactions had apparently been rather mixed.[265] Public opinion is never unanimous. The undeniable fact remains, however, that because there had been many eyewitnesses to the dramatic events, a current of sympathy for the hapless victims had welled up.

"Dear Marshal Pétain," wrote a woman living in the town of Saint-Girons in the département of L'Ariège on August 30, 1942,

> we respectfully beseech you to hear the echo of suffering caused for us here in our little town by the abduction that occurred on the morning of the twenty-sixth. We were waiting for the bus to Foix that leaves at about 8 A.M: the bus still had not come and we waited until 10:30. But ten buses went by loaded with gendarmes taking away foreign Israelite residents of the region who had been snatched out of their beds without warning and without any baggage. Among them we recognized a pregnant women with a small child, a charming family that had moved to the country and was determinedly cultivating a little field in order to have enough vegetables for the winter, and children that had played with our children. These ten buses were like carts that used to carry the condemned away to be executed. All who saw this scene were overwhelmed with pity and shame; even those who bellow out "Down with the Jews, death to the Jews" were moved to tears.
>
> But what everyone felt was that France had condemned and dishonored itself in applying such an unworthy and cruel treatment on people who had thought to have found asylum in our country. We are ashamed to be French, ashamed to be Christian, ashamed to be human beings, and our veneration for the person of

> Marshal Pétain has been shaken, if not swept away. We nevertheless hope that under your leadership, the spirit of charity and justice will be awakened in a country that was historically the land of chivalry and the eldest daughter of the Church, and it is here that we place all our respect for you, Marshal Pétain, Chief of the French State.[266]

Similar emotions can be found in many French villages,[267] at least in those that were located near one of the places used for grouping Jews together or along the route taken by the deportation trains. Such was the case in Pontcharra: after "a group of about fifty foreign Jews—men, women, children, and babies—that were being taken to Fort-Barraux before being handed over to the Germans"[268] had passed through the village, the local café was charged with emotion.

Public opinion was thus stirred by a spontaneous wave of indignation. Official stances taken first privately, then publicly by some French bishops echoed these feelings. And by conferring legitimacy on these spontaneous reactions of the public, the bishops' stances not only strengthened them but also widened their base and paved the way for acts that would aid or rescue threatened Jews.

The first such voice came from Paris, where the annual assembly of cardinals and archbishops had just happened to meet at the time of the Vel d'hiv roundup. On July 22, Cardinal Suhard took a letter to Marshal Pétain on behalf of this assembly. Stating that he was shocked to see the "mass arrests of Israelites" and the "harsh treatments inflicted upon them," Cardinal Suhard pleaded on behalf of the assembly for the "inalienable rights of the human person" and "made an anguished call to have pity in the face of such tremendous suffering, especially the suffering of so many mothers and children."[269] Although this text was only sent to priests and not read from the pulpit, it did, in spite of its moderation, use a new language in referring to governmental authorities.

But it was in the Southern Zone that the episcopate's attitude proved to be the firmest. The expression of these condemnations was marked by two phases. The first can be situated before the massive roundups of August 26, 1942. On August 17, Chief Rabbi Kaplan appealed personally to the primate of the Gauls, Cardinal Gerlier, in order to convince "the highest moral authority in the country [to intervene] in Vichy and protest against the delivery to the Germans of thousands of human beings that Germany wants to exterminate."[270] "These thousands of innocent people have been sent to Germany not to work there [as is the case for the French] but to be exterminated," argued the chief rabbi, who compared his action to that of Esther who had appealed to King Ahasuerus. To substantiate his assertions, Rabbi Kaplan provided Cardinal Gerlier with various documents about what had transpired in Paris and about the massacre of Jews in Romania. On the following day, Cardinal Gerlier received the visit of Pastor Boegner.[271]

Meanwhile, activists with the Christian Friendship and representatives of the Nîmes Committee were pressing the bishops to speak out publicly. On August 19, 1942, Cardinal Gerlier opted to send a message to Marshal Pétain. Gerlier reiterated his "faithful and respectful attachment" to the marshal, associated his appeal with Cardinal Suhard, and stated his awareness of the "complexity of the problem." He nevertheless "urgently requested that, if possible, these poor people be spared from the suffering that had already [afflicted] so many."[272]

Pastor Boegner proved to be more explicit in the letter he sent Marshal Pétain on the following day: "No French citizen can remain indifferent to what has been happening in the camps for lodging and internment since August 2. The truth is that men and women who had sought refuge in France for political or religious reasons have just been handed over to the Germans. Some of these refugees already know the terrible fate that is in store for them." Boegner reminded Pétain of the duties entailed by the right to asylum, the fundamental calling of Christian churches, and the inhumane conditions in which "these poor foreigners had been handed over" to the Germans. Boegner then pleaded for Pétain "to carry out the measures that are absolutely necessary for France to avoid inflicting on herself a moral defeat of incalculable dimensions."[273] Pastor Boegner was moreover in constant contact with the social activists who were onsite, trying to get those responsible for applying ministerial directives to show compassion. Pastor Boegner's letter was part of his continuous effort to appeal to Marshal Pétain to curb the antisemitic policies of the Vichy government.

The break with Pétain was nevertheless most clearly signaled by a pastoral letter from Cardinal Saliège, the archbishop of Toulouse: first, because it came from an eminent member of the Catholic Church, one of the pillars of the regime: and, second, because it made itself perfectly clear:

> My Dearest Brethren,
>
> There is a Christian morality, there is a human morality, which imposes duties and recognizes rights. These duties and these rights stem from the nature of man; they come from God. It is possible to violate them. . . . No mortal being has the power to do away with them.
>
> The sad spectacle of men, women, children, fathers and mothers being treated like a herd of animals, of members of the same family separated from each other and sent off to an unknown destination, has been reserved for our time.
>
> Why does the right of asylum no longer exist in our churches?
>
> Why are we the losers of the war?
>
> Lord, have mercy upon us.
>
> [Holy Mother of God] . . . , pray for France.
>
> In our own diocese, the most disturbing scenes have taken place in the camps of Noé and Récébédou. Jews are human beings. Foreigners are human beings. All is not permitted against them, against these men, against these women, against these fathers and these mothers of families. They belong to humankind; they are our brothers, as are so many others. A Christian may not forget this.
>
> France, our beloved country, our France who carries in all its children's consciences the tradition of respect for the human person, our chivalrous and generous France, I trust that you are not responsible for these errors.
>
> Rest assured, my dearest brethren, that I remain warmly devoted to your service.[274]

Furthermore, this was not the text of a letter to Marshal Pétain, but a pastoral letter read from the pulpit on August 23, 1942, in most parishes of the diocese, despite the prefecture's prohibition. It turned its back to the French authorities and spoke directly to Catholics. That it was read from the pulpit assured it a wide audience. And it came three days before the massive August 26 roundup: when the widespread arrests took place, many were mindful of the gravity of the event thanks to this letter that had been read in public. The letter was a first step that brought on other similar public appeals.

"I voice the indignant protest of Christian conscience, and I proclaim that all men, both Aryan and non-Aryan are brothers, because they were created by the same God; that all men, whatever their race or religion, are entitled to respect from individuals and states. The current antisemitic measures on the contrary disregard human dignity and violate the most sacred rights of the human person."[275] Such was the message that Bishop Théas of Montauban had priests in his diocese read from the pulpit on Sunday, August 30, 1942. As was true of the letter from Cardinal Gerlier on September 6, other messages were accompanied by a few concessions to the habitual rhetoric of the day, admitting that there was a Jewish question or stressing the authors' loyalty to the Vichy regime. On behalf of the National Council of the Reformed Church that had been called into an emergency session on September 22, Pastor Boegner wrote a letter that was read in the majority of Protestant churches. This letter stated that the Reformed Church was aware of "the extreme complexity of the situations" in which the authorities of our country [found] themselves, and reiterated the church's refusal to "intrude into the realm of politics," but it recalled that

> divine law [did not accept] for families desired by God to be torn apart, for children to be separated from their mothers, for the right of asylum to be refused and scorned, for the respect of the human person to be violated, nor for the defenseless to be made to suffer such a tragic fate. . . . The Savior of the world was born among the people whose children, according to the flesh, are the Jews. . . . These measures had also been hitting non-Aryan Christians who belonged to Protestant congregations.[276]

While there were appreciable nuances of difference among these letters, they reached an audience that stretched far beyond church circles, particularly in the case of the letters from Archbishop Saliège, Bishop Théas, and Pastor Boegner.[277] That was because an endless number of copies were made by the underground press and because the texts were cited in the broadcasts by De Gaulle's Free France over the BBC. Texts soon circulated throughout the Unoccupied Zone.[278]

Up until this summer of 1942, the majority of resistance newspapers had been rather discreet about the fate of the Jews. In December 1941, the first edition of *Franc-Tireur* had indeed denounced "the Hitlerian fable of a so-called Jewish conspiracy promoted by Hitler and the Vichy government at the Nazis' service."[279] *Libération* (south[280]) had stigmatized the ignominy of racism in February 1942. *L'Humanité* and *L'Université libre* had also spoken out, albeit in different styles and on different occasions. Clearer strains of protest had been heard during the spring of

1942 in *Le Populaire* and *Libération* (north),[281] when underground newspapers focusing on the fight against racism were created under the influence of Jewish Communists working with *J'accuse* (in the Northern Zone) and *Fraternité* (in the Southern Zone).[282] Meanwhile, Henri Hertz and Marc Jarblum were seeking to make an impact on public opinion with the "green document." Number 6–7 of the *Cahiers du témoignage chrétien*, "Anti-Semites," also came out at this time: it was a sequel to the preceding editions, and continued implacably to denounce not only the theoretical foundations but also the practical outcome of racist ideology. Outside of these highly specialized publications, however, the specificity of the plight of the Jews went largely unnoticed.

The imposition of the yellow star and later the massive Vel d'hiv roundup stirred many to write. "The yellow star is an emblem of the persecuted, the swastika a target for the patriots' bullets. That is the answer of French youth to the vile antisemitic campaign conducted by the Krauts and traitors." So wrote *L'Avant-Garde*, the paper put out by the Federation of Communist Youth in July 1942. The paper also called on French young people to demonstrate in every possible way their support for all who had to wear the yellow star.[283] *Libération* (south)[284] denounced what had transpired on July 16 in Paris as a new St. Bartholomew Day massacre, and, six weeks later, the "manhunt" that had extended into the zone controlled by Pétain and Laval led to descriptions of horror. Here again, the emphasis was on the separation of mothers from their children.[285] "Why?" asked the author of the article. "Because that's the sort of thing Nazi Germany does," he answered, adding: "But how could France accept this, even allowing for the fact that it has suffered a crushing defeat and domination . . . ?" "Show people the horrible things that have happened in Paris, show solidarity for all the victims, shelter them, hide them, do not let France be tarnished, and fight with the resistance movements against the Nazi executioners, their traitors, and their obedient dogs," added a tract put out by *Franc-Tireur*.[286] The August issue of the same newspaper would return to the subject of the "disgraceful tragedy of the Vel d'hiv."[287]

Issue no. 7–8 of the *Cahiers du témoignage chrétien*, which came off the press on August 16, had been revised to include the story of the Vel d'hiv roundup.[288] "We must cry out to the ignorant and indifferent world our disgust and our outrage that such a manhunt should be carried out in our land," added Father Chaillet in that issue.[289] "There is no Jewish confessional problem. . . . There is no Jewish racial problem. . . . [There exists no] issue of "Jewish blood" . . . [or] of "Jewish race," asserted *Combat* in October.[290] "Lodge, protect, hide Jewish children and their families, save the honor of France,"[291] pleaded one Communist tract. Along with the fight against the exchange of workers for prisoners of war and the call for sabotage, the campaign against antisemitic policies would represent one of the main themes of the Communist tracts listed by the judicial police in the Paris region.[292]

Condemnation was unanimous, and in all quarters—even in the Communist papers—the bishops' pastoral letters (often published in their entirety) were cited in support of protest. French voices speaking over the BBC in London echoed similar views. "So France is becoming a land of pogroms, a land of shame?" wondered André Labarthe on the evening of August 8, 1942.[293] Between July 1 and September 15, 1942, the plight of the Jews in France was mentioned on seven occasions.[294] At one moment, during the height of the massive police roundups and in the following weeks, all the voices of resistance repeated the views of a largely loyalist clergy, and public opinion in the Southern Zone became aware of the stark reality. In the Southern Zone, people saw the concrete link between the Vichy government and the German Occupation forces; in the Northern Zone, they realized to what extremes such servitude could lead.[295] *Libération* (north) spoke of the "harness of shame restraining powerless spectators," and concluded that it was now necessary to "take a stand."[296]

But after the fate of the Jews had been placed back into the general context of the war and the Occupation and once the shock and outrage had subsided, both the underground newspapers and the voices speaking for De Gaulle's Free French over the BBC returned to their usual concerns. Indeed, the focus of attention kept shifting. By the end of September, observed the author of the monthly report on postal communications, things had calmed down again.[297] In the months that followed, the subject disappeared from mail that was opened and read, just as it disappeared from the prefects' reports on the state of public opinion. During his visit to Aix-les-Bains, Chief Rabbi Kaplan made the same observation: "There is no longer the strong sense of indignation as there was last month. There is acceptance of an incident of war."[298]

The stubborn resistance of Soviet troops in Stalingrad was beginning to impress public opinion.[299] The law of September 4, 1942, worried and unsettled many. It required men between the ages of eighteen and fifty without a steady job of at least thirty hours a week to register in their local town hall. It also provided that the Office of the Secretary of State for Labor should designate a certain number of factory workers to be sent to work in Germany. It was the first step down the path to forced labor.[300]

And so workers were the object of a census, and then risked being "deported"—such was the term that quickly prevailed in common usage—to Germany. The plight of the Jews had come into public focus, but was soon blurred by the dominant larger picture. They were involved in a struggle against the same enemy, went the common wisdom, and victory would solve all the problems.

There was one exception, however. While on the whole the underground newspapers turned their attention away from the plight of the Jews to focus on other propaganda themes, there were two monthly papers specifically devoted to the Jewish issue. Jewish Communists had been regularly publishing *Notre Parole* (in the Northern Zone) and *Notre Voix* (in the Southern Zone), both in French and in Yiddish. Both were intended for Jewish readers. *J'accuse* and *Fraternité,* on the other hand, proclaimed themselves "fighting papers of the French forces battling against racist barbarity,"[301] and spoke to French public opinion in general. Beginning in October 1942, information about persecutions of the Jews in France and about the plight of Jews in various parts of Occupied Europe was published on its pages every month. Particularly noteworthy in this "official" publication of the National Movement Against Racism (MNCR, an organization devoted to rescuing Jews), was its repeated call to hide Jews on the run. Although the jolting of public opinion proved to be short lived, it did lead some to become aware of the crisis, and also to the creation of an underground infrastructure crucial to hiding a large number of Jews.

Moreover, the movement of public opinion had been significant enough for Vichy to take certain steps in the area of anti-Jewish propaganda. Vichy had already given in to Darquier de Pellepoix's insistent requests, granting him, in July 1942, two million francs for propaganda efforts.[302] During the mass roundups, newspapers had been ordered to remain silent: they were forbidden "until further notice [to publish] any information about the arrests of Jews in the Unoccupied Zone."[303] The same discretion was imposed on the Northern Zone. On the very day of the Vel d'hiv roundup, *Paris-Soir* published the list of public places off-limits to Jews wearing the yellow star, but nothing on the mass arrests. Not until August 16 could readers learn, in a front-page article, that four thousand stateless Jews had been deported from the Unoccupied Zone "[i]n order to check the Jewish invasion of the Occupied Zone." In the same issue was a reference to the "approximately similar number" of stateless Jews recently arrested in the Occupied Zone.[304] These figures were of course far short of reality: they revealed only about one-fourth of the actual number of Jews that had either been arrested and deported or else slated for deportation in the near future.

This deliberate underreporting was accompanied by an equally deliberate inflation of the number of Jews who were in the Southern Zone. More than a million Jews were said to have infiltrated the Aryan population. Over the following weeks, the numbers were inflated even more, swelling to two and a half million, a level necessitating a "delousing" operation.[305] Racism and antisemitism were equally prevalent among the Allies, insisted the papers in the Occupied Zone. The accent of antisemitic propaganda was shifting. Although papers continued to denounce either the Judeo-Bolshevik collusion, or the influence of the Jew Frankfurter on President Roosevelt, or the grip of the Jews over English political leaders, depending on political expediency, the United States had equally shown itself to be racist, and antisemitism was growing steadily both in Great Britain and in America.[306] The central themes of antisemitic propaganda were becoming defensive.

There was also an organized response to the bishops' appeal. On September 4, 1942, the Ministry of Information put out a memorandum on the general orientation of articles: it ordered papers to recall the traditional common doctrine of the church with respect to the Jewish problem based on Saint Thomas and the popes. Such a thrust was necessary in order to fight "against the cunning propaganda spread by the adversaries of the National Revolution" and against the "political maneuver" aiming to compromise the work of Marshal Pétain.[307] Some had "indeed taken advantage of the high clergy's gullibility" for a short time, but by reaffirming his fidelity to Pétain, the primate of the Gauls had put an end to what had only been a misunderstanding. Pro-Jewish propaganda had in the end failed. *Paris-Soir* published three long articles examining in detail the underpinnings of this plot put together by the rabbis.[308]

And then, with a slight twist of perversity, papers were asked to publish news about Jewish refugees turned away at the Swiss border.[309] One article by *Le Petit Marseillais* on September 23, 1942, carried the tame title "Too Many Emigrants Are Entering Switzerland."

The national radio also prepared a more aggressive propaganda campaign. Up until then, antisemitic programs had found their niche in the regular reports devoted to the Legion of War Veterans. They presented Jews as a subversive force working against France and as people that would always remain foreign. It was thus impossible for Jews to be assimilated into the general population because of the particularities of their race. Accordingly, went the message of these broadcasts, the Jews' intellectual and spiritual influence had to be stopped, and they were to be eliminated from the leadership of the country.[310]

Beginning in mid-September, the General Commission on Jewish Affairs also went on the radio three times a week to warn the public of the Jewish peril.[311] The programs elaborated on the basic notions of Jews as parasites and exploiters, spoke of a worldwide Jewish conspiracy, and drove home the necessity of maintaining absolute unity in face of the Jews.[312] They presented scenes from everyday life intended to strike the imagination: one involved a Jewish woman delighting in the good food found in France, another featured a Jew from Morocco who soon hoped to be an American, and yet another revealed the existence of an association of stateless Jews.[313] Although marked by numerous errors in pronunciation, the programs were spoken in a voice that Darquier termed "excellent" and with an "delivery inspired by the flame that carries conviction and [made Darquier] forget the minor details."[314]

This propaganda would intensify and continue until the end of the war: it was another sign that the Vichy regime was becoming increasingly harsh. A harmonization of propaganda was under way even before the Germans crossed the demarcation line to occupy all of France in early November 1942. Collaborationist newspapers were circulated more freely in the Southern Zone. One of the most virulent voices of antisemitism was the weekly publication of the French League, *L'Appel*, whose publication had been authorized in the Unoccupied Zone since August 6, 1942. In a open letter to Marshal Pétain published in the July 30, 1942, issue, the league's leader, Pierre Constantini, asked that Jews in the Unoccupied Zone be required to wear the yellow star. "Protect yourself against the Jews, Marshal Pétain, strike out against the Jews, Marshal Pétain, take France back from the Jews, Marshal Pétain."[315] And he would keep on writing articles of a similar nature.

Beginning on August 21, 1942, cinema newsreels shown in both zones were coordinated by a new company, France Actualités. The Francistes presented the exhibit

"Jews and Freemasons" from July 19 to August 20 in Nice.[316] Vichy had a more ambitious project: the Ministry of Information had planned for the exhibit "The Jew and France" to be shown in major cities under the sponsorship of the General Commission on Jewish Affairs.[317] However, the project was never brought to fruition. As in Paris, there was a proliferation of antisemitic incidents perpetrated by the PPF. During the nights of September 11 and 12, 1942, most Jewish-owned businesses in Grenoble had the Star of David and the word "Jew" painted in yellow on their storefronts.[318]

The mass arrests of Jews were the clearest indication that the term "Free" was illusory when applied to the Unoccupied Zone: the roundups were the price Vichy paid for an appearence of sovereignty. But it was from these events that the Jewish population and its leaders drew the lessons that would henceforth dictate or authorize other types of behavior both in the capital and in the south of France.

9
The Hunt for Jews in Paris

THE NOOSE TIGHTENS

The Jewish population in Paris had suddenly decreased. This rapid decline was of course brought on not only by the deportations but also by the flight of many to the Southern Zone, which was not yet occupied by the Germans. Given such a rapidly changing situation, then, how can the number of Jews still remaining in the capital be estimated with any reliability? It would seem rather risky to rely on the statistics carefully put together by the prefecture of the Paris police, which put the number of Jewish families present in Paris at the end of the month of August 1942 at 45,883.[1] We can observe the number of arrests and deportations to Auschwitz: 18,618 Jews from the greater Paris region were sent to an "unknown destination" in 1942, 6,300 in 1943, and 4,500 more in 1944.[2] As new categories of Jews were constantly being arrested and deported, however; any estimate given would only account for a fleeting reality. We know that thanks to the intervention of their respective embassies, just under three thousand Jews from countries that were either neutral or allied with Germany were successfully repatriated, and that between October 1, 1941 and June 7, 1944, just under fifteen hundred Jews reportedly died either in the camps or from natural causes.[3]

But people who had fled to the south had left clandestinely, and those who were still living in Paris increasingly avoided the rather careful verifications made by the prefecture of police. One year after the Vel d'hiv roundup, there were no more than about sixty thousand Jews in Paris and its immediate suburbs.[4] In view of the number of identity cards issued to Jews beginning in 1943, their number officially totaled no more than twenty-six thousand.[5] There were thus some twenty-six thousand Jews wearing the yellow star in August 1943, but how many were either living under an assumed name, working with a resistance movement, or hiding with the complicity of a friend, a neighbor, or a concierge? It was the immigrant population that had decreased the most appreciably. During the very first phase of the Occupation, the French Israelites had been the ones to flee the capital in the highest proportions. As they had been the main targets of the mass arrests, Jewish immigrants—or at least those who had avoided capture—henceforth sought to escape by all means possible, by changing their identity or by reaching some place they judged safer. One last check on the foreign Jews in the département of La Seine carried out in the first week of December 1943 put their number at 6,472,[6] less than ten percent of the figure given by the census taken in the fall of 1940.

The history of the Jews of Paris after the summer of 1942 is a story that unfolds around a manhunt. It was a manhunt that targeted ever-widening categories of Jews, but confronted a population increasingly aware of the dangers facing it. The hunt was conducted in the constantly evolving circumstances dictated by the military situation.

From One Massive Roundup to the Next

Those who ran the greatest risk were those who had managed to escape arrest even though they belonged to the category of Jews targeted. And so from August 10, 1942, on, foreigners who had been targeted by the recent measures taken in order to "regroup" "Jews of certain nationalities" (such were the terms officially used at the prefecture of the Paris police)[7] regularly found themselves added to the Jews who had gotten caught without their "special insignia": the French policemen turned them over to the "Occupation authorities." The efforts of the judicial police to hunt down Jews were bolstered by the addition of inspectors from the Section of Investigations and Inspections (SEC). The SEC had taken over the role of the Police for Jewish Affairs (PQJ) in mid-August 1942, and in the Northern Zone, had the power to carry out a temporary transfer: once they had seen an "infraction" committed by a Jew, they could take the individual to the police station.

Regardless of the cautious terminology, they actually had the power to arrest someone.[8] Now, any Jew who belonged to one of the nationalities targeted by the "regrouping measures" and who was walking around in Paris rather than staying penned up in Drancy was "in violation of the law." And the list of such nationalities was constantly growing: every time another national group was added, the municipal police would conduct a roundup. On September 14, 1942, some 208 Baltic, Bulgarian, Dutch, and Yugoslavian Jews were arrested in their homes.[9] Five hundred others named on the same lists were henceforth "in violation of the law."[10] On September 23, it was the turn of 1,594 Romanian Jews.[11] Five days later, 130 Jews from Luxemburg, Belgium, and Danzig were taken to Drancy. Then during the night of November 4 to November 5, a mass arrest of Greek Jews in their places of residence surpassed all expectations: out of the 1,426 Greek Jews listed by the prefecture's census data, 1,060 were apprehended.[12] After a two-month lull, another roundup took place on February 11, 1943.

There was no age limit on the persons targeted: 1,569 Jews, including almost 1,200 over the age of sixty, were led off to Drancy to be deported.[13] A group of elderly people who had suddenly been taken out of the Rothschild nursing home were slated for departure on the same day. Georges Kohn describes the scene.

> The buses parked right outside the door next to the departure stairwells so that the elderly would not have to be carried. . . . An elderly Jew wearing a long black bathrobe and a white cap embroidered with ornaments walked toward the bus. He had no baggage. No coat and not one blanket. He carried no food supplies, but on his two hands held out in front of him, he lovingly held his prayer books like an offering. Only his faith mattered to him.[14]

The group was completed on February 20, at which point the number of those arrested rose to 1,631.[15]

On March 19, two groups who had been previously spared suddenly saw their protection disappear.[16] One group was formed by the foreign Jews employed by the UGIF, who up until then had been protected by a "legitimation card" and exempted by order of the General Commission on Jewish Affairs. The other group was formed by the furriers carrying an *Ausweis*, whose work had been deemed indispensable. Indeed, it was so indispensable that they were released only three days after their arrest and enjoyed a reprieve of a few months. On March 22, Hungarian Jews joined the ranks of other foreigners destined for "evacuation." On July 19, 1943, time expired for the furriers, and 157 Jews bearing an *Ausweis* were arrested.[17] Then after another lull in action, a roundup of Romanian Jews was carried out on October 18. What followed was a schedule of arrests that continued relentlessly until February 1944: soon, not one single nationality was spared.[18] During the night of November 25 to November 26, some 275 Jews from neutral countries, including Hungarians, Spaniards, Italians, Swiss, Portuguese, Swedes, Danes, and Finns, were snared in the municipal police's nets.[19] On January 22, 1944, an operation targeting all nationalities wound up sending five hundred more Jews to Drancy.[20] And finally, 485 Turkish and Polish Jews were caught during one last roundup on February 4.[21]

This seemingly unending procession of arrests gives an idea of their cumulative effect on the daily lives of Jews in Paris: as time went on, they saw the gradual disappearance of the meager possibilities that they had managed to hold on to through so many hardships. The "lulls" that occurred between roundups in Paris corresponded to moments of political negotiation when the Germans were trying to set the stage for a more ambitious program of arrests. The Nazis were driven by three strategies: they planned to bring about a massive denaturalization of French Jews, push more aggressively into the Southern Zone, and concentrate on what had become the Italian Occupation Zone. But Jews in Paris now knew that these breaks in police activity would not last long; the mass roundups following a specific timetable only represented the most dramatic moments of a daily routine in which arrests were commonplace.

Daily Arrests

"Stateless Jews," "Polish Jews," "German and Austrian Jews," "Romanian Jews," and then "Hungarian, Belgian, and Luxemburgian Jews," "Greek and Argentinian

Jews"—such were the general names given to the mass arrests ordered by Röthke and obediently carried out by the prefecture of the Paris police. The considerable preparation necessary for these undertakings nevertheless provided favorable conditions for leaks. And since experience had taught Jews that threats were never empty, they were less hesitant to vacate their apartment when they knew the police were coming. Sometimes relatives presumed not to be in danger or a neighbor of a different nationality fell victim to police raids and wound up at Drancy. Concierges were doubtless the most solicited people in all of France at the time: at times they were summoned to inform the police; while in other cases they were tempted by property left for grabs; and at others they were implored to help Jews, who were risking arrest and deportation.

The dates of specific roundups only represent phases of the entire process of hunting down Jews in Paris. Between these mass arrests, there was one police check after another, and Jews were constantly being apprehended. Each week, the prefecture of the Paris police would receive from the German authorities a list of Jews to be arrested. After completing the necessary verifications, they proceeded to intern those so named.[22] Drancy kept on taking in its daily lot of Jews: roundups aside, there were seldom less than ten new internees each day, often thirty or forty, and sometimes many more.[23] The foreign Jews who naively went to have their identity cards renewed were sent off to Drancy. Such was the case of Jochteva Boruchowitz, held by the prefecture of the Paris police on October 1, 1942. Her husband had been arrested back in August 1941 and deported in June of 1942. She doubtless feared that she would put her five children in danger if she did not comply with administrative rules. Five children, including eighteen-month-old twins, were thus left to fend for themselves in their modest quarters on 52 Rue d'Angoulême in the Eleventh arrondissement.[24] Ailing Jews who had recovered to the point where hospitalization was no longer required were also sent off to Drancy.

Such was the fate of Jews in many other situations. Jews who had been convicted by a French court for a minor infraction of the law,[25] and Jews arrested for acts of resistance[26] landed in Drancy. The Jews living on Avenue Victor-Hugo and Avenue Kléber were all taken away to Drancy in reprisal for an act of terrorism in that section of Paris.[27] The Jews caught in police raids of various buildings located at 72 Rue Claude-Decaen (in the Twelfth arrondissement), at 58 Rue Crozatier (in the Twelfth arrondissement), and at 8 Rue Popincourt (Eleventh arrondissement), perhaps on the basis of denunciations, were all carted off to Drancy.[28]

All Jews found by the inspectors with the Section of Investigations and Inspections (SEC) "on public thoroughfares" and taken to a police station to be handed over to Mr. Permilleux at the prefecture of the Paris police "in order to have them interned" were whisked away to Drancy. These zealous inspectors furiously hunted for "specifically Judaic facial features" on the streets of Paris, with a diligence that even the offices of the prefecture of the Paris police found annoying.[29] Their efforts produced a little over eight thousand reports,[30] which reportedly led to about nine hundred arrests.[31] The vast majority of these reports were burned on August 17, 18, and 21, 1944, on orders from Joseph Antignac, then secretary-general of the General Commission on Jewish Affairs, in order to destroy all trace of this activity.[32]

Some reports escaped the rage of destruction, however: there were in particular about a hundred covering the period from March through July 1944 that were carefully filed away in the records of the General Commission on Jewish Affairs.[33] These reports show that denunciations brought results; action was always taken in response. They also testify to the dangers present in the sections of Paris commonly frequented by many Jews. Woe to those who ventured out on Rue de Belleville or Rue des Rosiers if they were "in violation of the law": the reports show that the slightest irregularity, such as having a job that involved contact with the public, wearing a yellow star that looked too new, carrying papers that had expired, making a purchase at the wrong time of day, consuming a beverage at the counter of some simple café or other public establishment, invariably resulted in the person being arrested and sent to Drancy. They also testify to the fact that Polish or stateless Jews, or Romanian Jews, and all sorts of other categories of Jews continued to be hunted down until the very last days of the Occupation. The same reports show that Jewish soup kitchens on Rue Richer, Rue Vieille-du-Temple, and Passage Charles-Dallery turned out to be a trap for those Jews who, even though they were in violation of the "regrouping measures" or some other law or ordinance, came to eat there because they probably had no other way of subsisting.[34]

For a long time, French Jews had only sporadically fallen victim to police roundups, such as the ones carried out in August and in December 1941. In other cases they had been arrested at random and detained because it had been discovered that they were married to foreigners or that they had violated one or more of the ordinances. Beginning in August 1943, however, they were sent to Drancy more frequently. Moreover, it was becoming increasingly risky for Jews to rely on their French citizenship. From 1940 to September 1943, some 7055 Jews had been denaturalized, and there were 9,801 cases in limbo, waiting for a ruling.[35] Beginning in November 1942, the General Commission on Jewish Affairs regularly received from the police the lists of "people presumed to be of non-Aryan race" who had been stripped of their French citizenship: it was then up to the Section of Investigations and Inspections to locate their addresses.[36] And whenever a French Jew's foreign spouse applied for French citizenship, the minister of justice always sent the dossier over to the general commissioner for Jewish affairs for a ruling. Invariably, the commissioner would reply: "I think it would be inappropriate to accommodate this request at this time."[37]

However, there were no massive roundups of French Jews. Röthke and Knochen had envisioned such an action and had called for large categories of Jews to be collectively stripped of their French citizenship. The cutoff dates to be used in this process of revoking the citizenship of naturalized Jews varied according to the plans under consideration: either 1927, or 1932, or 1933. Darquier de Pellepoix had pushed hard for the harshest measure. Then Bousquet, hoping for a new police agreement with the Germans, got involved in the matter. At first, Laval gave in to German demands and even signed the decree ordering the collective denaturalization of all Jews having acquired French citizenship after 1927.[38] But then he changed his mind and refused to support the plan, as did Marshal Pétain, who voiced his categorical opposition to the German demand on August 24, 1943. The plan had thus failed.[39] On a collective level, Jews who were French citizens continued to be "privileged" in comparison with those who were not. On an individual level, however, only chance determined their fate, as for the Germans there was only one valid classification: regardless of categories, all were Jews and were to be seized under any and every pretext.

Soon the meager safeguards that did exist scarcely protected anyone. In July 1942, the wives of Jewish prisoners of war—but neither their mothers nor their children—had benefited from the intervention of Ambassador Georges Scapini, head of the diplomatic office of war prisoners.[40] But whenever one of them got arrested, she was automatically suspected of having violated one of the ordinances concerning Jews: it was therefore out of the question to intervene on her behalf.[41] In March 1943, the furriers had been worried by a preliminary alert. They were arrested and interned, but then released. Those who had not seized on this occasion to clear out were apprehended on July 19. After a roundup of the foreign employees of the UGIF—which did not obtain the results expected because, as Röthke noted, the UGIF had sabotaged the operation[42]—the organization's leaders were arrested on July 21, 29, and 30. Patients at the Rothschild hospital and the elderly in the Rothschild nursing home (many of whom had come from Drancy[43]) were mercilessly rounded up, interned and deported in November 1942, and then in February, April, July, and November 1943, and again in January, March, and April 1944. On September 1, 1943, the Jewish mental patients hospitalized in asylums in Paris were also rounded up and taken in.[44] On January 5 and/or 6, 1944, the Jews who had thought they made it to safety by going to work for the Germans in the département of Les Ardennes were rounded up and sent to Auschwitz.[45] UGIF houses, soup kitchens, and synagogues gradually became traps for Jews.

Administrative Checks Increase

All of these roundups and arrests were facilitated by verification procedures that continued to pace the administrative life of Jews in Paris. In addition to the usual requirements for renewing expired documents, the Vichy government, "for reasons of domestic security," decided on November 9, 1942, to restrict the movements of foreign Jews even more: they were now required to stay in the town of their usual residence without leaving it.[46] "Nothing new here," commented Jacques Biélinky.[47] But on December 11, 1942, this measure was replaced by a new law that required all Jews in France to have the word "Jew" stamped on both their identity cards and their individual food ration cards.[48] Up until then, the food ration card had been free of any specific marking, but within the next month, Jews in Paris had to have it stamped. On January 7 and 8, 1943, more than a hundred Jews who had come to fulfill this new requirement and who belonged to categories designated for deportation, were sent off to Drancy.[49]

Beginning in May 1942, the Germans sought a way to mark Jews' identity papers indelibly.[50] At first, it was decided to perforate documents. On August 9, 1943, Jews in the département of La Seine were summoned to the annex of the prefecture of the Paris police on 10 Rue Bailleul (in the First arrondissement) in order to obtain an identity card in full compliance with the law.[51] The preceding day's *Paris-Soir* had reassured the French: contrary to "certain information," "the French identity card is at present only in the planning stages," the paper announced. But plans concerning the Jews were obviously at a very advanced stage. On February 23, 1944, the Ministry of the Interior declared itself satisfied: all of the prefectorates had received the devices that could "imprint the word 'Jew' in raised letters on the identity cards carried by Israelites," and in Paris, the process of issuing such cards to Jews had been completed.[52]

Constant administrative and police harassment kept pressure on Jews in Paris and created a huge rift between the Jews and the other inhabitants of the capital. The Jews were aware of this problem, but the specificity of their fate was not always evident to those who did not share their experience. Then in the summer of 1943, the hunting down of Jews in Paris was suddenly intensified: Aloïs Brunner had just assumed command of the Drancy camp.[53]

TERROR SETS IN AT DRANCY

The camp had become the hub for deporting Jews to the east, and new detainees kept on arriving there every day. As we have seen, they came in from the Paris region either in small groups every day or in large numbers, following massive roundups. The other cities in the Occupied Zone also sent in their lots of "deportable" Jews, who had been arrested during massive operations such as those that took place in rapid succession during the month of October 1942, when 1,965 Jews were thus taken in.[54] Mass arrests were also carried out as measures of reprisal. Such was the case after the attack against a German officer in the Rouen train station: in retaliation, 220 Jews in the département of La Seine-Maritime were arrested on January 13, 1943.[55] Throughout the entire Occupied Zone as in the Paris region, there were daily arrests that kept regularly sending Jews to Drancy. Large numbers of Jews from the Southern Zone were once again sent to Drancy in March 1943. From that time on, Jews from the Southern Zone were sent northward on a regular basis.

The Anxiety of Deportation

From the German perspective, Drancy was supposed to be just one stop along the route that was to lead all of these Jews to Auschwitz. As for the internees and their families, they continued to be haunted by the Germans' capricious use of ill-defined and expandable categories of "deportable Jews," which constantly changed according to the number of Jews arriving at Drancy and the number of trains ready to leave for Auschwitz. There was a lull in this activity in some months (during December 1942, and in January, April, and May 1943, for example). Other months, such as November 1942 and March 1943 were dreadfully intense. And then there were the months during which one or two trains would regularly leave from the Bourget station. Then, after the July 14, 1943, bombing, they used the Paris-Bobigny station.[56]

"Everything in the camp was measured according to deportations," testifies Georges Wellers.

> The optimists were those who, for one reason or another, hoped the deportations would slow down or stop. Any detainee caught carrying on clandestine correspondence feared, above all, that he might be deported. The ordeal for thousands of mothers was either the success or failure of all their efforts to have their children entrusted to the UGIF: if they failed, their children would be deported with them, and if they succeeded, they would face deportation alone. At certain times, thousands of ailing detainees lived with the anxiety that they might recover just in time for a deportation. Others assumed great risks and great expense trying to secretly notify their friends and family in hopes of receiving in time items thought necessary for deportation. Still others were content to set aside part of their meager daily rations in order to constitute a pitiful reserve of food for the upcoming deportation. And then there were those who drew sarcastic remarks from their fellow detainees with their naive hopes of sheltering themselves from deportation by mouthing platitudes to an inspector or even to a mere gendarme. Others, however, earned their comrades' admiration by remaining calm and dignified when facing imminent deportation: some even volunteered to go in order to stay together with friends or family. We always acted and judged others' actions with the idea of deportation constantly on our minds. All other concerns remained far behind. We courageously endured hunger, filth, bedbugs, lack of privacy, unpleasant neighbors, and even the lack of news from loved ones. But deportation was the leap into the unknown.[57]

The specific arrangements for the deportations were determined by what was most convenient and practical (that is to say, from the point of view of camp personnel). And so internees in categories designated for deportation were placed in deportation stairwells as soon as they arrived. When the order came to organize a departure, it was simpler to load detainees into the train. The personnel explained to the camp commander that this arrangement also made it easier to classify deportees. Never mind that it was psychologically unbearable for the deportees, who sometimes had to spend several days waiting. And never mind that, as a result, some families that were already separated—with the men on one side and women on the

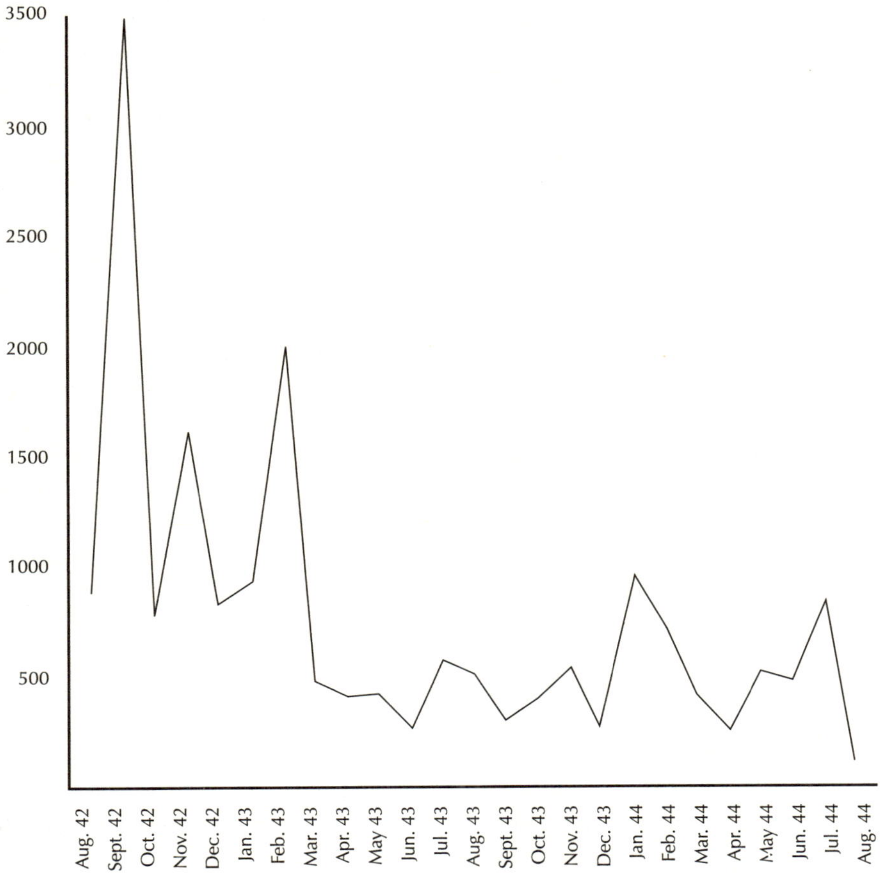

FIGURE 3. Number of arrests in the Paris region, August 1942–August 1944. Figures are according to Serge Klarsfeld, *Calendrier de la persécution des Juifs de France*. Paris: FFDJF, 1993.

other—experienced an additional dislocation, as family members of the same sex sometimes had been placed in different categories.[58] Deportees were loaded onto trains the day before their departure and would spend the evening and the whole night piled into cattle cars, just so the camp manager, who was responsible for supplying each deportation train with food, would not have to get up too early.[59] If one of these poor souls in the train died during the night, he was replaced by another internee in the early morning.

Between Deportations

For those who remained, life in the time between arrivals and departures settled into a certain routine dominated by the fear of deportation. At night, internees were plagued by omnipresent bedbugs; during the day, they spent their whole time looking for some relief from their hunger, since in November 1942 the already insufficient daily rations were suddenly cut even more.[60] Internees experienced a few moments of true happiness whenever a letter or package would arrive. For the sole month of May 1943, some 15,773 packages arrived for internees in the camp, who themselves sent out 3,000 letters. From their families 5, 614 letters arrived for loved ones at Drancy.[61] How could we convey here in these lines the joy of internees upon receiving a package of food that would ease their harsh daily regimen? Can we imagine the emotion that filled their hearts upon reading a few words that would evoke a bit of nostalgia and feed their dreams for the next few days?

The letters that have come down to us abound in descriptions of delicious food that was savored slowly. We also find expressions of great disappointment when certain food items had been confiscated or had spoiled during transport. Some letters list all the daily necessities and food supplies that were anxiously awaited: these included soap and shoes in particular, and also a piece of fabric, sugar, chocolate, and sanitary napkins for young women, who suffered from the lack of this item.[62]

There are also letters that show that internees were not fooled by the rosy picture of things that they received in their correspondence with the outside. "In short, I suspect that things are really not going all that well and that you have said all this so that I would not worry too much," wrote Hélène Felzenszwalbe on June 12, 1943. Even in such cases, however, internees did their part in trying to keep up courage. "My morale is excellent. We must clench our fists, grit our teeth, and hang in there," added Felzenszwalbe in the same letter. The imperative of "hanging in there" is one that is often found in these letters: internees at Drancy held firmly to this rule of conduct, even when they became depressed as the weeks kept going by without bringing the release that they were so anxiously hoping for.

The number of those receiving letters and packages was decreasing regularly, however; there were more and more arrests and thus fewer and fewer close relatives to send them. "Without packages, we are really miserable here," wrote Jules Lehmann about the Drancy camp, as he pleaded with Chief Rabbi Hirschler to send him food.[63] Each day, more and more internees were left with a feeling of complete emptiness, as most had seen their parents, their spouse, or some other member of their family sent away on a deportation train.

And so they tried as best they could to hold up, by working in one of Drancy's service departments at times or by taking advantage of the new freedom of movement within the camp confines, a recent improvement in living conditions obtained in late November 1943 after great effort.[64] They celebrated Christmas: the Drancy priest came to say mass, and on the afternoon of January 1, 1943, the UGIF even put on a circus performance for the three hundred children interned there.[65] These same children even received a semblance of schooling; there was no lack of teachers among the internees at Drancy. However, the activity was soon strictly prohibited and had to take on a different form: the children were secretly brought together in small groups, according to their instructional needs.[66] Out of a total of 2,476 internees in the camp on May 31, 1943, there were 25 children under the age of three, 17 others between the ages of three and six, 60 between the ages of six and thirteen, and 85 between the ages of thirteen and eighteen.[67]

When the pace of deportations slackened a bit, internees regained their confidence by attending one of the violin concerts or song recitals given by the talented people among them.[68] There were a particularly large number of these events in May 1943, after a month's lull in the deportations. Then networks were established that made it possible to carry on clandestine correspondence with one's family. One such network described by Georges Kohn operated from June 1942 to July 1943:

> For myself and about fifty other internees, I had organized a regular clandestine mail service. My fellow internees would give me their notes on Friday evening: these would be very small pieces of paper that nevertheless contained enormously long messages written in tiny letters. None of these papers carried any address, just a few distinctive signs. I would put all of them into one envelope, and Saturday morning, my liaison man (a nondescript employee in Guibert's office [police chief Guibert had been camp commander since August 1, 1942]) came to our meeting place to pick it up. On Sunday morning, he would take these messages to my residence, and my wife would take care of distributing them to their intended recipients. As for messages sent the opposite way into the camp, my wife would receive letters for us on Saturday evening and then place them all together into the large envelope and give it to the liaison on Sunday morning. At about noon on Monday, I in turn would receive this envelope: with the help of about two or three people, I was able to distribute this correspondence to intended recipients in the camp.[69]

Among the young people interned at Drancy, there were even a few tragedies of love: one such case involved a young man who took his own life in desperation in March 1943 after he was unable to win over the heart of a certain young woman.[70] And there were cases of swindling when some of those who had been in the camp the longest used their talents on those newly arrived: they took money from their victims by promising tobacco or a foolproof escape plan. There were some who received special privileges, such as the men married to Aryan women. On May 6, 1943, they were allowed a visit from their spouses: "six people at one time, in the same room, under the surveillance of the gendarmes."[71] This liberality, however, was short-lived. There were a tiny number who were able to spend a day in Paris to check some information at the prefecture of police. The luckiest ones of all were those who were set free: 1,191 Jews were released from Drancy between April 1, 1942, and the end of the same year.[72] Some 406 more internees would experience the same good fortune before July 1, 1943.[73] Some had been protected by their nationality—Turkish, Italian, or Swiss—once it had been firmly established. Others had doubtless finally managed to bring together all the documents necessary for them to be certified as "not belonging to the Jewish race." More than ten thousand such certificates had been issued by May 31, 1944: those who possessed such a document were thus able to "clear themselves."[74] For some, it was this all-powerful piece of paper that had saved them from Drancy and death. Some furriers had been deemed vital because of their work for the German army. A few upper-class French Israelites were released after someone had made a personal appeal on their behalf: such was the case of attorney Edmond Bloch, set free on November 17, 1942.

Finally, the UGIF managed to extricate a few children from Drancy, provided that their parents had not been deported: when this condition could not be met, it was simulated as best as could be. It was thanks to just such a stratagem that twenty-six children were to be sent to one of the UGIF's homes on October 24, 1942.[75] In November 1942, a group of about forty other children left the camp in similar circumstances: they were followed by thirty-one more in December.[76] In comparison with this total of about one hundred children (or 192, according to a report filed by division 14 of the UGIF, which handled relations with the German authorities),[77] 6,423 Jewish children under the age of seventeen had been deported by December 31, 1942.[78] Subsequently, the number of children freed by the UGIF dropped even more: on February 10, 1943, forty-two of them were rounded up from the UGIF's homes and taken back to Drancy to be deported.[79] They had only been given a short reprieve. Beginning on March 9, 1943,[80] camp authorities carried out more meticulous verifications, and it became even harder to fake matters.

The Arrival of Aloïs Brunner

On June 9, 1943, "a wind of anguish blew into the camp." It was, wrote Georges Kohn, "a major date in the history of Drancy"; for it was on this day that "Aloïs Brunner made his appearance in the camp," accompanied by Röthke and Röthke's assistant Ahnert. Brunner had already distinguished himself not only in the central office of Jewish emigration in Vienna under Adolf Eichmann's command, but also in Greece, where he played a decisive role in wiping out the Jewish community of Salonika.[81] With methods tested and proved in the German camps, he set about to transform Drancy as soon as he arrived. The first order was issued immediately: henceforth, only the spouses of Aryans would be able to be employed in the various departments of the camp.[82] Even more serious was that soon there were nothing but rumors of deportation: an "atmosphere of deportation"[83] pervaded the camp, and a reign of terror now prevailed in its administration.

Brunner proceeded to interrogate all the internees personally—thus preparing the upcoming loads of Jews to be deported—while seeking to widen the categories by every possible means and hunting down a few more Jews. To this end, he used simultaneously the carrot and the stick: the carrot fooled no one, but the stick made everybody shudder. On July 2, the Germans officially took over Drancy: only the business manager in charge of keeping the camp supplied with food and basic necessities was kept in his position for a few more days in order to give the UGIF enough time to assume the responsibility for feeding the internees. French gendarmes remained in charge of keeping watch over Drancy, which they now did from the outside.[84] The practice of using Jews to run the camp administration was renewed, and the "cadres" were more deeply involved in the application of all the Nazis' instructions: in particular, they were charged with maintaining discipline among their fellow internees. All the rules that had been in place up until then were changed. As announced in the July 30, 1943, issue of the *Bulletin de l'UGIF*, it was the end of individual food packages: henceforth their contents went to the camp's collective kitchens. Packages of clothing were still accepted: in order to reach their destination, however, they had to be taken to the office of the UGIF on 120 Boulevard de Belleville.[85] Correspondence was also suspended.[86] Both correspondence and individual packages were again authorized in mid-August 1943, but only for the "cadres."[87] Those internees who did take advantage of such liberalities took care to go through a non-Jewish intermediary in order not to divulge their loved ones' address.

In order to mark clearly their status as inferior beings, internees were required to maintain a respectful distance from Germans: whenever they crossed paths, the internee was to stand still until the German had moved away. In a stairwell, the internee had to stand flat against the wall in the corner. All signs and inscriptions in the camp were changed into German. Orders for these measures and for those that were to follow were only issued verbally. Other rules were communicated to internees in a more indirect, but violent manner. "Because of the sun," wrote Georges Kohn:

> many internees were wearing sunglasses. The German Brückler [second in command to Brunner] walked into the courtyard and slapped hard first one internee, then another, then still another. We realized that all those who were slapped were wearing sunglasses. The sunglasses all disappeared immediately and Brückler pointed out: "You people in France give written orders that are never respected. When we want something done, we do not need to write it or to say it, we use much more effective means." And indeed, from that day on, we have not seen any dark glasses in the camp. A few days later, Brückler would use the same method to get rid of all the beards in the camp.[88]

Thanks to the brutality of the sanctions used for any infraction of the rules, the new Nazi masters quickly succeeded in establishing the desired climate of terror in the camp. Internees were subjected to public beatings with a stick, collective punishments, imprisonment in horrible conditions, and physical brutality: nothing was spared in order to give the camp an aura of hell. At the same time, the "sadistic scatterbrain," as André Baur called Brunner,[89] had the internees dig embankments in the camp, for this hell was to be located in proper facilities. He ordered everything to be repainted and the courtyard to be smoothed out and covered with asphalt. He then added lawns and had new showers and model kitchens installed. He reorganized the infirmary and set up leather and sewing workshops, all the while bombarding the UGIF with orders and counterorders, and availing himself of the workforce at hand.[90] Georges Kohn describes the scene: "[The Krauts] walk around holding a cudgel, while the men labor bare-chested with picks and shovels under threats, blows and the burning sun. It is a real vision of hell."[91]

The French administration had problems financing these construction projects. The Office of the Prefect for the département of La Seine sought to get out of supplying funds by arguing that the management of the camp had been entrusted to the UGIF ever since June 30, 1943, after the camp had been seized by the Germans. Accordingly, the prefect's office tried to transfer over to the UGIF the entire financial burden that it had previously borne. Then the General Commission on Jewish Affairs stepped in to emphasize the absurdity of the prefect's argument: the role of managing the camp had not turned the UGIF into the owner or tenant of the Drancy camp, to which it did not even have access. In addition, the UGIF's aid came under the rubric of "optional assistance"; it was up to the French State to provide for the needs of the internees as usual (which was "legal assistance"), regardless of the particular administrative form used to manage each such center. This financial obligation was especially important as the internment of the Jews was in every way similar to the administrative internment of Aryans: both were preventive police measures. The Office of the Prefect for the département of La Seine had a special account to pay the costs related to German demands. The construction projects for Drancy, however, had been demanded verbally and the Germans had refused to issue a written order. Hence it was bureaucratically impossible for the prefect's office to cover the cost, while, as far as the UGIF was concerned, it was materially impossible to make up the difference.[92]

Jewish worship services were officially allowed in the camp while it was undergoing renovation; ceremonies were held in the children's refectory. Beginning on August 2, religious classes were organized.[93] For the 1943 Yom Kippur, there were even two different services held at Drancy: one was Ashkenazic and the other Sephardic.[94] Drancy nevertheless resumed its role as train station for sorting out Jews: the deceptively routine appearance that had come to prevail in the camp for the Jews had been shattered.

The first deportation to follow Brunner's arrival came after a hiatus of three months. This lull and the methods used by Brunner made all the internees expect the worst, and the protections that had previously existed suddenly seemed ridiculously fragile. Hélène Felzenszwalbe, who had up until then thought herself to be sheltered from deportation, asked her parents to supply her with a maximum of provisions for the big journey: bread, sugar, sausage, condensed milk, and as much chocolate as possible. She also wanted a package of underclothes, some sturdy shoes, and above all, a lot of money. "Be calm and strong," she added in a letter to her parents. "I am young, strong, and in good health."[95] Some 1,018 internees from Drancy were deported to Auschwitz on June 23, 1943. Hélène was not among them this time. "My dearest parents, A great joy to be still here today. Today, tomorrow, and for a long time yet, I hope," she wrote after the train had left.[96]

The relief she expressed was quite ephemeral, however; the deportations resumed.

Correspondence was now forbidden, except for one first letter that new internees were forced to send to their families in order to allow the Germans to locate their families' addresses. Internees were also allowed to write one last letter to their families before being deported, for the same reason. "This is the last time, this is it," wrote Hélène on July 30, 1943. "I firmly believe that we are not leaving France. Anyway, it won't be long now. You can be sure that we will soon be reunited. I am happy that this whole series of heavy blows has fallen on me and not you. . . . My morale is excellent." She had just turned nineteen.

Two final notes would follow. The first of these moving messages was sent from the Bobigny station, and it too sought to reassure her family.[97] "Morale is great," she wrote. "We have no regrets in leaving Drancy, which is presently a hellhole, given the violence and brutality that are now prevalent. And nothing could be worse. Some say that we are going to central Germany, others say Radom." In a postscript she spoke of another rumor: the train was supposedly heading for Sarrbrücken. The second note was thrown from the train while it was standing in the Revigny station. "The heat is stifling, I am dying of thirst," but "for me it does not matter because I have already had this experience. I traveled for 24 hours in cattlecars when coming from the Lalande camp. . . . Take heart my dear ones." The letter ended with these words. A passerby mailed it off after having kept a copy, perhaps in order to come some day and personally tell Hélène's parents what she had glimpsed as the train came through.[98]

"This is no longer a deportation, it is an evacuation"

The conditions of departure had changed: now Brunner designated the victims and deportees were no longer shorn. There were no more body searches, and deportees could now take all their baggage. "This is no longer a deportation, it is an evacuation," Brunner had announced.[99] The camp's office of social services moreover had to provide blankets, clothing, underwear, and shoes, all furnished by the UGIF, to those leaving. The Germans would take complete possession of all these personal effects when the deportation train arrived at Auschwitz. At Drancy, however, some gestures were intended to reassure deportees about what was in store for them. The deportees' savings were carefully counted and exchanged for a receipt; they were told that they would be reimbursed in zlotys upon their arrival. This was at the same time that the language of violence still prevailed, and blows would rain down on those the Germans judged to be too slow in getting into the deportation train.

Ernest, who was taken in a police roundup in Nice in October 1943, was a militant with the Jewish Army (AJ). He managed to convince the Germans that he was not a Jew and was released from Drancy on January 2, 1944. "The deportation trains are going to the ghetto in Auschwitz (in Upper Silesia)," he writes in his "testimony of a survivor." He goes on to describe living conditions as harsh but bearable and concludes: "And so, the information, all gathered firsthand from the soldiers escorting the trains back and forth between Drancy and Auschwitz, [is] rather reassuring."[100] These words were penned by someone who was hardly naive: Ernest had joined in clandestine militant activities and had succeeded in getting out of Drancy by adamantly insisting on his Aryan identity. He had nevertheless been fooled by the Germans, as had Hélène Felzenszwalbe.

Two militant Communist women who were deported in the same train with Hélène each independently expressed the same fears: each was concerned about the care her child would receive and about maintaining contact, so that they would be able to be reunited when they returned. "When fate will allow me to come back," said one; "when one day I will come back to life," wrote the other.[101] They had been fooled just as had Simone Weill, who in her last letter to her sister, describes a new camp near Dresden and supposes that the Germans want to bring in a new group of leaders.[102] The same was true of Georges Wellers, who thought that "Pitchipoï" (the term commonly used in the Drancy camp for the unknown destination) could only be one "huge, miserable ghetto" in which the Germans were isolating the Jews and brutally exploiting them. "The darkest imagination went no further," he testified just after the war.[103] The great majority of deportees thought the same thing.

The Germans were able to achieve two objectives by maintaining such confusion. First, they sought to keep in check any thought of resistance. Whether they had a keener awareness of what lay in store for them or whether they were simply more energetic and less worn down by conditions of their detention, some deportees did escape. Eleven internees loaded into the deportation train of February 9, 1943 tried their luck: using a saw, they opened up a hole in their sealed train car. Ten of them were recaptured. On February 9, eight other deportees had better luck, and escaped from the train. A group of about fifteen Jews escaped from the train headed for Sobibor on March 25 after having torn out floorboards in their train car. Only three of them managed to slip through the police dragnet, however.[104]

These escapes and a few other individual flights were in fact desperate attempts. Once the security guard had been tightened, such acts became even more risky, and required the mettle of a résistant. There were two other collective attempts to escape from deportation trains: nineteen deportees succeeded in fleeing on November 20 and a group of about twenty others escaped from the last deportation train to leave from France on August 17, 1944. Most of the latter group were résistants with the Jewish Combat Organization (OJC).[105] The other group had already distinguished itself by digging a tunnel from Drancy in mid-September 1943.[106] Using a cellar located under the office of the Jewish camp commander Lieutenant Colonel Robert Blum, some seventy internees patiently dug out a 32-meter tunnel in two months' time. Then, probably thanks to some indiscretion, Brunner found out what was going on. The underground passage had to be filled back up, the Jewish commander was stripped of his position and then deported, and camp security was tightened.

Nineteen leaders of the escape attempt were arrested, tortured, and deported: they were the ones who escaped from the deportation train on November 20, 1943.[107]

The confusion deliberately created by Brunner served another purpose: in order to hunt down more Jews, he used the tactic of "reuniting families," which consisted of calling on internees to urge their loved ones to join them in the Drancy camp. He attempted to use the UGIF to bring about these reunifications, but met with a refusal.[108] Brunner soon added threats to the incentives: if the family did not voluntarily report to the camp, the internee would be shot. And in order to have the message reach the families, Brunner organized a group of "missionaries"—internees chosen among those who had other family members in the camp. The Germans would send them to Paris to persuade the relatives of other internees to report to Drancy: the goal was to deport the entire "reunited" family.[109] Georges Kohn testified:

> Some "missionaries" would carry out their task by resisting, with all the risks that entailed: far from bring the families in to Drancy, they would manage to warn them or have them warned in such a way that when he came back to camp, he could say that he had found no one. Indeed, some "missionaries" never brought in one single Jew. On the contrary, however, other such "missionaries" followed the Germans' instructions zealously.

All in all, the results were rather meager. Some 150 "volunteers" apparently let themselves get caught in the trap set by Brunner in the first week.[110] In the month of August, only seventy-six Jews were arrested thanks to the work of these "missionaries,"[111] and Brunner decided to not to use them anymore.

Movements and transfers of internees were stepped up during Brunner's stint at Drancy. In addition to the trainloads of deportees sent eastward, 1,220 Jews who either had Aryan spouses or were French citizens born in France were transferred to Beaune-la-Rolande.[112] After a train carrying one thousand Jews had left directly for Auschwitz from Pithiviers on September 21, 1942, the Jews still interned there were transferred to Beaune-la-Rolande on October 1, and Pithiviers was given a new function: henceforth, it took in "undesirable French," Communists for the most part. Beaune became a sort of annex to Drancy: from then on, it was used to intern Jews who had been caught trying to slip across the demarcation line. The Beaune camp was also used to detain those that the Germans transferred in from Drancy because they were not (at least not at the time) "deportable."

At the time, the set of rules for packages was stricter at Beaune-la-Rolande than at Drancy. "It is less well organized than Drancy, but the air and food are better," wrote Renée Baumann three weeks after her arrival.[113] And families were not separated in different stairwells. Two weeks later, 690 of these internees found themselves back at Drancy. On June 20, another 113 returned. Brunner ordered for Beaune-la-Rolande to be closed down on July 12, 1943, and those still interned there also headed for Drancy.[114]

Indeed, for Brunner, the distinction between internees subject to deportation and those who were not was singularly blurred. He had divided them into several categories in order to exploit them as much as possible and to increase the number of those "deportable" to the maximum. There were of course the "workers for the East," those who would be sent to Auschwitz on the next train. "Workers for the West" were made up of both men and women married to Aryans: they were destined for the Todt organization's construction sites. Camp employees, whose numbers had increased,[115] were uniquely composed of French Jews and Jews with Aryan spouses: they were constantly subjected to being placed in another group and transferred back into the previously cited categories. There was a small minority of "releasable" people: they included internees who desperately strove to prove their Aryan identity and the wives and mothers of prisoners of war. A few months later, this latter group was sent to the Bergen-Belsen concentration camp.[116] There were also those who were "waiting for family": they were listed as "missionaries" before being classified as part of the category of "deportables." Finally, there were foreigners not deportable because of their nationality—provided, however, that their consulate had appealed to the Germans on their behalf.[117]

In addition to the flurry of arbitrary decisions that expanded a bit more each day the categories of Jews to be deported, there were two new practices. In the first place, French Jews were now subject to massive deportation. Second, Jews married to Aryans were being sent to destinations that had previously not been used. More than seven hundred internees were taken from Drancy to the island of Aurigny on July 9, 15, and 27, 1943.[118] The island's various nicknames—Adolf Island, Cursed Island, Devil's Island—testify to its sinister reputation.[119] There internees had to put in as many as thirteen hours of work each day, pouring concrete, digging ditches, carrying 50-kilogram sacks of cement, all while a German having earned the nickname "clubber" would rain down blows on them. They were given only meager portions of food and housed in ramshackle buildings infested with lice and fleas, with only a few dried fern leaves for bedding. Such was the fate suffered by a doctor, a pianist, a former county councilman, and many others. In May 1944, those who had withstood this regimen were sent back up north under conditions just as bad as those on deportation trains sent east: after reaching Cherbourg, they were taken to either Hazebrouck or Boulogne, where they were once again subjected to forced labor.[120] On July 17, 1944, a hundred of them returned to Drancy.[121]

Other "privileged" internees left Drancy on July 18, 1943 for Camp Lévitan on Rue du Faubourg-Saint-Martin. Wearing "uniform overalls with the yellow star," the Jews in this camp connected with *Einsatzstab Rosenberg* had to sort out the goods plundered from Jews' apartments and prepare these items for shipment to Germany.[122] At Lévitan, as at the Austerlitz camp opened in October 1943 in the Twelfth arrondissement and in the Bassano camp in the Seventh arrondissement, it was up to the UGIF to feed the internees. Conditions there were not so cruel as at Drancy, but the threat of deportation continued to hang over their heads. On a regular basis, a few would be sent back to Drancy, then deported to Auschwitz. However, a great number of them returned to Drancy at the time of the Paris insurrection, too late to

As required by the first German ordinance (dating from September 27, 1940), a fabric store displays the yellow placard, which has been surrounded by other "important details" in an attempt to dampen any negative effects. © Lohamei ha-getaot.

The word "Jew" stamped on a card. Did the bearer of the card have it renewed in October 1942, if he escaped arrest during the mass roundups of the previous summer? © CDCJ.

Spring 1941, before the massive roundups in Paris: a Jewish hairdresser in the Marais section. © YV.

Summoned by the "green card," these Jews—most of whom are Polish—do not know that this train will take them to one of the two camps in the département of Le Loiret. A year later, the vast majority of them will be deported to Auschwitz. © YV.

The Israelite Scouts of France attend class at a rural worksite in the Unoccupied Zone. © Lohamei ha-getaot.

At the Hôtel Bompard (one of the annexes to the Les Milles camp, near Marseille), children receive a supplement of food (1941–42). © Lohamei ha-getaot.

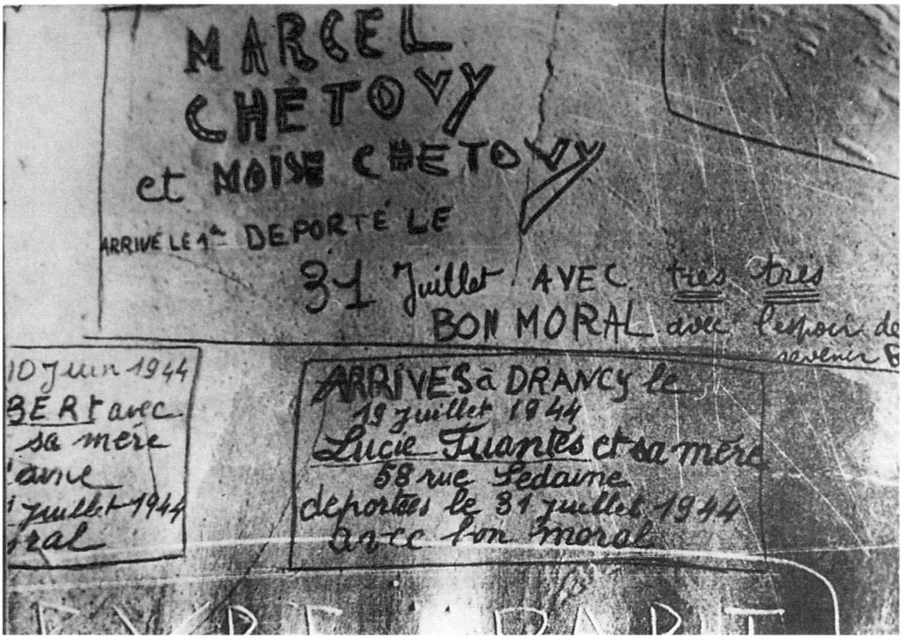

Graffiti on a wall in Drancy camp. © Lohamei ha-getaot.

In Bordeaux, a crowd of people at the entrance to the exhibit "The Jew and France" that began on March 29 and ended May 10, 1942. © YV.

As in Paris, signs point the way to the exhibit "The Jew and France." © YV.

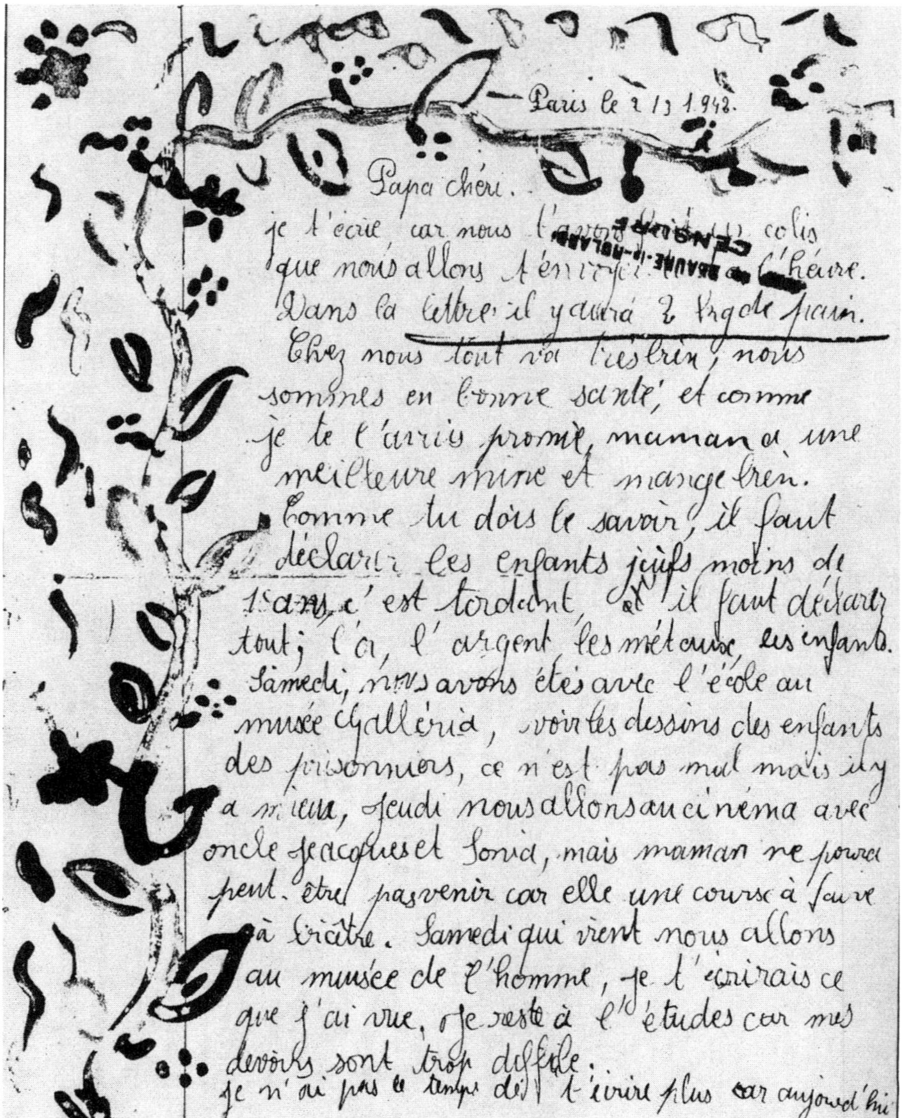

Paris le 2/3 1942.

Papa chéri.

je t'écrie, car nous t'[illegible] colis
que nous allons t'envoyer tout à l'heure.
Dans la lettre il y aura 2 [illegible] pain.
Chez nous tout va très bien, nous
sommes en bonne santé, et comme
je te l'avais promis, maman a une
meilleure mine et mange bien.
Comme tu dois le savoir, il faut
déclarer les enfants juifs moins de
15 ans, c'est tordant, et il faut déclarer
tout; l'or, l'argent les métaux, les enfants.
Samedi, nous avons étés avec l'école au
musée Galléria, voir les dessins des enfants
des prisonniers, ce n'est pas mal mais il y
a mieux, jeudi nous allons au cinéma avec
oncle Jacques et Sonia, mais maman ne pourra
peut être pas venir car elle une course à faire
à Créteil. Samedi qui vient nous allons
au musée de l'homme, je t'écrirais ce
que j'ai vue, je reste à l'études car mes
devoirs sont trop diffile.
je n'ai pas le temps de t'écrire plus car aujourd'hui

March 2, 1942: a letter from Lucienne Rodgold (age 14) to her father, interned at Beaune-la-Rolande.
Rodgold family, private collection.

je ne reste pas à la centre et je vais être en retard.
je t'écrirais, ainsi qu'à Salomon, jeudi tous les 6 nous t'écrirons.

Bons baisers, et ma devise c'est: « COURAGE—ESPOIR—

Ta fille Lucienne qui t'aime

reviens quand tu veux on t'attend toujours.

Bons baisers de la part de

maman
Jeanot
Héléne
Eva
Serge
Lucienne
Jacques
Sonia
oncle Maurice sa femme et ses enfants Sorlon et Anette

Je t'embrasse 1000 fois
Lucienne

on n'a plus d'enveloppes pour t'écrire — envoie-nous en —

Even at Drancy, the yellow star was compulsory. © Lohamei ha-getaot.

CCXVI-727

COMMISSARIAT GÉNÉRAL AUX QUESTIONS JUIVES

4,840

CERTIFICAT

DE NON-APPARTENANCE A LA RACE JUIVE

Sur le vu des pièces produites par l'intéressé, le Commissaire Général aux Questions Juives constate que Mr LACROIX Léon

né le 5 juillet 1912 à Bingen (Moselle)

ne doit pas être regardé comme juif aux termes de la loi du 2 Juin 1941.

Paris, le 9 avril 1943

- 7 JUIN 1943

LE COMMISSAIRE DE POLICE

The Office of the Status of Persons within the General Commission on Jewish Affairs issued about ten thousand of these certificates to Aryans facing "presumptions" or "suspicions" that they were Jewish. © CDJC.

The cover of a brochure put out at the same time as the Red Poster. © Lohamei ha-getaot.

The Carmagnole group in Lyon in September 1944, immediately after the Liberation. © Lohamei ha-getaot.

be deported: in the end, seven hundred Jews employed in these locations in Paris were thus saved.[123]

Word of the new regime in place at Drancy rapidly spread to everyone. The president of the Central Consistory and the chief rabbi were alerted by André Baur, who also wrote to Albert Manuel immediately on July 3, 1943, while at the same time officially notifying Pierre Laval and Marshal Pétain. "If the aforementioned facts are acknowledged to be true, we kindly ask that you appeal to the German Occupation authorities to reinstate more bearable and more humane living conditions for these poor prisoners," they requested in their letter to the head of the French government.[124] For his part, André Baur brought the matter to the attention of the general commissioner for Jewish affairs, the Office of the Prefect for the département of La Seine, the judicial police, and the gendarmerie. The French Communist Party put out a tract about the "Nazi atrocities in the Paris region" that revealed the "truth about the camp at Drancy."[125] A detailed report reached London, and on the evening of October 13, 1943, Roger Chevrier described the hell of Drancy to the French listeners of the BBC.[126] Everywhere, people had the same information, often transmitted in the very same terms; everywhere, people knew.

WAS IT STILL POSSIBLE FOR JEWS TO CARRY ON LEGALLY?

> For someone like me who has never personally been to the Occupied Zone nor, at least since June 1940, to Paris, it is truly stupefying to see the number of people walking around with the yellow star. . . . Upon arriving in Paris, I was surprised to see all these people displaying their Judaism so openly, to see Jews, both men and women, young and old, brushing up against Germans and members of the Milice in the métro, apparently without anyone even thinking of bothering them. I would not have been more surprised if I had seen people wearing the hammer and sickle or the cross of Lorraine by order of the authorities.[127]

In these terms, a young man named Maurice expressed his amazement as someone coming to Paris from the Southern Zone. It says much about the gulf separating the two zones, even though the Germans occupied all of France. It also helps us in perceiving the symbolic force of the yellow star. There were many people in the Southern Zone who maintained their true identity up until the end of the war. In the regions of France dominated by Vichy, however, this identity was not displayed so brazenly on the left side of the chest.

The Parisian Press

In the French capital spangled with yellow stars, there had been no letup in the virulently antisemitic propaganda since the summer of 1942. There were many items pertaining to Jews and their situation in major Parisian newspapers. There were laconic notices informing the general public about new measures taken against the Jews. On one day, all buildings belonging to Jews having fled to the Southern Zone were to be sold.[128] On another, Jews were forbidden to change residences. Then they were required to have their food cards stamped. Readers could learn about new institutes with rather revealing names: the Institute of Anthroposociology, with Claude Vacher de la Pouge as director, had been inaugurated on December 24, 1942,[129] and the French Union for the Defense of the Race followed on January 6, 1943. Finally, the Institute for the Study of Jewish and Ethno-Racial Issues was inaugurated on March 26, 1943 and placed under the direction of Georges Montandon. All of these institutes were sponsored by Darquier de Pellepoix, whose speeches at the ceremonies were duly recounted in newspapers.

The press also published threats against any Jews who might not comply with the new laws. In the article "They forget to wear the star," *Paris-Soir* informed Parisians on February 25, 1943, that since January 1 of that year, 517 Jews had been arrested for violating regulations. There were also appeals to turn Jews in to the police: on January 15, 1943, administrators, ministerial officers, managers, people having power of attorney, concierges, and renters were instructed to declare within a week any Jewish possession not already placed under the control of a provisional manager.[130] The proliferation in the Southern Zone of the constitutive assemblies of the Milice created two months before by Marshal Pétain was announced with a flashy title: "Citizens Have Risen Up Against Jews, Freemasons, and Gaullists."[131]

Meanwhile, antisemitic hatred reached new heights in feature stories. The front-page article in *Paris-Soir,* "The Crime of the Jews," published on March 2, 1943, speaks for itself. In his commentary on what he felt to be the most important point in Chancellor Hitler's most recent proclamation, Jean Bosc recalled the supreme goal "that should be achieved beyond the necessary victory": "above all, ensure the triumph of the Aryan race and destroy the Jews once and for all." Bosc asked: "Who are these men who are attempting to invade the European countries from the east and impose their harsh law?" This was a rhetorical question; Jean Bosc knew quite well the answer and was itching to share his knowledge with his readers.

> Before Stalin, a Jew, there were Lenin and Trotsky, also Jews, as well as a whole countless number of other Jews grouped together like a pack of wolves eager to satisfy their appetites. There were Jews, more Jews, and nothing but Jews at the origin of Communism. The Union of Soviet Socialist Republics is a band of adventurers and warped intellectuals from the ghettos of Russia, Poland, and certain Balkan countries: they are hords who have rallied together out of a common need for gratification at the expense of organized society. The rest are simply a bunch of ignorant, wretched, primitive people incapable of reason and perhaps even of thought.
>
> If we turn in the other direction and look at our American adversaries, we see the same unconscious masses: but behind them we once again find the Jews pushing them to fight for a cause that is obviously not theirs. The Jews of New York, Washington, Boston, and Philadelphia are pulling the strings of these democratic

> puppets just as the Jews of Moscow are pulling those of the Communist puppets. And it is once again Jews inciting people to engage in this senseless conflict.

For Bosc, there was only one possible conclusion: "What we must do is to save our race, the Aryan race, from Israel's domineering intentions. And in this battle to death that Hitler has undertaken against the Judaic monster, it is the duty of Christian France to be present, just as she has always been present in the world when the fate of civilization and humanity has been on the line."[132]

In the March 16, 1943, issue of *Le Matin*, Jacques Ploncard called for the "institution of a Ministry of Race" for the sake of France's "moral and material health." Then in the March 18, 1943, edition of *L'Appel*, Pierre Constantini loudly demanded a "ferocious purge." "If we want France to live," he proclaimed, "France must no longer be Jewish. Israel has taken the place of Satan, Israel is king, Israel is leading the bloody dance."[133]

The newspapers specifically committed to fighting against the Jews thus did not remain idle. First came an unrelenting series of calls for the French government to bring its antisemitic policies in line with those of the Third Reich: such a stance would be sure to bring political gains, they affirmed, for it would eliminate the uncertainty over Vichy's settlement of the Jewish problem. In addition, each newspaper gave its own commentary on the key events of the time. The occupation of the Southern Zone inspired Maurice de Séré to write for *Le Pilori* on November 19, 1942: "Filled with terror, you know what fate awaits you: you flee into the mountains and hide in secret corners. But just you wait, Jew, you will not miss anything by putting things off, and, as you know, your fate has been sealed, you will disappear right down to the last member of your race. And then, whether she is occupied or not, all of France will truly be a free zone."

When three age groups of French youth were required to go into the Forced Labor Service (STO), *Le Pilori* was outraged by the spectacle of "a large number of Jewish youth with and without the yellow star who smile as they watch our workers leave, just as they smiled the two times when our soldiers were mobilized." Accordingly, the paper advocated interning all Jews old enough to work.[134]

A few days later, when it became a question of stripping a large number of naturalized Jews of their French citizenship (as Darquier had already suggested), Jean Boissel writing for *Le Réveil du peuple* asked for "the pure and simple abrogation of the decree of the constitutional assembly of September 27, 1791, which criminally granted French citizenship to Jews." Boissel then added, "There is only one definitive, categorical solution, one that is the basis of the true revolution: the taking of blood and sterilization." Did *Le Réveil du peuple* have knowledge of the plans for a massive denaturalization of Jews that Bousquet was preparing? The accumulation of these virulent attacks in March and April 1943—which were carefully noted by the inspectors with the prefecture of the Paris police in their biweekly reports—suggest instead that the offensive was masterminded from afar, perhaps in order to extend a warm welcome to Heinrich Himmler, who came on a visit to Paris on April 3.[135]

Aerial bombardments were occurring more frequently and creating anxiety among the population. This gave ideas to Lucien Pemjean, who wrote in the July 29, 1943 issue of *Le Pilori*:

> Concentration camps for Jews should be spread out around factories, airfields, railways junctions, the barracks of German Occupation troops, and around every place threatened by squadrons of planes from overseas. That way, the bombs that fall astray on civilian populations will first of all strike the children of Juda. . . . At the same time, . . . a decree stipulating that for every civilian victim of the aerial bombardments, two Jewish adults will be shot, should be issued and rigorously put into application. First two, then three, then four, then five: the number of Jewish hostages to be shot should be increased by one with each new raid that hits our civilian population.[136]

Disseminated by marginal newspapers at the cutting edge of propaganda, and backed by the more "reasonable" antisemitism of the mainstream press, such virulent racial hatred was part of daily life for Jews in the capital. Groups of militant collaborationists added a few touches of their own. Sometimes they handed out antisemitic tracts, as did the French People's Youth [Jeunesse Populaire Française] on April 2, 1943, in the Fifteenth arrondissement. On other occasions, they provoked a scuffle in a café known for serving a large number of Jews: thanks to the initiative of a lieutenant with the Legion of French Volunteers, such incidents occurred on both March 17 and March 20, 1943, on Rue Popincourt and Rue Sedaine. In the noisy demonstrations that would sometimes take place as people left political rallies, the most common slogan seems to have been "Death to the Jews." After a sharp rise in the autumn of 1942, however, such incidents occurred less and less frequently.

A Population Totally Preoccupied with Daily Living Conditions

On the whole, however, if we are to believe personal testimony of those who experienced these events, the people of Paris remained more or less unsupportive of such expressions of extremism. The press complained about this indifference from time to time, castigating the "outbreaks of misguided sympathy" that the "elimination of the Jews" had aroused in the hearts of some Parisians.[137] The number of people joining various collaborationist groups had leveled off and their activists were increasingly ostracized, particularly after the Allied landing in North Africa.[138]

Shortages of basic commodities, extreme weather conditions, and the heating problems brought on by such occurrences left little place for other worries. The studies of public opinion carried out for the prefecture of the Paris police continued to emphasize first and foremost the recriminations of a population totally preoccupied by everyday living conditions. Having returned to Paris with a suitcase full of food after a short stay in Brittany, one lycée girl observed in her diary that "there, the main topic of conversation was the Germans. Here, it is food."[139] Three weeks earlier, she had noted: "I never talk about food in my diary, because I find that particularly annoying. But now, all the French talk about is grub, heating, and clothing. Shoes are particularly hard to find."[140] In face of the increasingly acute shortages, a rumor swept through Paris: a large number of people were supposedly going to be evacuated from the capital in order to make it possible to keep the city supplied in a more rational manner.[141]

In March 1943, the central sections of Paris had taken on a new look. Department stores, fashion shops, luxury boutiques, and florists had been requested by their respective trade associations to take luxury and high-priced items out of their storefront windows, as such displays might appear inappropriate to the majority of people, given the hardships imposed by the war. Some shopkeepers had even covered their display windows with an opaque veil, leaving only a small space for a few items to be displayed.[142] In June, some bakeries in the capital closed because they were out of flour.[143] In September and October 1943, Paris experienced a dire shortage of meat.[144] Large crowds of Parisians had come to get textile points in exchange for all rags, old clothes, woolen goods, and rugs at the ninety-seven exchange centers that opened in the capital during autumn of 1943.[145] People blamed the supply offices and especially the German requisitions for these widespread shortages.[146]

There was moreover growing anxiety over the young people who risked being sent forcibly to work in Germany; this fear made people hate the occupying forces even more. As for the law of September 4, 1942, authorizing the requisition of male French citizens between the ages of eighteen and fifty as well as females between the ages of twenty-one and thirty-five, it was generally seen as "a pure and simple requisition of French labor for Germany."[147] "The public seems to consider the Workers for POW's program [which since June 1942 had taken on the official appearance of reciprocity in that it provided for the release of one French prisoner of war for every three French workers volunteering for work in Germany] to be a deportation measure."[148] Families worried about what would become of those who had left and dreaded that they might be incorporated into the teams sent to build fortifications on the Russian front.[149]

February 1943 marked the imposition of the Forced Labor Service (Service du Travail Obligatoire, [STO]) and required young people who had been born in the years 1920, 1921, and 1922 to go work in Germany. It was widely seen as a disguised deportation of French youth.[150] From then on, every report on the public's mood would mention the anxiety connected with these departures, and the police were increasingly criticized for their efforts to seek out and apprehend those who tried to dodge the Forced Labor Service.[151] People's assessments of major political and military events were largely determined by their concerns about basic commodities and forced labor in Germany.

Public opinion in Paris became even more pro-American after the Allied landing in North Africa. Contacts between Marshall Pétain and Chancellor Hitler had given rise to "unfavorable" remarks in late 1942,[152] and people closely followed the unfolding events of the Battle of Stalingrad.[153] The population of Paris was completely behind the Allies, while collaboration was more and more despised. In his biweekly report of July 26, 1943, a police inspector did not hesitate to write that "the French [expected] the Russians and the Anglo-Americans to liberate them." And so people greeted the news of the Allied landing in Sicily with satisfaction. In this context, people were even resigned to the fact that they would suffer from English and American bombing. The air raid of April 4, 1943, claimed 392 victims in the département of La Seine, and over the first half of September, Paris and its suburbs recorded almost three hundred deaths, while some fifteen hundred people required hospitalization for their injuries. Fears were so great that *Paris-Soir* published a long front-page article on the possibility of using the sewers to shelter or evacuate people in case of aerial bombardment.[154]

Nevertheless, the public considered the bombing to be a "painful necessity of the war,"[155] the prelude to an Allied landing, and thus to the Liberation. The deep tendencies of public opinion in Paris would not change. The expectation of the Allied landing was at the forefront of people's minds, and they were less hesitant to come out and say what they had been thinking all along. In late December 1943, directors and managers of cinema halls were instructed to keep the lights on during newsreels in order to avoid incidents such as the loud round of applause that had greeted the footage on the destruction in Berlin caused by the English and American bombing, screened during the first matinee session on December 25, 1943.[156]

Thus everyday life for Jews in Paris went on not only in face of unceasing manhunts by the police and virulently antisemitic invective in the press, but also of chronic shortages of basic necessities and the swings of public opinion. In the very same police report, an inspector from the prefecture analyzed Parisians' reaction to the conscription of men born in 1920, 1921, and 1922 into forced labor in Germany; he also remarked that "the distribution made by the offices of basic commodities and supplies have never been so meager" and that "Russian military successes are raising many hopes for a quick end to the hostilities." And with respect to the more than sixteen hundred Jews of all ages arrested and sent to Drancy on February 11 and 20, 1943, the same report also noted that "the recent arrests of foreign Jews [had not] stirred any reaction" except for "a certain remonstrating at of the internment of elderly people."[157]

The public did not always perceive what made the mass arrests of Jews radically different from other events of the time, especially as some such police operations carried out during the same time hit social groups much more widely scattered in Parisian society. As Romanian Jews were being arrested on September 23, 1942, four hundred American citizens were apprehended by the Feldgendarmerie. This number represented two-thirds of those who had been subjected to weekly police checks after having declared themselves at the Kreiskommandantur in compliance with an order from the German military command in France issued on December

22, 1941.[158] The previous week, a massive police roundup of Communists had led to the arrest and internment of 1,614 people.[159] Anyone who gave the matter a bit of thought could have seen that the fate reserved for the Jews was in no way comparable to that of the others. But the typical Parisian was not necessarily aware of that: were not Americans, Jews, and Communists all sworn enemies of the Germans?

A Common Fate?

The gradual introduction of the Forced Labor Service blurred perceptions even more. When the law was first promulgated on September 4, 1942, Jews began to worry. "Condemned to do nothing, [they] will be the first victims" of this law, predicted Jacques Biélinky.[160] When French youth were drafted to go work in Germany, Jews were exempted—the Germans had other things in store for them. But just as the number of youth refusing to comply with the law kept increasing, so did the number of youth who were stopped by police and made to show their papers: in the spring of 1943, more than 130,000 such checks were made every two weeks.[161] As a result, Jewish youth found themselves doubly exposed, and the insecurity of their situation heightened. But in the eyes of most Parisians, "deportation" now threatened all French citizens, and the deportation of the Jews was just the first stage of a wider operation. What was thus perceived as a shared destiny (even though some people were outraged to see the Jews exempted from the Forced Labor Service) led to some new forms of aid and cooperation, that were both indispensable—and utterly illusory.

The relations between Jews and the general public of Paris were not limited to the question of whether or not people reacted to the police roundups. Both Jews and non-Jews suffered from shortages and the material hardships of everyday life. In his diary, Jacques Biélinky took careful note of the amounts he spent each month, and from February to November 1942, we observe that his food budget increased by 60 percent.[162] The last words that he wrote down in his notebook on December 17, 1942, were to observe that "the black market is snatching up everything and those who only live on their ration tickets are doomed to starve."[163]

But non-Jews did not actually suffer so severely from the shortages as did Jews: while unemployment was disappearing in France,[164] Jews continued to be barred from most professions. Aryanization was in full swing in 1943: the number of businesses aryanized doubled, while sales and liquidations of Jewish property increased by 60 percent.[165] And by that time, any savings they had were largely depleted. The fact remained that, in spite of the empty store shelves, the best way to obtain basic commodities was with money.

In his report, Maurice strives to define which Jews were carrying on their lives legally in Paris. The first group was made up of those who carried the "legitimation card" and their families. According to his estimate, there were about 3,500 such people: they either had the advantage of being protected by their job with the UGIF or by a number of specific circumstances. There was one person who provided for the needs of his entire family: he could not leave his job without forcing his family to go begging in the streets. There were invalids and people whose loved ones were either invalid or gravely ill, and could not be abandoned. And then there were French Jews who either had simply not understood the danger of their situation or who had resigned themselves to a sort of fatalism, and who were waiting their turn to be taken. "What do all these legal Jews live from?" wondered Maurice, who then answered his own question:

> Let us eliminate right away those who continue to draw on their inexhaustible reserves: they form an extremely small category whose numbers are dwindling as the war wears on. First of all, then, there are the young people who, if they were Aryan, would be old enough to fall under the requirement to go to Vichy's youth camps (Chantiers de Jeunesse), to be drafted into the Forced Labor Service, or to leave for Germany. But since there are no youth camps in the Northern Zone and since Jews cannot be sent to Germany as workers, these youth get requisitioned to go to factories in the Paris area producing goods directly or indirectly for the Wehrmacht. They are granted furloughs to visit their families in Paris or in the surrounding area; they are rather well treated; and they receive a salary proportionally high enough for them to support all their dependents. Then there are certain tradesmen (tailors, furriers) working for firms that protect them because they also produce goods for the German Occupation forces. Finally, there is the category of those spunky individuals clever enough to beat the system. They have an extremely unusual lifestyle, and enjoy an equally unusual tolerance. . . . Amongst themselves they sell and traffic in all sorts of merchandise, particularly fabrics, silks, haberdashery, hats, furs, rarely in hard currencies; and of course the reason why such trafficking is tolerated is because the merchandise, after going through a sort of vicious circle, is hard to obtain by any other means, and ends up being sold to the Germans.[166]

Maurice's description suggests that he did not particularly esteem those who had chosen to maintain a legal existence in Paris. His account nevertheless helps us profile such Jews. There were UGIF employees carrying their miraculous "legitimation card," immigrants carrying an *Ausweis* and working for a protected industry, Jews who had hung on to their job thanks to an exemption, merchants who had worked things out with their provisional manager, and tailors and other tradesmen who managed to eke out a living by maintaining a discreet clientele. We can bet that in addition to all those, a significant number of Jews were managing to survive only because of their clever, innovative methods of beating the system (which sometimes meant trafficking in contraband, but more often involved all sorts of barter). Existing laws left them few other options.

Jews also had to beat the system just to do their shopping. Since mid-July 1942, they had to make do with only one hour, from 3:00 to 4:00 in the afternoon, during which they could go to stores—and at that time of day, stores were generally closed. On October 31, 1942, newspapers announced that Jews could henceforth do their shopping between eleven in the morning and noon.[167] Granted, an internal memorandum from the prefecture had instructed agents not to arrest Jews who might have done their shopping during forbidden hours.[168] But the inspectors with the Section of Investigations and Inspections (SEC) did not see things that way, and in most cases, Jews managed to obtain food supplies thanks only to the kindness of a neighbor who took care of shopping for them (which was explicitly forbidden by the German ordinance) or to a storeowner who handled their purchases discreetly. Such indulgence was also required to make a phone call, as Jews were now forbidden from using any telephone, public or private. Such help was equally useful for corresponding with a relative interned at Drancy without revealing one's address. In short, Jews had to rely on the kindness of non-Jews just to take care of any one of a myriad of little everyday matters.

The illusion of a shared destiny between Jews and non-Jews is not limited to the incommensurable difference between those who had to go work in Germany under the Forced Labor Service and those deported by trainload to Auschwitz-Birkenau. The Jews were not fooled by that illusion, because they had to suffer the stigma of their difference in every activity of their daily lives. Not only did they suffer more severely from the shortage of everyday commodities and supplies; they also found it much harder to find any relief or escape. One sign among others of an "escape into and through culture,"[169] for example, was that cinema and entertainment halls in Paris still drew considerable crowds in spite of a 20 percent increase in ticket prices in early 1943: Jews, however, had to stay home because of the curfew. For many young people, it was this impossibility of participating in social functions organized by their friends that symbolized the gulf separating Jews from the rest of society. Of course Jews could still seek entertainment and escape by reading, but public libraries were off-limits, unless some non-Jewish friend provided indirect access to their books.

Jews continued to be singled out as the pariahs of the new society. When unhindered movement between the Northern and Southern Zones was reestablished on March 1, 1943, the newspapers did not fail to point out that "Jews and undesirables" did not enjoy this new freedom of movement. Any Jew who overlooked one of the provisions of the German ordinances and, for example, walked through and not around a public garden, risked at the very least the humiliation of being chased out by the caretaker, and at the worst, being arrested and sent to Drancy. This omnipresent threat represented the essential difference between the situation of Jews and non-Jews.

Each Jew either had at least one family member at Drancy or had learned that a loved one had been sent to some terrifying unknown destination. Each was anxiously awaiting some sign of life from a deported family member, which might come from the small number of letters that trickled through to the UGIF. There were relatively few letters that made it through, compared with the number of deportees: only about twenty letters as of late September 1942[170] and a few hundred in the spring of 1943.[171] "Ich bin gezund," (I am in good health) was invariably the message, as was written on the card received in January 1944 by the parents of Hélène. There were a few terribly empty, sterile sentences in German, and an official signature: it was no longer "Yours, Hélène" but "Hélène Felzenszwalbe" who had signed the note, and such a closing aroused as much anguish as it did hope.[172]

Beginning in the spring of 1943, it was theoretically possible to get through a message to deportees by the intermediary of the UGIF.[173] It remains difficult to determine the number of families fooled in this manner and the number of illusions thus nourished. This particular service of the UGIF doubtless maintained hopes that would not be proved futile until the end of the war. All the documents show, however, that the UGIF leaders shared similar hopes. The possibility of corresponding with deportees was cleverly granted in May 1943, with certain restrictions that made it seem even more credible: only two letters a month, in German, with no reference to political problems. And then, the possibility of sending packages of clothing, once again through the UGIF,[174] only thickened the smokescreen separating deportees from their families.

Moreover, the threat of deportation hung over all Jews. Anxiety clutched children's throats when their parents came back later than expected, and the same was true of parents when a child stayed late at school. Police checks regularly conducted at métro exits did not have the same significance for Jews and non-Jews. From the summer of 1943 on, whenever one family member got arrested, all the others were to go immediately into hiding in order to escape "family reunification" measures. Drancy and deportation were an integral part of all Jewish home life.

But even under those conditions, there were Jews who kept on living in absolute legality up until the Liberation, being careful to wear their yellow star properly and not violate any of the anti-Jewish ordinances. During the 1942–1943 school year, more than 7,700 Jewish children were enrolled in the Paris district, attending preschool, primary school, secondary school, middle school, and vocational school.[175]

Table 3. Jewish Pupils within the Paris School District, 1942–1943 School Year[1]

	Boys	Girls	Total
Preschoool	780	686	1,466
Primary School	2,323	2,500	4,823
Secondary School	234	268	502
Middle School	299	271	570
Vocational School	281	60	341
Total	3,917	3,785	7,702

1. AN, AJ 38, 1142 contains the responses given on July 16, 1943, by the main office of vocational schooling in the Ministry of National Education, on May 17, 1943, by the superintendent of the Paris school district, and in March 1943 by the office of general inspection of primary schools at the prefectorate for the département of La Seine. The information was sent subsequent to the March 31, 1943, request from the General Commission on Jewish Affairs.

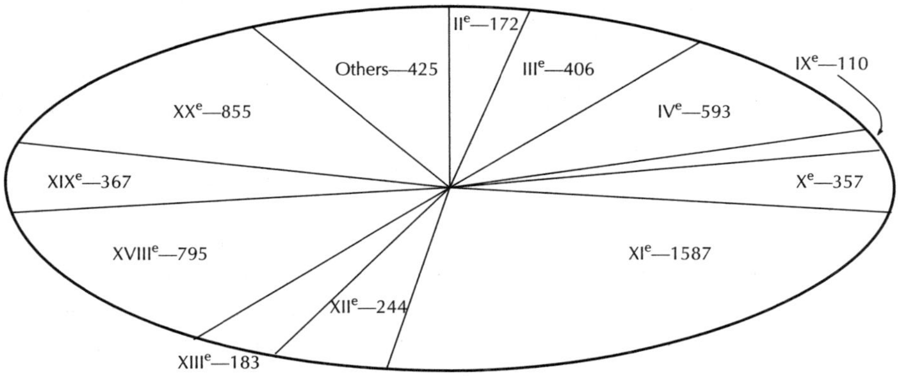

FIGURE 4. Distribution of Jewish students in primary and middle schools in Paris (for the 1942–1943 school year), according to arrondissement.

Nearly half of the Jewish children enrolled in primary and secondary school in the Paris region were in the Eleventh, Eighteenth, and Twentieth Arrondissements.[176] The largest groups of Jewish adolescents could be found in the Voltaire middle school (for boys) and Victor-Hugo middle school (for girls).[177] Given such a distribution, we can surmise that most of these schoolchildren came from families who were either of foreign nationality or naturalized French citizens.

We owe this wealth of information to the General Commission on Jewish Affairs, which had plans to "separate Aryan youth from Jewish youth and to provide to both groups a parallel course of instruction to be carried out under the continuous control of the state, but which would avoid direct contact between the two races as much as possible."[178] The General Commission thus considered the possibility of setting aside ten public schools for Jewish primary school pupils by dividing the Paris region into sectors and adding on two UGIF schools. It seemed more difficult

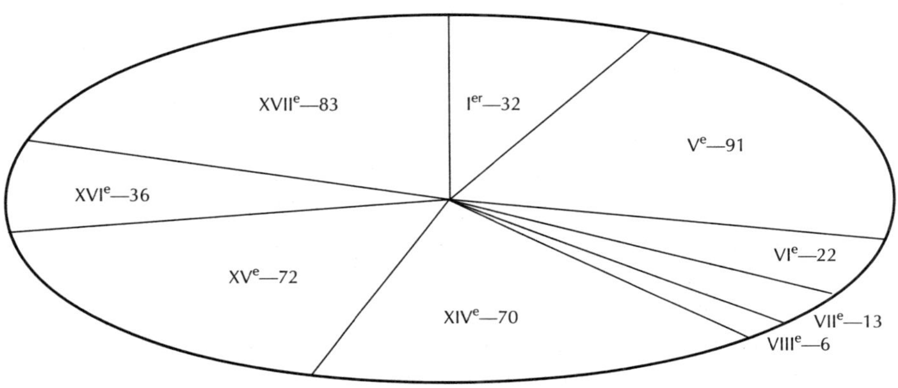

FIGURE 5. Distribution of Jewish students in primary and middle schools in Paris (for the 1942–1943 school year) in arrondissements I, V, VI, VII, VIII, XIV, XV, XVI and XVII.

to work out some way of regrouping children attending preschool (who moreover did not yet wear the yellow star). As for the secondary schools, the question was moot, as it was not a required part of the educational program and as it led to professions from which Jews were barred. These plans, however, were never brought to fruition: on a technical level, it was too difficult.[179]

As precise as they may be, the figures only sketch out a fleeting reality: the number of Jewish students duly enrolled in Paris area schools was constantly falling. Before the imposition of the yellow star, seventeen out of the forty-four children attending the neighborhood elementary school for girls at 82 Rue de Ménilmontant in the Twentieth arrondissement since the beginning of the Occupation no longer appeared on the institution's register in 1941. Over the course of 1942, fifteen other children left the school, ten of them in July. And 1943 saw the departure of nine other Jewish pupils. Some of them had been deported, and others had either fled to the Southern Zone or gone into hiding.[180] Extrapolating from these figures, one can easily imagine that if the General Commission on Jewish Affairs had conducted a survey for the 1943–1944 school year, it would have observed that the number of Jewish children attending school had decreased dramatically. The number of Jews carrying on their life legally in Paris was falling steadily, and often children were the first to be sheltered by being withdrawn from school.

A *Legal Jewish Organization*

The UGIF provided the organizational facade for Jews to carry on a legal existence: it was their only possible intermediary when a loved one was at Drancy, a recourse when they were penniless, and the only Jewish entity recognized by the authorities in a world increasingly closed to them.

As of December 1942, there were 815 employees with the UGIF[181] who enjoyed the benefits of a "legitimation card," which indicated that Monsieur X, serving the UGIF in such and such capacity, "is to be exempted from all internment measures. This protection is extended to his family members living with him. This legitimation card has been issued with the approval of the German Occupation authorities. The German administrative offices having jurisdiction in this matter have a copy of this card." The text of the card was also written in German and bore the stamp of both the General Commission on Jewish Affairs and the UGIF.[182]

However, foreign employees soon had to give up this protection. Previously, just before some of the police roundups, it had been possible, using information about the categories of Jews targeted, to protect those in danger by using the legitimation cards to quickly make them UGIF employees.[183] Only a small number of people had benefited from these quick transformations. In the autumn of 1942, however, the German Sicherheitsdienst ordered André Baur to fire all foreign UGIF employees (a decision actually suggested by Darquier de Pellepoix).[184] In an attempt to have the order revoked, André Baur, in a reversal of roles, tried to used the time-honored tactic of playing off the Germans—who had demanded that there be an equal representation of both French and foreign Jews in the "compulsory organization" constituted by the UGIF—against the General Commission on Jewish Affairs. Threats of resignation, equivocation, and delaying tactics succeeded in obtaining some concessions. The deadline for executing the order was postponed, and permission to keep some fifty employees in the UGIF-North organization was granted. Wherever possible, those forced out of the UGIF could be replaced by a family member of French nationality: in the case of the children's home at Montreuil-sous-Bois, the director's wife, who was French, thus served as a cover for her husband, who was Hungarian.[185]

In addition, the delay enabled some of those newly threatened to disappear just as the document protecting them was being withdrawn.[186] In spite of the reassurances given by Röthke, the police roundup targeting them was carried out two weeks before the day (March 31, 1943) their employment with the UGIF was scheduled to be terminated: as a result, more Jews—anywhere from 38 to 60 or 80, depending on the sources cited—fell into the hands of French and German police.[187] The Jews who managed to avoid capture suddenly found themselves vulnerable and without protection: they had no choice but to join the multitude who had gone underground. Once again, André Baur had only succeeded in limiting the damage.

And that was precisely the objective of his strategy for dealing with the many groups of children in precarious situations. Some children were now without parents and had come to the UGIF or the OSE (a branch of the UGIF) on their own. Others had been brought by neighbors and by parents, who were beginning to entrust their offspring to the UGIF. There were also those children that prefectures sent to the UGIF through the Red Cross (after having arrested their parents); these children had probably been born in France and were French citizens by declaration. Other children had, thanks to the efforts of the UGIF, been released from Drancy becaused they were "isolated": they had first transited through the centers on Rue Lamarck and Rue Guy-Patin. Finally, there were "isolated" Jewish children who had experienced the Poitiers camp: Rabbi Elie Bloch had gotten them out and placed them with a Jewish family in the region.[188] From 3,000 to 3,500 children stayed for what in some cases was a very short length of time in the various homes for them that had been set up by the social services division of the UGIF in former Jewish centers.[189]

That these children came out of so many different situations is indicative of the ambiguity of the UGIF's position. While providing a safety net for children who would have otherwise been deported, the organization was becoming Drancy's auxiliary. The total capacity of the UGIF's children's homes did not exceed 414 places.[190] There were always vacancies: while 386 beds were occupied on January 5, 1943, only 166 were in use on April 2, but on July 13, 1943, the number had increased to 374. Obviously these shelters were complemented by a system of placing children with families, a system required from the very beginning in order to take in as many children as possible. It is not possible to assess the number involved. At the outset, it seemed most important to spare these children from the hell of the camps and to save them from being deported. Bounced around from camps to centers and from one center to another, often separated from their families in traumatic conditions, these children found some semblance of a normal routine in these homes: they regularly attended a neighborhood or community school, scrupulously observed Jewish holy days, received medical care, and were as a general rule decently fed. All in all, they lived in a joyless atmosphere, but sometimes enjoyed a respite from the dramatic events unfolding around them.[191]

Beginning in January 1943, a new system of monitoring these children had been imposed on the UGIF: the homes in Paris and all the children with known addresses had been "blocked," and thus carefully inventoried. Forty-two children in UGIF homes were arrested and deported on February 10, 1943; the children "blocked" in the départements of L'Oise and La Seine-et-Oise suffered the same fate in July and August 1943.[192] In March 1943, moreover, the General Commission on Jewish Affairs ordered the UGIF to stop payments to non-Jewish wet nurses: the idea was to put an end to the practice of scattering children about in various locations and to make it easier to monitor them.[193]

Behind the Legal Organization (1)

Since the fall of 1942, certain UGIF leaders, but in particular activists with the OSE, had, under the direction of Dr. Eugène Minkowski and in conjunction with the Amelot Committee, begun systematically scattering children in various areas by sending them across the demarcation line and placing them with women who agreed to care for them and who most often lived in the country. As of September 1943, some eight hundred children had been spread about in "Aryan" families by the Amelot Committee and the OSE.[194] Beginning in January 1943, the UGIF's sociomedical commission, to which Minkowski belonged[195] and which worked closely with the Amelot Committee, decided to admit into its centers only children who were isolated and without parents.[196] Given the number of greatly distressed parents seeking at all costs to place their children somewhere, it was difficult to abide by this decision. After the police had rounded up the children in the UGIF's homes and when stricter monitoring began, Juliette Stern, who headed the UGIF's social services as well as the WIZO (an international organization for Zionist women), set up an underground system within the UGIF for placing children with families. Henceforth the clandestine 42b social services office duplicated the official 42 social services office: under the leadership of Madame Getting, it quietly placed about a thousand children, scattered about in various locations.[197] The UGIF office would refer parents to Aryan social workers, who would then take care of the placement.[198]

UGIF dispensaries were often a virtually mandatory first stop for children going from a legal to a clandestine existence. The OSE used the dispensary on Rue des Francs-Bourgeois to take in children brought by their parents. To get children out of UGIF homes, groups of social workers organized by the Israelite Scouts and working in close cooperation with Juliette Stern[199] would come get them in small groups and take them to the dispensaries for treatement. From there they would first be taken to a place where they would have to learn their new Aryan identity flawlessly before being placed with foster mothers who were scattered about in various locations and paid with UGIF funds. The social workers would come to check on the foster mothers each month and would fill out file cards describing their living conditions. When the operation went underground, the use of codes made it possible to put together all the information about the children, their families, and the places where they were being kept.

Similar file cards filled out by social workers with the OSE and the Amelot Committee give us an idea of what this responsibility for the well-being of several hundred children meant on a day-to-day basis. We can see how they reached the decision to discontinue the use of one foster mother whose household was particularly dirty, even though the children were well fed; how another nice, sweet foster mother let herself be controlled too much by a hidden child's mother, who would take the children on outings and thus put them in danger; how yet another used blackmail to get an increase of the stipend allotted for the children under her care and to ask for supplies (bread, potatoes, and soap); and how one such foster mother decided from one day to the next not to take care of children any more. Some of these foster mothers were good but rather simpleminded, while others were too cold. There were also some who pampered these children who had to be fed, clothed, fitted with shoes, and cared for when ill, and who surrounded them with warmth.[200]

These concise reports allow us to see the complexity of the task facing the activists with the OSE and the Amelot Committee, and at the same time point to the wide variety of trying experiences these young children had to face as they were bounced around from one place to another, then suddenly placed under the care of total strangers. We can imagine the difficulties encountered by these little city-dwellers suddenly transferred to a rural setting. Those who took on a new identity totally foreign to their previous surroundings had to learn and "play" the role of the character they were to become: for them, it was as if they had entered another universe. And those who had seen their parents taken away by the police suffered unspeakably from their loss.[201] And as danger drew ever nearer, it became ever more imperative to avoid all contact between parents and children, at least in the cases in which there were parents. This was no small problem either for the parents, who had no other choice, nor for the leaders of the aid organizations who were obliged to comply with the rule, nor for the children, who thus found themselves cut off from their families.

Such children often had to follow a long, tortuous path, as witnessed by the example of Robert Frank. Separated from his parents (Polish Jews subsequently arrested and deported to Auschwitz) at Angoulème, he was first taken in, along with ten other French Jewish children, by a priest who placed them in the hands of a Catholic charitable organization. There he felt threatened by the religious proselytizing, and so wrote to Rabbi Elie Bloch, who then placed the eleven children in Jewish families in the Poitiers region. A few months later, the children were taken from the families and sent to the UGIF's centers by the French police. Robert Frank thus arrived at the Rue des Rosiers vocational school in a state of tremendous distress and found an "atmosphere of deportation" there. Thanks to the intervention of Dr. Fred Milhaud, who was in charge of monitoring the health of the children in the school and one of the leaders of the Temporary Assistance (ET), Frank got out. Given false papers, Robert "François" was then taken in by a Parisian woman and attended a private school in the Eleventh arrondissement.[202]

The leaders of the Amelot Committee continued to favor the strategy of spreading the children about at various locations, and the Communist activists working together within the Solidarity organization and the National Movement Against Racism (MNCR) even managed to get sixty-three children out of UGIF homes on February 16, 1943.[203] Although UGIF leaders sometimes (but not always) agreed to look the other way when an aid organization "kidnapped" a child from one of its centers,[204] they maintained a close watch over the so-called blocked children and refused until the end to close down their houses, not only for fear of reprisals but also to avoid jeopardizing the whole range of their social work. This unswerving legalism was maintained at a heavy price: between July 21 and July 25, 1944, some 250 children along with those caring for them were rounded up from the various UGIF homes in the Paris region. Among them, some fifteen children of prisoners of war were deported to Bergen-Belsen and survived.[205] Seven children from three different families managed to be rescued by their parents, who came to pick them up at the gates of Drancy.[206] The rest were sent down the road to Auschwitz on deportation train number 77, which left on July 31, 1944. Two hundred of these children never returned.[207]

Compliance with the law prevailed in matters concerning both foreign employees of the UGIF and care of children, although in a few cases, after rounds of haggling that created the illusion of having room to maneuver, the rules were bent. This facade, which UGIF leaders intended to maintain at all costs, provided a cover for the operations of both the OSE and the Amelot Committee. Concretely, this strategy made it possible to provide monthly aid to thousands of Jews who depended on it for survival: there were 5,293 such persons in August 1942 and around 7,000 at the end of the year (figures that would have been higher if not for deportations).[208] In 1943, the UGIF came to the aid of an average of eight thousand Jews every month in Paris.[209] In addition to these official aid recipients, there were four hundred other Jews unofficially aided by the underground social service. There were moreover some nine hundred families in such a precarious situation that they did not dare contact the UGIF:[210] they were aided by the Amelot Committee, thanks to funds from the Southern Zone and even from the UGIF. Directly or indirectly, the official organization thus apparently provided financial aid to one-third of the Jews maintaining a legal existence in Paris on the eve of the Liberation.[211]

The UGIF also continued to finance the soup kitchens run by the Amelot Committee that had avoided being incorporated into the UGIF itself.[212] It did so by reimbursing their food coupons without the slightest oversight: the operation amounted to 25 percent of the UGIF's budget. When the Germans demanded to know why certain Jewish organizations in Paris were still functioning autonomously, UGIF leaders argued that the "groups that had not been disbanded enabled [their] members to assist each other, and that their activity [thus amounted] to zero."[213] On June 1, 1943, David Rapoport, who took the main responsibility for running the Amelot Committee's operations on a day-to-day basis, was arrested. Certain soup kitchens then closed, but those that remained open were henceforth entirely funded by the UGIF. Some 31,000 meals continued to be served in these kitchens every month during the first part of 1944.[214] Dr. Eugène Minkowski, who directed the clandestine service that placed Jewish children in private homes, testifies:

> On more than one occasion we were compelled to ask ourselves if it would not be better to close the soup kitchens that the Gestapo had raided several times. On that score, I recall the words of the director of one of these charitable programs: "Doubtless," he said, "that would be the most prudent thing to do, but my clients, and particularly the elderly ones, who have no defense and no place to sleep, have told me that if we closed down, they would go turn themselves in on their own in order to get sent to Drancy. Under those circumstances, I could not make such a decision."[215]

The fact that worship services continued in all circumstances during this time is probably due to a number of factors. There was a public demand from people for whom life without religious observance was inconceivable, and long-time Jewish leaders felt a certain responsibility toward them. Moreover, these leaders still believed such religious observance was one of the few areas that remained open for the expression of a Jewish way of life; freedom of worship had still not been threatened in official discourse. And so when in the summer of 1943, one of the two kosher butchers authorized in Paris was arrested and his butcher shop placed under the control of a provisional manager, the Consistorial Association of the Israelites of Paris (ACIP) considered making an appeal to authorities to allow a new butcher shop to open in the Fourth arrondissement.[216] Work was done on synagogues that had fallen into disrepair and worship services were regularly held.

Doubtless there were few people in the synagogues for the observances of *Tishri* in the fall of 1943. Services had been scheduled not according to the setting of the sun, as mandated by tradition, but in compliance with the curfew. On Rosh Hashana (which fell on September 30 and October 1), French police checked the papers of Jews who ventured out to the synagogue: four of those wearing the yellow star but who did not have their identity documents on them were arrested at the synagogue on Rue Notre-Dame-de-Nazareth. At Yom Kippur, on October 10, all the Jews who had come to worship at the Rue d'Enghien synagogue were arrested. The Gestapo raided the temple on Rue Saint-Lazare and carted everybody off to the Kommandantur installed in the Maisons-Laffitte department store. The eight persons ultimately detained—including three who had not sewn the yellow star on their coat and five foreigners—were sent off to Drancy.[217] Division 14 of the UGIF intervened on their behalf, hoping to have them released on the basis of freedom of worship: obviously, their efforts never stood a chance of having any effect.

The Consistorial Association of the Israelites of Paris nevertheless continued seeing to the preparation of unleavened bread, offering against all odds all sorts of religious instruction classes, and holding services in as many synagogues as possible, even when it meant repairing facilities and finding replacements for rabbis such as Joseph Sachs, arrested in February 1944.[218]

A *Financial and Political Cost*

The price paid for maintaining all of these activities, however, was very heavy, both in terms of money and of what had to be accepted from the authorities. In October 1942, seven million francs per month—a figure that included one million francs for satisfying German requisitions—were deemed necessary to cover expenses.[219] And the unofficial expenses incurred by the UGIF only kept mounting.[220] Soon it was no longer sufficient to draw upon the Solidarity Fund, as the UGIF had reluctantly been obliged to do, nor even to rely on the generosity of Jews who had taken refuge in the south. The UGIF was out of money. Faced with pressure not only from the Germans but also from the French authorities (who feared that the organization would collapse and that they would then have to take on the UGIF's burden of providing aid judged indispensable), the UGIF finally caved in and in the spring of 1943 accepted what it had always refused: to take part in the application of a compulsory tax on Jews. The law of May 11, 1943, henceforth required all Jews in the Northern Zone over the age of eighteen to pay an annual tax of 120 francs per person (the amount was 360 francs in the Southern Zone).[221] In addition, Jews were authorized to make financial donations to the UGIF by using funds from their accounts that had been frozen. The UGIF's coffers were also fed by a penalty of 5 percent levied on each financial transaction made by a Jew.

As a result of this law, Jews saw their meager resources diminished even further, especially as they were not allowed to draw from their frozen accounts the money needed to pay the annual tax; for that would have constituted "an unjustifiable favor for those Jews who have bank accounts."[222] And so we find the general commissioner for Jewish affairs demonstrating his concern for establishing a basis for equal treatment among Jews. More than fifteen hundred Jews in the Northern Zone requested exemption from the tax in 1943: 95 percent of these requests were granted at least in part.[223]

An equal number of requests for exemption from the tax was registered in March 1944: they speak eloquently of the dire poverty of those who dared ask to be exempted from the tax in spite of the dangers involved in such an appeal.

At the same time, the annual tax only tightened police control over Jews; they now were required to produce on demand still another card bearing a sticker testifying that they were in compliance. In January 1944, the General Commission on Jewish Affairs requested and obtained authorization from the minister of the interior to go ahead and intern those who had not paid their dues to the UGIF.[224]

As for the rule imposing a 5 percent fee on all financial transactions, it was not applied in cases where the provisional manager of an aryanized business had carried the operation out in order to meet the needs of the industry or store in question. After all, it was necessary to protect the interests of the French economy! If, however, the sum withdrawn went to a Jew holding the account (who was required to reimburse personal creditors, say) the 5 percent fee was levied.[225] Only a few months after the creation of the new tax, slightly more than 25,000 Jews had paid the required sum to the UGIF-North,[226] but the amount of money collected from the tax and from the mandatory fee still had not solved the organization's financial problems.

The price of keeping the UGIF running legally was not merely financial; Jews not having paid their UGIF dues risked being interned. The UGIF thus reluctantly found itself associated with police control. The organization's status, both within Jewish society and vis-à-vis the Germans, changed again when Brunner appeared on the scene. Brunner immediately took over as the UGIF's interlocutor, supplanting the General Commission on Jewish Affairs whenever possible. And as we have seen, French gendarmes at Drancy were limited to the perimeter of the camp and replaced by German police agents, while at the same time the UGIF's responsibilities were increased:

> As far as we are concerned, . . . we see [these changes] as the beginning of some sort of collaboration asked of us, to the most dubious of ends. . . . We have come to a very dangerous turning point, an extremely delicate one to steer through. I have the feeling that beneath the appearance of improved material conditions for internees and deportees, they are trying to make us into docile instruments of a new strategy. We are therefore going to have to maneuver and equivocate, accepting certain things while skillfully ducking out of others without, however, flatly refusing, as that could serve as a pretext for tightening down on us even more.[227]

So wrote André Baur to Albert Manuel on July 3, 1943.

The practical outcome of the strategy thus outlined by Baur was for the UGIF to accept the responsibility for taking care of the Jews interned at Drancy—for the sake of improving their living conditions—but to refuse to take part in the "family reunification" program pushed by Brunner. As the UGIF pointed out, it was impossible to convince families to cooperate.[228] At the same time, Baur availed himself of financial arguments in his constant efforts to use the General Commission on Jewish Affairs as a buffer between the UGIF and the Germans.[229] Brunner had no patience for such maneuvers and equivocation: using as a pretext the escape from Drancy of two internees, he had André Baur arrested.[230] And just to make sure that his message had been heard loud and clear, a week later Brunner summoned other UGIF leaders to Drancy and detained them there. On the following day, the office on Rue de la Bienfaisance was raided and sixty-seven UGIF employees were arrested.[231] Some were released a few days later, but Brunner came knocking on the door again on September 3, 1943: when he did not get the list that he had been asking for from Marcel Stora, he proceeded to arrest several of the UGIF leaders present.[232] On December 17, 1943, the UGIF leaders that had been detained at Drancy—including André Baur and his family—were deported to Auschwitz.

It was now clear that the time for hemming and hawing was over. But the UGIF was still caught up in the urgency of its social assistance programs—upon which, it argued, thousands depended—and so it refused to scuttle ship. And in spite of the threat hanging over their heads (the legitimation cards no longer provided protection), the UGIF employees remained on the job. The UGIF continued to function, even though that meant greater and greater submission to the German Occupation forces, and even though Resistance groups protested more and more vehemently that the official institution should be abolished.

FROM CLANDESTINENESS TO RESISTANCE

A report from the Section of Investigations and Inspections intended to give a synthesis of "elements of information bearing on certain illegal activities attributed to the UGIF" noted:

> A . . . Jewish self-defense fund reportedly used in a highly suspect manner has apparently been created from various officially disbanded charitable organizations that have been secretly maintained with the UGIF's complicity and outside financial assistance, doubtless by means of men who serve as a front while carefully hiding their origins. It is apparently by using these funds of unknown origin, for example, that it was possible for the "Mother and Child" dispensary, operating under the cover of the purely charitable enterprise suggested by its name, to be established and to actually serve as both as a center for fabricating false papers for Jews seeking to flee the Occupied Zone and as a source of funds large enough to provide them with the basic necessities. The entire operation is carried out with great caution, which would make it extremely difficult to audit. It has even been stated that the leaders of social services have given verbal instructions to social workers—many of whom have been reluctant to comply—to maintain the closest possible contact between this organization and those seeking secretly to flee: this fact apparently establishes a link between this illicit organization and the UGIF. Moreover, the dispensary in question is apparently not the only charitable organization under the UGIF umbrella that is working for Jewish self-defense, simply the most reprehensible. Another, formerly the OSE, has reportedly also been carrying on its activities, which are focused exclusively on Jewish children and youth—especially foreigners—and intended to shelter them from any eventual

> searches by placing them with reliable families. Room and board for these children are covered by funds coming from sources as dubious as those supporting the dispensary: in any case they are separate from the amounts that the UGIF budgets for the needs of children and youth.[233]

It was perhaps this report (which with all its deadly precision was quickly handed over to the Germans by the General Commission on Jewish Affairs) that was behind not only the arrest of David Rapoport,[234] but also the disbanding of the organizations run by the Amelot Committee within the UGIF.[235] In any case, the report bears witness to a chain of endeavors ranging from the official aid programs to underground activities and finally systematic rescue operations.

The specific points marking a break from legality still need to be defined. At one end of the spectrum we find the choice to engage in charitable undertakings in the strictest compliance with all rules and regulations, whatever the consequences might be. That did not keep leaders from engaging in haggling on certain occasions, even though it meant taking personal risks; those trying to finesse things in this way could have easily chosen the safety of anonymity and simply disappeared. At the next step along the way to underground activity, we find that the dominant objective was to save people, even if it meant bending the rules a bit: in short, it was a sort of resistance that continued to keep within the bounds of legality. Farther along, we find acts of resistance tied to specific cases, followed by the conscious choice of full-fledged political resistance.

Playing Games with Legality

This range of behaviors found within the Jewish organizations reflects the general set of stances taken by Jews in France in general. Everyone played games with legality in order to hold up and make it through, as can be seen in myriad concrete situations where incoherent combinations of obedience and disobedience were required. People would wear the yellow star during the day, but then go out in the evening after having taken it off. Young people excelled at defying authority; such behavior soon became a necessity for all who stayed out after the curfew. People kept the yellow star on while at home and in their neighborhood, but took it off to go to work. They would scrupulously follow all other German and French decrees, but would keep a radio hidden in the oven of the kitchen stove. They would climb in the last métro car while concealing the star under a handbag or sack. They would hurry across the Luxemburg gardens with their yellow star hidden behind a stack of books to attend a class at the Sorbonne with the insignia in full view: Claude Mossé remembers being the only Jewish girl in the whole amphitheater taking the course with the yellow star sewn on her clothes. People would maintain their legal existence, but after having hidden their children. They would destroy their identity papers without acquiring any other ones that would have provided a new identity.

They would walk through the neighborhood where they were known, concealing the place where, according to the regulation, the yellow star should have been sewn on. In other cases, people had succeeded in obtaining false papers attesting that they were Aryans, but still complied with the curfew applying only to Jews. Better yet, they would go to places reserved for Jews while carrying these false papers. Using the UGIF as an intermediary, people would send a package to Drancy, but only after having first gone to the Amelot Committee to get false papers. The most consistent Jews led a double life.

Among the Jews who maintained their legal existence, relates Maurice, there were those who lived out in the open with the star on their chests during the day, but never went back to their residence at night (as that was when most police roundups took place), and made use of a set of false papers to take on an Aryan identity.[236] It was no easy matter, under the very eyes of neighbors, the concierge, and local shopkeepers, to make the transition from being a Jew with the yellow star to being an anonymous Aryan. There were still plenty of people around who would inform authorities. Yet such a double identity was what could allow some to slip gradually into clandestine existence. For others, it provided a solution that would last until the Liberation.

Often people chose to go underground only after they had exhausted all other possibilities. In order to do so, they had to extricate themselves from the web of police files and verifications that had been set up in the fall of 1940 and become more and more sophisticated. In order to get food in this increasingly controlled society, one had to be duly registered with storeowners—which was no small matter. And if they hoped to blend anonymously into the crowd, families had to resign themselves to a painful separation and dispersion. The elderly and those who were destitute, ill, or invalids were too dependent on social assistance to risk such an adventure. It was even more hazardous for immigrants, who often spoke French haltingly and with a heavy accent and whose identity was betrayed by habits acquired in other lands. Money, which made it possible to pay for information and services, and political affiliation, which helped sharpen consciences and open up networks, were both determining factors.

The necessary resolve came easier for some groups than for others. Some French Israelites who had remained in Paris, for example, were able to make the leap thanks to chance acquaintances they had made before the war. Among immigrant groups, clandestine life was a kind of continuation of previous habits for militant Communists. In addition, there were many who went from their social aid work in Jewish circles into military action, from a life semi-clandestine to a totally clandestine life. Others, who had seen family members deported, no longer hesitated when contacted. Spurred on both by the Communist Party's strategy and the force of circumstances, a stream of militants came to strengthen the ranks of the second Jewish detachment of the FTP-MOI resistance group. From then on, they lived underground and faced the dangers that come with the choice of direct action.

Jews who had not managed to blend into Parisian society as discreetly as possible with the aid of a friendly neighbor could go to the Jewish social aid organizations, which would either provide them with what they needed to survive or help them go underground. The political organizations of the Resistance provided a social alternative as well as the possibility of taking action against those who had reduced them to pariahs. The same avenues of recourse had been there before the summer of 1942, but their number had increased as repression heightened and people distanced themselves more and more from the established order. More important, the needs were now of a different nature: the most urgent imperative for Jews at this time was to go into hiding.

Behind the Legal Organization (2)

Parallel to the double life of most Jews in Paris were the varied kinds of legal and extralegal activities conducted by Jewish organizations such as the Amelot Committee, the OSE, and the Israelite Scouts. While they strove to help those Jews who were willing to go into hiding and systematically scattered out as many children as they could, these same organizations also availed themselves of the UGIF's infrastructure when necessary. Ever since August 5, 1942, the leaders of the Amelot Committee had accepted the UGIF leaders' offer of legitimation cards, enabling them to resume their work after the Vel d'hiv roundup.[237] As we have seen, the UGIF kept on funding the soup kitchens until the Liberation. In an internal report of the Federation of Jewish Societies in France (FJSF), one of the few leaders of the Amelot Committee who had remained at his post in Paris wrote that, although they had been "materially detached" from what was left of the committee, the soup kitchens were still "morally linked" to it.[238] The Amelot Committee continued to receive money from the UGIF for all "official" public activities.

In addition to running soup kitchens, two dispensaries, and a cloakroom allowing the most indigent Jews to come get clothing and shoes three times a week, the Amelot Committee helped all who came to its offices to obtain false papers, get across the demarcation line, and hide their children. It also distributed its essential aid directly to people's homes, without ever asking beneficiaries to justify their needs.[239] All of these undertakings got off to a shaky start: one does not learn forgery overnight. With the complicity of a woman who worked in city hall and the aid of Communist activists, Henry Bulawko created, then perfected a false paper "factory" that operated on Rue Amelot.[240] When Bulawko was arrested in mid-November 1942, David Rapoport decided to take on the job of directing the operation.

One of the first requirements for any underground activity was having financial links with the Southern Zone. It was indispensable to have a secret fund to pay for aid to Jews who had gone into hiding in Paris and to remunerate the women who had in most cases accepted the task of caring for children for financial reasons (often they did not know that the children were Jewish). As we have seen, the UGIF appealed to the Consistory for unofficial funding. The Amelot Committee, on the other hand, could rely on the activists with the Federation of Jewish Societies in France, which received funds from the Joint; from July 1943 until the Liberation in August 1944, the Federation thus sent 600,000 francs per month from the Southern Zone to the Amelot Committee.[241] Within the Northern Zone, David Rapoport worked on the basis of an agreement with the Joint and collected funds by borrowing from certain Jews who wished to shelter their savings: those making the loans were given a receipt saying that "this sum, which ha[d] been used to save Jewish children from Paris, [would be] reimbursed [to them] in New York, at the latest, three months after the war officially ended and normal postal services between the United States and France were reestablished."[242]

A second prerequisite for underground activity was to establish ties with humanitarian organizations, Resistance networks, and Christian charity programs, as their work provided the infrastructure necessary for rescue operations: false identities had to be created, food coupons found, and "ideological" networks for taking in and sheltering Jews had to be located in order to complete the network of women who were paid to take care of children.

The example of the Temporary Mutual Aid organization (ET), which hid some five hundred children in scattered locations,[243] shows to what extent the work of one organization was inextricably tied to that of various others. Madame Chevalley was not just the president but the heart and soul of this underground interfaith group that had formed out of the pre-war Social Services for Emigrants (SSAE). She had also become the liaison between the Amelot Committee and the leaders of the Federation who had fled to the Southern Zone.[244] The pivotal role in the operation was played by Dr. and Madame Milhaud, who were employed by the UGIF and worked directly under Dr. Weill-Hallé, a member of the board of administrators and André Baur's uncle. Denise Milhaud served as a social worker and director of the UGIF's children's homes. Dr. Milhaud would take children from one of the UGIF's homes, to the Mutual Aid for children facility, the vocational school that was under his medical care. Within the centers used to lodge the children temporarily before spreading them out in different families, we find a preventive convalescence center at Trelon in the north, a center for children with special needs, and various hospital services (providing urgent housing for people pretending to be ill). The latter included the center run by Professor Debré and the La Clairière center run by Pastor Vergara, who at the time worked in collaboration with the National Movement Against Racism (MNCR), a Communist group. The false papers were provided through Dr. Milhaud: he would obtain them either at the Val-de-Grâce hospital or through his contacts with the clandestine CGT labor union.[245]

From a UGIF officially frozen in its legalism, we thus slip over toward organizations whose first priority was to rescue Jews, sometimes using a legal front and at other times turning to illegal methods. With the exception of the Communist organizations that were totally underground, the double link with an official facade and underground operations characterized practically all Jewish organizations. The UGIF and the Amelot Committee were at opposite ends of this symbolic spectrum, however. There were several organizations within both the UGIF and the Amelot Committee, and both focused on social work. There was a blend of legalism and disobedience to the law in both organizations, though at very different levels. The leaders of the Amelot Committee gave top priority to taking care of Jews coming to seek help: they sometimes used legal channels, but illegal means were the norm. It was just the opposite at the UGIF. Accordingly, the existence of these two organizations took on a completely different political meaning for each, even though they were for a long time often inextricably linked on the level of day-to-day operations.

The political divide between the two groups nevertheless widened after the summer of 1943: from then on, the activities of the Amelot Committee suffered an appreciable reduction. The following autumn was a time of reorganization. At the time, the Amelot Committee was financially supporting some three hundred families: one hundred officially, and the others unofficially.[246] Beginning in November 1943, while still under the leadership of Eugène Minkowski (who had already been arrested on August 23 of the same year, then set free thanks to Marcel Stora, who intervened on his behalf), the OSE limited its activities to keeping watch over the children who had been hidden by the Amelot Committee and to ensuring that their caregivers were paid.[247] Going completely underground had in fact meant that an active rescue strategy had been abandoned.

Jews in Paris were being hunted down more intensively. The Amelot Committee's independence had been curbed, and the UGIF's top leaders had been arrested; at the same time German control over the organization became more and more heavy-handed. The nexus of Jewish political activity had moved south of the demarcation line, while the UGIF-North, telecommanded by the Germans, pressed to make the UGIF-South, whose offices were more and more frequently raided by the Germans, submit to its authority. Under those circumstances, it was only inevitable that the divide between the UGIF and the other Jewish organizations should become deeper and wider.

The perspective and action of Jewish Communists were guided by strictly political reasoning. Any compromise with the UGIF was denounced as a collaboration enterprise and thus out of the question. The Communists had chosen to break with legal authorities at the time of the Coordinating Committee, and they stuck to their decision. The Vel d'hiv roundup had hit many a Jewish family, including many families of militant Communists: accordingly, it had three effects on the organization of Jewish Communists in the Paris region. First, it brought new topics to the fore in an underground press that was to grow rapidly. Second, it led to the creation of a structure aimed at fighting racism while at the same time pursuing the goal of rescuing both Jews and non-Jews. Third, it strengthened the number of Jews who had joined the immigrant worker Resistance group, FTP-MOI, by a hundred men.

Using Information as a Tactic

Given the official press's silence about the measures hitting the Jews and in view of the discretion shown by the underground papers (which had turned back to other problems after their outcries in the summer), the newspapers and tracts written, printed, and distributed by the Jewish Communists took on special resonance.[248] There were two types of such material: the texts published in either French or Yiddish and intended for the Jewish population, and the material meant to reach the general public in France. Texts of the latter category were put out under the auspices of the Liaison Voice of the French Forces United Against Racist Barbarianism (l'Organe de liaison des forces françaises contre la barbarie raciste), which in late December 1942 was to become the National Movement Against Racist Barbarianism, and then in June 1943 the National Movement Against Racism (MNCR).

The texts aimed at the Jewish population stemmed from two traditions. First, they were special adaptations of topics characteristic of the underground Communist press. They not only emphasized solidarity with the USSR and celebrated the heroism of the Red Army's soldiers; they also paid tribute to a country that had extirpated all the root causes of racism and antisemitism from its society. "Jewish masses have always had the warmest admiration for the country where all forms of national oppression have been eradicated," read one article in *Unzer Wort* in mid-November 1942, "[the country] where antisemitism has been wiped out, where Jews are really equal citizens, where Jews are workers and engineers, state employees, professors, soldiers, and officers. Never before, however, has the love of the Jewish masses for the Soviet Union been greater than it is today, when the Soviets' victory signals the destruction of Hitler."[249]

This hymn to the fatherland of socialism was accompanied with a reiteration of all the propaganda themes and claims used by the Soviet Union vis-à-vis the Allies: the Katyn massacre of Polish officers was attributed to the Germans, who were accused of having engaged in a disinformation campaign; and the Polish government in London was termed "reactionary and profascist." The necessity of opening a second front in Europe came up constantly in these pages.[250]

Within this general strategy of fidelity to the fatherland of socialism, the tactical watchwords of the Communist Resistance in France—on both the political and military levels—were adapted to the Jewish sociopolitical milieu and reiterated. For example, the Communists mobilized the widows, wives, and mothers of Jewish prisoners of war and incited them to demonstrate outside city halls, prisoner centers, and other institutions in the arrondissements of Paris, demanding protection for themselves and their children.[251]

First and foremost, however, was the call to immediate action along with an unequivocal condemnation of all forms of the "wait and see" attitude:

> At this very moment, by the blood of thousands, of tens of thousands of Jews, the blood of our brothers and sisters, and children, we are called to fight side by side with the nations involved in the struggle. As the decisive battles loom on the horizon, our desire for vengeance must not falter but burn with renewed passion. The sacred desire for sacred revenge must release new sources of fighting energy, resolution, and heroism. . . . The watchword "Every Jew, a résistant" must now become a reality. Waiting, fleeing, and hiding lead to disappearance, to death. Combatting, fighting, sabotage, taking up arms lead to life.[252]

Vengeance was becoming the driving force of the armed struggle. The political strategy of breaking with legal authority led naturally to a strategy of combat. The urgent need to achieve unity among all Jewish groups echoed the strategy of creating a national front.[253]

All of these writings, however, drew very heavily on a second traditional frame of reference: the past and present history of the Jewish people. The chronology of woes that had stricken the Jews during "one of the darkest periods of their long and painful history"[254] was unsparingly laid out and denounced. This was true first of all in France, but also in the rest of Occupied Europe, to the extent that the information reached militants. "For it is indeed the Jews as a people that are being targeted," wrote Jewish Communists celebrating their people's "contribution to the universal aura and prestige of French culture."[255] And each day, the Jewish people were proving their eagerness to contribute to the fight against the Nazis. Finally, with special reference to the great figures of Jewish history, this struggle was placed in the Jewish tradition of heroes fighting for "their existence as an independent nation."[256]

Out of the entire series of terrible events in Eastern Europe that militant Communists in France managed to get wind of, the news of the Warsaw ghetto uprising made the strongest impression on them. "Hitler's bands use tanks to push into the Warsaw ghetto. The heroic resistance of the Jews. Jews of France, let us strengthen our defenses! Let us hasten Hitler's defeat!" read the headlines of the May 15, 1943, edition of *Notre Voix*.[257] The Warsaw ghetto became the "tragic symbol of the ordeal of the Jews in occupied Europe." "The Jews in Warsaw have given a magnificent example of courage to all their brothers and to the world. Their sacrifice is not in vain," added the June 1, 1943, edition of *Notre Voix*.[258] Jewish Communist newspapers would henceforth make constant reference to the Warsaw ghetto uprising. The glorious history of Jewish resistance throughout the world had been enriched with a new episode.

It was this twofold frame of reference that was used directly to mobilize Jews and to incite them to join Jewish Communist organizations in order to step up the armed struggle against the Nazis and their "lackeys" in Vichy.

The solidarity that had arisen between the Jews and other oppressed peoples—the people of Occupied France in particular—bound up in a common destiny was another prominent theme. Resistance papers repeatedly explained that the deporations of Jews foreshadowed the "widespread deportation of hundreds of thousands of

French people."[259] They accordingly denounced the deportation of French youth to Germany in the context of the Forced Labor Service (STO); it was only setting the stage, they wrote, for the "massive deportation of all able-bodied French people" designed to "drive out and enslave the French population as ancient Asian tyrants would do."[260] It was only the logical sequel to a prediction that had haunted the pages of previous editions. The solidarity between Jews and French people was now constantly emphasized: "Maybe [the poor fellow who has been suffering far from his loved ones for over two years] speaks incorrect French with an accent that would make our own Hitler-lovers grind their teeth, but between the idea of France that he has loved and served and that of the Hitler-lovers, which is the truest and most beautiful?"[261] The various editions of the paper abound with examples of French people acting in solidarity with Jews: workers in a Parisian factory and families taking in Jewish children, among others.

The content of the July 5, 1943, edition of the new paper of the young Jewish Communists, *Jeune Combat,* testifies to such syncretism. Young Jews were urged to commemorate the Vel d'hiv roundup on July 16 by making it a day for sabotage and by creating a National Vengeance Fund. Young Jews were at the same time called to unite with all French youth on July 14 to make the national holiday an occasion for fighting against the Germans.[262]

> Young Jews, you who were and still are the Hitlerian monster's first victims, you for whom the deportations are linked to the memory of sulfur, asphyxiating gas, and electrocution chambers . . . you whose parents were savagely torn away from their homes and sent to the slaughterhouses in Poland, you shall join with all French youth on this July 14, 1943, for a day of fraternity in arms. In that manner, you will overturn the schemes carefully set up by our enemies, who are trying to use propaganda and antisemitic measures to create division among youth. Fraternally united with all French young people, you, as have your fathers who on many occasion shed their blood for France, will thus prove the strength of your ties with this country whose fate intimately concerns you and whose liberation is essential for your own freedom.

At the same time—and this is what constitutes the originality of these writings—we find a wealth of information about the fate reserved for Jews. In this area, the newspapers and tracts intended for Jews were complemented by *J'accuse* in the north and *Fraternity* in the south: instead of urging Jews to fight, they called on French people in general to help the victims.

Right after the Vel d'hiv roundup, there was a very thorough "personal testimony" explaining how it had been carried out and describing the conditions in the covered stadium used to detain those arrested.[263] There were henceforth a number of goals for Jews: to continue to resist, to take advantage of the sympathy for persecuted Jews now present among the French population, to transform the struggle against antisemitism into a springboard for uniting Jews with the rest of society, to denounce the Nazis' crimes, to carry out acts of sabotage everywhere, to "oppose all attempts to deport Jews with active resistance," to flee from the camps, and to join the Resistance.

Deportation was immediately understood as the equivalent of death.[264] Articles recalled the speeches in which Hitler spoke of the extermination of the Jews and compared them to the scenes of violence perpetrated against Jewish children and elderly people who had been mercilessly arrested, interned, and deported.[265] Granted, the same edition of *J'accuse* indicated in November 1942 that French workers in Germany were under the threat of "being deported to do forced labor alongside deported Jews in the salt mines of Poland," a statement that seems to contradict the threat of death. But there was an abundance of questions about deportees who were never heard from again, information reporting large-scale massacres, plans to exterminate the Jews, and the variety of means used to accomplish this massacre: forced labor and famine, poisonings and shootings, minefields and epidemics—but also gas chambers that were sometimes used as a form of torture and at other times as an experiment.[266] There were reports on the massacres of Jews in Vilno and Warsaw, in Ukraine and Byelorussia, and on the British Parliament's condemnation of these crimes. It was noted that the eleven Allied governments along with De Gaulle's Free France Committee had published a declaration that publicly denounced the horrible process in Poland of exterminating tens of thousands of Jews from various occupied countries. The declaration proclaimed that those responsible would have to answer for their crimes.[267]

From the roundup in Marseilles in January 1943 to the raid on the UGIF children's homes in February,[268] every episode of the hunt for Jews was described and denounced. "Hitler's monsters" were accused of "having declared a war of extermination on children, on babies in their cradles."[269] Even as early as the fall of 1942, it was revealed that toxic gas was being used, and such reports always concluded by noting the necessity of helping fugitives. Such an appeal was issued in one of the editions of *J'accuse*: "Every French family should take in a persecuted child." And with it came the same watchword: "Solidarity with the victims of Nazi barbarity."

But in late November 1942, when *J'accuse* announced that a "new wave of pogroms [posed a threat] to Jews throughout France," just what did these words conjure up in people's minds? And what did they imagine upon hearing of "signs foreshadowing a large-scale massacre that Hitler's desperate agents [were preparing]?"[270] A January 1943 appeal to the people of France spoke not only of the "methods of bloody repression" used by the Vichy government and its Gestapo bosses, but also of Hitler's systematic pursuit and extermination of the Jews. "Since November 1939, over 2 million Jews have been murdered in Europe," people learned in this appeal. "And each day brings the horrible echo of new massacres."[271]

Although those who wrote this appeal actually underestimated the scale of the killings, exaggeration is inherent in propaganda writings, particularly in times of war. Who could know that there was no exaggeration here? Beyond such shockingly brutal terms and descriptions of such incredible horror, the most frightening thing for us now is our awareness that people were actually systematically *under*estimating the number of victims. As was the case for all reports leaking out about the extermination of the Jews, reality always outstripped the descriptions in these newspapers. Ironically, however, they were interpreted as exaggerations linked to the circumstances of war and necessities of propaganda.

It is necessary to dwell on the content of these tracts and newspapers in order to understand their significance. Beyond the devices and manipulations inherent in any propaganda literature and in spite of their incoherences, contradictions, and errors, the picture one gets from reading them is clear. Jews were being deported from France to the slaughterhouse in Poland. And, warned these papers and tracts, all Jews should hide and escape from the arrest that threatened them, "use the help of the French, people who are in solidarity, to put their children in a safe place," join a patriotic combat organization, resist arrest by all possible means, "organize acts of resistance and revolts against deportation at Drancy and other assembly points," and always, everywhere, sabotage everything that might help the enemy, strike out in every way possible.[272]

The specificity of Hitler's plan to exterminate the Jews was indeed present in these texts, but it was not perceived as absolute. This may seem surprising, but we should not forget that Nazism was understood by all who were fighting against it to be a threat to the values of Western civilization in general: it was this acute awareness of an ideological war that dictated Allied strategy and eliminated any possibility of compromise with the Germans before total victory. The fate of the Jews was tied to this victory. The Jews had experienced persecution throughout their history and they had never been so fortunate as to have such powerful allies in the past. It is scarcely surprising that this confluence of interest should be continually reemphasized by the Jewish underground newspapers, especially as it was in perfect harmony with the Communist view that the end of antisemitism would come from a transformed society.

This twofold awakening of consciences was first and foremost intended to lead people to take up arms against the enemy. For it would have been inconsistent for these papers to advise Jews to hide, since the condemnation of the "wait and see" attitude was a central theme of Communist propaganda in France. Could they even think of spurring the French on to active combat while at the same time telling Jews to hole up and take shelter?

This position doubtless amounted to a tactical rather than a strategic use of information;[273] the main goal, however, was still to inform people. But what impact did it make, and how many Jews actually got to read one of these pieces? According to David Diamant, there were no fewer than seven underground printing presses—and a similar number of printing ink and paper depots—operating for Jewish Communist organizations in Paris. Between 3,000 and 15,000 copies of each such text were reportedly printed.[274] How many non-Jews made up their minds to provide shelter for their Jewish neighbors after having read an edition of *J'accuse*? That remains difficult to assess. Given the enormous number of these texts and the accumulation of information in Paris where groups of Jews remained concentrated, the papers' effect had to have been significant: we can suppose that they led many to become aware of the crisis.

Writing, printing, publishing, and distributing all this underground literature made it necessary to set up a highly complex infrastructure. Each step along the chain of actions that made it possible to distribute a tract involved a large number of dangers. Imagine using a handcart to deliver several hundred kilos of paper, making one's way through the streets of a capital city under heavy surveillance to an address where one might not be expected at this particular moment.[275] Just as when one was involved in organizational tasks or took part in the armed combat, engaging in this political activity and being part of a Jewish Communist network meant going completely underground and committing totally to resistance activity.

Every Jew, a Resistance Fighter

After late 1941 and early 1942, the young Jewish Communists who had previously been scattered about in the organization were assigned by party leadership to specific Jewish groups within the party, even though they were often perfectly integrated into French society.[276] This rather surprising decision was in a way the flip side of the persecutions targeting only Jews; those who made the decision, however, probably intended to make it easier to mobilize the troops. A new generation of Jewish Communist militants arrived on the scene following the Vel d'hiv roundup. This "generation of the police roundup"[277] was no longer made up of experienced and proven militants, but of young people who had been deeply shocked by those events in the streets of Paris, who had in some cases seen a loved one arrested by the French police, and who had consequently decided to commit themselves totally to resistance. A chance encounter or acquaintance would bring them into contact with Communist organizations.

The ranks of the resistance fighters of the Immigrant Worker group MOI thus found themselves suddenly reinforced. During the following months, moreover, the resistance fighters with the FTP-MOI under Boris Holban's military leadership were given a larger number of assignments, and the party leadership increasingly appreciated the importance of their work. For at the same time, the party's only armed group in Paris was put out of action by the arrest of one of its leaders in October 1942, and in January 1943, the entire command structure of the FTP resistance network fell captive to the Germans.[278]

Driven by their desire for vengeance, young Jews were at the forefront of military action. Spectacular raids on Jewish workshops producing goods for the Germans henceforth gave way to attacks on the German Occupation forces and their allies. They placed time bombs in a hotel occupied by the Germans, in an office hiring workers for the enemy, and in one of the Parti Populaire Français's offices. They attacked a German truck, threw hand grenades at a detachment of enemy troops, into a "Nazi" garage, and into a restaurant frequented by German officers. The second Jewish detachment of the FTP-MOI, which now counted some forty members, undertook fifty-nine operations between July 1942 and July 1943. Out of the 162 claimed in all by the various detachments of the MOI during the same period, 38 others were carried out by the first Romanian and Hungarian detachment (90 percent of whose members were Jews).[279] These actions reached their high point in the first half of 1943, before the Jewish organization was disbanded in July of the same year. There were in addition thirty-nine other operations carried out up until November 1943 by the so-called derailment detachment, in which Jewish resistance fighters constituted the overwhelming majority.[280]

These actions were not without risks, however. The "terrorists" were hunted down in the most professional way first by the police, then by the Special Brigades that had been reinforced after August 1941. An early police detective operation had resulted in thirty-eight arrests in December 1942.[281] The first detachment had to be reorganized. Three major series of arrests followed in 1943. First the organization of young Jews fell victim in March, with almost sixty arrested among them. Then in April, twenty-one leaders of the movement were captured.[282] And then, after a particularly well-executed three-phase police operation, the group of armed Jewish résistants was disbanded, when seventy-seven militants were arrested between June 29 and July 9, 1943. On July 19, 1943, the second detachment was dissolved after having thrown one last grenade at a German truck in Vanves. Those who had managed to slip through the cracks were scattered among the other groups, while the special team and the derailment detachment kept up the same level of military action in the Paris region.

In November 1943, however, it was the entire FTP-MOI group of resistance fighters, including their leader Missak Manouchian (who had been Boris Holban's replacement since August 1943) along with Joseph Epstein and Colonel Gilles (who was at that time the FTPF's interregional military leader) that fell to the enemy in Paris.[283] Some of those who managed to escape arrest were scattered out in the Southern Zone, while others were sent to the départements of Le Nord and Le Pas-de-Calais. These captures marked the end of the epic of the FTP-MOI resistance fighters in Paris and the beginning of the "Trial of the Twenty-three" as well as of the propaganda campaign that accompanied the widespread publication of the "Red Poster."

But for all these militants, capture meant being subjected to clubs and to savage blows that left marks all over their bodies, the threefold classification of "terrorist," Communist, and Jew (and often foreigner to boot) was hardly one that aroused the sympathy of the inspectors charged with interrogating them. They were spared neither physical nor psychological torture before being condemned to death and shot, or else sent to Drancy—which, as we know, was only a first step down the road to Auschwitz.

To engage in such a risky undertaking was to become part of the Resistance, as there was no possible legal facade for underground fighters. For the furrier-worker now handling explosives, the tailor now charged with placing bombs, and the young lycée student—some were no older than seventeen—suddenly transformed into a terrorist, the first need was to find a place to sleep. Often they set up quarters in the eastern part of Paris, sometimes near their parents. They had to obtain false papers (provided by a special division headed by a Jew from Romania who had fought in the Spanish civil war), avoid all contact with their families, eat in a different place every day, and be wary with each step and every movement.

But how was it possible to follow these security rules when members of a same family were militants in different branches of the organization? And how, in such circumstances, could they maintain the strict separation of branches that was constantly said to be indispensable? As for contact with the members of their families that, either because they were too old, too young, or ill, were not involved in the same type of activity, was it possible for them to keep their oath to break off all relations with persons outside the armed underground combat and deny them their moral and material support? For immigrant Jews in Paris, who were all threatened by their very identity as Jews, such instructions were impossible to follow to the letter. Yet Jews were nevertheless the most exposed to danger; unlike other immigrants, they had no safety zone to which they could retreat and blend in with the surroundings. Moreover, their militant activity proved to be all the more dangerous in that the necessity of recruiting people from an entire population in danger was in direct contradiction with their status as full-time resistance fighters.

They did receive a stipend from the organization: on the average, 1,600 francs per month in 1942 for those who were not married. This sum was subsequently increased.[284] Each was put into a group of three, to which was assigned a woman to act as a liaison. This female agent would first locate targets to be attacked (carefully noting, for example, the place and the time that a German patrol would pass by), and then transmit the information to the command group. She would also be responsible for transporting necessary munitions to the site of the planned operation: there she would give them to the resistance fighters and retrieve them after the attack was over.

The National Movement Against Racism (MNCR) provided for their families, furnished them with false papers, and hid their children. In order to accomplish this mission, the group Solidarity had recruited non-Jews: under this label, the new organization of intellectuals and doctors found lodging for the resistance fighters and hid their children. The circle of those on the run had widened, and when it was learned that the children in one of the UGIF's centers were in danger of being deported (as had happened in February 1943) or when there was a special individual case, a team took charge of the rescue operation. Between July 1942 and April 1943, Solidarity and the MNCR thus scattered 607 children about in Paris.[285] When a resistance fighter was wounded during an attack—or more prosaically fell ill—it was sometimes a doctor with the MNCR who was called in. However, the MOI resistance group also had its own medical service, led by a Jewish doctor from Bessarabia. The MNCR not only saw to the distribution of *J'accuse,* but also provided for the needs of those involved in both political and military action. It looked after their families and even extended its aid services to other groups in the Jewish community.

Those who committed themselves to such armed resistance were always a minority among the Jewish population in Paris, but they did constitute a sort of brotherhood, with family ties overlying ideological affinities and creating a very special microsociety. While seeking vengeance upon their persecutors, they were led by the conviction that they were helping to weaken the Nazi enemy. Theirs was not a strategy of rescue, but of combat, a combat that cost a great many of them their lives.

The fight was orchestrated by a Communist leadership that pursued its own objectives. In the first place, they firmly intended to hold a prominent position among the forces that would rule the country when the Liberation occurred. To that end, it was essential to carry on sustained military action in the capital. When Jewish resistance fighters who knew that they had been identified by police asked to be transferred to the Southern Zone in late April 1943, pointing out the Jewish masses that had taken refuge there, the party leadership flatly refused.[286] The MOI group was the most active at that time. They were disbanded by the forces of repression not only because of a particularly effective series of operations carried out against them in July and November 1943, but also because of defections and betrayals. The main reason why these losses were so heavy, however, was the Communist Party leadership's strategic choice to pursue military action in Paris at all costs.

There were also political objectives specific to the political microcosm of Jews. Jewish Communist leaders were hoping to represent the entire community. Here again, the focus was on preparing for the postwar period, when the redistribution of political influence would result from the balance of power reigning among the various institutions within the Jewish community. The umbrella organization called the Union of Jews for Resistance and Mutual Aid (UJRE) also reflected the French Communist Party's strategy that was initiated on May 1, 1942, and put into action in early 1943 with the goal of creating a national front of opposition. The organization, which brought together all the illegal Jewish Communist organizations (including Solidarity, the Union of Jewish Women, the Union of Jewish Youth, the People's Relief, a commission on labor unions, and all the groups of resistance fighters) was created in Paris in late April 1943.[287]

The creation of this organization marked the beginning of a strategic turn toward French Jews, as amply illustrated by an internal report written by Adam Rayski in December 1943: "We must succeed," he wrote, "in involving the majority of the Jewish population in the fight against the enemy, both in the Resistance and in defense of their own existence." At the same time—and this was new—Rayski thought it necessary "to widen [our] influence among French Jews" in view of "achieving the full unity of the Jewish population of France."[288] The new organization's platform announced that "the UJRE will do its utmost to establish a single representative entity for the Jews of France which will include representatives from all Jewish groups of resistance fighters."[289] This was indeed the first step of a political strategy that was supposed to put the Jewish Communists—with all the military and political activity of which they could boast—at the head of the entity representing all the Jews of France.

The following steps of this political endeavor involving all Jewish organizations took place in the Southern Zone, where the great majority of the Jews in France were then to be found. After the police intensified their efforts to hunt down Jews and crack down on resistance fighters in the summer and fall of 1943, the center of gravity of Jewish politics moved southward. The intracommunity work was to dictate that subsequent Jewish organization activities in the Paris region would henceforth stem from their political contacts in Vichy France.

10

The Occupied "Free" Zone

It is an extremely complicated matter to follow the evolution of the Jewish population in the Unoccupied Zone. French authorities tried to keep track of the situation up until 1944, but with little success. Historians generally fare no better. However, even if numbers and places remain imprecise, the general tendencies are clear. Judging from the figures provided by the various prefectures after the 1941 census, there were slightly fewer than 110,000 Jews (over the age of fifteen) in the Southern Zone in March 1942, not including the Jews interned in the camps.[1] Jews had subsequently continued to flee to the Unoccupied Zone, particularly in the summer. But the deportations had taken their toll and severely reduced the number of Jews appearing on the list for each prefecture. As in Paris, moreover, Jews were increasingly seeking the safety of anonymity. The first dispersion of Jews after the defeat was followed by a second dispersion after the summer of 1942; in the following months, the tendency was for Jews to scatter far and wide.

Here again, we can point out certain trends in this movement: Jews left cities for the country and poured into certain sheltered places—either Huguenot strongholds or the Italian Occupied Zone—that at times provided only temporary protection. For some Jews, this situation meant that they would bounce around from one place to another. Such was the case for the family who had to leave Lahourcade (in the département of Les Hautes Pyrénées) in May 1941 and who were sent to Sévignac-Meyracq, then to Thèze, then on to Eaux-Bonnes on November 11, 1942, and finally, on to Neuillat, in the département of La Creuse in January 1943. In each case, they were under house arrest.[2] And for an ever-increasing number of Jews, the overall situation also meant that they had to use a false identity. Arrests and deportations continued to hit hard: 6,628 Jews in 1943, and then 7,300 more in 1944 were taken to Auschwitz from the "Free" Zone, which no longer bore any resemblance to its name.

Based on the data collected in December 1942 and afterward, when Jews were required to have the word "Jew" stamped on their identity papers and food cards, a March 1943 report from the Division of Investigations and Inspections (SEC) put the number of Jews in the Unoccupied Zone at 140,000.[3] We learn in the same report that since the July 1941 census the number of Jews had decreased markedly in

Table 4. Distribution of the Jewish Population as Recorded in the Southern Zone, March 1942 –February 1943[1]

Region	March 1942	February 1943
Montpellier	8,849	8,000
Clermont-Ferrand	7,926	8,000
Limoges	17,197	12,000
Lyon	21,659	40,000
Marseille	22,659	32,000
Toulouse	18,820	25,000
Nice	12,873	15,000

1. The figures from March 1942 come from the Centre de Documentation Juive Contemporaine, LXXII–16, reprinted in Joseph Billig, *Le Commissariat général aux questions juives*, 2:209. The figures from February 1943 are taken from AN, AJ 38, 243, Vichy, March 8, 1943. Report no. 8 for February 1943, sent by the head of the Division of Investigations and Inspections (SEC) to the General Commission on Jewish Affairs.

the Limoges region, while at the same time almost doubling in the Lyon region, remaining steady in Montpellier and Clermont-Ferrand, and increasing in the Marseille, Toulouse, and Nice areas.[4]

These numbers, however, are only an indication of the actual situation. They do not enable us to account for the number of arrests, for example, nor do they enable us either to find those who had not declared themselves or to track the constant movements of those going from one place to another. In any case, there were probably no less than 150,000 Jews in the Southern Zone at the time of the Liberation: they tended to be increasingly scattered about and blended together with the rest of the population.[5]

Historians find themselves helpless to attack these problems, as the French government offices did not reach the objectives assigned to them. This failure, however, was not for lack of attempts to exert administrative and police control; indeed, we can follow such efforts up until the summer of 1944.

CONTROLLING AND MONITORING THE JEWS

Given the requirements connected with applying decidedly complex instructions, the Ministry of the Interior and the various offices of the General Commission on Jewish Affairs kept calling upon the prefectures, who then would call upon city halls and police stations to keep a tighter watch on the Jews. The Jews were not aware of all this correspondence aimed at establishing an accurate picture of the distribution of Jews in the Southern Zone. They did, however, experience the concrete results, as they were required to report their every move. For example, when they wanted to stay in a hotel, they were required to fill out forms and instructed to indicate their religion.[6] On January 22, 1943, the daily newspaper *La Dépêche de Toulouse* informed its readers that, in addition to the usual information (which included the religion or race of guests), the forms to be filled out by hotel guests now had to ask for the date when a declaration of Jewish identity had been made.[7]

So much for the increasingly sophisticated means of control. True, this measure was not put into application everywhere. On July 9, 1943, the State Council nullified a decree issued by the prefect of the département of La Haute-Savoie concerning this type of form, because it required everyone to declare their religion. However, it would have been perfectly legal to demand that travelers declare whether they were Jewish or not.[8] This type of formality forced Jews who intended to remain anonymous to change their identity. But a much more extensive measure was just entering into application.

Stamped with the Word "Jew"

Gazagne, the head of the office of the status of persons in the General Commission on Jewish Affairs for the Southern Zone, had sent Ziegler de Loès (in charge of the census office) on a mission in ten départements. Ziegler filed his report with Gazagne on June 17, 1942, and on June 23, Gazagne drew from it what to his mind were the obvious conclusions.[9] "The census was poorly executed," he wrote. "It is absolutely necessary to conduct a new census: only on this basis will it be possible to take the adequate measures needed to alleviate the dangers posed by their proliferation in the Free Zone." In order to prevent the next census from suffering the same setbacks as the first, he proposed that a liaison should be established "between the census offices and the food ration card offices in city halls: this is the only way to ensure an effective control." Gazagne moreover recommended that it be required for the identity cards to be stamped with the word "Jew."

As we have seen, this measure had actually already been decided in Vichy in mid-April 1942. On November 7, 1942, Robert Kiefe asked members of Marshal Pétain's entourage about the status of this plan. "No need to worry," one of Jardin's collaborators assured him, "the identity card will not be created any time soon." "The Germans have demanded the use of this identity card," Kiefe was told by René Bousquet, "but we are short on paper."[10] The solution for saving this precious paper was obviously found: all they had to do was to use the existing cards and stamp the word "Jew" on them.

One month later, on Monday evening, December 7, in the twenty-eighth program of the General Commission on Jewish Affairs' broadcast over Vichy's radio network, Darquier de Pellepoix laid out "his program of 'dejewification,'" which was to be the first step in a crusade for "our" race. He urged each to avoid all contact with Jews, "for [it was] a problem of contamination."[11] Newspapers then received instructions not to report the measures announced by the General Commissioner for Jewish Affairs.[12] The Jews, however, had heard the message: "With the usual eloquence of an impassioned rightwing huckster, Darquier has announced new measures against the Jews, whom the Statute has not succeeded in neutralizing," commented Raymond-Raoul Lambert in his diary.[13] "There is growing anxiety in our circles," he added. On the next day, December 8, a new law further restricting the movements of foreign Jews and threatening violators with internment appeared in the *Journal officiel*.[14] It was adopted on November 9, 1942.

Then on December 12, 1942, the *Journal officiel* confirmed for Jews that on the previous day, Pierre Laval had signed a decree stipulating that "all persons of Jewish race as defined by the law of June 2, 1941 [were] required to report within a month of the promulgation of this law to the nearest police station or else to the local brigade of gendarmes in order to have the word "Jew" stamped on their identity cards or on the document held in lieu of the identity card as well as on their individual food ration cards."[15] Less than a week later, prefects received the necessary instructions for the concrete application of this measure.[16] The measure applied to French Jews, foreign Jews, and Jews incorporated into a Foreign Worker Unit: no one was forgotten. The word "Jew" had to be stamped in one-centimeter-high letters on the part of the identity card showing the bearer's civil status. It was moreover recommended to call on the local newspapers to notify and summon Jews and to warn them of the sanctions they risked by not complying. It was left up to the prefects to determine the specific conditions in which Jews were required to report to police stations or brigades of gendarmes. In order to keep Jews from dodging this new requirement, however, it was stressed that verifications made on the basis of the June 2, 1941, census list were absolutely necessary.

Chief Rabbi Isaïe Schwartz and the president of the Consistory Jacques Helbronner sent a letter of protest to Pierre Laval on December 30, 1942, once again expressing their "outrage over a measure that [tended] to subject one category of French citizens to another humiliation, and [we protest] vigorously one more measure of harassment that came on top of so many others."[17] Honor was thus preserved, but the new law was applied. Attorney Robert Kiefe, Helbronner's emissary in Vichy, took up the subject with his usual interlocutor on January 6 and 7, 1943. Jardin distinguished himself in the art of ducking the question on this occasion. As for General Campet, he expressed his surprise: "Why are the Israelites so upset about this card" to be stamped? "Everyone has a card. Even officers have their special card. What good would it do you to have this measure postponed? The postponement would not be long enough to get you through until the end of the war anyway."[18] (Now *that* was most reassuring.)

"What can we do about it?" Jews wondered. "It keeps me from sleeping," wrote one Jew in a letter that was opened by Vichy.[19] "If I get my card stamped, I will be fired by my boss [but if I don't], "I am taking a big risk," explained one Jew from Mende (in the département of La Lozère) to another living in Toulouse.[20]

Such fears became even more acute after November 11, 1942, when the Germans rushed down to occupy the south of France in response to the Allied landing in North Africa. At the same time, Italian troops had pushed through to the Rhone.

"Stunned indifference on the part of the crowd. Heightened anxiety in Jewish circles," commented Raymond-Raoul Lambert in Marseilles.[21] "The activity of the Jews has almost completely disappeared in the départements newly occupied by Axis troops," we are told in a synopsis of postal, telephone, and telegraph checks made between November 10 and December 10, 1942.[22] The next month, the Germans were there and the new measures were made public: "the Jews dread the application in the Free Zone of the measures taken against their coreligionaries in the Occupied Zone," noted the person making the latest synopsis.[23]

On November 17, 1942, the regional secretaries the Central Consistory met in Lyon to assess what implications the German Occupation of the Southern Zone held for Jews. Measures had been taken in Marseilles to proceed with the removal of documentation. A few police roundups were reported in Toulouse, and the followers of Doriot in Toulouse along with the Toulouse office of the General Commission on Jewish Affairs had apparently made up lists of Jewish hostages. Elsewhere, however, things had apparently remained calm. Leon Meiss had been told confidentially that the Germans supposedly had no intention of harming either the Jews, nor the people from Alsace-Lorraine, nor the escaped prisoners. Meiss nevertheless suggested that all Jews who were in a position to do so abandon the large urban centers and seek refuge in the country.[24]

By the next meeting on December 1, 1942, fears had mounted noticeably. A certain number of Jewish refugees had left Marseilles, reported that region's delegate. Most Jews from Marseilles had remained in their city, but had often sent their families to live in the country. Certain rumors had created a panic: word had been that the Jews would have to hand over five thousand hostages. It was this fear of being used as a hostage that predominated. In Toulouse, where the minister of the interior had supposedly asked for the list of all foreign nationals considered to be Germans, people were particularly upset. The Jewish community in Brive had been shaken by a police roundup of foreign Jews that had targeted those who had crossed the demarcation line after September 5, 1942. And all foreign Jews in Pau had been sent to live in house arrest in Eaux-Bonnes.[25] The place was "sad, depressing, humid, and cold, and its people were of an awful mind-set, as they try to get the most they can while giving the very least possible," according to a Quaker's description.[26] The prefect and the police intendant in Lyon had told Helbronner that the Germans were only interested in foreign Jews and deserters from the German army.

Two weeks later, the requirement of having the word "Jew" stamped on identity cards was on the agenda of the meeting of the regional delegates of the Consistory. It was decided that "the Consistory does not have the right to recommend avoiding this obligation." Nevertheless, they spoke of new measures that were to be imminently taken against single foreign Jews between the ages of eighteen and fifty-five in Lyon. Jews in Marseilles and Toulouse had no thought of doing anything but hiding out. On December 12, the prefect of the département of La Corrèze had seen Rabbi David Feuerwerker and told him that the Germans had asked for the list of foreign

Jews and of all persons from the countries of the Greater German Reich. In Pau, Jews were beginning to panic.[27]

The ordeals of the summer were not far off. When the Germans came down into the Southern Zone, however, Jews had maintained a discreet profile while waiting to see the effects of the German occupation on the entire country. The most direct result of the new political situation as far as the Jews were concerned was the increased power of the German police,[28] but that was only one facet of the Jews' perception of things at that time. The French government seemingly continued to govern. "One month after the Free Zone has come under military control, I observe that the fiction of Laval and Pétain still remains," noted Raymond-Raoul Lambert in his diary.[29]

The word "Jew" had, however, been stamped on identity papers on Laval's orders. The alignment of the situation in the Southern Zone with the conditions prevailing in the Occupied Zone seemed to be on the agenda. Would the shadow of the yellow star fall over the southern part of the country? In view of such circumstances, then, it is hardly suprising that one committee chair for the Central Consistory who was trying to give a picture of the overall situation as of December 24, 1942, noted that every community had been severely shaken: "Some, including Montpellier, Nîmes, Béziers, Perpignan, and others, have become almost lifeless, while others are teeming with people: people in a panic are going in every direction and into every region."[30]

From November 11, 1942, until December of the same year, the tension had only mounted. Jews were encouraged to comply with the requirement of having their identity cards stamped by notices printed on the front page of newspapers during the month of January 1943. The people in Marseilles were thus notified that identity checks would be increased. "Do not go out without identity papers," warned the January 5, 1943, edition of *Le Petit Marseillais*. "Do not go around without your food ration card," added the same paper on January 27. This time, however, the notice was directly linked to the large police roundup that had begun a few days earlier. In the minds of Jews, papers stamped with the word "Jew," arrests, and deportation trains were becoming more and more clearly linked to each other and formed a terrifying chain of events.

A certain number of Jews clearly refused to comply with the required stamping of their papers. It was hardly a matter of conscience for those who had come clandestinely from the Northern Zone. But what was the response of those who had been duly registered as Jews in prefectoral offices since July 1941? As was the case in the Northern Zone, the decision to dodge the gauntlet of verifications constituted a leap into the unknown, especially since extensive steps seem to have been taken to ensure the full application of the new law.

The Administrative Machine

The offices of prefects, police stations, and city halls all worked for the Ministry of the Interior, but were also supposed to collaborate with the General Commission on

Jewish Affairs and its police, the Division of Investigations and Inspections (SEC), to hunt down those who refused to comply. The traditional administrative apparatus conscientiously fulfilled the mission assigned to it. The task of marking identity papers was briskly carried out by the offices of the prefecture and 140,000 Jews had their papers stamped: for some, this was the last act of compliance before finding a way to replace these documents.[31] But other long arms of the French State—in particular, the General Commission on Jewish Affairs and its Division of Investigations and Inspections (SEC)—stepped in to identify those who had not complied.

Those repression services had been transformed somewhat since Darquier de Pellepoix had taken over for Xavier Vallat. Driven by the most rabid, unbridled antisemitism to push incessantly for a complete alignment with German "Jewish policy," Darquier had undertaken a gradual replacement of his personnel. The new agents of the General Commission on Jewish Affairs were not only younger and more ideologically oriented, but also less integrated into the milieu of French administration than their predecessors.[32] Their authority and the impact of their action necessarily suffered accordingly. At the same time, however, their determination did not slacken, and they enjoyed significantly augmented financial means from the state to carry out their operations. As we shall see, Darquier strove to use special propaganda to create the climate he deemed necessary to get his policies accepted. He hustled and bustled about and set the tone.

From November 1942 on, the mainspring of the General Commission was Joseph Antignac, who had first headed the Police for Jewish Affairs in Limoges and then directed the entire Divison of Investigations and Inspections in Vichy before becoming the chief of staff at the General Commission. Antignac's professional background speaks volumes not only of his ambition but also of the depth of his antisemitism.[33] Although the General Commission on Jewish Affairs no longer had the same clout with the higher administration and the other bodies of the state as it had under Vallat, the power that it and its police exerted over the Jewish population had on the contrary increased. Granted, there were no new laws after December 1942, but the existing set of laws was formidable enough. The General Commission and the SEC could devote their attention to conducting to their "relentless job of ferreting about,"[34] an activity that made any evasion ever more problematic, as the Germans were now everywhere present and had resumed their deportations.

The framework of the SEC in every region consisted of a director supported by a secretarial staff and backed by two to four inspectors. On October 13, 1942, Pétain signed a retroactive decree providing for a personnel of a hundred agents.[35] The tasks assigned to them, however, were quite numerous. Top priority was given to investigations dealing with problems of aryanization.[36] The SEC's inspectors were also supposed to seek out Jews who had been stripped of their French citizenship and inform them of the General Commission's decision on reviewing citizenship status. As of October 6, 1942, some 1,500 decisions to strip Jews of their French nationality had not been communicated to the individuals concerned because they could not be located.[37] Inspectors were also sent to look for Jews that authorities were unable to locate in the Paris region.[38] They were also charged with seeing that the complex set of anti-Jewish laws was obeyed, as Jews were trying more and more to escape from their clutches.

In an effort to address the complexity of these tasks, a "Handbook of Legislation on Jewish Issues for the Use of Mayors and Gendarmerie Brigades" was put together. In eleven pages, it explained "how to recognize someone as a Jew" and laid out the various laws, decrees, and sanctions applying to Jews.[39] This handbook was written subsequent to the law of December 11 and distributed throughout the year 1943 by the regional offices of the SEC. The terms and conditions of cooperation between the SEC and the national gendarmerie had indeed been fixed ever since February 11, 1943.[40]

And to increase its personnel indirectly, there was a general directive referred to as "Recruiting informers" that emanated from the SEC in February 1943: it declared that the provisional managers of Jewish property should henceforth consider themselves as informers who could help the SEC, and act accordingly.[41] At the time 786 provisional managers were operating in the Southern Zone.

There was a proliferation of orders to initiate general inspections during the month of February. Agents were to determine the number of Jews working as lawyers, doctors, and pharmacists by contacting the local presidents of various professional associations.[42] They were also to check on all the Jewish students registered for classes in universities.[43] This monitoring of administrative offices and professional circles thus took on a collective nature and met with uneven success, as their interlocutors often took their time to respond. It is difficult to tell whether such delays were due to administrative laziness, to the fact that the General Commission on Jewish Affairs and the SEC were outsiders, or to a real reticence to comply with orders: probably all played a role. Such checkups also entailed individual investigations intended to reveal any lack of compliance with the rules imposed on Jews.

The SEC's inspectors thus conducted more than 6,600 investigations in the Southern Zone between December 1942 and November 1943.[44] They maintained a pace of 400 to 450 investigations per month until the end of July 1944, and in some cases up until the first days of August 1944.[45] In February 1943, for example, 435 investigations were carried out: 210 concerned economic cases, while 275 dealt with persons. They resulted in 85 requests to place a business under provisional management, turned up 16 failures to submit to the census, and caused 5 Jews to be expelled from urban zones, 5 to lose their citizenship, 5 others to lose their government benefits, and 16 to be incorporated into a Foreign Worker Unit. The investigations moreover turned up four cases of Jews using a pseudonym and seven failures to have the word "Jew" stamped on papers.[46] The inspectors' recommendations were not always put into effect, but they nevertheless made life even more precarious for the Jews.

These reports provide us with virtual biographies of Jews in this time of war: they deal with one person's racial origin, another's activity, and the search for still another.

Those who had left Paris at the time of the mass exodus in May and June 1940 and had not returned since were strongly supected of being Jewish. People who sent their children to a lycée showed that they enjoyed certain personal resources, which made them suspicious. Such was the case for W.P., who had taken refuge at Saint-Junien, where he was receiving money orders: he was placed under investigation after being reported by the head of the local post office. "It is regrettable to see most of the Israelites having taken refuge in the Unoccupied Zone enjoying their personal resources and living like parasites. While awaiting better days, they have neither the desire nor the intention of readapting to a life of gainful employment," complained one regional head of the SEC.[47]

In other reports, we can follow the tribulations of Jews who had been taken out of a camp and placed under house arrest, and then removed from their assigned residence and incorporated into a Foreign Worker Unit. We can empathize with the little forty-nine-year-old Polish craftsman who was managing to survive thanks to a mechanical knitting workshop where he had one employee doing custom orders: the inspector requested that he be incorporated into a Foreign Worker Unit and that his workshop be placed under provisional management. And so we see just how many Jews thought they could get by while living off their savings.[48]

Inspectors were guided by a twofold objective. First, aryanization was to be rigorously applied both economically and "socially" (referring to a purge of professional circles). Second, all movements and activities of the Jewish population—by definition suspect—were to be monitored. In May 1943, priority was given to the search for Jews reported to have disappeared or to be on the run. In order to remain operative while on the move, inspectors were instructed to carry with them at all times a pocket notebook containing an updated list of Jews wanted by authorities. "I ask you to consider this search mission to be of the utmost importance and to fulfill it in all good professional conscience," the head of the SEC in Limoges commanded his inspectors.[49]

The main objective was indeed now to track down Jews on the run or in hiding. The stakes had changed since the summer and even more since the end of 1942: the risk of social and economic exclusion had given way to the threat of deportation to an increasingly ominous destination. Arrests and deportations of Jews had resumed more vigorously, and a mere verification could lead to Auschwitz for Jews. Even with all that, the Ministry of the Interior decided on May 22, 1944, to establish a card file of Jewish consumers.[50] It was thus decided that "ration cards will henceforth be issued to Jews only at the city hall having jurisdiction over their home or usual place of residence." And "when time comes for the general renewal of food ration cards, a card file of Jewish consumers residing in each community should be established." From then on, three notecards had to be filled out for every Jew: one for the National Office of Statistics, one for the city hall responsible for establishing "[its] card file of Jewish consumers—which [was] to be carefully kept up to date," and one to be sent by the city hall to the prefectorate.[51] The General Commission thus relayed the ministerial directive to the various prectorates, who, due to the Allied landing and subsequent Liberation, never had the time to carry out this new mission.

The political determination to monitor and control thus never wavered, and this persistence in marking and keeping files on Jews facilitated police work. The authorities had not only excluded the Jews from society, but also insisted on keeping them under tight surveillance, and subjected them to systematic denigration. It was only logical that these same authorites do everything they could to make the Jews productive.

Putting the Jews to Work

"They won't think about Jews so much, now that they have to organize a manhunt," observed Raymond-Raoul Lambert on October 15, 1942.[52] He was watching a demonstration against the Prisoner for Worker Exchange program (la Relève) at the Perrache train station in Lyon. As we have already seen, Jacques Biélinky in Paris had instead feared that Jews might just be the first victims of the law of September 4, 1942, as they had been forced to remain idle. After having excluded them from a number of professions, however, the French State was intent on using them as it saw fit. On December 8—even though the telegram was dated December 6—the minister of the interior ordered that unmarried foreign Israelites of all nationalities who had entered France since January 1, 1933, be immediately incorporated into Foreign Worker Units.[53] On December 14, 1942, newspapers published a "Notice to Foreign Israelites" that directed them to report to various assembly points in order to undergo an examination that would determine their aptitude for induction into a Foreign Worker Unit.[54]

With the introduction of the Forced Labor Service (STO), all sorts of ideas proliferated. Indeed, Jews were terrorized by the law of February 1943. "What shall be the fate of young French Jews?" wondered Consistory leaders. "Will they be sent to Germany, and if so, will they suffer the same fate as our compatriots, or that of the poor deportees?"[55] In other words, would they leave as Jews or as French citizens? As it turned out, they did not depart with the trains of workers bound for Germany. Central Consistory leaders learned in June 1943 that the Germans were opposed to the departure of Jews and that they did not want any Jews either at the construction sites of the Todt organization or in factories under German command in France.[56] In the département of Le Puy-de-Dôme, government employees in the placement service assured Jews that they would be summoned individually and sent only to French firms.[57] We know moreover that the prefect for the Limoges region had issued directions stipulating that the young Jews drafted into the Forced Labor Service should replace the young Aryans sent to Germany. And so it was that eighty-two Jews from the département of La Dordogne were apparently employed at four different construction sites of the Guyenne Pétrole company in Bergerac.[58] Such "favoritism," however, was resented by zealous antisemites, who wanted to put an end to the practice. That resentment was probably behind the unimpeachable logic of the project concocted in March 1943 by the head of the SEC.

The fate of foreign Jews without financial resources was sealed by the decision of December 1942. (Except for those declared unfit for work: in that case, the individuals concerned were to be turned over to the Office of Social Services for Foreigners [SSE], which would see that they were retrained and given light tasks to carry out.) As for those Jews with financial resources, the head of the SEC proposed that "a provisional manager be placed in charge of their personal property, at which point we return to the preceding case: the Jew must be incorporated" into a Foreign Worker Unit. French Jews without financial resources were to be reported to one of the professional reorientation offices: they would be offered jobs, and if they refused, would no longer have any right to any assistance. For French Jews with financial resources, their property could simply be placed under provisional management, and once again, they would be sent to work.[59]

It seems that these fine propositions never saw the light of day, but that did not keep other ideas from emerging. Laval decided to place young Jews between the ages of twenty and thirty at the disposal of the Germans (in spite of their opposition?), who would then be responsible for putting them to work in France.[60] In the Occupied Zone, the general commissioner of the Forced Labor Service had sent instructions to this effect to regional prefects, recommending that they summon Jews individually.[61] Raymond-Raoul Lambert was then officially assured that no French Israelite nor any foreign Jew incorporated into a worker unit in the Free Zone would be transferred to Germany.[62] As for the Jews from the départements of L'Alsace and La Moselle, they were exempted from forced labor at the constructions sites of the Todt organization and relegated to working in peat bogs and logging sites.

Moreover, in late August 1943, regional prefects and the regional heads of the General Interministerial Commission on labor received orders from the General Commission on Labor mandating "the use of Jewish labor at the construction sites of the Todt organization."[63] To see to it that these new instructions were carried out, the regional delegates of the SEC in the Southern Zone were secretly summoned to Toulouse on September 7, 1943 and instructed to draw up lists of French and foreign Jews. But it was the French police that went ahead with the scheduled roundups of Jews two days later (which was too soon). In addition, the French police were content with apprehending foreign Jews, and did so in a conspicuous manner that resulted in the total failure of the operation:

> The upshot [of all this] is that the lists that had been secretly requested from the regional delegates of the SEC in the Southern Zone and that are still being drawn up will most likely amount to a lot of useless work, as both foreign and French Jews have now been alerted and are constantly on the watch, and as the prefects are moreover frankly hostile to this measure that they partially allowed to be imposed on foreign Jews: when it comes time for the French Jews [to be subjected to the same measure], they will hold back.[64]

In Toulouse, only eighteen out of the seven hundred persons listed had been arrested. In neighboring départements, however, 250 others got taken. News of the imminent roundup had indeed and spread throughout the Jewish population in the days preceding the operation. Moreover, police agents had displayed a distinct lack of enthusiasm. "Should we take this lethargic attitude to represent the general state of public opinion?" wondered one witness in recounting these events:

> It seems instead that we should interpret such an attitude as stemming from the policemen's weariness of pressure from the Germans: they felt fed up both as policemen and as French citizens. But it is also true that they had been influenced by the overt threats broadcast from London almost every evening and directed against policemen working for Vichy and the Gestapo. And then one has to think that the announcement of the armistice in Italy, which drew Allied armies dramatically nearer to French soil and seemed to hasten the date of an Allied landing in France, had an appreciable influence on opinion and contributed to the careful attitude of the police.[65]

How many Jews were picked up in all, and on the pretext of the Forced Labor Service, how many not so young Jews were "put to work?" We know that, until September 8, 1943, the Italian authorities refused to comply with Vichy's orders for their Occupation Zone, and that in certain places such as in Roanne, Jews summoned for induction into the STO generally preferred to join the ranks of the Jewish Resistance rather than to work for the Todt organization.[66] When all Jews in Capdenac between the ages of eighteen and fifty were called up "for the STO" on August 24, 1943, the inhabitants of the département of L'Aveyron were greatly upset, especially as the date and time of their summons were directly inscribed on their identity cards, making them unusable.[67] The aforementioned range of ages shows just how much confusion there was at the time between the departures for the STO and inductions into the Foreign Worker Units. Did orders concern foreign Jews or all Jews? Did they affect those between the ages of eighteen and thirty or between the ages of eighteen and fifty? Such "administrative disorder" increased the confusion among the Jews and fueled rumors, but in no way reduced their acute awareness of the danger stalking them, and only them.

And when Jews were identified as such by their German employers, it is not difficult to imagine what lay in store for them. One example on record is provided by three young Jews from the département of L'Indre who, because of the STO, were forced to sign contracts to work in La Rochelle. Identified as Jews by the Germans, they were immediately sent to the camp at Neuville-de-Poitou, where they were treated as civilian prisoners, underfed, and forced to do hard labor.[68]

There are in fact very few documents available to help us assess how Laval's plan was actually put into application, but one observer in the Southern Zone stated: "It was a manhunt for the STO and one more danger for the Jews."[69] The danger was unrelenting; in April 1944, the secretary of state for labor assured the General Commission on Jewish Affairs that there was no longer any reason to fear possible competition from Jews on the labor market. Henceforth, "all Jews liable to be called up under the conditions provided for by the law of February 2, 1944" would be sent to work for the Todt organization.[70] On May 16, 17, and 26, 1944, a group of about fifty Jews was arrested in the département of L'Indre. The operation was carried out by gendarmes in rural communities and by police in urban areas: both forces used a list drawn up by the prefectorate and sent to the STO. Twenty-nine of those arrested were sent to Cherbourg.[71]

And so Jews would no longer be a source of competition on the labor market: a most curious worry, as Jews were finding it quite difficult to find any work at all. The Ministry of the Interior was cognizant of this:

> When it comes to putting Israelite refugees back to work, the special sections of the labor offices in the various départements run into particular obstacles stemming from the application of the General Statute of the Jews, from the aptitude of the concerned individuals for certain jobs, and finally from a certain reticence on the part of employers, even when it comes to authorized positions, because of their fear that an extension of the Statute might suddenly deprive them of personnel still in training or having just completed a training period.

Employers were thus still displaying a good deal of caution in May 1943. Hence the logical conclusion: because "assisting this category of refugees indefinitely is out of the question," it was important "to notify able-bodied Israelites, both men and women between the ages of 15 and 60, that their government benefits would be terminated three months after they had been notified."[72]

The first to try to deprive the Jewish refugees from the départements of L'Alsace and La Moselle of their government benefits had been the prefect of the département of La Haute-Savoie in June 1942.[73] A few months later in Marseilles, the Office of Refugees in the Ministry of the Interior took a similar initiative, and met with the opposition of Raymond-Raoul Lambert.[74] On December 8, 1942, however, the UGIF received a new letter from the Office of Refugees explaining why the payment of a government benefit to Jews would be terminated. Arguing that the UGIF needed time to find ways of making up for the state's role in this domain, Raymond-Raoul Lambert requested on January 13, 1943, that this decision be delayed. The outcome of Lambert's appeal is not clear, but it was the very same functionary in the Office of Refugees that had been so diligently pursuing his objective since November 1942 who once again spearheaded the effort in May 1943.

In December 1943, the head of the SEC became particularly zealous. He denounced the granting of government benefits to Jewish refugees by prefectorates, as the UGIF was the "only entity authorized to provide aid to Jewish refugees and needy people," and instructed the regional delegates of the SEC to summon the delegates of the UGIF in their respectives regions "in order to instruct them to take care of all Jews receiving refugee benefits distributed through prefectorates, city halls," and so forth.[75]

However, this functionary was put back in line by his superiors at the General

Commission on Jewish Affairs. A memorandum dated January 14, 1944, sent to the regional heads of the General Commission and to the regional delegates of the SEC pointed out that "none of the legal texts forming the basis for government aid bear any trace of racial discrimination. . . . The UGIF is responsible only for optional aid."[76] At the time, the UGIF was struggling with insurmountable financial problems, and no one was in a better position than the General Commission to realize it. This was an instance in which the interests of effective administration prevailed over visceral antisemitism.

Certain city halls had nevertheless not waited for this clarification. They instead hastened to bar Jewish refugees from the lists of those receiving government benefits and, as was the case in January 1944, in the département of Les Vosges, instructed them to turn henceforth to the UGIF. On January 22, 1944, in the département of Le Var, the prefect sent to the General Commission on Jewish Affairs in Marseille the names of seventy-two Jews receiving government benefits in his département: they were to be cut off beginning on February 1, 1944.[77]

And yet even in 1944, there were still Jews who counted on government aid in order to survive. Because they remained visible to government administrative offices, they were vulnerable and must have been in a miserable state. Equally miserable were those who suddenly—within anywhere from a few hours to three days in the best of circumstances—received the to order leave a place where they had just begun to settle in or had even established roots for many long years.

DRIVING THE JEWS OUT

Authorities were indeed continuing to seize upon all sorts of pretexts to expel Jews. Expulsions sometimes resulted from one prefect's decision. Such was the case for all the French and foreign Jews living in hotels and family boardinghouses in the département of La Haute-Savoie: on the spur of the moment, they were forced out.[78]

On January 21, 1943, Vichy released a communiqué announcing that fourteen French départements had managed to escape from the invasion of Jews: L'Allier, Le Puy-de-Dôme, La Haute Savoie, Les Alpes-Maritimes, Le Var, Les Bouches-du-Rhône, Le Gard, L'Hérault, L'Aude, Les Pyrénées-Orientales, L'Ariège, La Haute-Garonne, Les Hautes-Pyrénées, and Les Basses-Pyrénées.[79] That was a rather hasty conclusion, as at least three of these départements came under the authority of the Italian Occupation forces, and since in Les Alpes-Maritimes, as we shall see, the prefect was not in a position to put Vichy's instructions into application.

Other "transfer-expulsions" did occur, however. The "foreign workers" living in Le Var and Les Pyrénées-Orientales were sent further inland, while foreigners that had been placed under house arrest in L'Hérault, L'Aude, La Haute-Garonne, L'Ariège, and Les Basses-Pyrénées were sent to the départements of La Creuse, Le Gers, Le Lot, and La Corrèze.[80] Approximately seven hundred people, mainly from the départements of L'Ariège and Les Basses-Pyrénées, thus came into La Creuse during this month of January 1943:[81] they were spread out in the towns of Bonnat, Champsanglard, Dun-le-Palleteau, Guéret, Naillat, Saint-Sulpice-le-Dunois, and probably other villages as well.[82] All of these measures were just the first steps in the application of a plan emanating from the SS and aiming to bring all the Jews together before deporting them.[83] René Bousquet had therefore signed off on it.

Authorities had thus begun to rid départements along the coasts and borders of Jews. Jews were once again driven away from Spanish border areas on February 18 and April 3, 1943.[84] On April 21, 1943, newspapers published a new communiqué about a reserved zone in the Pyrenees: three days later, there was another round of expulsions.[85] In late April and early May, nearly three hundred Jews from Bayonne, Biarritz, and the coastal area were sent to Pau, their first step on the road to house arrest.[86] A month later, it was the turn of 332 Jews from La Bourboule, but this time for a different reason: "On Monday, May 31, 1943, the foreigners and Jews (both French and foreign) living in La Bourboule were summoned by the town crier to report that very evening to city hall at 9 P.M." Interrogated individually (the last ones were questioned at 2:30 in the morning,

> they were summarily told they had to leave La Bourboule on the next train. They were forced to choose their new place of residence on the spot among fourteen different towns in the départements of Le Cantal and La Haute-Loire that were quickly read off to them: the town chosen was then immediately inscribed on their identity card along with the indication that they were not to leave it. . . . The reason for this measure was that Marshal Pétain was coming to set up his residence at La Bourboule.[87]

The villa of one of those expelled had been made available for the Marshal two days previously. Consistory president Helbronner and the Chief Rabbi Schwarz again sent another protest to Pierre Laval on June 6, 1943, since it was from his cabinet that this decision was said to have emanated. There were also fifty-two Jews and sixty-one foreigners expelled from Châtel-Guyon in May 1943, probably because some government employees had set their eyes on their homes.[88] And in August 1943, a group of about fifty families of Jewish refugees from L'Alsace and La Moselle were informed that they were to give up their places of residence in Saint-Amand-Montrond (in the département of Le Cher) because of plans to house a detachment of the First French Regiment: this idea was Guérard's, secretary-general with the Vichy government.[89] Because there was an increasing amount of complicity toward Jews in the ranks of government administrators, such instructions were carried out with little enthusiasm.[90]

Collective expulsions of Jews, some of whom had been living in the region for a very long time, also occurred in several towns in La Savoie, including Aix-les-Bains.[91] In the same département, at Brides-les-Bains, there were about three hundred Jewish refugees at the beginning of 1943. On October 8, a group of about one hundred were summarily informed that they were to be expelled.[92] The campaigns aiming to drive Jews out were thus focused on mineral water resorts, areas near residences of prominent members of the Vichy regime, and border and coastal regions. We cannot, however, reconstitute all the movements of Jews who were expelled and driven from one place to another in that manner. Given the political conditions that were henceforth to prevail, the obvious result was to place those whom the Germans were seeking to deport in an increasingly precarious position.

ARRESTING AND DEPORTING THE JEWS

The delivery of Jews to Drancy by the trainload had not actually stopped after September 15, 1942. Even before the Southern Zone was occupied by the Germans, four trains carrying 494 Jews (most of whom had first been grouped together in the Rivesaltes camp) had been transferred to Drancy before October 22.[93] The pace of such transfers had slackened significantly, however. Jews were no longer "being delivered like merchandise in a discount store, where you can take as many items as you wish at the same price"—to borrow an expression used by Laval in the talks he had had with Oberg on September 2, 1942.[94]

Events took a new turn on December 10, 1942, when Hitler ordered that all Jews and other enemies of Germany in France be arrested and deported.[95] Because they had only limited manpower to police the entire territory of mainland France (except for the Italian-occupied départements east of the Rhône River), the Germans had to count on the collaboration of the French to enter a new phase of the annihilation of the Jews in France. Trains would next be available in mid-February, and they needed to be filled. The largest operation was carried out in Marseilles in late January 1943: this was before the roundups were resumed in the Northern Zone and then extended to the entire Southern Zone.

The Roundup of Jews in Marseilles

On January 21, 1943, the people of Marseilles saw security police from Toulouse, Lyon, Nancy, and even Paris arrive in their city.[96] The operation got under way the next day on January 22: it was marked by arrests made in the vicinity of the train station and targeted in particular all whose identity papers bore the telltale stamp. The roundups of Jews seemed to have intensified during the night and in fact continued day and night up until January 27. French security police and German police patrolled the streets of certain sections of the city, mercilessly picking up every Jew they encountered. Apartment buildings were meticulously searched, and locksmiths had been requisitioned to force open the doors of those who pretended to be gone.

On January 26, Rue Sénac, Rue de l'Académie, Rue Saint-Saens, Rue Pisançon, and the center city commercial districts inhabited by Jewish families from Marseilles were targeted in particular. A train left the Arenc station in the early hours of the morning, carrying away the first load of Jews toward Compiègne. The train was guarded by the Germans and made up of cattle cars with groups of at least fifty persons penned up in each car. Every individual was given two hundred grams of bread, a half-can of sardines, a slice of cheese, and a piece of sausage. All had to relieve themselves in a corner of the car, right on the floor. Some people became desperate, while others remained silent, overcome with sadness. Among the passengers were some who had come to Marseilles just for the day and so had no extra underwear and no coat, even though the winter of 1943 was bitter cold. No social worker had been allowed to come near them.

It was on this same fateful day of January 24 that the evacuation of the northern section of the Vieux Port area was begun. The January 24–25 edition of the newspaper *Le Petit Marseillais* explained to its readers the rationale of these operations:

> For reasons of a military nature, and in order to guarantee the security of the general population, the German military authorities have issued to the French administration the order to proceed immediately with the evacuation of the northern section of the Vieux-Port area. . . . For domestic security reasons, the French administration has for its part decided to carry out a vast police operation in order to rid the city of Marseilles of certain people whose activities posed a serious danger for the general population.

The instructions contained in the police memorandum of January 18 ordering the operation specified more clearly who these "certain people" were: they commanded police agents to apprehend "chronic offenders, pimps, tramps, vagrants, vagabonds, all persons without a food ration card, all Jews, foreigners whose papers are not in order, those whose expulsion had been ordered, all persons who have not maintained any legal employment for one month."[97] And the communiqué put out by the prefectorate and also printed in *Le Petit Marseillais* added the following delightful sentence: "The French administration strove to avoid any possible confusion between these two operations." Nearly 30,000 people were thus evacuated, and 5,956 others arrested (3,977 of whom were released). How important were the Jews—dangerous criminals by definition—in this vast police sweep?

On the following day, there were a particularly heavy number of arrests in the vicinity of the train station. Even on January 26, entire sections of town were being ringed by police. On January 27, roundups were carried out in movie theaters and in some outlying sections of town. On January 29, the offices of the UGIF were swamped with relatives looking for family members arrested from January 22 through January 24. On January 31, two more trains, coming from the camps in Fréjus, headed out toward Compiègne, carrying 1,642 people. Of whom 782 were Jews; 745 of the 782 landed in Drancy on March 9. Most were deported to the extermination camps at Sobibor and Maïdanek on March 23 and 25, 1943, while a few others were ultimately sent to Auschwitz.[98] All French and foreign Jews had been arrested, whether or not their papers were in order. Some young children were spared, and elderly people were in a few cases released, but the stamped identity cards had proven effective.

The collaboration between French and German police in hunting down Jews was not new, but the massive police roundup in Marseilles nevertheless marked another step in a now well established submission. Nearly six hundred of the Jews arrested were French citizens, and that was indeed new. It is true that some French Jews had been arrested in Paris and even deported in September 1942. And it is also true that, on orders from the local German authorities angered by an attack on a German officer, French police in the Rouen region had just arrested 220 Jews, including French Jewish families.[99] But that was in the Occupied Zone, considered to be another world . . .

Prior to January 1943, French police in the Southern Zone had arrested French Jews only if they had violated the rules. But in Marseilles they had worked with German police in setting up a dragnet for any and all Jews. The action was a result of a new strategy adopted by the Gestapo, since Knochen had already contacted Eichmann on January 21, 1943 to inquire about the possibility of deporting French Jews:[100] the answer from the Reich's central security office (RSHA) had been affirmative.[101]

Stages of the Ordeal

Jewish leaders from the UGIF, the chaplain's office, the rabbinate, and the Central Consistory frantically tried everthing they could to bring a halt to the arrests of Jews, or at least shelter certain categories (French Jews, war veterans, Jews from the Alsace-Lorraine region, and Jews working with the charitable programs), and then later to have the train return from Compiègne. Some of these leaders went to the regional intendant of the police or to the prefect, others to Vichy, and still others to see Cardinal Gerlier or Pastor Boegner. "By using verbal instructions to transform a general police measure into a deliberately antisemitic measure, the chiefs of the Marseilles police acted consciously or unconsciously as the operatives or instigators of the German police," wrote Raymond-Raoul Lambert.[102] He thus places the responsibility for the mass arrests squarely on the shoulders of the local police, forgetting that he himself had written in his narrative of the events of January 24 that René Bousquet had been on the scene directing the whole series of operations and had refused to see him.

"We have been painfully shocked and deeply saddened by the news that has reached us from Marseilles," wrote Central Consistory president Helbronner to Premier Laval:

> During the operations carried out by French police in the city of Marseilles, thousands of French citizens of Israelite confession abiding perfectly by all the laws of our country were arrested. . . . All of these arrests *were apparently made only* [emphasis mine] because the persons apprehended were Israelites. . . . We

> indignantly protest this violation on French soil of the most elementary rights of French citizens who no longer have any protection even from their own country, and we send you our impassioned appeal to grant their release.[103]

"The painful measures taken against such a large number of law abiding French Israelites, I believe, can only be the result of an error, perhaps imputable to the confusion brought on by an operation of such considerable dimensions," wrote Cardinal Gerlier in a letter to the chief rabbi of France on February 1, 1943, after having received the latter's alarmed message.[104] Pastor Boegner was also deeply shocked, especially as he had been in Marseilles on January 29. He had only learned that French Israelites had been arrested, however, upon returning to Nîmes and receiving the chief rabbi's telegram.[105] On the following day he felt reassured, believing the news that those arrested had been released.[106] It was only an abuse of power by local police, said Lambert, while Helbronner stressed that the reports were unconfirmed. Gerlier considered the arrests to have resulted from a mistake, and Boegner concluded that the damage had been repaired. Their varied reactions reflect the widespread stupefaction in face of a new type of police operation that now threatened to upset the situation of Jews—all Jews—throughout France. At the plenary session of the Consistory meeting of February 28, 1943, Jacques Helbronner no longer hesitated to attribute the responsibility for carrying out the mass arrests in Marseilles to the French government, adding: "The different stops along the Jews' 'Via Dolorosa' are becoming ever harsher, as each new report is followed by accounts of even graver events."[107]

After these events in Marseille, on February 9, 1943, a new phase was indeed begun in Lyon. On that day, the Gestapo raided the UGIF facilities on Rue Sainte-Catherine, where were located both the offices of the Committee on Aid to Refugees and those of the Federation of Jewish Societies in France. Eighty-four Jews, including both office staff and aid applicants, were immediately carted off by Klaus Barbie's men.[108] The pretext invoked—namely, the use of illegal practices to aid Jews—was partially founded. The raid had in particular caught militants for the Bund who were holding a secret meeting in these offices. But B.A., who had come to get a free innoculation, was carted off along with them, as were all aid recipients present.[109] Such a roundup of Jews carried out in the very offices of the UGIF was not a good sign. And there were many others, with the next occurring three months later. In 1944, such raids were no longer the exception but the rule.

The raids were always carried out by the Gestapo, who never failed to terrorize entire villages and sections of cities when making individual arrests. Whenever the Germans seized people to use as hostages in reprisal for a terrorist attack, they always put Jews first on the list of those to be shot: such was the case in March 1943[110] in Saint-Etienne and again on June 26, 1943 in Le Puy-de-Dôme.[111] The French police had nevertheless not had their last say about hunting down Jews. French police services in Paris had offered to deliver a new load of stateless Jews to the Germans in order to avoid the massive deportation of French Jews already interned; Röthke and Knochen had set their sights on this group in hopes of filling the next deportation trains. The French police thus carried out the task that remained for them in the February 1943 roundups: the number of Jews demanded was to be met by using the so-called Free Zone to fulfill the quota.

On February 18, the Ministry of the Interior issued the order for the regional prefects to bring foreign Jews together and send them to Gurs before transferring them to Drancy for deportation.[112] The Rivesaltes camp had indeed already been closed down on November 25, 1942, and 1,565 women and children had been transferred to Gurs, which thus became the main transit camp in the Southern Zone, with Nexon second in line.[113]

As a result of these new instructions, there was thus a proliferation of arrests beginning on February 20. Between February 24 and February 27, some 509 Jews were arrested in the Limoges region and sent to Gurs.[114] During the same period, eighteen men were taken from small towns and villages in the département of La Corrèze and sent to Gurs.[115] Similarly, forty-eight foreign Jewish workers fell victim to these roundups in Montpellier and its outlying areas.[116] In the département of Le Tarn-et-Garonne, the number of foreign Jews arrested apparently reached several hundred.[117]

Jews thus met with a variety of fates during this time. The Central Consistory was moreover having trouble obtaining reliable information: Jews were reportedly being hunted down in the Montpellier region, while in the département of La Lozère only twenty-two out of the fifty men sought had been arrested, and in Chambéry, twenty-four had been apprehended. In Villefranche-de-Rouergue (in the département of L'Aveyron), eighty Jews had been "picked up" and transferred to Gurs in two operations carried out during the month of March.[118] Thirty-five Jews from Saint-Amand-Montrond were also deported at that time.[119]

Most of the places where there were large numbers of Jews were raided to fill the deportation trains. Beyond the (very fragmentary) figures given here, we can see the general contours of the massive roundup of Jews that was under way, even though the results did not match those of the police operation that had taken place in late August 1942. Perhaps the shortfall was due to a lack of enthusiasm on the part of those executing the orders. That the Jews had scattered out in anticipation of the arrests was certainly a major factor. There were certain places and certain milieus that provided refuge, and Jews henceforth made heavy use of them.

Some 925 Jews were nevertheless transferred from Gurs to Drancy on March 1, 1943.[120] On the following day, 775 more Jews who had transited in the Gurs camp followed the same route, along with 177 others who had passed through the camp at Nexon.[121] "We had thought that all those trying days of August were over and done with. . . . And now here we go again," wrote Laurette Monet, who was at the Nexon camp, to one of her friends.[122] Counting those in the trains that left from Marseilles, 2,622 Jews had been "delivered" to Drancy in ten days' time.

Beginning on April 10, 1943, Jews were delivered on a regular basis to "the Jews' camp" shortly after being arrested in the Southern Zone. They came from Toulouse, Nîmes, Marseilles, Lyon, Perpignan, and elsewhere in groups of two, three, five, ten or fifteen, and sometimes even more.

It was henceforth the Germans who conducted most of the arrests, as was the case in Marseilles during the night of April 9–10.[123] And for that reason, the distinctions previously made between foreign Jews and French Israelites were now disregarded. The latter, however, often enjoyed a more comfortable financial situation and, being better integrated, blended into the rest of the population more easily: in a few cases, appeals in their favor succeeded in obtaining their release. As of April 19, about forty Jews from the Nîmes, Avignon, Carpentras, and Aix-en-Provence area were taken to the Saint-Pierre prison in Marseilles, from where they were then sent on to Drancy.[124] Between April 28 and May 6, the Germans systematically "combed" trains from the southwest of France for Jews and took them into custody. During this time, a terrorist attack had seriously wounded two SS agents in Marseilles on May 1, 1943. In response, the local Gestapo raided the offices of the UGIF on 58 rue de la Joliette on May 6 and seized seventy-four Jews.[125]

This second raid into a UGIF facility in the Southern Zone was part of what began as a much more ambitious reprisal operation; the Germans had summarily ordered Raymond-Raoul Lambert to turn in a list of two hundred prominent Jews from Marseilles (Lambert refused.) The raid also spurred President Helbronner of the Central Consistory to register once more a formal protest with Marshal Pétain against these "cruel persecutions" that had been "carried out without the knowledge of the French authorities." Helbronner nevertheless pointed out that it had been the Jews' compliance with the law, and in particular with the requirement of having the word "Jew" stamped on identity cards, that had served as a basis for the arrests.[126]

As a result of all these expulsions, transfers, roundups, and spontaneous or planned dispersions, Jewish communuities were henceforth completely torn apart. In an attempt to get a grip on this new distribution of the population and its new needs, and in order to organize the collection of funds intended to relieve those in direst need, the Consistory sent an emissary, Albert Lévy, in early May 1943, and gave him the task of systematically visiting every place where Jews might have flocked together. Between May and November 1943, he wrote a series of highly valuable narrative accounts[127] of his travels that—as do the reports presented throughout the entire year by the various regional delegates of the Central Consistory—testify again and again to police roundups and the scattering of people in some communities and panic in others. There was no longer any point in conducting a detailed study of some new law or submitting a report about the encouraging development of cultural activity here and there or about the emergence of renewed religious fervor.

Seemingly striking at random, the Gestapo carried out police roundups in Nîmes and Avignon in April, again in Nîmes and then in Toulouse in June, and in Montauban in July: they were in most cases also accompanied by individual arrests.

Everywhere, rumors of imminent police roundups caused the local Jewish population to spread out a little more. On the eve of July 14, 1943, some 80 percent of the Jews still living in Limoges panicked and scattered about throughout the area.[128] In mid-August, the Jews in Périgueux experienced a similar type of terror.[129] The very same scenario occurred again in Pau one month later, and in many other places as well.

Arrests resumed more vigorously beginning in September 1943: the emphasis then was on the Occupation Zone that had just been abandoned by the Italians, as it was the Italian Zone—between November 1942 and September 1943—that had constituted a safe haven for a large number of Jews having fled the zone occupied by the Germans. But this haven was not accessible to all Jews, at least not the most destitute. And during this second phase of the war and the Occupation, when Jews were being deported, those who remained under the double control of the French and the Germans also had to deal with a propaganda campaign conducted in particular over the waves of the National Radio Broadcasting service: under the direction of the Ministry of Information, it brought the Vichy's official French antisemitism in line with what had been spewing out from Radio Paris for a long time .

FROM PROPAGANDA TO PUBLIC OPINION

Informing the French People about the Jewish Problem

Radio broadcasts had taken on a special importance during the Occupation, particularly in view of the war for public opinion waged between Vichy's official radio and the BBC.[130] Once he had returned to power, Pierre Laval was immediately interested in developing the National Radio Broadcasting service. And as soon as he was appointed General Commissioner for Jewish Affairs, Darquier de Pellepoix firmly intended to broadcast his ideas on the "Jewish question." It was not until December 1942 that he managed to set up a head office for propaganda at the General Commission on Jewish Affairs. But there was an urgent need to support the massive deportations under way with the specially focused propaganda, as public opinion had displayed its disgust: the result was an appeal apparently made by René Bousquet.[131] On September 10, 1942, Paul Marion, the secretary of state for information under Laval's authority, declared in Vichy to the accredited press that "the government [would respond] over the radio to the attacks of which it [had] been the target," and added: "The police roundups have only concerned the Jews that have come from Germany and Poland in recent years, and that we offered, to no avail, to export to the United States."[132]

Vichy thus defended its actions through the voice of Darquier and his acolytes who were then given the necessary time on the air: there were henceforth three ten-minute programs per week in the evening, then four per week in January 1943.[133] Two were broadcast on behalf of the General Commission, and two others on behalf of the French Union for the Defense of the Race (UFDR), an institution created, sponsored, and promoted by Darquier, and which officially presented itself as "a gathering of disinterested French citizens whose goal is to ensure France's racial integrity."[134] The primacy of the racial principle was set as absolute dogma. Beginning on June 14, 1943, the programs were aired from the studios of the National Radio Broadcasting service in Paris.[135] As was the case in many other domains, the heavy hand of German Occupation authorities was increasingly manifest. When we examine the content of these programs, we find a terrifying line of argument, given what we now know about what Nazi leaders had in store for the Jews.[136]

The first broadcasts contained a mixture of defensive and offensive arguments: the "so-called massive deportations" were reduced to "the expulsion of a few hundred families composed of foreign nationals from the Third Reich."[137] What was more, "the Jews [were] hoarding everything" and "[were] doing darned well."[138] Fortunately, the General Commission was there to "refute the errors of the propaganda spread by pro-Jewish elements and others tainted by Jewish influence." It would have been an "error," for example, to think of the Jewish problem as a religious one, as "the Jews do constitute a sect, but also a people and a nation." There were consequently no good Jews, and "to be anti-Jewish [was] to do one's national duty."[139] As for the supposed intelligence of the Jews, there were no Jews among the great inventors: that was the proof that the "spirit of creation, in other words the truly noble part of intelligence, is virtually atrophied in Jews." And although Jews seem to do particularly well in school, that was because Jews were Orientals, and consequently precocious in comparison with French children. At the end of their growth period, however, they reveal their true character as exploiters and parasites.[140] Jews were moreover ugly, as borne out by anecdotes taken from daily life.[141] But Jews were above all dangerous. As a result of their drive for domination, which formed the very basis of their religion, were they not at the bottom of all wars and revolutions?[142] Were they really a persecuted race? Don't kid yourself: "The oft-cited pogroms have never been anything more than the feeble reactions of long-oppressed Aryans, but when they cause thousands of Aryans to die, they proclaim it to be a holy war or a social experiment."[143]

The National Radio Broadcasting stations flooded the airwaves with historical examples of massacres, assassinations, and pogroms perpetrated through the influence of the Jews:

> The stateless Jews that our government had decided to send back to the government from whose territory they came were all instigators of revolution. The Jews bring on financial ruin, revolution, and war. Among the Jewish men whom they would have pity, there are monsters who would not hesitate to snatch up your possessions. The greatest danger to the world at present is the threat posed by the Jews."[144]

It was thus a dire moment. "Citizens of France, . . . do you want [France] to die or do you on the contrary want to recover that civilization that you carry in you, in spite of the filth with which the Jewish horde has covered you? Then be mindful of the mission of your race and, whatever your past or present opinions may be, rise up for this crusade and proclaim everywhere and always the Sacred Union against the Jews."[145] "It is urgent for the French to unite and stop the deadly work of these foreign troublemakers, the Jews."[146]

Once the emotional shock of October 1942 had passed, the subsequent series of broadcasts sought to elaborate and support the basic assertions voiced during these first radio talks. The register varied according to the specific program. When the broadcast offered a rewriting of world history in the vein of "the Jewish conspiracy" and its specific manifestations (in Russia, Hungary, Germany, Austria, and of course in France), it used the pseudoscholarly mode. Such phony erudition was also used to present truncated citations of one famous Jewish author or another: Theodore Herzl, the founder of political Zionism, but especially Bernard Lazare, one of the most famous advocates for Alfred Dreyfus, and Kadmi Cohen, were given prominence in these fanciful lectures.[147] Sometimes the program be devoted to explaining the central role of the Talmud, a "sort of code of the Jewish nation," in which "the collected directives of the Jewish horde" could be found.[148] Broadcasters made use of the crudest of terms, as when they referred to "the oily Jews with shady eyes,"[149] "the Jewish slime producing a stench," or "the hecatombs of thousands of young Christian girls, sacrificed to the Semitic Minotaur."[150]

And they were sometimes unwittingly funny, as in the following lines, which were supposed to support the idea of an irreducible opposition between Israel and France: "The most beautiful poems that the French people have written are the cathedrals, and they have built them not only during the Crusades but also during the Napoleonic wars. Jews, not having any roots, being nomads and vagabonds, are insensitive to true solidarity, and after the establishment of a national home for Jews in Palestine, they have never reconstructed the Temple of Jerusalem, even though they would have had plenty of time to do so."[151]

Two themes were constantly hammered home to listeners: the link between Jews and Bolshevism—both now and in the past—and the emphasis on the French race, "the only national wealth remaining for us." And they did not forget to mention all the characteristics of this chosen people: corruption and venality, parasitic behavior, perversion (as seen in the theories staged in *Le Mariage* by Léon Blum), cruelty, base sentiments, along with many other vices that made the evil incarnate.

Let us remember that this was the French State's official radio spouting such insane talk four times a week. Announcements of concrete measures (such as the law requiring that identity cards be stamped with the word "Jew") were given during these instructive presentations, with promises that others would follow. The programs were a far cry from the explanations given by Xavier Vallat in order to justify the formal adoption of the Jewish Statute, and it was doubtless because of their extremism that the Consistory did its utmost to have them stopped. They appealed through the usual channels: attorney Kiefe gave shorthand transcriptions of the programs to Jean

Jardin, while Consistory president Helbronner addressed a letter to Marshal Pétain, with General Campet, military chief of staff, acting as intermediary. And the result was the same as always: Jardin declared that he was disgusted by the programs and that Marshal Pétain certainly did not approve of these "harmful excesses." But in that case, the Marshal should step in and halt the practice! Yes, indeed, . . . but the division of information does not come under the authority of the chief of state, but rather under the authority of the head of the government.[152] Such discreet expressions of compassion invariably led to the same failures to act in earnest.

These radio broadcasts, however, represented just one facet of a propaganda campaign that took on several forms. It was the secretary-general for information that was in charge of the April 1943 distribution of five thousand copies of Jean de la Herse's *L'Eglise et les Juifs* in both the Northern and Southern Zones. A year earlier, he had circulated Gabriel Malglaive's *Juifs ou Français*, prefaced by Xavier Vallat.[153] The two books were closely linked: both stressed that deicide had condemned the Jews to an errant life, and their constant wandering from one place to another condemned them to be foreigners wherever they were, as they were so tied to their own peculiarities and obsessed with dominating the world. In sum, they were a cursed race. Other suggestively titled publications, such as Léon de Poncins's *La Mystérieuse Internationale juive*, were distributed far and wide at no cost.[154] Provisional managers were even used as distributing agents in this instance.[155]

There was also a more "subtle" propaganda exploiting associations that kept seeping into the public domain through other channels, and in particular through an anti-Bolshevism now more virulent than ever, as the Red Army's successes began to make the prospects for a Nazi Europe look ever dimmer.

The synopses of intercepted letters and wire-tappings prove that these propaganda efforts did not achieve the expected results—far from it. Instead people sought to glean information from foreign broadcasts, judged to be more reliable on military developments. The French radio and press, on the other hand, inspired "jeers and mockery from the public."[156]

The French and the Jews

In December 1942, the propaganda office of the General Commission on Jewish Affairs decided to conduct a survey of public opinion in order to determine the general view of the Jews, and in particular public feelings about the policies in this domain.[157] Within three weeks, a group of some ten pollsters had questioned 3,150 persons, according to a preestablished socioprofessional and geographical distribution.[158] The pollsters had been told that "the General Commission's goal in conducting this survey is not to obtain a majority of antisemitic responses," and so were accordingly instructed not to seek answers, but rather to interview people at random, guided only by the aforementioned socioprofessional and geographical quotas. Five questions were posed: Do you like the Jews? For what reasons? Are you in favor of the government's measures taken against the Jews in the Free Zone? If so, do you feel that they are sufficient? If not, what measures do you advocate?

Some 3,019 people responded to the first question: 51.44 percent of them declared themselves to be antisemitic, 12.05 percent philo-Semitic, and 36.51 percent said they were indifferent.[159] Further analysis shows that more women declared themselves to be philo-Semitic than men, that the owners of small and midsize stores did not have very kind feelings about Jews, that students and farmers turned out to be the most antisemitic, and that the largest number of philo-Semitics were to be found among those in the professions of law, medicine, pharmacy, and architecture. Finally, Montpellier and Limoges came in first among the most antisemitic areas, while Lyon and Grenoble had the highest number of favorable opinions about the Jews.

When we study the responses to the following questions, we discover that the image of Jews as exploiters and unassimilable foreigners was prevalent among antisemites who were little interested either by the racial arguments or by the revolutionary threat supposedly posed by the Jews. As for the philo-Semites, they most often took their stance "in reaction" (against Fascism or the Vichy regime, or because the Jews were victims of German measures). In some cases, people declared themselves to be philo-Semites "because of their [the Jews'] own qualities" or simply "because Jews are human beings like the others."

The indifferent make up a particularly interesting category. In the first place, 48.9 percent declared that they were opposed to the antisemitic measures, while 40.07 percent said they were indifferent to the matter: this gives us an idea of what their "indifference" really meant. Among those who were against the antisemitic laws, a large number again gave reasons similar to to a "reaction against" something. It was doubtless such responses that led one regional head of the SEC to conclude that the propaganda should henceforth aim "to show that the anti-Jewish measures are a policy of self-defense and not the result of German pressures."[160] There is one final curiosity worth examining in this survey. Among the minority of those stating that they would like to see stronger antisemitic measures, the most common suggestions involved forcing Jews out of all businesses and driving them out of France. The yellow star, on the other hand, enjoyed little popularity, although there were about ten persons who responded that "Jews should be purely and simply killed."

The results of this survey(whose information obviously cannot be accepted on face value) can be compared with a report emanating from an agent with the Central Bureau of Information and Action (BCRA), which was basically the secret service division of De Gaulle's Free France (or rather, after July 14, 1942, of his Fighting France). In this report, the agent gives an account of "public opinion in France" for this same month of January 1943.[161] He first observes "with sadness"—but in highly ambiguous terms[162]—that antisemitism had become widespread in rural areas where people had not had any contact with Jews before the war. But he added that "the deportations, dispersions of families, and the banning of all commercial activity that are tormenting the Israelites offend people's common idea of justice. These measures are not condoned by French public opinion and a large number of non-Jewish French citizens have generously provided refuge and hospitality to Israelites hunted down by the police.

Nevertheless, he added, one should not misinterpret these gestures of solidarity that were "completely to the honor of the French people."

> They are the mark of compassion, and not the mark of a high opinion of these people . . . The French public knows that it is true that in every society and in every group of people, the Jews know how to use both their recognized talents as well as their skill in dealing with people to occupy the key positions, leaving the subordinate positions to others. The necessity of driving the Germans out must therefore not appear as an effort to provide Jews the opportunity of resuming economic and even political activities that are not clearly maintained within proper proportions. This antisemitism must be taken into consideration, for to try to ignore it would be surely to risk the disaffection of the masses.

There follows in the report a long development on the need for a legal statute for foreigners and the necessity of distinguishing between Israelites having lived in France for a long time and those having recently immigrated, who should be subject to the Statute as should be any and all other foreigners. This was seen as the solution for getting rid of antisemitism.

The same themes were expressed in an shorter report made for the BCRA on May 3, 1943. "The persecution of the Jews has deeply hurt the French people and their principles of humanity: at times, it has even led the French to be almost fond of the Jews. One nevertheless cannot deny that there is a Jewish question: the present circumstances have even contributed to a making it more serious."[163] Similar ideas were echoed in December 1943:

> The French are not antisemitic: they are repulsed by racial persecutions. They do not cry out in cowardice that the death of the Jews is necessary for us to have our rightful place in life. But they do curse the banks of Israel (even though they do their best to copy them!) and would like to get rid of all the refugees from the ghetto who have gotten themselves kicked out everywhere and who have invaded our country with no hope of assimilation.[164]

While these two sets of documents emanated from politically opposite sources and made use of different methods, they ultimately point in the same direction. The French clearly disapproved of the persecutions endured by the Jews, but a massive wave of antisemitism, tied to the stereotypes of Jews as unassimilable foreigners or as exploiters a bit too bright for commerce continued to haunt the imagination of a large number of people in France. That these two currents ran parallel is sufficient to account for both the antisemitism of French society and the assistance that French people provided to persecuted Jews. Either one or the other tendency would dominate, depending on the time, the political and economic circumstances, the context, and the more general attitude of public opinion on the evolution of the worldwide conflict. And then there was a third tendency, doubtless the most widely shared among all societies: indifference.

The Vichy government was becoming increasingly unpopular, however, and its policies were increasingly felt to be German-inspired. Both the massive roundups and the occupation of the Southern Zone had made Jews in both zones share a common fate. Shortages and difficulties in obtaining basic commodities had continued to preoccupy people, particularly in poorer regions. On July 1, 1943, bakeries in Marseilles and surrounding areas were informed that they would henceforth be required to close one day a week and one month out of the year on a rotating basis.[165] In September, an exchange of old rags and used clothes for textile points was organized for the entire Southern Zone as well as in Paris.[166] Montluçon was hit by a bombing attack for the first time on September 18, 1943. Other strikes would follow. Meanwhile, administrative controls over French youth were tightened in efforts to hunt down those who refused to be incorporated into the STO.

In sum, the majority of people were beginning to grow weary,[167] wishing for a rapid end to the war, hoping for an Allied victory, which now seemed certain. The STO was often the first of their worries. People "were vehemently indignant about the massive deportations to Germany" ("deportations" meaning the departure of those forced to go work in Germany because of the STO).[168] It was feared that the STO might be extended to women. Such constant threats of forced labor were now weighing on all sectors of the population,[169] and projected outcome of the war after the Battle of Stalingrad and then the liberation of North Africa caused the "balance to sway" decisively in the summer of 1943. Now "Vichy's cause [was] completely lost and definitively identified with that of Germany. Public opinion [was] in its phase of clear and unmistakable hostility."[170] The swaying of opinion in Occupied France is present between the lines on the front page of *Le Petit Marseillais* on July 4 and 5, 1943: the headlines story "Is a landing possible?" was followed by two highlights of the speech delivered by Premier Laval, "The German army will not be defeated" and "Our ancient administration represents the continuity of France." These words were in fact an acknowledgment of the failure evident in all the reports reaching the executive offices of Vichy.

Vichy's illegitimacy was that its own measures, and in particular of those most clearly bearing the stamp of the Germans—in other words, all of the anti-Jewish laws. With a slight delay, the population of the Southern Zone had come in line with that of the Occupied Zone. That probably explains why the agents of the General Commission on Jewish Affairs were finding it increasingly difficult to recruit provisional managers or people interested in acquiring Jewish property. For the latter group, the future was too uncertain; thus certain Jewish businesses managed to avoid aryanization.

Such was the case for the family store "A la femme chic," which sold women's clothing in Montluçon. The Police for Jewish Affairs was asked to conduct an investigation in April 1942, and the ensuing report had been submitted to the General

Commission on Jewish Affairs on June 30, 1942. A provisional manager was therefore appointed and the sale of the business was begun, but it was not put up for public bids until the spring of 1943. As of June 1943, no one had yet stepped forward to acquire the store, in spite of the ads placed in the local papers.[171] Too late! Pierre Tissier had already issued a clear warning over the BBC on September 1942 for those who might have been tempted to acquire Jewish property. The sales of Jewish property, stated Tissier, "are null and void. The properties involved in such sales will in principle be restituted in kind to their rightful owners. Persons acquiring such property can thus in any case be sure that they will be dispossessed of it and in most cases will also lose the money paid."[172] As the military situation kept on evolving in favor of the Allied forces, this threat became increasingly substantive.

The same was also true for the threat issued in August 1943 over the same BBC channel that the French were tuning in so diligently in their homes: "Members of the Milice! Security Police! Gendarmes! Government employees! You whose job it is to carry out deportations to Germany, don't forget that people come back from Germany. . . . Don't forget that the return of our deported ones is drawing near, as is the Liberation [of France] and that they will demand that you answer for your acts."[173]

When the German police stepped in and took over the job of hunting down Jews, the general population provided more aid to an ever-larger number of Jews. The types of threats mentioned above doubtless curbed the technical collaboration of certain undecided individuals and dissuaded opportunists from collaborating. But let us not overlook the confusion contained in these warnings that "the return of our deportees is drawing near," since "deportees" referred both to the Jews deported "to the East" and those sent off to work in Germany by the STO. There was a widespread sympathy and complicity with all those avoiding either deportation or induction into forced labor, and this sympathy created a favorable terrain for rescuing all those on the run. The number of such fugitives was rising dramatically: the rate of those dodging the STO had risen from 20 percent in May 1943 to anywhere from 50 to 70 percent in July and August, and then again to 80 or 90 percent in the last few months of the year.[174] The ensuing development of resistance groups hidden in the countryside created even more places of refuge for a good number of young Jews. On the other hand, the specific urgency of rescuing the Jews was no longer apparent. What now prevailed was not really indifference, but a sort of fatalism: as everyone was threatened and all had a common enemy, it was only natural that opposition should take on a general character and eschew all particularism.

These tendencies became even more pronounced in the fall of 1943, with the gradual installation of a police state by the Milice, which dominated Vichy in its final stages. Up until then, Jews could move from one zone to the other when looking for a safe haven. Prior to the summer of 1942, the general tendency had been to flee the German-occupied Northern Zone for the so-called "Free" Zone in the south. But the massive roundups in the summer of 1942, followed by the occupation of the Southern Zone, had created largely similar conditions on both sides of the demarcation line. But before the situation became relatively homogeneous, there had remained one geographical loophole: the Italian occupation of French territory east of the Rhône.[175]

THE ITALIAN SAFE HAVEN

The Italian Jews in the Occupied Zone

The Italians had already had occasion to protect their Jewish nationals in France, particularly in the Occupied Zone. Not that they renounced the antisemitic policies that they themselves had independently put into effect in Italy subsequent to their alignment with Hitler's regime in 1938;[176] but the considerations of sovereignty that for a time prevailed led them to step in between "their" Jews and the Germans.[177] There were some 1,500 Italian Jews residing in France at the outset of the war, 499 of whom were concentrated in the département of La Seine.[178] Italian authorities stepped in after having been alerted by Italian Jews whose possessions had been slated for aryanization: these authorities strove to recover this property for Italy and keep it from falling into French hands. In January 1941, these Italian authorities obtained permission for provisional managers who were Italian to take over aryanized property from Italian nationals—the same type of arrangement that had been adopted for Jews that were nationals of Spain, Cuba, Brazil, Switzerland, Hungary, Romania, Turkey, Portugal, and Mexico.[179] Proceeds from any sales conducted were to be paid to the Italian Consulate.

The bureaucratic activity occasioned by these transfers aligned the Jews and the Italian Consulate in Paris against the Germans, who were administratively responsible for handling these arrangements. Thus when the Italian consul in Paris, Gustavo Orlandini, was notified of the adoption of harsher anti-Jewish measures in France in May 1941, he requested instructions from Rome and offered to plead with the Germans to exempt Italian Jews. Orlandini met with refusal, however. After several months, he did succeed in obtaining the release of the dozen or so Italian Jews—including Nissim Calef—who had been arrested in Paris in August 1941.[180] He also forced the hand of the central authorities in Rome by issuing to all Jews who came to him a pass allowing them to be repatriated to Italy, in spite of Rome's refusal to organize such a repatriation. Consequently, the Jews who availed themselves of Orlandini's liberality often remained blocked by border police in the little border village of Bardoneccia. Orlandini also obtained the permission for Italian Jews to be exempted from wearing the yellow star.

But when the objectives of German policy concerning the Jews became clearer, the Italians strove to stand apart from their allies. Thus when the fate of Italian Jews residing in France came up for discussion, the Germans—spurred on by Abetz—kept insisting that they be given a free hand, while the Italians hemmed and hawed.

When the Germans demanded a firm decision from Mussolini, he refused to accept the terms of the two choices put before him on September 17: namely, that he either let the Italian Jews be deported or else organize their repatriation to Italy before January 1, 1943. At the same time, by way of concession, he withdrew his opposition to the yellow star,[181] while Consul Orlandini tried—to no avail—to pressure Röthke into releasing a few Italian Jews who had been snared by French police during the summer 1942 roundups.

The evolution of the military situation reduced the Italians' room to maneuver vis-à-vis the Germans even more, and forced them to make a decision. In late January 1943, Count Ciano had the Germans informed that the Italian Jews residing in France, Belgium, and Holland would be repatriated: a few days later instructions reached the consulates involved. Until September 1943, those who requested to do so—including the Italian Jews who had been interned at Drancy—were thus able to leave France for Italy or the Italian Occupation Zone in France.

But it was in November 1942, when the Italians moved in to occupy a part of French territory, that they were obliged to decide on a clear policy regarding the Jews who then came under their authority.

East of the Rhone River

As was the case in the zone occupied by the Germans, relations between authorities in Vichy and those of the Italian Occupation rested on a fundamental ambiguity. The Germans and Italians had seized control of these zones "militarily," officially for security reasons, in order to protect them from an Allied landing. The French civilian power remained in place. On December 17, 1942, however, the Germans, followed on January 15, 1943 by the Italians, granted themselves all the powers of an armed Occupation force in their own zone, irrespective of the armistice agreements. The Italians had moreover not relinquished their ambition to annex a portion of the area that they occupied, which explains why they were keen on demonstrating their sovereignty each time they were given the opportunity. The political rivalry between the French and Italian authorities that grew out of this situation worked in favor of the Jews. It was a unique case in the history of the period.[182]

The Italians let the Germans know right away that they themselves would take care of monitoring "undesirable" people of all sorts within their Occupation Zone. The first occurrence of friction with the French authorities at the prefectoral level came in short order. On December 6, 1942, the French prefects were instructed to keep foreign Jews having come to France after January 1, 1938, at a distance of at least thirty kilometers from the coastline, and also to move them to the départements of La Drôme and L'Ardèche. Concretely, that meant that the foreign Jews in the Italian Zone were to be taken to the German Occupation Zone. It seemed rather obvious that those expelled in that manner would then be put on the next deportation trains headed for the east. On December 20, Marcel Ribière, prefect for the département of Les Alpes-Maritimes, followed Vichy's instructions and notified the foreign Jews under his jurisdiction having come to France after January 1, 1938, that they should be prepared to be evacuated inland within seventy-two hours.[183] The Italian Consul in Nice, Alberto Calisse, immediately demanded that Italian Jews be exempted from this measure, and then he appealed to Rome.

Was the intervention of the Italian Jewish banker Angelo Donati (who had been interceding with the Italian authorities on behalf of the Jewish community since November 1942) decisive in compelling Calisse to act in this manner?[184] For it was Donati who had once again come before him to plead the Jews' case. At any rate, the response from Rome came without delay: the French administration was informed that the fate of foreign Jews in the Italian zone would remain the exclusive prerogative of Italy. As we have seen, there were other anti-Jewish measures looming on the horizon, namely, the forcible induction of foreign Jews into Foreign Worker Units and the stamping of the word "Jew" on identity papers. But once the Italian Consul had received confirmation from Count Ciano on January 2, 1943, that the Jews in the Italian Zone were to be exempted from such French measures, he let Prefect Ribière know on Janaury 14, 1943, that it was out of the question to apply the most recent instructions, except with respect to French Jews.[185] This exemption was applicable in the area extending out from the département of Les Alpes-Maritimes to all the rest of the Italian Occupation Zone. "The Italian authorities are presently stymieing the three major measures that the French government had adopted against foreign Jews," wrote Prefect Ribière to Premier Laval.[186] Vichy could only give in, and none of these three measures was applied to Jews in that area.[187]

The rumor that the Italian military authorities were protecting Jews spread like wildfire, and thousands of refugees who had been without any legal identity for weeks went all-out to reach what the secretary-general of the Consistory Albert Manuel termed the new Land of Canaan.[188] The young people with the Zionist Youth Movement (MJS) moved to Grenoble and transferred their center for fabricating false papers as well as all their rescue operations to Nice. It was also in Nice, in the facilities of the synagogue on Rue Dubouchage, that a Refugee Aid Committee came together. This committee's work became ever more extensive once it had taken on the task of working with the Italian military authorities and supplying Jewish refugees in the Italian Zone with an officially stamped card attesting to their legal status. More than four thousand Jews were thus able to reacquire a legal identity that provided them with some semblance of the tranquillity that had been lacking from their lives for several months.

Nevertheless, German demands and French claims had not vanished. And it was at this point that Rosario Barranco, an Italian police officer, concocted a clever plan: he proposed transferring foreign Jews out of coastal areas to assigned residences within the territories under Italian control.[189] That showed that the Italians took seriously the job incumbent on them to monitor the Jews.

The French deeply resented the effects of this opposition to their authority. In their view, it amounted to a violation of their sovereignty, and their image was beginning to suffer from this comparison of French and Italian policies concerning the Jews. Moreover, the Italian policy threatened to impose on French Jews measures that no foreign Jew would have to fear: such a situation was very delicate. René Bousquet first approached the subject with Oberg on January 8, 1943, and Laval took it upon himself to complain to the Germans by sending Jean Leguay to see Knochen.[190] These appeals, along with the others that followed, brought on a more energetic reaction from the Germans who pressured the Italians to comply with the French demands. The German Minister of Foreign Affairs Von Ribbentrop appealed directly to Mussolini. But even though some high-level Italian political personnel had been replaced,[191] they were all quite determined not to give an inch on this question—especially as a report sent to Rome from Dino Alfieri (the Italian ambassador in Berlin) had reported in great detail the massacres of Jews in Eastern Europe.[192]

Deportations had been scheduled to resume ever since December 1942. When the police roundup operations began on February 20, 1943, in the south of France and extended into the départements occupied by Italy, they provoked the Italians' anger: indeed, the Italians would constantly step in to secure the release of the Jews that the French had arrested in the "Italians'" area and then taken to Gurs. In spite of increasing pressures from the Germans, brigadier general Avarna di Gualtieri, representing the Italian high command in Vichy, sent a curt letter to Admiral Platon. In it, he demanded the release of the eight Jews arrested in Annecy and transferred "to the Pyrenees," and recalled that the issue of the foreign Jews fell "exclusively under the jurisdiction of the Italian military Occupation forces." He also requested that the French government order prefects in the départements concerned "[to refrain] from adding any measure whatsoever involving the arrest or internment of Italian, French, or foreign Jews residing in the aforementioned territory."[193] In response, Laval once again contacted the Germans and expressed his surprise over this Italian initiative.[194]

The Germans' patience was beginning to wear very thin; such "resistance" by the Italians hampered the execution of the Final Solution and could only encourage other partners to mark their differences with the Germans' treatment of the Jews. In early March, Von Ribbentrop presented Mussolini with an ultimatum of choosing between three possibilities: Mussolini could (1) order the Italian high command not to stymie the efforts of the French police; (2) take these matters out of the hands of the Italian military authorities and assign them to Italy's civilian police; or (3) do neither, and the SS working in collaboration with the French police would take over.[195] Possibly acting out of indifference, Mussolini first informed the German ambassador delivering the ultimatum that he would order his generals to no longer get in the way of the French police.

An immediate appeal from Giuseppe Bastianini (Mussolini's assistant for foreign affairs since the firing of Count Ciano) however, led the Duce to reconsider his position and choose instead to accept the second of the choices put before him. Guido Lospinoso was thus appointed inspector general of the Racial Police for the occasion and sent to Nice in late March 1943. His official mission was to use the support of Italian high administrators and organize the transfer of foreign Jews from coastal areas further inland in order to save the Jews. The Germans, however, expected him next to collaborate with them in deporting these same Jews.[196] Obviously, they had not caught on that the Italian police bore little ressemblance to their own.

Lospinoso got to work as soon as he arrived. With the aid of the Rue Dubouchage Committee, which provided both the lists of refugees to be brought together as well as the necessary trucks—a train trip would have forced them to pass through areas under German control—he proceeded to have hundreds of Jews taken to Mégève, Saint-Gervais, Saint-Martin-de-Vésubie, Vananson, Barcelonnette, and Vence. Some four thousand Jewish refugees thus headed out for their "assigned residences" in areas inland from the coast, where the Jewish organizations took complete care of them.[197] Other *carabinieri* were posted in front of the central portion of the Rue Dubouchage to prevent French police from coming to arrest Jews who might not have been in compliance with some of the special rules and regulations governing their status.[198] The Italian government had pledged to limit its protection to those Jews who been in their zone prior to March 26, 1943, a theoretical deadline to which the Italian authorities paid no attention. At the same time, Lospinoso, with the help of his superiors, managed to avoid all contact with the Germans, who strove unsuccessfully to meet with him in hopes of hammering out a common policy.

However, after first German then Italian troops were routed in Tunisia (on May 11 and 13), and after the Allies landed in Sicily (on July 10), Mussolini was deposed by the Fascist Grand Council during the night of July 24–25, and the prospect that the Italians would soon have to evacuate their zone of occupation loomed on the horizon. The Italian authorities were inundated with requests for repatriation from Jewish nationals and so to that end expedited the necessary administrative formalities. They then also expedited the return of former Italian nationals who had given up their Italian citizenship after their "fatherland" had enacted racial laws. The Ministry of the Interior, on the other hand, was hardly enthusiastic about taking in thousands of utterly destitute Jewish refugees at a time when the country was not only being bombed, but was also suffering from social and economic disorder and facing a rather uncertain future.

During the night of July 28–29, 1943, a German motorized division arrived in Nice and was stationed in various barracks in the area.[199] There was now no doubt as to the switch from Italian to German Occupation forces: the only question was about the date, and Jewish circles were put in a state of panic. Here again, rumors of a large-scale general roundup of Jews came to be part of daily life.

Some Jewish leaders argued that Jews should immediately scatter out into inland rural areas. Joseph Fischer thus asked the Consistory to have Vichy step in and give instructions to the prefect of the département of Les Alpes-Maritimes so that the prefect could issue passes without first having to obtain the consent of the départements taking in the refugees.[200] For its part, the OSE focused its efforts on placing as many children as possible in safety, and put 150 of them in scattered locations within a few weeks.[201] Parents had to pledge not to try to contact their children, in order to avoid putting them in danger.[202] Others worked tirelessly to get the Italian authorities to organize an evacuation of all Jews.

A meeting between the two commanders of the Axis armies was held in Bologna on August 15, 1943.[203] It was thereupon decided that the Italians would retain control over a portion of French territory in the Nice area. A few days later, during an interministerial meeting in Rome, it was decided to take the Jews from all the rest of the Italian Zone and put them all together in this area.[204] With an escort of forty *carabinieri*, forty trucks transported some 1,800 Jews from Saint-Gervais and Mégève to Nice on September 6 and 7. The original plan had been to take them to Saint-Martin-de-Vésubie, the point closest to the border, but the town lacked sufficient room to house them.[205] With the help of the young Zionists and the Scouts, the Rue Dubouchage Committee did the best it could to put them up in Nice's hotels.[206] In any case, Jews from Vence and elsewhere were now pouring in to the Nice region on their own. They were met by the young volunteers at the train station.[207] They kept themselves prepared to leave, when leaving might be possible.

During the forty-five days of the Badoglio government's rule in Italy, various plans for a possible evacuation of the area remaining under Italian control were put forward. Angelo Donati, aided by Father Pierre Marie-Benoît, sought to obtain the relocation of the Jews from Nice to North Africa: with the official backing of the Italian government, he carried out secret negotiations to this end in Vatican palaces with the Allies. For his part, the Chief Rabbi of Geneva, Salomon Poliakof, pleaded for the Swiss borders to be opened.[208] But both the Allies and the Swiss failed to take action.[209] According to a report emanating from the Division of Investigations and Inspections, a yacht anchored in Cannes and carrying one thousand Jews, supposedly left the city for Corsica on September 8.[210] But just how credible is the report? On this same day of September 8, 1943, General Eisenhower created quite a surprise—along with joy and panic—when he announced publicly and prematurely, that Italy had signed an armistice agreement with the Allied powers. The Italian troups were thrown into confusion and chaos: as a result, some 25,000 Jews found themselves caught in a trap that prevented a large number of them from escaping.

Brunner and His Physionomists

The "happy days" had indeed been "numbered," to borrow the terms used by the head of the SEC who, on September 3, 1943, was preparing to serve as an auxiliary to the Germans in the grim task they had assigned themselves.[211]

A special commando led by Aloïs Brunner arrived in Nice on September 10 and carried out one of the most vicious manhunts that France would see during the war. All the subtle distinctions formerly made between French Jews and foreign Jews no longer held any validity for Brunner. He knew that there were somewhere between 20,000 and 25,000 Jews in the region, some of whom had just come to Nice, and he had strong hopes of seizing the better part of them. He received no list to facilitate his job: Prefect Chaigneau claimed he had turned all such lists over to the Italians, while Lospinoso, before clearing out of his offices, had burned the ones he had drawn up. But Brunner recruited paid informers, "physiognomists"—experts on the infamous "specifically Judaic facial features"—who assisted the Gestapo's units as they went up and down the streets, going from hotel to hotel, building to building, casting their nets far and wide and arresting as many people as they could. Those arrested were made to drop their pants, and all who were circumcised were once and for all considered to be Jewish. It was an effective alternative to the identity card stamped with the word "Jew."

After having been rounded up and grouped together in the synagogue, all were taken to the Excelsior Hotel, where Brunner had set up his headquarters. The Feldgendarmerie stopped all cars on the road from Nice to Menton.[212] Some train stations were closed, while passengers were screened in others. Between September 10 and September 14, 1943, there were 1,819 Jews arrested (including 1,100 in Nice)[213] in these operations: they were sent to Drancy in twenty-seven trains. It was a heavy toll. "From time to time, we count and recount ourselves. Someone is always missing." Such was the message received in October by Marc Jarblum, who had taken refuge in Switzerland, from one of his correspondents.[214]

An activist with the Federation of Jewish Societies estimated that out of the 3,000 Jews then receiving aid from his organization, 800 had managed to leave on their own, while a few hundred others had scattered themselves out by their own designs, and about 1,300 were still in Nice. The latter group were without the slightest resource. There had been increasingly urgent calls sent from Nice to Marc Jarblum in Switzerland, but all the offices that might have distributed such aid—which was vital for Jews to find lodging—had been mercilessly raided. The Rue Dubouchage Committee no longer existed, nor did the OSE, which had remained in operation for a time, nor did the UGIF.[215]

It was indeed a heavy toll, but little in comparison with what Brunner had had in mind. The relative "failure" can be explained by a number of factors. It should be stressed in the first place that the Germans did not have a sufficient number of men to carry out their ambitions. And the factors coming into play in Nice would henceforth weigh heavily on the outcome of subsequent operations all over France. The French government offices no longer lent their previous level of support to the Germans, and the French prefectoral authorities performed their functions with enough laxity to allow Jews to slip through. Jews sought to go into hiding by all possible means, the local population cooperated, and religious authorities lent their support. Jewish organizations—especially the young Zionists, the Scouts, and the activists with the OSE—had become increasingly better organized in their totally illegal activities of providing false papers and distributing material aid. In three months, the Zionist Youth Movement, had furnished 6,000 identity cards, 200 food cards, 1,000 work cards, and 1,000 demobilization papers. They had moreover evacuated hundreds of Jews further inland and toward the Swiss border.[216]

There were also hundreds of Jews who managed to flee to Italy: two hundred of them gathered in Turin.[217] At the same time that the forty trucks carrying Jews from Saint-Gervais and Mégève to Nice were heading out, a train had been made available for Jews living under assigned residence in order that the elderly, the sick, and the children—in short, all those who could not have endured the long ride on the back of an open truck—might be taken to Nice more comfortably: some 240 such individuals availed themselves of this transportation.[218] Due to the publication of the armistice agreement, however, the train was rerouted and sent to Italy.[219]

Others were less fortunate. Take for example the case of the 345 Jews who had fled Saint-Martin-de-Vésubie on September 8, 1943, and followed the retreating Italian troops on foot. A report written at the time describes "the endless line of people that set out for the mountains" on that day, spending the nights out in the open in the rain that "soaked them to the bone," reaching mountain passes "by abandoned roads devoid of all vegetation and water, shivering in the freezing cold," suffering from hunger, total exhaustion, and panic at the approach of the Germans.[220] They were indeed caught by the SS after having crossed the border, and were taken back to Nice.[221]

Another three to four hundred fugitives who had set out for Italy succeeded in escaping such a fate. Utterly destitute and in a state of indescribable misery, they "lived in abandoned shacks or with farmers," isolated and separated kilometers apart on the inhospitable mountainsides, spending "their day[s] hoping for a visit that [would] rescue them."[222] As for those who had remained in Saint-Martin-de-Vésubie, they were supplied with false papers thanks to the efforts of the Zionist youth. On September 21, the Germans had it announced "by the public crier that all Jews were to gather at the town square" three hours later. "A few came and [were] deported, others stayed at home without hiding and were taken into custody there. Still others went to hide in the mountains. . . . There are still some wandering about in the mountains in all sorts of weather with no papers, no food card, and no money," wrote a young Zionist activist on October 6, 1943.[223]

In early December 1943, activists with the Federation estimated the number of Jews having found refuge in Italy at about one thousand: 250 were hiding with farmers around Antrax, a little border town; 350 had been interned—in conditions termed bearable—by the Italian authorities in the Bargo camp; 250 were scattered about in the mountains; and 70 others hospitalized in Bargo.[224] Some refugees were able to reach Switzerland thanks to Italians.[225] Some six hundred others wound up in Rome in February 1944: utterly destitute, they sent urgent appeals for aid to the leaders of the Federation in Switzerland.[226] They then shared a plight similar to that of the Italian Jews in Occupied Italy and suffered the ravages of an Italian militia that (as would be the case in France), would not hesitate to snatch a group of Jews out of prison and execute them: such was the fate of six refugees from Saint-Martin-de-Vésubie on April 25, 1945.[227]

There was no longer any area in France that was safe for Jews. However, in addition to the fact that some thirty thousand Jews had found protection for several months, the "Italian interlude"[228] had had a certain number of effects. During the time that the Germans were focusing on their efforts in the Italian Zone, the pressure was relaxed in other regions. And after having first sought support from the German authorities, Laval ended up using the Italian position as a pretext for curbing the assistance lent by the French police and administration to the hunt for Jews. The signal for this posture was given in May 1943, when the fervently Pétainist prefect of the département of Les Alpes-Maritimes was replaced by Jean Chaigneau, who set about to legalize the status of all foreign Jews in his département.[229] The extra time afforded to Jews before the Germans swept in was invaluable. Finally, there was a widening gap between the legal state and the civilian population of France: Jews took advantage of the situation to scatter out in rural areas, while Jewish leaders and activists organized their efforts.

11
Scattering Far and Wide in France

THE SUCCESSIVE DISPERSALS

"When the German forces crossed the demarcation line, one of the immediate consequences was the disappearance of three communities along the Mediterranean coastline: those in Montpellier, Béziers, and Perpignan," declared Chief Rabbi Schwartz to the Central Consistory on February 28, 1943.[1] And he added that most of the members of these worship organizations had gone mainly to small towns and villages in the départements of L'Aveyron, La Lozère, and L'Isère.

A Spontaneous Dispersal

The dispersal was widespread. It was a movement that had begun immediately after the roundup operations of August 1942, grown larger in November with the arrival of the Germans, and continued regularly. It had been encouraged by both the regional delegates of the Consistory[2] and by the UGIF, which sought out the most favorable sites—such as the département of L'Isère—for relocating Jews.[3]

On October 25, 1943, Albert Lévy took stock of his trips to the dozens of places where Jews had gathered. Since April of the same year, he had undertaken these travels to check on the conditions and attitudes prevailing in these now scattered communities. "When the Germans moved into the Southern Zone, [there were] as a result two major movements of the Jewish population," he wrote. "One movement involved the majority of the well-to-do, who emigrated to the zone occupied by the Italians. The other was marked by the large numbers of Jews who abandoned the cities and spread out in rural areas. Due to the only too real dangers posed by the presence of the Germans, our fellow Jews everywhere have been compelled to hide out and try to make authorities lose track and forget about them. We found a vacuum, as it were, in just about every city."[4] Those who had remained in the cities were generally the poorest, but they too spared no effort to go into hiding.[5]

The SEC complained bitterly. "The Jewish subject migrates so much that about 30 percent of the information from the census is already out of date," observed one inspector for the Marseilles region.[6] The information gathered in Arles a few months earlier at the request of the German security police confirm that assessment: out of the 108 Jews identified by the census, thirty-two had left without giving any future address.[7] The same was true everywhere. As a general rule, Jews would decide to leave whenever something new occurred: rumors of an imminent roundup would immediately cause all Jews in a section of town or in an entire city to scatter. Such was the case in Avignon in May and again in Montauban in late July 1943.[8] An official summons could have a similar effect: when A.F., a leather-goods dealer in Avignon, received from the foreign nationals office in the prefectorate of the département of La Vaucluse the order to leave the city and go live under house arrest in Flassan, he chose to go into hiding.[9] An increasing number of Jews were leaving both the Foreign Worker Units and assigned residences into which they had been placed. Such flights occurred both individually and collectively. In December 1942, one group fled Saint-Léonard-de-Noblat and crossed over the border into Spain.[10] And a large number left the département in which they were staying, after first having their papers stamped, so that they could get new residence papers.[11]

When it seemed likely that the Italian Zone would lose all its advantages, Jews once again began streaming back to the French Southern Zone. In Périgueux, for example, some Jewish families were seen returning in early August 1943.[12] The movement would only intensify: the Jewish community was henceforth completely broken up and scattered apart. By the summer of 1943, the chaplain's office was serving not only the internment camps but also shelters and all sorts of institutions, plus nearly seventy Foreign Worker Units and dozens of centers where people were under house arrest, all of which were scattered throughout the country.[13] But if we could take a count of the places where Jews had come together, sometimes by random chance and sometimes only for a short period, we would have to number such places in the hundreds; we are really dealing with a series of continous movements that led people to set out in all directions. And each of these moves was surrounded by uncertainty.

In the Southern Zone as in Paris, we can gauge the importance of this new dispersal of Jews thanks to the diligence of Antignac, who on March 31, 1943, asked that all prefects provide a table of all Jewish schoolchildren in their respective départements. His intention was to see if it were possible to set up an elementary school system just for Jews.[14] All but ten responded. The resulting "table of the population of Jewish schoolchildren" for the 1942–1943 academic year bears witness first of all to the fact that Jewish schoolchildren were widely scattered out among départements: 53 here (in L'Ain), 41 there (in L'Ardèche), 77 elsewhere (in La Drôme), and so on. A survey was also made of middle schools and the results confirmed the various individual testimonies on the subject: the youngest children were sent to school, but adolescents, who were considered to be at greater risk, were often, or more readily, withdrawn.

The table also provides evidence of the importance of the Italian Zone: there were 317 children in the département of Les Alpes-Maritimes, but significantly larger numbers remained in the départements of Le Rhône (748 children) and Les Bouches-du-Rhône (with 416). We can also see from this table that most of the Jewish children legally attending school at the time were living in the départements in the center of France: La Corrèze, la Creuse, L'Indre, Le Puy-de-Dôme, and L'Allier accounted for almost 1,350 of those enrolled, while 424 others were registered in La Haute-Vienne. Such a distribution leads us to suppose that the children of the French families from the départements of L'Alsace and La Moselle were proportionally the largest group among those accounted for.

These are fragmentary data, however, and we must bear in mind that, as was the case for Paris, such information was only valid for a certain time, namely, until the fall of 1943, when another scattering of the Jewish population took place. The data's validity is even more limited when we recall that, in the Southern Zone as in Paris, children were the first ones families would seek to protect by giving them a false identity.

The Stages of an Organized Dispersal

In addition to these spontaneous scatterings of the Jewish population, an organized movement to spread out was begun shortly after the summer of 1942. The different phases in the evolution of the OSE, which had first backed up and then completely replaced its network of children's homes by a system of individual placements, provide a good illustration of this transition from life in full public view to the plunge into anonymity. In this respect, the events that occurred one night in Vénissieux had marked an important turning point. There was an almost natural slide toward illegality; although the operation aimed at saving the children in Vénissieux had begun under the cover of following the law, when in action, everything suddenly changed. All those involved in the rescue effort at Vénissieux, including the Christian Friendship organization, the OSE, the Scouts, the local population, and the hierarchy of the Catholic Church (in the person of Cardinal Gerlier) had worked together to achieve success. "You won't get the children!"[15] read a tract distributed at the time. The Jews now had allies in the general population.

The idea of secretly spreading out the endangered children took concrete form in the fall of 1942, when the German forces extended their occupation to the Southern Zone. The initiative came from Dr. Joseph Weill, who had for several months already been urging his fellow workers with the OSE to intensify their clandestine activity. When Archbishop Saliège in Toulouse lent his support to the operation aimed at saving children, he also advised Georges Garel to seek support from existing institutions and provided him with a letter of introduction opening the doors of Roman Catholic institutions: the rescue operation was thus able to get under way. Twenty-four children were first placed with families, then placement for three hundred others was found in the Toulouse region.

When it was learned in the Southern Zone that the German authorities in Paris had been using a system to block children, to keep them under surveillance, since January 1943, and that, in February of that same year, children in the UGIF houses in the Northern Zone had been arrested, efforts to disperse them over a wide area were stepped up. The movement became structured: beginning in the summer of 1943, it was divided into four regional operations, which included the entire Southern Zone. Two networks were gradually put into place: one was a network of social workers responsible for dealing with the parents, while the other maintained contact with the hidden children.[16] There were Aryan social workers, the "pure" ones, but there were also the "official" ones, those prevented by their marked accent or physical appearance from passing themselves off as non-Jewish. And then there were the "a-specific" or "synthetic" ones who, although Jewish, could pass for Christian. All had specific places in the network, which became more and more sophisticated as months went by. Both religious and nonreligious institutions and charitable programs provided refuge for children as well as a front for the twenty-nine social workers[17] who officially worked for them. The true identities of the hidden children were sent to Switzerland so that, whatever might transpire, they could be located at the end of the war.

It is difficult to grasp the magnitude of work involved in hiding these children. The tasks included giving everyone false Aryan identities, food ration cards, and textile cards, finding a place to stay for each child, maintaining contact with both parents and children, transporting children from one place to another, and providing clothing for the small children. All this could only be accomplished through the collaborative efforts that were developed with the other Jewish organizations and charitable programs, especially with the young people.[18]

At the same time, however, there were still hundreds of children officially under the OSE's care, either in its children's homes or with the Jewish families, where Andrée Salomon had placed them under their real name. Were these children considered to be in less danger, or were they children who were harder to hide because they could not easily have assumed an Aryan identity? Or perhaps it would have been inconceivable to interrupt their strict observance of religious rites. All of these factors probably entered into the equation, along with another that is rarely mentioned: that the number of children in distress did not remain constant thoughout the long months of this ordeal. Children kept on pouring in from the Occupied Zone: there were some twelve hundred of them during the summer of 1942 alone.[19] Each new wave of arrests brought on another group of children. The dual structure was, for a long time, necessary in order to take them in and provide them temporary shelter until another solution could be found.

In May 1943, the OSE's budget was equally divided between its legal operations and its clandestine activities. There were then 1,500 children hidden in the Southern Zone, while another 2,000 were duly registered and living in children's homes, and 1,000 others had been placed with Jewish families.[20] The OSE was experiencing serious financial difficulties at the time. Money from Switzerland had to be used first for official activities in order not to arouse the suspicions of Vichy and the Germans. But in the context of so many restrictions and of often insurmountable difficulties in obtaining basic supplies and commodities, hiding children required large amounts of money. Moreover, children kept pouring in,[21] and parents were continuing to look for safe places for their children. But the local populations' capacity to absorb these additional residents were reaching their limits at the very time when the number of families having to hide loved ones—those avoiding induction into the Forced Labor Service—was constantly increasing.

As of July 9, 1943, there were officially 840 children still staying in the OSE's ten homes.[22] On the same day, however, the Gestapo opened a house for children who were "blocked": thirty children whose parents had been deported were placed there in La Verdière near Marseilles. On October 20, 1943, all—including the personnel—were arrested and deported.[23] Consequently, the OSE leadership decided that all the children still in its homes should be scattered out. In order to achieve this end, it was necessary not only to find safe places for the children to stay but also an official pretext to account for their disappearance from these homes that had previously been so prominently established. The first such children's home to be closed was Chabannes center, in the département of La Creuse. It had been officially requisitioned by local French authorities, upon the request of OSE leaders: this was a trick that would prove useful subsequently. Times had changed: first the Catholic hierarchy, and then the local populations had lent their aid to the Jews. Now, even government offices were at times in complicity with organizations trying to save the Jews.

These efforts to spread the children out throughout the country were undertaken with an unprecedented sense of urgency. Practical matters of logistics, however, dictated their pace. At the end of 1943, there were still 450 children in the OSE's homes, and several hundred others were being monitored by offical social workers in various départements. OSE leaders were hoping to have completed scattering these children out by February 1944.[24]

It was precisely at that point that the OSE gave up all efforts to maintain a legal facade. But here again, the OSE was reacting to a new calamity that had struck the organization. Alain Mossé, who in October 1943 had written that the Gestapo was close on his heels,[25] had just been arrested along with his entire office staff in a Gestapo raid in Chambéry, which had been the OSE's headquarters since the time of the Italian Occupation. From February 1944 until the Liberation, the OSE continued in a totally clandestine manner to care for some six thousand children. It was actually not until April 1944 that they closed their last official homes. The Gestapo from Lyon raided the home at Izieu and arrested the forty-four children staying there just before the dispersal that the director was in the process of preparing.[26] Some one thousand children had been placed in families since the month of October 1943. There were still fifty children under the protection of the Red Cross in the home at Chaumont and in the nursery at Limoges. But the deportations continued, and children in need of protection kept pouring in. Three hundred "new" children whose parents had just been deported were still waiting for a place to take refuge.[27]

The Jewish children who had found some semblance of stability in the OSE's homes once again saw their world turned upside down. Such was the case not only for those under the care of the OSE, but also for those who had been individually placed by their parents, who at times availed themselves of chance encounters.[28] In their new farming families or in the convents that had taken them in, Frida was changed to Françoise, Sarah to Geneviève, Jojo to Jean. But the transformation also often included learning the Lord's Prayer and the rosary. It was an initiation to a clandestine life. For adolescents, who kept within their hearts precious memories of a different family atmosphere, it meant the beginning of a double life. For the smaller children, it meant gradually abandoning a world that they could scarcely grasp. For some, it meant hard work in the fields, while for others it was a safe haven. Some were subjected to subtle or not so subtle religious pressure, as in the boarding school Saint-Paul Béranger in Montluçon, where Pavel-Paul Friedländer, who had become Paul-Henri Ferland, was for a while destined for the priesthood.[29]

But there was often a deep respect for an identity that was other, as was the case in the center in Chamonix. There, two fervently Catholic leaders of the Aid to Family Mothers organization saw to it that the Jewish holy days were strictly observed by the small children entrusted to them. The OSE's social workers continued to see after the children that had been scattered about, giving money for room and board to those who had taken them in, monitoring their material conditions, and seeing to it that they "[kept] within them the meaning of Jewish values."[30] In that respect, this organized dispersal of the children was quite different from individual rescue efforts. For all of these children, it was this break from their previous situation that saved their life. But at the same time and in spite of all the precautions taken, the aftermath of the war would be painful and difficult to face.

We can see to what extent the OSE, which specialized in bringing relief to children, was dependent on the other Jewish and non-Jewish organizations in carrying out its work. The OSE was able to hide children in France thanks to the various charitable institutions and programs throughout the Southern Zone that were willing to take in them in. In addition to the support of the Christian Friendship organization and the Cimade, one must list the Saint-Germaine charitable society in Toulouse, the Aid to Mothers of Families in Saint-Etienne, Pastor Monod's charitable organization in Lyon, the National Relief agency in Limoges and Périgueux, and the Compensation and Family Benefits Bank in Grenoble, not to mention a good number of private charities.[31] And there were many others.

It would moreover have been inconceivable to finance all of this clandestine activity if the American Jewish Joint Distribution Committee and its representatives in France, Dika Jefroykin and Maurice Brener, had not been willing to supply the funds.[32] But the OSE was not the only organization to move from open legality to clandestine operations. The Israelite Scouts of France followed an almost identical path, and for very similar reasons.[33] There were, however, two important differences. The first was the presence of Robert Gamzon (Castor) as a member on the board of administrators of the UGIF, which connected the Scouts to the legalist strain. The second was Darquier's decree of January 1943 ordering the Scouts to disband, which hastened their conversion to clandestine activity.

The Period of the Double Game

The link with the authorities led to a relationship of trust between Gilbert Lesage with the Office of Social Services for Foreigners (SSE) and Robert Gamzon. It also afforded Gamzon two days warning about the mass arrests that the French police planned to carry out on August 26, 1942: in each of the rural worksites, the young foreign Jews targeted by the roundups were hidden in the surrounding area while the roundup was occurring.[34] Among those hidden were adolescents who had just left the camps at Rivesaltes and Gurs. "Their happiness only lasted a short time," observed Isaac Pougatch in Charry.[35] "The house that we set up with such love, the land that we cleared so peacefully, the very companions who little by little became bonded through their joint efforts, will all be torn away from us just as it happened elsewhere, just as it has always happened."

At that point, the decision to disperse was inevitable. It was to be a methodical, progressive dispersal: those who had had to take refuge in neighboring forests for a few days or rather a few nights were the first to leave, and the girls were next. Subsequently, after the Germans had moved in to occupy the Southern Zone, everyone was disheartened, watching for the slightest sign of dangers, and harboring no illusions as to their future prospects. As of the summer of 1943, there were still some three hundred youths, most of them French, in these rural worksites: they disbanded and scattered in the fall of 1943.[36]

The unceasing work of the Scout units had given them a firsthand experience with scenes of deportation. The Scouts had also played an important role in scattering out the children from Vénissieux. The counterpart to the OSE's Garel Network was the "sixth," or the Office of Social Services for Youth, which was the clandestine version of the sixth division called "Social Assistance" within the fourth "Youth" leadership division of the UGIF. Its first goal was the rather obvious mandate of hiding the young people whose parents had been deported. Priority was given to those located in the rural worksites. Some eighty-eight young boy and girl Scouts took on the sacred vocation of fabricating false papers and rescuing adolescents.[37] They set up their headquarters in Grenoble, which was at the time in the Italian Occupation Zone, but then spread out rapidly into all seven regions of the Southern Zone beginning in the spring of 1943. As a cover, the Scouts used the profession of commercial traveler, which was one of the very few jobs that Jews could still hold. Such was the case for Henri Wahl, the head of the "sixth" who held a fictitious job in a freight company.[38] At the same time, the Israelite Scouts of France pursued the activities that had always been a part of scouting in the past. And so the efforts to scatter youth out into rural areas conveniently coincided with the organization of vacation camps, curiously dubbed "mass camouflages." The various steps marking the evolution of the Israelite Scouts of France are analogous to those that we observed for the OSE.

Unfortunately, the continuing endeavors of the Israelite Scouts of France did not find favor with the General Commissioner for Jewish Affairs. On January 5, 1943, he decreed that the fourth directorship for youth within the UGIF should be closed down: the Scouts, he charged, had since November 29, 1941 been using a fictitious integration into the UGIF as a cover, and had in fact continued their activities as before. This time, he was ordering that they actually be disbanded immediately, and that they should be prohibited from coming back together under any pretext whatsoever.[39] Raymond-Raoul Lambert immediately made an appeal to Antignac and managed to limit the decree to the Scouting movement and other youth organizations: the professional retraining and social aid office (the "sixth" division) was placed under the administrative authority of the other directorships of the UGIF (for "work" and "health").[40] As a result, the "sixth" found itself administratively linked to the OSE, an arrangement that made for an even closer coordination between the two movements.

This time it was the former president of the Scouts, Edmond Fleg, who protested to Marshal Pétain. In a dignified letter that did not request any favor nor even any delay in the decision that had been taken, Fleg wrote:

> In subjecting themselves to preliminary training in wholesome agricultural and handcraft activities aimed to prepare for the future, in seeking to relieve all present forms of human misery in a diligent and effective manner, in helping their fellow Scouts of foreign origin to become more and more deeply integrated into the French tradition, in providing for our armed forces a larger than normal contingent of soldiers and officers (many of whom figure among those decorated, taken prisoner, wounded, and killed in this war), in stirring up and deepening their religious faith through ritual and prayer, the Israelite Scouts of France have, in their modest place but with all their soul, served their religion and their motherland in keeping with their promise.[41]

Pétain had been moved by the "nobility and dignified suffering" expressed in these lines, answered André Lavagne, the Marshal's civilian chief of staff, three months later, but "such matters were being handled outside the domain of the chief of state."[42]

"My dear Scout brothers," wrote Castor to his disciples, as he informed them of the order to disband and asked them to comply "with discipline." "Our Scouting has no need to be displayed by any uniform or insignia. Each of us has freely and personally made before God the promise to serve Judaism and France, to obey the Scout's law, and to serve in every occasion: this promise is still totally valid, and no human force shall ever be able to tear it away from our hearts."[43]

Strangely, once Darquier had signed his decree, he never checked to see how it had been put into application. In Moissac and elsewhere, life went on for the Scouts, as they continued to benefit from the complicity of local administrative offices. As for groups of Israelite Scouts in large cities, they turned to the Unionist Scouts and the Scouts of France for support:[44] everyone found the necessary assistance in society for the activities they were developing. On February 26, 1943, Marc Haguenau, who handled relations with the UGIF as well as with other contributing organizations for the Office of Social Services for Youth, submitted a report to Consistory treasurer André Weil on activities completed since mid-August 1942. Except for uniformed outings, not one single Scouting activity had ceased, wrote Haguenau. What was more, 950 children and adolescents had been looked after, 350 had been able to enjoy a few weeks of rest or vacation, and as of then, placement had been found for some 400 (15 percent were taken care of by charitable organizations, 10 percent had been given various jobs in towns and cities, and 75 percent were working on farms). The group of 400 received regular visits from four social workers.[45]

This high percentage of potential "farmers" among the adolescents cared for by the Scouts testifies not only to the necessities tied to that particular moment but also to the persistent, widespread ideas for making Jews productive that, as we have seen, were so prominent in the ideology of their organization. It was in the rural areas that it was the easiest to place Jewish youth, and it would become even more so with the development of the Forced Labor Service. In all, the Office of Social Services for Youth reportedly took complete care of 853 children, while at the same time the Scouts watched over some two thousand others.[46]

With the Scouts, we once again find the same breakdown into chronological phases that characterized the evolution of the OSE, with the transitions clearly marked by the dates of major turning points in the life of the Jews. The decision to scatter the children staying in the organization's centers was made by Castor in the autumn of 1943, when the Italian Occupation came to an end and when the "sixth's" team in Nice, including Claude Gutman ("Griffon"), was arrested by the Gestapo in Nice. When the "sixth's" mainspring Marc Haguenau and his secretary Edith Pulver were arrested in February 1944, the organization broke with the UGIF.[47]

The OSE and the Israelite Scouts of France (EIF) were also coordinating their efforts with the Zionist Youth Movement (MJS). At the very moment when the General Commission on Jewish Affairs was so closely scrutinizing the Scouts' very existence, the leadership of the MJS and the national Scouts team sent a joint letter to the local leaders of both organizations. "Now more than ever, we feel that unity among all the vital forces of Jewish youth in France is necessary," they wrote in this letter.[48] In May 1943, the formal agreement between the MJS and the EIF was ratified, resulting in the integration of the two movements' executive ranks and the coordination of the leadership of their rural groups, urban units, and social work.[49]

We have been speaking of the Garel network, also known as the Office of Social Services for Youth or the "sixth." The analogous entity for the youth of the

Zionist Youth Movement was called Physical Education. It proved to be particularly effective in Nice and Grenoble, and distinguished itself in the fabrication of high-quality false papers. Once again, the watchword was to scatter out. According to the reports sent to Zionist leaders by Joseph Fisher, there were, out of the 2,000 members of organizations under the MJS umbrella, some 1,500 that were grouped together and 500 that were spread out in early 1943. By the end of the year, the proportions had been reversed.[50] In the end, all of these organizations worked together. Social aid and rescue operations had almost completely taken the place of the propaganda and education efforts more prominent during the first two years of the Occupation. They focused more and more on the common goal of hiding those most at risk.

Going to "Nystar's" House

Spreading out meant going into hiding or, in the language used in the endless correspondence sent to Marc Jarblum, who had taken refuge in Switzerland, "going to *Nystar's* house." As was the case for all code words used in these letters, *nystar* was a Hebrew word meaning "hidden." The device was both sublime and naive, and doubtless not very safe, but any historian who knows a bit of Hebrew can only take pleasure in it. However, before one could even think of changing one's identity, one first had to do something about the word "Jew" stamped on one's papers before crossing over into illegality. The personnel in the General Commission on Jewish Affairs had realized how a large number of Jews were skirting the law: they would have several sets of identity papers but would only have one set stamped, or they would present for stamping another card (a commercial traveler's card, for example) in lieu of the identity card. The inspector for the Division of Investigations and Inspections complained that as soon as their food card had been stamped, Jews would declare they had lost it and would get the offices of the city hall to issue them another.[51]

Such was the scheme used by Denise Caraco, among many others: she went crying to the police station in Marseilles, claiming she had lost her purse with all her papers. Then, having kept the old set of documents which were free of all stamp marks, she had the new identity papers stamped. Others, having managed to procure a completely compliant Aryan identity, kept on using their stamped food ration card. A new identity meant a whole set of documents that had become increasingly complex as the state sought to tighten its control over the entire French population and hunt down increasingly larger groups of people.

For those not lucky enough to have an Aryan-sounding name, the best solution was to swap it off for another. The September 16, 1942, edition of the newspaper *Le Matin* had provided the solution when it denounced the ease with which Jews could inexpensively change their identities:

> Almost all Jews have had a Marie Dupont working for them at some time or another. Rachel Lévy writes to the municipal administration in the city where the aforementioned Marie was born in order to obtain a birth certificate. Armed with this document, she establishes her place of residence in a hotel where she registers under this new identity. Two weeks later, she has the proprietor issue her a certificate of residence. All she has to do now is to go to the local police station and request an identity card.[52]

This method was indeed widely used, except that there was no need to have recourse to a former employee: one could glean an abundance of information from the *Journal officiel*. It was there that one could find the names of non-Jewish foreigners who had become naturalized French citizens, and such names could be used as a cover by foreign Jews who would have had a hard time selling themselves off as native French. It should be noted that the Central Consistory went to the trouble of distributing this interesting article, which was included in the press clippings given to the regional delegates in October 1942 so that they might put its information to good use: it was a brilliant feat of turning the tables on the enemies of the Jews, and one that turned out to have a great future.

In foreign-born Jewish families, it was often the elder children who took charge of the conversion to a clandestine life. Lea Minczeles, for example, chose to use for her parents the name of an ex-associate, who was a naturalized French Jew. Unfortunately, however, the man was sought by his provisional manager, and Minczeles's father was arrested. He hastened to confess that he was using false documents, and got off with four and one-half months of prison for use of forgery. This was in Nice: he was released two weeks before the Germans rolled in. It is difficult for us to weigh the respective importance of such factors as random chance, luck, and destiny (those two weeks), as they combined in this case with a more tangible factor: the possibility for a Jew in the Italian zone to be released from prison once his term had been served.

But the safest way to slip into clandestine life was to work through channels that had been organized by the "sixth" and the Zionist Youth Movement (which was particularly efficient in producing false papers) and that worked in collaboration with the Federation of Jewish Societies in France and the Jewish Army (AJ). It was these groups that provided the life-saving documents.

The methods used were becoming more and more sophisticated.[53] At first, all sorts of solvents were used to wash off the information inscribed on the documents and replace it with information creating a fake Aryan identity. Then the various underground services that entered into operation began to make their own false seals: pencil erasers or pieces of linoleum carved out with a razor blade would do the trick. With the complicity of people in local administrative offices, it was more and more often possible to "borrow" authentic seals that were well broken in. For the place of birth on fake identity papers, abundant use was made of a certain city in the north of France whose archives were known to have been destroyed. Stamps were regularly exchanged between regions in order to avoid any accumulation of identical papers in any one given spot, and similar exchanges were made with non-Jewish resistance groups.[54]

These false identity papers varied as to their quality. The most common were the "strikeouts" *(les bifs),* which were totally artificial and most often could not withstand any verification. The "synthies" conferred an authentic Aryan identity (that of a willing accomplice in the Occupied Zone, of a prisoner of war, or even of a deceased person, for example) and were much more reliable, but were reserved for militants within the organizations. Such was the case for the new identity acquired by Robert Gamzon in the autumn of 1943. Henry Paul Lagnès, a farmowner born in 1908 in Moissac really did exist, but his double was Castor, armed with papers that had been duly registered in the town hall in Moissac: the numbers, date of issue, and all other details of these papers corresponded exactly to the originals. Only the photo and the mention of distinctive marks had been modified.[55]

Those receiving these false identity papers were a heterogeneous group, to say the least. They included foreigners that no magic wand could transform into native French. And we are not talking about some young man avoiding the Forced Labor Service or some isolated individual involved in resistance activity, but rather entire families. Added to all that was the need to act quickly, as during Brunner's mass arrests in Nice, when the local organizations had to provide new identities for thousands of Jews of all origins, ages, and appearances in just a few days. Jewish organizations were not the only ones carrying out this work: all of the Resistance was involved in making false documents. Whether or not they were actively involved in any of these movements, a large number of French Jews often availed themselves of their services. But for foreign Jews who were not so well integrated into French society, such "Jewish contacts" were often essential in order to cross over into a clandestine existence. The established organizations that had at a very early point opted to "lay low" sent those who came to them over to these underground groups. This was the case for the Federation (officially integrated into the UGIF) as well as for the members of the Jewish Army, who were all active in one or another of the organizations distributing aid and rescuing Jews.

The Jewish Army also had its own division for fabricating false papers: it was so efficient that the man in charge, Maurice Cachoud-Loevenberg, later became the head of the division of false papers for the National Liberation Movement resistance group in Paris. The young militants in these organizations frequented all the places where Jews continued to congregate: a synagogue, a social aid office, or the facilities of the OSE in Marseilles. It was there that contacts were made. There were also certain independent groups such as the "André division" that Joseph Bass developed in the Nice area. It is extremely difficult to determine precisely which organization did what. They overlapped, often working in conjunction with each other in spite of their efforts to seal themselves off: such barriers proved ineffective, as the same people were often involved in several organizations.

Seeking Safety beyond the Borders

The year 1943 produced a heavy number of all sorts of refugees, who often found they had to escape the confines of mainland France. In April, OSE leaders began to turn systematically to another way to help Jews escape danger: clandestine emigration. Switzerland was the first destination for such escapes; later Spain became a secondary, although less preferred, option.

Periodically, there were renewed efforts to develop channels of legal emigration for the children. After the desperate attempt in the autumn of 1942, a new effort to have the visas validated was made in November 1943,[56] if for no other reason than to soften the position of the Swiss authorities, who displayed little eagerness to accept these potential emigrants. Nevertheless, the unyielding positions taken by the Swiss authorities during the summer and winter of 1942 were giving way under the pressure of the hundreds of refugees trying to get across the border. Authorities in the cantons became conciliatory at times, and although people were frequently denied entry into Switzerland,[57] the children taken there secretly by Jewish organizations found a shelter.

It was in particular the "aspecific" children, those who could not easily blend into a Christian environment because of their religious convictions, who were chosen for emigration. Georges Loinger was the leader of the operation: it was thanks to the efforts of a resistance network, the "réseau Bourgogne," that he was able to contact mountain guides and smugglers in the Annemasse area. The Italians' "soft" occupation had made it easier to perfect techniques for getting people across the border. The first "passengers" led by Loinger into Switzerland in this manner were children over the age of sixteen sponsored by the Scouts. Later, such crossings would take place without the assistance of guides. Loinger estimates that he personally helped some seven hundred children get into Switzerland in this way.[58] From autumn 1943 to July 1944, some 1,069 children were able to get into Switzerland thanks to the OSE's efforts.[59] The Israelite Scouts of France and the Physical Education group led hundreds of others to Switzerland: here again, all three of these groups worked together.

The escape route to Spain was much more problematic, largely due to topography: crossing the peaks of the Pyrenees posed serious problems for groups of children. Andrée Salomon was nevertheless informed by Ernest Lambert, one of the members of the Jewish Army (AJ), that it was doable. The AJ was on the verge of becoming the military branch of the Israelite Scouts of France to be known as the Jewish Combat Organization (OJC).[60] In order to get Jewish children across the border into Spain, it created an organization called the Division for the Evacuation and Grouping Together of Children (SERE), and placed it under the leadership of Gisèle Roman. From April 6, 1944 until the Liberation, the SERE got between 85 and 134 children—it is not possible to determine which source has provided the accurate figure[61]—that had been taken to Toulouse by Andrée Salomon out of

France and into Spain. In October 1944, seventy-nine of them boarded the *Guinée* sailing for Palestine.[62] The AJ was a Zionist organization, and in creating the SERE, it was pursuing a twofold objective: to rescue the children and send them to Palestine. While it is difficult for us to determine exactly which group did what in all the varied activities so hastily outlined here, we can clearly attribute these crossings into Spain to efforts of the AJ.

The interdependence of these various organizations, both Jewish and non-Jewish, could be found at all levels. It was thanks to a resistance network that it was possible to set up an underground channel for getting children to Switzerland.[63] The OSE would not have been able to ferry children to Switzerland and supply them with false papers without the aid of the young Israelite Scouts of France and the Zionist Youth Movement. The quality of these false papers depended entirely on the complicity of people working in the offices of a town hall or prefectorate. And finally, it was only possible to set up an escape route to Spain after the Jewish Army had created a logistical infrastructure to get people across the Pyrenees.

During the early war years, collective structures of socialization had made it possible to bolster a community targeted for its very identity; those structures had been transformed in order to respond to an emergency and, to the extent possible, rescue those whose physical existence was now in jeopardy. This transformation was rarely the result of anticipation: rather, it was the gradual response to a whole series of shocks that had a cumulative effect. At the same time, however, it followed the same progression as the evolution experienced by French society in general. Both the OSE, which focused on social aid, and the Israelite Scouts of France, who had educational aims, were linked to French society in a thousand ways. And by virtue of their commitments to the Jewish population, they occupied a pivotal position not only between Jews and French society, but also between the two main subgroups of the Jewish community: they had been formed by French Jews and focused their efforts on foreign Jews. When the persecution of the Jews changed in nature, their transformation became urgent. The change became possible when the geopolitical divisions of the French mainland and the heterogeneity of French society provided places of shelter and refuge for the Jews. It is in these very locations and milieus that one finds—at least partially—those who had no recourse whatsoever to any of these organizations, but instead blended individually into some microsociety here and there: they were doubtless a majority.

PROTECTED PLACES AND SHELTERING MILIEUS

Under the Protection of the Italians

We shall now turn our attention back to the Italian Occupation Zone. As we have seen, not only the protection it afforded to thousands of Jews, but also the political bargaining sessions that alleviated pressure in other areas and the time thus gained were all crucial. And the reprieve had importance consequences, as it was the very thing that allowed the Jewish aid groups to get organized. In Nice, Moussa Abadi took on a new identity as Monsieur Marcel and disguised himself with the priest's habit given to him by Bishop Paul Rémond, who also had Abadi named inspector of the Catholic schools in his diocese. Abadi was thus able to organize a network for hiding children. Aided by advice from Garel and funded by the Joint, he succeeded in rescuing more than five hundred Jewish children by disguising them as Christian boys and girls and scattering them in various convents, orphanages, and religious schools after the Germans had taken over control of the area from the Italians.[64]

The Zionist Youth Movement had transferred its headquarters from Montpellier to Grenoble. The "sixth" left Moissac and moved there also. After the police roundup on Rue Sainte-Catherine, the activists with the Bund moved to an alternate location in the Italian Zone. An elite commando of the Jewish Army, which was subsequently to become one of the most active, was put together in Nice. The OSE henceforth directed its operations out of Chambéry, and the groups of children headed for Switzerland used the Savoie region as their point of departure. The prevailing climate in the Italian Zone was less that of a police state, and Jews enjoyed a certain degree of protection there. The Italian Zone moreover provided the opportunity for many Jews to take on a false identity on an individual basis.

It was here in the Italian Zone and through this rescue activity that was carried out the cultural and educational work that strengthened the internal cohesion of these groups and armed them to face the final, most difficult phase of the war. The postwar phase was in fact already emerging here: what was later to become the Centre de Documentation Juive Contemporaine was created in Grenoble on April 29, 1943, in the apartment of Isaac Schneersohn.[65]

It was also here, in the Italian Zone, that societies making it possible to lead a Jewish life and forget the outside world for a time were created and maintained. The members of the *gdoud* (group) with the Zionist Youth Movement in Grenoble,[66] for example, gathered around Jeanne Latchiver in a small village near the city, and then in Grenoble itself. They fabricated false papers, put up children headed for Switzerland, and joyously celebrated the Sabbath. "Each Saturday was an extraordinary event," remembers Toto Giniewski, who speaks of an entire series of lecturers, the Hebrew and gymnastics classes, and the songs and danses that rhythmed these meetings.[67]

Whether they occurred there around Jeanne Latchiver or in a kosher restaurant—where Jews usually came armed with a false Aryan identity—or in the youth camps that functioned in the summer of 1943, such gatherings created various sorts of protected Jewish milieus. The term "protected milieus" may seem a poor choice of words, but these were indeed veritable oases or havens that allowed participants to break out of isolation and made it possible for Jews to forget the outside world while the gathering were being held. They were far from providing any protection from the dangers of underground action, however. These young men and women paid dearly for their dedication to the cause of rescuing Jews. Marc Haguenau, Claude Gutman, Jacques Waintrob, David Donoff, Mila Racine, Marianne Cohn, and many others lost their lives in this endeavor when they were caught with a suitcase full of false papers or intercepted while ferrying children to Switzerland.

As for the four thousand Jews who had been taken by bus to the residences that had been assigned to them by the Italians, the precariousness of their refuge had nothing to do with any dangers associated with their activity, but with the provisional nature of their shelter. Before everything suddenly plunged into chaos in autumn 1943, however, these little enclaves were absolutely amazing. The whole situation seems surrealistic in comparison with the situation that prevailed for Jews in the rest of France. There were thousands of foreign Jews on the run who were being completely taken care of by the Jewish organizations and whose papers had been put in order, often after weeks of wandering about: they had been lodged in these former tourist resorts and were organizing into veritable communities. The only thing they were required to do was to report to the Italian police authorities every day. In June 1943, there were just over 600 foreign Jews in Mégève,[68] between 800 and 900 in Saint-Martin-de-Vésubie, and a similar number in Saint-Gervais: the others were scattered about in Vence, Castellane, Barcelonnette, and elsewhere.[69]

In every case, only those who could afford it paid for their trip and for their daily living expenses. These individuals were moreover required to pay a "solidarity tax."[70] However, they were a small minority. In Saint-Martin-de-Vésubie, for example, only twenty-five families were living on their own financial resources.[71] According to various reports, there were seven hundred needy people out of total of eight hundred refugees in Saint-Gervais.[72] But they were provided a place to live and a monthly allowance, and there were soon cafeterias serving from three hundred to four hundred meals a day.

And in all of these places we can observe various forms of self-administration, with all the advantages that come with it: a central purchasing office was set up in Saint-Gervais not only in order to keep down the costs of providing for all the refugees there, but also to avoid "disturbing the regional economy"—or in plain language to avoid stirring up antisemitism in the neighborhood with unexpected crowds of buyers. The Professional Training and Reorientation Organization (ORT) set up shoe- and clothing-repair shops, both to take care of needs and to provide an occupation for some of the refugees.[73] They also tried to find work on local farms for the younger, stronger ones. The OSE looked after their medical needs and saw that the children received proper care. In Saint-Gervais, two doctors barred from practicing because of their status as foreign Jews ran an infirmary: their prescriptions were officially signed by the town's doctors.[74] The OSE and the Federation also organized kindergartens. Older students were called upon to give lessons to the younger ones. Religious rites were practiced everywhere. Cafeterias providing kosher food were opened and a synagogue was established; in Mégève, the holy days of Passover were observed according to custom, even though the "residents" had just arrived.[75]

In addition, the Zionists energetically took the matters of organizing cultural and educational activities into their own hands. The young people with the Zionist Youth Movment were not idle in Saint-Martin-de-Vésubie: they set about giving classes in Jewish history, talks on Zionism and the land of Palestine, and classes in Hebrew that some attended five days a week. Nursing classes were also given to a group of about twenty girls, while at the same time a laboratory for producing false papers was being set up.[76]

There was one rather comical aspect to all this activity: the formation of all sorts of committees that did indeed proliferate once given free rein. A report on Saint-Martin-de-Vésubie written in October 1943 by a young Zionist lists no fewer than nine of them: the UGIF had its own committee, as did the Federation; the Zionists formed another, those involved in setting up cafeterias put together their own, and so on.[77]

But life was not a paradise in these "residences." Food remained meager, and the approach of winter made people anxious about their need for warm clothing in these resorts perched 3,300 hundred feet above sea level. However, all reports echo the same sentiment: "in the midst of all our hardships, it is a comforting sight to see. If only we felt more secure about the future."[78] Using more colorful language, another compared the refugees in Saint-Gervais to "shipwreck survivors on a boat at high sea." "The sea is still rough," the writer added, and "an iceberg has been spotted nearby. The collision might happen at any instant, but it might also be avoided. Uncertainty and anxiety."[79] We know how things turned out. There was really neither the mad scramble that the author of these lines feared, nor the organized rescue operation that was so ardently desired. But the respite provided in the Italian Zone had not been for nought. These few months of hiatus in the hunt for foreign Jews in France in 1943 give us a real sense not only of the longing for security gripping these refugees as they were bounced around from one place to another, but also the precariousness of their situation, and even the strength they displayed whenever they were given the opportunity to organize a bit.

What appears here under the double patronage of the Italians and of the Jewish aid organizations can be seen elsewhere in other forms, and in particular in the regions with a strong Huguenot presence.

In the Land of the Huguenots

The formation of the bond that would unite the largely Protestant villages to the refugees—and in particular to Jews on the run—can be situated on September 6, 1942, during the annual meeting of the French Protestants at the Musée du Désert, near Mialet in the département of Le Gard. The CIMADE was an organization that grew out of the Protestant Youth Movements. It first focused on aiding refugees from the départments of L'Alsace and La Moselle, then turned its attention to providing aid in the internment camps, and finally devoted itself entirely to rescue work. The leaders of the CIMADE in Nîmes used buses that the Reformed Church in Nîmes had chartered for the occasion and hid in them Jews being pursued by the authorities.[80] They practiced what they preached: speaking to the four thousand Protestants gathered at the meeting, Pastor Boegner stressed the good Samaritan's obligations to the Jews. In closer confidence, he was even more explicit when addressing the sixty-seven pastors in attendance.[81]

A network of people of goodwill immediately began to organize on several levels, with particularities specific to each of the Protestant communities. Jews were integrated into these communities in two ways. The first involved integration on an individual basis, which occurred when a community offered refuge to a large number of French and foreign Jews who would come and blend in with the local population: the specific modes of integration were as varied as the individuals involved. It was this sort of integration that characterized the community of Sainte-Agrève in the département of L'Ardèche and Dieulefit in La Drôme as well as scores of other villages, particularly in the Cévennes, where 40,000 inhabitants sheltered 1,200 refugees.[82] But there were also communities such as Le Chambon-sur-Lignon in the département of La Haute-Loire that provided shelter to large groups of Jews.

Several factors came into play in the relationship between the Protestants and the Jews that developed at that time. The theologian Karl Barth in Bâle had stigmatized Nazism as a new paganism and issued warnings about the dangers it posed: his message had been widely disseminated among the Protestants in France.[83] In addition to this ideological preparation, one can also make a case for an almost natural union of the persecuted—in the past as well as in the present—and a similar attachment to the Bible. But we can also follow Pierre Vidal-Naquet's more sociological analysis and stress the solidarity between the two minorities that had developed over the course of time: this argument is indeed more convincing than the others. It should nevertheless not be forgotten that some Jews, believing they shared a destiny with the Protestants, went to ask them for help. "For us, the Protestants were like England: they were a safe haven," writes Pierre Vidal-Naquet in his *Mémoires*.[84] Vidal-Naquet's family had decided to enroll him with the Unionist Cub Scouts, and he was not the only one in this situation. "There was obviously one minority that sought protection from another minority that was not being persecuted, but who believed in the God of Israel," he explained.[85]

The expectations of those who turned to the Protestants for help were not disappointed. There were no organized networks bringing fleeing Jews to Protestant areas, and there was no need for any sophisticated plan: they came individually and spontaneously.[86] The first to come to the Cévennes were the foreign Jews who had escaped from the mass arrests of the summer of 1942. When the Germans swept down to occupy the Southern Zone in November 1942, there were those who decided it was wiser to leave the cities of Nîmes and Narbonne for the outlying rural areas, where they had friends.[87] In addition to the summer homes that were the first used to lodge refugees, there was also the space available due to the marked population drain of the early war years, which had left one residence in six uninhabited. These vacancies were soon filled by Jewish refugees, who in the local collective memory would be first and foremost remembered simply as refugees.[88]

Everywhere they found a pastor to welcome them, a large portion of the community willing to help, and a law of silence among all the others. In some cases, a secretary or even a mayor in the town hall would provide false papers, while in others (such as in Saint-Germain-de-Calberte)[89] the proprietor of a hotel would give them a place to live. And in some places, cooperative storeowners did not require food ration cards. In each of these places, there was a family having a strong spiritual authority that played a central role. Pastor Boegner writes in his diary of Pastor Henri Eberhard in Dieulefit, saying how glad he was to have found someone he could trust to handle delicate matters.[90] One also thinks of pastors André Trocmé and Edouard Theis in Le Chambon. The collegial ties between pastors made it possible for refugees to be transferred from one place to another when one particular site became too risky. And in all of these Protestant communities, the strong social cohesiveness, that of a "minority bonded together by a dominant religion,"[91] prevented denunciations.

Jews lived semi-clandestinely in these places. As a general rule, they had false identities: they did not hide from the local population, but would flee at the sight of a gendarme. Some participated in local religious activities. The children attended school without being enrolled as Jews. A Jewish doctor could teach there under his own name. In other communities, Jews helped with work on farms, and the most well-to-do lived on their savings. While living in Dieulefit, Flo, the daughter of Clara Malraux, said one day to her mother: "You know, they all have a secret they tell to everybody."[92] The woman in charge of the school had made a point of showing the girls in her classes the caves in the forest where they could hide in case of danger. Danger indeed existed, and even if the local people had discouraged French gendarmes from being too zealous, some police roundups nevertheless did succeed in capturing Jews who would be sent to Auschwitz.

In Le Chambon-sur-Lignon,[93] the community took in refugees in a more collective, organized way. In addition to the efforts of Protestant families and individuals to help Jewish families and individuals, entire homes sheltering groups were sponsored by the Swiss Relief agency, the CIMADE, and the Protestant students relief office. Even before the summer of 1942, these centers had taken in Jewish children and adolescents that relief organizations had managed to get out of the internment camps.

Obviously, this area had avoided falling into the mind-set of the times and coming under the thumb of Vichy. Georges Lamirand, Vichy's secretary of state at the youth ministry was greeted rather coldly when he came to pay an official visit to Le Chambon. Pastor Trocmé, who moreover distinguished himself by his sermons against antisemitism, encouraged this independent spirit: at the ten o'clock service on August 16, 1942, at the very time when the roundups were occurring throughout the Southern Zone, and well before the summons that would follow, he spoke out against the cruelty inflicted on the Jews, calling the Vel d'hiv roundup and the events looming on the horizon in the Southern Zone acts of barbarity. "The Christian Church must kneel down and ask God to forgive its present failings and cowardice," he added.[94]

As was the case at the Scouts' rural worksites, efforts to camouflage what was going on began with the news of the roundups in August 1942. At first these were spontaneous, makeshift operations: foreign Jews risking arrest were hidden in neighboring forests for the duration of the roundup. Gradually, a well-oiled rescue apparatus was put into place.[95]

From then on, Jews came to Le Chambon on an individual basis, informed by word of mouth. Each day, the afternoon train would bring a few more Jews seeking to hide out, and local activists would meet them at the station. In addition, the CIMADE and the Jewish organizations (in particular, the OSE and the "Service André") also went about the region systematically, prospecting for new hiding places. Some set up bases in the area for clandestine departures to Switzerland: Mireille Philip, the wife of the representative to the National Assembly from Lyon, organized an escape route between Le Chambon, Annemasse, and Switzerland. There were two things, however, that made Le Chambon and the surrounding area truly special among Huguenot hideouts: the seven homes lodging a large number of Jewish children and adolescents "completely blended in with the others"[96] and the way that the rescue organizations in the area took advantage of these shelters. When the Italian Zone turned into a trap for those who had found refuge there, some—at times led by the "Service André"—fell back in the direction of the plateau surrounding Le Chambon.

As was the case in the villages of the Cévennes, the solidarity displayed by the entire population made it necessary for the gendarmes to proceed with caution and to issue indirect warnings when they had received orders to conduct a search of a farm or a boarding house. When the Germans took over the task of making such arrests, there were even more direct warnings that allowed Jews in hiding to scatter immediately. The director of the public school, Monsieur Darcissac, had set up an increasingly effective unit for fabricating false papers, and nobody asked any questions: they were happy to take fiction for reality. Some people were working actively to create such fictitious covers, while others were happy to let themselves be duped. As for the Jews that had been taken in, some could live off their savings, while others helped the families putting them up by chopping wood or using the sewing skills, or performing other services in line with their talents.

Pastors Trocmé and Theis were not allowed to stand up to the Vichy authorities in this way with impunity. In mid-February 1943, Pastor Boegner learned they had been arrested and immediately appealed to René Bousquet.[97] They were released five weeks later. But they soon had to go into hiding, leaving the authority over this enormous rescue operation with Magda Trocmé, the pastor's wife, while the rest of the local population took care of logistics. As for the German authorities stationed in the neighboring town of Le Puy-en-Velay, they were rarely seen in Le Chambon, for reasons that still are unclear.[98] The Gestapo nevertheless raided "La Maison des Roches" in May and June 1943, arresting all students who were present there along with the director Daniel Trocmé, Pastor André Trocmé's cousin.

When Albert Lévy set out on a tour of the region in October 1943, he noted that there were several hundred Jews living within a radius of about twenty kilometers from Tence and Le Chambon. He specifically tallied three hundred Jews in Le Chambon and some fifteen Jewish families in Tence. Most were widely scattered throughout the area.[99] He could have spoken of thousands, although some were only passing through the area. Pastor Trocmé estimated that the two thousand inhabitants of Le Chambon region saw some twenty-five hundred Jews come through their various little communities.[100] Albert Lévy observed that a good number of these Jews had, more or less sincerely, become Protestant. Trocmé was nevertheless encouraging Jews to attend Jewish worship services. The Consistory had been worried about rampant proselytism in a place where religious life was lived out so intensely on a daily basis.[101] As was the case in the Cévennes, however, respect for the other was the norm in Le Chambon. Life in the area was paced by religious observances that everyone attended: as it was a practice that help conceal the presence of such a large number of refugees from outside the community, it helped maintain the appearance of normalcy.

Thus it was that Jews seeking safety and shelter from the mass arrests found protection not only from the Italian public authorities but also from Protestant communities welded together by common spiritual values. The Italians and the Protestants were more or less encouraged by sometimes discreet and sometimes massive and overt appeals from aid organizations and Jewish groups. But there were other types of social milieus that played an identical role.

A Multitude of Microsocieties

Schools played an essential role in both Dieulefit and Le Chambon. At La Roseraie in Dieulefit as well as at Le Collège Cévenol in Le Chambon, Jews such as the orientalist Georges Vajda, as well as many other less famous teachers and professors who had been removed from posts and stripped of their titles because of the Jewish Statutes, openly carried out their academic functions.[102] Integration on the professional level was part of the refuge offered to Jews by these communities, but it was often the latter that led to the former.

Such was the case at the medical school in Montpellier, in spite of the cap instituted by the second Jewish Statute of June 21, 1941, which limited the number of

Jews enrolled in every institution of higher learning to three percent of the total number enrolled.[103] After consultation with the General Commission on Jewish Affairs, the minister of education Jérôme Carcopino had nevertheless stipulated in a memorandum dated October 7, 1941, that it was up to regional school superintendents and university deans to see to the "application of this categorical rule" and to ensure that "the spirit and the letter of the law [were] applied."[104] And just to make Vichy's intentions perfectly clear, Carcopino put out a memorandum dated March 14, 1942, specifying that even when the fixed number of Jewish students allowed had not been reached, universities should not accept applications from Jewish students who had managed to enroll in an institution in the Occupied Zone in spite of the restrictions but who had finally decided to cross over into the Unoccupied Zone in order to escape the increasingly repressive measures in the north.[105]

But at the medical school in Montpellier—and the same was also true both of the University of Strasbourg in Clermont-Ferrand and of the University of Lyon law school—Jewish students pursued their studies outside of the fixed number by auditing courses without having their names appear on the lists of Jewish students that the General Commission on Jewish Affairs periodically demanded from university authorities.[106] They took their exams secretly, with the announcement of their grades postponed "until better times." Or, with Dean Giraud's complicity, they were able to use the proper seals and stamps and receive the diplomas that they had earned. Behind this operation one finds not only the dean but also Professor Antonin Balmès. Professor Balmès was also the one who signed the prescriptions given by one of his fellow doctors who had been barred from practicing medicine because he was a foreign Jew. Then during the period of roundups and mass arrests, Balmès availed himself of his network of relations in the medical world, helping a doctor get across the border into Spain, placing a patient in a sanatorium run by one of his friends, warning a family about an imminent police roundup, among other things.[107] One could cite hundreds of other examples.

We can identify another network in medical circles that was integrating Jews into society. Doctor Sigismond Hirsch ("Djigo") was a refugee from Paris. Thanks to the friendships and admiration gained through his competence in the field of medicine, he had been able, over time, to find places in the Auvillar region (situated where the départements of Le Tarn-et-Garonne, Le Lot-et-Garonne, and Le Gers meet) for eighty foreign Jewish young people who had escaped arrest during the roundups. The problem of identity papers was solved thanks to the complicity of people in administrative offices, and the Scouts provided equipment and supplies. Even after Dr. Hirsch and his wife were arrested on October 18, 1943, and deported, the Scouts' organization continued secretly to find places in the region for agricultural workers.[108]

It is practically impossible to detect each one of these networks, but their number increased with time, as the Germans took over the task of hunting down the Jews, while French society distanced itself from Vichy, and concrete, personal ties developed between Jews on the run and non-Jews who were willing to help them.

We can take the following example from a different area. Le Malzieu-Ville was a little village in the département of La Lozère. By chance, it had become a rallying point for a group of about one hundred Jews, all of whom had come from the Sterdyn *shtetl* in Poland, a few kilometers from Treblinka. Most were knitters by profession who had gradually come down from Paris beginning August 1941, but especially after the mass arrests of the summer of 1942. The type of solidarity at work here was that of the *Landsmanschaft*: just as those who had just come to Paris from Poland were welcomed and taken in before the war, so now those fleeing the police roundups in Paris were greeted and taken care of when they came to Malzieu. This group of a hundred Jews in Malzieu lived in isolation, and the children played among themselves. Only the youngest went to the primary school, while the older ones wandered about and gave lessons to the little ones. Most parents did not work: the wealthiest helped the others. Two tailors made it possible for local farmers to take advantage of their talents. And the village doctor, a Protestant who was later to become mayor, gave medical care to those who fell ill.

Outside of these two meeting points, the Jews' contacts with the local population were limited to getting their supplies: indeed, this little Jewish community provided the village's livelihood by buying basic necessities on local farms. When French gendarmes came looking for the foreign Jews in February 1943, some were able to flee. Lea's father hid out temporarily in the home of a French Jew. The people of a small village could quietly accept a group of Jews in their midst, but the French gendarmes sent by authorities were nevertheless a dreadful threat. After spending a few months in Nice (in the Italian Zone) and after having acquired a good set of false papers (provided by the Dubouchage Committee, which shows the sophistication of Jewish organizations in this area), Léa's family returned to Le Malzieu. Times had changed, and the gendarmes reassured them: they would be forewarned if a police roundup loomed on the horizon. It was there that they remained up until the Liberation. For them, taking refuge there meant a daily routine of inactivity, waiting for the Liberation, and receiving protection (in most cases passive). From our contemporary perspective, a change in the gendarmes' attitude symbolizes the transformations that had occurred to a various extent in French administrative offices.

The widespread practice of scattering themselves in rural areas most often meant that Jewish families were separated, as it was always the children that were the first to be put in some safe hiding place. Some of the young (and in some cases the not so young) did at times find an opportunity for growth and personal enrichment in rescue work in the Jewish societies that continued to function in connection with a synagogue, a study circle, or some social assistance office. Others, however, found a substitute for their social milieu in the political world that was springing up around opposition to Vichy. The Communist circles offered a specific framework to Jews collectively; all the movements of the Resistance took in Jews who were willing to contribute to their action.

A Political Integration

"To be accepted into the Communist Resistance," wrote Annie Kriegel,

> after one had lost family, residence, home, neighborhood, school, career, and home, was also to gain back a sense of belonging. . . . Thanks to the warmth of an underground homeland that existed tenuously somewhere between shadows and catacombs but that in any case was alive and animated with the certainty of a brighter tomorrow, being a member of this resistance movement drove out the unspeakable sadness of losing the meaning of daily life, which had resulted from the persecutions.[109]

What the historian Kriegel brings back to life for us here is the same social reality that can also be found in the Jewish organizations and in the resistance movements.

There was nevetheless an originality specific to the Jewish Communist resistance organizations: they incorporated Jews into resistance operations that shared the general objectives of the other movements, without losing sight of the specificity of the Jews' situation. This particularlity, as we have seen, was expressed in the underground newspapers circulated in the Northern Zone. In the Southern Zone, *Notre Parole* was called *Notre Voix*, while *J'accuse* was known as *Fraternité*. "Jews in the Unoccupied Zone!" reads the September 1942 edition of *Notre Voix*, "The extermination of the Jews is being rapidly carried out in the Unoccupied Zone. Thousands of families interned in the camps have been delivered to the Nazis. The entire Jewish population of certain towns and villages has been suddenly torn out of their homes and deported. Trucks and trains filled with Jews are heading out in the direction of the demarcation line every day."[110]

Once again, we find the main themes of the underground newspapers in the Occupied Zone. Every Jew was threatened, and the "climate of pogroms and murders" thus created was aimed at "terrorizing the French people by threatening to make them endure the same fate as the Jews if they did not bow down under the yoke of the Germans and their lackeys." The French people were on the side of the Jews, and Jews should resist arrest with all their might: "Barricade yourself up in your homes. Make them break down the doors. When they drag you off, make a struggle and cry out to alert your French neighbors!" Referring to such watchwords, Nina Gourfinkel concludes that, from a tactical perspective, this was the best possible advice. However, she observes that "this exhortation was not heeded" and doubts that she herself would have been able to do so: "To shout, to vociferate, and to struggle with all my might, even if it cost me my life. I think it would have been almost impossible for me, as well as for a multitude of others, to do so. Our upbringing, our sense of self-respect, our distaste for such behavior, and then too, our pride indicated to us that one does not humiliate oneself in such a manner in front of one's executioners."[111]

It is true the word "extermination" cited above was part of the rhetoric of propaganda. Only a small number of Jews would have been able to physically oppose the

French police officer who came to arrest them. But there was more in such writings: "The Jewish people can only be saved by joining the French people in the common struggle against the Krauts and their agents." This call to fight could only resonate deeply with Jews. By investing their energy in the production of such papers, a large number of young Jews who were eager to act found a way of participating in a common enterprise. As in Paris, these papers had to be put together and distributed: the details of their contents were less important than the conviction of working together with others, with Jews exposed to the same dangers, joining in a larger endeavor that involved other French people.

This underground press grew up later in the Southern Zone than in the North, and for a long time remained dependent on technical support from Paris. It was only in May 1943 that the first printing press was set up in Lyon,[112] and in July 1943, there were twice as many copies printed of *J'accuse* than of *Fraternité*. From then on, however, the tendency went in the opposite direction, as the publications of the Jewish Communists diversified and began to be put together in the Southern Zone: such was the case of *Jeune Combat*, which had its first printing in June 1943 and served as a voice for young people. The main themes voiced by these papers were hardly different from those expressed by their counterparts in the north, and for the scores of militants involved in putting them out, they fulfilled a similar social function. Each city had its own particularities: Lyon served as the center for political activity in the Southern Zone; Grenoble, due to the special conditions it enjoyed under the Italian Occupation, saw the development of several types of clandestine activity; in Toulouse, the makeup of Jewish Communist groups was heavily influenced by the proximity of the Spanish border and of the internment camps.[113] While these regional specificities were tempered by the transfers from one region to another made by the leadership of the MOI resistance movement, they nevertheless had a direct influence on the development of the armed struggle headed by the FTP-MOI groups.

The first such group to appear was the formation of the Carmagnole unit in Lyon, which came together for its first meeting in early June 1942. It initiated its action by throwing a grenade—that did not explode—at a group of Wehrmacht soldiers on November 11, 1942.[114] It was the German Occupation of the Southern Zone that spurred the development of guerilla activity. Under the Italian Occupation in Grenoble, the armed struggle was initiated in the spring of 1943.[115] There again, it was the group Liberté (founded in March 1943 by Marcel Gaist and made up initially of four Polish Jews) that played the main role.[116] And once again, it was the replacement of the Italians by the German Occupation forces that led to an intensification of armed resistance activity. From September 1943 until March 1944, this group in Grenoble was responsible for three-fourths of the armed operations carried out in the département of L'Isère.[117] While it subsequently played a less prominent role, it remained at the forefront of the combat right up until the Liberation. The ranks of the FTP-MOI movement were decimated when many of its members had fallen into the hands of the Germans in Paris: subsequently a number of those who had escaped were assigned to Lyon, Grenoble, and Toulouse.

Jews thus figured prominently in each of these formations of the Resistance, often forming coherent groups within the various units. And in the case of Carmagnole-Liberté, to cite the most famous example, they were even dominant in the original organization. Contrary to the situation in Paris, however, they did not constitute a specifically Jewish detachment. In Lyon as in Grenoble and Toulouse, Jews worked side by side with Italians, Spanish, and anti-Nazi Germans. Everywhere, veterans of the International Brigades occupied the key positions. The group in Toulouse was called the 35th Marcel Langer Brigade in honor of one of its founders who had been guillotined by Vichy authorities on July 23, 1943, after having been caught with a suitcase full of explosives.[118] The Langer Brigade was distinct in two respects. First, it included a group of internationalist militants originally from Russia and Poland: Yacov Insel, Marcel (Mendel) Langer, Joseph Waschpress, and a few others had gone to Palestine, gotten expelled, and then had fought in the ranks of the International Brigades in Spain.[119] And then there was another group, in which Claude Lévy, Catherine Varlin,[120] and Yehuda Leib Gorzyczanski (Gorans) participated. All were newcomers to path of armed resistance. The consequence of the Jewish Statutes as well as chance encounters with activists had first oriented these individuals toward the camps organized by the Israelite Scouts of France, and their determination to take on a more active role had ultimately compelled them to join the military units of the MOI.

As in Paris, there were only a few men in each one of these FTP-MOI units: on the eve of the Liberation, there were somewhere between thirty to sixty in each group. There were only a small number of these *sportifs*, as these hardy individuals were called, but they were determined to make as much noise as possible, and carried out one spectacular operation after another. They concentrated their efforts on transportation and communication links; derailing trains and destroying gas depots, electric pylons and transformers; and attacking German convoys, facilities of French collaborationists, over zealous collaborators, and businesses working for the Germans. Together, Carmagnole and Liberté logged 413 operations before the Liberation.[121] All led the life of terrorists, with their dangers, anxieties, unavoidable acts of imprudence, rendezvous ("the central part in the ritual of the conspirator's life"), and casualties: the Carmagnole-Liberté units lost almost a hundred men. They had become marginal elements in society; terrorists always live in the margins. They had even become marginal with respect to the leaders of the FTP-MOI, who were a bit frightened by the audacity of some of their operations, most of which were decided upon autonomously.

But the members of these units had chosen this life on the very edge: it was no longer the result of persecution to which they had been subjected. By taking personal responsibility for their marginality, they had a sense of working for the liberation of France and for an ideal that would guarantee a place for them in society.

They were moreover acting within a sort of brotherhood that was socially comfortable for them: they had come from the same neighborhood or from a similar family setting and shared the same ideal, along with their Spanish and Italian comrades. The MOI had provided them a structure for social integration.

As was the case in Paris, the activity of these Jewish Communists included many other operations beyond the political action entailed by underground newspapers and the armed attacks carried out by the FTP-MOI units. They set up centers for fabricating false papers: the one in Lyon was particularly productive. The groups of the National Movement Against Racism (MNCR) specialized in rescue operations. The magnitude of this work, however, remains difficult to assess. In mid-May 1945, the Central Commission on Children founded by the Jewish Communist organizations had almost four hundred children under its care.[122] These were orphans among the children who had been retrieved from their hiding places: the figure can only be an indication of the number of children who had been hidden.

In addition to the small minority of resistance fighters, there were then many more—the MNCR in Grenoble had some two hundred members in April 1943[123]—belonging to the Jewish Communist Resistance who found in their action a way to integrate specifically Jewish concerns into a broader strategy that aimed to build an ideal world and thus eliminate all traces of segregation. It is true that Jewish Communists were at the forefront of the armed resistance. But in addition, they helped create in their families—or what remained of them—and among their friends an ever keener awareness of what deportation really meant. At the same time, they could provide the contacts necessary to get false papers and go into hiding. In that respect, they each formed a nexus of aid and support within the Jewish immigrant population: their intervention led a significant number of Jews into hiding.

A number of bundist militants wound up in the Southern Zone, often thanks to the help of Jewish social organizations. Such was the case for Fayvel Shrager, who managed to contact his friends on one of the ORT's farms in the Agen area.[124] Bundist millitants' organizational efforts in the Southern Zone followed the same pattern. These reconstituted social networks were ideologically oriented toward the Jewish "masses," which included a much wider group of people than the central group of militants. The bundists were not so highly structured as the Communists, and their underground newspaper, *Unzer Shtime,* was less prolific. Plagued by misfortune, they had been severely diminished by the mass arrests, particularly the one on Rue Sainte-Catherine. But they constituted another political microsociety of immigrant Jews. They were motivated by a keen political awareness and developed ways of coming to the aid of fellow Jews. Both of these qualities bolstered the defenses against the dangers of arrest and deportation.

For Jews who came from long-established French families or from families that had immigrated to France long ago, it was not necessary to be part of some collective Jewish structure in order to be socially integrated: the various movements of the Resistance provided the desired countersociety.

Individual Paths

It is a well known fact that Jews figured prominently in the various resistance movements, even though it would be impossible to measure their participation with precise numbers.[125] Their commitment came very early. From Raymond Aron, to André Weill-Curiel,[126] and René Cassin,[127] they were among the first to join de Gaulle in London. They figured among the founders of the Musée de l'Homme network, that came together in 1940 and published the first edition of the paper *Résistance* on December 15, 1940.[128] There were three Jews among the founders of *Libération* in July 1941.[129] Robert Salmon was one of the two founders of *Défense de la France*, and it was he who suggested that the new resistance paper first published in July 1941 be given the same name.[130] We could also cite Jean-Pierre Lévy, Daniel Mayer, Léo Hamon, Serge Ravanel, Raymond Aubrac, Maurice Kriegel-Valrimont, Pierre Villon, and many, many others. Thus, Jews participated in all the movements of the Resistance and held important positions on all levels.

It was only natural that the initial decision to resist was an individual rather than a collective decision for French Jews.[131] Such a political commitment was right in line with the political tradition of Jews in France: whenever they took sides, they did so as individual French citizens without letting their Jewish identity have any influence over their political choices. And they joined the Resistance as French citizens. "To join the Resistance," writes Léo Hamon, "was to consciously choose France, the French nation, with its woes, its grandeur, its struggles."[132] Jews deliberately blended in with their compatriots in the French Resistance: their personal war against Hitler and Vichy's antisemitic regime was absorbed into the general struggle.

In a sense, this was another way of refusing the enemy's efforts to single them out. Léo Hamon (then Goldenberg) would take this attitude to the extreme of refusing to talk about the specific problems of the Jews in his family conversations in order to avoid getting penned up in a "moral ghetto of anxiety."[133] And he was not the only one to adopt such an attitude. As patriots, the French Jews who had joined the Resistance at this time were mainly concerned with bringing an end to the German Occupation; as lovers of democracy, they were offended by the Vichy regime; and as Jews, it was the threat of ghettoization that they dreaded above all else.

It seems that some were also fearful that the Resistance might be perceived as an essentially Jewish movement, which would have provided an easy target for Vichy propaganda. In a February 11, 1942, meeting that Roger Stéphane (Worms) had arranged with Stanislas Mangin (who had joined the Free French forces in February 1941), and Pierre-Henri Teitgen, Stéphane was "happy to see the crucifix always displayed on Teitgen's desk, so that Mangin would be convinced that there were 'also, and even mainly'" Catholic militants in the Resistance."[134] When Raymond Aron was criticized after the war for having devoted to the plight of the Jews only a tiny part of the newspaper *La France libre* for which he was responsible in London,[135] he argued that he had acted first and foremost as a French citizen; he added that it was precisely because he was Jewish that he had spoken so little of the Jews.[136] He further specified that it was for the very same reason that he had so rarely voiced his views over the radio:[137] being Jewish, he did not want to fuel enemy propaganda.[138]

In the daily action of the Resistance, however, the Jewish background of some of its militants did exert a certain influence. Take the case of Daniel Mayer, whose name is synonymous with the socialist branch of the Resistance that he organized: up until March 1943, he worked in a UGIF office in Marseilles, thus earning his living and having at his disposal a secret meeting place (which says a great deal about the security people thought they enjoyed in the UGIF facilities). According to Mayer's own testimony, it was the bundist militants who taught him the ins and outs of clandestine activity. Moreover, the socialist action committees were generously financed by Marc Jarblum, who had always been a socialist Zionist, and at the time held the office of president of the Federation, the largest Jewish immigrant organization in the country.[139]

And then we have the case of Léo Hamon, the author of what is doubtless the most important study of the Jews in the Occupied Zone, written in April 1941.[140] The report resulted from a survey that he had conducted upon the request of Marc Jarblum: it shows how groups of Jewish social activists interacted with groups of the French Resistance through the intermediary of these same French Jews who had joined the Resistance.[141] It would therefore be improper to speak of any split between the two types of involvement in public events. It sometimes happened that within one family there would be one person involved in the "sixth's" efforts to rescue children while another had joined the resistance group "Combat": such was the case of Madeleine and Simone, Alfred Dreyfus's two granddaughters.[142]

At the same time, however, that Jews were able to take on so many leadership positions in the various resistance movements proves that in spite of Vichy's attempts to segregate Jews from the rest of French society, the French Republic's logic of assimilation had not been eradicated. If the Resistance was the true embodiment of France, Jews could still be integrated into it even though they had been rejected by its official institutions.

Nonetheless, although these Jewish résistants could repress any reference to their origins and refuse to give them any signficance for their identities, they still could not change an objective reality: that in the eyes of the Germans and of the Vichy government, they remained Jewish. They were sometimes the subject of specific instructions. "All Israelites holding leadership positions in the movement must immediately go underground . . . , and no longer live in their usual place of residence. . . . They must take on a new identity. Duty consists not of going to the slaughterhouse, but rather of escaping from it," one "Combat" resistance group was told in late 1942.[143] Even when they managed to conceal their Jewish identity by using an assumed name, their families were still more at risk than those of their friends. One of their first concerns was thus to provide their families with a false identity, although such families were often reluctant to use it. When Jewish members of the Resistance were captured, the fact that they were Jews exposed them to greater danger. When Madeleine Dreyfus-Lévy was arrested because of her resistance activity, she was sent first to Drancy and then to Auschwitz, where she died of typhus, weighing less than sixty-six pounds at the time of her death.[144]

All Jewish résistants were familiar with this danger, even though they tried not to let it affect their lives. They found themselves in a situation that was doubly precarious: they were at risk not only as résistants, but also as Jews. On January 28, 1944, in a handwritten personal letter to Emmanuel d'Astier, Raymond Aubrac remarks incidentally in the middle of a long political analysis that "my parents have been arrested." One can easily imagine, behind these simple words, the unspoken suffering and rage drowned in the brotherhood of the Resistance.[145]

As important as it was—and Jewish participation in the French Resistance was indeed extensive—it remained the action of only a minority of the Jewish population, just as those who committed themselves to an organized effort to rescue Jews constituted a minority. The vast majority of Jews—and in particular those who were French citizens and all those whose age would not have enabled them to participate in armed operations—simply found some niche of shelter in French society, blended into the woodwork, and waited for France to emerge from the long tunnel.

Some were able to find refuge thanks to friendships dating from prewar years. Lucie Dreyfus acquired an assumed identity through her friends in the Resistance and took refuge in a retirement home run by "nuns from Valence": she had located the home thanks to family acquaintance with nuns in the convent.[146] A friend and a fellow doctor offered Dr. Lucien Simon the hospitality of his home in the Cévennes in the summer of 1943. A few months later, the subprefect for the département of L'Aveyron found a hiding place for him.[147] A country home in the Jura provided a solution for Léon Werth until he rejoined his wife—who was not Jewish—in her appartement in Paris: he hid there in this apartment, which also took in a large number of résistants and Jews wanted by authorities. Here again, we find a concrete example of all the unspoken things that weighed so heavily on the mind of Jews. Among the reflections recorded in his *Journal* on October 13, 1943, he jotted down without any other commentary: "The atrocities in Poland, at Drancy."[148] It was as if everything but that could be described: its horror was so great that it could only find expression after the end of hostilities.

There were many such silences in the lives of all these Jews, even those who were perfectly integrated into non-Jewish society. Four months later, Léon Werth termed intolerable the "risk we carry within ourselves, which becomes part us, and which has no other purpose or limit than our very persons. Such is the case for Communists, or so-called Communists and Jews. They bear their dangers within themselves, they and their dangers become one. They cannot escape from them one minute."[149] On the same day, he bitterly criticized "these faithful friends who are waiting—without, moreover, really desiring it—for the return of a world in which [he, Werth, would have] the right to live, and who tolerate so well this world that excludes [him]."[150] Coming from an intellectual who was so well integrated into French society, married to a non-Jew, and in such close contact with resistance circles, this remark testifies to a distance that would prove difficult to reduce. And then there were also some Jews, such as Lucie Varga, who never found any suitable niche in French society, and who finally let herself die from illness.[151]

How the Jews in France adapted to their lives as fugitives in society can often best be described on an individual basis. The fate of many was determined by their degree of social, professional, or political integration, by chance encounters or connections, by the audacity of young people in their families, or by the ailments connected with old age. Parallel to this social fragmentation, which was a sign of a growing alternative society, Jews maintained a facade of legality. For a while, synagogues kept on providing spiritual solace to those Jews who turned to them. Monetary aid was still being given by the southern branch of the UGIF, even though its legitimacy could only continue to decline. Meanwhile, both the military and political situation continued to evolve.

THE PRECARIOUSNESS OF LEGAL CHANNELS

Should the Synagogues Be Closed?

Religious life was no longer what it had been before the massive police roundups of Jews in the summer of 1942. The scattering of Jews also scattered the worship organizations, many of which had been newly constituted. In the reports of regional delegates, we find that previous plans to take advantage of the religious renaissance had given way to observations on the growing indifference of the majority of Jews, now too preoccupied with hiding out to be interested in religion.[152] Except in the city of Nice (at least until the fall of 1943), there had been a sharp decline in the participation of youth in the study groups led by rabbis. The chaplain for youth, Samuel Klein, concluded that this lull should be used to provide greater spiritual training to those who were to constitute the new leaders "of a Jewish youth organization worthy of the name" after the war.[153]

Like Nice, the département of La Dordogne was also an exception to the general trend: there, "the Alsatian Jews in exile" continued to send their children to classes in Hebrew, the Bible, and other religious subjects organized by Rabbi Elie Cyper. The number of children in attendance had even increased between February 1942 and May 1943. There were 162 children enrolled in ten classes right in Périgueux, and 278 children under the age of thirteen scattered about in twenty-seven towns and villages in the same département were regularly attending classes in religious instruction. One teacher reached forty-two other children while making his rounds.[154] But this situation was the exception to the rule.

Attendance of synagogue services was also heavily influenced by the changing circumstances. At the height of the massive police roundups, they often served as rallying points, information centers, and shelters for those who ran the greatest risk of being taken. "At the time of the roundups in August 1942," testifies René Kapel, "the Jewish community in Toulouse left the synagogue on Rue Palaprat open around the clock in order to allow those sought by the police to find refuge there. In order to justify the constant crowd of people pouring into the synagogue in full view of the authorities, a pastoral letter signed by the Chief Rabbi of France was posted at the entrance: it exhorted the faithful to 'recite prayers night and day, because of the situation of French Judaism.[155]

The same initiative was undertaken in other cities, including Lyon, where in one night 550 people were thus given food and lodging and then sent by various Jewish organizations to places less exposed to the dangers.[156] In September 1942, the local police intendant became worried about the situation. "Rumor has it that the synagogue is putting up a large number of Israelites without proper documents: [I have] been told that there were 150 of them," he complained to Rabbi Schönberg on October 11, 1942. Rabbi Schönberg responded,

> In a time of persecution, we have in our rituals of worship, as is the case for other faiths, the custom of telling people either to fast or to pray publicly. The Chief Rabbi of France wrote to me on August 29 requesting that I organize round-the-clock prayers in the synagogue of Lyon in order to beseech God that the ordeals of our fellow Jews might come to an end and that France may take a hold on herself again. These services are more or less heavily attended, depending on the time of the day. It is possible that some foreigners who perhaps without proper documentation have taken advantage of these services to come to our Temple and stayed longer than other worshipers, perhaps even resting for several hours. But absolutely nobody has been given lodging there.[157]

The authorities' legal tolerance of religious practices was not discontinued. And when a local initiative—such as the ones undertaken in the autumn of 1942 in the département of La Dordogne and in the spring of 1943 in Limoges—resulted in the prohibition of the ritual Hebraic slaughter, an appeal from the Consistory or the chief rabbi was sufficient to have the measure repealed.[158]

But synagogues were increasingly targeted in raids carried out by the Gestapo, PPF collaborationists, the hatchet men of the Milice, and even by French police: a few days after the conversation between the Lyon police intendant and Rabbi Schönberg, the synagogue was subjected to a search that led to the arrest of somewhere between thirty to fifty people, fifteen of whom were kept in detention.[159] In Nice, seventy men belonging to the Pétainist war veterans group known as the Service d'Ordre Légionnaire stormed into the synagogue on Rue Gustave Deloye on September 14, 1942, and demanded the payment of a million francs in reprisal for attacks on propaganda centers for the Révolution Nationale.[160] The synagogue was also raided by the Gestapo during the same month. In Marseilles, the number attending synagogue services had decreased markedly after November 1942 and fell even more after the police roundup of the following January. On March 6, 1943, however, two plainclothes German agents burst into the oratory on Rue des Convalescents and carted off some twenty worshipers, including a fourteen-year-old boy.[161] On April 8, it was the turn of the synagogue on Rue de Breteuil to be raided by the Germans.

On August 25, 1943, a group of about twenty members of the Milice burst into the synagogue in Toulouse, profaned the sanctuary, and detained the ten or so worshipers who had gathered there for the evening prayer (the *minha*) in isolation until the following day.[162] In October 1943, members of the Parti Populaire Français targeted the same synagogue with their invective, making it the subject of repeated threats.[163] On December 2, 1943, the synagogue in Grenoble was also vandalized.[164] On December 10, five armed men entered the synagogue on Quai Tilsit in Lyon and threw two bombs.[165] And as we have seen with Brunner's operation in Nice, the Germans no longer spared synagogues when they decided to carry out mass roundups. One could always find a few elderly people who had come there seeking solace in the observance of ritual.

After this series of unofficial, uncoordinated attacks on synagogues came the time when prominent figures of French Judaism were targeted for arrest, including leaders of the Consistory and of the chaplain's office and those who served as rabbis. On October 23, 1943, Jacques Helbronner and his wife were arrested in their home. Rabbis Bernard Schönberg, Josué Pruner, Léon Berman, and Robert Meyers had already been sent to Drancy. On December 22, the second day of the festival of Hanukkah, Chief Rabbi René Hirschler was also taken into custody.[166] On January 9, 1944, Chief Rabbi Isaïe Schwartz narrowly escaped arrest and went underground.[167] Everywhere in France, the most important personalities in the local communities—or groups—of Jews had become vulnerable: presidents of worship associations, former presidents of a community, perennial figures of importance, and new social or religious activists. The number of such victims continued to increase in the months that followed.

In view of the deteriorating situation, the assembly of French rabbis that met on January 11, 1944, adopted by a vote of five to four the motion put forward by Chief Rabbi Jacob Kaplan who was to be named a few days later to be Isaïe Schwartz's interim replacement): Kaplan's motion recommended closing the synagogues,

> in view of the fact that the continuation of public services in the synagogues is a danger for the worshipers. . . .
>
> Whereas the continuation of public services in the synagogues, far from serving the spiritual interest of our religion, was conducive to the pernicious actions of the enemies of Judaism who, behind the facade that the respect of the Israelite worship service constitutes for them, continually harm the life and liberty of our fellow Jews,
>
> Whereas the continuation of public services in the synagogues is giving a false sense of security to our fellow Jews,
>
> Whereas from a religious perspective, it is not forbidden to suspend regular services in case of an emergency . . . there are grounds for deciding that temples should, in principle, be closed.[168]

Most synagogues actually continued to function normally, and closings only increased gradually. As a general rule, these closings were usually done in reaction to rather than in anticipation of the police roundups that kept on taking worshipers to be deported until July 1944. After the roundup that hit the Quai Tilsit synagogue in Lyon the Consistory finally decided to close its own offices as well.[169]

Those who had opted to live out in the open struggled with the decision to make the break from such a life and go underground. They sometimes had the feeling that they were abandoning responsibilities that they were obliged to assume in all circumstances. Such reluctance to take self-protective steps often reflected a lack of political foresight. Leaders who wore such blinkers did not escape the tragic results of those shortcomings, as many of them also fell victim. This was true for both rabbis and other persons designated to officiate at religious services: all of them were well aware of the dangers to which they were exposed. Such was also to be the case for the leaders of the UGIF.

The Southern Branch of the UGIF Loses Its Legitimacy

The southern branch of the UGIF was quite different from its counterpart in the Occupied Zone. There was no official *Bulletin* to relay the German ordinances and the UGIF's primary interlocutor was Vichy; indeed, the southern branch had been formed because of the General Commission on Jewish Affairs' concern for maintaining French authority over policy in the Unoccupied Zone. In addition, the various charitable organizations that had regrouped after their flight from the north and were incorporated into the new organization had maintained almost complete autonomy in their operations. And it was precisely that autonomy that kept the French authorities constantly worrying. Had the Federation of Jewish Societies in France been truly disbanded in keeping with the law? So wondered the Ministry of the Interior, for such did not seem to be the case.[170]: "The General Union was not intended to be a patchwork quilt of what used to be charitable groups whose dissolution would be purely one of form, but rather one unique, centralized entity," protested the general commissioner for Jewish affairs in May 1943.[171] And he returned to the same subject on June 30, 1943:

> The southern branch of the UGIF continues to look like a regrettable juxtaposition of the former charitable groups that have been disbanded by law. Under a new name, these groups are continuing to pursue their operations in their respective domains, with their own peculiar tendencies and usual methods and without having achieved the least bit of internal cohesion.

This is what accounted for a "chaotic functioning."[172]

The UGIF was indeed nothing but a supple centralizing structure that allowed for all sorts of institutional developments. Only the council, actually dominated by Raymond-Raoul Lambert, spoke on its behalf, but this council did not play any role in the daily operations of the assistance programs. The OSE, the Israelite Scouts, and the Federation acted not only inside the UGIF, but with it, behind it, and finally against it, with each group following its own agenda. The financial management of these organizations was also based on the autonomy of the member institutions known as "directions" (directorships) that Lambert kept under a veil of secrecy, away from the watchful gaze of the General Commission on Jewish Affairs. This method of financial management also reinforced the autonomy of each unit within the organization.[173]

The General Commission's auditor of the UGIF was nevertheless not fooled. He found advantages in this anomalous setup that had made it possible for the UGIF to receive subsidies for which it would have otherwise been ineligible. If the UGIF had strictly complied with the law and had used only the solidarity funds, it would not have been able to continue functioning for more that two weeks, observed the auditor, who also added that his

> primary concern [had] always been to forestall as long as possible the time when the southern branch of the UGIF would request official funds: that is why [he] had postponed the application of the centralizing measures. Although the law obviously provided for these measures, everything indicates that their first effect would be to cut off the generous sources of money upon which the various aid programs depended.

Out of "strictly administrative caution," the auditor had therefore simply "responded to the Jewish organization's camouflage by camouflaging the intentions of the General Commission, in order to gain enough time for a financial plan to be put in place."[174]

The southern branch of the UGIF had also managed to avoid dipping into the Solidarity funds for its operations. Supported by local loans that were to be repaid after the war, the Joint had made it possible to meet the most essential needs. But now, that was no longer sufficient, and as we have seen, the General Commission was worried. According to the law of May 11, 1943, all Jews in France were to pay a mandatory annual tax of 360 francs to the southern branch of the UGIF. But this tax solved none of the financial problems, and in order to collect this money, UGIF leaders would have had to have lists of all Jews subject to the tax, along with their addresses. The General Commission on Jewish Affairs had been working up such lists since late August 1942: prefects were instructed to send the UGIF detailed records (including indications about nationality) of the census files that had been compiled on Jews in their respective départements. This measure was (1) to facilitate the collection of a one billion–franc fine levied on Jews in the Occupied Zone, and (2) to provide the basis for mandatory contributions stipulated by the law that had created the UGIF.[175] The process was so long and drawn out that even as late as the summer of 1944, partial, incomplete, and inaccurate lists were still being sent in every direction, without really meaning anything.

At the same time, however, the law had been adopted and its application had become imperative. As in the Northern Zone, the UGIF had, following the same process, and in spite of its resistance, become an auxiliary used to maintain control over the Jews. Nevertheless, Raymond-Raoul Lambert had vigorously protested the imposition of this tax from the very beginning,[176] and the UGIF made no effort to increase the number of people paying it. For the year 1943, some 13,190 Jews paid their tax in full, while 444 made partial payment. As of mid-May 1944, only 3,105 Jews had paid the tax for 1944, while 483 had made partial payment. On the other hand, almost 7,000 Jews had requested an exemption from the tax.

In the same file from the archives of the General Commission, one finds a whole series of such requests that were sent to the UGIF accounting agent. Monsieur H.W., for example, eked out a living from doing a little gardening and raising rabbits. He was refused an exemption for 1943. He was still waiting for the response to his request in 1944, and was fearful of the threats of punishment prominently printed in newspapers. On April 12, 1944, he offered to pay fifty francs a month in order to liquidate his debt. Monsieur B. was a Belgian refugee living in Marseilles who suffered from a heart condition: he pleaded for the tax to be reduced to the sum of ninety francs. Madame D., whose husband had been arrested by the Germans on January 23, 1943, in Marseilles, had taken refuge in Carmaux with her nine-year-old son. For a time, she had received a subsidy of six hundred francs every two months from the UGIF in Toulouse. But after having found a job as a typist and stenographer, she no longer got any such aid. Her request for exemption was rejected.

"I paid my tax in 1943," wrote Madame G. from a little village in the département of L'Aude on March 21, 1944. "My husband was with me, he was working. But he has been deported." Left without any source of income and a fourteen-month-old baby, she was receiving aid from the UGIF in Carcassonne and was requesting an exemption. "I have been a refugee for four years and my husband was deported fourteen months ago. I have to take responsibility for my seven-year-old daughter and my mother, who is elderly and ailing. I am living only with the funds granted to me by the UGIF in Montpellier," wrote B.L. from a small town in the département of La Lozère. Most of the other letters in the file were also sent by people receiving financial assistance from the UGIF. They were often refugees from Alsace or elsewhere and had borrowed money in order to pay their tax for 1943. Some had sold personal belongings to meet the requirement, while others found themselves responsible for paying the sums levied on family members (in many cases a sister or a mother having suddenly found themselves alone) who had become their dependents. Along with their poignant requests for exemption, they often enclosed certificates of residency, dire poverty, or medical conditions.[177]

Nearly 50 percent of the Jews in Paris had paid their tax, but less than 10 percent of those in the Southern Zone had done so. Conversely, the percentage of Jews daring to send in an official request for exemption was twice as high as in the Northern Zone. As in the Northern Zone, the vast majority of such requests were at least partially granted, albeit to a somewhat lesser extent: 73 percent were honored in the Southern Zone as opposed to 95 percent in the Northern Zone.[178] And as was the case in the Northern Zone, failure to pay the tax was punishable by internment in the camps. The number of those not having paid nevertheless kept increasing, and such threats were difficult to carry out. In 1944, there were even fewer who complied with the requirement. Jews were increasingly reluctant to maintain contact with the organization that was now subjected to Gestapo raids.

And indeed, the offices of the UGIF had been raided several times by the Gestapo: its facade of protection was crumbling. In addition, Raymond-Raoul Lambert was having to cope with the same problems that we have already referred to in the Northern Zone, in particular, the problem of the foreign Jews who had been fired. Granted, this measure did not have the same ramifications in the Southern Zone; it did not necessarily lead to the immediate arrest of those who had lost their jobs. And that is what accounts at least in part for the conciliatory attitude of the secretary-general of the UGIF's southern branch. André Baur, by contrast, was greatly upset by Lambert's stance and fought vigorously to have the decision repealed.[179]

This is only one instance of a growing divergence betweeen the twin organizations. The unification of France under the thumb of the Germans was also making its effects felt. Finances were at the heart of the disagreement between the northern and southern branches of the UGIF. André Baur had to struggle with tremendous financial difficulties and expected monetary aid from the sister organization. And though the southern branch promised to help out, it rarely sent anything, as it was hardly rolling in money either. This tension between the two branches led to a conflict over the structure of the UGIF. Pointing to the fact that the German move to occupy the entire country had created a new set of conditions, André Baur argued that the UGIF should be centralized in Paris (which would have given him control over the entire organization and thus over its financial resources). At the same time, he added, the negotiations that would inevitably occur with the Germans would be easier: ultimately, the fate of the Jews would be decided in the north.[180] Lambert countered that such a unification would only accentuate the mandatory nature of the UGIF's representation, which was exactly what he was striving to avoid.

Changing circumstances settled the question before the two leaders could come to an agreement. The one branch's delegates and the other's council were unable to iron out differences in the meetings they held over the course of 1943. Following the massive police roundup in Marseilles, Lambert leaned more and more toward illegal activities. He accordingly sent Robert Gamzon, Maurice Brener, and Dika Jefroykin to the Northern Zone in May 1943 to resolve the dispute with the UGIF council. Lambert's choice of representatives was not innocent. Gamzon headed up the "sixth," while Brener and Jefroykin were using most of the funds received from the Joint to fund the clandestine activities of a number of organizations, some of which had not been placed under the UGIF umbrella.[181]

UGIF offices nevertheless continued to distribute official aid. UGIF reports even recorded a growing number of aid recipients in 1943, due both to the migration of a significant portion of the Jewish population and "the rapid and almost total impoverishment of an ever-increasing number" of foreign Jews.[182] Whenever one of the UGIF offices was raided during a police roundup, the number of requests for aid would drop dramatically for a while, but would pick up again once normal operations had been restored. The new office that replaced those on Rue Sainte-Catherine registered the "normal resumption of operations" on May 10, 1943.[183] The only restrictions noticed were those of a financial nature: there was not enough money to respond to all the needs. In June 1943, only two-thirds of the families in need were able to receive aid from the regional delegations, and what they did get covered only a small portion of their needs.[184]

The summer of 1943 nevertheless marked a new phase in the life of the southern branch of the UGIF. One month after André Baur had been arrested in Paris, it was Raymond-Raoul Lambert's turn to be led down the dark road to Drancy: he had unfortunately bumped into Röthke in the halls of a government ministry during one of his visits to Vichy to register his protest with Laval. Like Baur, he would be deported with his wife and his four children in December 1943. The UGIF began to lose credibility rapidly. During his trips to cities in the Southern Zone, Albert Lévy would more and more frequently observe a growing feeling of mistrust and downright hostility toward the UGIF. It is interesting to note that people were criticizing the UGIF above all for maintaining a bloated administration instead of seeking first to provide ever more indispensable aid.[185] The UGIF's loss of legitimacy could thus be seen in two complementary ways: organized Jewish forces leveled increasingly substantive political criticism at the official institution, while Jews not involved in any organized opposition condemned the UGIF's inability to meet their needs.

Here again, we find the same chronological breakdown of events. The autumn of 1943 marks a cutoff point: on October 20, 1943, the Gestapo stormed into the UGIF's Rose à la Verdière center and carted off ten mothers and twenty-nine "blocked" children, along with the center's director, Alice Salomon, who had refused to abandon those under her protection.[186] Gaston Kahn, Lambert's replacement at the UGIF, had been warned the day before, but had refused Brener's suggestion to let the children be scattered in rural areas by members of the Resistance; the Gestapo had threatened to carry out a massive roundup of all Jews living in Marseilles if the children were not present at the center.[187] From then on, the option of trying to forestall German demands was radically divorced from the choice of clandestine activity. As noted previously, it was at that point that the OSE decided to take the children in its homes and scatter them in rural areas.[188] Raymond Geissmann, now in charge of the southern branch of the UGIF, suggested that the agency's office be closed and that the regional leaders be responsible for distributing aid, but his advice was not heeded: Georges Edinger with the northern branch stood in his way. On May 26, 1944, however, Geissmann overcame this opposition: from then on, aid was delivered to people's residences or sent by post.[189] The UGIF's fate was sealed, and the Jewish political world was in the midst of a recomposition: there would be no place for the UGIF in the new landscape.

THE RECOMPOSITION OF THE JEWISH POLITICAL LANDSCAPE

From the spring of 1943 on, all political developments in France would be dominated by the prospects of the aftermath of Liberation. This was particularly true for the French Resistance: in 1943, it set about to unify all its movements and established the National Council of the Resistance (CNR). Placed under the authority of General de Gaulle, the CNR was to represent all the forces fighting against the Germans in France, including political parties.[190] In the months that followed, one after another of the UGIF's offices and centers were raided by the Gestapo: after being arrested in Sisteron, Marseilles, Chambéry, Brive, Limoges, Périgueux, and Toulouse, UGIF employees and their clients were taken to Drancy.

The new political legitimacy that was being created would be that of the postwar. The Communists were determined to occupy a predominant place, and so once more set out to form a National Front.[191] This front was an organization of the masses entirely dominated by the Communists: it was supposed to recruit a wide number of people and thus play a role in the political domain similar to the role played by the FTP resistance fighters on the battlefield.

The impact of all these developments was soon felt in the Jewish political world, whose protagonists were feverishly preparing for the postwar period, which was to follow this era in which Jews were being hunted down and carried off to Auschwitz. Throughout 1943, new pieces of information kept coming in, making it possible to have an increasingly clear idea of just what deportation meant. In addition to the underground newspapers put out by the Jewish Communists, the voice of London was making itself heard. The BBC had already announced the declaration signed on December 17, 1942, by the eleven Allied governments along with the Free French Committee: the document denounced "the application of Hitler's oft-repeated intention to exterminate the Jewish people in Europe" and promised to punish the guilty parties.[192] On July 8, 1943, the BBC broadcast Jan Karski's testimony[193] on the systematic extermination of Jews "coming from all over Nazi-dominated Europe" to camps where they were "asphyxiated with gas, burned alive with steam, or electrocuted."[194] This was the direct testimony from a member of the Polish Resistance who was convinced that he had personally witnessed the gassing of Jews in Belzec. The massacre of Jews in Kiev was also described over the radio on November 29, 1943.[195]

All this information was carefully noted by the Jewish leaders in the Consistory. However, nothing indicates that they really grasped the true meaning of this news. The same was true of Jews involved in the Resistance. Toward the end of the Italian Occupation, the Jewish groups in Nice that were working in conjunction with the Dubouchage Committee received a rather traumatizing visit. Two men who had taken refuge in Belgium, Mr. Honig and Haïm Salomon, were brought back to Nice at their own request. There, they told of being deported from Nice in 1942. But they especially told of how they had escaped from Auschwitz and described the reality of the death camps. But who believed them? At the time, people thought they were madmen.[196]

But even though people were not fully aware of the implications of such news, they nevertheless more and more closely associated deportation with certain death in the fall of 1943. News of the revolt of the Warsaw ghetto had made an impression, and the arrival of all these pieces of information was begining to have a cumulative effect. "The camp at Auschwitz. One would like to respond in kind with similar tortures, with a death that would be an eternal torture. And then one is overwhelmed, numbed by such extreme horror, by such sadism to the nth degree. The punishment will never equal the crime. Brutes suffer less and die faster. And nothing will do away with what has been done."[197] Léon Werth wrote these lines on November 4, 1943. But once Jews were in the Drancy camp and faced with inevitable deportation, they clung to the faintest hope and repressed the horror: they were no longer able to believe it.

But even allowing for such a jumbled or repressed perception of things, how can we explain the emphasis on rebuilding the Jewish community after the war, given the fact that, all around, Jews were being hunted down, arrested, hauled off to Drancy and then deported to Auschwitz? In the first place, such a perspective is part and parcel of the vocation and dynamics that characterize every representative political organization. Second, it testifies to the widespread conviction that the end of the conflict was drawing near and that a large number of Jews would escape the fate held in store for them by the Nazis. But there is more. During the first phase of the Occupation, which was marked by laws excluding Jews from French society, Jews kept trying to adapt to the circumstances and make it through. At the same time there was a renewed desire to seek out their distinctive character and to transform what for many Jews had until then been a neutral identity into something more specific. They complemented their adaptation to current circumstances by plunging into a past that conferred meaning and value.

During the second phase of the Occupation, when Jews were systematically hunted down, their priorities changed. They now had to scatter themselves out in sparsely populated areas, go into hiding, and avoid being arrested. The constructive part of their strategy no longer consisted of deepening their Jewish identity, but in making plans for the postwar period. Because they were no longer in a position to organize a collective life for Jews in the present, they took refuge in a future that afforded them hope.

The Jewish Communists had initiated this movement of political recomposition by creating the Union of Jews for Resistance and Mutual Aid (UJRE), which was for all Jews, be they French citizens, foreigners, Communists, or non-Communists, for "all were targeted by the persecutions."[198] Though not totally void of political intent, such language was not merely part of a political tactic: it was too close to tangible experience to be reduced to political rhetoric. Moreover, such a unifying strategy in the

Jewish Communist circles was in many ways analogous to a similar strategy among the resistance movements and was the result of pressures exerted on both milieus from the outside. In the political landscape that was taking shape in France, no one would have understood a proliferation of formations claiming to represent the Jews.

For its part, the Central Consistory devoted its entire September 23, 1943, meeting to the question of postwar Judaism in France. Their goal was to spell out the doctrine that the Consistory would be called on to support during peace negotiations. At the center of their discussions was the question of what attitude should be adopted with respect to Zionism. Various scenarios were considered, including a Vatican state in Palestine, a British dominion, and a land of refuge.[199] A lengthy survey on the subject of "wartime Judaism and the problems of the postwar period" was conducted subsequent to the meeting.[200] In the background, there indeed loomed the question of how French Judaism was to be represented with the government of a liberated France.

For their part, the Zionists were tending to unify their efforts. We have already observed several stages of this process, including the constitution of the Zionist Youth Movement (MJS), which brought together all Zionist young people, and the joint action carried out by the MJS and the Israelite Scouts of France. It was leaders such as Dika Jefroykin, active in both groups, who coordinated their joint efforts. However, the movement toward unity did not proceed without difficulty. The youth who had previously been with the far-left Zionist *Ha-shomer ha-tsaïr* movement were particularly wary of the Jewish Army, and sent to their movement's world leadership in Switzerland virulent reports complaining about the Jewish Army's methods and describing them as a den of revisionists.[201] But the response from the *Ha-shomer ha-tsaïr* leaders categorically instructed the youth to continue the work of joining forces: the most important thing in these leaders' eyes was to maintain contact with Jewish youth in order to be in a leadership position at the outcome of the war.[202] These contacts were also encouraged by the Zionist Organization in France, whose steering committee set up a special council in December 1943 to oversee the Jewish Army and calm similar apprehensions.[203]

The final episode in this internal movement of those connected with Zionism was the agreement signed between the Israelite Scouts of France and the Jewish Army on June 1, 1944: on the one hand, it placed the military branch of the Scouts under the authority of the Jewish Army; on the other, the Jewish Army pledged not to interfere with the political, social, and religious stances elaborated by the Scouts.[204] It had once again been necessary to overcome apprehensions on both sides: the Jewish Army was rather wary of these French Israelites who had been under the UGIF umbrella, while those Scouts who were not Zionists were worried by the Jewish nationalism within the Jewish Army.

With the exception of the Communists, all Jewish immigrant organizations worked together within the framework of a coordinating committee that was a replica of the Amelot Committee in Paris.

As was the case in the French political arena, the legitimate Jewish power established after the war could only emerge from the Resistance. The image of disunity among Jewish leaders that had marked the aftermath of the First World War moreover had not been forgotten,[205] and all Jewish leaders were strongly convinced that this time it was imperative to present a united front. It was in this context that all the organized Jewish "political" forces participating in Jewish Resistance joined ranks in July 1943 in Grenoble to put together a General Defense Committee (Comité général de défense [CGD]). This body brought together representatives of the Coordinating Committee with those from the Union of Jews for Resistance and Mutual Aid: in other words, it included Communists, Zionists of all sorts, and bundists. It was a first step toward an organization that would offer an alternative to the UGIF.[206]

Of course, the political differences between the various groups had hardly disappeared. The bundists were uncomfortable with giving the Communists an "entry ticket to Jewish society."[207] The Communists continued to lash out against the "wait-and-see attitude of the Zionists."[208] At the same time, however, they expressed their satisfaction over the unity thus achieved. "The unity of Jewish parties and organizations has been sealed in order to organize the resistance of the Jewish masses in France and save their existence," wrote *Notre Voix* on September 1, 1943.[209] Political differences nevertheless prevented a Jewish Youth Action and Defense Committee[210] from acting in a unifying manner.

The General Defense Committee requested membership on the National Council of the Resistance (CNR):

> Our resistance actions did not arise at the same time, and, in the beginning, were not of the same nature. . . . The law condemned us . . . to be irremediably stripped of everthing we had, which for most people meant dire poverty with no chance for support. Our first form of resistance was therefore one of mutual aid. [Then came the time of a second form of resistance] the resistance of escape and defense. It brought us closer to you. Our methods were the same as yours. We hid people, disguised their identities, and snatched them from the clutches of a slow death, while you snatched them away from a violent death. We wrote, and sent out watchwords. You helped us. We helped you. . . .
>
> By becoming members of the National Council of the Resistance, we pledge to perservere even more ardently and tenaciously in the work of aid and protection carried out alongside your work. We pledge to provide all the support we can muster to carry out our joint task. We pledge to share your propaganda, to engage in it and disseminate it in agreement with you. We pledge to participate in all joint actions and to be in harmony with the common front of the Resistance on all points.
>
> We ask the National Council of the Resistance to support us in the areas in which we lack resources and to reinforce our defense where there are breaches. And when the time shall come to establish the future status of the country, we ask that you address the issue of repairing the blatant injustice committed against the Jews.[211]

The authors of the letter explained that they had delayed their request for membership in order to avoid providing a target for enemy propaganda: "We would not have liked for anyone to be able to say that the resistance movement was governed by the purposes and instigation of the Jews or that the Jews' action was purely political. If we had openly declared our solidarity with you at any earlier time, our adversaries would not have failed to take advantage of the situation both to our detriment and to yours."

Reflecting on the history of the General Defense Committee in face of the sister organization that had been created in Paris, Fayvel Shrager pointed out on October 4, 1944, that the National Council of the Resistance had never responded to their request.[212]

The General Defense Committee managed to publish a joint newspaper, *Unzer Qempf*, in November 1943. In preparing the next step in the recomposition of the Jewish political world, Léo Glaeser, the committee's secretary-general, stressed the many things that French and immigrant Jews shared, particularly on the level of social work. And Glaeser added:

> Nowadays, many French Jews understand that scattered treasures of a Jewish culture are buried away deep within the consciousness of peoples. It is the heritage handed down to us by our parents and great grandparents. . . . But immigrant Jews must not underestimate the importance of a certain way of thinking, feeling, and acting that French Jews have acquired over the course of their prolonged contact with the French nation. It is a reflection of one of the most important civilizations in the world. . . . A unified representation of the Jews will open a new page in the history of Jews in our country, a time characterized by effective efforts to defend the interests of the Jewish masses and to achieve equal rights for the citizens of all countries.[213]

The emphasis here is on the unity of the Jewish people—a cultural notion.

As for the Communists, their voice was more clearly political, but the idea was the same: "We must untiringly strive to create a great representative body for Jews in France, one that will include all the organizations of both French and immigrant Jews." Such was what one internal letter advocated.[214]

The General Defense Committee and the Central Consistory made contact in October 1943 and laid out the basis for the establishment of a unified representative body of Jews.[215] That Léon Meiss had replaced Jacques Helbronner as interim president[216] may account for the Consistory's conciliatory attitude toward the General Defense Committee. Joseph Fisher served as the mediator between the two parties: he was a member of both the Consistory and of the Federation, and also was the secretary-general of the steering committee of the Zionist Organization in France.[217] These discussions ultimately led to the establishment of the Representative Council of Israelites in France (Conseil représentatif des Israélites de France" [CRIF]), whose charter was signed in May 1944.

For the first time, there was one representative body in which immigrant Jews, religious leaders, Zionists, bundists, and Communists held seats along with French Israelites. It was the Communists' official entry into the organized Jewish community. The CRIF's charter officially affirmed the non-Zionists' support of the Jewish Agency's demands relative to Palestine.[218] Only the Bund's delegate abstained when this article was brought up for vote.[219] The creation of the CRIF was indeed a revolution for the institutions of Jewry in France: for the first time in its history, they had adopted the principle of a unified representation that was not based solely on religion—even though, according to the charter's statutes, the president of the Central Consistory was to serve as the ex officio president of the new organization.

While this organizational reconfiguration was occurring, the Jewish population kept scattering far and wide. Some of the communities of support and assistance that were only partially organized also disappeared. The process set in motion by the massive police roundups was everywhere the same. Such was the case in Vals-les-Bains in the département of L'Ardèche, where a group of about sixty Jewish refugees from Alsace had settled in June 1940. At dawn on September 30, 1943, fifteen of them were arrested by German soldiers accompanied by French civilians. On the pretext an identity check, they were all taken to the Hôtel du Vivarais, where the Milice stripped them of their belongings. Following a short stay in the Saint-Pierre de Marseille prison, they were sent to Drancy.[220]

Similar operations proliferated everywhere, causing those not arrested to scatter immediately. Such was the case in Chambéry, where the number of Jews receiving aid from the UGIF in December 1943 had dropped by 50 percent in three months: from then on there were no more religious instruction classes and no worship services.[221] The same was true elsewhere. In November 1943, it was decided to disperse the little rabbinical seminary in Limoges, where twenty-one students divided into six classes were still taking preparatory courses at the rabbinical school in March 1943.[222] This time the turning point was decisive.

12
Liberation: Before and After

Due to the Germans' increasingly tighter grip on Vichy, the end of 1943 had been marked by a greater similarity between the situation in the Northern and Southern Zones. At the same time, everyone knew that the end of the conflict was drawing near, and all were fearful of the excesses that might accompany the Liberation. The rift separating Vichy from both Paris and the majority of the French people was widening, and repression was becoming the essential feature of a French State ferociously determined to maintain its existence at all costs. The situation of the Jews in France during the months preceding the Liberation was directly shaped by all of these developments.

THE ACCELERATION OF EVENTS IN THE LAST MONTHS OF THE OCCUPATION

For the Sake of State Continuity

Although the sweep of events left Laval and Pétain in a highly diminished role, their intent to maintain state continuity at all costs—in order to ensure at the very least a peaceful transition[1]—meant that their antisemitic policies would continue. The offices of the General Commission on Jewish Affairs had been centralized in Paris since December 1943. After the Germans had asked that Darquier, whom they considered ineffective, be revoked as head of the Commission, a brief interim was filled by Charles Mercier du Paty de Clam, a descendent of the army officer in the high command who had arrested Alfred Dreyfus in 1894. In the spring of 1944, the commission was placed in the hands of Joseph Antignac, who had already proven his fanaticism.[2] Even after the Allies had landed in Normandy, Laval ordered all government employees "to remain on the job without worrying about present events." This applied to those working at the Commission as well as in other government offices. When the Commission's regional delegate in Dijon worried about what action to take in case the Allies were victorious, he was sharply reprimanded by Antignac.[3]

That meant not only that all the legal measures remained in effect up until the very last moments of the Occupation, but also that some provisions were actually intensified and that, even though they were increasingly isolated from society, some branches of Vichy continued to see to it that these measures were vigorously enforced. On August 11, 1944, the director of economic aryanization in Toulouse wrote again to ask that Jewish property be put up for sale.[4] The Office of Inspections and Verifications (SEC) continued to wreak havoc: even though the regional head of the SEC in Limoges complained that his inspectors had been lagging in their work since the beginning of 1944, he nevertheless instructed them, "now that Jewish influence [had] practically been eliminated, to systematically check up on the situation of persons [who were] Jews or presumed to be Jewish."[5] The SEC conducted a whole succession of investigations during the months of May, June, and July 1944, seeking to find out the true nature of activities or racial origins of various persons. They also aimed at locating particular Jewish individuals and determing the racial origins of various business and store managers. The SEC continued to request that more provisional managers be appointed and that certain small stores be liquidated. In Montpellier, the SEC filed reports on fifty-three investigations in July 1944, indicating moreover that 135 others were still pending.[6]

Even as late as July 31, 1944, it was still possible for a couple in violation of the census law to be rigorously prosecuted.[7] And denunciations were still providing the basis for new investigations, such as the one targeting a certain professor at the University of Clermont-Ferrand who handled correspondence courses and awarded scholarships: he had been denounced as a Jew and accused of favoritism toward Jews in March–April 1944.[8] It is true, however, that since April 1944 the SEC's police inspectors had had to use a pseudonym instead of their family name "for security" reasons, which says a great deal about the evolution of their status in French society.[9]

The number of Jews convicted of violating antisemitic laws in criminal courts was declining, but there were new convictions—most by default—during the very last weeks of the Occupation.[10]

Moreover, as we have already noted, it was in April 1944 that Vichy decided to force "all Jews eligible for conscription according to the conditions laid out by the law of February 2, 1944" to go and work on the Todt organization's construction sites.[11] And in May 1944, the Ministry of the Interior decided to create files on Jewish consumers. It was also in the spring of 1944 that Jews were informed that they had to pay their UGIF dues for that year.[12] Since February 1944, Jews failing to fulfill this requirement could be interned in camps, as authorized by Vichy's secretary-general for the maintenance of order. And if the local UGIF office was closed due to a police raid leading to the arrest and deportation of its employees (as was more and more frequently the case), the SEC had the solution: "As the UGIF maintains a postal account in each region, all Jews will have to pay their UGIF dues to this account."[13]

Finally, on May 4, 1944, the *Journal Officiel* published the law of March 23, 1944, which doubled the amount of the Solidarity Fund stipulated by the law of July 27,

1941: the sum was to be taken from businesses, property, and financial holdings belonging to Jews.[14]

But as was true in most other areas, the administrative offices involved were thinning out and becoming obviously ineffective. The higher level political will continue, however, had not diminished, and was asserting itself in a context of widespread repression: this was the final phase of the Vichy regime, characterized by the predominance of the paramilitary police, the Milice.

The Paramilitary Police State

Toward the end of 1943, the paramilitary police state took on ever-increasing importance. The Milice had been created in January 1943 in the Southern Zone, and since June 1944, was backed up by an elite guard in uniform, "geared toward civil war combat."[15] Extended to the Northern Zone in January 1944,[16] the French State's Milice hunted down with ever greater vengeance all "anti-French" elements, including Jews, Communists, and "terrorists" of all sorts—in other words, all résistants and all Jews. In the fall of 1943, a political crisis during which Pétain tried to "disinherit" Laval brought on a German intervention. In early January 1944, Vichy became a totally obedient vassal of the Germans: the head of the Milice, Joseph Darnand, who had enrolled in the Waffen SS, was first named secretary-general for the maintenance of order and then given authority over all French police forces. Philippe Henriot became secretary of state for information and propaganda. While political repression brutally increased, propaganda broadcasts over the radio were intensified.

Henriot, "the most prestigious orator France has known for years,"[17] wrote regularly for the daily newspaper *Je suis partout* and had been doing a weekly news chronicle over the radio since February 1942.[18] Now he would hold forth daily for the benefit of listeners all over France on the "French Radio News" (Radio-Journal de France) at 12:40 in the afternoon and 7:40 in the evening. He cultivated an obsessive fear of Communism with an unequaled ardor and a persuasive force that made these editorials the highlight of the day for the great majority of French people, whether they approved of or hated his ideas.[19] In the course of its fight to drive out all undesirables, Vichy gave free rein to the most virulent antisemitism. Henriot's invective lashed out against the "terrorists" of every stripe who were supposedly part of the "diabolical plot of The City's plutocrats who had joined forces with the Judeo-Bolsheviks of Eastern Europe."[20]

Such was the formula used to depict the forces of evil. For its part, the daily paper *Paris-Soir* offered another version in its January 1, 1944, edition: taking a cue from Gauleiter Sauckel, it denounced "the Jewish plutocracy of the West allied with the Bolshevik nihilism of the East."[21] On June 28, 1944, the talented editorialist was executed by Liberation's elite commandos, who were the National Liberation

Movement's shock troops. He would be replaced by Paul Marion and Xavier Vallat.[22] Throughout all this time, the General Commission on Jewish Affairs' program had been regularly broadcast over the radio. The 197th was aired on August 15, 1944, and denounced "the Bolshevik killings, which bore the trademark of the Jews." Three days later, the 198th program attacked "Jewish racism."[23]

Equally unabated was antisemitic rhetoric of the Parisian newspapers, which continued to denounce "the international Jewry [carrying out] their age-old plan to clutch capitalism and communism, two sides of the same coin, in their crooked hands and dominate the world."[24]

In addition to the usual news articles, however, such propaganda was increasingly integrated into what was becoming the newspapers' main rubric: the fight against terrorism and the repression of banditry. "While it is deplorable for the French to be killing each other, it is even more regrettable that foreigners are meddling in this anti-national activity," read one article in *Paris-Soir*. Among the agitators referred to, the role of Polish Jews was particularly highlighted, even more than that of Spanish Communists and a few "isolated Soviets and those sent out to prepare the revolution on their own."[25]

The press had a field day with the Judeo-Communist "bandits" or "terrorists" and their misdeeds during the trial of the Manouchian Resistance group, which began in mid-February 1944 with the German war court proceedings conducted under the authority of the German commander for the Greater Paris area.[26] "No sign of emotion on the faces of these brutes," observed *Paris-Soir*, adding that "one notices the sly, hateful looks of the Jews," and describing "this horrible gallery of terrorists" in similar terms.[27] The twenty-three accused were condemned to death and twenty-two of them executed a few days later.[28] The climax of the propaganda campaign was the infamous red poster. Again from *Paris-Soir*:

> A vivid and most timely poster presents us with the hideous hit parade of the army of criminals' most famous "liberators." No commentary accompanies this poster: there are only photos, the identity of these wretches, along with their nationality and the record of their crimes. There is not one Frenchman among them. Polish Jews, however, are featured prominently everywhere. Next in line come the Hungarian Jews, the Spanish Communists, the Italians, and the most dreadful of these bandits, an Armenian. And so there we see what sinister brutes and what nightmarish faces we have as our "liberators" for today and our masters for the future if ever this anti-French plot had succeeded! And let me emphasize the point, they are all foreigners![29]

And so everything fit perfectly: the Jews were arming the Bolsheviks, who were preparing to invade France, just as they were the ones who were sending the British and American bombers on raids that were claiming a considerable number of victims in France in these recent months of the Occupation in 1944. All of these external enemies were allied with foreigners within the country: these were the stateless people (in other words the Jews) who made up the army of criminals. In response to this menace from the outside, death sentences handed down by German courts as well as by the newly instituted French courts martial were featured in lengthy newspaper reports and commentaries.

Cinema newsreels made their own contribution to this depiction of things. In the week of February 10, 1944, moviegoers learned about "the crimes committed by terrorists—all of them foreign Jews—in Chalon-sur-Saône, Grenoble, and Bourg-en-Bresse, and then saw Premier Laval and Joseph Darnand attend the funeral in Vichy for the guards with the Mobile Reserve Group (GMR), who had given their lives in the line of duty."[30] In late March, a cartoon showed the Nimbus family gathered around the radio to listen to the broadcast from London with a Jewish voice announcing "We're on our way." At that very moment, the house came under bombardment and the entire family was killed.[31]

For its part, newspapers strongly focused on antisemitism continued to argue that Jews should be used as hostages. "Let the Jews pay with their hide for every member of the Milice and for every militant assassinated," read Pierre-Antoine Cousteau's article written for the April 7, 1944 edition of *Je suis partout.* Cousteau proposed to "shoot one hundred Jews chosen at random for every French soldier executed in Algiers."

This type of discourse, which was particularly virulent in Paris, no longer resonated with a population weary from lack of basic commodities, preoccupied by the bombing, worried about the threat of civil war, and increasingly supportive of the Allies. Nevertheless, the groups disseminating such rhetoric coupled their "ideological delirium" with efforts to organize paramilitary units capable of carrying out the counterterrorism they were advocating.[32] As each side asserted its position more forcefully, police roundups and arrests sent an ever-increasing number of Jews to Drancy to be deported. There was also a proliferation of acts of reprisal against the Jews in response to every successful strike by the Résistance. The time of the massacres had come: Jews were not the only victims, but they were often the first.

Roundups and Massacres

The last mass arrest carried out by French police in Paris was on February 4, 1944. This time the conditions were harsher: French wives and children of foreign Jews (Poles and Turks on this occasion) targeted were no longered spared the fate that struck the head of the family.[33] Individual arrests continued beyond that time, however, and were conducted by either the Feldgendarmerie or the SEC's inspectors hunting out "specifically Judaic facial features."[34] Even as late as July 26, 1944, R.H. was stopped at eleven in the morning by inspectors on watch on Rue Faubourg Montmartre, because her yellow star was attached by pins. When an identity check showed that she was living with a relative (her own apartment had been sealed off) and that she had tried to dodge the laws and regulations in effect by not declaring her change of residence, she was taken to the Judicial Police to be interned.[35]

From November 1, 1943, to July 31, 1944, municipal police arrested 2,198 Jews in the Paris area.[36] The last report of the General Bureau of Information available to us dates from August 7, 1944, and reports that seventy-seven Jews were transferred to Drancy. The last deportation train left the camp for Buchenwald on August 17, 1944. There had been no "empty months" since September 1943, and deportations had been particularly numerous from February to May 1944. A total of 14,833 Jews were deported from France in 1944:[37] this amounted to an average of 550 more deportees per month than in 1943.

The last few months of the Occupation were thus characterized by an acceleration of the deportations. French police no longer provided the same level of logistical support, but Jews were now being targeted wherever they grouped together, including in children's homes, hospitals, homes for the mentally ill, and even soup kitchens, UGIF centers, and synagogues. Except for 400 elderly persons lodged in nursing homes and 450 Jews located in centers run by the Office of Social Services for Foreigners (SSE), there were no longer any Jews in the internment camps in the south of France in April 1944: they had all been deported.[38] Even one of the SSE's centers was emptied of its sixty-some residents, who were also sent off to an "unknown destination" on February 15, 1944.[39] In the spring of 1943, some 173 Polish Jews had been taken directly from the Warsaw ghetto to the Vittel camp: they had been arrested while carrying passports issued by various Latin American countries. On April 18, 1944, they in turn were sent down the road leading first to Drancy and then on to Auschwitz.[40] Sixty other Polish Jews in a similar situation were sent down the same path on May 16, and a few more were to follow in early August.

The first of these three deportation trains carried Itzhak Katzenelson, author of the *Song of the Murdered Jewish People*, a work that he wrote during his detention in the Vittel camp.

> Fear, anxiety, horrible terror hold me tightly in their clutches
> The railroad cars are there, again!
> Gone yesterday, and back again today, they are there,
> once again there, on the quay:
> Do you see their gaping maw?
> Their maw open in horror!
> They are still hungry!
> Once more, again. Nothing satisfies them.
> They are there, they are waiting for the Jews.
> When will they be brought?
> Famished, as if they had never swallowed up their Jew. . . .
> Never. . . . But yes they have! They want more, still more.[41]

Katzenelson, whose wife along with two of their children had been gassed in Treblinka, wrote these lines on October 26, 1943. Six months later, it was his turn to be swallowed up in the railroad cars that left from French territory.

French Jews no longer benefited from any protection either. Aided by members of the Milice, Doriot's followers, or other collaborationists, the Gestapo conducted its operations onsite in the various regions. Prefectorates did sometimes still provide lists of Jews to be arrested when the German authorities demanded such documents, but such was not always the case; at any rate, these lists were no longer of much use. The situation varied enormously from one département to another. Beginning in early July 1944, the SEC's agents in the Southern Zone were given the same powers as those in the north: they were now granted the authority to take people into custody.[42] Although they never had much time to use this power, roundups and mass arrests were now decided on and carried out by fervent ideologues, which meant that there was no longer any chance for leaks to give forewarning of planned raids. Small communities of Jews could only scatter in response to rumors.

Each city in turn supplied its contingent of Jews. In October 1943, the Normandy region was particularly targeted; the German Sipo-SD forces in the provinces were ordered to have the French police arrest even more Jews. But it was Bordeaux that first felt the impact of Darnand's appointment as the head of Vichy's forces of repression. After the German Sipo-SD had seized 108 Jews in the area on December 20, 1943, the prefectorate, after having first procured Darnand's approval, complied with German orders and apprehended 228 French Jews during the night of January 10 to 11, 1944.[43] From then on, the number of French Jews sent to Drancy on French trains would continue to increase. Such was the case in the Poitiers area (in the Poitou-Charentes region), where 484 Jews were rounded up by French police in January 1944.[44] On April 1, 1944, eight hundred Jews that had been arrested by German police in the départements of La Moselle, La Meuse, and La Meurthe-et-Moselle were sent down the road to Drancy, after having been incarcerated for almost a month in the internment camp at Ecrouves.[45] Toulouse and the surrounding region would supply a significant number of Jews for the trains to Drancy throughout these first few months of 1944.

And there were scattered groups from elsewhere: one day, 60 Jews were arrested in the département of La Sarthe, another day 62 were apprehended in Reims, 44 in the Limoges regions and 96 in Vesoul and the surrounding area (in the département of La Haute-Saône), 109 in Belfort, 86 in Dijon, and then 60 in Nice. Scores of Jews were thus rounded up and sent off to "the Jews' camp" at Drancy, which took in more Jews from the provinces than from the greater Paris area during the first trimester of 1944. And large numbers of Jews continued to be shipped to Drancy in these conditions in the following months: 2,000 arrived from the provinces in April 1944 along with 250 from Paris, followed by 2,000 more from the provinces with 500 from Paris in May, and then another 1,000 from all over France in June.[46] The last massive roundup was directed against the 250 children arrested on the orders of Brunner in the UGIF's homes in the Paris region between July 21 and 25, 1944.

Underneath all these figures we must follow a story of incessant anxiety. Periods of calm would give way to times when Jews were terrorized by manhunts. This was the case in every region, as uncertainty reigned. Sometimes roundups were triggered by specific events, such as the attack carried out in Toulouse on March 1, 1944, by the 35th Brigade of the FTP-MOI resistance group against Les Variétés, a moviehouse that had screened *Le Juif Süss* the previous day.[47] Other roundups were conducted for no specific reason, and totally arbitrarily: sparing the elderly, say, while carting off young children and invalids. Jewish communities were overcome with panic. Such was the case in Limoges and the surrounding area, where the Gestapo was carrying out a large number of individual arrests: rumors of an imminent expulsion of all Jews kept everyone deeply anxious.[48]

Hunted down so intensely, the Jewish population closely heeded watchwords telling them to scatter. They increasingly acted in accordance with what Chief Rabbi Maurice Liber termed a "Marrano syndrome." Liber observed this phenomenon while visiting every Jewish family that he managed to locate in his area. As he took orders for unleavened bread for the 1944 Passover, people often told him: "It is better not to attract neighbors' attention" or "I am afraid of being noticed by the baker."[49] It was indeed safer to maintain a low profile; in the context of the civil war that was brewing in France in the summer of 1944, Jews offered an easy target.

It was henceforth no longer unusual for members of Vichy's Milice and collaborationists (including Doriot's followers and others) to be the target of attacks. In previous months, a bomb placed in one of the facilities of the Legion of French Volunteers (LVF) or of some similar group would bring on a raid on a synagogue. Now, Jews were made to pay directly with their very lives for the death of right-wing collaborationist militants and members of the Milice. "Counterterrorism" had been part of Vichy's agenda since the fall of 1943.[50] Thus when members of the Milice were gunned down by local resistance groups in Annecy, two of the six men murdered in reprisal by the Milice were Jews.[51] And when Joseph Lécussan, accompanied by Lieutenant August Moritz murdered Victor Basch (the eighty-year-old president of the League of Human Rights) and his wife in cold blood on January 11, 1944, the text placed on their bodies bore the inscription: "Terror for terror: the Jew is always made to pay. This Jew has paid with his life for the assassination of a Frenchman."[52]

An oft-used method of carrying out such reprisals consisted of taking detainees from a prison and shooting them. Jewish prisoners were the first to be selected. Such was the fate of fifteen Jews taken out of the Caffarelli military barracks by the Germans in Toulouse in May 1944.[53] And on June 28, 1944, in Rillieux-la-Pape, the Lyon Milice led by Paul Touvier arrested seven Jews and slaughtered them with machine guns at dawn on the following day. Prominent Jewish figures were also taken out of detention and shot: such was the case of former government ministers Jean Zay and Georges Mandel, who had been favorite targets of antisemitic diatribes in the press ever since July 1940. Others, such as the banker Pierre Worms, father of Roger Stéphane, who was killed on the evening of February 6, 1944, were simply taken by surprise in their homes and shot.[54]

The danger would only increase during the fighting that followed the Allied landing in Normandy. When the Bron airfield was bombed on August 15, 1944, German authorities in Lyon took seventy-two Jews from the "Jew shack" at the Montluc prison and killed them.[55] From March to August 1944, there was a proliferation of individual murders perpetrated against Jews by the Germans in the départements of La Dordogne and L'Ain.[56] The same was true in the Limoges region. "In the year 1944, and particularly from May to August, the Milice's men committed numerous crimes and acts of violence in the Limoges region," noted the chief of the regional office of the Judicial Police in his report of April 27, 1945, adding: "As far as we can tell, 42 people were killed in various circumstances during that time period by the members of the Milice, and 106 others were victims of arbitrary arrests, acts of violence, thefts, and looting of apartments carried out by the Milice's men. The majority of the plaintiffs are Israelites."[57] Hunting down Jews had become the specialty of certain heads of the Milice, such as the sinister Joseph Lécussan, to whom we shall return, and Dagostini, who ordered several Jews to be arrested and killed in Voiron in the months of April and June 1944.[58]

This was indeed a time of revenge-taking and sneak attacks. Many French people were targeted because of their staunch support of the Resistance. As for Jews, they were by definition the enemy, as illustrated by the massacre of the Jews at Saint-Amand-Montrond in the département of Le Cher.[59] When members of the local Resistance prematurely attempted to liberate the town, they entered into a confrontation with members of the Milice, leading to a fatal chain of events. Both sides took hostages: captured résistants were handed over to the Germans and deported to concentration camps in the east, while some of the Milice's men taken by the résistants were hanged.

But the worst atrocity of these "scenes of civil war" was committed against the Jews. On July 21 and 22, seventy Jews were rounded up on the orders of Joseph Lécussan, who had formerly served as the regional agent of the General Commission on Jewish Affairs in Toulouse and had just been named the head of the local Milice. The heads of the regional Gestapo decided to kill them on the spot, as shipping them to Drancy by train had become difficult in these troubled times. Except for twenty-five women and nine children who survived the roundup, they were thrown down three wells located at Le Guerry by groups of six. In case some might have escaped death, construction blocks and sacks of concrete were thrown down on top of them to shatter their skulls. There were 36 victims in all, 28 men and 8 women, all Jewish. Some were involved with the Resistance, but all were chosen as hostages because they were Jewish. Was this really a "French Tragedy"?

The Jews and the French in 1944

Though they were doubtless more vulnerable than the rest of the population, Jews were now indisputably on the same side as the vast majority of the French people, which was very soon to be the side of the victors. In autumn 1943, Maurice Martin du Gard noted in his diary that "in Vichy, everyone [was preparing] their dossier" in view of the Liberation:

> As for me," says one government minister, "I saved so and so many workers." "I," says one police chief, "secured admission to a police academy for the sons of generals who supported de Gaulle." "I," says another, "saved so and so many Jews."[60]

Such efforts to lay the basis for a safe future without surprises also took other forms: the French Association of Owners of Aryanized Property, for example, was formed on September 25, 1943. Its

> purpose was to group together Aryans who, by virtue of the application of the ordinances, laws, decrees, and statutes governing Israelites, had become owners . . . of all possessions or holdings having formerly belonged to Jews.
>
> This group's basic goals are to defend the rights of the aforementioned property acquirers against all criminal pursuits and all civil and fiscal claims made by Jews. By bringing these acquirers of Jewish property together in one organization, the association intends to make it possible to defend them against any future pressures and attempts to eliminate them that might directly or indirectly be made by Jews formerly owning such property or by their defenders. . . .
>
> Finally, this association intends to use all possible means to provide special help to entities striving to create a favorable moral climate for aryanized businesses.[61]

The idea for such a group had been put forward by Marcel Déat in the September 9, 1943, edition of the newspaper *L'Oeuvre*.[62] It would garner the support of a number of people even after the Liberation.

Such rear-guarding efforts were more and more apparent among those who had in one way or another been involved with either Vichy's policies or, more specifically, with the application of the anti-Jewish measures. It was doubtless such efforts that made it possible for some Jews to find a helping hand in places where they would have been met with either a cold reception or indifference only a few months earlier. However, during these same months of 1944, the majority of the French population was still obsessed with the difficulty of procuring basic commodities and fearful of the bombings that, beginning in March 1944, had become massive. They were waiting for the Allied landing that would liberate them, but feared the foreseeable excesses of civil war.

For a French population generally weary of the war and the Occcupation,[63] Jews were a nonissue. The subject of the Jews is virtually nonexistant in the letters that were opened and read by postal control during this time: they are not mentioned in relation to the complaints about procuring basic commodities, nor in relation to worries about the aftermath of the war, nor in relation to the forms of opposition to terrorism, nor as participants in the war that was raging.[64] Only 0.026 percent of the letters opened and read in January 1944 in Lyon attacked Jews.[65] When expression was given to various forms of xenophobia, it was usually aimed against the Germans, and in rare cases against the English. It is true that reports on this surveillance of mail sometimes refer to expressions of antisemitism in their introductory synopsis—mainly in relation to the problem of the black market—but one never finds in the quotations used any precise reference that would support this claim.[66] What references there were occurred in insignificant proportion: for example, in Perpignan in April 1944, there were only thirteen such references out of more than 65,000 letters analyzed by the commission.[67] When one looks at the details of these letters, the thing most often stigmatized in matters involving the black market was the greed of farmers.

Rarely did these letters mention the mass arrests of Jews. Out of the 40,000 letters opened in May and the 50,000 read in June 1944, there were ten in May and twenty in June that approved of the roundup of Jews in Néris-les-Bains.[68] Out of the 20,000 letters intercepted in Saint-Amand-Montrond in July 1944, only twenty made mention of the arrests of Israelites, without any further comment.[69]

We can easily surmise that if a similar analysis had been conducted of the letters written specifically by Jews, one would have found—in addition to the common worries about procuring basic commodities, fears of bombing raids, and general weariness with the war and Occupation—profound anxiety about arrests and deportation. And that is indeed what is seen in the reports and letters written by various Jewish social and political activists. The letters received in Switzerland by Marc Jarblum in mid-February 1944 are unmistakable on this point:

> While in the battered city of Grenoble, Jews are subjected to the common rule of terror, and can seek shelter, hide, and try to flee—this time, not "like all the Jews," but "like everybody else"—isolated sneak attacks on Jews have not stopped. Right in the middle of Grenoble, on Rue Bonne, the Gestapo came in mid-December and rounded up the entire family of Monsieur Salomon, who was a storekeeper in Paris before the war. The Gestapo even laid a trap for 24 hours: 18 of our fellow Jews were taken. Such hits occur every two or three days even in the surrounding area, in Eybeus, Domène, Seyssinet, and elsewhere.[70]

And each one saw the ranks thinning all around. "After a day like that, we summarize: nothing to report," wrote another of Jarblum's correspondents on February 1, 1944:

> Yes, we publish communiqués that long quite often, every day. Even so, some are missing when we call the roll, and more will be missing tomorrow, and so it will go every day until the communiqué has to be written by somebody else. . . . If this continues at the same rate, I wonder if we will make it to the end of the war. And it is always under the rubric "those who have left." And it is always the best who leave.[71]

The Jews were indeed on the same side as the majority of French people, but the two groups still occupied different positions. The Jewish population had made its choices: for the most part, they had scattered out. Now they had to hold out until the liberation of French territory. Random chance, good fortune, or bad luck would decide the fate of those who had anonymously blended into French society in hopes of remaining undetected. The hazards of combat would determine the plight of those who had joined one of the branches of the French Resistance. Those in the specifically Jewish resistance groups were becoming more and more sophisticated in living a totally clandestine existence: partly because of the intensification of efforts to hunt down Jews, but also because their political strategy was increasingly dictated by the prospects of the reconstruction that would follow Liberation.

THE JEWISH RESISTANCE: BETWEEN SPECIFICITY AND ADAPTATION

Be they French citizens, immigrants, Zionists, or other, all groups comprising the Jewish Resistance now shared a twofold objective. It was important not only to organize the defense of the Jews, but also to incorporate Jewish Resistance into the general resistance movement in order to lay the groundwork for reintegrating Jews into French society as full-fledged citizens. In addition to the specific tasks to be accomplished, then, various formes of adaptation developed: some by mimetic influence, others by strategic choice.

Earning Our Rights as Free Citizens in the France of Tomorrow

Directly attacked by the Red Poster that had been disseminated throughout the country, the Communists responded with their own publicity campaign by using tracts that justified the struggle carried on by the Jews, presenting it as part of the combat of the French people fighting to liberate their country. "Why they fight, why they die," read one of the tracts put out by the Union of Jews for Resistance and Mutual Aid (UJRE) in March 1944:

> Yes, both French and immigrant Jews are fighting side by side with the French people in the struggle to liberate France. . . . Within the tremendous forces of the French Resistance, their numbers are considerable. . . . But they are doing their duty, their full duty. French Jews are serving just as are their fellow French citizens, while immigrant Jews are paying their debt of gratitude.

The tract absolved the French people of the crimes committed by "the Pétains and the Lavals who have transformed this land of freedom into a land of slavery" and who were thus the "detractors of the true France." It also described the plight of tens of thousands of deportees and observed that this "ridiculous anti-Jewish and xenophobic maneuver" had failed to accomplish its objective. The tract continued:

> The blood of Jewish fighters has been abundantly shed on French soil, and every day is mixed with generous blood of the finest sons of the French people. . . . Out of this community of sacrifice, out of this community of struggle by all the oppressed against the vicious oppressor of all peoples and all free men, tomorrow will emerge a country reborn, a country that will once again become a land of liberty that shines throughout the world, a country that will guarantee equal rights for all its children.[72]

The ties with a glorious era in the relations between the French people and the Jews were thus reaffirmed. Mindful of these bonds sealed by the blood shed together, the French people would restore full rights to the Jews once the usurpers had been driven out of power.

For those who might stray from Jewish organizations once the imposed segregation was ended, such arguments were used to emphasize the necessity of a specifically Jewish struggle. A new tone of voice was thus heard in the underground press: "The [UJRE's] struggle is a patriotic struggle," stated the organization's platform. "By the battle they are waging today, [the Jews of France] are acquiring the right to demand the France of tomorrow to give them their human and civil rights."[73] Just as the blood shed for their country by French Israelites in past wars had strengthened the alliance between France and its Israelite citizens, so their present participation in combat for the Resistance would solidify the foundations of a new alliance. This theme was henceforth always present in the Jewish Communist press. After the Allies had landed on the southern shores of France in mid-August, the UJRE struck up the same tune to call upon the Jews in Marseilles to rise up in large numbers and join in the battle for Liberation: "The sacred duty for each one of us is to take an active part in the struggle to kick the Nazi invaders out of France and to regain our rights as free citizens in the France of tomorrow and to be worthy of these rights."[74] To be worthy, indeed . . .

At the same time, there were increasingly insistent instructions to hide out:

> Jewish brothers, . . . abandon your legal residences and do not return there under any pretext. Be discreet in your illegal place of residence, and do not take anyone there if you do not know them well. Do not keep your papers stamped with the word "Jew" or with a foreign name. . . . Do not go to cafés, cinemas, or any other public places. . . . Do not speak Yiddish in public places or in the street.

Such was the advice of one of the UJRE's tracts distributed in Paris in January 1944.[75] "Jews of Lyon!" advised another tract put out one month later in the south of France:

> Be on your guard! Avoid assembling in public places. Leave your legal places of residence (the most recent roundups in Paris have once again shown us that the enemy makes no distinction between foreign and French Jews.) Put your children in a place where they are out of reach of the Gestapo's rage and hole up yourselves, too. Help each other out. Gather secretly around the Union of Jews for Resistance and Mutual Aid. Organize ways of helping the needy. Use all possible means to resist the extermination enterprise.[76]

These instructions were based on the specific fate dealt to Jews, especially in the most recent strategy of terror developed by the Gestapo and the Milice. The tracts continued their efforts to make the situation clear. "Several thousand German soldiers aided by Darnand's filthy rabble have invaded the départements of La Dordogne, La Corrèze, la Haute-Vienne, and L'Ain, and have established a regimen of desolation and crime," revealed one of the National Movement Against Racism's tracts dated April 1944. The same tract went on to describe the massacres of Jews isolated from the rest of the population in Brantôme, Château-L'Evêque, and elsewhere, and then issued the same call that had been sent out in all of the MNCR's publications since the summer of 1942 in various forms adapted to the situation of the moment: "Provide shelter for Jews and those refusing conscription into forced labor. Take in the Jewish children who have tragically been left to fend for themselves; stand in for the mother who has been deported, the father who has been sent before a firing squad. . . . Use every available means to oppose mass arrests!"[77]

The number of publications sponsored directly or under the table by Jewish Communists significantly increased during this time, and each was addressed to a specific audience: new titles such as *Le combat médical, Lumières, Clarté, Droit et liberté*, and *Résister* spoke to such groups as doctors, intellectuals, and students, while others were of a regional orientation (*Résister* was published by the UJRE in the département of Les Bouches-du-Rhône). And their distribution had become more efficient, if we are to judge by the number of editions intercepted by the Division of Postal Inspections.[78] In accordance with the strategy adopted by the National Front, this increased variety of underground newspapers was aimed at reaching all professional circles while at the same time diluting the pro-Communist bent of their publishers. Furthermore, their featured themes corresponded more closely to the day-to-day preoccupations shared by the entire Jewish population.

In addition to these efforts to strengthen their propaganda, Jewish Communist leaders intensified military action to an unprecedented level, complemented by surprise attacks on targets chosen to further political goals. Such was the case of the attack on the UGIF office in Marseilles in late 1943 and the UGIF office in Lyon on January 25, 1944.[79] In both instances, the destruction of the files kept on Jews was at the heart of the action: the personnel was not harmed, only neutralized for the time necessary to carry out the operation. The sums of money retrieved onsite were confiscated. Money found on employees, however, was returned to them. Employees also received a letter signed "The Resistance": it admonished them to maintain "the highest discretion about the operation that had been carried out in order not to incur the most severe sanctions against them and their families."[80]

The political meaning of these raids is clear: as a logical sequel to the attacks made by the underground newspapers, the raids were intended to take away any and all legitimacy from the UGIF. Those who carried them out doubtless thought that by destroying the files they were saving the lives of hundreds of Jews, and that if the Germans had decided to seize the files, they could have quite easily snatched the poor people receiving UGIF assistance. The Germans, however, were armed with the prefectorate's lists established from the census and benefited from the assistance of collaborationist informers: they had no interest in the UGIF's files.

Combat units from Lyon executed both a traitor who had handed Jews over to authorities as well as Carrel, the regional director of the General Commission on Jewish Affairs, in July 1944. Both of these executions were cases in which Jewish résistants carried out actions having become so common as to constitute the norm in relations between résistants and collaborationists. The Zionists had also been emboldened, doubtless encouraged by this prevailing atmosphere: in Nice they too carried out attacks on individuals who had turned in Jews to authorities.

From France to Eretz-Israel

The "Groupe-franc," an elite combat unit of the Jewish Army in Nice, had been constituted during the Italian occupation. A tough, highly determined nucleus of young men had emerged at the time when Brunner was on the rampage. This was after a large number of adults who had formerly handled assistance and rescue work had left, and after the "sixth" and the MJS group had been disbanded by bad luck and betrayal.[81] As was the case for the other groups of the Jewish Army that had been formed in Lyon, Toulouse, and Grenoble during 1943, a large part of their work was devoted to gathering information about informers and government employees who had proved particularly zealous in carrying out anti-Jewish measures.

The young men of the Jewish Army in Nice concentrated their efforts on a group of White Russians who had worked with Brunner's team of "physiognomists" and who had proved themselves particularly effective in identifying Jews. The Jewish Army unit began by blowing up the antique shop where the informers met. Then after one of the informers was wounded and another executed, the whole team was disbanded.[82] In Nice, such strikes against informers in general seem to have constituted one of the major activities of various resistance groups. For other operations, such as the execution of a woman informer and of the head of Vichy's Milice in Saint-Martin-de-Vésubie and an attack on a nightclub, the young men in the Jewish Army worked in conjunction with other groups of the local Resistance.[83]

The Jewish Army was a Zionist organization, and as such, entirely oriented toward the prospect of the emigration of Jews to *Eretz-Israel* (Palestine or the Land of Israel) where a Jewish state was to be created. On a tactical level, however, it remained essential to harmonize their action with the current political situation in France and to maintain their influence over the Jewish population, which was far from being won over to this notion of emigration. In June 1944, the Jewish Army changed itself into the Jewish Combat Organization (OJC), a name that corresponded more with the French political situation, made it possible to recruit a greater number of Jewish youth, and allowed it to claim its place among the various groups forming the Resistance.

At the same time, and in view of the long-term prospects, negotiations were conducted with a certain Charles Porel, whom the Jewish leaders believed to be a member of London's Intelligence Service. From England, which held the mandate over Palestine, they thus hoped to gain recognition as a National Jewish Group registered under the name of "Autonomous Jewish Legion" by the authority of the Interallied Command. They also hoped to obtain a status identical to that of the

Jewish Palestinian units and Palestinian citizenship "upon request, and as soon as they joined" for all "soldiers in this unit." "At the end of hostilities," stated point 7 of the projected agreement prepared by the leaders of the Jewish Combat Organization, "within six months, the Autonomous Jewish Legion shall be transported to Palestine by the British governement."[84]

The man claiming to be an agent of the British Intelligence Service was in fact an officer in the Abwehr, the intelligence service of the German army, whose real name was Karl Rehbein. Thinking they were going to leave for London, two members of the Jewish Combat Organization were arrested on July 17, 1944, in Paris, led first to Rue de la Pompe and then imprisoned at Fresnes. As a result of this incident, the Jewish Combat Organization's entire group in Paris was disbanded.[85] Brunner had the "dangerous terrorists" loaded into the last deportation train to leave Drancy on August 17, 1944. Almost the entire group managed to escape during the night of August 20 to August 21 in Morcourt, near Saint-Quentin. For still unexplained reasons, the only ones not to make it were a group of young Dutch Zionists who had helped fellow prisoners escape from the Westerbork camp in Holland and get into Spain: they had been working in close collaboration with the Jewish Army since the spring of 1943.[86]

The Jewish Army made other efforts that furthered the Zionist ideal while at the same time remaining in harmony with current political imperatives of the Resistance: they undertook the organization of a Jewish maquis and used their military authority and financial aid to back the maquis formed by the Scouts.

Jewish Maquis Groups

The constitution of Jewish maquis groups provides the most convincing illustration of the Jewish Resistance's twofold efforts intended not only to achieve specifically Jewish objectives but also to contribute to ending the Occupation and expediting France's Liberation. In the autumn of 1943, a time when Jewish organizations were deciding to go completely underground, the "maquis system" had developed in France, first as a refuge for a growing number of young men refusing to be conscripted into the Forced Labor Service (STO), then as a base for combat.[87] The fighters with the FTP-MOI groups also had a maquis system, consisting in many cases of bases providing refuge for those whose identity had been discovered. Carmagnole created its own bases in the Lyon area, Liberté had maquis in the mountains around Grenoble, and the 35th Brigade had maquis in the département of Le Tarn.[88]

The creation of a Jewish maquis had appeared to the Scouts an obvious necessity when Castor had decided that the rural worksites had to be closed down. While some were scattered out on the farms and in the maquis already existing in the region, a small group from Lautrec and Fretteserpes went to live at La Malquière, a farm located northeast of the town of Castres.[89] Along with another group from

Lautrec that moved to Lacado in the spring of 1944, they were to be the core group for the maquis of the Israelite Scouts of France. Then in May and June 1944, the group split up into three encampments, La Farasse, Laroque, and Lacado, totaling about sixty persons:[90] by virtue of the June 1, 1944, agreement, they were placed under the military authority of the Jewish Army. Financing was provided by the Jewish Army, and military training was handled by Jewish Army military instructors, and in particular Jacques Lazarus (called "Jacquel").[91]

These Israelite Scouts of France groups were then directly incorporated into the French Secret Army (AS) under the command of Pierre Dunoyer de Segonzac, the "old leader."[92] These maquis, which after the Allied Landing were to become the Marc Haguenau unit, engaged the Germans in a fire fight and lost three men during a parachute drop. They also took part in an attack on a German train in Mazamet and were among those who obtained the surrender of the town of Castres. "It was a Jewish second lieutenant just out of the Polytechnique military academy who led the charge, at the risk of being buried or swept away by the nearby explosion. It was a machine gun manned entirely by Jews that became embroiled in a terribly unequal duel with the German cannons. After the confrontation, when the guns had jammed, it was the Jewish patrols who went out every hour to remind the Germans that they had not been forgotten." So wrote Hubert Beuve-Méry in his account of the attack on the train in Mazamet, in which he also participated.[93]

For its part, the Jewish Army also set about to create a maquis in the fall of 1943, first at Le Roc (near Saint-Jean-du-Jeaune), then on the farm at Le Bic (twelve kilometers from Alban),[94] before finally going to Lacaune. "From the Jewish Army's standpoint, it is preferable to keep the youth together in order to be able to give them a special Zionist training," reported lieutenant RL (Raymond Levy-Seckel, called "Leblond") to his superiors in the Jewish Army in January 1944.[95] It was he who concerted his efforts with the Secret Army in the département of Le Tarn and took charge of this first unit. The location had been specifically chosen in order to protect the groups of adults, and later children, being led out of France into Spain: it was their last stop before they crossed the border.[96] Once it had moved farther south to Espinassier, the Jewish Army's maquis was incorporated into the special Black Mountain Fighting Unit (Le Corps-franc de la Montagne noire [CFMN]), in which it would make up the Fourth Levy-Seckel squadron, or Jewish Trumpeldor platoon.[97] The Black Mountain Fighting Unit was in direct contact with London: one of its leaders was a British officer (Commander Richardson) who distinguished himself by an independent mind-set that the local command structure of the FFI did not particularly appreciate.[98] Given the "Palestinian" perspectives of the Jewish Army leaders, this direct link with London—even though it was to a large degree fortuitous—was doubtless much to their liking.

Another Jewish maquis was put together in the département of La Haute-Loire by Joseph Bass: it, too, received subsequent military instruction from the Jewish Army. It was formed, however, according to a different logic. Bass had organized a rescue network in Le Chambon, and the leadership of what was later to become a maquis was put together from the small groups charged with protecting the social aid workers.[99] The self-defense groups that the Russian Jews had begun to organize after the Kishinev pogrom in 1903 served as a reference for Bass. Through the intermediary of Maurice Brener, who financed his activities, he contacted Lucien Lublin, one of the leaders of the Jewish Army. From this meeting was born the maquis at Le Chambon-sur-Lignon, which both Bass and Lublin claimed to have created after the Liberation.

There were never more than two or three hundred men in these Jewish maquis. They were involved in all the Liberation battles, and those who won them shared the common lot of all those in the maquis.[100] However, except for Joseph Bass, those who formed these groups were not only seeking to participate in the combat: the leaders were politically coherent groups that had come together in a common struggle against persecution. The maquis of the Jewish Army and the Israelite Scouts of France maintained a Jewish way of life as much as possible. In the Marc Haguenau unit, the Sabbath was scrupulously observed, although sometimes disturbed by a parachute drop or interrupted by a general alert: vigils with hymns and readings from the Bible alternated with military exercises. The Jewish Army maquis wore a blue- and-white badge and a Star of David on the shoulder of their uniforms, which surprised the local batallion head.[101] Reconciling the specific goals of the Jewish maquis with the general objectives of the Resistance was not something that occurred naturally. In the reports that have come down to us about the predominant mind-sets of the new members of the Jewish Army's maquis, we often find a desire for autonomy and regrets at seeing Jewish goals buried under one of the Secret Army's strategies.[102] We also find complaints about the weakness of the some individuals' ideology: these criticisms concerned young Jews who had joined it in a somewhat happenstance manner.

As far as the Jewish Army was concerned, the maquis was specifically intended to serve as a base to provide military training to young Jews heading for the Spanish border. As already pointed out, the location of the Jewish Army's maquis had been determined by the desire to create a stop along the route leading through the Pyrenees, into Spain, and on to Palestine. When, in October 1942, Spanish authorities became aware of the stream of Jewish refugees heading for the border between France and Spain, they were tempted to expel all those who crossed over into their territory. But until the end of the war, Britain and the United States kept pressuring them to allow those wanting to join the Allied forces to cross the border. This policy equally benefited Jewish refugees, who were thus not sent back to France.[103] However, that still did not prevent them from being interned for varying amounts of time at the Miranda de Ebreo camp: the authorities intended to make them leave Spain as soon as possible.

There were in all some fifty networks helping people secretly cross over the border from France into Spain.[104] While the Jewish Army was not the only group to seek out such escape routes, it was the only Jewish organization to undertake the task in spite of all the difficulties involved: the shores of Palestine awaited those who made it.

Given the region's harsh climate and rugged terrain, those who helped them make these border crossings—often mountain guides, smugglers, or shepherds—played an crucial role. Members of the Jewish Army turned to professionals. Crossing the Pyrenees was a very strenuous undertaking lasting several days, and only young people in good physical condition were able to endure the harsh conditions. And while the young men that the Jewish Army wanted to get over the mountains were those who would go on to fight with the Jewish units from Palestine incorporated into the Allied forces, the need to save Jews from being arrested and deported nevertheless forced them to include other categories of people along with the military recruits. Approaching the border held by the Germans (off-limits to anyone who did not have a special pass) posed yet another difficulty. The problem was resolved when the Jewish Army developed ties with a group of young Dutch Zionists who were seeking ways of getting members of their organization who escaped from the Westerbork camp across the border into Spain. They had become experts in making fake German papers, such as those that made it possible to pose as employees of the Todt construction sites.[105]

When Castor decided to disperse the people at the worksites, he also ordered youth with the Israelite Scouts of France to mobilize. He gave them three choices: they could join the Scouts' maquis or another resistance group, join the "sixth," or cross over the border into Spain and continue on to Palestine.[106] The decision to accelerate the closing of rural worksites increased the number of those choosing to leave for Palestine.

Between May and October 1943, the Jewish Army succeeded in getting forty-two men (including thirty from the Dutch group) across the border into Spain. Also among them were two Jewish Army envoys charged with discovering what was available for sustaining those who made it into Spain and for organizing the departures of groups headed for Palestine.[107] Then in October 1943, the Jewish Army created the Evacuation and Regrouping Unit (SER) under the leadership of Jacques Roïtman: its task was to oversee the entire operation of getting Jews out of France, through Spain, and into Palestine. After several unsuccessful attempts, the first group led by the SER made it to Spain on February 28, 1944. Others would follow. The entire operation was hampered when the system set up by the Dutch group was broken up following the April 1944 arrest of one of its members in Paris. In mid-May 1944, the Gestapo arrested Jacques Roïtman along with five others heading for Spain at the train station in Toulouse. Nevertheless, the SER reorganized its network and continued to work with the remaining members of the Dutch group : thanks to their joint efforts, some 225 adults (at the lowest count) finally were able to get across the Pyrenees and into Spain.[108] Some eyewitness accounts speak of five hundred such people (including eighty Dutch). The last ones left on August 26, 1944.[109]

Each one of them had to be taken to Toulouse, housed, fed, given gear for the hike in the mountains, and provided with identity papers that could withstand any and every verification. Whenever a trip was canceled at the last minute or a group had to turn back, the needs of the entire team had to be clandestinely met until it was once again possible to attempt a crossing. One can imagine all the efforts required just to get hold of a pair of sturdy walking shoes, not to mention the security problems.[110] All adults had taken an oath of fidelity to the Zionist organization and had pledged to join one of the Jewish combat units in Palestine. Out of the 313 (or 600?) adults and children that the Jewish Army sent over the Spanish border through the intermediary of the SER or SERE, 272 ultimately made it to Palestine: 18 boarded the *Nyassa* in February 1944 and 254 got on boarded the *Guinée* in October 1944.[111] A few more probably left during the weeks that followed. The others committed themselves to other causes or else, being sheltered from the dangers that stalked them, waited there in Spain for conditions that would allow them to return safely to France.

There was furthermore an agreement that had been signed on July 21, 1944, by Jules (Dika) Jeffroykin, representing the Jewish Army, and Eliahu Dobkin, representing the Jewish Agency in Spain: the document placed the Jewish Army under the authority of the worldwide Zionist Organization and the Jewish Agency.[112] Even though it had transformed itself into the Jewish Combat Organization (OJC) and had accordingly joined in the armed conflict in France, the Jewish Army was consistent in its ideological choices. Some 7,500 Jews reportedly managed to flee France by crossing over the Pyrenees into Spain: most of them either made it on their own or benefited from the assistance of the HICEM.[113] Among that number, the 313 (or even 600) with the Jewish Army constituted only a tiny minority. Nevertheless, the collective saga and the motives that drove them to undertake the crossing give them a special place in the wider movement.

In France, military preparations were the top priority. At the same time, however, it was often thanks only to subsidies provided mainly through underground channels that the Jewish population managed to survive. And so while such topics as the various maquis groups, the action of elite commandos, police roundups, and massacres dominated the news at the time (and also garners the most prominent place in historians' accounts), efforts to furnish aid in increasingly trying conditions continued. As obscure as it may have been, the support secretly provided to hundreds of Jewish families by members of the Federation in particular) allowed them to make it until the end of the war.

The final phase of the war and the Occupation demanded military action; the situation facing many Jews made it urgent to provide secret assistance, and certain Jewish organizations compelled them to engage in ideological struggles. It was only natural for all of these efforts to find their expression in political demands.

POLITICS RETURNS IN FULL FORCE

From 1944 on, the Jewish organizations all sought to return to Paris. This institutional return to the capital, however, was not the result of a new migration of the

Jewish population back to Paris. It instead foreshadowed their return and was another indication that the end of the war was drawing near. In order to set up the political structure for the post-Liberation period, it was imperative to be in Paris. That was where everything would ultimately be decided, and the Jews indeed streamed back into Paris as soon as the situation allowed it. The UJRE reestablished its organization in Paris in early 1944, and in compliance with the Communist Party's directives, began organizing patriotic militia groups as early as February 1944.[114] While helping Scouts in Paris go completely underground, Simon Lévitte did all he could to facilitate contacts between the various components of the Jewish community and create there in Paris the same unity that had been established in the Southern Zone. The Committee for the Union and Defense of the Jews (CUDJF) was established in January 1944.

In the spring of 1944, the Jewish Army sent some of its leaders to Paris, where it set up a dynamic group that operated in collaboration with the Dutch group, doing intelligence work for the most part, executing some who had turned Jews in to be arrested,[115] and putting together the Jewish Legion (later to go to Palestine).[116] It nevertheless collapsed over the course of the summer, after most of its militants had been set up by the German Abwehr agent and arrested.

In Paris as in the south, each one of the ideological components of Jewish umbrella organizations such as the CGD, the CUDJF, and the CRIF tried to strengthen its position by taking advantage of the organizations under its authority and seeking to get acceptance of its sway. Such was the case of the UJRE: even though the Communists held key positions with the General Defense Committee (CDG), the UJRE fought to be institutionally joined to the CGD, which would have placed the unifying (umbrella) organization under Communist control.[117] For its part, the Zionist Organization in France kept on insisting, for equally obvious reasons, that the CRIF should accept a delegate from the youth organization (the Jewish Youth Steering Committee, mostly made up of young Scouts and MJS Zionists).[118]

However, in addition to these internecine struggles, which were only to be expected, the main problem facing the united Jewish organizations at that time was still the UGIF. Ever since it had been established, the Committee for the Union and Defense of the Jews had tried—to no avail—to convince the UGIF to abolish itself. Similary, in the south, the newly constituted CRIF was looking for ways to close down the UGIF. The ones who were the most intent on doing away with the UGIF were the Communists, who had always fought against it, and Jewish immigrants linked to the Federation.

At the same time, however, immigrant Jews were well aware of the concrete ramifications of abolishing the UGIF. In the south, pratically all of the organizations under the UGIF umbrella had gone almost completely underground by the spring of 1944; this was due not only to their leaders' decision, but also to the Gestapo raids on a number of UGIF facilities. The only function still existing was that of providing aid to individuals. Even so, closing down a UGIF office could bring on unprecedented hardships. "You know that the meager subsidies provided to them are just barely enough to prevent them from dying of hunger, and you can easily imagine how distressed the recipients of such aid can be when the subsidies don't reach them on time," protested Rabbi Apeloig to the director-general of the UGIF on June 5, 1944, after the closing of the UGIF office in Châteauroux and the ensuing delay in the distribution of monthly assistance.[119]

The situation in Paris was quite different. There the UGIF continued to run soup kitchens and children's homes; it had also retained its responsibility for the Drancy camp. There were moreover some twenty thousand Jews going about in Paris prominently displaying their yellow star on their chests: they were a favorite target for the Germans, more than ever present on the scene. "Now more than ever before, it is urgent to close down Raoul home," [the UGIF] wrote one correspondent to Jarblum on July 11, 1944. However, "once this has been done, those closing it down will have to cope with the tremendous responsibility of having to feed nearly 5000 clients. Where then will they find the money?"[120] Regardless of its actual function, however, the continued existence of an institution that had been created by Vichy to serve the Germans was no longer politically viable. Endless discussions on this subject rocked the meetings of the new umbrella organizations, and no conclusion was to be reached before the Liberation. Throughout the second half of July and on into the first week of August 1944, the CRIF's special committee headed by Léon Meiss, held sessions aimed at elaborating a stance on the UGIF.[121]

Everyone attending these meetings agreed that a procedure for shutting down the UGIF had to be found, but there were several rival positions. The Communist delegate stigmatized the UGIF as a "shameful blemish on the Jews in France" and asked that it be immediately done away with once and for all. "Regardless of the honesty and goodwill of some of its leaders," the UGIF "had been placed in circumstances such" that it "was objectively collaborating with the Nazis." Jews in general disapproved of the UGIF, which had been a trap for many and which perpetuated a legalistic illusion that prevented Jews from going into hiding and joining the Resistance.

While the Federation's representative Ruben Grinberg was also in favor of doing away with the UGIF, he took a more moderate approach. Grinberg distinguished between the men that had taken charge of the UGIF and the organization itself: reasoning from both a moral and political perspective, and pointing out that the situation had evolved, he argued that the UGIF should be shut down immediately in the Southern Zone, but that there should be a procedure for its gradual elimination in the Northern Zone.

Raymond Geissmann, who was the director-general of the UGIF–Southern Zone, first responded to the Communist delegate's accusations. It was true that the UGIF had been created at the request of the Germans, but even though it operated under the official authorities, all of its work was aimed at responding to the needs of the Jewish population. Geissmann offered several examples to back up his assertion. First, he cited the development of underground activities that had been carried out behind this protective screen. Next he recalled that the aid programs in the Southern Zone were autonomous. He also pointed out that the Consistory had lent its support to the UGIF throughout the last twelve months and reminded those present that the number of Jews apprehended in UGIF facilities was nothing compared to those who had been arrested in the street, at home, in cafés, and elsewhere. Geissmann furthermore retiterated the efficacity of the lists put together by the French administrative offices. Finally, he defended the honor of those who had totally committed themselves to the UGIF's work and described the drawbacks—and especially the dangers—of a sudden liquidation of the organization. Geissmann said he would trust the Consistory to make the proper decisions, with which he pledged to comply.

For his part, Léon Meiss offered a less political, more practical approach. While advocating a gradual closing of the UGIF, a process that was moreover already well under way in the south, he was nevertheless fearful of what might happen to the 16,000 to 18,000 thousand recipients of UGIF aid if the organization were suddenly shut down. He was even more fearful of a possible retaliation against the UGIF–Northern Zone or against Jews in Paris. He therefore suggested that the UGIF be phased out gradually, as that would make it possible to compensate for any possible negative consequences. The roundups of children occurring on July 20 and July 25 struck a nerve in this debate, but it was ultimately the Liberation that imposed the decision.

Shortly after the Allied landing in Normandy, in a tract dated June 10, 1944, the UJRE called on all Jews to take part in the liberation of France: "So that we may enjoy freedom and dignity in a liberated France . . . let us prepare ourselves to fight.[122] The Jewish Army was also prepared to issue its own directives for the course of action to be followed once the Allies had landed. They too called on all Jews to mobilize, but they relieved any members who were French citizens of all obligations to the Jewish Army if they were to be incorporated into service under the overall Resistance military command that was to be established. In the meantime, however, they assigned specific tasks for their soldiers to carry out; now was the time to put to use all the various pieces of information so patiently gathered for months by the intelligence services. They were therefore to seize all documents connected with the administration of Jewish matters, arrest all individuals having participated in the persecution of Jews, place them "in the custody of those charged with maintaining order during the Liberation," and carry out sneak attacks against the concentration camps in view of freeing all detainees and bringing to justice all those who had zealously performed "their jobs in service of the enemy."[123]

The Communist groups were assigned to military action, and played a particularly important role in traditional strongholds such as Villeurbanne. The elite commandos of the OJC took over the offices of the General Commission on Jewish Affairs in a number of places including Lyon: in each case they seized any documents found onsite. The Communists often chose to occupy UGIF facilities. In Paris, what remained of the Jewish Army group that had been disbanded in mid-July returned to military action under the orders of Captain Charcot. Six groups of the UJRE's patriotic militia made up of some 200 men[124] took part in all the battles.[125]

On August 17, 1944, Brunner and the other Germans left Drancy on one last train carrying fifty-one deportees. The internees cried out "Take off your stars" in celebration of the Nazi commander's departure.[126] Police Commissioner Permilleux, head of the division of Jewish Affairs at the Paris police prefecture, came onsite to assess the situation, but did not seem to be in any hurry to release those interned.[127] The camp was nevertheless placed under the authority of the Swedish Consul, Raoul Nordling, who had been alerted about the situation by local résistants: Nordling entrusted the Red Cross with the task of releasing the detainees.[128]

Armed with a mission order issued by Colonel Rol Tanguy (called "Rol"), the Parisian group of the OJC came to Drancy.[129] Mademoiselle Monod, a social worker with the Red Cross since 1941 who had devoted herself to relieving the suffering of those interned in Drancy and the camps in the département of Le Loiret, had notified Edinger at the UGIF of the need to find some way to lodge a good portion of the 1386 people, including 64 children,[130] still remaining in "the Jews' camp." Each had to be given a small amount of money, identity papers, food ration cards, and release certificates. Those married to non-Jews left without worrying about all these formalities. The others received one thousand francs from the UGIF and the required papers from the municipality at Drancy. Six hundred of them were lodged by the UGIF. The entire operation was completed on Sunday, August 20. After the National Council of the Resistance had called for a general insurrection on August 19, the city hall in Paris and the mayor's offices in most of the arrondissements were taken over by the Resistance on August 20. The CUDJF—or rather the patriotic Jewish militia acting in its name—occupied the offices of the UGIF on the next day.[131] On August 23, 1944 Raymond Geissmann took it upon himself to decree the self-liquidation of the UGIF.[132] The UGIF North and South no longer existed.

On August 26, 1944, General de Gaulle led a triumphant procession down the Champs-Elysées, and on September 2, 1944, the Provisional Government of the French Republic assumed power over a liberated France. Vichy's days were over.

"We can bid adieu to the specter of deportation," wrote Jeanine Auscher when she had been set free from Drancy. With the yellow stars ripped off, Drancy shut down, and the threat of deportation removed, the most tangible signs of the specific fate suffered by the Jews throughout the last years of the Occupation disappeared. But these changes were not enough to eliminate all their problems, as Jews quickly realized when it came time to rebuild a normal life in a country that was still nursing its war wounds. The foreigners in the maquis were the first to be disillusioned: when they were to be incorporated into what had become the regular army, they were offered places in the Foreign Legion. The Marc Haguenau company's ranks quickly thinned out.[133]

"At the time of the Liberation," wrote Marc Jarblum on December 1, 1944,

> no-one thought about the problems that we were going to have to face right away. We were happy to have emerged from the nightmare, to be rid of the Germans and the SS, and to have been freed of the fear of being arrested and deported: we had forgotten just what our situation was. . . . For each one of us, our joy was first dampened by the thought of parents, children, companions, and friends who had died. . . . Reality once again prevailed. And [most] found themselves at the edge of an abyss. Everything had to be started over again from nothing. . . . The vast majority [of Jews] had lost everything: their possessions, the possibility of working, their stores, and their homes.[134]

There were indeed so many "parents, children, companions, and friends" among the eighty thousand Jews formerly living in France who were no longer alive: one-fourth of the prewar Jewish "community" had disappeared.[135] At the time, however, it was thought that the number of Jews who had fallen victim was as high as 120,000. It was during the spring of 1945 that the newspapers published lengthy accounts of the return of deportees and of the horrors suffered by those who would never come back. As we know, only 3 percent of the 75,721 Jews deported from France ever came back, as compared to 59 percent of the 63,085 résistants, hostages, political prisoners, or common criminals.[136] "They say that most of the Jews deported were exterminated," wrote Marie-Thérèse Gadala in her diary on April 25, 1945.[137] Indeed.

As a general rule, returning deportees would first come to stay at Le Lutétia, a hotel that had been used as the headquarters of the Abwehr during the Occupation. Although the place does not seem to have made much of an impression on those coming back from the camps—the return to French soil overshadowed all other references to a specific place[138]—it no doubt left an indelible impression on those who would crowd into the hotel every day in hopes of gathering the slightest piece of information, to post a photo, or to consult a list—all anxiously waiting for loved ones to return. For Jews, the wait was often in vain. From then on, the daily lives of many Jewish families were marked by the absence of loved ones who would never return, sometimes shrouded in a silence that would not be broken until many years later.

We must be aware of this terrible feeling of emptiness within each family before we can understand the problems faced by those who had survived and were trying to return to a normal life.

THE AFTERMATH OF THE LIBERATION

In denouncing (over the waves of the BBC) France's share of responsibility for the massacre of the Jews, André Gillois saw well to add: "Now I know quite well that there are other martyrs, and we certainly do not want to fall into the trap of racism by setting crimes against Jews apart from others. But the policemen, civil servants, and prison guards should know that in accepting to take part in the massacre of Jews, they have no more excuse than [they have] for lashing out against all other victims of Nazism."[139] What a strange way of expressing things, as if it were necessary to justify himself for focusing on the particularly deadly fate dealt to the Jews during the war. As if it were necessary to convince people that Jews were human beings like others and that a murder committed against them was still an act of murder.

At the Liberation, France emerged as a wounded nation. A million French prisoners of war were still detained in Germany, in addition to some 800,000 volunteers or conscripts for the Forced Labor Service. Allied bombing had destroyed or seriously damaged one and one-half million buildings; shortages of basic commodities and supplies were still routine; scenes of civil war haunted people's minds, and a purge was under way. An elite group of Resistance leaders assumed power and began the reconstruction of the country on a mythified vision of the Resistance. In the France of that time, Jews naturally returned to the place that was theirs. They took part in this glorification of the Resistance, thereby defending their reintegration into French society. Responding to pressure from the Communists, they even went so far as to try to carry out an internal purge by sending a questionnaire to the former UGIF employees. Nothing, however, came of this initiative.[140] Nor did anything ever come of the Jewish Communists' renewed demands for "the UGIF and its deleterious action" to be "publicly condemned."[141] But the tacit—and sometimes specifically stated—condition for being reintegrated into the national community was conforming to prevailing conditions and toning down any specific demands.

There Is No Longer Any Jewish Problem

Already in early June 1943, Maurice Martin du Gard cited the following declaration, supposedly made by Jean-Jacques Bernard upon being released from the camp at Compiègne: "Even so, we better not say anything about their outstanding debts to us!" Martin du Gard went on to add: "For their sake, one hopes that his fellow Jews will be as sensitive and intelligent as he is."[142] In October 1944, Gabriel Marcel went even further: in an article published in *Témoignage Chrétien*, he beseeched the Jews to display "discretion in their demands" after emerging from persecution.[143] The same thoughts are echoed by the disillusioned remarks of André Weill-Curiel, who had spent the war with General de Gaulle. Weill-Curiel offered the following advice "for one of his young Jewish friends": "Do not display your rights conspicuously, that would be an abuse; do not wear your war medals, that would be a provocation. . . . Act in such a way that the blueblooded French in France who hoped never to see you again forget that you exist."[144]

"We are emerging from four years of racism, do not engage in it yourself." Such was the argument presented to the leaders of Jewish organizations in their contacts with the French authorities: whenever they made an appeal, they were told that the French government did not recognize any distinctly Jewish problem.[145] When the Toulouse Press Committee planned to discontinue *Renaissance*, because "in speaking of the 'Jewish people' the newspaper was liable to arouse antisemitism," the director of the OJC's official publication had to explain that *Renaissance* supported both assimilation and Zionism.[146] And when the OJC sought certification as a resistance organization, its leaders stressed the fact that "at no time [had they] thought of creating a Jewish separatist movement; [they had been] compelled to create this Resistance group by the circumstances and the previous regime."[147]

Elsewhere, one government employee criticized the Jews for maintaining a "Jewish defense" organization now that the antisemitic laws no longer prevailed.[148] As if the new French government had magically done away with the aftermath of four years of persecution simply by declaring, as stipulated by article 3 of the law of August 9, 1944, that "all acts establishing or applying any discrimination whatsoever based on the fact that a person was a Jew" were null and void! "Be careful not to arouse antisemitism," seemed to be the most generously given advice offered to Jews immediately after the Liberation.

Moreover, while the purge had brought in a new set of political leaders, it had had a much lesser impact on the lower levels of government, within the bureaucracy.[149] In the daily life of Jews, there thus arose a discrepancy between an official discourse that restored their full rights and the application of a public policy that had to win the approval of large sectors of the population.

Now a good number of French people had taken advantage of the plundering of Jewish property occasioned by the antisemitic laws. Those plunderers who feared they would now suffer put themselves, under the pretext of defending their rights, at the forefront of a new antisemitic campaign that erupted in the fall of 1944, when a dozen associations defending the acquirers of Jewish property were created.[150]

The National Interprofessional Commerce Association of industry and handcrafts, for example, brought together thirty-two trade groups and published a tract that was unsettling, to say the least. "Irrespective of all controversy and any antisemitism," the association based its arguments on the legality of the sale of Jewish property, the modest economic status of the buyers, the perennial nature of French law, and on the illegality of retroactive laws. The association claimed that acquirers of Jewish property had acted in the national interest, as they had kept these goods (which constituted a valuable patrimony for the French economy) from disappearing, and that these sales had put into the state's coffers large amounts of back taxes from several years owed by Israelites. Along the way, the tract also recalled that "Israelites eagerly took part in the flight of capital" out of France, and added that the vast majority of working people dreaded the return of the Israelites who had exploited them. Moreover, contended the tract, these acquirers of Jewish possessions had contributed to the Resistance, for they had not gone to Germany with the Forced Labor Service. It was thus imperative to see that the purge was thoroughly carried out among Jews: they had after all been the first to collaborate, had they not? Finally, the tract argued that all victims of the war should be considered together, without singling out any one category: "Could one imagine asking the Allied armies to rebuild or return to their owners in one way or another the businesses destroyed as a result of necessary war operations?" asked the tract candidly.[151]

Other tracts of a similar nature appeared. The virulence of their language varied, but the theme common to all of them is illustrated by the following title: "No Special Victims." This tract, signed "A group of average electors," went on to state:

> "JEWISH COMPATRIOTS, who have returned to your place after four years of suffering you are overdoing it a bit, let us say so to you without animosity, for your own personal good as well as for the general good. . . . YOU MUST CONSIDER YOUSELF TO BE VICTIMS OF THE WAR and get it into your head that all victims of the war will not be compensated. It is extremely regrettable, but that's the way it is. . . . Do not leave yourself open to the criticism that you are seeking revenge on your compatriots for what the Germans did to you! ACCEPT WHAT IS IRREPARABLE JUST AS FRANCE'S OTHER SONS ACCEPT THE DAMAGE CAUSED BY THE WAR. There must not be any category of SPECIAL VICTIMS; you would stir up a wind of antisemitism that is perhaps already rising."[152]

Such was the advice so kindly offered to the Jews for their own good. However, another tract titled "The Other Peril" made no claims to such generosity and did not hesitate to ask: "Are you trying to put out in the street our poor war victims who are occupying residential facilities that had been so bravely deserted by Jewish tenants during the Occupation?" The tract concluded: "No! The French people do not have to decide whether they want to suffer from either Hitler's plague or the Jews' cholera. In order for France to be free, happy, and prosperous, there must be not one single Kraut, traitor, or Jew on its soil."[153]

A new uprising of antisemitism occurred in the spring of 1945, and anti-Jewish demonstrations disturbed the peace and quite of the Third, Fourth, Eleventh, and Twentieth arrondissements in Paris.[154]

How can we assess the true extent of such grassroots antisemitism? It was doubtless the expression of a minority within French society and was not echoed by the government. At no time did it threaten the status of Jews in France. But after these years of persecution, it represented a painful experience for the Jews; it revived sinister memories of a past that had been pushed to the back of their minds. Moreover, it unquestionably weighed on the process of concretely restoring full rights to Jews, a process that the Jewish organizations had nevertheless approached with considerable precaution. In one of the first texts to examine measures to be taken, the Jewish Defense Committee (Comité de défense des Juifs) displayed moderation in the requests it made to public authorities:

> After so many massacres, so many ruins, one cannot hope for or even imagine any true reparation for such suffering and such dire human misery. Countless Jews will never come back! Countless others will wind up in utter destitution upon their return: their apartments have been emptied, their furniture and their wardrobes have disappeared, their stores and businesses have been liquidated, and their buildings have been sold. What reparation can be granted to them? The Defense Committee understands that the problem is first and foremost of a political nature. The question is to determine what can be done for the Jews without

> jeopardizing peace and order, without bringing about too serious economic problems, and without putting public finance in difficulty.[155]

And without arousing a wave of antisemitism either, the text implies.

While they were often quite firm in stating their demands, Jewish leaders often found themselves on the defensive: it was as if they were obliged to provide justification whenever they made an appeal in favor of the Jews. On that score, a long letter sent by the UJRE to the secretary-general of the MLN in December 1944 is emblematic:

> We think that it would be wrong to try to remedy the situation facing the Jews at present by saying that there is no Jewish problem." Unfortunately, the facts of the matter refute this assertion, and those who think that the Jewish question only existed because of the presence of the enemy on our territory are mistaken, for there are specific problems concerning the Jews. Remaining silent about the subject can only serve the cause of the racists and antisemites who for four years were allowed to poison public opinion with a carefully orchestrated propaganda campaign, supported by the most powerful resources.[156]

Jews retrieved their possessions in a manner that was irregular and incomplete, to say the least. In the provinces, thanks to the work of the local Unity Committees and to their relations with the new regional authorities, certain situations were corrected right away; this was during the period of transition when everthing was possible. On a national level, however, it was not until November 14, 1944, that two ordinances were issued, ordering that property held by provisional managers should be returned to its Jewish owners and that Jews be admitted back into the places of lodging from which they had been driven out. The law was nevertheless very restrictive in its application: war victims, evacuees, and refugees could not be expelled, nor could their wives, their parents, their descendants, wards of the state who had been mobilized, prisoners of war, or those who had been deported as political prisoners or conscripts into the Forced Labor Service. In addition, persons filing a request had to provide proof that they had been evicted from their apartment without their consent.[157]

One can easily imagine that in these circumstances, the process allowing Jews to return to their former residences was long and only partially effective. But that did not keep the Confederated Union of Tenants in France from appealing to government authorities in August 1945 in order to limit the application of this ordinance, "at the risk of otherwise strengthening the current of antisemitism that already existed in France."[158] The ultimate argument . . .

The ordinances of November 14, 1944 provided for the restitution of property that had been placed under aryan provisional management. The catch, however, was that the law applied to property that had not yet been subsequently sold. As for the property that had been sold or liquidated, however, the problem was not even addressed before spring 1945. The situation was such that as of 1951 only half of the Jews from Paris had recovered their property.[159] And that was only one of the difficulties of returning to a normal life.

A Return to Normal Life?

During the final months of the Occupation, there were between fifty and sixty thousand recorded Jews officially living in France. Two-thirds of the Jewish community were thus concealed in more a or less completely underground existence. The first concern of those who had escaped arrest and deportation was to resurface. They had to get their identity back, obtain food ration cards, try to get information about the plight of those deported, retrieve their children, and receive a bit of money in order to make ends meet. For all these needs, Jews turned to the Jewish organizations that had sprouted from the Resistance. In Toulouse, for example, once the local Jewish Committee had been recognized, a letter written on its stationery could be used to gain entry to the prefectorate and made it possible for Jews to put their administrative situation in order.[160]

But Jews urgently wanted to return to their households as soon as possible; for most, that meant returning to Paris. The Jewish organizations that had not preceded this return hurried to follow their constituency, sometimes after having tried in vain to provide some order or slow down the new migration. In September 1944, the Jewish Communists' youth organization, the Union of Jewish Youth (UJJ) asked its activists to hold back the leaders of its various provincial sections as long as necessary.[161] Soon, however, their role would be confined to providing for the daily needs of Jews who were only waiting for their chance to return to Paris.

Nevertheless, both in Paris as well as in the provincial cities where Jews were still seeking refuge, their situation everywhere was one of dire poverty and tremendous hardship. From thirty to thirty-five thousand Jews depended directly on the aid supplied by the Jewish charitable programs. After the UGIF had been shut down, the Unity Committees had to assume the responsibility for all these people, without always having the financial means to do so. On October 18, 1944, the General Defense Committee pointed out that the number of those receiving aid had risen threefold since the Liberation: "Most of the Jews that had hidden out in the country and in small villages, and who, for their own personal safety, had not dared give any notification of their whereabouts are now pouring in to the big cities and flooding our Relief Committees with requests," explained Ruven Grinberg.[162] A month later, the number had risen another 10 percent.[163] Between fifteen and sixteen thousand of them were in Paris, where they also had to solve the problem of housing. Those who were lucky enough to get their apartment back in most cases found all their furniture gone. Craftsmen found their tools gone; funds needed to begin a new business were lacking; other people now occupied Jews' shops and jobs: a thousand things stood in the way of resuming regular work. In early May 1945, a group of Jewish storeowners tried to physically drive out the French people who had taken over their booths at Le Carreau du Temple: this was seemingly an isolated incident.[164]

Jews could sometimes find a bit of aid from the Resistance Organizations' Committee for Social Aid (COSOR), but such aid was not provided on a regular basis and foreign Jews seldom received any.[165] In the end, the Joint continued, as during the Occupation, to fund all of this aid, which for the most part was soon distributed by a new umbrella organization, the COJASOR, created in March 1945 as the social branch of the CRIF.[166]

For families, returning to normal life also meant retrieving the children that had been scattered and hidden in family homes or religious institutions. For their part, organizations did all they could to take in the children whose parents had not come back from deportation.

Retrieving the Children

In the first two months following the Liberation, the OSE managed to return about one thousand of the Jewish children that it had hidden during the war to their parents.[167] But the situations for the families were not always so clear. There were families that had been decimated, with only one parent still alive. There were others that could not afford to take their children back right away. Some adoptive families had become attached to the children for whom they had assumed responsibility. The most critical situation of all was that presented by the children whose parents had been deported. As of mid-December 1944, the OSE estimated their number at 2,500. Of these, 540 were in children's homes, 310 in various institutions, and the rest in adoptive families.[168] The best solution for taking care of these children was thought to be the extension of the network of children's homes, but that would take time. As of January 1, 1945, there were some one thousand children in the OSE's homes, and twenty-seven of the OSE's social workers continued to monitor children placed with families. It was planned to transfer all these Jewish children into a collective setting by the spring of 1945.

In addition to the OSE's efforts, there were some 700 Jewish children in the care of the SERE, 200 adolescents with the Israelite Scouts of France, 600 children with the School Colony (Rue Amelot), 400 others with the UJRE, and about 60 with the Bund.[169] Some of these were in children's homes while others were spread out among individual families.

All of these organizations agreed that they should be the ones to have custody of the Jewish children whose parents had not returned from deportation, and were unanimous in protest when voices from various quarters insisted that, until they reached the age of legal majority, such children should be left with the Christian families and organizations that had taken them in during the Occupation.[170] Taking custody of these children was no simple matter. They first had to be located, then taken out of religious institutions that were not very eager to provide information. When in November 1945 one social worker with the School Colony conducted her investigation in Le Petit-Bourg, where Jewish children had been reported to be in one of the town's convents, she ran into a stone wall of silence in every quarter. Sometimes, she explained that she was searching for these children on behalf of their parents. In other instances, she invoked the ordinance of April 20, 1945, which stipulated that, be they of French or foreign nationality, the children of those deported for political or racial motives were to become wards of the state, and that, in such cases, a family council should be appointed for them. Once she was onsite, however, she realized the considerable risks that had been taken by those who had helped save Jewish children in a region where the Germans had been particularly brutal, and so concluded "that it [was] impossible to pursue the matter."[171]

This was just one example, among many others, of the silent struggle that had begun immediately after the Liberation, and which pitted Jewish organizations against certain institutions or families that had become attached to the children they had sheltered.[172] The most dramatic was the case, in the early 1950s, of the Finaly children, baptized by the guardian to whom they had been entrusted and who refused to let them go join their aunt in Israel.[173] All Jewish charitable programs that looked after children set up special task forces to track them down and work with public authorities to settle matters concerning their future.[174] Even now, however, it would be impossible to provide a statistical assessment of those whose provisional place of refuge had become their permanent home.

This unanimity among Jewish organizations quickly vanished when the issue of the children's future was taken up. The Organization for the Protection of Jewish Children (OPEJ) was created in June 1945: as the descendant of the SERE, it was a Zionist organization that wished to see the children emigrate to Palestine. It had been encouraged by the Jewish Agency's Palestinian envoys who, as soon as they arrived in France, had created a commission in charge of children.[175] Such was certainly not the goal pursued by the OSE, which, in its own children's homes, opted either for a liberal manner of raising the children or for strict religious observance, depending on the particular case. Nor was it the objective of the UJRE, which in April 1945 created its own children's homes and entrusted them to a new Central Committee for Children.[176] The UJRE's homes raised children according to secular, progressive (Communist, in the terminology of that time) values, combined with the teaching of Yiddish and non-religious Jewish culture. These methods were inspired by the theories of Anton Semenovitch Makarenko, the Russian pedagogue who insisted that children and adults should share responsibilities.

It was only to be expected that these divergences of an ideological nature should also be reflected in the political formations of a Jewish community under reconstruction.

Building a Community

The leadership of the Jewish community had been decimated. Nineteen out of the sixty rabbis in office before the war had been either deported or sent before a firing squad.

Several prominent figures of the prewar Jewish world, including Jacques Helbronner, Raymond-Raoul Lambert, Nahum Hermann, and Léonce Bernheim, among many others, were now dead. The ranks of the younger generation who had played such an active role in the Jewish Resistance had also been considerably diminished.

Nevertheless, it soon became necessary to reorganize in order to take care of the entire set of problems facing the Jewish population. The CRIF, now joined by the Universal Israelite Alliance, represented the new, innovative force in the construction of an organized community. René Cassin presided over the AIU: from the outset, it had been agreed that the Consistory's delegate would be president and that the various institutions representing French Jews would have one more delegate than would the organizations representing immigrant Jews.[177] The CRIF was a concrete sign of the institutional rapprochement between the various components of Jewry in France; its creation and daily operations had been possible because the links between French and immigrant Jews had over the course of the war developed into a real will to work together. Both groups had been hit hard by an antisemitism officially endorsed by Vichy, even though immigrant Jews had been more intensely targeted. In spite of all the differences that continued to separate them, the leaders of the various Jewish organizations had come together in the fight against persecution. Those at the head of the Consistory found it unimaginable to ignore the immigrant Jews' organizations. And it was clear to the leaders of the immigrant Jews that their integration into French society depended on their ties with French Jewry. In most of the tasks related to reconstruction, Jews were thus in a position to present a united front before French authorities.

Within this umbrella organization, however, the Jewish community in France remained pluralistic in its ideological options. Zionists, bundists, Communists, and "Consistoralists" continued energetically to jockey for position and defend their own conception of the future of Jewry and Judaism. Within the Jewish circles' own political struggles, one can at the same time identify the major features marking French political developments in general, including the rivalry between traditional organizations and those having sprung out of the Resistance, the splitting up into factions of movements that had been unified during the war, and so on.[178]

There were a considerable number of Jews who, in order to facilitate their reintegration into French society or to put the nightmare of the Occupation years out of their mind, chose simply to seek refuge in the anonymity of assimilation. "French Jewry has changed," wrote Joseph Fisher on October 13, 1944. "The issue dividing us is no longer that of Palestine, but the tragic question of whether or not to remain Jewish." Assimilation, he added, was not an issue that concerned only those born into French families.[179] Many Jews were changing their names at the time, a practice denounced by Jewish newspapers.[180] There were also a good number of Jews who chose to keep their underground name. We can appreciate the extent of this phenomenon when we observe that 85 percent of the name changes occurring between 1803 and 1957 took place after the year 1945.

The Central Consistory was worried about this trend. "Nothing stands in the way of such a procedure from a religious point of view," observes one report taking position on the subject. It was perfectly understandable "that certain persons whose names are difficult to pronounce for native speakers of French individually request to change or to gallicize their names," just as it was entirely legitimate for "résistants, members of the maquis, who are justly proud of the names they bore in those critical years and heroic times to want to keep them and hand them down to their children." The problem, however, was that these name changes were in fact symptoms of a desire to abandon Judaism or even to convert to Christianity.[181] Along with an increase in conversions (difficult to assess statistically) and a decline in the observance of Jewish rituals (recorded by the Central Consistory), the name changes were one sign among others that many Jews wanted to do away with all ties to their roots, which had caused them so much suffering.

Others, however, chose to rally around "the glorification of a mythified resistance"[182] that constituted not only a unifying force within the Jewish political world but also a path to integration into French society. Certainly, the French Revolution was still the ultimate reference for all components of the Jewish community in France. In the 1920s and 1930s, the Jews' participation in World War I had been the most concrete expression of the value attached to defending the French institutions born of the Revolution.[183] A large number of immigrant Jews, however, had come to France after World War I, and in 1945, the France of human rights was embodied by a more familiar saga in which all had taken part: the epic of the Resistance. Just as in the past, the Jews' participation in France's major wars[184] had been carefully recorded, so in the immediate postwar era there was a proliferation of works devoted to Jews in the Resistance. The Jewish press, including such Zionist newspapers as *Renaissance*, *Quand même*, and *La Terre retrouvée* featured the widest variety of personal testimonies that, implicitly or explicitly, stressed the contribution made by all forms of Jewish Resistance to the French Resistance.

Jews who had fought in one of the Resistance movements either in mainland France or in London could close the "parenthesis"[185] that Vichy represented and return to the traditional notions of emancipation following an individual path. When David Diamant's book *Les Héros juifs de la Résistance française* was published, the Union of Jews for Resistance and Mutual Aid gave a reception and put out a brochure.[186] "This moving book is a testimony to the major role played by French citizens of Israelite origins in the grand national epic that was also simply a human and particularly antiracist story,"[187] wrote André Tollet, who had been the president of the Paris Liberation Committee. He added: "Their blood has once and for all consummated the complete integration into the French nation of thousands and thousands of immigrants who up until then had been denied all rights."

Be they French or foreign Jews, Communist or non-Communist, their attachment to France had remained intact: the "heroic attitude of the French people" had made this possible. The fact that Jews in general rallied around this mainstream discourse provided the concrete sign of their attachment to France, although there were several variations on the main theme. For French Jews, it was essential to reaffirm their ties to the past. For others, it was a matter of integrating into French society. For Zionists, it was this very reference to the Resistance that would make it possible for them to win over French public opinion to the cause of the Jews in Palestine.

In late August 1945, *La Terre Retrouvée*, which had become the official voice of the Zionist Organization in France, provided the following assessment of the year that had gone by since the Liberation of Paris:

> One year ago, when General de Gaulle entered the city hall of Paris and church bells rang loudly, for an instant the City of Lights became its old self again, as Paris and all of France hailed the dawn of a new era, an era of resurrection, victory, and liberty. For us, this liberation of Paris in which so many young Jews had taken part marked the end of our misery, the end of daily fears, the end of separations and deportations. It marked—or was supposed to mark—the beginning of moral and material restitution: the restitution of our freedom, of our rights, and of our duties as well. It was supposed to mark our total reintegration into the mainstream of French society.
>
> Should we go ahead and take stock of the situation as it is now? Should we recall all of our unabated suffering, all of our returned deportees who are now homeless, our storeowners deprived of their shops, our unemployed workers? Should we recall all of the decrees that have not been applied, all of the court decisions that have failed to render justice, all the unending delays? Alas! Should we recall that some wretches have again had the audacity to engage in antisemitic demonstrations, without fearing to perpetuate the most abject demonstrations of the Nazi doctrine in a France that has been liberated and renovated?
>
> On this glorious anniversary, however, there must be nothing but joy everywhere. Let us forget our bitterness and rancor and tremble joyfully with France—and let us above all trust the nation that was the first to have the audacity to shake off the abject yoke of oppression and to show its desire to live a free and noble life.[188]

In the same edition, Henri Hertz published the text that he had submitted to the prosecutor Mornet on behalf of all Jews in France in order that the Jews might be represented at Pétain's trial, as no Jew had been called as a witness.[189] "It must be hoped," wrote Hertz, "that this trial, one of the most important in France's purge, will lift the veil of the secrecy which, since the Liberation, has surrounded the Jewish problem that was once again posed in 1940 and then for five years elaborated upon by crime and defamation, and then enclosed in silence." Henri Hertz demanded a place for the Jews in Pétain's indictment. He concluded,

> We Jews in France find that virtually all of our families have been wounded, that our friends and relatives are suffering from this loss of loved ones whose names were besmirched before they were snatched away from us. In addition to the grief over their deaths, we shall forever carry in us the even greater grief over the degradation they suffered and the bitterness of not ever having the possibility of doing anything to console and heal their suffering. We shall testify that by remaining silent when he could have spoken, by doing nothing when he could have made a gesture, by lying when he now says that he did not know, he accepted and sponsored

> these unusual tortures, which were only the inevitable result of the set of special laws that he knowingly and deliberately elaborated and coordinated for five years.[190]

The two texts that we have just cited summarize the relations between the Jews and France one year after the Liberation. Henri Hertz asked the French people to take the Jews' memory into consideration and stressed the responsibility of Marshal Pétain—and thus that of the Vichy regime in general—for the persecution of the Jews. The editors of *La Terre Retrouvée* pointed out the active participation of Jews in the Resistance and cleared the French people from guilt, but nevertheless dwelled on the Jews' disillusion over their incomplete reintegration into French society, a problem that weighed heavily on their day-to-day lives. Echoes of what was already history, what constituted the hardships, what was left unspoken, and finally, what constituted the bases of memory then in its embryonic stage can be heard throughout the pages of this Zionist newspaper.

Conclusion

It was no accident that the cornerstone for the historiography of the Jews in France during World War II was laid by the Centre de Documentation Juive Contemporaine. The center was secretly established under the Occupation, and when the Shoah became a central point of reference in the memory of the Western World in general and France in particular, it became, for the Jews in France the principal depository for the memory of the genocide, as well as the principal forum for the expression of this memory. This conjunction attests to the inextricable relationship between history and memory for anyone who ventures into this period of the history of France and/or of the Jews.

TWO DIFFERENT FRANCES?

Because these studies touch on issues so vital to both French and Jewish identity—and to the relation between the two—it is hardly surprising that the historiography of the Jews in France begins with the concerns of the postwar era: the reconstruction of France around the consensus of Resistance and the reinsertion of the Jews into French society. In the pioneer works published as early as 1945 by the Centre de Documentation Juive Contemporaine, Vichy was thus represented as a servile regime that had caved in to the victor's pressures.[1] The people of France and Italy were thus celebrated for having managed, in face of Nazi barbarity, "to resist antisemitism in spite of the leaders of the time and their corrupt means of government."[2] The existence of two distinct Frances was posited from the very outset: the France of Vichy was set apart from

> the France of democracy, the France of the Republic, the France of generosity, and the France of the Resistance [. . . the France that had] preserved the honor of the country and [to which . . .] the crimes of collaboration could in no way and at no time ever be attributed.[3]

This dichotomy was the scholarly side of the general tendency of the Jewish public to rally around the mainstream discourse which, by performing a twofold marginalization of Vichy (seen as an anomaly in French history, divorced from the majority of the population) and by clearing French society in general of responsibility for the egregious offenses committed by the state, made it possible to preserve the paradigm of emancipation.

Thus influenced by the prevailing mood of the time, but highly documented, these studies nevertheless remained confined to the limited audience that had taken out subscriptions. At the same time, the general historiography of the era either ignored the antisemitic side of Vichy or else drowned it under an entire series of repressive measures and thus wiped out all specificity of the question.

The 1970s saw not only the shocks of memory transmitted through the media[4] but also the arrival on the scene of historians from the other side of the Atlantic who shattered this reassuring representation of Vichy France.[5] The Paxtonian revolution, fleshed out and completed by Michael Marrus and Robert Paxton's *Vichy France and the Jews,* brought about a total revision of the ends and means of the French regime's antisemitic policies during the Occupation. Thanks to these works, the French origin and the autonomous nature of Vichy's earliest anti-Jewish laws promulgated independently of any German pressures were now firmly established. The laws fit not only into a pattern of exclusion that was part and parcel of the "National Revolution," but also into the context of an overall policy of a collaboration desired by Vichy, and finally, in the continuity of an antisemitism rooted in French society. Marrus and Paxton showed that French and German collaboration in the persecution of the Jews was particularly extensive: the massive roundups of 1942 and the deportations appeared as the sequel to a series of measures that, in the eyes of leaders, served the national interest.

There was thus a clear answer to one of the primary questions: How were 25 percent of the Jews in France deported and exterminated? The stain that now marred the French political regime of this time of war and Occupation seemingly spread out over French society in general. But once the responsibility of the French government, the Germans' accomplice, had been well established, substantiated by archives, and integrated into a consensus among historians, it was possible for another question to surface: How had 75 percent of the Jews in France been saved? To find the answer, we must refer back to the pace of arrests and deportations as fixed by the Germans according to the means they decided to deploy.[6] The liberation of French territory interrupted the extermination process: if it had occurred a few months later, the results would have been different.

Later, others changed the question and in its place posed one that is seemingly quite similar but, due to its particular formulation, leads to a very different type of answer. *Who* saved 75 percent of the Jews in France? asked these historians. Two answers then prevailed. Lucien Lazare explained that the organizations of the Jewish Resistance took charge of the rescue of the Jews in France.[7] For his part, Serge Klarsfeld[8]—later seconded by Asher Cohen[9]—argued that it was the French people, in diametric opposition to Vichy, that saved 75 percent of the Jews in France.

There is no lack of evidence to support each one of these three theses. On the eve of the Liberation, there were more than twenty thousand Jews legally residing in Paris with the yellow star firmly attached to their chest. All the Germans had to do to snatch them up was to make the decision and provide the technical means: had they done so, the question would have been formulated quite differently, as clearly demonstrated by the increase in the number of deportations in the first few months of 1944. Certainly, no one could deny that the Jewish Resistance organizations helped thousands of Jews obtain false identity papers, concealed thousands of children, and that it was thanks to them that hundreds of adults and children managed to cross the border and reach more clement environments. And no one can doubt that this work could not have been accomplished without the active assistance of a good part of the French population: there are thousands of individual accounts testifying to various forms of assistance and complicity, or at least silence instead of denunciation. But to give precedence to any one of these factors is to ignore equally decisive elements that could be used to support the opposing thesis: for example, Brunner's relentless determination (which actually "paid off" less than he had hoped), or the delay of most Jewish organizations in coming to grips with the situation, or the undeniable antisemitism of a good part of the French population. One faces the eternal debate: is the glass half-empty or half-full.

Such responses ultimately lead to a twofold problem: the relations between Jews and French society, and the question of the Jewish Resistance, a subject which in turn leads us back to life within the Jewish world and thus raises still other issues. Every study of the Jewish organizations and their leaders' response to persecution inevitably raises explicitly or implicitly the question of heroism, passivity, and the real contribution to the rescue of the Jews made by one group or another of the Jewish Resistance. Each of these possible interpretations becomes a weapon used in the internal struggles of the community.[10]

From whichever perspective the analysis is conducted, any study of the Jews in France during World War II always centers on the number of victims, which provides a basis for determining the various responsibilities. Another number stems from comparing France with other countries: France has one of the lowest percentages of victims in Western Europe, which overall lost an average of 40 percent of its Jews to the process of extermination (75 percent in the Netherlands, 40 percent in Belgium, 16 percent in Italy, and 25 percent in France). (The figures for Central and Eastern Europe are of course much higher.) Yet another approach raises the towering question of the Jews' response first to the persecutions, then to the manhunts.

Conducted "from the bottom up," the study of life for the Jews in France, can, I think, shed light on these questions, without necessarily providing ultimate answers. While the Vichy government decided on matters of policy and promulgated its laws accordingly, it was French society—in other words both administrative offices and public opinion—that determined the application of these measures. It was thus French society that translated policy into the concrete reality experienced by the

Jews. We now have an approach to public opinion that goes beyond the sole question of French antisemitism. Placing the emphasis on the Jewish population—its needs, its reactions, and its processes of anticipation—makes it moreover possible to detect the pressures exerted from below on Jewish organizations as they elaborated their strategies.

FROM THE STATE TO SOCIETY

Viewed from this perspective, however, Vichy is not seen through the mechanisms of its general political strategy or specific antisemitic policies, nor through its relations with the Germans. I have chosen instead to avail myself of the historical framework already laid out by Michael Marrus and Robert Paxton. In observing the day-to-day application of Vichy's antisemitic laws, we can grasp a certain number of features, first of all the complexity of these measures. The *Handbook for Mayors and Gendarmerie Brigades On the Laws Concerning the Jews,* which provides a most concise summary of the rules with which Jews had to comply, contained no fewer than eleven pages. And, as clearly demonstrated by the Consistory's reports, one of the major concerns of the Jews was simply finding their way through the maze of restrictions that had been placed over them. One can also see how the various exclusionary mechanisms actually worked: the corps of government employees was entirely "cleansed" of its Jews and most Jewish storeowners were plundered. Although there were a few glitches here and there, they were all in all negligible: the administrative machine lived up to its reputation. The censuses—especially those ordered by the Germans and carried out by the French in the Occupied Zone—appear as a dynamic, uninterrupted process beginning in the autumn of 1940 and continuing through the first few months of 1944; they were designed for monitoring the Jews and keeping files on them.

This process was also characterized by an escalation of bureaucratic control in other areas. It was much harder to escape from this bureaucracy than from highly focused police operations; when people chose to go underground, they literally had to extricate themselves from an entire chain of control. We are taken aback by the determination of this administrative manhunt pursued in conjunction with the police's efforts to track down the Jews—and that Laval's government even tried to reinvigorate in the spring of 1944. The arrests and deportations did not take the place of the exclusionary policies, but were simply laid on top of them. The former set of policies did not just lead to the latter: the policies of exclusion and persecution continued to constitute an active basis for arrests and deportations.

While in the Southern Zone the exclusionary policies were one of the Jews' primary concerns, these measures were superseded by German ordinances in the Northern Zone. However, Jews in the Northern Zone were also directly affected by Vichy's policies. In June 1941, they had to declare all their possessions at the prefectorate, and

French authorities recognized as Jews categories of people who had been exempted from such status by the Germans. Even as late as January 1943, Jews in Paris who had gone to have their food ration cards stamped in order to comply with the new French law wound up at Drancy. The high level political will to apply thorough, consistent antisemitic policies everywhere never slackened at any time nor in any place, even when such polices contributed to the support of German measures of which the French did not necessarily approve.

In the specific application of the rules and laws that governed the life of the Jews, as well as in the arrest orders that followed, we observe attitudes that vary from one département to another. In one place we find a relatively easygoing prefect, elsewhere we find a zealous inspector with the Police for Jewish Affairs or from the Division of Inspections and Verifications, and still elsewhere gendarmes more or less conscientious in carrying out their task. Practices also varied greatly from one region to another: the search for Jews trying to dodge the census requirement, the issuing of a permit to circulate, the attitude toward refugees and the government benefits to which they were legally entitled, the requisitions for the Forced Labor Service, the application of expulsions that had been decreed (and sometimes a decision to expel that had been initiated locally), and the degree of cooperation of the General Commission on Jewish Affairs with the Police for Jewish Affairs, and then with the Division of Inspections and Verifications.

But while there was sometimes some flexibility, it was always of local origin: it was never encouraged by ministerial memoranda, which always pleaded for a more rigorous application of rules and regulations. This rigor of application changed over time: there was the period of "chaos" in the aftermath of the defeat as well as the deterioration that in some places marked the final phase of the Occupation beginning in autumn 1943. There was all in all an entire range of administrative behaviors that account for certain spontaneous movements of the Jewish population.

The difference in Vichy's treatment of French and foreign Jews, the role of Vichy policy in the various stages of the deportation of Jews from France, the nature and limits of the relative protection granted to French Jews by Vichy are all questions that have been analyzed first by Marrus and Paxton, then by Serge Klarsfeld. On that score, the figures for the extermination speak volumes: approximately 24,500 French Jews (one-third of them were children born of foreign parents and another third naturalized French citizens),[11] as opposed to 55,000 foreign Jews. Clear signs of this difference can of course be observed when we follow the day-to-day existence of the Jews. Foreign Jews were the first victims of the mass roundups; French Jews, on the other hand, often found in administrative offices or in their social milieu a comprehension rarely encountered by foreign Jews. If they fled the Northern Zone, French Jews were not turned away when they came to the line of demarcation, and in the Unoccupied Southern Zone, they ran little risk of being arrested by the French police—at least not before the roundup in Marseilles.

There was indeed an obvious difference, but the so-called safety net for French

Jews still had a good number of holes. First, any Jews found in violation of one of Vichy's regulations ran the risk of being interned in a camp, with all the consequences that entailed. Second, Jewish children born of foreign parents were not considered to be full-fledged French citizens. Third, the exclusionary measures had made them vulnerable and paved the way for their capture, especially as their identity papers and food ration cards had been stamped with the word "Jew": this made it easier to lay hands on Jews when the Gestapo and the French Milice increasingly replaced the French gendarmes. French Jews were thus excluded from the national community, shaken in their identity, driven out of the workplace, often reduced to financial ruin, and left to the Germans by the Vichy regime. We can better appreciate this total upheaval of their existence when we remember their high degree of integration into French society before the defeat of June 1940, instead of simply observing their smaller proportion of losses to the annihilation machine.

All in all, this entire set of policies, which sometimes stemmed from Vichy's autonomous initiatives and sometimes were conceded to the Germans or inspired by them, seldom alleviated the plight of Jews and aggravated the fate of the vast majority. In its desire to articulate its own coherent, autonomous brand of antisemitism, and its desperate efforts to seize a few tidbits of sovereignty, Vichy determined what was and what was not legitimate with respect to the Jews. It was Vichy that advocated the internment of foreign Jews, and then helped deport them. It made Jews pariahs in French society, made outlaws of those who did not submit to their new status, and made society frown on all who helped Jews.

It is in this context that we must pose the question of the denunciations. Indeed, there were hundreds of them and they were dreadfully effective, for they were always followed up with investigations carefully conducted by a police force that had been set up specifically to catch violators of the antisemitic laws. Although these denunciations can be attributed to a minority in French society, they had infinitely greater impact on the fate of their victims than did the active or passive complicity of an entire bataillon of other French citizens. Many Jews thus lived with the ever-present anxiety of denunciation. But one can above all observe that acts of denunciation proliferated when official communiqués published by the newspapers presented them as a service rendered to Marshal Pétain in his struggle against anti-French activities. Nevertheless, they should in no way be considered as emblematic of the public's attitude toward the Jews. On the contrary, the responsibility for such acts comes back to the public authorities who made acceptable such an outlet for all sorts of resentment.

Public opinion and the public's attitude toward both the Jews and the policies enacted against them has become the focus of much current debate. How are we to interpret the general silence that greeted the legislative phase of persecution? To what extent was there a sudden awakening of conscience in the summer of 1942? How much assistance was given to the Jews hiding from police during the period of the roundups and mass arrests? I should first of all point out that these three questions are closely tied to two larger issues covering the entire Occupation period: (1) amount of traditional or newly imported antisemitism in French society and (2) the extent of public support for Marshal Pétain and the "National Revolution."

When a whole series of laws made Jews pariahs in French society and at a time when foreign Jews were being interned in the south of France, the public remained silent. This silence was probably a reflection of both the "apathy that dominated public opinion during the first few months of the Vichy regime"[12] and the public's general support of Marshal Pétain. Beyond these two factors, there was probably also a good measure of indifference and a sort of inward withdrawal brought on by the hardships of everyday life; nonetheless, there was also a tacit approval that attests to the normalization of an antisemitism heavily tainted with xenophobia. Religious authorities in France also remained silent during this first phase of persecution. The underground newspapers that were just beginning also displayed a great deal of discretion, while the official press's commentary on the subject explained the reasons for the policy and the collaborationist papers unleashed torrents of antisemitic hatred.

Such was the silence of the public stemming from indifference or from a vague approval. However, when one reads the reports written at the time by Jews who were trying to fathom the depth of French antisemitism and thus approach the question through people's concrete reactions to victims of the antisemitic laws, one is struck by these victims' indulgence. Although indifference is certainly evident, the interpretation of this indifference varies according to the phase of the Occupation in question. For the contemporary analyst, this indifference set the stage for the promulgation of the antisemitic laws that were conducive to the Final Solution. Throughout the war, Jews in the Occupied Zone viewed this indifference as a relief in comparison with the virulently antisemitic propaganda being spewed out from various Nazi fronts under both German and French labels. Events in Paris are not unfolding as they are in Warsaw, wrote Léo Hamon in April 1941.[13]

Thus, comparisons with other places were also made at this time. The frame of reference was that of wartime, during which things are measured by war; that is, the worst events are heard about. In peacetime, the perspective is just the opposite. So from one perspective, indifference is seen as proof of a rejection of Nazi antisemitism; from the other, indifference is viewed as having facilitated the application of the plan to exterminate the Jews. So two different sensitivities were distinctly present in the French public's indifference: the transplant of Nazi racism had not taken root in French society as a whole, but a "respectable" form of antisemitism did not necessarily arouse people's indignation.

That dichotomy also partially explains the differences that can be observed between the zones. In the Northern Occupied Zone, a fundamental hostility to the Germans was present from the very beginning, although it did not prevent people from cooperating with the Germans on a day-to-day basis. Anti-Jewish measures, especially those visible to the public eye, met with disapproval in the north, for they were marked with the seal of the Germans: as a result, all antisemitism took on a Nazi tint. In the Southern Zone, however, another form of antisemitism, marked by economic fear and xenophobia was clearly prevalent and quite French. Condoned by the state, it could give itself free rein. All observers concurred in emphasizing the differences between the forms of grassroots antisemitism visible in the Northern and Southern Zones.

Equally important in these "surveys" conducted by Jews during the Occupation were the signs of warmth and friendship from their non-Jewish friends, neighbors, and colleagues. Such gestures were often noted with emotion: what was important, in other words, was that their day-to-day relations had not changed. People who theoretically approved of the anti-Jewish laws could still be friendly with victims of these measures with whom they were in daily contact. People continued to buy goods in stores displaying the yellow placard. It must be pointed out, however, that a goodly number of French people stepped forward to take advantage of the liquidation of these same stores.

The essential fact remains that the policies of exclusion were carried out implacably, particularly when they were profitable for certain individuals. No-one spoke out publicly to condemn these measures. Jews did take comfort in the fact that these policies often had no effect on their personal contacts and that their personal networks of daily relations were for the most part not disturbed. At the same time, however, they were not always wary of this discrepancy between the political measures and their personal milieu. And while the smokescreen created by this relative normality alleviated the effects of some measures, it also created a false sense of security.

Certain voices among the religious authorities and the Resistance—albeit discreetly, privately, and often in guarded terms—began to speak up, first in the spring of 1941, and then again after the adoption of the second Jewish Statute. But it was not until the summer of 1942 that a nerve was struck in the public's conscience: the yellow star, the massive Vel d'hiv roundup, and then the extension of mass arrests to the Southern Zone caused a general wave of indignation: the Germans were displaying their barbarity in the Northern Zone, and it was to these same Germans that Vichy was handing over the Jews who had trusted France to protect them. To my mind, the sequence of events beginning at the' Vel d'hiv in occupied Paris and proceeding on to the Southern Zone was essential in creating this heightened awareness of the situation of the Jews, revealing, like a flash of lightning, Vichy's complicity with the Germans. These were no longer abstract laws, but poignant scenes of families torn out of their homes and children separated from their parents, nightmarish sights that left few indifferent.

A nerve had been struck in the public's conscience, but the effect was in several ways short-lived, particularly with respect to public outrage. This spontaneous and natural human reaction was nevertheless deepened and strengthened by appeals (this time public and unequivocal) from some of the most eminent members of Catholic hierarchy, and it was encouraged by the voices of both the mainland Resistance and de Gaulle's Free French in London. Politically, Léon Werth was rightly indignant over the corrections that Cardinal Saliège thought he needed to publish on September 27, 1942, in *La Semaine religieuse* (put out by his diocese): in it, Saliège reaffirmed his "perfect loyalty to Marshal Pétain and to the political authorities in his country."[14] And the concessions to the prevalent mood of the time and to the Vichy regime characterizing some pastoral letters doubtless mitigated the force of their message. Nonetheless, I think that Pierre Laborie is right in contending that the message was nevertheless "heard on the whole, and what struck people and remained in their minds were the themes of indignation and reproval."[15]

From then on, there developed a dialectical relationship between the evolution of public opinion toward Vichy and the evolution of public opinion toward the Jews. The mass arrests of the summer of 1942 had revealed the moral cost of collaboration. The Resistance took on an ethical dimension,[16] while the legitimacy of the Vichy government was seriously shaken: the public's hostility to the German Occupying forces began to spill over on Vichy.

This gradual disenchantment with the Vichy regime brought growing doubts about the legitimacy a whole series of its measures—and even more serious doubts about measures that obviously came from the Germans. From then on, the visible aspect of persecution of the Jews was not "the purge," but rather relentless manhunts aimed at deporting Jews to a destination that was surmised to be quite deadly. These operations clearly bore the stamp of the Germans. These tendencies only grew stronger as the military scene kept evolving and an Allied victory became more and more likely. Solidarity with the victims of German persecution did not, however, wipe out an old wellspring of antisemitism, which had been both muted and strengthened in certain rural areas, and which resurfaced as soon as the reconstruction began after the war. In addition, the underlying idea of an entire community of destiny including all victims of the Germans and of "deportation" had several effects: it blunted the specificity of the Jews' fate; it sometimes prevented people from understanding the urgency of rescuing the Jews; and it clearly fueled a certain fatalistic attitude.

Efforts to provide aid to all the victims of the Germans—not only Jews, Communists, Freemasons, and foreigners, but now also all those who refused to submit to conscription into the Forced Labor Service—nevertheless kept on developing as the number of victims continually increased and as alternative social milieus began to form. In this context of a society no longer reluctant to organize itself outside the legal government of France, the Jewish and non-Jewish organizations who devoted themselves to rescuing Jews were able to function. This same context made possible the many personal networks and individual rescue efforts that, by the scale of their numbers, took on collective significance.

Indeed, individual rescue efforts such as the one revealed by the following exchange of letters, illustrate the differences between the public mind-set—meaning that of simple people—and the mind-set of those who believed that the administrative function makes the man. On June 14, 1943, a country woman (Henriette Gourhant aux Fraîches, La Bazoche-Gouet), who according to her own terms just loved children, wrote to the prefect of her département, L'Eure-et-Loir. She had taken in two Jewish children whose parents had disappeared, but in order to feed them, she had to have food ration cards. She had been denied all forms of relief in her local area. "I have become attached to them and it would hurt to have to be separated from them," she wrote, "so I appeal to your kindness and your justice in order that these children who are in no way responsible for all this human misery might have their ration cards for basic commodities and supplies." On June 25, she sent another letter to the prefect to thank him for the coupons she had received. She did not know that on June 18, 1943, the prefect had written to the subprefect in Châteaudun to request that he conduct an investigation, and if the story proved to be accurate, to have ration cards issued to them, but "at the same time reminding them that the word "Jew" [had to be] stamped on the food card and on the textile card by the gendarmerie brigade before they could be issued to these people."[17]

Clearly, such dossiers of administrative correspondence between French government employees and Jews, whose honor, possessions, or persons had been attacked, reveal a generalized case of administrative autism. This callous behavior sharply contrasts with the utterly dignified attitude of many French Israelites who, while complying with the law, made a point of openly expressing their deep disagreement with the law's underlying principles.

JEWISH RESPONSES

Whatever reactions the Jews had to the measures targeting them, we should recall here that their fate remained largely out of their hands, regardless of their defensive strategy. The reaction of a state should in no way be confused with that of a powerless minority. The fate of most Jews was ultimately dictated by supposedly "overriding" national interests: their plight was little more than a card for Laval to play when negotiating with the Germans. On the other hand, the territorial rivalry between the French and the Italians played in favor of the Jews and was a key factor in the protection they enjoyed in the Italian Zone. Similarly, it was because the Allies were interested in using the border between Spain and France that they pressured Franco's government: the border thus remained open, even for Jews.

What was true on a state level was no less true on a societal level. When Jews become the prime victims of the French Milice in the civil war developing between the members of the Milice and the résistants, their fate still remained out of their control. The essential point, however, is that Jews were intrinsically connected to French society. Accordingly, the ways of thinking that they had interiorized dictated their behavior no less than for French people: the only strategies for their own defense, survival, and opposition were those that were in harmony with certain types of structures in the host society.

For that reason, we can best understand the behaviors followed by different categories of French Israelites by remembering that they were totally integrated into French society. Often the only Judaism they retained was that of faithfulness to their origins. That explains, for example, why Roger Stéphane felt so humiliated, furious, and disgusted at having to lie to the police about being Jewish in order not to put the directors of the newspaper *Mot d'ordre* (who had obtained a press card for him) in a difficult position.[18] It also explains why Clara Malraux could not bring herself to dodge the census requirement and why Léon Werth so loudly proclaimed his Judaism when complying with this same census requirement.

Such bold acceptance of Jewish identity turned out to be a trap for some, but to renounce it and blend in completely with an Aryan identity would have meant losing the only tie linking them to Judaism, which thus represented their memory of a legacy of persecution tied to the refusal to renounce their origins. This stubborn fidelity was lived out as the specific feature of the history of the Jews: to interpret it as passivity is to engage in ideological manipulation. "Paradoxically, by depriving us of any sort of Judaic training, our parents forbade us from forgetting that we were Jewish," wrote the Russian immigrant Nina Gourfinkel on this subject. She was linked to Judaism by the same sort of attachment. "We had to proclaim that we were Jewish, because Jews were being humiliated and offended and no-one has the moral right exempt themselves from this suffering. Such was the foundation of my Judaism, the only one I can articulate and that comes right out of the Russian intelligentsia's creed."[19]

The choices made by Jewish leaders were based on the logic of the political and social positions they occupied before the war. Upper-class French Israelites managed to shelter themselves by taking advantage of their network of social contacts and adopting a prudent wait-and-see attitude, or by joining one of the Resistance organizations, or by joining an effort to represent the French Israelites. They were above all mindful of preserving their honor, which meant repeatedly protesting the very principle of the persecutions while at the same time stressing their loyalty to France—which in practical terms meant total compliance with the law.

There were nevertheless some Jews associated with the Consistory who before the war had not been connected in any way with any of the various Jewish institutions. Among them, it was often the Zionists, for whom the term "Jewish people" held real substance, that led the efforts to provide social aid to Jews in difficulty. To do this work, they were often compelled to operate within the UGIF. Among the French Israelites, personalities as diverse as Marc Bloch and Jacques Helbronner were united in opposing the UGIF: their stance did not stem from the alternative of collaboration versus resistance but rather from their conception of the future of Judaism in France, a future that the UGIF had put in jeopardy.

Of particular concern was that the UGIF replaced the fundamental distinction between French citizens and foreigners—a distinction fundamental in the hierarchy of their identity—with a distinction between Jews and non-Jews. Without denying their duty to show solidarity with fellow Jews who were less fortunate, French Israelites were first and foremost attached to France. All these French Israelites, including not only those who joined the Resistance as French citizens, but also those who found a way to blend into French society, and those who continued to protest that they were attached to France even when France heaped scorn on them, remained true to their prewar stances and bore witness to the strength of their cultural and social roots.

Foreign Jews and those who had recently immigrated to France were infinitely more vulnerable. However, their type of social integration was not individual but collective, and quite often political; in this sense, they were less isolated in face of the dangers threatening them. Thanks to various political organizations already in existence that went to work immediately, they were able to receive support from social aid programs: these programs were for the most part provided by the circles connected with the Federation of Jewish Societies in France, which in turn was supported by the financial infrastructure of the Joint or by the political activities led principally by the Communists, who took advantage of their party's political infrastructure. For the many Jews involved with them, they constituted a link with the Communist Resistance. Collectively, this connection was also a link with a sector of French society. The bundists and Socialist-Zionists (gathered around the Federation) were in a close but noninstitutionalized relation with socialist circles.

Aid received first from the Coordinating Committee in Paris, and then from the UGIF allowed those not connected with one of the networks cited above to hold out for a while. For some, however, this situation created a fatal illusion. For others, the contacts made in UGIF facilities on the contrary paved the way to the organizations working behind the scenes.

For immigrant Jews, the decision to deal with the UGIF also stemmed from a feeling of solidarity. But the keener their political awareness, the more they opposed the official Jewish organization, even though there were differences between the occupied Northern Zone and the so-called free Southern Zone. The "social" Zionists—in other words, those concerned with social aid—agreed to cooperate for a time with the UGIF, while the more "political" Zionists refused. Both social and cultural dimensions were nevertheless present in the immigrant Jews' organizations, even if they were sometimes subordinated to political objectives.

Although the types of aid provided differed from one zone to the other, similar motives compelled a considerable portion of the Jewish population to seek support from these organizations. Their priority was survival; as the exclusionary laws and plundering of Jewish property kept on, an ever-larger number of Jews were suffering from dire poverty. But that is not all. We must not forget that most of the measures persecuting the Jews were met with silence, especially at the time of the roundups and mass arrests. It is difficult to imagine both the wave of hatred that swept in from the "specialized" papers and the major newspapers in the Occupied Zone, and, at the same time, the silence of these publications when words were put into action.

This dichotomy can be found everywhere else and it is key to understanding the conditions in which the Shoah took place. And it is this same dichotomy that explains why some historians have argued that everything had been announced ahead of time, while others have found just as many arguments to support the contention that "people didn't know anything."

Such was the case in France, where uncertainty about the matter reigned. There were a number of contradictory sources of information and disinformation, including silence from the official press, then sudden outbursts of antisemitism, antisemitic pressures from certain special newspapers, and the important announcements of the *Journal Officiel*. And then there were news and rumors spread by "outhouse Radios" (doubtless known by other names outside the camps), and also the news spread by the underground newspapers (although it remains difficult to gauge the real extent of their dissemination). Finally, the dossiers sent by the Consistory through their regional delegates to prominent local Jewish community leaders also responded to the need to know. And it was also in order to break the silence that the Consistory made a point of getting out precise information about the extent of the persecution to those it considered to be its allies among France's spiritual and cultural leaders.

It is in this context that we can appreciate the importance of places of social interaction. People do not think ahead in a vacuum. When their anxiety is mixed with uncertainty, their most natural reaction is to go find out what is happening. Soup kitchens in Paris, synagogues all over France, dispensaries, and the facilities of all the well-established Jewish organizations provided places where Jews could go and catch up on the news. The cultural development observed during the first two years of the Occupation sprang from such gatherings around synagogues and made it possible to reinvigorate a bruised identity. When roundups and mass arrests intensified, it was necessary to disperse, and priorities changed. Cultural activities became less attractive: to go to a café or a synagogue where Jews were in the habit of congregating was to reveal that one was Jewish and thereby risk being arrested. On the other hand, if one was not abreast of all the latest developments in detail—and how was that possible without going somewhere to find out what was going on?—one risked not being able to make the best decision when necessary.

A striking case in point is provided by the mass roundup of Jews carried out over several days in Nice by Brunner and during which S. Majerowicz wrote a diary, recording everything he did. Majerowicz's *Journal* confirms the impression we get from Biélinky's:[20] even though Biélinky was writing at a different time (the beginning of the Occupation) and in a different place (Paris), he points to the same uncertainty about tomorrow that compelled Jews to go out in the street and seek out other Jews who just might be better informed about what was in the making.

Cultural concerns nevertheless gave way to the imperatives of providing social aid, and the most visible aspects of such gatherings increasingly concealed some sort of underground rescue activity. Pivotal organizations such as the Israelite Scouts of France (EIF) and the Children's Relief Agency (OSE) took on a key role in this transition. They were to play an ever more important role for several reasons: they were both made up of French Jews; the EIF had close ties with the Scouting movement, while the OSE was well connected with other French charitable organizations; they both benefited from friendship with people inside government bureaucracies; and they both were quick to look after foreign Jews. They attracted a large number of young people, and the pressure of events along with spontaneously initiatives gradually led them first to the edge of legality and then to clandestine activities when it became imperative for Jews to disperse.

At the same time, the Jewish Communist organizations, which by necessity had already gone underground, made political action their priority. The Communists were led down separate paths: they emphasized armed struggle more than mutual aid (although aid programs also existed among the activities of the Jewish Communists, they were subordinated to political work). The rapprochement between the Communists and other organizations took place when politics once again became a primary concern near the end of the war, and people began rebuilding the community. During this reconstruction period, Zionists gained entry into the official community by their emphasis on rescuing Jews threatened with extermination. The Jewish Communists achieved the same result by contributing a large number of Jews to the armed struggle. While the Zionists obtained their legitimacy directly from Jewish issues, the Jewish Communists gained their acceptance as part of the Communists' overall acquisition of legitimacy in the French political arena.

During the final phase of the war, the southern branch of the UGIF had discontinued most of its operations, largely due to the decision of the organizations under the UGIF umbrella, but also because its French interlocutor, Vichy, was administratively disintegrating. The northern branch of the UGIF, however, was under the thumb of the Germans and continued to carry out a large number of tasks. The organization was nevertheless politically condemned, as the time for the primacy of social aid had passed.

The chronology of events can help us characterize the UGIF other than by defensive slogans and anathema. Those who assumed positions of responsibility in the UGIF opted for a technical collaboration in order not to jeopardize aid programs that were making it possible for a large number of Jews to survive. None of them supported either the Nazis' plans or the objectives of the "National Revolution." Their aim was to maneuver to limit the damage and to salvage whatever was possible. Even if they did not encourage them, they did not stand in the way of the use of other methods by both organizations that belonged to the UGIF and those outside its umbrella: they either passively provided cover or sheltered them from authorities.

In so doing, they in no way guaranteed their own personal safety; each one of them could have easily fled across the border or blended into French society. The main leaders of the UGIF paid dearly for their commitment, losing both their lives and their families. In accepting these positions, however, they involved themselves in a fatal chain of events from which it proved hard to extricate themselves: such was the result of their granting priority to social aid over politics. While Brunner was tightening his grip in the summer of 1943 and showing by a whole series of arrests that there was no longer the slightest room for maneuver, the logical political choice for the UGIF would have been to scuttle ship. Honor would have been saved, but at the price of how many lives sacrificed? In face of an enemy driven by an ideology of destruction, only a political response is truly effective but only for the long term. The UGIF was neither a Gestapo front nor a Resistance organization. It was the Germans' whipping boy in the Occupied Zone, an interlocutor for the French authorities, and a social safety net for a large number of Jews. It fostered an illusion of normality, but provided cover for rescue efforts. Some of its leaders conducted themselves valiantly, while others proved cowards. The UGIF was also a trap for those who were arrested in its facilities: the children deported by Brunner come to mind. Any assessment must take all of these facts into consideration.

The Jews' responses to their persecution thus reflected both the diversity of their "community" and the influences of their equally diverse social backgrounds.

HOW DID THREE-FOURTHS OF THE JEWS IN FRANCE SURVIVE?

A preliminary answer to the question of Jewish survival in France is found not by studying Jewish organizations or French society, but rather the modes of social integration specific to each component of the Jewish population in France. In spite of the exclusionary measures, the French Israelites, who tended to be integrated on an individual basis, found networks of complicity in French society that provided them with alternatives when they were driven from their jobs and when it became necessary to go into hiding. The latter necessity cropped up just when most people in France had become disaffected from the Vichy regime. On a collective level, moreover, the legitimacy of the Jewish religion, which had traditionally been recognized and never denied, made it easier for Jewish religious leaders to make their countless appeals to religious authorities in France, in order either to inform them about what was happening or to plead that they intervene. These appeals played a key role in the wave of pastoral letters sent out in the summer of 1942. While the French State could peremptorily strike off the legal texts emancipating the Jews, it could not wipe out the effects of these laws that had taken root in French society for one hundred fifty years. These lasting effects are what we have seen at work in each of the social milieus, for the French Israelites were found throughout.

For their part, the immigrant Jews from Central and Eastern Europe were characterized by a particularly high rate of political awareness and involvement. Jewish organizations constituted a basis of support for the Jewish immigrant population first of all by means of their social aid programs, as had traditionally been the case. Both Zionist and Communist organizations, along with activists with the Federation or the

Bund helped Jews first to survive economically, then to go into hiding. This type of collective integration, combined with a high level of political awareness, saved more than one life.

All of these developments, including the persecution, the evolution of public opinion, and the Jews' responses, are linked to a chronology that, combined with France's geographical features, largely determined the fate of the Jews in France.

We have seen that the persecutions gradually became more severe, being progressively applied to different categories of people. Moreover, situations Jews faced varied from one region to another. This combination of factors sometimes provided loopholes in the system until the autumn of 1943. Although ostracized, French Jews were at first spared deportation, and were able to find refuge in the Southern Zone where, even though second-class citizens, they did not risk being targeted by a German-initiated roundup, as had been the case in Paris in August and December 1941. The existence of this large category of Jews remaining out of their reach drew the fixed attention of the Germans for several months: hoping to snare a large number of Jews with a minimum of effort, the Germans pressured Vichy to denaturalize a large number of these French Jews. These efforts failed, as Marshal Pétain backed off at the last minute and refused to sign the denaturalization decree.

When the Germans occupied the Southern Zone, the Italian Zone became a place of refuge. There again, the efforts of the Germans to rip open the safety net stretched out by the Italians were in vain. This allowed Jews to gain time, especially as, in view of the Italians' attitude, Laval had to curb the collaboration of the French police. Because of the diversity of the Jews in France (including French Jews, foreign Jews, and Jews of certain protected nationalities) and the division of French territory (into the Northern Zone, the Southern Zone, and the Italian Zone), the Germans had to spread their efforts out in several areas.

When the Germans took over everywhere in September 1943, public opinion had matured, Vichy's enthusiasm for collaboration in this domain had waned, French bureaucrats were no longer so cooperative, the Resistance had developed, the Jewish population had become aware of the necessity of going into hiding, and Jewish and non-Jewish rescue networks could function better—they had taken advantage of the Italians' reprieve in order to become organized. In dealing with what he calls defensive resistance, the Swiss historian Werner Rings[21] describes the time necessary for its development: the time needed to recruit, organize, plan, find hideouts, and to make contact. But time was often lacking, and police roundups were the most successful when one followed on the heels of another in rapid succession. In France, time and loopholes made a crucial difference in determining the fate of Jews.

This chronology of events also accounts for the different steps leading the Jews and their organizations from legality to clandestine existence. While these steps are directly tied to the persecution, one must nevertheless remember the various stages in the overall evolution of events in mainland France. Jewish Communist militants were quickly forced to go more or less completely underground. However, it was the proliferation of police roundups that incited them to encourage first their families, then all those they managed to convince to follow them into secrecy. Faced directly with the Occupation in Paris, but partially protected by the Germans' having chosen the leaders of the Consistorial Association of Israelites in Paris (ACIP) as their interlocutors, the Amelot Committee used both legal and clandestine channels according to the needs of the Jewish population.

In the Southern Zone, the problem did not pose itself in the same terms. There again, however, it was a strongly ideological organization, the Jewish Army in Toulouse, that immediately chose clandestine channels for its activities but not for its militants. The creation of the UGIF provided the starting point for a gradual transition to secrecy, at which point the Federation began setting up a parallel structure. But Zionist leaders of the Federation then decided to distribute far and wide a tract denouncing the exclusionary policies directed at the Jews, they did so because the widespread disapproval of Vichy was conducive to such a message. A large number of social activists were once again compelled to act first by the mass arrests of the summer of 1942 and then by the Occupation of the Southern Zone. At that point, however, the top priority was for the Jewish population to go into hiding. After the Germans came and occupied the Italian Zone, it was decided everywhere to scatter out, and the series of raids on UGIF offices and synagogues in the first few months of 1944 convinced the undecided to go into hiding.

During the early part of the Occupation, clandestine methods had begun to develop in the north, while in the Southern Zone the choice of legality prevailed. During the final months of the war, the intervention of the Southern Zone compelled those who were still playing by the rules in the north to go underground. There we have an example not only of the differences between the two zones, but also of the interaction between the ways of functioning in each zone and even of each zone's influence on the other.

All in all, it is perhaps heterogeneity that provides us the key to the survival of a large number of Jews in France. There was a pluralistic "community" that made the Germans' task more difficult in the first place. There was a diversity of organizations that ultimately determined the nature of the UGIF. The Amelot Committee was thus able to function autonomously in the Northern Zone, while in the Southern Zone the UGIF maintained the structure of a federation. There were different modes of integration, each having their own affiliations in French society. To summarize, there were the effects of one hundred and fifty years' emancipation: while a particular government might do away with the attributes of this freedom, it cannot, even if immensely popular, remove its deep roots, especially when it attempts to do so in the shadow of enemy occupation.

On August 22, 1944, at the very height of the Parisian insurrection and as the Allied troops were approaching the capital, Léon Werth confided his new fears to his Journal:

> Imagination anticipates; they have left. And already you can feel the coming lapse of memory. The war is going to be lined up beside other past wars. The war is nothing more than two dates that children will recite. There no longer remains anything of the war other than what one has to know to complete elementary or secondary education. Will what was incredible in the midst of the most horrible also be forgotten? Yes, as will be the rest. What can one do so that people do not forget?[22]

People were certainly encouraged to forget at first, but this turning away is no longer appropriate. Vichy now haunts the memory of the French people and occupies a number of historians. Because crimes against humanity do not come under any statute of limitations, court cases continue to flare up, and, along with a now militant Jewish memory, have placed French policies toward Jews at the very heart of this memory. "What was incredible in the midst of the most horrible" cannot so easily be wiped out, and the centrality of this issue owes much to the entire Western World's awakening to the absolute horror represented by the Shoah.

On July 21, 1945, the Committee for the Understanding of the Associations for the Defense of the Victims of Oppression organized at the Parc des Princes a "commemoration of the separation of mothers from their children on July 16, 1942, in Paris." "One of the most barbarous acts committed by the Germans during their occupation," said the circular announcing the demonstration on May 25, 1945.[23] On February 4, 1993, President François Mitterrand decreed July 16 (or the following Sunday) to be a "national day for commemorating the racist and antisemitic persecutions committed under the authority of the "government of the French State (1940–1944)," in order to commemorate the Vel d'hiv roundup.[24]

More than fifty years had passed and times had changed. A private organization had been replaced by the state, the separation of mothers from their children was placed in the general context of racist and antisemitic persecution, and the responsibility for the event had been transferred from the Germans to the government of the French State. The memory of the genocide is now no longer diluted by the more general memory of deportation.[25] A rivalry of memories, reflecting divergences over the nature of Jewish identity, sometimes prevails. When he brought together all the elements that compose the heartrending story of the children of Izieu—seized by Klaus Barbie on April 6, 1944—Serge Klarsfeld subtitled his book *A Jewish Tragedy.* When Tzvetan Todorov recounted the "scenes of civil war" in the summer of 1944 that led to the massacre of Jews thrown into wells in Guerry, however, he entitled his book *A French Tragedy*. If such competition of memories occurs, it is indeed because the ordeal suffered by the Jews in France during World War II was both a Jewish *and* a French tragedy.

Notes

Preface (pages xv–xxii)

1. Renée Poznanski, "Vichy et les Juifs. Des marges de l'histoire au coeur de son écriture," in *Vichy et les Français*, ed. Jean-Pierre Azéma and François Bédarida (Paris: Fayard, 1992), 57–68. The most important book is Michael R. Marrus and Robert O. Paxton's *Vichy France and the Jews* (New York: Basic Books, 1981; reprint, Schocken Books, 1983), which is nicely supplemented by Serge Klarsfeld, *Vichy-Auschwitz*, 2 vols. (Paris: Fayard, 1983 and 1985).

2. Among the numerous works on this subject, see Richard I. Cohen, *The Burden of Conscience* (Bloomington: Indiana University Press, 1987); Jacques Adler, *The Jews of Paris and the Final Solution: Communal Response and Internal Conflicts, 1940–1944* (New York: Oxford University Press, 1987); Stéphane Courtois, Denis Peschanski, and Adam Rayski, *Le Sang de l'étranger* (Paris: Fayard, 1989); Lucien Lazare, *Rescue as Resistance: How Jewish Organizations Fought the Holocaust in France* (New York: Columbia University Press, 1996); Annette Wieviorka, *Ils étaient juifs, résistants, communistes* (Paris: Denoël, 1986); and finally, Asher Cohen, *Persécutions et sauvetages, Juifs et Français sous l'Occupation et sous Vichy*, with a preface by René Rémond (Paris: Cerf, 1993).

3. This change was pointed out in *Vichy et les Français*, ed. Azéma and Bédarida. Concerning the Jews themselves, one finds some of these questions in André Kaspi, *Les Juifs pendant l'Occupation* (Paris: Seuil, 1991); Adam Rayski, *Le Choix des Juifs sous Vichy* (Paris: La Découverte, 1993); and Susan Zucotti, *The Holocaust, the French, and the Jews* (New York: Basic Books, 1993).

4. These are problematics that resemble the approach taken by Pierre Laborie, *L'Opinion française sous Vichy* (Paris: Seuil, 1990).

5. Citation from Vidal-Naquet's preface to Michael R. Marrus, *Les Juifs de France à l'époque de l'affaire Dreyfus* (Paris: Calmann-Lévy, 1972), which is reprinted in Pierre Vidal-Naquet, *Les Juifs, la mémoire et le présent* (Paris: Maspéro, 1981), 88.

6. Saul Friedländer, "Some Reflections on the Historicisation of National Socialism," *Tel Aviver Jahrbuch für deutsche Geschichte* 16 (1987): 310–324.

7. Renée Poznanski, "Simon Doubnov, l'homme et son époque," introduction to Simon Doubnov, *Lettres sur le judaïsme ancien et nouveau*, translated from Russian, annotated, and presented by Renée Poznanski (Paris: Cerf, 1989), 11–80.

8. I regret that some documents reproduced are truncated or that their sources are not indicated, which makes it risky to use them.

9. These archives pose an additional problem: they were brought together by Maurice Moch and one finds thrown together both authentic documents and others that were recopied by Maurice Moch in the early 1960s. I used them on the same basis as the originals, for each time that I found the original and the copy made by Moch, the copy was a faithful reproduction.

10. Jacques Biélinky, *Journal, 1940–1942: Un journaliste juif à Paris sous l'Occupation*, established, edited, and with an introduction by Renée Poznanski (Paris: Cerf, 1992).

11. Noël (Nissim) Calef, *Drancy 1941, Camp de représailles*, ed. and intro. Serge Klarsfeld (Paris: Fils et filles des déportés juifs de France, 1991).

12. Raymond-Raoul Lambert, *Carnet d'un témoin, 1940–1943*, annotated and with an

introduction by Richard I. Cohen (Paris: Fayard, 1985). There are numerous other diaries listed in the Bibliography.

13. Léo Hamon, Renée Poznanski, *Avant les premières grandes rafles; les Juifs à Paris sous l'Occupation (juin 1940–avril 1941)*, in *Cahiers de l'IHTP* 22 (December 1992).

14. For a discussion of the subject, see Danièle Voldman, ed., *La Bouche de la vérité, la recherche historique et les sources orales, Cahiers de l'IHTP* 21 (November 1992).

1. 1940: *Jews and Israelites in France (pages 1–29)*

1. Dominique Schnapper recalls and elaborates on this most useful distinction in *Juifs et israélites* (Paris: Gallimard, 1980), 155. The book has been published in English as *Jewish Identities in France: An Analysis of Contemporary French Jewry* (Chicago: University of Chicago Press, 1984).

2. On the history of this group of Jews in the nineteenth century, see Paula E. Hyman, *The Emancipation of the Jews of Alsace* (New Haven: Yale University Press, 1991).

3. Paula Hyman, *De Dreyfus à Vichy* (Paris: Fayard, 1985), 134. The book has been published in English as *From Dreyfus to Vichy: The Remaking of French Jewry, 1906–1939* (New York: Columbia University Press, 1979).

4. Simon Schwartzfuchs, *Du Juif à l'israélite* (Paris: Fayard, 1989); Michael Graetz, *Les Juifs en France au XIX siècle* (Paris: Seuil, 1982); and Patrick Girard, *Les Juifs de France de 1789 à 1860* (Paris: Calmann-Lévy, 1976).

5. Michel Roblin, *Les Juifs de Paris* (Paris: Editions A. et J. Picard, 1952), 137.

6. On the Jews in public service, see Pierre Birnbaum, *Les Fous de la République* (Paris: Fayard, 1992). The book has been published in English as *The Jews of the Republic: A Political History of State Jews from Gambetta to Vichy* (Stanford: Stanford University Press, 1996).

7. Leroy-Beaulieu's statement is found in *La Semaine politique et littéraire*, March 3, 1900.

8. David Weinberg, *A Community on Trial: The Jews of Paris in the 1930s* (Chicago: University of Chicago Press, 1977), 26.

9. Lambert's statement dates from May 22, 1936, and is cited in Michel Abitbol, *Les Deux Terres promises* (Paris: Olivier Orban, 1989), 181.

10. Simon Epstein, *Les institutions israélites françaises de 1929 à 1939. Solidarité juive et lutte contre l'antisémitisme*, Ph.D. diss., University of Paris-I-Sorbonne, 1990, 205.

11. See Pierre Birnbaum, "La citoyenneté en péril: les Juifs entre intégration et résistance," in *La France de l'Affaire Dreyfus*, ed. Pierre Birnbaum (Paris: Gallimard, 1994), 505–542; see also Michael Marrus, *The Politics of Assimilation, A Study of the French Jewish Community at the Time of the Dreyfus Affair* (Oxford University Press, 1971), and Dominique Schnapper, "Une mémoire de l'enracinement: les Juifs français avant 1940," *Revue des Sciences Humaines* 62, no. 191 (July–September 1983): 96.

12. Vicki Caron, *Between France and Germany, the Jews of Alsace-Lorraine, 1871–1918* (Stanford University Press, 1988), 191.

13. Albert Memmi first introduced this most useful distinction between *Judaism* (the entire set of Jewish doctrines, beliefs, and institutions), *Jewishness* (the fact and manner of being Jewish), and *Jewry* (the entire set of Jewish people) in *Portrait d'un Juif* (Paris: Gallimard, 1962), 16–17.

14. Weinberg, *Community on Trial.*, 25.

15. Raymond Aron, *Mémoires, 50 ans de réflexion politique* (Paris: Julliard, 1983), 18–19.

16. François Bédarida and Denis Peschanski, editors. "Marc Bloch à Étienne Bloch, Lettres de la "drôle de guerre," *Cahiers de l'IHTP (Institut d'histoire du temps présent* 19 (December 1991): 104, September 13, 1942.

17. Robert Aron, *Fragments d'une vie* (Paris: Plon, 1981), 132.

18. Lucien Vidal-Naquet, *Journal* ("15 septembre 1942–29 février 1944"), in *Annales: Economies, Sociétés, Civilisations*, 48–3 (1993), 513–543.

19. Pierre Vidal-Naquet, "Protestants et Juifs pendant la Seconde Guerre mondiale. Souvenirs d'un témoin," in *Les Juifs, la mémoire et le présent* (Paris: La Découverte, 1991), 2:181ff.

20. Joseph Weill, "Déjà!. . . Essai autobiographique," typewritten manuscript, undated, 166.

21. Annie Kriegel, *Ce que j'ai cru comprendre* (Paris: Robert Laffont, 1991).

22. Thus when Marc Bloch describes for his son the military office to which he has just been assigned, he takes care to specify that there was no antisemitism there. Letter of October 22, 1939, in "Marc Bloch à Étienne Bloch," ed. Bédarida andPeschanski, 49.

23. This number comes from a report from Röthke on June 14, 1943, and cited by Serge Klarsfeld in *Vichy-Auschwitz* (Paris: Fayard, 1985), 2:288. It represents 10 percent of the total number of foreigners who took advantage of this law.

24. Barbara Vormeier, "La République française et les réfugiés et immigrés d'Europe centrale," in *De l'exil à la Résistance*, ed. Karel Bartosek, René Gallissot, Denis Peschanski (Paris: Arcantère, 1989), 13–26.

25. Ralph Schor, *L'Opinion française et les étrangers* (Paris: Publications de la Sorbonne, 1985), 562.

26. Ralph Schor, *L'Antisémitisme en France pendant les années trente* (Brussels: Complexe, 1992), 38ff.

27. Schor, *L'Opinion française et les étrangers*, 631.

28. Archives of the Russian Center for the Conservation and Study of Contemporary History, Moscow, collection 517, catalog 1, 1,811, June 1936, "Rapport sur les problèmes des cadres dans les immigrations."

29. Michel Roblin, *Les Juifs de Paris*, 127–128.

30. On the Pletzl during the Belle Epoque, see Nancy Green, *Les Travailleurs immigrés juifs à la Belle Époque* (Paris: Fayard, 1985), 92–93.

31. Rita Thalmann, "Topographie de l'émigration du III Reich à Paris," in *Le Paris des Étrangers*, ed. André Kaspi et Antoine Marès (Paris: Imprimerie nationale, 1990), 92–93.

32. Weinberg, *Community on Trial*, 32ff.

33. Joseph Klatzmann, *Le Travail à domicile dans l'industrie parisienne du vêtement* (Paris: Armand Colin, 1957), 120–121.

34. Nina Gourfinkel, *L'Autre Patrie* (Paris: Seuil, 1953), 69.

35. CRCEDHC archives, Moscou, collection 517, catalog 1, 1523, January 1933, "Rapport d'organisation sur la MOI en France."

36. CRCDEHC archives, Moscow, collection 517, catalog 1, 1653, "La section centrale de la MOI, aperçu sur sa composition et son travail," May 11, 1934.

37. CRCEDHC archives, MOscow, collection 517, catalog 1, 1523, January 1933, "Rapport d'organisation sur la MOI en France."

38. Ibid.

39. CRCDEHC archives, Moscow, collection 517, catalog 1, 1811, "Rapport sur les problèmes des cadres dans les immigrations," June 20, 1936. At that date, out of the 6,635 immigrant members of the party, 495 of them were controlled by the language groups.

40. Rita Thalmann, "Topographie de l'émigration du III Reich à Paris," and Nancy Green, "Les Juifs étrangers à Paris," in *Le Paris des étrangers*, 95–96 and 116–117 respectively.

41. Renée Poznanski, "Un journaliste juif à Paris sous l'Occupation," introduction to Jacques Biélinky's, *Journal, juilllet 1940–décembre 1942*, established, annotated, and with an introduction by Renée Poznanski (Paris: Cerf, 1992).

42. Edgar Morin, *Autocritique* (Paris: Seuil, 1975), 15–16.

43. Léon Poliakov, *L'Auberge des musiciens* (Paris: Mazarine, 1981).

44. Boris Holban, *Testament* (Paris: Calmann-Lévy, 1989).

45. Dolly Steindling, *Vienna, France, Vienna, The Story of a Jewish Refugee and Resistor* (in Hebrew) (Jerusalem: Hebrew University and Rubin Mass Publishing, 1990).

46. Noël (Nissim) Calef, *Drancy 1941, Camp de représailles*, ed. Serge Klarsfeld (Paris: Fils et filles des déportés juifs de France, 1991), 261ff.

47. Marseilles, March 19, 1942, report on the situation of young people, AIU, CC-42.

48. Jean Giraudoux, *Pleins Pouvoirs* (Paris: Gallimard, 1939).
49. Jean-Pierre Bertin-Maghit, *Le Cinéma sous l'Occupation* (Paris: Olivier Orban, 1989), 73–74.
50. Schor, *L'Antisémitisme en France pendant les années trente,* 149ff.
51. Pierre Birnbaum, *Un mythe politique: "la République juive"* (Paris: Fayard, 1988).
52. Archives of the Paris police prefecture (PP) report of July 26, 1933, BA-1814.
53. Vicki Caron, "Jewish Refugees in France before Vichy," *Journal of Contemporary History* 20 (1985): 157–176.
54. Jean-Pierre Azéma, "La France de Daladier," in *La France des années noires,* ed. Jean-Pierre Azéma and François Bédarida (Paris: Seuil,1993), 1:26.
55. Michael Marrus, "The Strange Story of Herschel Grynszpan," *American Scholar* 62, no. 1 (1987–1988): 69–79.
56. According to a police report in the archives of the Paris police prefecture (PP), BA-1814.
57. Catherine Nicault, "L'accueil des Juifs d'Europe centrale par la communauté juive française," in *De l'exil à la Résistance,* 53–59.
58. On the special attachment of Jews to the French Revolution, see Pierre Birnbaum, *Les Fous de la République* (Paris: Fayard, 1992), 143–161.
59. From the December 29–January 5, 1940, edition, in a reprint "Le judaïsme et la guerre," from *L'Europe Nouvelle* of Geneva.
60. Jacques Biélinky, "La communauté juive reste digne de son passé," *L'Univers israélite,* September 15, 1939.
61. Weinberg, *Community on Trial,* 204–205, and Stéphane Courtois, Denis Peschanski, and Adam Rayski, *Le Sang de l'étranger* (Paris: Fayard, 1989), 71.
62. The *Naïe presse* of September 2, 1939, cited by Annette Wieviorka in *Ils étaient juifs, résistants, communistes* (Paris: Denoël, 1986) 40–41.
63. Holban, *Testament,* 60.
64. Joseph Ratz, *La France que je cherchais* (Limoges: 1945), 64–65.
65. Zionist Archives (CZA, Central Zionist Archives), Jerusalem, reports sent by Albert Cohen to Dr. Weizmann, Z. 4–15167. Albert Cohen immediately set out for London on June 18, 1940 (see Albert Cohen, *Hommage à l'Angleterre* (La France libre [1941]). There, both the Jewish Agency as well as the Jewish World Congress put him in charge of handling relations with De Gaulle's Free France.
66. Kalman Stein, "Jewish Soldiers in the Polish Army," *Jewish Frontier,* May 1944, 18, cited by Zosa Szajkowski, *Jews and the French Foreign Legion* (New York: Ktav Publishing House, 1975), 67.
67. Philippe Landau, "France, nous voilà! Les engagés volontaires juifs d'origine étrangère pendant la `drôle de guerre,'" *Pardès* 16 (1992). 20–38, and Jean Delmas, "Les étrangers dans l'armée française durant la Seconde Guerre mondiale," in *Les Étrangers dans la Résistance en France,* ed. Philippe Joutard and François Marcot (Besançon: Musée de la Résistance et de la Déportation, 1992), 34–38.
68. Anne Grynberg, *Les Camps de la honte* (Paris: La Découverte, 1991), 66ff.
69. Archives of the Central Consistory during World War II, Rue Saint-Georges, Paris, 26.
70. Grynberg, *Les Camps de la honte,* 83.
71. F. and J.-B. Joly, J.-P. Mathieu, "Les camps d'internement en France de septembre 1939 à mai 1940," in *Les Barbelés de l'exil* by Gilbert Badia et al (Grenoble: Presses universitaires de Grenoble, 1979).
72. Hanna Schramm and Barbara Vormeier, *Vivre à Gurs, un camp de concentration français, 1940–1941* (Paris: Maspero, 1979), 13.
73. Arthur Koestler, *La lie de la terre* (Paris: Calmann-Lévy, 1973), 146. (English version: *Scum of the Earth* [New York: Macmillan, 1941]).
74. David Vogel, *Et ils partirent pour la guerre,* translated from Hebrew by Rosie Pinhas-Delpuech (Paris: Denoël, 1993), 88–89.
75. André Fontaine, *Le Camp d'étrangers des Milles, 1939–1943* (Aix-en-Provence: Edisud, 1989), 289ff.

76. Grynberg, *Les Camps de la honte*, 76.
77. Vogel, *Et ils partirent pour la guerre*, 112ff.
78. Ibid, p. 82–83.
79. Ibid., p 106.
80. Barbara Vormeier, "La situation des réfugiés en provenance d'Allemagne (septembre 1939-juillet 1942)," in *Zone d'ombre, 1933–1944*, by Jacques Grandjonc and Theresia Grundtner (Paris: Alinea, 1990), 193–194.
81. Noël Calef, *Drancy 1941*, 262ff.
82. Jacques Biélinky, "Lettre de Paris," YIVO, coll. 239, 3.
83. According to Cohen, *The Burden of Conscience*, thirty thousand Jews returned home to Paris.
84. Roger Langeron, *Paris, Juin 1940* (Paris: Flammarion, 1946), 131.
85. Robert Debré, *L'Honneur de vivre* (Paris: Stock, 1974), 214.
86. Archives of the Paris Police prefecture (PP), biweekly reports entitled "Situation à Paris," July, August, September, and October 1940.
87. Annie Kriegel, *Ce que j'ai cru comprendre*, 118.
88. Aron, *Mémoires*, 164–165.
89. Philippe Erlanger, *La France sans étoile* (Paris: Plon, 1974), 99.
90. Biélinky, "Lettre de Paris," September 26, 1941, p. 151, and "Dossier constitué par Edouard Schneeberg pour le Lieutenant Moritz," December 20, 1940, Archives of the Central Consistory during World War II—43/44.
91. Georges Wormser, *Français israélites* (Paris: Editions de Minuit, 1963), 121–122.
92. Archives of the Paris Police prefecture, "Situation à Paris," July 29, 1940.
93. Biélinky, "Lettre de Paris, July-August 1940.
94. Langeron, *Paris, Juin 1940*, 134.
95. Archives of the Paris Police prefecture, "Situation à Paris."
96. Archives of the Paris Police prefecture, "Situation à Paris," August 19, 1940.
97. Gérard Walter, *La Vie à Paris sous l'Occupation* (Paris: Armand Colin, 1960), 177–178.
98. Pierre Audiat, *Paris pendant la guerre* (Paris: Hachette, 1966), 79. See the August 29, 1940. edition of the newspaper *Paris-Soir*.
99. *Paris-Soir*, July 25, 1940.
100. Michael Marrus and Robert O. Paxton, *Vichy France and the Jews*, 3.
101. José Corti, *Souvenirs désordonnés* (Paris: 1983), 190.
102. Archives of the Paris Police prefecture, "Situation à Paris," August 5, 1940.
103. Pascal Fouché, *L'Edition française sous l'Occupation* (Paris: Bibliothèque de littérature française contemporaine de l'université Paris 7), 64.
104. "Résumé d'impressions d'un Juif résidant à Paris depuis l'entrée des troupes allemandes," October 18, 1941, AIU, CC-4.
105. Report on the situation of Jewry in France, unsigned and undated (probably written between June and November 1941), AN, AJ 38–1142. It remains difficult to provide reliable numbers for these fluctuations of the Jewish population. In all, there were probably between 18,000 and 20,000 Jewish refugees in these regions.
106. Report of Chief Rabbi Schwartz on his activity since 1940, doubtless written during the winter of 1940, AIU, CC-4.
107. "Le sionisme et le *Keren kayemet leisrael* en France pendant la dernière guerre—Souvenirs," unpublished document written by Joseph Fischer (Ariel), Yad Vashem Archives (YV).
108. Raymond-Raoul Lambert, *Carnet d'un témoin, 1940–1943*, introduced and annotated by Richard I. Cohen (Paris: Fayard, 1985), 72.
109. Weill, *Déjà!... Essai autobiographique*, 183.
110. Special series, number 19b, cited by Jacques Polonski in *La Presse, la propagande et l'opinion publique* (Paris: Editions du Centre, 1946), 34.
111. This was the conclusion already reached on August 31, 1940 by Herbert Katzki, the representative of the Joint Archives in France (Joint, General, France). The Zionist institutions in

Geneva concurred. (CZA, S 26–1 452, Geneva, October 14, 1940, Kahany to Zionist Executive Council).

112. Bernard Laguerre, "Les dénaturalisés de Vichy, 1940–1944," *Vingtième Siècle, Revue d'histoire* (October–December 1988): 11–12.

113. Archives of the Paris Police prefecture, "Situation à Paris," August 5, 1940.

114. Such was the case of Thomson-Houston and the Messageries Hachette. Geneva, October 14, 1940, Kahany to the Zionist Executive Council in Jerusalem, CZA, S 26–1452.

115. Handwritten diary by Tcherikower, YIVO, Tcherikower Archives, folder 1238, and the August 7, 15, and 20 editions of the newspaper *Paris-Soir*.

116. Henry Rousso, "L'aryanisation économique—Vichy, l'occupant et la spoliation des Juifs," *Yod* (1983): 15–16, and (1982): 52ff.

117. Memorandum from the administrative headquarters, Centre de Documentation Juive Contemporaine, LXXV-70, cited by Joseph Billig, *Le Commissariat général aux questions juives* (Paris: Editions du Centre, 1960), 1:29.

118. Kahany to the Zionist Executive Council at Jerusalem, Geneva, October 14, 1940, CZA, S 26–1452.

119. Paris, September 20, 1940 (confirmation of a telegram dating from September 10, 1940), CDJC, XXIV-12.

2. *The Occupation Sets In (pages 30–65)*

1. Roger Langeron, *Paris, Juin 1940* (Paris: Flammarion, 1946), September 23, 1940, pp. 168–170.

2. Jacques Biélinky, *Journal, juillet 1940–décembre 1942*, annotated with an introduction by Renée Poznanski (Paris: Cerf, 1992), "12 octobre 1940," pp. 59–60.

3. Léon Poliakov, *L'Auberge des musiciens* (Paris: Mazarine, 1981), 79.

4. Adopted on October 27, 1940 (but published in the *Journal officiel* on Novembre 20), the law was modified on March 28, 1942 (*Journal officiel*, March 29, 1942), while the application decree dated from April 12, 1942 (*Journal officiel*, April 14).

5. AN, AJ 38, 117, Paris October 13, 1940, head of the German military administration for the Paris region to the Paris police prefect.

6. Jospeph Lubetzki, *La Condition des Juifs en France sous l'occupation allemande* (Paris: Centre de Documentation Juive Contemporaine, 1945), 184ff; and Roger Errera, "La législation antisémite de Vichy," *Yod* 15–16 (1982): 48.

7. Archives of the Paris police prefecture, "Situation à Paris," October 21, 1940, and AN, AJ 38, 70, M 85, Paris police prefect to Commissariat Général aux Questions Juives (CGQJ), April 4, 1942.

8. Jean Jérôme, *Les Clandestins, 1940–1944* (Paris: Acropole, 1986), p. 16, but also Boris Holban, Adam Rayski, and many others.

9. Gérard Israël, *Heureux comme Dieu en France* (Paris: Laffont, 1975), 93.

10. The October 8, 1940 edition of the newspaper *Le Matin* thus asked, "Les Juifs renieraient-ils leur origine?" (Would the Jews renounce their origins?)

11. Maurice Martin du Gard, *La Chronique de Vichy, 1940–1944* (Paris: Flammarion, 1948), 152.

12. Pierre Birnbaum, *Les Fous de la République* (Paris: Fayard, 1992), 446.

13. See, for example, the letter written by four of them on June 9, 1942: accompanied by a very complete dossier, it was intended to show that in Russia, they were not considered to be Jews. AN, AJ 38, 148.

14. Léo Hamon, "Etude sur la situation des Juifs en zone occupée" [1941], in *Avant les premières grandes rafles; Les Juifs à Paris sous l'Occupation (juin 1940-avril 1941)*, by Renée Poznanski, *Cahiers de l'IHIP*, no. 22 (December 1992): 59.

15. AN, AJ 38, 5, CGQJ to the Paris police chief, April 16, 1942.

16. CDJC (Centre de Documentation Juive Contemporaine), LXXIXa-10 and archives of the Paris police prefecture, "Situation à Paris," October 21, 1940. According to the census of foreigners taken on August 6, 1940, there were at that time 197,913 foreigners in Paris and its suburbs (ibid, October 7, 1940).

17. According to the biweekly reports (which were in fact weekly until June 29,1942) known as "Situation à Paris" and written by inspectors from the police prefecture, these declarations numbered 2,521. But the report for November is missing. See figure 1.

18. Archives of Paris police prefecture, "Situation de Paris," December 30, 1940, and subsequent reports.

19. Biélinky, *Journal*, January 14, 1941, p. 93.

20. Douelle, October 24, 1941, Apeloig to Albert Manuel, CC-10 to 12.

21. Louis Joinet, "Affaire dite du `Fichier des Juifs'," in *Il y a cinquante ans, le statut des Juifs*, ed. Serge Klarsfeld (Paris: CDJC, 1991), 105–135.

22. "La charte des Juifs établie à Vichy va entrer en vigueur," *Le Matin*, October 18, 1940.

23. Cited by Daniel Cordier, "La Résistance française et les Juifs," *Annales*, 48–3, 1993, p. 622.

24. Archives of the PP, "Situation à Paris."

25. According to the table of Jewish businesses in AN, AJ 38, 538 (without date). See table 1.

26. CDJC, LXXIXa–10, November 14, 1940, memorandum from the office of the head of the German military administration in France. (There were, more precisely, 7,737 businesses owned by individuals and 3,456 Jewish companies.)

27. Biélinky, *Journal*.

28. *Le Matin*, November 1, 1940.

29. Biélinky, *Journal*, October 25, 1940, pp. 63–64.

30. Letter from the *Militärbefehlshaber* in France to the Ministry of Industrial Production and Labor, dated December 9, 1940, cited by Michael R. Marrus and Robert O. Paxton, *Vichy France and the Jews*, 8.

31. Instruction given by the MBF to the steward-administrator, dated November 12, 1940. AN, AJ 38, 117.

32. According to a ruling issued by the MBF on December 12, 1940. Billig, *Le Commissariat général*, 3:76–80, and *Les Juifs sous l'Occupation*, 32–33.

33. Archives of the Paris police prefecture, "Situation à Paris."

34. According to the figures given by a report of the Auditing Office of Berlin. This report was based on the data provided by the SCAP in February 1942. CDJC, LXXV-19, cited by Billig, *Le Commissariat général*, 3:288.

35. Ibid., report dated May 8, 1942 (CDJC, CIV-79) cited by Billig, *Le Commissariat général*, 3:295.

36. Ibid., 291.

37. Biélinky, *Journal*, December 19, 1940, p. 83.

38. Ibid., December 30, 1940, p. 86.

39. Ibid., January 5 and 6, 1941, pp. 90–91.

40. A good number of these denunciations can be found in the National Archives, AJ 38, 6.

41. N.N., July 25, 1941, CDJC, XIa-431, cited by Adam Rutkowski, ed., *La Lutte des Juifs en France à l'époque de l'Occupation* (Paris: Editions du Centre, 1975), 55.

42. Max Heilbronn and Jacques Varin, *Galeries Lafayette—Buchenwald—Galeries Lafayette* (Paris: Economica, 1989), pp. 73–77.

43. Hamon, "Etude sur la situation," 72.

44. Ibid., 70.

45. These cases are reported in a long text written by Jewish Communists, called "Deux ans de persécution antisémite." It was never published. Archives of the Musée de la Résistance, Champigny, Diamant Collection.

46. Biélinky, *Journal*, July 18, 1941, p. 130.

47. Dominique Veillon, *La Mode sous l'Occupation* (Paris: Payot), 80ff.

48. Archives of the Paris police prefecture, "Situation à Paris," April 7, 1941.

49. Archives of the Paris police prefecture, "Situation à Paris," May 19, 1941. To be precise, there were 326 shoemakers and 384 shoe sellers in Paris, according to the list of Jewish businesses (AN, AJ 38, 538, undated).
50. Veillon, *La Mode sous l'Occupation*, 80.
51. Archives of the Paris police prefecture, "Situation à Paris," July 28, 1941.
52. Archives of the Paris police prefecture, "Situation à Paris," August 11, 1941.
53. Ibid., April 28, 1941.
54. Archives of the Paris police prefecture, May 19, 1941. These facts are also reported in "Deux ans de persécution antisémite," Archives of the Musée de la Résistance, Champigny, Diamant Collection.
55. Archives of the Paris police prefecture, June 3, 1941.
56. "Deux ans de persécution antisémite," archives of the Musée de la Résistance, Champigny, Diamant Collection.
57. Jewish businesses under provisional management, AN, AJ 38, 538, December 3, 1941.
58. Henri Michel, *Paris Allemand* (Paris: Albin Michel, 1982), 181.
59. AN, Aj 38, 197, mail and investigations of the Police des Question Juives, October 18, 1942.
60. Police prefecture, head office of the general administration, memorandum for the local police chiefs, February 26, 1941, signed François. AN, AJ 38–538.
61. *Les Juifs sous l'Occupation*, a collection of official French and German texts, 1940–1944, Paris, CDJC-FFJF, 1982, pp. 41–44.
62. AN, AJ 38, 70, M 85, October 7, 1941, message from the Commissariat Général aux Questions Juives to the Paris police prefect.
63. Ibid., 54.
64. "Les Juifs à Paris sous l'Occupation allemande," report doubtless written by Ruven Grinberg, July 30 1941, AIU, CC-4 and YIVO, Tcherikower holding, dossier 1650.
65. AN, F 60, 490, message from La Laurencie sent to the head office of the Armistice Bureau in Vichy.
66. See Jean Massot, "Instruments, relais et cadres du régime: Le Conseil d'État," in *Le Régime de Vichy et les Français* (Paris: Fayard, 1992), 312–328, and in particular Jean Marcou, *Le Conseil d'État sous Vichy, 1940–1944*, diss., 1984, 231ff.
67. Their exemptions were granted by a decree dating from January 5, 1941, which was never published in the *Journal Officiel*. CDJC, CXV-100, cited by Carole Fink, *Marc Bloch: a Life in History* (New York: Cambridge University Press, 1989), 252.
68. Message from Darlan to the Commissariat Général aux Questions Juives, August 7, 1941, AN, F 60 491.
69. CDJC, CXV-100, Vichy memorandum dating from January 30, 1943, cited by Billig, *Le Commissariat général*, 3:21.
70. This example and those that follow are found in the report on "the present situation of French Jews," which was distributed in the second half of 1942 by the Central Consistory to its delegates, AIU, CC-17. This document is complemented by another document: "Quelques exemples tragiques de situation faite à de nombreux israélites," AIU, CC-10.
71. This waiting period had been established thanks to the proposal of General de La Laurencie; see the affirmative response given by Baudouin on November 4, 1940. AN, F 60 490, from the office of the Président du Conseil.
72. AN, AJ 38, 1145.
73. Jérôme Carcopino, *Souvenirs de sept ans* (Paris: Flammarion, 1953), 360.
74. AN, F 60, 490.
75. Vichy, January 12, 1941. Memorandum to the generals and to the commanders of fifteen military divisions. CC, dossier 1940–1942, laws, ordinances, decrees.
76. AN, F 60, 490. Minutes of the meeting of December 16, 1940 at the Hôtel Thermal, in which were examined the questions raised by the law of October 3, 1940.
77. There were to be exact 2,919 such cases. AN, AJ 38 146 Ministry of the Interior, "Jewish agents and employees of the government fired under the application of the laws of October 3,

1940 and June 2, 1941," March 23, 1942, cited by Denis Peschanski, "Les Statuts des Juifs," in *Il y a cinquante ans: le Statut des Juifs,* ed. Serge Klarsfeld (Paris: CDJC, 1991), 32.

78. Claude Singer, *Vichy, l'Université et les Juifs* (Paris: Les Belles Lettres, 1992), 106.

79. Ibid., 165.

80. Ibid., 158.

81. Jean-Richard Bloch, Moscow, May 3–5, 1941. Confidential report on intellectuals: resistance to racism. CRCEDHC, holding 517, catalogue 1, 1931.

82. Ibid., 172.

83. Memorandum number 2008/SG, dating from December 21, 1940, addressed to government ministers and secretaries of state, AN, AJ 38, 1145.

84. AN, AJ 38, 1145, message from the minister of justice to the Commissariat Général aux Questions Juives, May 23, 1941.

85. AN, AJ 38, 158, individual dossiers.

86. Jean-Pierre Bertin-Maghit, *Le Cinéma sous l'Occupation* (Paris: Olivier Orban, 1989), 70 ff., and AJ 38, 1137, Vichy, April 23, 1941, memorandum from the chief of staff of the Commissariat Général aux Questions Juives concerning the application of the Jewish Statutes to the film industry.

87. The law pertaining to lawyers dated from September 10, 1940. See Marrus and Paxton, *Vichy France and the Jews,* 17–18, and Hamon, "Etude sur la situation," 75.

88. AN, AJ 38, 1 146, figures communicated to the Commissariat Général aux Questions Juives by the chancellery on April 18, 1941.

89. Hamon, "Etude sur la situation," 87.

90. Archives of the Paris police prefecture, "Situation à Paris," January 1941.

91. Hamon, "Etude sur la situation," 62.

92. "Les Juifs à Paris sous l'Occupation Allemande" (see note 64).

93. On this question, see Renée Poznanski, *Avant les premières grandes rafles; les Juifs à Paris sous l'Occupation (juin 1940–avril 1941), Cahiers de l'IHTP,* no. 22, December 1992, 32ff.

94. This was the decision made on May 31, 1941, at a meeting of the heads of the various offices and departments of the Commissariat Général aux Questions Juives, AN, AJ38, 2. The numbers are given in the undated table of Jewish businesses in Paris having posted the yellow placard. AN, AJ 38, 538, SCAP and Office of Economic Aryanization.

95. Hamon, "Etude sur la situation," 62.

96. Biélinky, *Journal,* 104, 11 avril 1941 and Hamon, "Etude sur la situation," 118.

97. French police forces at first arrested thirty-seven people responsible for this action, but released them once it was established that the operation had been carried out in agreement with the German Occupation authorities. Archives of the Paris police prefecture, "Situation à Paris, April 14, 1941. In a letter dated April 28, 1941, Admiral Darlan regretted that this takeover was not carried out "in an orderly manner, with a properly issued requisition order." AN, F 60 490, premier's office.

98. Archives of the Paris police prefecture, "Situation à Paris," December 2, 1940, December 9, 1940 and following.

99. There are numerous such examples in AN, AJ 38 6.

100. Roger Langeron, *Paris, Juin 1940,* January 2, 1941, p. 216. Hamon, "Etude sur la situation.," 81.

101. Archives of the Paris police prefecture, "Situation à Paris," December 30, 1940, January 6, 1941, January 13, 1941, and following.

102. Archives of the Paris police prefecture, "Situation à Paris," October 7, 1940, January 13, 1941.

103. Hamon, "Etude sur la situation," 77.

104. Singer, *Vichy, l'Université et les Juifs.*

105. Its creation had been announced in *La Terre retrouvée* dated September 15, 1940. It had set up an office on Rue Elzévir.

106. "Les Juifs à Paris sous l'Occupation allemande" (see note 64).

107. Ibid.

108. One thousand of them were served by the soup kitchen on the Rue de Saintonge and the one run by the ACIP. Jacques Adler, *The Jews of Paris and the Final Solution: Communal Response and Internal Conflicts, 1940–1944* (New York: Oxford University Press, 1987).

109. Report on the activity of the Joint in Paris, December 31, 1940. Herbert Katzki, Joint, General and Emergency, 609.

110. To learn more about these first few months of the Occupation in Paris and the Amelot Committee, see memoirs of Henry Bulawko, *Les jeux de la mort et de l'espoir* (Paris: Encres, 1980).

111. Adler, *The Jews of Paris and the Final Solution*, 60.

112. Gestapo inspections of the Central Consistory, from the minutes of the meetings held between December 19, 1940 and March 28, 1941, AIU, CC-4.

113. *Informations juives*, no. 3, May 1, 1941.

114. On the subject of Jewish organizations and German Occupation authorities in Paris, see Poznanski, "Avant les premières grandes rafles," 39–51.

115. Paris, January 21, 1941, "Office central juif à Paris," Dannecker, CDJC, V-59.

116. Undated report on the state of Jewish affairs, probably written toward the end of June 1941, AIU, CC-57.

117. AIU, CC-48.

118. "Les Juifs à Paris sous l'Occupation allemande" (see note 64).

119. *Informations juives*, no. 2, April 25, 1941, AIU, CC-48.

120. Report by Marcel Sachs cited by Maurice Moch in "Tentative de création d'un *Judenrat* en France; l'action de défense en zone nord des dirigeants du Consistoire et du Comité de coordination," *Pardès* 16 (1992): 55.

121. Hamon, "Etude sur la situation," 106.

122. Adler, *The Jews of Paris and the Final Solution*, 173–174.

123. Reports kept at the Bibliothèque nationale, under the shelf mark Res. G 1470 (1020 bis). The last edition to be analyzed was that of March 14, 1941.

124. The paper of A. Bekerman, cited in *La Presse antiraciste sous l'Occupation hitlérienne* (Paris: UJRE, 1950), 26.

125. Archives of the Paris police prefecture, "Situation à Paris." This tract was reported on June 9, 1941.

126. "A bas les mesures racistes prises contre les petits et moyens commerçants juifs," in *La presse antiraciste sous l'occupation hitlérienne* (Paris: UJRE, 1950), 261–268.

127. See Annie Kriegel, "Résistants communistes et Juifs persécutés," *Réflexions sur les questions juives* (Paris: Hachette, 1984), 29–58.

128. "A bas les mesures racistes" (see note 126), 267–268.

129. Surveillance of Jewish groups by the *Section des Renseignements généraux et des jeux*, May 8, 1941, CDJC, LXXVII-7. The French translation of some excerpts of these reports and an analysis of their contents can be found in Annette Wieviorka, *Ils étaient juifs, résistants, communistes* (Paris: Denoël, 1986), 82ff.

130. Alain Michel, *Les Eclaireurs israélites de France pendant la Seconde Guerre mondiale* (Paris: Editions des EIF, 1984), 135–140.

131. David Diamant, *Le Billet Vert* (Paris: Editions du Renouveau, 1977), 26. The same text has also been cited by Serge Klarsfeld, ed., *1941, Les Juifs en France* (Paris: FFDJF, 1991), 27.

132. CDJC, LXXVII-12, "Israelites sent to the concentration camps in the Loiret department." Paris police prefecture mentioned 3,747 Jews who were thus sent to the Loiret camps. "Situation à Paris."

133. Gérard Walter, *La Vie à Paris sous l'Occupation* (Paris: Armand Colin, 1960), 180.

134. Archives of the Paris police prefecture, "Situation à Paris."

135. Biélinky, *Journal*, beginning on May 14, 1941, pp. 112ff.

136. "Les Juifs à Paris sous l'Occupation allemande" (see note 64).

137. AJ 38, 67.

138. For a description of living conditions in these two camps, see Laurence Appelbaum-Rosengart, *Qui est Juif? L'oeuvre législative du régime de Vichy*, diss., Paris, 1990.

139. Biélinky, *Journal*, June 1, 1941, p. 118.

140. Archives of the Paris police prefecture, "Situation à Paris," June 30, 1941.

141. The deputy prefect of the Loiret département had issued a ruling on the matter on May 24, 1941. See AN, AJ 38, 229, message on security in the Pithiviers camp, sent by the deputy prefect of the Loiret to the minister and secretary of state for the interior, Orléans, March 25, 1942.

142. Diamant, *Le Billet vert*, 176.

143. Such was the case of the father of Madeleine. Claudine Vegh, *Je ne lui ai pas dit au revoir; des enfants de déportés parlent*, with a preface by Bruno Bettelheim (Paris: Gallimard, 1979), 57.

144. Jacques Ravine, *La Résistance organisée des Juifs en France, 1940–1944* (Paris: Julliard, 1973), 85.

145. M. Vilner-Fanstein, June 25, 1942, reproduced in David Diamant, *Par-delà les barbelés* (Paris, 1986).

146. Diamant, *Le Billet vert*, 84ff. M. Vilner (N. Fanstein), editor of the *Pithiviers Concentrationlager Zeitung*, was to become chief editor of the Communist daily newspaper *Naïe presse* after the war.

147. Biélinky, *Journal*, June 9, 1941, p. 120.

148. Ravine, *La Résistance organisée*, 55.

149. CDJC, LXXV-238, pp. 3–5, report of a German police agent for the month of July 1941 dated August 4, 1941 and reproduced in Adam Rutkowski, *La Lutte des Juifs en France à l'époque de l'Occupation* (Paris: Editions du Centre, 1975), 63–64.

150. "Note sur les manifestations des femmes des internés civils," YIVO, UGIF, I–13, and Biélinky, *Journal*, August 1 1941, p. 134.

151. Archives of the Paris police prefecture, passim.

152. AN, F 60 502, message from the Paris police chief to Darlan, July 3, 1941.

153. According to a report by Dannecker, CDJC, XXVI-1.

154. Annie Lambert, *Les Juifs dispersés de quatre départements bretons face à l'antisémitisme institutionnalisé*: 1939–1945, diss., Université de Haute-Bretagne, Rennes-II, 1990, 29.

155. Ibid, p. 8.

156. Christophe Capelle, *La Destruction des Juifs de Seine-Inférieure*, Rouen, 1991, 1:34.

157. Daniel Cordier, "La Résistance française et les Juifs," *Annales, ESC*,48–3, 1993, p. 622.

158. AN, AJ 38, 1157.

159. AN, AJ 38, 1157, September 1, 1941, message from the special police prefect to the director of the Supervisory Office of Provisional Managers (SCAP) in Paris.

160. AN, AJ 38, 229.

161. AN, AJ 38, 147.

162. AN, AJ 38, 1147, message from the prefect of the Allier département to the regional representative of the police for Jewish Affairs of Dijon.

163. AN, AJ 38, 1147, January 10, 1944, overall report on Jewish businesses in the Jura made by an inspector for the Office of Investigation and Inspection (Section d'enquête et de contrôle, SEC).

164. See Claude Tocze, *L'Antisémitisme économique, aryanisation de l'économie et spoliation des Juifs en Bretagnede 1940 à 1944*, diss. Université de Haute-Bretagne, Rennes-II, 1990.

165. AN, AJ 38, 1152, Many 30, 1942, message from the secretary-general of the prefecture to the police for Jewish Affairs on the status of Jewish businesses.

166. Centre de Documentation Juive Contemporaine, CCCLXIX-22.

167. Michel Slitinsky, "Les spoliations à Bordeaux et dans la région, 1940–1944."

168. Hamon, "Etude sur la situation."

169. Report on Bordeaux and Bayonne, undated, AIU, CC-4.

170. Roger Berg, *La Persécution raciale* (Paris: Office français d'édition, 1947), 194ff.

171. YIVO, UGIF, XCII-57, p. 7, cited by Zosa Szajkowski, *Analytical Franco-Jewish Gazetteer, 1939–1945* (New York, 1966), 210.

172. According to the testimony of Henri Kriesher.

173. Françoise Job, *Gustave Nordon (1877–1944)* with a preface by André Kaspi (Nancy: Presses Universitaires de Nancy, 1992).

174. December 16, 1940. Narrative account of the arrest of the Jews in Boulogne, AIU, CC-16.

175. Centre de Documentation Juive Contemporaine, LXXV-249, Letter from the German military commander for the Dijon area to the local command office in Troyes, reproduced in Rutkowski, *La Lutte des Juifs en France*, 48. See also YIVO, RG 343 22, Troyes, April 3, 1941, report submitted by Mademoiselle Panas to Monsieur Rapoport.

176. Paris, March 28, 1941, unsigned document, Joint, General and Emergency, France, 609.

177. "Renseignements sur le camp de La Lande," AIU, CC-4, and YIVO, archives of the Rue Amelot, 23, cited by Zosa Szajkowski, *Analytical Franco-Jewish Gazetteer*, 203–204.

178. Robert Aron, *Fragments d'une vie* (Paris: Plon, 1981), 132.

179. AN, AJ 38, 152, August 30, 1941, message from the prefect of the Gironde region to the Commissariat Général aux Questions Juives. See also AIU, CC-18, "Affaire d'Arcachon," report by Monsieur Cohen, chief rabbi in Bordeaux, undated but doubtless written in early August 1941.

180. Report by the rabbi of the département of La Moselle, submitted to the prefect on August 4, 1941, AIU, CC-31 and AIU, CC-7: "Rapport sur un camp de la Haute Vienne," undated and unsigned. See also Zosa Szajkowkski, *Analytical Franco-Jewish Gazetteer*, 284, and YIVO, RG 34329, visit to the camp at Poitiers on the Limoges highway, September 11, 1941, Madame Valensi, social worker.

181. This was at the La Sansonnerie center. YIVO, RG 343 29, agreement signed by Monsieur and Madame Roux, Madame Valensi, and Rabbi Elie Bloch.

3. *The State, Society, and the French Israelites in the Unoccupied Zone (pages 66–103)*

1. Nina Gourfinkel, "Le problème de l'aménagement des Centres d'accueil vu de Lyon," October 25, 1940, YIVO, France during World War II, 3–43.

2. *Procès de Xavier Vallat*, with an introduction by his friends (Paris: Editions du Conquistador, 1948), 104.

3. Clara Malraux, *Le Bruit de nos pas*, vol. 5, *La fin et le commencement* (Paris: Grasset, 1976), 200.

4. Message from Kahany to the Zionist Executive in Jerusalem. Geneva, October 14, 1940, CZA, S 26–1452.

5. Philippe Landau, "Religion et patrie: les prières israélites pour la France," *Pardès* 14 (1991): 11–32.

6. As did the prefect for the Alpes-Maritimes region in his message to Darlan dated May 10, 1941, AN, F 60, 502.

7. Ernst Papanek and Edward Linn, *Out of Fire* (New York: Morrow, 1975).

8. Léon Werth, "October 4, 1942," in *Déposition, Journal, 1940–1944* (Paris: Viviane Hamy, 1992), 352.

9. Herbert Katzki, August 31, 1940, Joint, General, France, 594.

10. Memorandum dated January 1941, Centre de Documentation Juive Contemporaine, V-59.

11. Marrus and Paxton, Ivichy France and the Jews, 82–83.

12. Pierre Birnbaum, *Un Mythe politique: "la République juive"* (Paris: Fayard, 1988), 327.

13. Raymond-Raoul Lambert, *Carnet d'un témoin, 1940–1943*, with an introduction and notes by Richard Y. Cohen (Paris: Fayard, 1985), May 10, 1941, p. 101.

14. For the government minister, the secretary of state for the interior, the state counselor, and the secretary-general for the administration, Maurice Sabatier, AN, AJ 38, 146.

15. Vichy, September 2, 1941, message from the secretary of state in charge of basic necessities and supplies to regional and departmental prefects and others, AN, AJ 38, 289.

16. According to a report made by the minister of the interior on March 23, 1942, AN, AJ 38, 146. Cited by Denis Peschanski, "The Statutes on Jews—October 3, 1940 and June 2, 1941," *Yad Vashem Studies* 22 (1992): 65–88.

17. AN, AJ 38, 1145 contains the minutes of this meeting, as well as the responses from the various ministries to the question of candidates for such reassignments and possible new positions. See also Marc-Olivier Baruch, *Servir l'État français* (Paris: Fayard, 1997), 137ff.

18. AN, AJ 38, 1145.

19. AN, AJ 38, 61, M 49.

20. Centre de Documentation Juive Contemporaine, LXI-42, cited by Joseph Billig, *Le Commissariat général aux questions juives* (Paris: Editions du Centre, 1960), 2:213.

21. Henry Rousso, "L'aryanisation économique; Vichy, l'occupant et la spoliation des Juifs," *Yod* 15–16 (1982):58.

22. AN, AJ 38, 117. The memorandum has been printed in *Les Juifs sous l'Occupation* (see note 64 to chapter 2), 75–78.

23. AN, AJ 38, 1147. Memorandum on the modifications introduced by the laws of November 17, 1941.

24. Marrus and Paxton, *Vichy France and the Jews,* 135ff.

25. AN, AJ 38, 242, July 22, 1941, message from the secretary-general in charge of police to the General Commission on Jewish Affairs.

26. AN, AJ 38, 242. Mains office of the National Police, October 28, 1941.

27. AIU, CC-6, message from Georges Cahen to Helbronner, Vichy, June 14, 1941.

28. CC-7, memorandum issued by the regional office of the state police in Clermont-Ferrand in response to a letter from Benjamin Holzmann, a leader of Jewish worship who had been ordered to leave the Allier département by July 18, 1941.

29. AN, AJ 38, 242, reports from the meetings of the special commission.

30. AN, AJ 38, 244, head of the police for Jewish Affairs in April 1942 to the secretary-general for the police.

31. AN, AJ 38, 261, inspector's reports.

32. AIU, CC-22, letter from Rabbi Robert Meyers to Albert Manuel, March 3, 1942.

33. Lublin Archives, dossier 26. Handbook for mayors and gendarme brigades on laws concerning Jews.

34. Anne Grynberg, *Les camps de la honte,* 94. Claude Laharie gives the number of 6,538 Jews detained in the Gurs camp in *Le Camp de Gurs, 1939–1945; Un aspect méconnu de l'histoire du Béarn* (Pau: Infocompo, 1985), 168.

35. Forty thousand is the number given by Grynberg, *Le camps de la honte,* 12.

36. Report written by a delegate from the Central Consistory in early 1942, AIU, CC-20.

37. Marrus and Paxton, *Vichy France and the Jew,* 137–138.

38. *Le Petit Marseillais,* October 18, 1940.

39. Vichy, October 18, 1940, power of attorney Guérard, cited by Serge Klarsfeld, *Le Statut des Juifs de Vichy* (Paris: FFDJF-CDJC, 1990), 27.

40. October 19, 1940, cited by Jacques Polonski, *La Presse, la propagande et l'opinion publique* (Paris: Editions du Centre, 1946), 34.

41. AIU, CC-16.

42. December 22, 1941, excerpts from the diary of Isaïe Schwartz, in his account of Vladimir d'Ormesson's visit. AIU, CC-32.

43. The terms are those of General Boris, in a memorandum dating from November 1941. AIU, CC-57.

44. Raymond-Raoul Lambert, *Carnet d'un témoin,* August 16, 1941, p. 126.

45. On the subject of radio propaganda, see Hélène Eck, ed., *La Guerre des ondes,* with preface by Jean-Noël Jeanneney (Paris: Armand Colin, 1985).

46. Henri Sinder, "La situation des Juifs depuis l'armistice en juin 1940," undated but most probably November 1942, YIVO, France during WWII, 4–56.

47. Christian Font and Henri Moizet, *Les Juifs et l'antisémitisme en Aveyron pendant la Deuxième Guerre mondiale* (CRDP de l'Aveyron, 1994), 10ff.

48. These declarations date from April 13, 1941. Jacques Adler, *The Jews of Paris and the Final Solution*, 18.

49. Declaration made by Xavier Vallat on the French State's radio on December 20, 1941. AIU, CC-49. On the subject of Xavier Vallat's objectives, see Marrus and Paxton, *Vichy France and the Jews*, 96ff.

50. Nahum Hermann, CZA, KH 4B 2378. Nahum Hermann was the leader of the *Keren ha-yessod* in France. Thanks to his American press card, he was residing in Vichy at the time (according to the report received in Geneva on April 13, 1942 from Joseph Fisher, CZA, KKL 5 12149).

51. Lambert, *Carnet d'un témoin*, June 22, 1941, pp. 107–112.

52. On this subject, see Pierre Laborie, "The Jewish Statutes in Vichy France and Public Opinion," *Yad Vashem Studies* 22 (1992): 89–114.

53. October 6, 1940, Marie-Thérèse Gadala, *A travers la grande grille, mai 1940-october 1941* (Paris: Editions du Grand Siècle, 1946), 127.

54. Marc Ferro, *Pétain* (Paris: Fayard, 1987), 241.

55. Reports from Georges Leven, March 18, 1941, AIU, CC-5.

56. Meeting of March 16–17, 1941, AIU, CC-1-b.

57. Jacques Helbronner related his May 30, 1941 meeting with Pétain during the meeting of the Central Consistory held on June 15, 1941. AIU, CC-1-b.

58. The text of Pétain's pronouncement appears in Marie-Thérèse Gadala, *A travers la grande grille*, 2:29. There was, however, no protestation after the execution of the hostages at Châteaubriand.

59. AIU, CC-14, notes taken by Robert Kiefe from the meeting of December 16, 1941.

60. Andrzej Bobkowski, *En guerre et en paix, Journal 1940–1944* (Paris: Editions Noir sur Blanc, 1991), 243–244.

61. AIU, CC-10.

62. Lambert, *Carnet d'un témoin*, December 20, 1940.

63. Ibid., July 16, 1941.

64. Joseph Barthélemy, *Ministre de la Justice, Vichy, 1941–1943, Mémoires* (Paris: Pygmalion-G. Watelet, 1989), 319–320.

65. AN, AJ 38, 61-M 46.

66. Lambert, *Carnet d'un témoin*, July 16, 1941, p. 116.

67. AIU, CC-5, Central Consistory meeting of April 20 and 21, 1941.

68. AIU, CC-59.

69. Jean-Louis Panicacci, *Les Juifs et la question juive dans les Alpes-Maritimes de 1939 à 1945, Recherches régionales, Côte d'Azur et contrées limitrophes*, 1983, 3:239–327.

70. AIU, CC-36 contains the invitation to the ceremony and the letter sent by Raymond Bloch, president of the Worship Association to the president of the Central Consistory on November 4, 1941.

71. AIU, CC-34, report given by Chief Rabbi Schilli on his rabbinical activities in Montpellier from January 1 through May 1, 1941.

72. Claire Andrieu, "Démographie, famille, jeunese," in *La France des années noires*, 1:455ff. See also Alain Michel, *Les Éclaireurs israélites de France pendant la Seconde Guerre mondiale* (Paris: Editions des Éclaireurs Israélites de France, 1984), 86ff.

73. AN, AJ 38, 265, PQJ, Vichy, "Report on the activity of Doctor Weill in Terrasson," Périgueux, October 27, 1941.

74. "There must be no group leaders or managers, but the General Commission on Jewish Affairs has no problem with allowing Jews to stay in youth hostels," wrote the General Commission on Jewish Affairs to the Office of the Secretary-General for Youth on May 30, 1941. On September 17, the situation brought into line and "in compliance with German Occupation authorities, Jews must be banned from youth hostels," AN, AJ 38, 64.

75. Rabbi Samuel Klein, report on his activities since September 1940, Vichy, June 12, 1941, AIU, CC-39.

76. Letter from "Building Grounds" head Rebiquet to Rabbi Schönberg, AIU, CC-35.
77. Centre de Documentation Juive Contemporaine, XXXI-128.
78. "Organisations de secours," undated, but probably summer 1941, CC, dossier on associations.
79. AN, AJ 38, 261, report number 557 filed by Inspector Lathière on July 6, 1942.
80. Jacques Helbronner pronounced these words at the meeting of the Central Consistory on June 15, 1941. AIU, CC-1-b.
81. Letter from Bernard Schönberg to Isaïe Schwartz, February 27, 1941, CC-35.
82. AIU, CC-11, August 16, 1941.
83. *Carnets du Pasteur Boegner, 1940–1945,* with an introduction and notes by Philippe Boegner (Paris: Fayard, 1992), 107 passim.
84. AIU, CC-3.
85. Jean-Louis Crémieux-Brilhac, ed., *Les voix de la liberté, Ici Londres, 1940–1944* (Paris: La Documentation française, 1976), 1:217.
86. Cited by Daniel Cordier, *Jean Moulin, l'inconnu du Panthéon,* vol. 1, *Une ambition pour la République* (Paris: Lattès, 1989), 25–26.
87. Indomitus, "Lettre au Maréchal," no. 9, January 25, 1942, cited by Olivier Wieviorka, *Destins d'un mouvement de Résistance: Défense de la France,* diss., University of Paris I-Sorbonne, 1992, 52. See also *Une certaine idée de la Résistance. Défense de la France, 1940–1949* (Paris: Seuil, 1995).

The most extreme example of contamination of Resistance circles by such strains of diluted antisemitism is found in the first edition of the *Cahiers de l'OCM* (Organisation Civile et Militaire [Civil and Military Organization], whose civilian branch was directed by a Jew, Maxime Blocq-Mascart) in June 1942. It was so extreme that it stirred up a controversy in other Resistance newspapers. I thus prefer to support my case by using other examples.

88. Daniel Mayer, *Les Socialistes dans la Résistance* (Paris: Presses Universitaires de France, 1968), 28–30.
89. Werth, *Déposition,* June 20, 1941, 218–219.
90. According to Claude Vigée, in a letter to his uncle dated May 4, 1942 and printed in *La Lune d'hiver* (Paris: Flammarion, 1970), 110.
91. Henri Sinder, "La situation des Juifs depuis l'armistice" (as in note 46).
92. AIU, CC-17, July 1942. Brive, report by the Consistory's regional delegation.
93. AIU, CC-23, message from Robert Meyers to Albert Manuel, Annecy, June 18, 1942.
94. Gadala, *A travers la grande grille,* 1:139.
95. AIU, CC-18, Nîmes, notes submitted by Boris.
96. Jean-Louis Panicacci, *Les Juifs et la question juive,* 243.
97. Font and Moizet, *Les Juifs et l'antisémitisme,* 8.
98. Laborie, "The Jewish Statutes," 89–114.
99. January 23, 1942, message from the public attorney in the Riom appeals court to the minister of justice, AN, AJ 38, 7.
100. Henri Sinder, "La situation des Juifs depuis l'armistice" (as in note 46).
101. CDJC, CCXII-28, reprinted in Adam Rutkowski (editor), *La Lutte des Juifs en France à l'époque de l'Occupation* (Paris: Editions du Centre, 1975), 45–46.
102. Ibid., October 2, 1940.
103. AIU, CC-1-b, proceedings of the meeting.
104. February 20, 1941, AIU, CC-49.
105. CC, boxes 10 to 12.
106. The president of the Central Consistory, Edouard de Rothschild, had left France for the United States. He was followed a few weeks later by Robert de Rothschild, president of the Paris Consistory. See Maurice Moch, *L'Etoile et la francisque,* ed. Alain Michel (Paris: Cerf, 1990), 48.
107. Minutes of the meeting, AIU, CC-15.
108. Edgar Morin, *Autocritique* (Paris: Le Seuil, 1975), 30.
109. Werth, *Déposition,* 129.
110. Ibid., December 9, 1940, p. 128.

111. Roger Stéphane, *Chaque homme est lié au monde, Carnets août 1939/août 1944* (Paris: Sagittaire, 1946), October 6, 1940, p. 51. "Already before the war," writes Edgar Morin, "I was fearful of reacting to political events on the basis of being a Jew. . . . If I had not been a Jew, I would have reacted to this filthy antisemitism from the very beginning of the Occupation—at least, I hope I would have. But in striving to remain clear-headed on one point, I made myself blind on another. I was even ready to accept the sacrifice of the Jews if that was what it took to save the rest of the French people, if such were the fate of history." *Autocritique*, 30.

112. CDJC, CCCXXI-8 and CCXIX-14, reprinted in Rutkowski, *La Lutte des Juifs en France*, 57ff.

113. AIU, CC-5.

114. Speech made by the vice president of the Central Consistory on October 19, 1941, AIU, CC1-a. "Objections have been raised for the sake of honor and for the future," declared the chief rabbi of France at the general assembly of French rabbis at Chamalières on September 10 and 11, 1941, AIU CC-31.

115. AIU, CC-32.

116. AN, F 60, 490, file 1940.

117. AIU, CC-49.

118. CDJC, LXXII-2, cited by Adam Rutkowski, *La Lutte des Juifs en France*, 52–53.

119. AIU, CC-1a, record of the deliberations of the Central Consistory from March 16, 1941 through May 6, 1943.

120. June 17, 1941, AIU, CC-9.

121. Letter from Jacques Helbronner to Pétain, June 25, 1941, CC-7.

122. Périgueux, October 27, 1941, Report on the activities of Dr. Weill, AN, AJ 38, 265, report from inspectors with the Police for Jewish Affairs.

123. Speech given by the vice president of the Central Consistory on October 19, 1941, AIU, CC-1a.

124. The form requested its recipients to "provide information as soon as possible about the genealogy of Jewish families having lived in France for several generations," AIU, CC-44.

125. AIU, CC-6.

126. In his memoirs, *La brisure et l'attente, 1930–1955* (Paris: Seuil-La Découverte, 1995).

127. Ibid., 109.

128. Ibid., 107.

129. The text of this letter has been printed in Moch, *L'Etoile et la Francisque*, 45–46.

130. Such was the report written by General Boris in February 1942 and of a study of antisemitism done in July 1942. AIU, CC-57.

131. AIU, CC-24, instructions for general distribution, September 1942. This text is a revised version of a prior document.

132. AIU, CC-32.

133. AN, AJ-38, 61, M 46, general inspection division of the offices of the Renseignements généraux.

134. "This evening the decree against the Jews was published in the *Journal Officiel*. There are no more copies of it anywhere, since every Jew has bought three or four of them," wrote Marie-Thérèse Gadala, *A travers la grande grille*, 1:140.

135. Concise report on the survey carried out by the delegates of the Leadership Council of Jewish Youth, Marseilles, July 18, 1941, AIU, CC-39. It was presented to the permanent delegation of the Central Consistory by Pierre Dreyfus on July 20, 1941, AIU, CC-15.

136. Werth, *Déposition*, 225–226.

137. July 8, 1941, Lambert, *Carnet d'un témoin*, 117.

138. These examples are taken from CC-1.

139. Lucien Simon, *Les Juifs à Nîmes et dans le Gard durant la Deuxième Guerre mondiale* (Nîmes: Lacour libraire-éditeur, 1985), 17.

140. CDJC, LXI-40, memorandum sent by Chavin to prefects, July 12, 1941, cited by Joseph Billig, *Le Commissariat général aux questions juives*, 2:207.

141. CC, genealogy file—1941.

142. AN, AJ 38, 70. Annecy, October 18, 1941, report filed by Captaine Gresset with the General Commission on Jewish Affairs, concerning individual declarations made in compliance with the census requirement.

143. CDJC, XVII-23, Hautes-Pyrénées, report on the inspections conducted in the town of Tarbes, August 25–27, 1941.

144. January 2, 1942, report on a new census form, sent by the director of the police for Jewish Affairs in the Unoccupied Zone for study by the Ministry of the Interior. Response sent to the secretary-general of the police, February 11, 1942. AN, AJ 38, 1157.

145. There were a large number of lists, including those, for example, emanating from the prefecture for the département of La Haute-Garonne on November 4, 1941, AN, AJ 38, 60.

146. Letter sent to Lécussan, director of the General Commission on Jewish Affairs in Toulouse, November 20, 1941, concerning a list sent on November 12, AN, AJ 38, 60.

147. There again, numerous examples can be found in AN, AJ 38, 60.

148. AIU, CC-49. These words were also cited in Michel, *Les Éclaireurs israélites de France*, 89.

149. CC, 7.

150. October 4, 1940, in the file containing the reactions of the Consistory to the anti-Jewish measures.

151. Denise Baumann, *Une famille comme les autres* (Paris: Albin Michel, 1985), 229–230.

152. Lambert, *Carnet d'un témoin*, February 11, 1942, p. 126.

153. Limoges, July 16, 1943. Report from an inspector with the SEC, AN, AJ 38, 262.

154. AN, AJ 38, 61.

155. AN, AJ 38, 172.

156. Ibid.

157. According to an evaluative report dated September 15, 1941 and sent to the General Commission on Jewish Affairs by the secrectary-general of the police on October 3. AN, AJ 38, 60.

158. CDJC, LXXII-16, statistical report dated March 15, 1942, cited by Joseph Billig, *Le Commissariat général aux questions juives*, 2:209.

159. Robert Aron, *Fragments d'une vie* (Paris: Plon, 1981), 135.

160. Werth, *Déposition*, 225.

161. Clara Malraux, *Le Bruit de nos pas*, vol. 6, . . . *Et pourtant j'étais libre* (Paris: Grasset, 1979), 105–110.

162. CDJC, LXI-38, Vichy, July 10, 1941, cited by Josph Lubetzki, *La Condition des Juifs en France sous l'Occupation allemande* (Paris: CDJC, 1945), 54.

163. October 8, 1941, AN, AJ 38, 60.

164. The large number of cases found in AN, AJ 38, 262, involving undeclared Jews investigated by the police for Jewish Affairs is consistent with this hypothesis.

165. John F. Sweets, *Choices in Vichy France* (New York: Oxford University Press, 1986), 119.

166. February 28, 1942, message sent by the prefect for the département of Les Bouches-du-Rhône to the General Commission on Jewish Affairs, AN, AJ 38, 60.

167. Henri Sinder, "La situation des Juifs en France depuis l'armistice" (as in note 46).

168. AIU, CC-49.

169. CC-6.

170. Letter from René Hirschler to Isaïe Schwartz, Marseilles, June 17, 1941, AIU, CC-35.

171. Vichy, July 10, 1941, CDJC, LXI-38, cited by Rutkowski, *La Lutte des Juifs en France*, 54.

172. Léon Hamon, *Vivre ses choix* (Paris: Laffont, 1991), 105.

173. Clara Malraux, *Le Bruit de nos pas*, 6:61–63.

174. These words are taken from the diary that he had started to keep. Lucien Vidal-Naquet, *Journal* (September 15 1942-February 29, 1944), *Annales, ESC*, 48–3, 1993, pp. 513–543.

175. Lambert, *Carnet d'un témoin*, June 22, 1941, 105–106.

4. *From Shock and Dismay to Adaptation (pages 104–135)*

1. Raymond-Raoul Lambert, *Carnet d'un témoin,* August 2, 1941, 121.
2. Léon Werth, *Déposition,* 216.
3. AN, AJ 38, 1145.
4. After the minister and secretary of state for the national economy and finance had ruled on the question, the same answer was given by the office of the General Commission on Jewish Affairs to the head of secondary education, the secretary of state for youth and national education on December 27, 1941.
5. "It seems to me excessive," wrote the secretary of state for family and health to the General Commission on Jewish Affairs on August 25, 1941, "that people be dismissed without any form of indemnity when they have family to support; at the very least, family subsidies should be maintained for a period of three months." On August 29, 1941, the minister and secretary of state for the national economy and finance sent his response to the legislative division of the General Commission on Jewish Affairs. AN, AJ 38, 1145.
6. AN, AJ 38, 64, Vichy, July 2, 1941, message from the General Commission on Jewish Affairs to Marion, secretary-general of information.
7. AN, AJ 38, 67, procedure to be followed for a request for special exemption, sent by the General Commission on Jewish Affairs, July 30, 1941. See also the page of explanations provided by the Commission on such requests, CC-7.
8. AN, F 60, 490, "Dismissals or terminations of professional service or employment must take effect immediately, even in cases where a request for special exemption has been filed, except in the rare cases in which such a request would appear to be clearly justified," read the ruling issued on August 7, 1941.
9. Decree number 975, AN, AJ 38, 117.
10. June 16, 1941 session of the Central Consistory, AIU, CC-1b.
11. Such was the case in Lyon, for example, of a graduate of the prestigious Ecole Polytechnique, who wrote to Xavier Vallat on July 31, 1941. AIU, CC-49.
12. See dossier found in AN, F 1bl, 919. I would like to take this occasion to thank Marc-Olivier Baruch for having drawn my attention to this case.
13. Werth, *Déposition*.
14. AIU, CC-49.
15. Letter from René Guastalla to Jérôme Carcopino, Lyon, October 23, 1941, AIU, CC-22. This letter has also been printed in Singer, *Vichy, l'Université et les Juifs,* 384–388.
16. AJ 38, 150, contains a list of requests for special exemptions filed between May 10 and August 30, 1941.
17. AN, AJ 38, 146, Vichy July 24, 1942, message from the head of the Office of the Status of Persons to the General Commission on Jewish Affairs.
18. AN, AJ 38, 150, June 23, 1942. Joseph Billig cites a memorandum drawn up in Vichy on January 30, 1943 (CDJC, CXV-100) and which reported nineteen exemptions to the first Jewish Statut, eighteen to the second, and seventeen government employees in subordinate positions who did not correspond to the terms of the law, *Le Commissariat général,* 3:21.
19. Singer, *Vichy, l'Université et les Juifs,* 253.
20. CDJC, XXIII-66, and CXV-39, also cited by Billig, *Le Commissariat général,* 3:21.
21. CC-7.
22. AN, AJ 38, 60.
23. AN, AJ 38, 1147.
24. Ibid.
25. *Pilpoul* is a Hebrew word that refers to a discussion over the Talmud.
26. AN, AJ 38, 1,090, January 12, 1943, message from the General Commission on Jewish Affairs to the regional office for the Toulouse region.
27. AN, AJ 38, 19, message from the General Commission on Jewish Affairs to the head of the Agence Fournier in Vichy, May 21, 1942.

28. The commissioner was responding to a letter sent by the secretary on February 17, 1942. AN, AJ38, 1146.
29. AN, AJ 38, 150 provides a list of Israelite doctors barred from medecine: application of the prohibition, May 5 or June 22, 1942, département of La Seine.
30. CC-7.
31. Panicacci, "Les Juifs et la question juive," 246.
32. AN, AJ 38, 58. This undated, unsigned report gives figures on the number of Jewish lawyers reported by the chancery on April 18, 1941.
33. Marc Knobel, "L'élimination des magistrats juifs sous l'Occupation," *Le Droit de vivre* (June–July 1992), and "De la loi du 2 juin 1941, de ses dispositions et de son application quant aux magistrats juifs," typewritten manuscript.
34. Lucien Vidal-Naquet, *Journal (15 septembre 1942–29 février 1944)*, 513–543. "In spite of their distinction in practicing their profession, none of these lawyers, in my judgment, has achieved the eminence required by the decree. I am therefore issuing an unfavorable ruling on the requests for their exemption," wrote Xavier Vallat on April 4, 1942 to the minister of justice. AN, AJ 38, 146.
35. Attorney Vidal-Naquet was Millerand's collaborator. See Pierre Vidal-Naquet, "Présentation d'un document, le journal de Maître Lucien Vidal-Naquet," *Annales, ESC*, 48–3, 1993, pp. 501–512.
36. AN, AJ 38, 67.
37. Lambert, *Carnet d'un témoin*, February 24 and 25, 1941.
38. Ibid., June 4, 1941.
39. Ibid., September 7, 1941.
40. AN, F7, 14929.
41. From a letter addressed to J. Helbronner, AIU, CC-5.
42. AN, AJ 38, 58, Périgueux, November 25, 1941, letter from the prefect of the département of La Dordogne to the General Commission on Jewish Affairs.
43. CC-7, correspondence from the months of April and May 1942.
44. "La condition des Israélites en France en 1942," AIU, CC-17.
45. Lambert, *Carnet d'un témoin*, July 8, 1941, p. 115.
46. Xavier Vallat reiterated this point in a letter dated September 16, 1941. Henri Boulange, a industrial magnate from the north who had moved to Marseilles and who was the patron of several budding performers in the music hall and cinema, was indignant over their exclusion and had complained about it to Vallat in a letter dated September 9, 1941. AN, AJ 38, 1147.
47. These cases can be found particularly in AN, AJ 38, 192.
48. Letter from Lécussan, August 24, 1942, AN, AJ 38, 1075.
49. July 6, 1942, letter from the head of economic aryanization in the département of La Corrèze to the area Prefect. AN, AJ 38, 1051.
50. CC-7 contains the undated letter from Dobrine Nathan as well as the text of the classified ad to which he was responding.
51. Vichy, March 3, 1941, letter from Picard, employed in the office support staff, to Pétain, CC-7.
52. Henri Sinder, "La situation des Juifs en France."
53. Letter intercepted on January 7, 1942, AN, AJ 38, 265.
54. CDJC, SVII-29, intercepted mail, "Doléances d'un médecin juif," intercepted on November 13, 1941.
55. Henri Sinder, "La situtation des Juifs en France depuis l'Armistice en juin 1940."
56. Letter from the General Commission on Jewish Affairs to the head of the government and reporting the number of people working for the commission, Vichy, August 28, 1942. AN, AJ 38, 61.
57. Billig, *Le Commissariat général*, 3:300.
58. Henry Rousso, "L'aryanisation économique," 73. The exact figure for these provisional managers in April 1944 was 825, according to Joseph Billig, *Le Commissariat général*, 3:300.

59. According to Marrus and Paxton, *Vichy France and the Jews*, 153, who base their figures on "Spoliations et restitutions," *La Documentation française*, number 1107, April 12, 1949.

60. Henri Sinder, "La situation des Juifs en France."

61. General Commission on Jewish Affairs, September 3, 1942, memorandum on the dismissal of Jewish employees by provisional managers, AN, AJ 38, 123.

62. See the numerous letters devoted to the subject in AN, AJ 38, 20.

63. AN, AJ 38, 20 September 1942.

64. Letter from the General Commission on Jewish Affairs to the regional head of the commission in Clermont Ferrand, January 31, 1942, AN, AJ 38, 20.

65. General instruction number 15 for the Division of Investigations and Inspections, December 15, 1942, AN, AJ 38, 243.

66. CC-7, correspondence between IB.R. and the Central Consistory, March 19 & 23, 1942.

67. AN, AJ 38, 1075.

68. AN, AJ 38, 259.

69. Vichy, August 30, 1941, letter from Romain Roussel, chief of staff in the Office of the Secretary-General for Information and Propaganda to the General Commission on Jewish Affairs. Roussel points out twenty-three such individuals. AN, AJ 38, 19.

70. Numerous examples of these initiatives can be found in AN, AJ 38, 158.

71. The entire file can be found in AN, AJ 38, 1153, from August 1942 to January 1943.

72. AN, AJ 38 1075.

73. There are a large number of these reports, from early 1942 to May of the same year. AN, AJ 38, 265.

74. AN, AJ 38, 19.

75. There are numerous examples of such letters in AN, AJ 38, 158.

76. AN, AJ 38, 6, May 26, 1942.

77. Vichy, November 13, 1941, report on the Jews in Saint-Géraud-le-Puy, AN, AJ 38, 60.

78. The director of the post office in Limoges would systematically report such cases. AN, AJ 38, 261.

79. Examples can be found in AN, AJ 38, 262.

80. Limoges, March 16, 1943, AN, AJ 38, 262.

81. Marseilles, June 16, 1942, AN, AJ 38, 243.

82. From a report dated October 5, 1942, AN, AJ 38, 261.

83. According to the reports on the investigations dated March 10 and March 17, 1943, AN, AJ 38, 262.

84. The complete file on this case (going from April to June 1942) can be found in AN, AJ 38, 25.

85. AN, AJ, 261.

86. The term is that of Marrus and Paxton, *Vichy France and the Jews*, 245.

87. CC-22–23.

88. February 27, 1942, Saint-Etienne, Rabbi Champagne, CC-7.

89. The completed forms can be found in CC-7.

90. This example was cited by Singer, *Vichy, l'Université et les Juifs*, 193.

91. Clara Malraux, *Le Bruit de nos pas*, vol. 5, *La Fin et le commencement* (Paris, 1976), 215–216.

92. Joseph Fisher-Ariel, "Le Sionisme et le Keren kayemeth le-Israel en France pendant la dernière guerre, Souvenirs," typewritten manuscript, Yad Vashem archives, Fisher collection (henceforth referred to as "Fisher-Ariel, "Souvenirs." This agreement made possible the distribution of some twelve million dollars, according to Joseph Fisher, "*Hagana atzmit u-meri yehudi bimey hashoa*," (Jewish self-defense and revolt during the Shoa [in Hebrew]) *Gesher* 34 (March 1963): 171. The reimbursement was made according to the rate of the parallel market, which practically doubled the sum that was thus made available to the Joint. For every dollar thus transferred, the Joint pledged to deposit ten French francs in the account of the *Keren kayemeth* of New York.

93. All these examples and more can be found in AN, AJ 38, 262.

94. AN, AJ 38, 265, B.S., Châteauroux, June 24, 1943.

95. Carol Iancu, "Les Juifs à Montpellier pendant la Deuxième Guerre mondiale," in *Les Juifs à Montpellier et dans le Languedoc, Du Moyen Age à nos jours,* ed. Carol Iancu (Montpellier: Centre de recherches et d'études juives et hébraïques, 1988), 376.

96. Sweets, *Choices in Vichy France,* 129.

97. Limoges, December 21, 1941, AN, AJ 38, 262.

98. The entire file can be found in AN, AJ 38, 130.

99. Iancu, "Les Juifs à Montpellier," 364.

100. See Jean-Pierre Bertin-Maghit, "Les Juifs dans l'économie du cinéma français," paper delivered at the colloquium Les Juifs et l'économique: Miroirs et mirages (Toulouse: UTM-CIREJ, January 1989).

101. Ibid.

102. Limoges, November 13, 1942, report on a survey, AN, AJ, 38, 261. In *La France que je cherchais* (Limoges: 1945), 109–132, Joseph Ratz relates the ups and downs of relations between this organization and the Vichy administration.

103. Ruff's case is cited in Singer, *Vichy, l'Université, et les Juifs,* 278.

104. Report dating from July 28, 1943, AN, AJ 38, 262.

105. Letter from Xavier Vallat to the regional head of the General Commission on Jewish Affairs in Limoges, December 29, 1941, AN, AJ 38, 1051.

106. February 25, 1942, AN, AJ 38, 1051.

107. The entire dossier with all the ups and downs of this authorization can be found in AN, AJ 38, 1051.

108. Julien Benda, *La jeunesse d'un clerc, Un régulier dans le siècle, Exercice d'un enterré vif* (Paris: Gallimard, 1968), 346.

109. Cited by Singer, *Vichy, l'Université et les Juifs,* 287.

110. Renée Poznanski, "The Jews of France and the Statutes on Jews, 1940–1941, "*Yad Vashem Studies* 22 (1992): 136ff., and Claude Singer, "L'engagement des intellectuels juifs face à Vichy," *Pardès* 16 (1992): 106ff.

111. He did so, however, not without at first arousing the opposition of the General Commission on Jewish Affairs. But then he received support from the Ministry of Agriculture. See the correspondence about the matter (dating from February and March 1942) in AN, AJ 38, 61.

112. According to the minutes of the meeting devoted to the dissolution of the OSE on September 22, 1942. AN, AJ 38, 1141.

113. OSE, Montpellier, December 15, 1941, CC, 22–23.

114. Letter from the secretary-general of the first section of the UGIF to the head of the first direction. Centre de Documentation Juive Contemporaine, CDXVI-152.

115. Letter from Marc Bloch to Etienne Bloch dated September 13 in François Bédarida and Denis Peschanski, eds. "Marc Bloch à Etienne Bloch, Lettres de la 'drôle de guerre,'" *Cahiers de l'Institut d'histoire du temps présent* 19 (December 1991): 102.

116. Léon Poliakov, *L'Auberge des musiciens, Mémoires* (Paris: Mazarine, 1981), 84–85.

117. Letter from René Guastalla to André Baruch, October 29, 1941, CC-24.

118. Report submitted by M. Weill, "L'activité de l'ORT en face des lois et réglements actuels," undated, Centre de Documentation Juive Contemporaine, CCXIII-84.

119. Over the course of the year 1941, some 2,200 school children attended one of the institutions of the ORT. Centre de Documentation Juive Contemporaine, CCXIV-10a, William Oualid, *Bulletin de la Fédération des sociétés juives d'Algérie,* no. 77 (February 1942), cited by Adam Rutkowski, *La Lutte des Juifs en France,* 82–83.

120. CC, file on associations, Union-OSE, July 31, 1941.

121. AIU, CC-39, "French Jewish Youth and the Head Council on French Jewish Youth, from June to December 1941," report written in early 1942.

122. Report on French Israelite Mutual Aid association (EIF), undated, Centre de Documentation Juive Contemporaine, CCCLXVI-17.

123. Orange, April 17, 1942, letter from Olmer to the Consistory's office in Marseilles, CC-7.

124. AN, AJ 38, 259, "Brive—census of the Jews, law of June 2, 1941," application of the provisions of the prefect's memorandum of July 17, 1941, followed by lists.

125. Herbert Katzki, Lisbon, March 22, 1941, memorandum number 356, Joint, General, France, 595.

126. Ibid., and AIU, CC-40, letter from Raymond-Raoul Lambert to Albert Manuel.

127. Report on the activity of the Israelite Social Aid Program among evacuees from the Alsace-Lorraine region, 1941, CC, dossier on associations.

128. Joint, 607, General statistics on the aid distributed by the Federation of Jewish Societies in France (FSJF) in 1941.

129. Herbert Katzki, Lisbon, March 22, 1941, memo number 356, Joint, General, France, 595.

130. AIU, CC-39, report from the central commission of the Central Commission on Jewish Aid Organizations (CCOJA), presented at the meeting of June 4 and 5, 1941.

131. On the steps leading to the creation of the UGIF, see Szajkowski, *Analytical Franco-Jewish Gazetteer*, 39–52, Adler, *The Jews of Paris and the Final Solution*, 37ff, and Richard I. Cohen, *The Burden of Conscience*, 24ff. For the Occupied Zone, see Poznanski, "Avant les premières grandes rafles," 39–51.

132. The law of July 22, 1941, governing the aryanization process in the Southern Zone provided for 10 percent of the funds gathered from the sale of Jewish property to be taken by the General Commission on Jewish Affairs and used to pay for the cost of provisionally managing and inspecting businesses in the red and to constitute "a solidarity fund for aiding indigent Jews."

133. Lambert, *Carnet d'un témoin*, December 2, 1941, 134–135.

134. On the subject of the UGIF in the Southern Zone, see Lambert, *Carnet d'un témoin*, passim, and Richard I. Cohen, *The Burden of Conscience*, passim.

135. AJ 38, 242, wiretap of the telephone conversation between Joseph Weill in Terrasson (in the département of La Dordogne) and Fanny Schwab, contained in a report filed by the Police for Jewish Affairs on March 23, 1942.

136. Centre de Documentation Juive Contemporaine, CDXX-18, Vichy, March 19, 1942, French Scouts memorandum (signed Lafont) on the situation of Israelite Scouting, and Moissac, March 30, 1942, letter from Gamzon to the leaders of the Israelite Scouts.

137. CZA, S6/4565, March 1942.

138. On Marc Bloch in general, see Carole Fink, *Marc Bloch: A Life in History* (New York: Cambridge University Press, 1989). On Marc Bloch the résistant, see Carole Fink, "Marc Bloch: l'historien et la Résistance," in *Marc Bloch aujourd'hui, histoire comparée et sciences sociales*, ed. Astma Haratmut and André Bruguière (Paris: Editions de l'EHESS, 1990), 51–64.

139. The text of this letter and the list of the twenty-nine individuals who signed it on March 31, 1942 can be found in Marc Bloch, *L'Etrange défaite* (Paris: Gallimard, 1990), 314–321.

140. Quoted in Bloch, *L'Etrange défaite*, 307–310.

5. *Seeking Refuge in Social Interaction (pages 126–170)*

1. AIU, CC-39, report from the Central Commission of the CCOJA, presented at the meeting of June 4–5, 1941.

2. Ibid. By June 1941, the search office opened on February 16 of the same year had found 332 of the persons out of the total number of 528 that it was looking for. Classified ads can be seen in *Le Petit Marseillais* in particular, toward the end of 1940.

3. See the report on the activity of the Israelite Scouts of France since June 1940. Report dated September 1, 1941. YV, 09/11–3.

4. CC-16. Report by Rabbi Samuel Klein, dated May 20, 1941, and dealing with the camp for leaders held at Beauvallon in the département of Le Var from April 28 to May 14, 1941.

5. Paula Hyman, *From Dreyfus to Vichy: The Remaking of French Jewry, 1906–1939* (New York: Columbia University Press, 1979), 196.

6. All of this information has been drawn from various reports that date from 1941 and that are located at Yad Vashem under the shelf-mark 09/11–3. See also Centre de Documentation Juive Contemporaine, DLXI-30, interview of Anny Latour by Isaac Pougatch.

7. Robert Gamzon, *Les Eaux claires, Journal, 1940–1944* (Jerusalem: EIF, 1981), 27.

8. Isaac Pougatch, *Charry* (Paris: Oreste Zeluck, 1945), 24–26.

9. AIU, CC-39, report on the cultural activities of the rural group at the Charry estate, October 1941.

10. See Centre de Documentation Juive Contemporaine (CDJC), CCXX-52 on the subject. See also the partial list of the works available at the Moissac documentation center, CCXX-44.

11. Pougatch, *Charry*, 106.

12. Robert Gamzon, *Les Eaux claires*, 16–17.

13. AIU, CC-39, report on the Jewish Youth of France and the governing board of the Jewish Youth of France from June to December 1941.

14. Paula Hyman, *From Dreyfus to Vichy*, 179–198.

15. On the subject of the OSE during the war, see Renée Poznanski, "L'OSE de l'action philanthropique à la résistance humanitaire," in *Au secours des enfants du siècle; regards croisés sur l'OSE*, ed. Martine Lemalet (Paris: Nil Editions, 1993), 57–82.

16. CDJC, CCCLXVI-11, report on the activity of the Union-OSE for the months of June, July, and August 1941.

17. Report on the six months of work carried out by the OSE from January to June 1942, printed in *Au secours des enfants du siècle; regards croisés sur l'OSE*, ed. Martine Lemalet (Paris: Nil Editions, 1993), 187–206.

18. Archives of the OSE (AIU), Ha2, Centre OSE de Marseilles, undated, unsigned, typed report.

19. Ibid.

20. CDJC, XXXI-127 to 132, March 28, 1942.

21. Archives of the OSE (AIU), Rivesaltes-Gurs, 1939–1945, report on the activity of the Coordinating Committee in charge of evacuating children for the OSE, November 1939.

22. AIU, CC-39, report from the OSE, March–May, 1941.

23. CC-22/23, OSE, Montpellier, December 15, 1941, and AIU-CC, 27, November 25, 1941, message from OSE to CCOJA, report on the activity of the OSE's emigration office from April to October 1941.

24. There were 1,349 children in the OSE's homes in the Southern Zone as of May 1, 1942. Joint Archives, New York, 611, May 1, 1942, "Memorandum" from Joseph C.Hyman to Henrietta K. Buchman.

25. Centre de Documentation Juive Contemporaine, CCCLXVI-11, report on the activity of the Union-OSE for the months of June, July, and August 1941.

26. For a perspective of such family situations, see the archives of the OSE (AIU), Vivette Samuel, "Journal d'une internée volontaire," typewritten manuscript, 23.

27. Laurence Rosengart, "Les maisons d'enfants de l'OSE: parcours d'une enfance fragmentée," in *Au secours des enfants*, ed. Lemalet, 83–106.

28. Archives of the OSE (AIU), October 1941, "Émigration d'enfants," report on the organization and activity of this special office.

29. AIU, CC-32.

30. AIU, CC-1b, a speech by Helbronner dating from March 1942.

31. AIU, CC-11.

32. "These disgraceful acts are a violation of the most sacred feelings. At a time when the Israelite community is experiencing sufferings for which I have expressed my entire sympathy, such attacks are particularly odious," wrote Gerlier to the chief rabbi of France on December 5, 1941. AIU, CC-6.

33. Visit of Chief Rabbi Kaplan in Aix-les-Bains, September 17, 1942, AIU, CC-33.

34. CC-16, letter from Chief Rabbi Kaplan to Grünewald dated September 30, 1941.

35. Archives of the OSE, Yeshouroun collection, Friends of the Jewish Tradition, "A Few Rabbinical Instructions for the Observance of Passover 5701—1941—."
36. Archives of the OSE (AIU), Yeshouroun collection, Friends of the Jewish Tradition, "The Miracle," *tishri* 5702.
37. Archives of the OSE (AIU) Yeshouroun collection, Friends of the Jewish Tradition, "The Spirit of Sacrifice," *kisslev* 5702, "A Few Facts to Recall about our Time and its Restrictions," November 1941.
38. AN, AJ 38, 262, Limoges, March 3, 1943, investigation conducted by Inspector Borde at "Chez Vitrat" (ritual baths), Palais Road, Limoges.
39. AIU, CC-19, Vichy, August 12, 1942, letter from Hirtz Weill to the Central Consistory.
40. Léon Poliakov, *L'Auberge des musiciens*, 90.
41. AIU, CC-19, questionnaires sent to various rabbis by the Central Consistory on April 24, 1942, and CC-15.
42. Iancu, "Les Juifs à Montpellier," 359.
43. AN, AJ-38, 123, for an example, see the letter sent by the prefect for the département of La Dordogne to the chief of the Police for Jewish Affairs in Limoges, Périgueux, September 5, 1942.
44. AN, AJ-38, 123, message sent from the minister and secretary of state to the Ministry of Agriculture, the Ministry of Commodities and Supplies, and to the General Commission on Jewish Affairs, August 25, 1943.
45. Archives of the OSE (AIU), Yeshouroun collection, report on the camp for leaders of Yechouroun, Montintin, August 7–17, 1941.
46. The *bar mitzvah* is the ceremony marking the entry of a young Jew into the Jewish community when he turns thirteen: from then on, he is required to observe Jewish ritual.
47. AIU, CC-13, report on the sacking of the temple on 24, Avenue Dubouchage on June 2, 1942, undated, unsigned.
48. Report by Chief Rabbi Léon Berman, AIU, CC-19.
49. AIU, CC-36, summary of the reports received from varioius rabbis about activities in the Unoccupied Zone in 1941, from the March 2, 1942, meeting of the Central Consistory.
50. See the questionnaires sent to the various rabbis by the Central Consistory on April 24, 1942, AIU, CC-19.
51. CC-15, responses given to questionnaires sent out from Lyon on April 24, 1942, about the organization of worship services.
52. Iancu, "Les Juifs à Montpellier," 342–343.
53. AIU, CC-31, minutes of the meeting.
54. AIU, CC-36, rabbinical activity in 1941 as laid out in the oral report made by Dr. André Bernheim in March 1942.
55. CC-15, Châtelguyon, August 3, 1941.
56. CC-15, Lyon, July 29, 1941.
57. AIU, CC-19, report from Chief Rabbi Berman.
58. The exact number was 6,065, according to the Police for Jewish Affairs for the Unoccupied Zone. Letter to the Interior Ministry dated April 13, 1942, AN, F 7, 1–887. The letter has been cited by Serge Klarsfeld, *Le Calendrier de la persécution des Juifs de France* (Paris: FFDJF, 1993), 197.
59. CC-15, Périgueux, February 1, 1942, report by Rabbi E. Cyper on religious instruction and the organization of worship services in the département of la Dordogne.
60. AIU, CC-4, Nîmes, July 13, 1942, letter from the board of directors of the worship association in Nîmes to the president of the Central Consistory, Helbronner. At that date, only five out of the thirty-five families contacted had become registered members.
61. AIU, CC-19, Toulouse, July 22, 1941.
62. FSJF, financial report for the third trimester 1941, report from Toulouse, Joint, 607.
63. Claude Vigée, *La Lune d'hiver* (Paris: Flammarion, 1970), 50.
64. CC, folder on spiritual matters, 1942, report on the Commission on Confessional Information presided by Jacques Meyer (with the participation of General Boris, Professor

Olmer, Jules Isaac, René Mayer, Georges Wormser, René Lehmann, Roger Weill, Pierre Dreyfus, Samy Lattes, André Weill, Raymond Lindon, Claude Hirsch, Edmond Fleg).

65. AN, AJ 38, 262, December 18, 1942, head of the Division of Investigations and Inspections in Limoges.

66. AN, AJ 38, 60, June 28, 1941 and August 7, 1941, message from the General Commission on Jewish Affairs to the secretary-general of police; November 14, 1941, memorandum sent to the Police for Jewish Affairs.

67. CC-10 through 12, Vichy, March 3, 1942, the secretary-general of the police to the chief rabbi of France. The members of the B'nai B'rith are a sort of Jewish freemason group.

68. To learn more about the little seminary in Limoges, that as of May 1942, had taken over from the lycée Maïmonide in Paris (where 130 pupils were pursuing their secondary school instruction before the war), see the reports made by Rabbi Moïse Liber, AIU, CC-30.

69. AN, AJ 38, 262, Limoges, December 18, 1942, inspector's report.

70. AN, AJ 38, 60, December 19, 1941, head of the Police for Jewish Affairs in the Unoccupied Zone to the General Commission on Jewish Affairs.

71. AN, AJ 38, 265 Périgueux, January 8, 1942, message from the chief commissioner, head of the General Information Bureau (Renseignements Généraux) in the département of La Dordogne to the prefect of the département, providing information about the activity of Jewish associations in the département.

72. AN, AJ 38, 261, inspector's report made on the request of the prefect of the Limoges region, Limoges, February 26, 1942.

73. Archives of the OSE (AIU), Yeshouroun collection, report on correspondance courses (January 15 to April 15, 1942).

74. CC-22/23, and AN, AJ 38, 61. Marseilles, May 31, 1941.

75. AN, AJ 38, 64, Vichy, February 13, 1942.

76. AN, AJ 38, 261, Limoges, February 10, 1942, investigation into the French Israelite Mutual Aid (EFI) in Périgueux, conducted by Antignac.

77. Centre de Documentation Juive Contemporaine, XXXI-127/132, Limoges, August 18, 1941.

78. For more on Zionism in France during the war, see Renée Poznanski, "Le sionisme en France pendant la Seconde Guerre mondiale: développements institutionnels et impact idéologique," in *Les Juifs de France, le sionisme et l'État d'Israël,* ed. Doris Bensimon and Benjamin Pincus, Proceedings of the International Colloquium, 1987 (Paris: Publications Langues Orientales, 1989) 193–226. And on Jews in France before the war, see Michel Abitbol, *Les Deux Terres promises* (Paris: Olivier Orban, 1989).

79. Fisher-Ariel, "Souvenirs."

80. *La Terre retrouvée,* issue dated November 1, 1944, Joseph Fisher.

81. *La Terre retrouvée,* issue 8 dated April 15, 1945, Joseph Fisher.

82. Fisher-Ariel, "Souvenirs."

83. David Knout, *Contribution à l'histoire de la Résistance juive en France* (Paris: Editions du Centre, 1947), p. 74.

84. Report sent by Joseph Fisher to the Zionist Executive body in Jerusalem and received in Geneva on April 13, 1942, CZA, KKL 5–12.149. See also examples of newsletters sent out by Fisher between September 1941 and November 1942, Centre de Documentation Juive Contemporaine, CCXX-67, 72, 75, 85, 86, 87, 88. Sometime near the middle of 1943, these mailings ceased for a while because of the interruption of postal service between France and Switzerland, but Marc Jarblum managed to start them up again toward the end of the year. See the report from Lyon, dating from December 29, 1943, YV, P.7/3, and CZA, A. 303/19.

85. More than 4,000 dollars were thus transferred to the *Keren kayemeth* in New York, Fisher-Ariel, "Souvenirs," chap. v.

86. Centre de Documentation Juive Contemporaine, XXVIIIa-48, and XXXI-120/122, correspondence between the secretary of state for the national economy and finances and the General Commission on Jewish Affairs, and letter from Xavier Vallat to Raymond-Raoul Lambert, October 1941 and March 1942.

87. CZA, S5/811, Joseph Fisher to the Zionist Executive body in Jerusalem, received in Geneva on April 13, 1942.

88. "Do not publish this news," recommended Joseph Fisher to his interlocutors with the *Keren kayemeth* in Jerusalem in a telegram sent from Geneva on April 10, 1942. CZA,S5/811.

89. Centre de Documentation Juive Contemporaine, CCXIV-14, Lyon, June 1, 1942, Fisher (on behalf of the Zionist Organization of France) to R. Grinberg, on the call for the meeting of the Jewish conference on education, to be held on June 28, 1942.

90. For example, see the narrative of an AJ résistant, undated, Centre de Documentation Juive Contemporaine, XI-36.

91. On the subject of the objectives of the AJ (Jewish Army)—which was renamed the Jewish Combat Organization (Organisation juive de combat, [OJC]) at the end of the war in order for it to be integrated into the French Resistance—the version given in a report dated October 25, 1944, and aimed at gaining official recognition ("The purpose [of the movement]is to fight against Germany in conjunction with the French Resistance," Centre de Documentation Juive Contemporaine, CCXV-12) can be compared with the report sent to Jules Jefroykin by David Ben Gourion on August 27, 1945 ("The basis [of everything we do] is provided by one overarching idea: the Jewish State in Palestine. The action of the Jewish Army thus had to be defined by this aim and focused on achieving this goal." Polonski archives, D. 10-III/9).

92. Testimony given by Avraham Polonski, Paris, 1980.

93. Pierre Vidal-Naquet, "Du bon usage de la trahison," introd. to Flavius Josephus, *La Guerre des Juifs* (Paris: Editions de Minuit, 1977).

94. Vigée, *La Lune d'hiver*, 53.

95. According to the testimony of Arnold Mandel, which has been cited by Anny Latour in *La Résistance juive en France* (Paris: Stock, 1970), 93.

96. The manifesto has been printed in Vigée, *La Lune d'hiver*, 404ff.

97. From the archives of Lucien Lublin, 20, instructions for the introduction of a new member of the Jewish Army. See also the archives of Polonski, D 7–22.

98. René S. Kapel, *Un Rabbin dans la tourmente, 1940–1944* (Paris: Centre de Documentation Juive Contemporaine, 1986), 117.

99. Centre de Documentation Juive Contemporaine, CCXIV-117, August 1944, provisional report on the Zionist Youth Movement, written by Simon Lévitte. See also CZA, Z.4/10.300.

100. See the report on the meeting of the delegates from the Zionist Youth, Centre de Documentation Juive Contemporaine, CCXX-53. Eight others had not been able to come.

101. To this list of reasons could be added that Denise Lévitte, Simon Lévitte's spouse, handled Joseph Fisher's secretarial work throughout the war.

102. CZA, Z4/10 300, December 1942, ideological charter adopted at the second convention of the Zionist Youth Movement in La Grivolée, near Grenoble.

103. Centre de Documentation Juive Contemporaine, CCXX-54, Moissac, June 10, 1942, memorandums from Simon Lévitte on a "Summer stay in the *hakhsharot*," and on a "Training session at the school for the preparation of leaders."

104. AIU, CC-2, Central Consistory commission on youth, July 27, 1942.

105. Henri Hertz, "Le document vert" (the green document), CZA, A/303/19, p. 2. This is a most valuable testimony written by Henri Hertz himself on the circumstances in which he wrote the tract.

106. Renée Poznanski, "Des Juifs parlent aux Français: 1942—Le document vert," in *Transmission et passages en monde juif*, ed. Esther Benbassa (Paris: Cerf, 1994). The entire reprinted document can be found in this work.

107. Léo Glaeser, who became the secretary-general of the General Defense Committee as soon as it was created, was one of the seven Jewish hostages shot by the Milice in Rillieux-la-Pape on June 29, 1944. He was killed in reprisal for the assassination of Philippe Henriot, Vichy's secretary of state for information and propaganda, which had occurred on the previ-

ous day in Paris. The guilt of Paul Touvier in this sinister affair was established in mid-April 1992 by the Paris Court of Criminal Appeals. Touvier was convicted of a crime against humanity for this deed in April 1994.

108. Report on the first six months of the CDF, 1-V/30-X-1942, Centre de Documentation Juive Contemporaine, CCXIII-68, and Knout, *Conribution a l'histoire,* 75.

109. Pierre Birnbaum, *Les Fous de la République* (Paris: Fayard, 1992). Because the Jews were mixed in with every nation, it was only inevitable that they should become hostages of the "nationalistic convulsions amid which the peoples of the earth are slaughtering each other," wrote Henri Hertz at about the same time. Lyon, June 1942, "La France et la Palestine," CZA, A/68/19, p. 3.

110. Centre de Documentation Juive Contemporaine, CIX-21 and CII-27, repr. in Rutkowski, *La Lutte des Juifs en France,* 86–87. The original text can be found in AN, AJ 38, 7.

111. Centre de Documentation de Juive Contemporaine, Lubetzki Collection.

112. Laborie, *L'Opinion française sous Vichy,* 264ff.

113. Henri Hertz, "Le document vert," 3.

114. Renée Bédarida, *Pierre Chaillet, témoin de la résistance spirituelle* (Paris: Fayard, 1988), 162ff.

115. "Rapport. Témoignage Chrétien et l'Amitié chrétienne (1941/1942)," six typewritten pages, cited by Renée Bédarida, *Pierre Chaillet.*

116. Bibliothèque nationale, Paris, Res. G. 1490/186.

117. Centre de Documentation Juive Contemporaine, XXII.

118. Such was the case, for example, in Toulouse, according to the testimony provided by Fela Insel in an interview dating from May 1987.

119. Renée Poznanski, "Résistance juive, résistants juifs: Retour à l'Histoire," acts of the colloquium "La Résistance et les Français" (Université de Toulous-Le Mirail, December 1993), 241–264.

120. AIU, CC.

121. AIU, CC-24.

122. *Le Petit Marseillais,* July 25, 1940, in the commentary (provided by the news agency Havas) following the notice of the law stripping those who had left France between May 10 and June 30, 1940 of their French citizenship.

123. Gadala, *A travers la grande grille,* August 2, 1940, 1:70.

124. Fink, *Marc Bloch,* 249.

125. Vichy, October 28, 1941, informational memorandum from the general inspection division within the offices of the General Bureau of Information, AN, AJ 38, 61.

126. "Les Juifs à Paris sous l'Occupation allemande," Ruven Grinberg, report probably written by Ruven Grinberg, July 30, 1941, AIU, CC-4 and YIVO, Tcherikower collection, dossier 1650.

127. AN, AJ 38, 1,142, report on the situation of Jews in France (unsigned and undated, written between June and November 1941); there were 2,006 such emigrants during the first nine months of 1941, Centre de Documentation Juive Contemporaine, CDXIV-39, report from the HICEM, October 1941.

128. July 1942, Nîmes Coordinating Committee, report from the committee on emigration, AIU, CC-39.

129. *L'Activité des organisations juives en France* (Paris: Centre de documentation juive contemporaine, 1947, repr. 1983) 94.

130. Varian Fry, *Assignment: Rescue* (New York: Four Winds, 1968), 95.

131. July 1942, Nîmes Coordinating Committee, report from the Committee on Emigration, CC-39.

132. Report from the HICEM, October 1941, Centre de Documentation Juive Contemporaine, CDXIV-39.

133. Centre de Documentation Juive Contemporaine, CCXIII-42, Marseilles, July 17, 1942, message from the chief of the Police for Jewish Affairs in Marseilles to the chief of the Police for Jewish Affairs in the Unoccupied Zone.

134. Nahum Hermann, CZA, Jerusalem, KH 4B 2378.
135. Fry, *Assignment: Rescue*, 107.
136. The total number was twelve hundred according to Daniel Bénédite, *La Filière marseillaise* (Paris: Editions Clancier-Guénau, 1984). Varian Fry himself was expelled from France in August 1941.
137. Centre de Documentation Juive Contemporaine, Lesage collection, the camp at Gurs, from June 9 to June 25, 1941, account given to the head of the Police of the Territory and Foreigners by Jean Pochard, chief of the inspection team for the Social Division of Groups of Foreigners.
138. May 23, 1941, cablegram from Manuel Siegel in Havana to Robert Pilpel in New York, Joint; Joint, 616.
139. AIU-CC, 39 and Centre de Documentation Juive Contemporaine, CCXIX-69, December 15, 1941, report on the activity of the emigration service of the OSE during the period extending from April through October 1941.
140. Hillel J. Kieval, in "Legality and Resistance in Vichy France," *Proceedings of the American Philosophical Society*, nos. 124–125 (October 1980): 353, gives the figure of 311 children. A handwritten evaluation, deposited in the archives of the OSE (AIU) Hb2 II, undated and unsigned, gives the figure of 285 children.
141. Joint, 611, Memorandum, May 1, 1942, from Henriette Buchmann to Joseph C. Hyman.
142. Archives of the OSE (AIU), Hb 2II, 1941–1942, March 1942, report on the makeup of the next convoy of children.
143. Vichy, August 5, 1942, message from Cado to the regional prefects, cited by Serge Klarsfeld in *Vichy—Auschwitz* (Paris: Fayard, 1983), 1:318–319.
144. Michael R. Marrus, "Vichy et les enfants juifs," in *Etudes sur la France de 1939 à nos jours, L'Histoire* (Paris: Seuil, 1985), 102–105.

6. *Living in a Camp, in a Foreign Worker Unit (pages 171–201)*

1. Barbara Vormeier, "La situation des réfugiés en provenance d'Allemagne (septembre 1939–juillet 1942)," in *Zone d'ombres, 1933–1944*, ed. Jacques Grandjonc and Theresia Grundtner (Paris: Alinea, 1990), 197.
2. Zosa Szajkowski, *Jews and the French Foreign Legion* (New York: Ktav, 1975).
3. Ratz, *La France que je cherchais*, 83.
4. YIVO, France during WWII, 3043, Lyon, October 25, 1940, Nina Gourfinkel, "Le problème de l'aménagement des centres d'accueil."
5. *Le Petit Marseillais*, October 15, 1940.
6. Marrus and Paxton, *Vichy France and the Jews*, 10–11.
7. Interview with Gilbert Lesage, January 1988, Paris.
8. According to a statement by Henri Maux, who was assistant commissioner for the Fight Against Unemployment from October 1940 until February 1943. See also the overall report on the Office of Social Services for Foreigners (SSE) from 1941 through 1944. December 7, 1944, Centre de Documentation Juive Contemporaine, Gilbert Lesage Collection.
9. Anne Grynberg, *Les Camps de la honte*, 236ff.
10. Marrus and Paxton, *Vichy France and the Jews*, 171.
11. Archives of the OSE (AIU), notes for the minister of the interior, Vichy, "On the Subject of the Internment Camps." The same information can be found in AN, F7, 15 089.
12. AN, F7, 15 086.
13. Anne Grynberg, "L'action de l'OSE dans les camps de la zone sud," in *Au secours des enfants du siècle*, ed. Martine Lemalet, 135 n. 19.
14. Mechtild Gilzmer, "Blanche-Neige à Rieucros ou l'art de créer derrière les barbelés," in *Les Camps du sud-ouest de la France, 1939–1944; exclusion, internement, déportation*, ed. Monique-Lise Cohen and Éric Malo (Toulouse: Privat, 1994), 61–69.

15. An inventory of all the various sites used for internment in the Southern Zone from September 1939 until August 1944 was made by Christian Eggers, Theresia Grundtner, and Odile Morvan: according to this list, there were almost four hundred. André Fontaine, "L'internement au camp des Milles et dans ses annexes (septembre 1939—mars 1943)," in *Zone d'ombres*, ed. Jacques Grandjonc and Theresia Grundtner, 228.

16. On the subject of the shelter at Brens and its beginnings, see YIVO, France during WWII, 3–43, Nina Gourfinkel, Lyon, October 25, 1940 "Le problème de l'aménagement des centre d'accueil." On later developments at this shelter, see Kapel, *Un rabbin dans la tourmente*, 25ff. and Grynberg, *Les Camps de la honte*, 116ff.

17. Claude Laharie,*Le Camp de Gurs*, 175.

18. Marrus and Paxton, *Vichy France and the Jews*, 168.

19. AN, F7, 15 086, Office of the Secretary-General for the Police, Vichy, February 17, 1941: report concerning the guarded long-term occupancy camps, which came under the authority of the Ministry of the Interior.

20. Report on the Coordinating Committee's first meeting in Nîmes on November 20, 1940, Musée de la Résistance in Besançon, papers of Joseph Weill. I thank François Marcot for having a copy of these documents sent to me.

21. AIU, CC-28, internment camps as of July 31, 1941.

22. See the accompanying table. The figures given by Anne Grynberg are slightly different (*Les Camps de la honte*, 12).

23. Claude Laharie, *Le Camp de Gurs*, table of the different types of internment, 177.

24. Ibid., 221 and 234: the number 1,340 includes five hundred escapees.

25. AIU, CC-25, Vichy, January 2, 1942, message from the minister of the interior and secretary of state to regional prefects in the Unoccupied Zone.

26. First published in the newspaper *Le Matin*, this communiqué from the secretary-general of the vice premier's office has been reproduced in Klarsfeld, *Calendrier*, 167–168.

27. Pierre Limagne, *Ephémérides de quatre années tragiques* (Lavilledieu: Editions de Candide, 1987), December 9, 1941, 1:326.

28. AN, AJ 38, 244, December 19, 1941, memorandum on the conditions for incorporating Israelites into Foreign Worker Units. See also AIU, CC-22, Vichy, January 12, 1942, message from the secretary-general for the police to prefects in the Unoccupied Zone, concerning "the incorporation of organizations of foreign youths residing in France."

29. For the text of this placard, see AN, 72 AJ 266.

30. AIU, CC-25, Vichy, January 15, 1942, memorandum from Tavernier to the directors of the Foreign Worker Units.

31. Vichy, March 27, 1942, message from the secretary of state for the police (acting in the name of the secretary of state and minister of the interior) to the prefects of the Unoccupied Zone.

32. AIU, CC-25, Vichy, January 2, 1942, message from the secretary of state, minister of the interior to the regional prefects in the Occupied Zone, and Vichy, January 10, 1942, memorandum from Tavernier to the directors of the Foreign Worker Units.

33. Friedel Bohny-Reiter, *Journal de Rivesaltes, 1941–1942* (Geneva: Editions Zoé, 1993), 100.

34. AIU, CC-27, report from Rabbi Langer on the camp at Les Milles, January 1942.

35. AIU, CC-36, August 11, 1942, report from the regional delegation of the Central Consistory in Toulouse on its trip to Montauban.

36. AIU, CC-28, list of centers known to the general chaplains' office as of May 15, 1942; Marrus and Paxton, *Vichy France and the Jews*, 171, basing their estimate on a memorandum sent to the General Commission on Jewish Affairs in 1941 (AN, AJ 38, 1144), give the figure of twenty thousand Jews, or in other words, one-third of all the foreign workers in the units. The other two-thirds were made up for the most part of Spanish refugees. But as for 1942 . . . ?

37. Joseph Weill, *Contribution à l'histoire des camps d'internement dans l'Anti-France* (Paris: Editions du Centre, 1946), 28.

38. AIU, CC-39, reprinted in Weill, *Contribution à l'histoire des camps*, 27–49.

39. Ibid., 28.

40. Centre de Documentation Juive Contemporaine, CCXIX-39, February 1941, report on Gurs, René S. Kapel.
41. Schramm and Vormeier, *Vivre à Gurs*, 77.
42. Vogel, *Et ils partirent pour la guerre*, 107.
43. Centre de Documentation Juive Contemporaine, Gilbert Lesage collection, report on the Gurs camp from June 9 to June 25, 1941, written for the head of the police in charge of territorial security and foreigners.
44. Friedel Bohny-Reiter, *Journal de Rivesaltes*, November 29, 1941, p. 39.
45. Ibid., 118.
46. AIU, CC-28, the internment camps as of July 31, 1941, memorandum sent to the general chaplains' office, and Weill, in his report of May 1941, 2ff.
47. Schramm and Vormeier, *Vivre à Gurs*, 95.
48. AN, F7 15086. On the subject of conditions in the camps, see Anne Grynberg, *Les Camps de la honte*, passim, and the report of Joseph Weill cited above.
49. CC-17, report on the activity of the Commission on Camps for the month of May 1942.
50. Claude Laharie, *Le Camps de Gurs*, table on p. 221.
51. Weill, *Contribution à l'histoire des camps*, 55.
52. Bohny-Reiter, *Journal de Rivesaltes*, January 8, 1942, p. 63.
53. AIU, CC-39, conference in Nîmes, December 10, 1940.
54. CC-10 to 12, Montpellier, May 22, 1941: report from the general chaplains' office, stemming from a visit to the Rivesaltes camp, made on May 20, 1941.
55. Bohny-Reiter, *Journal de Rivesaltes*, 63.
56. Archives of the OSE (Children's Relief Organization) (AIU).
57. Weill, *Contribution à l'histoire des camps*, 47.
58. Schramm and Vormeier, *Vivre à Gurs*, 53.
59. An order from the prefecture dating from January 10, 1941 stipulated: "Foreign nationals and suspicious individuals staying in the unoccupied zones of the départements of Les Landes and Les Basses-Pyrénées must be kept at a distance of thirty kilometers around the Gurs camp." Cited by Laharie, *Le Camp de Gurs*, 343–344.
60. AIU, CC-22, correspondence between the heads of the camps, the president of the commission on monitoring mail, local postal clerks, and so forth, in January and February 1941.
61. AIU, CC-27, Rabbi Langer, visit of January 24, 1941 to the camp at Les Milles.
62. André Fontaine, *Le Camp d'étrangers des Milles, 1939–1943* (Aix-en-Provence: Edisud, 1989), 263.
63. Archives of the OSE (AIU), E 2, report on the Rivesaltes camp, undated, written by Doctor Isa Malkin, probably in June 1942.
64. Gret Arnoldsen, quoted by Anne Grynberg, *Les Camps de la honte*, 208.
65. Eric Malo, "Le camp de Noé (Haute-Garonne) de 1941 à 1944," *Les Annales du Midi* 100, no. 183 (July–September 1983): 341.
66. AIU, CC-28, the internment camps as of July 31, 1941.
67. Schramm and Vormeier, *Vivre à Gurs*, 119–120.
68. This is the term used by Anne Grynberg, "L'action de l'OSE dans les camps," 116.
69. Nina Gourfinkel, *L'Autre Patrie* (Paris: Seuil, 1953), 224.
70. Archives of the OSE (AIU), Vivette Samuel, "Journal d'une internée volontaire," typewritten manuscript, November 8, 1941, p. 14.
71. Schramm and Vormeier, *Vivre à Gurs*, 116.
72. Archives of the OSE (AIU), E 2, report on the Rivesaltes camp, undated, written by Doctor Isa Malkin, probably in June 1942.
73. On the subject of the Nîmes Committee, see Anne Grynberg, "Le Comité de Nîmes ou les limites de la philanthropie," in *Zone d'ombres*, ed. Jacques Grandjonc and Theresia Grundtner 433–450.
74. The sum allocated to the Commission on Camps was doubled between the beginning

of 1941 and May 1942. Anne Grynberg, "Une découverte récente: le fonds d'archives de la Commission des camps (1941–1943)," *Le Monde juif* 131 (1988): 111.

75. August 31, 1940, report by Herbert Katzki, Joint, General, France, 594.

76. Archives of the OSE (AIU), E 2, memorandum to the minister of the interior, Vichy, on the subject of internment camps. See also Weill, *Contribution à l'histoire des camps*, 157 and 177.

77. AIU-CC, 39, Report from the OSE, March–May 1941.

78. Anne Grynberg, "Une découverte récente," 111.

79. AIU, CC-27, visit to the camp at Les Milles by Rabbi Langer, October 9, 1941.

80. On this subject, see Grynberg, "L'action de l'OSE dans les camps de la zone sud," 118–120.

81. The letters of André Jean-Faure to the president of the Coordinating Committee for Camp Aid, February 4, 1942, and to the heads of the camps in the Unoccupied Zone, February 5, 1942, printed in Weill, *Contributions à l'histoire des camps*, 119–122.

82. Weill, *Contributions à l'histoire des camps*, 101.

83. Schramm and Vormeier, *Vivre à Gurs*, 132.

84. Weill, *Contributions à l'histoire des camps*, 130ff, report from the education committee, January 14, 1942.

85. AIU, CC-22, message from Kapel to Hirschler, Toulouse, April 15, 1942, and AIU, CC-28, the internment camps as of July 31, 1941.

86. Schramm and Vormeier, *Vivre à Gurs*, 136.

87. This is the version taken from the original and printed by Grynberg, *Les Camps de la honte*, p. 256–257. Slightly different versions can be found in Weill, *Contributions à l'histoire des camps*, 102, and Schramm and Vormeier, *Vivre à Gurs*, 138–139.

88. AIU, CC-22, report from René S. Kapel, January 1942.

89. The Sukkoth festival (Feast of the Tabernacles) recalls for seven days that the sons of Israel lived in huts (*sukka*, in the singular) after the flight from Egypt: hence the commandments to eat all one's meal in a *sukka* during this time.

90. AIU, CC-27, Rabbi Langer, visit to the camp at Les Milles, September 19, 1941.

91. Bohny-Reiter, *Journal de Rivesaltes*, 51.

92. AIU, CC-27, Rabbi Langer, visit to the camp at Les Milles, February 1942.

93. Weill, *Contributions à l'histoire des camps*, 101.

94. Gourfinkel, *L'Autre Patrie*, 216.

95. Hillel J. Kieval, "Legality and Resistance in Vichy France," 349–350. Kieval bases his analysis on Zosa, *Analytical Franco-Jewish Gazetteer*, 34.

96. Joint, SM 35 A-2, report on the activity of the UNION OSE, February 1942.

97. Archives of the OSE (AIU), Vivette Samuel, "Journal d'une internée volontaire," typewritten manuscript, 17.

98. "Oeuvre de secours aux enfants," in *L'Activité des organisations juives en France sous l'Occupation* (Paris: CDJC, 1947) (repr. 1983), 126.

99. Samuel, "Journal d'une internée volontaire," 27, and archives of the OSE (AIU), E 2, report on the Rivesaltes camp, undated, written by Dr. Malkin, probably in June 1942.

100. Joint, 611, Montpellier, April 20, 1942.

101. Weill, *Contributions à l'histoire des camps*, 154.

102. Report from the OSE, January-June 1942, in *Au secours des enfants du siècle*, ed. Martine Lemalet, 199.

103. Centre de Documentation Juive Contemporaine, DLXI-35, testimony by Andrée Salomon.

104. Samuel, "Journal d'une internée volontaire," 20.

105. AIU, CC-22, Report on shelters, unsigned and undated, probably written in the spring of 1942 by one of the leaders of the consistory. The name Léon Meiss is handwritten on the document. In the same box are found the minutes of Lesage's meeting with the Central Consistory on February 6, 1942.

106. Joint, 601, Marseilles, January 27, 1942, telegram from Jefroykin to Lisbon.

107. Interview with Gilbert Lesage, Paris, January 1988.

108. Who was at the time representing Relico, the Aid Committee for the Jewish population hit by the war, in Geneva and New York.

109. Weill, *Contributions à l'histoire des camp*, 158–159.

110. Centre de Documentation Juive Contemporaine, CCXVII-41a, Report on the activity of the DCA (Main Office for Shelters), 1941–1944, and Gourfinkel, *L'Autre Patrie*. About Abbot Glasberg, see the biography written by Lucien Lazare (Paris: Cerf, 1990).

111. Gourfinkel, *L'Autre Patrie*, 248.

112. Ibid., 252.

113. Sweets, *Choices in Vichy France*, 122.

114. Yehuda Bauer, *American Jewry and the Holocaust. The American Jewish Joint Distribution Committee, 1939–1945* (Detroit: Wayne State University Press, 1981), 163.

115. Jeanne Merle d'Aubigné, Violette Mouchon, and Emile Fabre, eds., *Les Clandestins de Dieu, CIMADE, 1939–1944* (Paris: Fayard, 1968), 29–38.

116. Stéphane Courtois, Denis Peschanski, and Adam Rayski, *Le Sang de l'étranger* (Paris: Fayard, 1989), 96.

117. Centre de Documentation Juive Contemporaine, Lesage Collection.

118. CC-17, report on the activity of the chaplains' general office from May 15 to June 16, 1942. But see especially AIU, CC-20, where one finds reports on several Foreign Worker Units. Except where other sources are referred to, subsequent descriptions are all based on these reports written by the camp chaplains. See also Centre de Documentation Juive Contemporaine, CCXIII-123, FSJF, Report on the Palestinian camps, undated.

119. On the subject of the Foreign Worker Unit no. 665 at Soudeilles, see also the report by Inspector Lathières from the Police for Jewish Affairs, Limoges, April 17, 1942, AN, AJ 38, 261.

120. AIU, CC-20, "Foreign Worker Camps," undated and unsigned study written after the war, probably by Maurice Moch. See also Zosa Szajkowski, *Analytical Franco-Jewish Gazetteer*, 166.

121. AN, AJ 38, 261, Report by Inspector Lathières, Limoges, August 28, 1942. The report points out that the group had great artistic talent and conducted itself without reproach in spite of the intense surveillance to which it had been subjected. At the same time however, Lathière expresses satisfaction in seeing the group disappear, and adds that Captain Jouassin, who intends to reorganize his unit, should avoid recruiting Jews. "His artistic group from the Foreign Worker Units will thus reflect the value of the Aryan workers who have a different demeanor and greater fervor in their work than the Jews who only seek clumsily to avoid all manual labor."

122. CC-17, meeting of the regional chaplains, July 7 & 8, 1942.

123. AN, AJ 38, 261. Limoges, March 17, 1942.

124. Zosa Szajkowski, *Analytical Franco-Jewish Gazetteer*, 83.

125. AJ 38, 64, M 791, Joint Commission on postal and telephone control in Foix, Foix, May 30, 1942, Report covering the period from May 24 to May 30, 1942.

126. On Aulus-les-Bains, see Kapel, *Un rabbin dans la tourmente*, chap. 6, 89ff.

127. Zosa Szajkowski, *Analytical Franco-Jewish Gazetteer*, 160.

128. Ibid., 27.

129. Centre de Documentation Juive Contemporaine, LVII-61, Bellac, May 8, 1942, message from A. Adler to Rabbi Soil.

130. AN, AJ 38 1141; this directive came in application of a decree dating from February 27, 1940, which was modified by the decree of April 14, 1941.

131. Centre de Documentation Juive Contemporaine, CCXIII-123, FSJF, report on the camps of Palestinians, undated.

132. Lublin Archives, 4, Israelite Scouts of France in Toulouse.

133. Lublin Archives, Grenada, April 4, 1942, message from Jacques Marburger to Lucien Fayman.

134. Vigée, *La Lune d'hiver*, 58.

135. Samuel, "Journal d'une internée volontaire," 21, February 10, 1942.
136. Gamzon, *Les Eaux claires*, 54ff.
137. AN, AJ 38, 229.

7. *From Drancy to the Yellow Star (pages 202–250)*

1. AN, AJ 38, 2, ruling of June 20, 1941.
2. AN, AJ 38, 162.
3. AN, AJ 38, 117, communiqué from the CGQJ.
4. Archives of the Paris Police prefecture, "Situation à Paris," reports from the months of June, July, and August 1941. See figure 1.
5. AN, AJ 38, 182.
6. AN, AJ 38, undated message from Ditte to Dannecker.
7. AN, AJ 38, 146, from June 14, 1941 until June 19, 1944. Part of this correspondence has been printed in Joseph Billig, *Le Commissariat général des questions juives*, 1:337ff.
8. The facsimile of certificate no.15, issued on June 23, 1941, can be found in Serge Klarsfeld, *Calendrier*, 116.
9. AN, AJ 38, 182, December 16, 1941, message from the CGQJ to Ministerialrat Schneider.
10. On the subject of Georges Montandon, see Pierre Birnbaum, "*La France aux Français*," *Histoire des haines nationalistes* (Paris: Seuil, 1993), 187–198.
11. This measure was published in the *Journal Officiel* on March 27, 1942. See *Les Juifs sous l'Occupation*, 140–142.
12. Jean-Jacques Bernard, *Le Camp de la mort lente* (Paris: Albin Michel, 1944), 10–11.
13. Biélinky, *Journal*, September 3, 1941, p. 145.
14. AN, AJ 38, 9, memorandum from Obersturmführer Dannecker to Xavier Vallat, September 8, 1941.
15. Archives of the Paris police prefecture, "Situation à Paris," report of September 29, 1941.
16. Biélinky, *Journal* 155.
17. *Vichy-Auschwitz* (Paris: Fayard, 1983), 1:20–21.
18. Belchatovski's testimony can be found in Serge Klarsfeld, *Vichy-Auschwitz*, 1:518ff.
19. *Les Juifs sous l'Occupation*, 148, *Le Matin*, March 2, 1942.
20. I thank Lucienne for permission to quote this passage from her letter and from her letter of June 9, 1942.
21. This episode was related to me by Fanny Fuks. About the controversy with Darlan, who followed down the radio sets confiscated from Jews in the Occupied Zone and sent to Germany, see AN, AJ 38, 64.
22. This was by virtue of an ordinance from the Paris police prefecture. See *Les Juifs sous l'Occupation*, 106.
23. Alfred Sauvy, *La vie économique des Français de 1939 à 1945* (Paris: Flammarion, 1978), 182.
24. AN, AJ 38, 117, message from the German commander for the greater Paris region to the prefect of the Paris police on February 16, 1942. These instructions were rigorously applied, according to the reports made at the Paris police prefecture. See "Situation à Paris," passim.
25. Biélinky, *Journal*, March 4, 1942, p. 193.
26. Jean-Pierre Azéma, *From Munich to the Liberation, 1938–1944* (London and Paris: Cambridge University Press and Editions de la Maison des Sciences de l'Homme, 1984), 102.
27. *Le Petit Marseillais*, March 21, 1942.
28. AN, AJ 38, 69, minutes of a conference held on March 12, 1942 and devoted to aiding the craftsmen and storeowners devastated by the bombing of Boulogne-Billancourt.

29. According to the table of Jewish stores displaying the yellow placard (AN, AJ 38, 538), there were in the Boulogne section four food stores, one café, twenty-four specialized clothing stores, three shoe repairers, five shoe stores, and two electricians' shops.

30. Biélinky, *Journal*, May 14, 1942, p. 208.

31. Archives of the Paris police prefecture, "Situation à Paris," report dated June 30, 1941.

32. Biélinky, *Journal*, June 23, 1941, p. 123.

33. AN, AJ 38, 67 (and F 60, 490), summary of the weekly meeting of the secretaries general of the French delegation in the Occupied Zone, August 26, 1941. About the police roundup, see also Klarsfeld, *Vichy-Auschwitz*, 1:25–28.

34. AN, AJ 38, 67, Vichy, August 20, 1941, message from the General Commission on Jewish Affairs to Darlan.

35. See F 60, 490, exchange of letters on the matter between the office of the vice premier and the General Delegation of the French Government in the Occupied Territories.

36. AN, F 9, 5579, memorandum number 311.5, 1941 from the General Bureau of Information, dealing with the camp at Drancy.

37. Paris, August 21, 1941, report of the prefect of the Paris police sent to Prefect Ingrand, who was also the delegate to the Ministry of the Interior in the Occupied territories. This document has been printed in Klarsfeld, *Vichy-Auschwitz*,1:26.

38. Centre de Documentation Juive Contemporaine, CCXXI-18, report written at the time of the events on the police roundup and Drancy, in the holding of the FSJF.

39. The precise number was 2,894 according to the report of the prefect of the Paris police Ingrand, who was also prefect and delegate to the ministry of the interior in the Occupied territories (Paris, August 21, 1941). This document has been reprinted in Klarsfeld, *Vichy-Auschwitz*, 1:27. However, without citing his sources, Klarsfeld speaks of 3,022 arrests a few lines after having reproduced the above text.

40. Archives of the Paris police prefecture, "Situation à Paris," report dating from September 1, 1941. See also Klarsfeld, *Vichy-Auschwitz*, 1:27.

41. According to the list attached to the report of August 21 that dealt with the execution of the operation. See also Klarsfeld, *Vichy-Auschwitz*, 1:27.

42. Biélinky, *Journal*, from September 14 to October 2, 1941, pp. 148–152.

43. Biélinky, *Journal*, August 22, 1941, p. 141.

44. Centre de Documentation Juive Contemporaine, CCXIII-85. The report can also be found at the end of Biélinky, *Journal*, p. 291–301.

45. Biélinky, *Journal*, November 12, 1941, p. 163. .

46. On the subject of these arrests that occurred on December 12, 1941, see also the testimony provided by Jean-Jacques Bernard, *Le Camp de la mort lente*; by Henri Bloch (August 13, 1951), archives of the Institut d'histoire du temps présent; and by Henri Jacob, "Journal de Compiègne, 11 décembre 1941–11 avril 1942," unpublished manuscript entrusted to his daughter Claude Bloch. See also the excerpts from the daily notes taken by Georges Kohn from 1941 to 1944, AN, F 9 5579.

47. Klarsfeld, *Vichy-Auschwitz*, 1:32.

48. Of the 1,007 shot, 174 were Jews. See Serge Klarsfeld and Léon Tsevery, *Les 1007 fusillés du Mont-Valérien parmi lesquels 174 Juifs* (Paris: Fils et Filles des déportés Juifs de France, 1995).

49. Archives of the Paris police prefecture, "Situation à Paris," December 8, 1941.

50. Ibid., October 27, 1941.

51. Guy Crousset, "Obstacles à vaincre," *Les Nouveaux Temps*, December 23, 1941.

52. Archives of the Paris police prefecture, "Situation à Paris," December 8, 1941.

53. Philippe Burrin, *La Dérive fasciste, Doriot, Déat, Bergery (1933–1945)* (Paris: Seuil, 1986), 428.

54. Archives of the Paris police prefecture, "Situation à Paris," January 5, 1942.

55. Ibid., March 30, 1942. The event took place on March 29, 1942.

56. Ibid., June 1, 1942. The RNP screened *Le Juif Süss* in its quarters in the Third Arrondissement (26, rue de Saintonge) with 120 people in attendance. It also screened the film in the Salle Bulgarelli (22, Boulevard Colbert) to an audience of 180 people.

57. Joseph Billig, *L'Institut d'étude des questions juives* (Paris: Editions du Centre, 1974) and Marrus and Paxton, *Vichy France and the Jews,* 211.

58. Archives of the Paris police prefecture, "Situation à Paris," report dated May 26, 1941.

59. AIU, CC-27, and Centre de Documentation Juive Contemporaine, XXVI–1, global report from Dannecker dating from July 1, 1941.

60. A photo of this poster appearing both on the walls of the métro and on those of the Rue de la Boétie at the time when the institute was inaugurated can be seen in Serge Klarsfeld, *1941, Les Juifs en France; préludes à la solution finale* (Paris: FFDJF, 1991), 25–26.

61. See Joseph Billig, *L'Institut d'études des questions juives,* 155–179, and André Kaspi, "Le Juif et la France: Une exposition à Paris en 1941," *Le Monde juif* 79 (1975): 8–20. The latter piece can for the most part be found in André Kaspi, *Les Juifs pendant l'Occupation* (Paris: Seuil, 1991), 104–110.

62. Cited by Henri Amouroux, *La Grande Histoire des Français sous l'occupation,* vol. 5, *Les Passions et les Haines* (Paris: Laffont, 1981), 294.

63. Archives of the Paris police prefecture, "Situation à Paris," report dated September 15, 1941.

64. Archives of the Paris police prefecture, "Situation à Paris," report dated October 6, 1941.

65. Archives of the Paris police prefecture, "Situation à Paris," report from January 12, 1942.

66. Archives of the Paris police prefecture, "Situation à Paris," report dated April 20, 1942. On the subject of this exhibit, which was sponsored by the offices of Vichy's ministry of information, see Dominique Rossignol, *Histoire de la propagande en France de 1940 à 1944* (Paris: PUF, 1991), 275–281.

67. AIU, CC-13, reports on these bombings dating from October 7 and October 15. The latter has been printed in Biélinky, *Journal,* 303–305.

68. Archives of the Paris police prefecture, "Situation à Paris," October 6, 1941.

69. AN, AJ 38, 7, report from the inspector general's office in the General Bureau of Information, Vichy, October 4, 1941.

70. Heydrich personally took full responsibility for this event. See Roger Berg, "Les attentats contres les synagogues en 1941," *Le monde juif* 1 (1946);, and Philippe Burrin, *Hitler et les Juifs* (Paris: Seuil, 1989), 140–141. Burrin's book has been published in English as *Hitler and the Jews: The Genesis of the Holocaust* (London, Arnold; New York, Routledge, Chapman and Hall, 1994)

71. Centre de Documentation Juive Contemporaine, LXXV-236, undated report made either at the end of 1941 or in early 1942. It has been cited by Lucien Steinberg, *Les Autorités allemandes en France occupée* (Paris: CDJC, 1966), 83.

72. Archives of the Paris police prefecture, "Situation à Paris," October 6, 1941.

73. This theme comes up again and again in all reports stemming from the Bureau of Technical Verifications (involved in wiretapping and intercepting mail) in the Southern Zone and in the biweekly reports made at the prefecture of the Paris police.

74. These words came from the pen of André Chaumet in *Paris-Soir,* September 12, 1941. Chaumet moreover added: "The difference being that the latter [French POWs] are innocent while the others represent a vast army of agitators and speculatorings working for foreign powers."

75. This is the conclusion that can be reached by reading a report made by the General Bureau of Information. The document has been reprinted in Klarsfeld, *Vichy-Auschwitz,* 1:27–28.

76. Micheline Bood, *Les Années doubles* (Paris: Robert Laffont, 1974), December 28, 1941, p. 127.

77. Archives of the Paris police prefecture, "Situation à Paris," reports dated December 22, 1941, and February 9, 1942, passim.

78. Archives of the Paris police prefecture, "Situation à Paris," February 2, 1942.

79. Annie Kriegel, "Résistants communistes et Juifs persécutés," *Réflexions sur les questions juives* (Paris: Hachette, 1984), 39–40.

80. I thank Claude Lévy for having provided me with a photocopy of this article.
81. *Libération* (north), no. 38 (August 29, 1941), and *Liberté,* no. 3 (January 10, 1941). All of these examples are dealt with in Asher Cohen, "La presse clandestine face à la question juive de 1940 à 1942," *Le Monde juif* 117 (1985): 1–6.
82. *Libération* (north), no. 78 (May 29, 1942). Cited by Asher Cohen, *idem.*
83. Jean-Louis Crémieux-Brilhac, Ed. *Les Voix de la Liberté, Ici Londres, 1940–1944* (Paris: La documentation française, 1976), 2:100–101.
84. Excerpts of the text that was given to Xavier Vallat during this visit can be found in Rutkowski, *La Lutte des Juifs en France,* 59–62.
85. Calef, *Drancy 1941,* 91.
86. Biélinky, *Journal,* September 2, 1941, p. 144–145, and archives of the Paris police prefecture, "Situation à Paris," reports dated February 9, 1942 and March 16, 1942.
87. Archives of the Paris police prefecture, "Situation à Paris," report dated January 26, 1942.
88. Maurice Rajsfus, *Drancy, un camp de concentration très ordinaire, 1941–1944* (Paris: Manya, 1991).
89. See figure 2.
90. AN, AJ 38, 7, August 27, 1941, minutes of a meeting held at Drancy and attended by the German authorities, the headquarters of the gendarmes, and the prefecture of the département of La Seine and the prefecture of the Paris police.
91. AN, AJ 38, 7, message from Prefect Magny to the Secretary of State for the Interior, Paris, August 21, 1941, and message to Xavier Vallat on September 10, 1941.
92. Centre de Documentation Juive Contemporaine, CCXXI-18, undated report (probably written in July 1942) from the Federation of Jewish Societies in France (FSJF), and AN, AJ 38, 7, letter sent from the département of L'Indre to the United States, intercepted and seized on November 25, 1941.
93. AN, AJ 38, 4 October 5, 1941, message from the secretary of state for communications to the General Commission on Jewish Affairs.
94. Calef, *Drancy 1941,* 49.
95. Ibid, 274.
96. AN, F 9, 5579, report from the General Bureau of Information number 311/5, 1941, on the camp at Drancy.
97. George Wellers, *L'Etoile jaune à l'heure de Vichy* (Paris: Fayard, 1973), republished under the title *Un Juif sous Vichy* (Paris: Editions Tirésias, 1991), 103; and Centre de Documentation Juive Contemporaine, CCXXI–18, undated report (probably written in July 1942) from the Federation of Jewish Societies in France (FSJF).
98. Centre de Documentation Juive Contemporaine, CCXXI–18, undated report (probably written in July 1942) from the French Federation of Jewish Societies.
99. An, F 9, 5579, memorandum from the General Bureau of Information number 311/5 on the camp at Drancy.
100. Centre de Documentation Juive Contemporaine, CCXIII–106, testimony taken and recorded by the Amelot committe from sixteen internees released from Drancy in November 1941.
101. Centre de Documentation Juive Contemporaine, CCXXI–18, undated report (probably written in July 1942) from the FSJF.
102. Calef, *Drancy 1941,* 103.
103. AN, AJ 38, 7 contains a large number of photocopies of letters written by Jews interned at Drancy.
104. Centre de Documentation Juive Contemporaine, CCXIII–106, reports made by the Amelot Committee from the testimony of sixteen internees released in November 1941. See also Calef, *Drancy 1941,* 188.
105. Calef, *Drancy 1941,* 94ff.
106. Centre de Documentation Juive Contemporaine, reports made to the Amelot Committee by sixteen internees released in early November. Testimony no. 6.
107. Calef, *Drancy 1941,* 118–119.

108. Biélinky, *Journal*, September 26, 1941, p. 151.
109. Calef, *Drancy 1941*, 138–140.
110. Ibid., p. 57.
111. AN, AJ 38, 9, report from Dr. Tisné, September 7, 1941.
112. AN, AJ 38, 7, August 27, 1941, minutes of a meeting at Drancy between the German authorities, the office of the gendarmes, the prefecture for the département of La Seine, and the prefecture of the Paris police.
113. Calef, *Drancy 1941*, 323.
114. Centre de Documentation Juive Contemporaine, CCXXI–18, undated report (probably written in July 1942) from the FSJF. Jacques Adler, in *The Jews of Paris* (118), speaks of the release of nine hundred internees.
115. Drancy, April 2, 1942, list established by Captain Richard, commander in the office of the gendarmes at Drancy, and printed in Rutkowski, *La Lutte des Juifs en France*, 88–89.
116. From August 21, 1942 to March 30, 1942, there were a total of thirty escapes from Drancy, according to Klarsfeld, *Calendrier*, 195.
117. AIU, CC-22, memorandum from Dr. Worms on the functioning of one of the medical branches for Drancy internees at the Rothschild hospital, December 1941 and July 1942.
118. Calef, *Drancy 1941*, 247.
119. Translated by David Diamant in *Par-delà les barbelés*, 170.
120. Centre de Documentation Juive Contemporaine, CCXXI–18, undated report (probably written in July 1942) from the FSJF.
121. *Bulletin de l'UGIF* 2 (January 30, 1942). This edition announced that 5,658 packages had been sent since January 12, 1942.
122. AN, AJ 38, 9, message from Magny, prefect for the département of La Seine to Xavier Vallat, September 10, 1941.
123. Many examples of such letters can be found in AN, AJ 38, 6. Also to be found in this dossier of the archives of the General Commission on Jewish Affairs (up until mid-August 1942) are the French authorities' responses, which invariably read as follows: "The offices of Marshal Pétain have forwarded your letter to me. . . . It is impossible for me to accommodate your request, as the measures forbidding such action emanate from German Occupation Authorities." No response was sent subsequent to mid-August 1942.
124. Calef, *Drancy 1941*, 225ff.
125. Klarsfeld, *Calendrier*, 184–186.
126. Archives of the Paris police prefecture, "Situation à Paris," March 30, 1942.
127. Adam Rutkowski, "Le camp de Royallieu à Compiègne, 1941–1944," *Le Monde juif*, 101 (1981): 121–150.
128. As a result of a ruling by the German military command in France dating from December 16, 1941, all American nationals present on French territory were required to declare themselves at the *Kreiskommandantur*. A weekly verification procedure was planned in the communities where they resided.
129. A. Alpérine, in *L'Un des trente-six, David Rapoport* (Paris: Kyoum, 1946), 4.
130. According to some estimations, the story of the Jewish detainees in the Compiègne camp comes to an end in May 1943, while others situate the final chapter in November of the same year. See Rutkowski, "Le Camp de Royallieu à Compiègne," 131.
131. Ibid., 128–129.
132. AN, F 9, 5579, excerpt from daily notes taken by Georges Kohn from 1941 to 1944.
133. A detailed statistical analysis has been done by the Masse brothers and by Georges Kohn in AN, F 9, 5579. These numbers have been taken from the daily notes written down by Georges Kohn from 1941 to 1944.
134. Bernard, *Le Camp de la mort lente*, 131ff.
135. "Journal de Compiègne, 11 décembre 1941—11 avril 1942," p. 26, unpublished handwritten manuscript kept by his daughter, Claude Bloch. My thanks to Denis Peschanski for having entrusted me with a copy of the valuable notes and to Claude Bloch for have authorized their use.

136. The list of lectures can be found in AN, F 9, 5579, an excerpt of the daily notes taken by Georges Kohn from 1941 to 1944.
137. Bernard, *Le Camp de la mort lente*,157.
138. Jacob, *Journal de Compiègne*.
139. Ibid., 34.
140. Rutkowski, "Le Camp de Royallieu à Compiègne," 138.
141. AN, F 9, 5579, excerpt of the notes taken daily by Georges Kohn from 1941 to 1944.
142. Bernard, *Le Camp de la mort lente*, 237.
143. These observations have been taken from the notes of Georges Kohn, AN, F 9 5579, and from the testimony of Henri Bloch given on August 13, 1951, Institut d'histoire du temps présent.
144. YV, M 25/23, "Déclaration," and YIVO, France During WWII, 1, *Massada; discours des camps de concentration*.
145. AN, AJ 38, 148. Biélinky reported this attempt to elaborate a theory of Aryan, non-Semitic Sephardites as early as July 29, 1941; *Journal*, p. 133.
146. Centre de Documentation Juive Contemporaine, CCXIII–138, letter (from the federation in Paris) to the Southern Zone, December 19, 1941. It was perhaps written by Rapoport.
147. Richard I. Cohen, *Burden of Conscience*, 139.
148. When Kadmi Cohen was set free from Compiègne, he designated Tuvel as his assistant along with David Levinson de Philippe Dziakowski, who would later replace him at the head of the Massada movement. YV, M 25/23.
149. See Jacques Biélinky, "Colonie scolaire, comité de coordination," reproduced in Biélinky, *Journal*, 284. See also "Le comité Amelot," YIVO, France during WWII, I-64 and the minutes of the meeting held on August 18, 1941, YIVO, RG 343, 8.
150. YV, P7/8, January 28, 1942, minutes of a meeting between the appointed members of the board of directors for the UGIF-North and representatives of the Amelot Committee.
151. Maurice Rajsfus, *Une Terre Promise? Des Juifs dans la collaboration (II)* (Paris: L'Harmattan, 1989), 73ff.
152. AIU, CC-42, Mr. C., October 8, 1941, activity of the youth in Paris.
153. The texts of theses appeals dating from July and August 1941 can be found in YIVO, UGIF, I-32 and YIVO, RG 343–8.
154. CC, dossier concerning the Occupied Zone.
155. CC-41/42.
156. AIU, CC-4, Marseilles, March 4, 1942, letter from Professor Olmer to Helbronner.
157. Centre de Documentation Juive Contemporaine, CCXIII–138, letter (from the FSJF in Paris, probably written by Rapoport) to the Southern Zone, December 19, 1941.
158. Adler, *The Jews of Paris*, 112.
159. AN, AJ 38, 9, November 4, 1942, message from the General Commission on Jewish Affairs to Dr. Stenger, Beauftragten with the German military command in France. André Baur, Georges Edinger, Marcel Stora, Albert Weill, and Madame Stern advanced nearly 260,000 francs (André Baur alone contributed 170,000 francs to this effort) between November 30, 1941 and February 28, 1942.
160. AN, AJ 38, 1141.
161. AN, F 60, 491, April 2, 1942, report by Chomel de Jarnieu. It was because of this delay that the chief of staff for the General Commission on Jewish Affairs, Cabany, was reportedly arrested by the Germans. See also Richard I. Cohen, *Burden of Conscience*, 74.
162. AIU, CC-1a, message from the permanent delegation of the Central Consistory, January 16, 1942.
163. YV, P 7/8, January 28, 1942, minutes of a meeting between the appointed members of UGIF-north's board of directors and representatives of the Amelot Committee.
164. Centre de Documentation Juive Contemporaine, CCXIII-45, November 16, 1941, handwritten letter sent to the Southern Zone, FSJF.
165. YV, P 7/8, January 28, 1942, minutes of a meeting between the appointed members of the board of directors of the UGIF-North and representatives of the Amelot Committee.

166. Centre de Documentation Juive Contemporaine, CCXIII–48, "Our Relations With the UGIF," January 1942, probably written by David Rapoport, and YV, P 7/8, January 28, 1942, minutes of a meeting between the appointed members of the board of directors for UGIF-North, and representatives from the Amelot Committee.

167. Zosa Szajkowski, *Analytical Franco-Jewish Gazetteer*, 41 n.84.

168. *Solidarité*, no. 3 (April 1, 1942), trans. Annette Wieviorka; *Le Monde juif* 125 (1987): 32–33.

169. *La Presse anti-raciste sous l'Occupation hitlérienne*, 41.

170. Archives of the Paris police prefecture, "Situation à Paris," report of May 4, 1942.

171. *Le Sang de l'étranger*, 87.

172. Louis Gronowski-Brunot, *L'Antisémitisme, le racisme et le problème juif* (Editions du Parti Communiste Français, SFIC, underground publication from November 1941, 79. BN, Rés. 16 Lb 58 676 (erroneously attributed to Georges Politzer). See also Adler, *The Jews of Paris*, 187. Louis Gronowski-Brunot, *Le Dernier Grand Soir; Un Juif de Pologne* (Paris: Seuil, 1980), 164ff.

173. Archives of the Resistance Museum in Champigny, David Diamant Collection.

174. David Diamant, *Le Billet vert*, 53.

175. Bergelson's appeal has been reproduced in *La Presse anti-raciste*, 37–38.

176. Adler, *The Jews of Paris*, 181–183.

177. Dated November 29, 1941, the issue has been reprinted in *Das vort fun vidershtand und zig* (Paris: UJRE, 1949), 59–60.

178. Adler, *The Jews of Paris*, 204.

179. This passage was translated by Annette Wieviorka in *Le Monde juif* 125 (1987): 29.

180. *Le Sang de l'Étranger*, 155.

181. Descriptions of this activity can be found in Annette Wieviorka, *Ils étaient juifs, résistants, communistes* (Paris: Denoël, 1986), 124ff.

182. Centre de Documentation Juive Contemporaine, V-120, April 22 and May 9, 1942, excerpts from the reports made by the secretary-general for propaganda of the Front Social du Travail, R. Eloy, and addressed to Dr. Gross, at the German embassy in Paris. Reproduced in Adam Rutkowski, *La Lutte des Juifs en France*, 92–93.

183. Adler, *The Jews of Paris and the Final Solution, op. cit.*, p. 185–186.

184. David Diamant, "Les Juifs de Paris dans la Résistance," handwritten manuscript, archives of the Musée de la Résistance in Champigny.

185. *Le Sang de l'étranger*, 122ff.

186. Abraham Lissner, *Un franc-tireur juif raconte*, with a preface by Henri Rol-Tanguy (Paris: 1969), 21.

187. Archives of the Paris police prefecture, "Situation à Paris," report dated April 27, 1942. See also *Le Sang de l'étranger*, 155. They were shot at the Mont Valérien on August 13, 1942 along with eighty-two other hostages.

188. Archives of the Paris police prefecture, "Situation à Paris," passim.

189. Archives of the Paris police prefecture, "Situation à Paris," May 18, 1942.

190. *La Presse anti-raciste sous l'occupation hitlérienne*, 39–40.

191. AN, AJ 38, 5.

192. AN, AJ 38, 67. Letter transmitted "by a Christian opposed to the Jewish domination but disgusted by human savagery," and bearing the stamp of the General Commission on Jewish Affairs, April 9, 1942.

193. AN, AJ 38, 7.

194. As to the circumstances in which the decision to impose the yellow star was made, see Marrus and Paxton, *Vichy France and the Jews*, 234ff. The main elements in this case can be found in Serge Klarsfeld, *L'Étoile des Juifs* (Paris: L'Archipel, 1992).

195. Langeron, *Paris, Juin 1940*.

196. See Léo Hamon and Renée Poznanski, *Avant les premières grandes rafles, Les Juifs à Paris sous l'Occupation (juin 1940–avril 1941), Cahiers de l'IHTP* 22 (December 1992): 81.

197. On behalf of the Sepharadite Worship Association of Paris, for example, Sam Lévy wrote to Marshal Pétain on September 9, 1941: "Parisian newspapers have recently announced

that the government of the Third Reich has required all German Jews to wear the little round insignia. This news seems to foreshadow the adoption of a similar measure with respect to the Israelites of the Occupied Zone." AN, AJ 38, 148.

198. Report from one of the women volunteers for the UGIF, July 1942, Centre de Documentation Juive Contemporaine, CCXIV-5.

199. Centre de Documentation Juive Contemporaine, XLIXa 4 and 5, memorandum from Best to Knochen on March 31, 1942, and memorandum from Dannecker on April 17, 1942. Dannecker doubted that it would be possible.

200. *Les Juifs sous l'Occupation*, 155.

201. These figures have been provided by Léon Poliakov, *L'Etoile jaune* (Paris: Editions du Centre, 1949) and cited again by most authors on the subject. For his part, Serge Klarsfeld talks about the distribution of some 92,600 such yellow stars in late June 1942: although he refers to Tulard, he does not indicate the source of this figure.

202. Biélinky, *Journal*, June 1, 1942, pp. 213–214.

203. His testimony was taken by Anny Latour, and can be found in the Centre de Documentation Juive Contemporaine, DLXXII-30.

204. AN, AJ38, 172.

205. Marrus and Paxton, *Vichy France and the Jews*, 237–238.

206. Examples of such requests can be found in AN, AJ 38, 162.

207. Previously cited report made by one of the volunteers for the UGIF, Centre de Documentation Juive Contemporaine, CCXIV-5. "Wear the yellow star with pride" was the watchword issued by Robert Welsh, editor of the German-language Zionist newspaper *Judische Rundschau* (published in the immediate prewar period). Cited by A. Margaliot, "The Struggle for Survival of the Jewish Community in Germany in the Face of Oppression," in *Jewish Resistance during the Holocaust* (Jerusalem: Yad Vashem, 1971), 106.

208. This practice can be seen in Jacques Doillon's film *Un sac de billes*, which was made after Joseph Joffo's autobiographical novel. The walk was intended to prove to passersby that Jews such as Joffo assumed their Jewish identity with pride.

209. AN, F 9, 5, 579. Excerpt from the daily notes taken by Georges Kohn from 1941 to 1944: June 15, 1942.

210. According to a report cited by the propaganda section of the German Military Command, printed in *L'Etoile des Juifs*, 89–92.

211. Previously cited report from one of the volunteers for the UGIF, Centre de Documentation Juive Contemporaine, CCXIV-5.

212. *J'accuse*, special issue (May–June 1942); BN, Rés. G 1470–186. Reprinted in *Qui savait quoi?* ed. Stéphane Courtois and Adam Rayski with the collaboration of Philippe Burrin, Claude Lévy, Denis Peschanski, and Renée Poznanski (Paris: La Découverte, 1987), 140.

213. Maxime Steinberg, *L'Etoile et le fusil* (Brussels: Vie Ouvrière, 1984), 2:125–128.

214. Werth, *Déposition*,303.

215. Georges Wellers, *L'Etoile jaune* p. 113.

216. Jean Guéhenno, *Journal des années noires* (Paris: Gallimard, 1947), 266.

217. Ernst Jünger, *Premier journal parisien, Journal II, 1941–1943* (Paris: Christian Bourgeois, 1980), 137.

218. AN, AJ 38, 70, October 14, 1942, message from the General Commission on Jewish Affairs to the Paris police prefect.

219. See the testimony given by Annette Müller in Klarsfeld, *Vichy-Auschwitz*, 1:508ff.

220. Cited by Marrus and Paxton, *Vichy France and the Jews*, 235; repr. *L'Etoile des Juifs*, 23–24.

221. Archives of the Paris police prefecture BA-1813, Paris, June 6, 1942, memorandum number 140–42, repr. *L'Etoile des Juifs*, 72–75.

222. Poliakov, *L'Etoile jaune*.

223. AN, F7, 14 929, Bureau of Technical Inspections, synthesis of intercepted letters between June 10 and July 10, 1942, and others.

224. Reports dated June 8, 1942 and June 22, 1942, archives of the Paris police prefecture, "Situation à Paris."

225. Archives of the Paris police prefecture, report dated June 15, 1942.

226. Archives of the Paris police prefecture, reports dated June 15 and June 22, 1942.

227. Poliakov, *L'Etoile jaune*, 79ff.

228. Micheline Bood, *Les Années doubles*, 141–142.

229. CC-24, lettre from André Baur to Albert Manuel, Paris, June 7, 1942.

230. June 16, 1942.

231. See also the previously cited report from one of the volunteers for the UGIF, Centre de Documentation Juive Contemporaine, CCXIV-5.

232. Claudine Vegh, *Je ne lui ai pas dit au revoir; des enfants de déportés parlent*, with a preface by Bruno Bettelheim (Paris: Gallimard, 1979), 33.

233. Excerpt of Rolland's diary in André Spire, *Souvenirs à bâtons rompus* (Paris: Albin Michel, 1961), 209.

234. See for example Henri Sinder, "La situation des Juifs,"

235. Alice Courouble, *Amie des Juifs* (Paris: Editions Bloud and Gay, 1946), 68–71.

236. There were three Aryans wearing the yellow star and twelve non-Jews bearing a whimsical insignia. Archives of the Paris police prefecture, "Situation à Paris," report dated June 8, 1942.

237. Centre de Documentation Juive Contemporaine, XLIXa-33, report dated June 16, 1942 and signed by Knochen (but apparently written by Röthke, according to Serge Klarsfeld) and repr.*L'Etoile des Juifs*, p. 118–121).

238. *L'Etoile des Juifs*, 87–89.

239. Courouble, *Amie des Juifs*, 86.

240. Report made on June 10, 1942 by Heinz Röthke; repr. *L'Étoile des Juifs*, 106–107.

241. Archives of the Paris police prefecture, "Situation à Paris," June 8, 1942.

242. All of these examples have been taken from press reviews carried out in the context of the bi-weekly reports at the Paris police prefecture, "Situation à Paris," passim.

243. Archives of the Paris police prefecture, "Situation à Paris," July 13, 1942.

244. Press review, July 21, 1942, AIU, CC-10.

245. Many examples of these denunciations can be found in AN, AJ 38, 6 dossier 1. They often refer explicitly to calls for such denunciations issued by the press.

246. See also Renée Poznanski, "Avant les premières grandes rafles; les Juifs à Paris sous l'Occupation (Juin 1940-avril 1941)," in *Avant les premières grandes rafles*, 32–39.

247. M. F. Gordon, "Protégeons la race," in the paper *Le National Populaire*, June 20, 1942.

248. Guy Crouzat, "La leçon de l'étoile jaune," *Les Nouveaux Temps*, June 16, 1942.

249. Archives of the Paris police prefecture, "Situation à Paris," June 8, 1942.

250. Archives of the Paris police prefecture, "Situation à Paris," June 15, 1942.

251. Previously cited report by one of the women volunteers for the UGIF (see note 231).

252. *L'Etoile des Juifs*, 104.

253. AIU, CC-21, police reports 913, register no. 42.

254. Léon Poliakov, *L'Etoile jaune*, 52–53.

255. Centre de Documentation Juive Contemporaine, XLIXa-69, report from the *Feldgendarmerie, Trupp* 923, Paris, June 8, 1942. This case has also been cited in *L'Etoile des Juifs*, 150.

256. Examples of such cases can be found in AN, AJ 38, 62.

257. AN, AJ 38, 1 154, SEC Paris, March–July 1944, arrests of Jews on the street, and Centre de Documentation Juive Contemporaine, XXXIII. Examples of such arrests have been reprinted in Rajsfus, *Drancy*, 135–137.

258. AN, F 7, 14 895, June 10, 1942, message from the prefect for the département of La Seine to the head of the Vichy government. The last paragraph of this memorandum indicates that these measures simply represent the concrete application of the order concerning "Negroes and Jews" given by the German authorities on November 8, 1940: in practice the order had not been put into effect for the Jews, for lack of means to identify them. Cited also by Poliakov, *L'Etoile jaune*, 54. See also archives of the Paris police prefecture, BA-1813, general appeal, number 18–6.

259. Charles Braibant, *La Guerre à Paris* (Paris: Corréa, 1945), 401.
260. CC, Consistory dossier, 1942, confessional information commission, Sunday, June 21, 1942.
261. AN, AJ 38, 117, message from the German military commander in France to the secretary-general of the French posts, telephone, and telegraph service.
262. "Frères," May 14, 1942; repr. Diamant, *Par-delà les barbelés*, 45–46.
263. Ibid., Pithiviers, May 16, 1942, p. 47.

8. *The Massive Police Roundups (pages 251–302)*

1. On the subject of Laval's return to power, see Robert O. Paxton, *Vichy France, Old Guard and New Order, 1940–1944* (New York: Columbia University Press, 1972), 133ff, and Azéma, *From Munich to the Liberation, 1938–1944*, 116ff. About Laval himself, see the biography written by Pierre Kupferman, *Pierre Laval, 1883–1945* (Paris: Flammarion, 1988).
2. Jean-Paul Cointet, *Pierre Laval* (Paris: Fayard, 1993), 381.
3. Robert Frank, "Pétain, Laval, Darlan," in *La France des années noires*, 1: 310–311.
4. Marrus and Paxton, *Vichy France and the Jews*, 220.
5. Ibid,. 218ff.
6. See Pascale Froment's biography, *René Bousquet* (Paris: Stock, 1994).
7. On the subject of Vallat's fall from power, see Marrus and Paxton, *Vichy France and the Jews*, 115–119.
8. Ibid., 228. See also the subsequent pages on Darquier and his appointment to the head of the General Commission on Jewish Affairs. See also Serge Klarsfeld, *Vichy-Auschwitz*, 1:50–51.
9. AN, AJ 38, 61, appointment decision.
10. For more on this question, see Burrin, *Hitler and the Jews: The Genesis of the Holocaust*, on the various interpretations (given the absence of a written order from Hitler) of the origins of the Final Solution, see Michael R. Marrus, *The Holocaust in History* (Hanover, N.H.: University Press of New England, 1987), 31ff.
11. Centre de Documentation Juive Contemporaine, LXXI-64, 65, October 8, 1941, message from Zeitschel to Dannecker, cited by Steinberg, *Les Autorités allemandes en France occupeé*, 104–105.
12. Centre de Documentation Juive Contemporaine, XXVI-31, memorandum by Dannecker dated June 11, 1942 concerning this meeting, cited by Steinberg, *Les Autorités allemandes*, 111. Cited also by Klarsfeld, *Vichy-Auschwitz*, 1:63ff., and by Marrus and Paxton, *Vichy France and the Jews*, 228. See also Robert O. Paxton, "La spécificité de la persécution des Juifs en France," *Annales, ESC*, 48–3 (1993); 605–619, and Maxime Steinberg, "Le paradoxe français dans la solution finale à l'ouest," *Annales, ESC*, 48–3 (1993): 583–594.
13. Courouble, *Amie des Juifs*, 37.
14. Centre de Documentation Juive Contemporaine, XXVb-103, June 29, 1942, letter from Kds Orléans to Bds about the deportation of June 28, 1942 and reporting the arrest of 107 Jews in order to fill the train that was only carrying 930 Jews from Beaune-la-Rolande; cited by Steinberg, *Les Autorités allemandes*, 114. Cited also by Klarsfeld, *Vichy-Auschwitz*, 1:70–71.
15. On the subject of these negotiations, see Klarsfeld, *Vichy-Auschwitz*,1:89ff.
16. Marrus and Paxton, *Vichy France and the Jews*, 263ff.
17. Message from Dannecker to the Central Security Office of the *Reich*, IV B 4, Berlin, Paris, July 6, 1942, repr. Klarsfeld, *Vichy-Auschwitz*, 1:237.
18. Marrus and Paxton, *Vichy France and the Jews*, Klarsfeld, *Vichy-Auschwitz*, 1:328. Message from Ahnert to the Central Security Office of the *Reich*, August 11, 1942.
19. Pierre Laval, Vichy, September 30, 1942, cited by Klarsfeld, *Vichy-Auschwitz*,1:455–456.
20. Cited by Marrus and Paxton, *Vichy France and the Jews*, 266. The account of Boegner's visit can be found in *Carnets du Pasteur Boegner, 1940–1945*, introd. Philippe Boegner (Paris: Fayard, 1992), p. 199–200.

21. On the subject of Laval's motives, see Marrus and Paxton, *Vichy France and the Jews,* 268–269.

22. Paris, June 15, 1942, Dannecker, on the "Practical execution of other transfers of Jews from France," repr. Klarsfeld, *Vichy-Auschwitz,* 1:203–204.

23. Annie Lambert, *Les Juifs dispersés de quatre départements bretons face à l'anti-sémitisme institutionnalisé:* 1939–1945, diss. University of Haute-Bretagne, Rennes-II, 1990, 38.

24. Ibid., 39.

25. Klarsfeld, *Calendrier,* 181.

26. AN, AJ 38, 1152, March 16, 1942, report sent from the interim delegate of the police for Jewish affairs in Dijon to the chief of police for Jewish affairs in Paris.

27. AN, F 7, 14,898, Angoulême, July 9, 1942, central police chief to the prefect for the département of La Charente.

28. Capelle, "La Destruction des Juifs," 1: 62ff.

29. Even though 2,626 Jews had registered with the census in the fall of 1940. François Job, *Gustave Nordon (1877–1944),* with a preface by André Kaspi (Presses Universitaires de Nancy, 1992), 76.

30. AN, AJ 38, 1142.

31. AN, AJ 38, 1152.

32. AN, AJ 38, 1157.

33. AN, AJ 38, 117.

34. AIU, CC, letter from Chief Rabbi Hagenauer in Nancy to the president of the Central Consistory in Grenoble, June 1942.

35. Klarsfeld, *Vichy-Auschwitz,* 1:114ff.

36. The description of this train full of deportees can be found in Klarsfeld, *Calendrier,* 287–288. Except for twenty-eight Jews dropped off at Drancy, the others were sent to Auschwitz.

37. AN, AJ 38, 229.

38. Klarsfeld, *Calendrier,* 277.

39. AN, AJ 38, 1 142, instruction from the German authorities and memorandum number 772/2 dated July 12, 1942; Dijon, July 14, 1942, list of foreign Jews arrested in the district of La Compagnie de la Côte d'Or, commander of the compagnie de gendarmerie.

40. AN, AJ 38, 1142.

41. Klarsfeld, *Calendrier,* 277.

42. Ibid., 278.

43. Lambert, *Les juifs dispersés,* 71.

44. Klarsfeld, *Vichy-Auschwitz,* 1:115.

45. Françoise Job, *Gustave Nordon,* and AIU, CC-21, July 22 and 24, 1942, postcards from the Chief Rabbi of Nancy.

46. AN, AJ 38, 152, M.S., March 18, 1943, message sent to the chief of police for Jewish affairs in Paris and also to the Prefect delegated to the Ministry of the Interior.

47. AN, AJ 38, 229.

48. AN, AJ 38, 229, message from the mayor of Logron dated July 19, 1942 to the subprefect of Châteaudun (who would refer the problem to the chief of police in the office of the prefect in Chartres on July 21). The children finally left Logron on their own toward the end of July to join their mother (perhaps released?) in Paris.

49. AIU, CC-21, July 21 and 22, 1942, postcards from the Chief Rabbi of Nancy.

50. AN, AJ 38, 1152, July 18, 1942, chief of the police for Jewish affairs to the assistant delegate, Dijon.

51. *L'Université libre,* July 5, 1942, number 63.

52. On the subject of this request and the response of André Baur, see Cohen, *The Burden of Conscience,* 76ff.

53. Adler, *The Jews of Paris,* 123.

54. Translated by Annette Wieviorka, *Le Monde juif* 127 (1987): 118–119.

55. On this point, see the analysis of Wieviorka, *Ils étaient juifs,* 150–151.

56. He was to stay there one month. Biélinky, *Journal,* July 12, 1942 and August 13, 1942, p. 232 and p. 242.

57. Claude Lévy, who puts the number of French agents mobilized for the massive roundup at nine thousand, gives an estimate almost twice as high as that of Serge Klarsfeld. See Claude Lévy and Paul Tillard, *La Grande Rafle du Vel d'hiv* (Paris: Robert Laffont, 1967, repr. 1992), 25. The book was also published in English as *Betrayal at the Vel d'hiv* (New York: Hill and Wang, 1967).

58. PP, message from the office staff on duty to the police prefect's staff, July 16, 1942, 8 A.M. Reprinted in Serge Klarsfeld, *Calendrier*, 323.

59. Centre de Documentation Juive Contemporaine, XXVb-80, July 18, 1942, cablegram from Röthke to the central security office of the Third Reich (RSHA). Cited by Lucien Steinberg, *Les Autorités allemandes*, 119, and by Klarsfeld, *Vichy-Auschwitz*, 1:118ff.

60. This figure includes 3,118 men, 5,919 women, and 4115 children. Archives of the Paris police prefecture, "Situation à Paris," report dated July 27, 1942.

61. Jacques Adler, *The Jews of Paris*, 122.

62. Among these books are the pioneer work of Claude Lévy and Paul Tillard, *La Grande Raffle*, and the most recent publication, Maurice Rajsfus, *Jeudi noir, 50 ans après; la rafle du 16 juillet 1942* (Levallois-Perret: Manya, 1992).

63. Situation as of August 25, 1942, unsigned document, Centre de Documentation Juive Contemporaine, XCVI-31, Joint, France, General and Emergency, 614, and YIVO, France during WWII, box 2, 23, reprinted in Biélinky, *Journal*, 310–319.

64. Archives of the Paris police prefecture, "Situation à Paris," report dated September 21, 1942.

65. Archives of the Paris police prefecture, "Situation à Paris," report dated July 27, 1942.

66. July 17, 1942, report of the Paris police prefecture, repr. Klarsfeld, *Calendrier*, 327.

67. Biélinky, *Journal*, 233.

68. YIVO, RG 343, 4, Paris, July 18, 1942, message from the head of office no. 5 to the "La mère et l'enfant" dispensary.

69. On the subject of these children, see Eric Conan, *Sans oublier les enfants; les camps de Pithiviers et de Beaune-la-Rolande, 19 juillet–16 septembre 1942* (Paris: Grasset, 1991). Some 7,618 or 7,816 Jews were thus transferred from the Vélodrome d'hiver to the camps in Le Loiret. Some 344 or 542 had either escaped, been taken to Drancy, or released, Klarsfeld, *Calendrier*, 369.

70. AN, 2 AG 495, Vichy, July 24, 1942 (confidential) memorandum on the subject of the National Relief agency's action in favor of the foreign Jews arrested on July 16, 1942.

71. The document is quoted in its entirety in Conan, *Sans oublier les enfants*, 32–36.

72. This letter has been reprinted in ibid., 68–71.

73. Klarsfeld, *Calendrier*, 279–281.

74. AN, F7 14,895, Paris, August 3, 1942, message from Leguay to the regional prefect in Orléans.

75. Conan, *Sans oublier les enfants*, 119.

76. Berlin, August 13, 1942, message from the RSHA (signed *SS-Sturmbannführer* Guenther) to the PdS of the Sipo; repr. Klarsfeld, *Vichy-Auschwitz*, 1:330.

77. Cited by Conan, *Sans oublier les enfants*, 153.

78. Here again, Conan's book is invaluable for establishing the chronology of these departures.

79. July 20, 1942, message from the director of the city police to the police prefect; repr. Klarsfeld, *Calendrier*, 331.

80. AN, F 9, 5 579, excerpt from notes taken daily by Georges Kohn from 1941 to 1944.

81. Ibid., April 24, 1942.

82. Ibid, April 24 to April 29, and Klarsfeld, *Calendrier*, 205–207.

83. Wellers, *L'Etoile jaune*, 194.

84. Georges Kohn, excerpt from his daily notes, July 21, 1942.

85. Georges Wellers, *L'Etoile jaune*, 114ff.

86. Ibid., 116ff.

87. AN, F 9, 5 579. In addition to the daily notes taken by Georges Kohn, various documents concerning Drancy can be found in this box of archives.

88. AN, F 9, 5 579, Drancy, August 14, 1942, memorandum from the police chief and camp commander, Guibert.

89. Courouble, *Amie des Juifs*, 74–75. It was in this group that there was the highest rate of suicides.

90. Biélinky, *Journal*, July 27, 1942, p. 237.

91. Archives of the Paris police prefecture, "Situation à Paris," report dated June 22, 1942.

92. Archives of the Paris police prefecture, "Situation in Paris," report dated July 27, 1942, Biélinky, *Journal*, July 26, 1942, p. 237, and AIU, CC-5, letter from Jacques Helbronner to Jardin, Laval's head cabinet, Lyon, July 29, 1942.

93. Archives of the Paris police prefecture, "Situation à Paris," report dated August 24, 1942.

94. These same terms can be found in all the memoranda indicating the categories of Jews targeted by the arrests, archives of the Paris police prefecture, BA/1813.

95. Paris, November 4, 1943, police prefecture, main office of the judiciary police, subbureau of Jewish affairs, AIU, CC-21.

96. Situation as of August 25, 1942, unsigned, Centre de Documentation Juive Contemporaine, XCVI-31, Joint, France, General and Emergency, 614, and YIVO, France during WWII, Box 2, 23.

97. Hennequin, August 11, 1942, archives of the Paris police prefecture, BA/1813.

98. *Les Juifs sous l'Occupation*, 106.

99. Adler, *The Jews of Paris*, 129.

100. Biélinky, *Journal*, August 3, 1942.

101. Undated, unsigned report on the Vel d'hiv roundup, Joint, SM 32.

102. Centre de Documentation Juive Contemporaine, Lubetzki source, undated and unsigned document, written before the mass arrests in the Southern Zone.

103. "Among Jewish circles, people are expecting the systematic destruction of all synagogues in Occupied France along with a new exodus of Israelites toward the Unoccupied Zone," observes an inspector with the General Bureau of Information, Vichy, October 4, 1941, AN, AJ 38, 7.

104. AN, AJ 38, 258.

105. *Le Petit Marseillais*, November 27, 1941.

106. Lambert, *Les Juifs dispersés*, 60.

107. Memorandum number 118 pol. 7 and 9, dated January 26, 1942, sent to all prefects in the Unoccupied Zone.

108. Memorandum number 4 from the national police, dated August 6, 1942, Centre de Documentation Juive Contemporaine, CCXX-31, reprinted in Adam Rutkowski, *La Lutte des Juifs en France*, 106.

109. The information available to me is too fragmentary to advance any figures. Nevertheless, to cite one example in the département of La Haute Vienne, there were for the dates of March 21 and 26, 1942 alone, 238 late declarations reported from Jews having secretly crossed over into the Southern Zone. AN, AJ 38, 60.

110. Biélinky, *Journal*, June 15, 1942, p. 223.

111. AN, F 7, 14 929, from July 10 to August 10, 1942.

112. Vegh, *Je ne lui ai pas dit au revoir*, 60.

113. AIU, CC-3, meeting of the commission of the office of the secretary of the Central Consistory, March 11, 1942. This was a request from Marcel Stora.

114. AIU, CC-67, handwritten notes taken by Robert Kiefe after each of his meetings with officials in Vichy.

115. AIU, CC-68, handwritten notes taken by Robert Kiefe, May 27, 1942.

116. AIU, CC-1a, register of the deliberations of the Central Consistory, June 22, 1942.

117. AIU, CC-2, meeting of the permanent commission of the Central Consistory, July 27, 1942, and AIU-CC-5, July 29, 1942, message from Helbronner to Jardin suggesting that he organize a meeting of the prefects of the Unoccupied Zone devoted to the problem of Jewish refugees from the Northern Zone.

118. AIU, CC-6, November 6 and 7, Robert Kiefe's discussions first with General Campet, then with Jean Jardin, and finally with René Bousquet.

119. Centre de Documentation Juive Contemporaine, Lubetzki collection, unsigned, undated document relating this discussion. See also AIU, CC-21.

120. Centre de Documentation Juive Contemporaine, CCXIII-59, Limoges, August 23, 1942.

121. AIU, CC-22, minutes of the meeting of the Commission on Social Aid and the chaplain's central office on July 26, 1942.

122. As of August 18, 1942, according to a document cited by Klarsfeld, *Calendrier,* 415–416.

123. YIVO, UGIF, XCII-57, p. 7, cited by Szajkowski, *Analytical Franco-Jewish Gazetteer,* 210.

124. Centre de Documentation Juive Contemporaine, XXVI-51, cablegram from the SD in Vierzon to the BdS, cited by Steinberg, *Les Autorités allemandes,* 122.

125. Centre de Documentation Juive Contemporaine, correspondence between the KdS in Poitiers and BdS, July 29 and 30, and August 4, 1942, cited by Steinberg, *Les Autorités allemandes,* 122, document number 410 (no shelf mark).

126. Centre de Documentation Juive Contemporaine, XXVb-142, Angers, August 26, 1942, report from the Sipo/SD in Angers to the Sipo/SD in Paris, reprinted in Rutkowski, *La Lutte des Juifs en France,* 109–110; AN, F 9, 5 579, excerpt from the daily notes taken by Georges Kohn from 1941 to 1944, September 1942, and Klarsfeld, *Calendrier,* 626.

127. Centre de Documentation Juive Contemporaine, CCXIII-59, Limoges, August 1942.

128. Centre de Documentation Juive Contemporaine, CCXIII-108, report by M. P.

129. Bohny-Reiter, *Journal de Rivesaltes,*125.

130. AIU, CC-26, telegrams from the national police on July 29 and August 4, confirmed on August 8, 1942.

131. Joint, 596, Lisbon, August 11, 1942, Joseph Schwartz to the AJDC in New York.

132. Joint, 596, Lisbon, August 11, 1942, Joseph Schwartz to th AJDC in New York, and Centre de Documentation Juive Contemporaine, CDXXX-13, September 1942, report on the situation of Jews in France (doubtless written by Raymond-Raoul Lambert). Raphaël Spanien was one of the leaders of the HICEM. See also Lambert, *Carnet d'un témoin,* 177.

133. Lambert, *Carnet d'un témoin,* 152–153.

134. AN, F 7, 14, 930, monthly report number 39, March 1942.

135. AIU, CC-3, commission of the main office of the Central Consistory, March 11, 1942, excerpts of discussions between André Baur, Marcel Stora, and members of the Vichy government.

136. AIU, CC-67, Vichy, April 15, 1942, secretary of state for the interior to the prefects—General instructions for the application of the law of October 27, 1940 making mandatory a French identity card.

137. Sweets, *Choices in Vichy France,* 122.

138. About the expulsion notices, see AIU, CC-18. On the subject of Helbronner's efforts to intervene, see AIU, CC- 19.

139. JO, July 19, 1942, *Les Juifs sous l'Occupation,* 37 and 162.

140. AN, AJ, 38, 1145, correspondence on the subject.

141. July 28, 1942, Centre de Documentation Juive Contemporaine, CCXIX-94 and CCXIV-6, reprinted in Rutkowski, *La Lutte des Juifs en France,* 102–103.

142. AIU, CC-67, handwritten notes by Robert Kiefe on his discussion with Jardin.

143. Cited by Klarsfeld, *Calendrier,* 272.

144. AIU, CC-26, H. Cado, main office of the police for national territory and foreigners, Vichy, August 4, 1942; repr. Klarsfeld, *Vichy-Auschwitz,*1:318–319, but for the date of August 5.

145. AIU, CC-26, main office of the police for the national territory and foreigners, summary of actions involved in handing over the Israelites to the German authorities, undated, probably written on August 26.

146. AN, F 15 088, train of August 24, 1942.

147. These figures are by necessity only approximate. The documents do not always agree. Some 6,584 Jews had supposedly been arrested just during the day of August 26. Centre de Documentation Juive Contemporaine, XXVI-58, August 29, 1942, message from Giessler to

Knochen; cited by Steinberg, *Les Autorités allemandes*, 127, and Ministry of the Interior, Vichy, August 28, 1942, number of foreign Israelites gathered together by region, repr. Klarsfeld, *Vichy-Auschwitz*, 1:373–374). But according to the information provided by the offices of the prefects, the number of Jews apprehended rose to 7,293 as of September 1. Some 1,408 of them had avoided deportation after going through a selection process; Vichy, September 1, 1942, the regrouping of the Israelites, reprinted in Klarsfeld, *Calendrier*, 590.

148. Klarsfeld, *Vichy-Auschwitz*, 1:158–159, puts the number of internees from the camps at 3,429 and the number from the Foreign Worker Units at 1,184. Grynberg arrives at different figures: according to her, 3,904 internees and 758 foreign workers were deported in August 1942 before the mass arrests of August 26, 1942; *Les Camps de la honte*, 309.

149. If we use these numbers, the final figure was 11,456, plus the 842 Jews counted by Serge Klarsfeld in the two trains that arrived at Drancy from the Unoccupied Zone on September 15 and 22. Basing his assessment on the number of Jews having arrived at Drancy, Klarsfeld gives a range of somewhere between 10,176 and 10,314 Jews that were thus handed over to the Germans during this time period (*Calendrier*, 470–475).

150. Instructions dating from July 29 sent by Cado to regional prefects in Perpignan, Pau, Toulouse, Marseilles, and elsewhere; repr. Klarsfeld, *Calendrier*, 493ff.

151. Centre de Documentation Juive Contemporaine, CCXIII-60, report written on August 13, relating the deportations from the camp at Les Milles. See also Christian Oppetit, ed. *Marseille, Vichy et les nazis; le temps des rafles; la déportation des Juifs*, with a preface by Pierre Vidal-Naquet (Marseilles: Amicale des déportés d'Auschwitz et des camps de Haute-Silésie, 1993), 100ff. See also Fontaine, *Le Camp d'étrangers*, 137ff.

152. Bohny-Reiter, *Journal de Rivesaltes*,130.

153. Ibid., 133–134.

154. AN, F 7, 15 088, Pau, August 11, 1942, message from the prefect of the Basses-Pyrénées to the secretary-general for the police concerning the trains having left Gurs on August 6 and 8 for Chalon-sur-Saône.

155. AIU, CC-26, report from the commission on the camps, August 7, 1942.

156. AN, F 7, 15 088, Pau, August 11, 1942, message from the prefect of the Basses-Pyrénées to the secretary-general for the police concerning the trains having left Gurs on August 6 and 8 for Chalon-sur-Saône.

157. AIU, CC-26, report on the deportations and on the activity of the chaplains' office, August–September 1942. See also Centre de Documentation Juive Contemporaine, CCCLXVI-38.

158. AIU, CC-26, report on the deportations and on the activity of the chaplains' office, August–September 1942. See also Centre de Documentation Juive Contemporaine, CCCLXVI-38.

159. AIU, CC-26, report on the camp at Les Milles, August–September 1942, by Chief Rabbi Salzer; repr. Grandjonc and Grundtner, eds., *Zone d'ombres*, 393–399.

160. AIU, CC-26, report on the deportations and on the activity of the chaplains' office, August–September 1942.

161. Oral presentation on the deportations from the camp at Les Milles given by Chief Rabbi Salzer, Marseilles, August 17, 1942, meeting of the regional chaplains, AIU, CC-25. See also his report, AIU, CC-26, and the report on the deportations and the activity of the chaplains' office, AIU, CC-26, August–September 1942. Lambert, *Carnet d'un témoin*, 184. Seventy children between the ages of two and fifteen were thus saved from deportation. An unsigned report also mentions seventy children between the ages of five and eighteen; Centre de Documentation Juive Contemporaine, CCXIII-60.

162. Lambert, *Carnet d'un témoin*, 184.

163. Klarsfeld, *Vichy-Auschwitz*, 1:158–159.

164. AN, F 7, 15 088, August 19, 1942, message from Bousquet to the commissioner for the fight against unemployment.

165. AIU, CC-26, message from Paul David to Chief Rabbi Hirschler, Montflanquin, August 31, 1942.

166. AN, F 7, 15 088, August 8, 1942, message from the secretary-general for the département of Les Pyrénées Orientales to the inspector general of the camps, on the subject of Rivesaltes.

167. AN, F 7, 15 088; response to a request made by telephone on July 21, 1942.

168. Response to a letter dated August 17, 1942. AN, F 7, 15 088, Vichy, August 19, 1942; message from the army general, secretary of state for the war ministry to the main office of the national police.

169. AN, F 7, 15 088. André-Jean Faure, August 12, 1942, report for the secretary-general of the police, member of the State Council.

170. AN, F 7, 15 088, telegram from the prefect in Limoges, August 12, 1942. The regional prefect in Limoges had suggested this action on August 1, 1942.

171. AN, F 7, 15 088, exchange of correspondence on this subject on August 15, 1942, between the police intendant and the Head of the second office of the secretary-general of the police at the office of the secretary of state for the ministry of the interior.

172. AIU, CC-26, Montpellier, October 2, 1942, Rabbi Schilli's report on events occurring between August 25 and September 4, 1942.

173. AIU, CC-26, Rabbi Eichiski, Grenoble, August 30, 1942.

174. AIU, CC-26, excerpts from the rabbis' reports, Léon Bermann for the Nice region, September 14, 1942.

175. *Journal de Berne*, September 1942, cited by Fontaine, *Le Camp d'étrangers*, 154.

176. Gourfinkel, *L'Autre Patrie*, 267–268.

177. AIU, CC-26, report from Rabbi Joseph Bloch, Clermont-Ferrand, September 3, 1942.

178. AIU, CC-26, September 1942, report from Rabbi Kahlenberg.

179. Thus out of the 6,701 Israelites arrested, 5,293 were kept in detention. Vichy, September 1, 1942, regrouping of Israelites (information provided by the prefectorates on the morning of September 1, 1942), ministry of the interior. Repr. Klarsfeld, *Calendrier*, 590.

180. Telegram from René Bousquet to the regional prefects of the Unoccupied Zone, August 18, 1942; repr. Klarsfeld, *Vichy-Auschwitz*, 1:339.

181. AIU, CC-22, Hirschler, efforts made to intervene at Vichy from August 31 to September 2, 1942.

182. AIU, CC-26, and Centre de Documentation Juive Contemporaine, CCCLXVI-38, report on deportations and on the activity of the chaplains' office, August–September 1942.

183. Marseilles, August 17, 1942, regional meeting of chaplains, AIU, CC-26, and Centre de Documentation Juive Contemporaine., CCXIX-8.

184. Henri Manen, *Au fond de l'abîme, Journal*, repr. Grandjonc and Grundtner, eds., *Zone d'ombres*, 353–375, quotation on 362.

185. Hans Fraenkel, "Les déportations des Juifs en zone non occupée," report written on August 21 and 22, repr. Grandjonc and Grundtner eds., *Zone d'ombres*, 377–391), quotation on 388.

186. According to the calculations of Klarsfeld, *Calendrier*, 475.

187. "Ever since the rumors of coming deportations were confirmed by official sources, the teams of UGIF social workers prepared notecards on Jews who were threatened by these measures in order to preserve the greatest possible number from the deportations planned. The greatest focus is on war veterans and children," Lambert, *Carnet d'un témoin*, 183.

188. AIU, CC-26. Report on the deportations and the activity of the chaplains' office, August–September 1942.

189. Kieval, "Legality and Resistance in Vichy France," 355.

190. AIU, CC-26, message from David Berman, Chief Rabbi of Brussels (temporarily living in Perpignan) to Chief Rabbi René Hirschler, September 14, 1942.

191. August–September 1942, excerpts from reports by rabbis and chaplains, AIU, CC-26.

192. AIU, CC-26, Alpes-Maritimes region, report on the arrests of foreign Israelites (Léon Berman, September 14, 1942).

193. Report on the events occurring between August 25 and September 4, 1942, AIU, CC-26.

194. Weill, *Contribution à l'histoire des camps d'internement dans l'Anti-France* (Paris: Editions du Centre, 1946), 206ff.

195. About Abbot Glasberg, see Lucien Lazare, *L'Abbé Glasberg* (Paris: Cerf, 1990).

196. Centre de Documentation Juive Contemporaine, CCXIII-116, report on Vénissieux; August–September 1942, excerpts from reports by rabbis and chaplains, AIU, CC-26; Lucien Lazare, *Rescue as Resistance*, 188. There were 110 children and 60 adults according to the testimony of Georges Carel, Centre de Documentation Juive Contemporaine, CCVIII-104. On this subject, see François Delpech, "La persécution des Juifs et l'Amitié chrétienne," in *Sur les Juifs* (Presses Universitaires de Lyon, 1983), 245ff; and the comments of Abbot Glasberg in Xavier de Montclos, Monique Luirard, François Delpech, Pierre Bolle, eds. *Eglises et Chrétiens dans la IIe guerre mondiale*, proceedings of the colloquium of October 1976 in Grenoble (Presses Universitaires de Lyon, 1978), 204–205.

197. Centre de Documentation Juive Contemporaine, CIX-117, "Why the Christian Friendship organization participated in screening operations at the Venissieux camp."

198. The specific figures were 25.3 percent for the Lyon region, 60 percent in the Montpellier area, and between 35 and 45 percent elsewhere, according to the rough draft of a report prepared for the head of the police of the national territory and of foreigners, AIU, CC-21.

199. AN, F 7, 15 088, message to regional prefects in Unoccupied Zone, number 13 224/13 226, August 30, 1942.

200. AN, AJ 38, 61, Vichy, August 18, 1942, information report number 3 271/16b.

201. AIU, CC-26, and Centre de Documentation Juive Contemporaine, CCCLXVI-38, report on the deportations and on the activity of the chaplains' office, August–September 1942.

202. Ibid.

203. AN, AJ 38, 2, Vichy, August 31, 1942, message from Bousquet to Darquier de Pellepoix; repr. Klarsfeld, *Vichy-Auschwitz*, 1:380–381.

204. AIU, CC-26, September 7, 1942, report by Rabbi Deutsch on the events in the département of La Haute-Vienne.

205. Lambert, *Carnet d'un témoin*, 189.

206. Châtelguyon, September 2, 1942, message from St. Zabiello, director-general of police offices in France to the minister of foreign affairs, London, "The Polish government in exile and the Jews." The document was translated and introduced by Jacques Burko and Pawel Korzec, *Pardès* 16 (1992): 121–133.

207. AIU, CC-8, message from André Baur to Albert Manuel, post card between the two zones, August 22, 1942; Gourfinkel, *L'Autre Patrie*, 260.

208. AIU, CC-26, Lyon, August 11, 1942, Chief Rabbi Kaplan.

209. Christian Lazard, *Journal*, AN, 72, AJ 287. A copy can be found at the Institut d'Histoire du Temps Présent.

210. AN, F 9, 5 579, excerpt from the notes taken daily by Georges Kohn from 1941 to 1944.

211. Ibid., 46.

212. Centre de Documentation Juive Contemporaine, XXVb-86, message from Röthke to Eichmann, July 20, 1942, cited by Steinberg, *Les Autorités allemandes*, 120.

213. AN, F9, 4, 579, excerpt from the notes taken daily by Georges Kohn from 1941 to 1944.

214. Christian Lazard, *Journal*, AN, 72, AJ 287. A copy can be found at the Institut d'Histoire du Temps Présent.

215. See also the testimony of attorney Henri Bloch, given to the Institut d'Histoire du Temps Présent on August 13, 1951.

216. Klarsfeld, *Vichy-Auschwitz*, 1:191.

217. The first time people were gassed at Auschwitz was in December 1941: the victims had been sick people judged beyond recovery and Soviet prisoners. On July 4, a trainload of Slovakian Jews were the first to undergo selection, with those unfit for work being sent to be gassed immediately. See Jean-Claude Pressac, *Les Crématoires d'Auschwitz. La machinerie du meurtre de masse* (Paris: Editions du CNRS, 1993), 34 and 43.

218. Maxime Steinberg, "Le paradoxe français dans la solution finale à l'ouest," *Annales, ESC*, 48–3 (1993): 490.

219. According to Maxime Steinberg, "the permissiveness of French authorities . . . re-

moved all restraints from the SS in the deportation of the Jewish population from the territories of Western Europe to the killing centers" (*le paradoxe français,* 590–592).

220. Klarsfeld, *Vichy-Auschwitz,* 1:191.

221. Henri Amouroux, *La Grande Histoire des Français sous l'Occupation,* vol. 5, *Les Passions et les Haines* (Paris: Robert Laffont, 1981), 226.

222. See Philippe Burrin's analysis, "Que savaient les collaborationnistes?" in *Qui savait quoi?* 76ff.

223. July 29, 1942, message from Henri Cado to regional prefects; repr. Klarsfeld, *Calendrier,* 493–497.

224. August 22, 1942, recommendations concerning the transfer of certain categories of Israelites into the Occupied Zone; Klarsfeld, *Vichy-Auschwitz,* 1:349–353.

225. Paris, September 4, 1942, Hagen, report on a meeting, "Agreement on language about the deportation of Jews from the Unoccupied Zone to the East"; repr. Klarsfeld, *Vichy-Auschwitz,* 1:410. See Denis Peschanski, "Que savait Vichy?" in *Qui savait quoi?* 53–66.

226. See also Marrus and Paxton, *Vichy France and the Jews,* 346ff.

227. Philippe Burrin, "Que savaient les collaborationnistes?" in *Qui savait quoi?* 75.

228. Renée Poznanski, "Que savait-on dans le monde?" in *Qui savait quoi?* 21–43.

229. *Verschickung zur Zwangsarbeit,* Centre de Documentation Juive Contemporaine, RF 1215 and XXVI-21, May 12, 1942, telex-memorandum from the MBF; cited by Steinberg, *Les Autorités allemandes,* 111.

230. *Umsiedlung*—June 15, 1942; documents cited by Steinberg, *Les Auorités allemandes,* 111–112, Marrus and Paxton, *Vichy France and the Jews,* 351.

231. The report emanated from the Polish Jewish *Bund.* It was transmitted to London in May 1942, probably by Swedes from Warsaw. The complete text can be found in Yehuda Bauer, "When did they know?," *Midstream* 4 (1968): 54–58.

232. Jean-Louis Crémieux-Brilhac ed., *Les Voix de la liberté,* 2:159–160.

233. Centre de Documentation Juive Contemporaine, XXXVc-184, correspondence on the subject cited by Lucien Steinberg, *Les Autorités allemandes,* 135.

234. AIU, CC-67, Robert Kiefe's notes on his talks with these two men.

235. Geneva, August 10, 1942, memorandum from Donald A. Lowrie to Tracy Strong, secretary-general of the World Committee of the YMCA; repr. Klarsfeld, *Vichy-Auschwitz,* 1:324–327.

236. AIU, CC-68, notes of Robert Kiefe, August 14 and August 20, 1942.

237. Marrus and Paxton, *Vichy France and the Jews,* 355.

238. The letter has been reprinted in *Carnets du Pasteur Boegner,* 191.

239. Louis Roché, "Les Français parlent aux Français, August 23, 1942," in *Les Voix de la liberté,* ed. Crémieux-Brilhac 2:196.

240. See the original manuscript in AIU, CC-1a. The document has been reprinted in Klarsfeld, *Vichy-Auschwitz,* 1:360–361.

241. AIU, CC-68, Lyon, August 28, 1942, message from Robert Kiefe to Albert Manuel, Adolphe Caen, and Jacques Helbronner.

242. AIU, CC-68, notes of Robert Kiefe on this meeting with Jardin.

243. AIU, CC-7, consistory session of August 23, 1942.

244. See also the message from Helbronner to Albert Lévy, July 24, 1942, and Geneva, August 27, 1942, message from the Committee for the Assistance of the Jewish Population Hit by the War to Chief Rabbi Hirschler, AIU, CC-22.

245. AIU, CC-21, message from General Verdier, general delegate for the French Red Cross in the Unoccupied Zone, to Madame K.

246. A transcription of these broadcasts can be found in the archives of the Consistory: see, among other documents, AIU, CC-21, 22.

247. AIU, CC-7, Consistory session of August 23, 1942.

248. Châtelguyon, September 2, 1942, St. Zabiello, 121–133 (as cited in note 206).

249. Ibid.

250. Gourfinkel, *L'Autre Patrie*, p. 260.

251. Written on October 15, 1942. Christian Lazard, *Journal*, AN, 72 AJ 287. A copy can be found at the Institut d'Histoire du Temps Présent.

252. Ibid.

253. Pithiviers, July 16, 1942. I thank Henri Minczelès for having entrusted me with a copy of this letter.

254. Archives of the Paris police prefecture, "Situation in Paris," August 10, 1942.

255. Archives of the Paris police prefecture, "Situation in Paris," August 24, 1942.

256. Ibid.

257. Bobkowski, *En guerre et en paix*, August 4, 1942, p. 344.

258. Gadala, *A travers la grande grille*, July 16, 1942, p. 60.

259. Biélinky, *Journal*, July 24, 1942, p. 236.

260. Werth, *Déposition*, 338.

261. Châtelguyon, September 2, 1942, St. Zabiello, "The Polish government in exile and the Jews," 121–133 (as cited in note 206).

262. Jean-Marie Guillon, "La France du Sud-Est," in *La France des années noires*, 2:174.

263. AN, F 7, 14 929, Monthly synopses of the monitoring of telegraph, telephone, and postal communications, synopses of July 10 through August 10 and August 10 through September 10, 1942; AN, F 7, 14 930, monthly report from the Central Commission on the monitoring of postal communication, no. 44 (August 1942) and no. 45 (September 1942).

264. AN, F1a, 3 705, Synopses and analyses of reports from the prefects from April 1941 to August 1944, August 1942. See also AN, F 60, 504.

265. Marrus and Paxton, *Vichy France and the Jews*, 276. Some excerpts of these reports from the prefects have been reprinted in Klarsfeld, *Vichy-Auschwitz* 1:305–307.

266. AN, AJ 38, 6, Saint-Girons-d'Ariège, August 30, 1942, Françoise Ditté d'Arrien.

267. Many examples are cited by Asher Cohen, *Persécutions et sauvetages, Juifs et Français sous l'Occupation et sous Vichy*, with a preface by René Rémond (Paris: Cerf, 1993), 300ff.

268. Roger Stéphane, *Chaque homme est lié au monde*, 142.

269. AIU, CC-26; repr. Klarsfeld, *Vichy-Auschwitz*, 1:280. On this same subject, and more generally, on the reactions of the episcopate, see Marrus and Paxton, *Vichy France and the Jews*, 270ff; and François Delpech, "Les Eglises et la persécution raciale," (1982) in Delpech, *Sur les Juifs*, 265–292.

270. AIU, CC-6, Monday, August 17, 1942, discussion between Chief Rabbi Kaplan and Cardinal Gerlier.

271. *Carnets du Pasteur Boegner*, 192.

272. AIU, CC-26; repr. Klarsfeld, *Vichy-Auschwitz*, 1:342.

273. Reprinted in Klarsfeld, *Vichy-Auschwitz*, 1:344–345.

274. AIU, CC-26, repr. Klarsfeld, *Vichy-Auschwitz*, 1:355.

275. AIU, CC-26, cited by Marrus and Paxton, *Vichy France and the Jews*, 270.

276. Quoted in Marc Boegner, "Le combat de l'Eglise à Vichy," in *Les Clandestins de Dieu*, 25.

277. To the surprise of Pastor Boegner, apparently. See *Carnets du Pasteur Boegner*, 206.

278. "Some [activists] had in their pockets four or five copies of [Archbishop Saliège's] letter, that they were distributing," remarked one "neutral" observer conducting a study throughout France in his (undated) testimony. AIU, CC-21.

279. *Le Franc-Tireur*, December 1941, cited by Dominique Veillon, "Franc-Tireur et les Juifs," in *La France et la question juive, 1939–1944*, ed. Georges Wellers, André Kaspi, and Serge Klarsfeld, Actes of the Colloquium sponsored by the Centre de Documentation Juive Contemporaine and held on March 10–12, 1979 (Paris: Editions Sylvie Messinger, 1981), 321.

280. *Libération*, no. 6 (February 15, 1942); Laurent Douzou, *Le Mouvement de résistance Libération sud (1940–1944)*, diss., University of Paris, 1993, 562.

281. Asher Cohen, "La presse clandestine face à la question juive de 1940 à 1942," *Le Monde juif* 117 (1985): 5.

282. Number 1 of *J'accuse* dates from April 1942, BN, Rés. G, 1, 470186.
283. Musée de la Résistance in Champigny, no. 94 (July 1942).
284. *Libération*, no. 16 (August 1, 1942); Douzou, *Le mouvement de résistance*, 587.
285. *Libération*, no. 18 (September 15, 1942); Douzou, *Le mouvement de résistance*, 587.
286. Centre de Documentation Juive Contemporaine, CCXIV-46; cited also by Dominique Veillon, *La Collaboration* (Paris: Le livre de poche, 1984), 244–246.
287. Dominique Veillon, "Franc-Tireur et les Juifs," in *La Collaboration*, 324. *Franc-Tireur*, no. 10.
288. François Delpech, "Les églises et la persécution raciale," in *Sur les Juifs*, 279.
289. Renée Bédarida, *Pierre Chaillet* (Paris: Fayard, 1988), 172.
290. *Combat*, no. 35 (October 1942), cited by Asher Cohen, "La presse clandestine," 8.
291. Centre de Documentation Juive Contemporaine, CCXIV-9a.
292. Urman archives, October 27, 1942, message from Inspector General Buffet in the offices of the judicial police to Dr. Ménétrel, cabinet head for Marshal Pétain.
293. Jean-Louis Crémieux-Brilhac, ed., *Les voix de la liberté*, vol. 2.
294. On July 1, 8, and 23, August 23 and 31, and September 9, 12, and 15. Ibid.
295. On the link between public opinion and the Vichy regime, and the effects of the Vel d'hiv roundup on public opinion, see Pierre Laborie, *L'opinion française sous Vichy*, 280.
296. *Libération* (north), 85 (July 17, 1942).
297. AN, F 7, 14 930, no. 45 (September 1942).
298. AIU, CC-33, Chief Rabbi Kaplan's visit to Aix-les-Bains, September 17, 1942.
299. Archives of the Paris police prefecture, "Situation in Paris," report of September 21, 1942.
300. Archives of the Paris police prefecture, "Situation in Paris," report of October 5, 1942. And for the Unoccupied Zone, see AN, F 1A, 3705, synopses and analyses of reports from the prefects, September 1942.
301. BN, Rés. G., 1 470 (186), *J'accuse*, no. 1 (October 10, 1942). Extensive excerpts of the two papers can be found in *Qui savait quoi?*.
302. AIU, CC-24 and *JO*.
303. Order no. 663, August 26, 1942; cited by Pierre Limagne, *Ephémérides*, 737.
304. *Paris-Soir*, August 16, 1942.
305. *Paris-Soir*, August 6, August 18, and October 6, 1942.
306. *Paris-Soir*, August 18, 19, and 26, and September 17, 1942.
307. The memorandum can be found in AIU, CC-21.
308. *Paris-Soir*, October 23, 27, and 28, 1942.
309. Order no. 723, September 14, 1942, and order no. 802, October 4, 1942, cited by Limagne, *Ephémérides*, 2:776 and 818.
310. See for example the programs of February 14, April 25, and May 2, 1942, AIU, CC-49.
311. AN, AJ 38, 61, Vichy, September 8, 1942, message from the General Commission on Jewish Affairs to the head of the national radio broadcasting, confirming the conversations of recent days about airing a ten-minute program by the commission three times a week.
312. AIU, CC-61, broadcasts of October 5 and October 7, 1942.
313. AIU, CC-61, broadcast of October 9, 1942.
314. AN, AJ 38, 64, September 26, 1942, message from the General Commission on Jewish Affairs to the head of national radio broadcasting.
315. Archives of the Paris police prefecture, "Situation in Paris," report dated August 10, 1942.
316. AIU, CC-17.
317. Centre de Documentation Juive Contemporaine, CIX-84, August 18, 1942, message from Paul Marion to Creyssel, cited by Billig, *L'Institut d'étude des questions juives*, 178–179.
318. AIU, CC-16, meetings of the regional delegates of the Central Consistory on September 1, 16, and 29, 1942.

9. *The Hunt for Jews in Paris (pages 303–355)*

1. Klarsfeld, *Calendrier,* 643.
2. According to the syntheses provided in the form of numerical tables in Klarsfeld, *Calendrier,* 1,109, 1,111, and 1,113.
3. Adler, *The Jews of Paris,* 13.
4. Centre de Documentation Juive Contemporaine, I-54, cited by Adler, *The Jews of Paris,*13.
5. AN, F 7, 14 930, Vichy's wiretapping service, November 1943.
6. Centre de Documentation Juive Contemporaine, XXVc-252, cited by Lucien Steinberg, *Les Autorités allemandes,*155.
7. Archives of the prefecture of the Paris police, "Situation in Paris," report dated August 10, 1942, and following reports.
8. AN, AJ 38, 1 153, July 8, 1944, message from the chief of staff in the central office of the national police to the regional prefects in the Southern Zone. On the subject of the SEC, see Billig, *Le Commissariat général aux questions juives,* 1:294ff.
9. According to the list provided in a report assessing the "General Arrest Operations ordered by the Occupation Authorities [the Germans]," dated November 4, 1943, and emanating from the office of the assistant director for Jewish affairs at the prefecture of police, AIU, CC-21.
10. These are the figures given by Klarsfeld, *Calendrier,* 639.
11. Centre de Documentation Juive Contemporaine, XXVc-175, IV J, September 24, 1942.
12. Klarsfeld, *Calendrier,* 684.
13. AN, F 9, 5 579, excerpts from the notes taken daily by Georges Kohn between 1941 and 1944, February 11, 1943.
14. Ibid.
15. Archives of the Paris police prefecture, "Situation in Paris," February 22, 1943.
16. Archives of the Paris police prefecture, "Situation in Paris," March 22, 1943.
17. AN, F 9, 5 579, excerpts from the notes taken daily by Georges Kohn from 1941 to 1944.
18. This schedule (AIU, CC-21) ran until February 4, 1944.
19. Klarsfeld, *Calendrier,* 916.
20. Ibid., 943.
21. Ibid., 954.
22. AN, F7, 14 895, November 26, 1942, message from Permilleux to the secretary-general of the police.
23. See figure 3, illustrating the number of arrests in the Paris region from August 1942 to August 1944.
24. Centre de Documentation Juive Contemporaine, II-202: two letters sent by the eldest child, Madeleine, to Marshal Pétain on October 3 and October 9, 1942, as well as information about the family, sent by the National Relief agency to Brinon. Rue d'Angoulême is now Rue Jean-Pierre-Timbaud.
25. AN, F 7, 14 895 and AN, AJ 38, 5 November 5, 1942, message from the prefecture of the Paris police to the General Commission on Jewish Affairs.
26. Centre de Documentation Juive Contemporaine, CDXXXIV-3, memorandum relaying orders from Knochen, May 29, 1943.
27. AIU, CC-4, October 17, 1943, report on Paris by Édinger.
28. These raids were conducted on December 21, 1942, and January 4, 9, and 18, 1943 respectively. Cited by Klarsfeld, *Calendrier,* 709, 715, 717, 719.
29. Billig, *Le Commissariat général aux questions juives,* 2:88ff.
30. Maurice Rajsfus (*Drancy,* 137) cites report no. 8,042, filed by an inspector with the SEC on July 27, 1944: this was doubtless one of the last.
31. Billig, *Le Commissariat général aux questions juives,* 2:75.

32. Ibid., 75.
33. AN, AJ 38, 1,154. Others are kept at the Centre de Documentation Juive Contemporaine, XXXIII, and are abundantly cited by Billig, *Le Commissariat aux questions juives*, 2:76ff.
34. Arrests were made in these cafeterias on June 12 and July 12 and 15, 1944, AN, AJ 38 1 154.
35. Some 1,904 Jews had been allowed to retain their French citizenship in the same process, according to the message from Gabolde, minister of justice, to Brinon, September 8, 1943; cited by Klarsfeld, *Calendrier*, 883.
36. AN, AJ 38, 242, SEC, Vichy, correspondence with police bureaus, 1941–1943. The first such request in the dossier is dated November 16, 1942.
37. Specific requests and replies can be found in AN, AJ 38, 4; AN, AJ 38,69; and AN, AJ 38,162.
38. This document has been reprinted in Serge Klarsfeld, *Vichy-Auschwitz*, 2:284–285.
39. Marrus and Paxton, *Vichy France and the Jews*, 323–326. It was apparently a plan by Darquier dating from December 31, 1942, that had been at the origin of the constant pressure that the Germans had put on Vichy about this matter. See also Klarsfeld, *Vichy-Auschwitz*, 2:19 and passim.
40. Centre de Documentation Juive Contemporaine, XXVb-104, 110, 114, XXVI-52, NG 1 968, correspondence dating from July and August 1942 on this subject; cited by Steinberg, *Les Autorités allemandes*, 122–123.
41. AN, AJ 38, 192, correspondence between the National Union of War Widows and the High Commissioner for Prisoners of War and the General Commission on Jewish Affairs, March–April 1943.
42. Centre de Documentation Juive Contemporaine, XXVI-72, annotation of the order to arrest them dated March 15, 1943, made by Röthke on April 25, 1943; cited by Steinberg, *Les Autorités allemandes*, 142. See also AN, Z 6 1 380.
43. Such was the case of the thirty-eight elderly Jews who had been sent to the Rothschild nursing home from Drancy on October 8, 1942. Klarsfeld, *Calendrier*, 672.
44. Georges Kohn, excerpt of daily notes, September 1, 1943 (as cited in chapter 8, note 80).
45. Rajsfus, *Une terre promise?* 271.
46. Published in the *Journal Officiel* on December 8, 1942, *Les Juifs sous l'occupation*, 169.
47. Biélinky, *Journal*, December 8, 1942, 271.
48. Published in the *Journal Officiel* on December 12, 1942, *Les Juifs sous l'Occupation*, 172.
49. AN, F 9, 5 579, excerpt from daily notes taken by Georges Kohn from 1941 to 1944, January 8, 1943. See also Klarsfeld, *Calendrier*, 716.
50. AN, F 7, 14897, discussions with the Germans on this subject.
51. CC-5, and Centre de Documentation Juive Contemporaine, XXVII-34a; cited by Steinberg, 150.
52. AN, F 7, 14897, February 23, 1944, message from the Ministry of the Interior to the Northern Zone's representative of the secretary-general for maintaining order.
53. Didier Epelbaum, *Aloïs Brunner*, with a preface by Serge Klarsfeld (Paris: Calmann-Lévy, 1990), and Mary Felstiner, "Commandant de Drancy: Aloïs Brunner et les Juifs de France," *Le Monde Juif* 128 (1987): 143–172.
54. The number established by Röthke in his overall assessment of this entire series of roundups; cited by Klarsfeld, *Calendrier*, 679.
55. Klarsfeld, *Calendrier*, 718.
56. See figure 3.
57. Wellers, *L'Etoile jaune*, 129.
58. AN, F 9, 5 579, excerpt from the notes taken daily by Georges Kohn from 1941 to 1944, January 11, 1943.
59. Ibid, November 3, 1942.

60. Ibid., November 18, 1942.

61. AN, F 9, 5 579, prefecture of the Paris police, head of the general police, internment camp at Drancy, month of May 1943.

62. An example of such correspondence can be found in Denise Baumann, *Une famille comme les autres*, a collection of letters introduced by the author, 2d ed. (Paris: Albin Michel, 1985). But I have also taken examples given in this paragraph from the letters sent out of Drancy by Hélène Felzenszwalbe to her family. My thanks to her brother Maurice, who entrusted me with copies.

63. AIU, CC-28, January 4, 1943.

64. AN, F 9, 5 579, excerpt of notes taken daily by Georges Kohn from 1941 to 1944, November 22, 1942.

65. Ibid., 56–57.

66. Ibid., January 15 and 27, 1943.

67. AN, F 9, 5 579, prefecture of the Paris police, main office of the general police, Drancy internment camp, month of May 1943.

68. Such performances were given, for example, on January 24, March 16, April 11, May 2, 8, 11, 17, and 18, and June 8, 1943, Georges Kohn, passim.

69. Georges Kohn, excerpt from daily notes, March 8, 1943.

70. Ibid., March 28, 1943.

71. Ibid., May 6, 1943.

72. Serge Klarsfeld, *Calendrier*, 711. That brought the total of those released since the opening of the camp to 2,454.

73. This recapitulation was calculated on the basis of the daily statistics recorded at the camp and reprinted in Klarsfeld, *Calendrier*, passim. For his part, Jacques Adler speaks of a total of 2,399 releases in *The Jews of Paris*, 266, n. 100.

74. AN, AJ 38, 162. Certificate number 10,336 was issued on May 31, 1944.

75. Georges Kohn, excerpt of daily notes, October 23, 1942.

76. According to the figures given by Klarsfeld, *Calendrier*, passim.

77. Cited by Adler, *The Jews of Paris*, 129.

78. There were 1,102 under the age of six, and 2,807 between the ages of six and twelve. Those are minimums, as Serge Klarsfeld determined these figures on the basis of the 70,870 deportees whose ages he was able to determine; *Calendrier*, 1121.

79. Ibid., 745.

80. Georges Kohn, excerpt from daily notes, March 8, 1943.

81. Raul Hilberg, *The Destruction of the Europeans Jews*, rev. ed. 3 volumes (New York: Holmes and Meier, 1985), 692ff, and Leni Yahil, *The Holocaust, The Fate of European Jewry, 1932–1945* (New York: Oxford University Press, 1990), 408ff.

82. Georges Kohn, June 9, 1943.

83. Hélène Felzenschwalbe, June 18, 1943.

84. AN, F 7, 14,895, message from the prefect of the Paris police to the secretary-general of the police, July 2, 1943.

85. YIVO, RG 210, XCII-100, "Instructions concerning the rules for packages in the Drancy camp," and AIU, CC-28, September 27, 1943, "New rules for packages in the Drancy camp."

86. AIU, CC-46, message from André Baur to his uncle Albert Manuel, secretary-general of the Central Consistory, July 3, 1943.

87. Simone Weill, Drancy, August 13, 1943, Denise Baumann, *Une famille comme les autres*, 163–165.

88. Georges Kohn, July 8, 1943.

89. AIU, CC-46, message from André Baur to Albert Manuel, July 8, 1943.

90. AIU, CC-46, message from André Baur to Albert Manuel, July 3, Sunday morning, then July 8, 1943. See the minutes of the meeting of June 30, 1943 between Brunner and Brückler on the one hand, and André Baur and Léo Israélowicz on the other, AIU, CC-22.

91. Georges Kohn, July 5, 1943.

92. AN, AJ 38, 1 141. See the correspondence on this subject in January 1944 between the General Commission on Jewish Affairs and the Head Office for Economic and Social Affaires (under the prefect for the département of La Seine).

93. AIU, CC-35, two reports made by Rabbi Bernard Schönberg to Lieutenant Colonel Blum, camp commander at Drancy, one dated July 22, 1943 and the other undated.

94. Rajsfus, *Drancy*, 274.

95. Hélène Felzenszwalbe, June 20, 1943.

96. Hélène Felzenszwalbe, June 26, 1943.

97. Hélène Felzenszwalbe, July 29 or 30, 1943.

98. The letter was sent from Bar-le-Duc on July 31, 1943.

99. According to the account given by an escapee who had been in Drancy from June 19, 1943 to July 16, 1943, and published in *France d'abord*, May 15, 1944, AIU, CC-21.

100. Archives of Lucien Lublin, Jewish Army reports.

101. Cela Perla and Eva Golgevit (Rozencwaig by her maiden name), letters printed in David Diamant, *Par-delà les barbelés*, 156–157.

102. Baumann, *Une famille comme les autres*, December 15, 1943, p. 184.

103. Wellers, *L'Etoile jaune*, 185ff.

104. The accounts of these escape attemps can be found in Rutkowski, *La Lutte des Juifs en France*, 147–166. According to recent research done by Jean-Claude Pressac, the train wound up in the camp at Maïdanek.

105. The account of this episode can be found in Jean-Francois Chaigneau, *Le Dernier Wagon* (Paris: Julliard, 1981).

106. XXVc-249, report from the head commander of the escort to Röthke, Strasbourg, December 3, 1943; repr.Rutkowski, *La Lutte des Juifs en France*, 211.

107. See the account given by Rachel Cheigam, *La Terre retrouvée*, no. 9 (May 1, 1945), and Rajsfus, *Drancy*, 323ff.

108. AIU, CC-22, minutes of the June 30, 1943, meeting between the Germans Brunner and Brückler on one side and UGIF leaders André Baur and Léo Israelowicz on the other.

109. Georges Kohn, excerpt from daily notes, July 7, 1943. See also Drancy, situation as of July 15, 1943, YV, P/7, 37, and Centre de Documentation Juive Contemporaine, CCXXI-19.

110. YV, P/7, 37, and Centre de Documentation Juive Contemporaine, CCXXI-19, situation in the Drancy camp as of July 15, 1943.

111. According to Klarsfeld, *Calendrier*, 877.

112. Georges Kohn, excerpt from daily notes, March 9, 1943, and Baumann, *Une famille comme les autres*, letters 75ff.

113. Baumann, *Une famille comme les autres*,March 29, 1943, p. 95.

114. Georges Kohn, excerpt from daily notes, July 13, 1943.

115. According to YV P/7, 37 and Centre de Documentation Juive Contemporaine, CCXXI-19, situation in Drancy as of July 15, 1943, there were 117 such employees. André Baur, who was ordered to prepare armbands that would distinguish them from the other internees, estimates their number at 600 or 700; AIU, CC-46, Baur's letter to Albert Manuel, Sunday morning, July 1943.

116. On May 2, 1944, Klarsfeld, *Calendrier*, 1,017.

117. Georges Kohn, excerpt from daily notes, July 9, 1943.

118. Ibid., and Klarsfeld, *Calendrier*, 843 and 846.

119. AIU, CC-21. See the testimony of Dr. Uzan as well as the other testimonies contained in this dossier. See also Szajkowski, *Analytical Franco-Jewish Gazetteer*, 223.

120. AIU, CC-21, "Les camps de travail du nord de la France," probably written by Maurice Moch.

121. Kurt Schendel, August 31, 1944, "Report on the discussions having taken place after the arrest of children, including the last discussion before the Germans' departure."

122. Testimony about Lévitan from Mira Lessovoï and Michèle Bonnet, *Le Monde juif* 146 (1993):42–44.

123. Lucien Steinberg, "Austerlitz, Lévitan, Bassano: trois camps annexes de Drancy," *Le Monde juif* 146 (1993): 34–37.

124. AIU, CC-46, reprinted in the Central Consistory's report for the month of October 1943.

125. Archives of the Resistance Museum in Champigny.

126. Crémieux-Brilhac, *Les voix de la liberté*, 4:72–73.

127. Joint, SM 33, Maurice's trip, from May 3 to May 17, 1944.

128. AN, AJ 38, 117, press release from the General Commission on Jewish Affairs, August 27, 1942.

129. *Paris-Soir*, December 24, 1942. The creation of this institute "upon the decision of the Commission on Jewish Affairs" had been announced one month before. Biélinky, *Journal*, November 24, 1942, p. 269.

130. CC-24, and *Paris-Soir*, January 15, 1943.

131. *Paris-Soir*, March 2, 1943.

132. *Paris-Soir*, March 2, 1943, "Le crime des Juifs," Jean Bosc.

133. Noted in the March 22, 1943 report "Situation in Paris," in the archives of the prefecture of the Paris police.

134. "Situation intolérable, *Le Pilori*, March 25, 1943, noted in the April 5, 1943 report "Situation in Paris," archives of prefecture of the Paris police.

135. About this visit, see Klarsfeld, *Vichy-Auschwitz*, 2:54–55.

136. Pemjean would reiterate this idea in the September 23, 1943, edition of *Le Pilori*.

137. *Paris-Soir*, July 4, 1943, P.-A. Cousteau, "La Lettonie s'éveille du cauchemar soviétique."

138. Philippe Burrin, "Le collaborationnisme," in *La France des années noires*, ed. Azéma and Bédarida, 1:378–382.

139. Bood, *Les années doubles*, December 15, 1942, p. 179.

140. Ibid., Sunday, November 8, 1942, p. 166.

141. Archives of the prefecture of the Paris police, "Situation in Paris," January 11, 1943.

142. Archives of the prefecture of the Paris police, "Situation in Paris," March 22, 1943.

143. Archives of the prefecture of the Paris police, "Situation in Paris," June 28, 1943.

144. The October 15, 1943, edition of *Paris-Soir*.

145. These centers were open from October 6 to October 16, and then, in view of the success of this recovery campaign, they were opened for an additional week. Archives of the prefecture of the Paris police,, "Situation in Paris," reports of October 18 and November 2, 1943.

146. Ibid., March 22, 1943.

147. Ibid., November 2, 1942.

148. Ibid., December 14, 1942.

149. Ibid., January 25, 1943.

150. Ibid., February 22, 1943.

151. Ibid., July 12, 1943.

152. Ibid., December 28, 1942.

153. Ibid., February 8, 1943.

154. *Paris-Soir*, September 23, 1943.

155. Archives of the prefecture of the Paris police, "Situation in Paris," September 6, 1943.

156. Ibid., December 28, 1943.

157. Ibid., February 22, 1943.

158. Ibid., October 5 and 19, 1942. Subsequent to the report of February 2, 1942, the number of United States citizens living in Paris was put at 650.

159. The operation took place over the night of September 14–15, 1942. Archives of the prefecture of the Paris police, "Situation in Paris," October 5, 1942.

160. Biélinky, *Journal*, September 25, 1942, p. 252.

161. Archives of the prefecture of the Paris police, "Situation in Paris," April 5, 1943.

162. Renée Poznanski, "Jacques Biélinky, un journaliste juif à Paris sous l'Occupation," in Biélinky, *Journal*, 30ff.

163. Biélinky, *Journal*, 274.

164. Sauvy, *La vie économique des Français*, 173–174, and Henry Rousso, "L'économie: pénurie et modernisation," in *La France des années noires*, 1:433.

165. AN, AJ 38, 108, yearly statistics from the aryanization files sent to the Germans, from May 1941 to July 1944.
166. Joint, SM 33, Maurice's Journey from May 3 to May 17, 1944.
167. Biélinky, *Journal*, 263.
168. Memorandum number 190–42, confirmed on October 15, 1942 (by number 225–42), archives of the prefecture of the Paris police, BA-1813.
169. Jean-Pierre Rioux, "Ambivalences culturelles," in *La France des années noires,* 1:534.
170. Biélinky, *Journal*, September 22, 1942, p. 255.
171. AIU, CC-22, Lyon, April 19, 1942, message from Helbronner to Madame Jacques Lantz.
172. The card is dated January 30, 1944.
173. AIU, CC-8, report from Albert Manuel, Lyon, May 7, 1943.
174. AIU, CC-24, May 15, 1943, "mailings to be made to deportees."
175. AN, AJ 38, 1 142, subsequent to a request from the General Commission on Jewish Affairs made March 31, 1943, response dated July 16, 1943 from the main office of vocational schooling in the Ministry of National Education, on May 17, 1943, from the superintendent of the Paris School District, and in March 1943, from the office of General Inspection of Elementary Schools at the prefecture of the département of La Seine. See figure 4.
176. See figure 5 and table 2.
177. There were 39 and 43 students, respectively, enrolled in these schools; AN, AJ 38, 1 142, May 17, 1943, message from the superintendent of the Paris school district to the General Commission on Jewish Affairs.
178. AN, AJ 38, 1 142, March 29, 1943, report to the General Commission on Jewish Affairs on the organization of a Jewish primary school system.
179. However, a fixed quota limiting the number of Jewish school students had been instituted in Algeria. See Singer, *Vichy, l'Université et les Juifs,* 86ff; on the plans for Jewish school children in mainland France, see 130ff.
180. Marc Knobel, "Etude d'un registre d'inscription d'une école parisienne, Fanny, Béatrice, Esther, Rose et les autres," *Le Monde juif* 134 (1989): 60–65.
181. This number includes 282 foreigners, message from André Baur to the General Commission on Jewish Affairs, February 3, 1943.
182. A photocopy of one of these cards can be found at AN, 72 AJ 266.
183. Based on testimony from Catherine Jarreau, 1987.
184. Cohen, *The Burden of Conscience,* 166ff., and Adler, *The Jews of Paris,* 134ff.
185. Jean Laloum, "L'UGIF et ses maisons d'enfants: le centre de Montreuil-sous-Bois," *Le Monde juif* 116 (1984): 159.
186. Adler, *The Jews of Paris,* 133ff. There were a dozen such cases in the UGIF-South: see Cohen, *The Burden of Conscience,* 170.
187. A handwritten memorandum from Röthke, Centre de Documentation Juive Contemporaine, XXVI-72, repr. Billig, *Le Commissariat général aux questions juives* 1:384–385, speaks of sixty to eighty arrests. According to the entry register at Drancy, 388 Jews were arrested on that day, including 350 furriers and their families who were set free three days later. In that case, then, the number of foreign employees of the UGIF arrested would not have exceeded thirty-eight. About Röthke's reassurances, see YIVO, RG 210, IV-4, report on the special meetings of the UGIF on February 22 and 23, 1944.
188. Such was the case, for example, of David Amzel (Dan Amit).
189. Centre de Documentation Juive Contemporaine, CDXXX-39, memorandum on the UGIF's children's homes, written after the war. The list of these homes can be found in Laloum, "L'UGIF et ses maisons d'enfants," 154.
190. Message from André Baur to the General Commission on Jewish Affairs, January 5, 1943; cited by Serge Klarsfeld, *Calendrier,* 715.
191. About the life of the children in the Montreuil-sous-Bois center, see Jean Laloum, "L'UGIF et ses maisons d'enfants," 161.
192. YIVO, RG 494, 20, Geneva, November 25, 1943, report sent by the OSE Union in Geneva to the American Committee of the OSE in New York.

193. Centre de Documentation Juive Contemporaine, XXVIII-159, interministerial ruling of March 18, 1943. Adler, *The Jews of Paris*, 155, places the dates of this restriction in April 1943. In her personal testimony, Juliette Stern places it in June 1943: Centre de Documentation Juive Contemporaine, CDLXIX-53, "Rappport sur le SF—Service familial clandestin de placement des enfants," Juliette Stern.

194. Joint, SM 35 A-2, September 22, 1943, "Die augenblickliche Kinderhilfe in Frankreich."

195. Szajkowski, *Analytical Franco-Jewish Gazetteer*, Annex XV, note on the organizational structure of the UGIF, 143.

196. Centre de Documentation Juive Contemporaine, CDXXII-26, January 20, 1943, memorandum from the Socio-Medical Commission adressed to the directors of the Neuilly, Lamarck, Guy Patin, and Montreuil children's centers; cited by Laloum, "L'UGIF et ses maisons d'enfants," 155.

197. Centre de Documentation Juive Contemporaine, CDXXX-39, memorandum on the UGIF's children's homes.

198. Centre de Documentation Juive Contemporaine, CDLXIX-53, "Rapport sur le SF," Juliette Stern.

199. Michel, *Les Eclaireurs israélites de France*, 150.

200. These file cards can be found at YIVO, RG 494, 20.

201. Read the testimonies bearing witness to these points in Sabine Zeitoun, *Ces enfants qu'il fallait sauver* (Paris: Albin Michel, 1989), 15–65.

202. See Robert Frank's testimony given on January 11, 1984, in *L'entraide temporaire, Sauvetage d'enfants juifs sous l'Occupation*, typewritten booklet, Centre de Documentation Juive Contemporaine, p. 26–31.

203. Ravine, *La Résistance*, 111.

204. Jean Laloum, "L'UGIF et ses maisons d'enfants: l'"enlèvement" d'une enfant," *Le Monde juif* 124 (1990): 172–176.

205. See the personal testimony of Paulette and Rosette Widawski in Jean Laloum, "L'UGIF et ses maisons d'enfants: Témoignages," *Le Monde juif* 139 (1990): 121–145.

206. Centre de Documentation Juive Contemporaine, CDXXX-39, report on the UGIF's children's homes written after the war.

207. Klarsfeld, *Calendrier*, 1,058.

208. Adler, *The Jews of Paris*, 128.

209. AN, Z 6, 1,382, March 20, 1944, report to the General Commission on Jewish Affairs on the results of the exercise 1943 and plan for the 1944 budget, Duquesnel.

210. "The activity of aid programs depending on the Amelot center," YIVO, RG 343, 116.

211. Cohen, *The Burden of Conscience*, 103.

212. Ibid., p. 102.

213. AN, AJ 38, 9, message from the UGIF to the *Befehlshaber der Sicherheitspolizei und des SD im Berreich des MBF*, November 2, 1942.

214. Ibid.

215. Dr. Eugène Minkowski, in *L'un des trente-six*, 46.

216. AIU, CC-15, record of the meetings of the Paris delegation, July 27, 1943.

217. AIU, CC-4, Edinger, report dated October 17, 1943.

218. AIU, CC-15, record of the meetings of the Paris delegation from July 10, 1943 to July 20, 1944.

219. AIU, CC-45, October 1942, report on the financial situation of the UGIF North.

220. CC, Dossier ZO/UGIF. In his appeal to the Central Consistory for aid, André Baur referred to the sum of 653,450 francs unofficially spent during the month of February 1943.

221. *Les Juifs sous l'Occupation*, 175–177.

222. AN, AJ 38, 1 141, December 14, 1943, message from the General Commission on Jewish Affairs to the minister and secretary of state for the national economy and finance.

223. AN, AJ 38, 1141. The count was made by using the seventeen (out of the total of twenty-seven that were made) monthly reports (which list 1,043 requests) found in the dossier.

224. AN, AJ 38, 4, January 29, 1944, message from the General Commission on Jewish Affairs to the minister and secretary of state of the interior, and AN, AJ 38, 1 141, Paris, March 3, 1944, message from Antignac to the secretary-general for the maintenance of order thanking him for his agreement (February 28).

225. AN, AJ 38, 1 141, June 21 and 28, 1943, exchange of letters between the director in charge of monitoring the UGIF and the director-general of economic aryanization.

226. The exact number was 25,555 according to Duquesnel (November 11, 1943), AN, Z 6, 1 382. See also AIU, CC-15, Léon Edinger, September 29, 1943.

227. AIU, CC-46, July 3, 1943, letter from André Baur to his uncle Albert Manuel.

228. AIU, CC-22, minutes of the June 30 meeting of Brunner and Brückler with André Baur and Israelowicz.

229. Cohen, *The Burden of Conscience*, 91.

230. Joint, SM 32, minutes of the meeting at the Drancy camp on July 30, 1943.

231. Klarsfeld, *Calendrier*, 859. Adler, *The Jews of Paris*, 152, speaks of forty-six arrests.

232. YIVO, France during WWII, 2-F 23, report dated September 10, 1943, and Cohen, *The Burden of Conscience*, 92–93.

233. Centre de Documentation Juive Contemporaine, XXVIII-159, XXVIIIb-72a, and XCVI-29, April 22, May 11, and May 18, 1943: the report and the letters from Antignac to Röthke can be found in these sources.

234. It was thought at the time that he had been arrested because one of those receiving aid from the Amelot Committee who had been apprehended by the police had broken down and revealed the source of his false papers (Eugène Minkowski in *L'un des trente-six*, 48). It is difficult to determine which of these two explanations is correct.

235. The organizations disbanded by a decision made on June 23, 1943; published in the *Journal Officiel* on July 15, were the "School Colony," located on Rue Amelot in addition to the three soup kitchens on Rue Elzévir, Rue Richer, and Rue Vieille-du-Temple. See *Les Juifs sous l'Occupation*, 148. See also YIVO, RG 210, IV-4, reports on meetings of the UGIF's board of administration from June 15 and 22, 1943.

236. Joint, SM 33, Maurice's trip from May 3 to May 17, 1944.

237. Adler, *The Jews of Paris*, 198.

238. Joint, SM 32, Paris, October 16, 1943, Feder (sent to Marc Jarblum in Switzerland).

239. On the subject of the Amelot Committee, see not only Adler but also Yehuda Jakoubowicz's *Ri Amelot, hilf und viderstand* (Rue Amelot, aid and resistance) (Paris: Editions Colonie scolaire, 1948 [in Yiddish]), as well as *L'un des trente-six*.

240. Bulawko, *Les jeux de la mort et de l'espoir*, 39–40.

241. Adler, *The Jews of Paris*, 214.

242. Examples from May 1943 can be found in YIVO, RG 343, 9.

243. *L'entraide temporaire*.

244. L. Chevalley-Sabatier, "En souvenir de David Rapoport," in *L'un des trente-six*, 25.

245. For the most part, this information has been gleaned from Dr. Milhaud's personal testimony (Paris, January 1984) published in *L'entraide temporaire*, 11–24. This intertwining of various organizations is also noted by Lazare, *Rescue as Resistance*, 179–180.

246. Joint, SM 32, Paris, October 16, 1943, Feder (the letter was sent to Marc Jarblum in Switzerland).

247. Sabine Zeitoun, *L'oeuvre de secours aux enfants (OSE), sous l'Occupation en France* (Paris: L'Harmattan, 1990), 57.

248. There are a large number of such texts, in many cases published, that can be consulted today. See *Das vort fun vidershtand und zig; La Presse anti-raciste sous l'occupation hitlérienne;* and also *Qui savait quoi?* as well as the documents translated from the Yiddish by Annette Wieviorka in *Le Monde juif* (1987): no. 125, 19–33, no. 126, 43–57; and no. 127, 117–127.

249. *Unzer Wort*. The edition is officially dated September 1942, but it makes reference to the occupation of the "Free" Zone by Italian and German troops; translated by Wieviorka, *Le Monde juif*, no. 127 (1987): 123–124. For examples of defenses of the USSR written during the first six months of 1942, see Wieviorka, *Ils étaient juifs, résistants, communistes*, 142–144.

250. Renée Poznanski, "La résistance juive en France," *Revue d'histoire de la Deuxième Guerre mondiale* 137 (1985): 18ff. Examples can be found in the publications cited in note 248.

251. Centre de Documentation Juive Contemporaine, CDLXXIII-77; Yiddish tract repr. Rutkowski, *La Lutte des Juifs en France*, 119–120.

252. *Unzer Wort*, Paris, dated November 20, 1942, but written and disseminated a month later; trans. Wieviorka, *Le Monde juif*, no. 127 (1987): 125–127.

253. Stéphane Courtois, "Le Front national," in *La France des années noires*, 2:91–104.

254. *Notre voix*, May 1, 1943, repr. *La Presse antiraciste*, 83.

255. "Qu'est-ce que l'Union de la jeunesse juive?" *La Presse antiraciste*, 121–123.

256. Centre de Documentation Juive Contemporaine, CDLXXI-42, *Notre voix*, June 20, 1943.

257. *La Presse antiraciste*, 87.

258. Centre de Documentation Juive Contemporaine, CDLXXI-41; repr. Rutkowski, *La Lutte des Juifs en France*, 177–178.

259. "Paris, août 1942: En avant pour la victoire en 1942, notre politique," trans. Wieviorka, *Le Monde juif*, no. 127 (1987): 119–123.

260. The April 1944 edition of *J'accuse*, BN, Res. G 1 470, 186.

261. *J'accuse*, no. 3, November 11, 1942, BN, Rés. G 1 470, 186.

262. Centre de Documentation Juive Contemporaine, XXII-7, no. 2 of *Jeune Combat*, July 5, 1943. The first edition dates from June 1943.

263. Personal testimony, reprinted in *La Presse antiraciste*, 45ff.

264. *J'accuse*, no. 3, November 11, 1942, BN, Rés. G 1 470, 186.

265. *J'accuse*, no. 4, November 20, 1942, BN, Rés. G 1 470, 186.

266. Extensive excerpts of such news can be found in *Qui savait quoi?* 37.

267. On the subject of that declaration, see Renée Poznanski, "Que savait-on dans le monde?" in *Qui savait quoi?* 37.

268. *J'accuse*, nos. 11, 12, and 13 dating from February 15 and 25 and March 15, 1943. BN, Rés. G 1 470, 186.

269. Centre de Documentation Juive Contemporaine, XLIX-13, "Hommes et femmes de coeur," Paris, November 15, 1942; repr. Rutkowski, *La Lutte des Juifs en France*, 121–122.

270. No. 4, November 20 and no. 5, November 27 editions of *J'accuse*.

271. Centre de Documentation Juive Contemporaine, XXII-12, January 1943, appeal Sent Out by the Movement of Solidarity and Resistance to the racist persecutions and deportations; repr. Rutkowski, *La Lutte des Juifs en France*, 140–141.

272. *Notre parole*, no. 355, March 8, 1943, BN.

273. Such is my view of the thesis put forward by Stéphane Courtois and Adam Rayski in *Qui savait quoi?*

274. David Diamant, "Les Juifs de Paris dans la Résistance," typewritten article, archives of the Resistance Museum in Champigny.

275. See the description provided by Abraham Lissner, *Un Franc-tireur juif raconte* (Paris, 1969), 25–26.

276. *Le Sang de l'étranger*, 160–161.

277. Wieviorka, *Ils étaient juifs, résistants, communistes*, 139–159.

278. *Le Sang de l'étranger*, 164–165.

279. See the communiqués and the "Bilan des actions jusqu'à la grande chute de novembre, par détachement et par période," published at the end of Boris Holban's *Testament*, 296ff. The operations of the second detachment from March 1942 to April 1943 can be found in the file MOI at the Resistance Museum in Champigny. Some of these operations are corroborated by the reports of the General Bureau of Information in the archives of the prefecture of the Paris police, and, concerning the Paris region from June 1942 to August 1944, in the Urman archives.

280. Holban, *Testament*, 283–295, report on the numbers of FTP-MOI resistance fighters, June 1942–August 1944.

281. *Le Sang de l'étranger*, 178.

282. Ibid., p. 250.
283. Ibid., p. 352.
284. Lissner, *Un Franc-tireur juif raconte,* 23–24.
285. David Diamant, "Les Juifs de Paris dans la Résistance," typewritten manuscript, Resistance Museum in Champigny.
286. This refusal was given on May 24. See *Le Sang de l'étranger,* 278–279. See also Adam Rayski, *Nos illusions perdues* (Paris: Balland, 1985), 144ff.
287. David Diamant, *Les Juifs dans la Résistance française* (Paris: Roger Maria, 1971), 174–175; Adler, *The Jews of Paris,* 209ff.
288. Centre de Documentation Juive Contemporaine, CDLXXXIII-93, December 1943, internal report written by Adam Rayski. The report stresses "the importance of the armed struggle, both in order to save and defend Jews and to hasten the defeat of the enemy."
289. See the UJRE's manifesto in *La Presse antiraciste,* 155–160, in a version dating from April 1944.

10. *The Occupied "Free" Zone (pages 356–393)*

1. AN, AJ 38, 243. There were, to be exact, 109,983, including 59,344 French citizens and 50,639 foreigners; census of Jews in the Unoccupied Zone, according to the figures provided by prefectures in March 1942. In *Le Commissariat général aux questions juive.* Joseph Billig provides a region-by-region breakdown (2:208ff). On the subject of censuses in France, see Szajkowski, *Analytical Franco-Jewish Gazetteer,* 85–88.
2. This example was given by Szajkowski, *Analytical Franco-Jewish Gazetteer,* 89.
3. AN, AJ 38, 243, Vichy, March 8, 1943. Report no. 8 for the month of February 1943, message from the Division of Investigations and Inspections to the General Commission on Jewish Affairs.
4. See table 3.
5. Out of the 330,000 Jews who were in France in 1940, 80,000 fell victim while some 60,000 remained in the Paris region and 6,500 left the country before the end of 1942, through the efforts of the HICEM. An undetermined number of others left by other means. Between 1942 and 1944, there were 25,000 who left illegally for Switzerland and Spain; (Cohen, *The Burden of Conscience,* 148. These figures include approximations and data from other regions of the Occupied Zone. A more accurate assessment will only be possible through a thorough examination of archives in the various départements.
6. Lambert, *Carnet d'un témoin,* October 15, 1942, p. 190: "At the hotel, a form upon which you have to indicate your religion. Did they ask me this when I was on the Chemin des Dames [during World War I]?"
7. Reprinted in CC-5.
8. Lubetzki, *La Condition des Juifs en France,* 115.
9. AN, AJ 38, 147, June 23, 1942, report from Gazagne for the General Commission on Jewish Affairs.
10. AIU, CC-68, report on talks with Vichy officials on November 7, 1942, Robert Kiefe.
11. CC-4 contains an outline of the contents of the General Commission on Jewish Affairs radio broadcasts.
12. Instruction number 65; Limagne, *Ephémérides,* 2:932.
13. Lambert, *Carnet d'un témoin,* December 18, 1942, p. 201.
14. The text can be found in *Les Juifs sous l'Occupation,* 169. A violation punishable by a mere fine became an offense to be judged by a criminal court and punishable by imprisonment, followed by administrative internment.
15. The text of the decree can be found in *Les Juifs sous l'Occupation,* 172
16. AN, AJ 38, 242, Vichy, December 18, 1942, head of the government to prefects, application of law no. 1,077 of December 11, 1942, concerning the stamping of the word "Jew" on identity papers issued to French and foreign Israelites.

17. CC-24.
18. AIU, CC-68, talks recorded in the notes of Robert Kiefe, January 6 and 7, 1943.
19. AN, AJ 38, 1 090, January 8, 1943.
20. Ibid., January 9, 1943.
21. Lambert, returning to the events of November 11, *Carnet d'un témoin*, November 29, 1942, p. 197.
22. AN, F 1, 14 929, monthly synopses of wire tappings and opened letters.
23. Idem, from December 10, 1942 to January 10, 1943.
24. AIU, CC-17, meeting of the regional delegates of the consistory, November 17, 1942.
25. Ibid., December 1, 1942.
26. November 9, 1942 from the Quakers, cited by Szajkowski, *Analytical Franco-Jewish Gazetteer* 241.
27. AIU, CC-17, meeting of the regional delegates of the Consistory, December 15, 1942.
28. Marrus and Paxton, *Vichy France and the Jews*, 302.
29. Lambert, *Carnet d'un témoin*, December 18, 1942, p. 202.
301. AIU, CC-8, unsigned report, December 24, 1942.
31. Marrus and Paxton, *Vichy France and the Jews*, p. 304, and AN, AJ 38, 243, Vichy, March 8, 1943. Report no. 8 for the month of February 1943, sent by the head of the Division of Investigations and Inspections to the General Commission on Jewish Affairs.
32. Marrus and Paxton, *Vichy France and the Jews*, 287.
33. Ibid., 288–289.
34. The phrase is that of Billig, *Le Commissariat général aux questions* juives, 2:108.
35. AN, AJ 38, 243, decreee no. 3,085, October 13, 1942.
36. Centre de Documentation Juive Contemporaine, XXXIII-33, February 5, 1043, Division of Investigations and Inspections in Vichy to the regional offices; repr. Billig, *Le Commissariat général aux questions juives*, 2:110.
37. AN, AJ 38, 243, report from the Division of Investigations and Inspections, Southern Zone, no. 1, October 6, 1942.
38. One finds in AN, AJ 38, 259, some twenty lists running from December 1941 to May 31, 1944, containing 922 names. These lists, however, are clearly incomplete.
39. A copy of the handbook can be found in the archives of Lucien Lublin, now stored in the Centre de Documentation Juive Contemporaine.
40. Centre de Documentation Juive Contemporaine, CXCIV-51, memorandum from the main office of the national gendarmerie, February 11, 1943; repr. Billig, *Le Commissariat général aux questions juives*, 2:93–94.
41. AN, AJ 38, 243, Feruary 11, 1943, general directive for recruiting informers.
42. Ibid., number 26.
43. Ibid., general directive no. 29.
44. Centre de Documentation Juive Contemporaine, CV-110; cited by Billig, *Le Commissariat général aux questions juives*, 2:99.
45. The review of these investigations can be found in AN, AJ 38, 243.
46. AN, AJ 38, 243, Vichy, March 8, 1943, report no. 8 for February 1943, sent by the head of the SEC to the General Commission on Jewish Affairs.
47. AN, AJ 38, 261, inspector's report, Limoges, November 21, 1942.
48. All of these examples have been taken from inspectors' reports from the Limoges region, AN, AJ 38, 262.
49. AN, AJ 38, 265, Limoges, May 7, 1943.
50. Reference is made to this memorandum in AN, AJ 38, 147, July 28, 1944, message from the prefect of the Département of Les Bouches-du-Rhône to the General Commission on Jewish Affairs.
51. AN, AJ 38, 146, memorandum from the General Commission on Jewish Affairs, June 15, 1944.
52. Lambert, *Carnet d'un témoin*, 190.
53. AN, AJ 38, 244, December 19, 1942, memorandum on the specific application of instructions to incorporate Israelites into Foreign Worker Units.

54. *Le Petit Marseillais*, December 14, 1942.
55. CC-5, and AIU, CC-1b, Lyon, February 28, 1943, Helbronner's speech at a Consistory meeting.
56. Moch, *L'Étoile et la francisque*, 185. Attorney Robert Kiefe had apparently found this out during one of his visits in Vichy.
57. AIU, CC-17, Albert Lévy's trip to Clermont-Ferrand from May 19 to May 25, 1943.
58. AN, AJ 38, 265, Limoges, August 6, 1943.
59. AN, AJ 38, 243, March 4, 1943, informational memorandum number 14, signed by the head of the SEC, on the subject of putting Jews to work.
60. Marrus and Paxton, *Vichy France and the Jews*, 327–328.
61. AN, AJ 38, 1 157, telegram from the regional prefect to the prefect of Chartres, August 23, 1943. The response sent back to him on the same day read: "Only one French Jew fits the description—he has already been transferred to Drancy."
62. Lambert, *Carnet d'un témoin*, August 20, 1943, pp. 237–238.
63. YIVO, France during WW II, I, 6, 93, Toulouse, September 28, 1943, "Report on the rounding up of Jews," SEC. It refers to the instruction number 10-M-7 from August 21, 1943 as well as to the telegrams of August 19 and 26, 1943.
64. Idem.
65. Joint, SM 32, report sent to Marc Jarblum, September 1943, "The Latest Roundups of Jews in . . ." According to the information contained in this report, it refers to Toulouse.
66. Rabbi Champagne about the community of Saint-Etienne, written after the Liberation, undated.
67. AIU, CC-17, Albert Levy's liaison and information mission: Roanne, Toulouse, Villeneuve-sur-Lot, Périgueux, Brive, Capdenac, Limoges, Châteauroux, Roanne, August 18–28, 1943. Report on Capdenac, August 24, 1943.
68. AIU, CC-25, report on the Département of La Haute-Vienne by M. Freund, October 15, 1943.
69. See Biélinky, *Journal*, September 15, 1942, p. 252, and CZA, KH, 4 B 2 377, Madame Goldstein, Montpellier, December 11, 1944.
70. AN, AJ 38, 1 142, message from the secretary-general for labor to the General Commission on Jewish Affairs, April 14, 1944.
71. AIU, CC-22, Châteauroux, May 31, 1944, message from G. Apeloig to the administrative secretary of the Central Consistory.
72. AN, AJ 38, 1 142, Vichy, May 19, 1943, message from the main office of refugees (in the Ministry of the Interior) to the prefect of the Département of Les Basses-Alpes. Also YIVO, RG 210, XCIV-9, message from F.G. Fraisse, for the main office of refugees, to the prefect of La Savoie.
73. AIU, CC-23, leter from Rabbi Robert Meyers to Albert Manuel, June 18, 1942. And AIU, CC-17, report to the meeting of the regional delegations of the Central Consistory, July 1942.
74. Lambert, *Carnet d'un témoin*, November 3, 1942, p. 1994.
75. AN, AJ 38, 1 142, December 28, 1943, message from the head of the SEC to the head of the SEC for the Southern Zone.
76. AN, AJ 38, 1 141, memorandum from the General Commission on Jewish Affairs, January 14, 1944.
77. AN, AJ 38, 1 153.
78. AIU, CC-16, report of the general delegation of the consistory of Grenoble for the month of September 1942.
79. CC-24.
80. AIU, CC-25, report from the General Chaplain's Office, January–February 1943.
81. Marrus and Paxton, *Vichy France and the Jews*, 305.
82. Szajkowski, *Analytical Franco-Jewish Gazetteer*, 178–180.
83. Marrus and Paxton, *Vichy France and the Jews*, 305.
84. Szajkowski, *Analytical Franco-Jewish Gazetteer*, 83.

85. CC-5, Lyon, May 7, 1943, report from Albert Manuel.

86. Idem, based on a letter from André Baur dated April 30, 1943.

87. AIU, CC-12, "Report on the trip to La Bourboule," by Albert Lévy, June 3, 1942. See also Sweets, *Choices in Vichy France*, 125.

88. Sweets, *Choices in Vichy France*, 125.

89. AIU, CC-17, Albert Lévy's trip to Châteauroux on August 9, 1943.

90. Tzvetan Todorov, A *French Tragedy: Scenes of Civil War, Summer 1944* (Hanover: University Press of New England, 1996), 97.

91. *Jewish Telegraphic Agency Bulletin*, July 13, 1943; cited by Szajkowski, *Analytical Franco-Jewish Gazetteer*, 257.

92. CC-5, report by Rabbi Sin Avram from Chambéry, October 17, 1943.

93. Klarsfeld, *Calendrier*, 653, 667, 672, and again 677.

94. According to Hagen's report of the talks reprinted in Klarsfeld, *Vichy-Auschwitz*, 1:407–409.

95. Marrus and Paxton, *Vichy France and the Jews*, 304.

96. The story of the roundup has for the most part been taken from the account given by Raymond-Raoul Lambert (AIU, CC-46 and YIVO, France During WWII, 2–25, 1/5); repr. in *Carnet d'un témoin*, 206–215. I have completed it by using both the report of an escapee from the Compiègne deportation train, written on February 1, 1943 (AIU, CC-46) and the additional report given by Chief Rabbi René Hirschler on February 3, 1943 (also AIU, CC-46).

97. Cited by Klarsfeld, *Calendrier*, 721.

98. Serge Klarsfeld, "La déportation dans le camp d'extermination de Sobibor des Juifs raflés à Marseille en janvier 1943: histoire des convois 52 et 53 des 23 et 25 mars 1943," in *Marseille, Vichy et les nazis; le temps des rafles; la déportation des Juifs*, ed. Christian Oppetit, with a preface by Pierre-Vidal Naquet (Marseilles: Amicale des déportés d'Auschwitz et des camps de Haute-Silésie, 1993), 113–114. According to Jean-Claude Pressac, these trains actually wound up in the camp at Maïdanek.

99. They were arrested between January 13 and January 16, 1943; Klarsfeld, *Calendriet*, p. 718.

100. Centre de Documentation Juive Contemporaine, XXVc-195, January 21, 1943, message from Knochen to Eichmann, cited by Lucien Steinberg, *Les Autorite's allemandes*, 137.

101. Centre de Documentation Juive Contemporaine, XXVb-70, January 25, 1943, Günther's response, idem.

102. Reprinted in Lambert, *Carnet d'un témoin*, 213.

104. Centre de Documentation Juive Contemporaine, CCCLXVI-45, January 27, 1943.

104. AIU, CC-46.

105. *Carnets du Pasteur Boegner*, 230, Nîmes, January 29, 1943.

106. AIU, CC-46, Nîmes, January 30, 1943, message from Pastor Boegner to Isaïe Schwartz.

107. AIU, CC-1b, plenary session of the Central Consistory, February 28, 1943.

108. Centre de Documentation Juive Contemporaine, XLVI-A, Lyon, February 11, 1943, message from the Sipo/SD in Lyon to the Commander of the Sipo/SD in France; repr. Rutkowski, *La Lutte des Juifs en France*, 169.

109. AN, AJ 38, 152.

110. AIU, CC-18, Rabbi Champagne on the community of Saint-Etienne after the Liberation, undated.

111. Sweets, *Choices in Vichy France*, 128.

112. Marrus and Paxton, *Vichy France and the Jews*, 306.

113. Nexon had taken in the ailing and the elderly when the Récébédou camp was closed down on October 26, 1942. The camp at Les Milles was also closed on December 10, 1942, when the 170 last internees were incorporated into the Foreign Worker Unit in La Ciotat; Klarsfeld, *Calendrier*, 678, 697, and 706. See also the report for the month of October 1942 from the General Information Bureau, cited by Laurette Alexis-Monet, *Les Miradors de Vichy* (Paris: Les éditions de Paris, 1994).

114. Marrus and Paxton, *Vichy France and the Jews,* 307.
115. Klarsfeld, *Calendrier,* 759.
116. Iancu, "Les Juifs à Montpellier," *loc. cit.,* p. 373.
117. From 500 to 700, according to Albert Lévy, July 1, 1943, AIU, CC-17.
118. Christian Font and Henri Moizet, *Les Juifs et l'antisémitisme en Aveyron,* 16.
119. Todorov, *A French Tragedy,* p. 95ff.
120. Klarsfeld, *Calendrier,* 764.
121. Ibid., 766.
122. February 27–28, March 1, 1943; repr. *Les Miradors de Vichy.*
123. CC-5, Albert Manuel, May 7, 1943.
124. AIU, CC-46, Raymond-Raoul Lambert, report on the events transpiring in Marseilles between April 28 and May 9, 1943; also repr. *Carnet d'un témoin,* 222–229.
125. Idem.
126. AIU, CC-15, May 12, 1943, message from the president of the Central Consistory to Marshal Pétain.
127. All of these reports can be found in AIU, CC-17.
128. AIU, CC-17, Albert Lévy's trip to Limoges on July 30 and 31, 1943.
129. AIU, CC-17, Albert Lévy's trip to Périgueux, August 22, 1943.
130. On the subject of this radio war, see Jean-Louis Crémieux-Brilhac and Hélène Eck, "France," in Hélène Eck ed., *La Guerre des Ondes,* p. 14, and Jean-Louis Crémieux-Brilhac and Georges Benshimon, "Les propagandes radiophoniques et l'opinion publique en France de 1940 à 1944," *Revue d'histoire de la Deuxième Guerre mondiale* 101 (1976): 3–18.
131. Centre de Documentation Juive Contemporaine, 65, memorandum from the Sicherheitsdienst dated September 4, 1942; cited by Billig, *Le Commissariat général aux questions juives,* 2:324.
132. Limagne, *Ephémérides,* 2:769.
133. AN, AJ 38, 61, Vichy, September 26, 1942, memorandum for the personnel of the General Commission on Jewish Affairs, and Vichy, January 16, 1943, message from the General Commission on Jewish Affairs to Bessieux.
134. Centre de Documention Juive Contemporaine, CXCV-95, November 1942, authorization request submitted to the German military command; cited by Billig, *Le Commissariat général aux questions juives,* 2:316. On the UDFR in general, see ibid., 315–321.
135. AN, AJ 38, 61, Vichy, June 12, 1943.
136. Between the holdings of CC-24, 25, 26, and 31, and AIU, CC-14, 17, 49, and 61, we have on hand the transcription or the summary of about seventy broadcasts running from September 1942 to November 1943.
137. September 15, 1942.
138. October 9, 1942.
139. October 5, 1942.
140. October 7, 1942.
141. October 9, 1942.
142. October 16, 1942.
143. October 21, 1942.
144. Idem.
145. October 7, 1942.
146. October 19, 1942.
147. See *L'Etat des Juifs* by Théodore Herzl, ed. Claude Klein (Paris: La Découverte, 1990). See also two biographies entitled *Bernard Lazare:* one by Nelly Wilson, subtitled *Antisemitism and the Problem of Jewish Identity in Late Nineteenth-Century France* (Cambridge: Cambridge University Press, 1978) and the other by Jean-Denis Bredin, subtitled *De l'anarchiste au prophète* (Paris: Editions de Fallois, 1992). On Kadmi Cohen, see Marrus and Paxton, *Vichy France and the Jews,* 310ff. A biography of Kadmi Cohen is currently under preparation by his son, Jean-François Steiner.
148. November 4, 1942.

149. December 28, 1942.
150. May 11, 1943.
151. June 15, 1943.
152. AIU, CC-68, attorney Robert Kiefe's notes, October 23 and 25, November 2 and 6, 1942.
153. Rossignol, *Histoire de la propagande en France,* 212–215.
154. AN, AJ 38, 1,075, Toulouse, April 10, 1943.
155. AN, AJ 38, 1 075, Vichy, December 12, 1942.
156. AN, F 14 929, see in particular the synopsis of the period between February 10 and March 10, 1943.
157. An account of this survey can be found in Léon Poliakov, "An Opinion Poll on anti-Jewish measures in Vichy France," *Jewish Social Studies* 15, no. 1 (1953): 135–150, and in Billig, *Le Commissariat général aux questions juives,* 2:340–346. See also AN, AJ 38, 61, December 3, 1942, report on the organization of the survey of the population's attitude toward the Jews.
158. AN, AJ 38, 1 075, Marseilles, January 11, 1943, propaganda office, General Commission on Jewish Affairs for the men conducting the public opinion survey, and AN, Z 6, 1 391, "Report and conclusions from the public opinion poll conducted in the Free Zone in the first trimester of 1943 for the propaganda office of the General Commission on Jewish Affairs."
159. All the results presented here have been taken from AN, Z 6, 1 391, ibid.
160. AN, AJ 38, 1 075, Pau, June 18, 1943, memorandum sent by the regional head of the Pau subdivision of the Police for Jewish Affairs to the regional head in Toulouse.
161. Archives of the Musée de la Résistance in Champigny, mail message dated January 28, 1943, 000 B, NM 19.
162. "The victims were throwing their money around carelessly, and, in addition to an unbridled penchant for speculation, this unreserved and immodest display joined with a rather conceited flippancy and the certitude of their asserted superiority, has led to a deep feeling of antisemitism. This feeling is particularly strong because of the Jews' propensity for grouping together and supporting each other, which creates the appearance that they are determined not to accept any life in common with the other citizens of this country." Ibid.
163. Musée de la Résistance in Champigny, May 3, 1943, 5 811, source: Fouquet.
164. Ibid., Inf: December 8, 1943, reference 13 426.
165. *Le Petit Marseillais,* July 1, 1943.
166. *Le Petit Marseillais,* September 10, 1943. The method had been first used in Marseilles on August 18.
167. Laborie, *L'opinion française sous Vichy,* 280–281.
168. AN, F 7, 14 930, monthly report from Vichy's Central Commission on Postal Control, May and June, 1943.
169. Roderick H. Kedward, "STO and maquis," in *La France des années noires,* 2:279.
170. Laborie, *L'opinion française sous Vichy,* p. 286.
171. AN, AJ 38, 30, file on the aryanization of the store.
172. *Les Voix de la liberté,* 2:215.
173. Ibid., 4:22.
174. Kedward, "STO and maquis," *loc, cit.,* p. 286.
175. This territory included seven départements: La Haute-Savoie, La Savoie, La Drôme, Les Hautes-Alpes, Les Basses-Alpes, Le Var, and Les Alpes-Maritimes. Also included were a large portion of the départements of L'Isère and La Vaucluse, a small portion of L'Ain, and the island of Corsica. Daniel Carpi, *Between Mussolini and Hitler: The Jews and the Italian Authorities in France and Tunisia* (Hanover: Brandeis University Press, University Press of New England, 1994), 79ff.
176. For a comparative analysis of German, French, and Italian anti-Jewish laws, see Laurence Rosengart, "L'originalité du statut du Juif en France dans l'Europe hitlérienne," *Communauté nouvelle* 47 (1989). As for the relations between Italian Fascism and the Jews, see Pierre Milza, "Les Juifs dans la zone d'occupation italienne," *Yod* 15–16 (1982): 134–140, and

Meir Michaelis, *Mussolini and the Jews: German-Italian Relations and the Jewish Question in Italy, 1922–1945* (Oxford: Clarendon Press, 1978).

177. Here I am following Daniel Carpi's exhaustive *Between Mussolini and Hitler*.

178. And 464 in Paris itself. Centre de Documentation Juive Contemporaine, files from the General Consulate of Italy in Paris, 794, November 21 and December 6, 1941, message from Orlandini to the General Commission on Jewish Affairs and handwritten response; cited by Lucien Steinberg *Los Autorités allemandes*, 216.

179. AN, AJ 38, 70, December 11, 1942, General Commission on Jewish Affairs to the minister of foreign affairs, referring back to a memorandum from the latter dating from July 31, 1942.

180. Carpi, *Between Mussolini and Hitler*, 32–34. Orlandini went to the German embassy in Paris on August 22, 1941. His requests were finally granted on December 9.

181. The German proposal (Martin Luther) dated from September 17, 1942, and Mussolini's twofold refusal from October 10; Carpi, Between Mussolini and Hitler, 45–49.

182. Ibid., 82–84.

183. Ibid., 87–88. On May 11, 1943, Marcel Ribière was replaced by Jean Chaigneau, much more accommodating toward the Italians and the Jews.

184. Most authors think this to be the case, based on the testimony given by Angelo Donati in 1944, Centre de Documentation Juive Contemporaine, CCXVIII-22 and I-65. Carpi, however, takes exception to the idea. Not that he questions the veracity of Donati's actions nor minimizes the importance of Donati's efforts throughout these long months: however, he doubts that the intervention of one individual could have swayed the balance in a matter involving state interests; *Between Mussolini and Hitler*, 97–98.

185. Ibid., p. 90–91.

186. Centre de Documentation Juive Contemporaine, XCVI-22, Nice, January 14, 1942.

187. Numerous documents on these developments can be found in Léon Poliakov, *La Condition des Juifs en France sous l'Occupation italienne* (Paris: Editions du Centre, 1946) and Klarsfeld, *Vichy-Auschwitz* 2:passim. See also Klarsfeld's analyses in the work just cited. More on the subject can also be found in Jean-Louis Panicacci, "Les Juifs et la question juive dans les Alpes-Maritimes" 239–327, and in the testimony of Philippe Erlanger, *La France sans étoile* (Paris: Plon, 1974), 253ff.

188. CC-5, Albert Manuel, Lyon, May 7, 1943.

189. Carpi, *Between Mussolini and Hitler*, p. 99–101. Barranco did not include the elderly, the invalid, nore unaccompanied women and children in his plan.

190. Ibid., 103.

191. Count Ciano and chief of staff Ugo Cavalerro had been dismissed; Carpi, *Between Mussolini and Hitler*, 109.

192. Ibid., p. 106–107.

193. Reprinted in Klarsfeld, *Vichy-Auschwitz*, 2:229.

194. Carpi, *Between Mussolini and Hitler*, 123.

195. Ibid., 125ff. The document has been reprinted in Klarsfeld, *Vichy-Auschwitz*, 2:236–237.

196. Carpi, *Between Mussolini and Hitler*, 128–135.

197. Ibid., p. 144–145.

198. Centre de Documentation Juive Contemporaine, CCXVIII-22 and I-65, oral report from Angelo Donati.

199. Joint, SM 32, letter from Joseph Fisher to the Central Consistory, Nice, August 1, 1943. See also YVS, P 7/10, and AIU, CC-12.

200. Ibid., and another letter from Joseph Fisher dating from August 8. YV, J. Fisher collection, 3. Léon Meiss, vice president of the Consistory, sent such a request to the secretary-general of the police on August 11 and 12, but I found no response. AIU, CC-12 and YIVO, RG 210, as well as Centre de Documentation Juive Contemporaine, CVIII-18.

201. Archives of the OSE (AIU), "Living under watch in the Italian Zone," report from a social worker.

202. YIVO, France during WWII, 3–45, the *Journal* of S. Majerowicz, Nice. September 3–12, 1943 (in Yiddish).
203. Carpi, *Between Mussolini and Hitler,* 170–171.
204. This decision was made on August 28, 1943. Daniel Carpi says that no concrete steps were taken to put the plan into action; ibid., 212.
205. AIU, CC-16, September 26, 1943, report from Joseph Fisher on the situation in Nice. Also archives of the OSE (AIU), dossier on the Italian Zone, "Under house arrest in the département of La Haute-Savoie," report from a social worker.
206. Lublin archives, 5, Nice, report dated December 20, 1945, obviously written by a young member of the AJ, probably Henri Pohorylès. See also Centre de Documentation Juive Contemporaine, CCCLXVI-64.
207. YIVO, France during WW II, 3–45, S. Majerowicz's *Journal,* Nice, September 3–12 (in Yiddish).
208. Carpi, *Between Mussolini and Hitler,* 180–181.
209. This is Carpi's conclusion; idem. In his testimony, Angelo Donati speaks of a favorable response from the Allies and attributes the failure of the plan to Eisenhower's premature announcement of the armistice. In a report dated September 26, 1943, Joseph Fisher specifies that the plan was to evacuate the three thousand Jews living under assigned residence. AIU, CC-16.
210. AN, AJ 38, 243, Nice, October 5, 1943.
211. Centre de Documentation Juive Contemporaine, XXXVII-1, Vichy, September 3, 1943, head of the SEC to the SEC's regional delegate in Nice.
212. Centre de Documentation Juive Contemporaine, XXXVII-1, Nice, September 14, 1943, regional delegate of the SEC to the head of the SEC in Vichy.
213. Klarsfeld, *Vichy-Auschwitz,* 2:124.
214. Joint, SM 32, October, unsigned, adressed to "My dear friend."
215. Joint, SM 32, December 5, 1943, letter addressed to Marc Jarblum, "From the Feder" (i.e., the Federation of Jewish Societies in France).
216. Lublin archives, 5, Nice, report dated December 20, 1943, Henri Pohorylès. See also Centre de Documentation Juive Contemporaine, CCCLXVI-64.
217. AIU, CC-16, September 26, 1943, report from Joseph Fisher on the situation in Nice.
218. Archives of the OSE (AIU), dossier on the Italian Zone, "Living Under House Arrest in the Département of La Haute-Savoie," report from a social worker.
219. Joint, SM 47, Furmanski, Kasterztein, and Dr. Léon(?) to Jarblum, Natan, and Raffal, Rome, February 10, 1944.
220. Archives Lublin, 5, Nice, "Report on crossing the border and on living conditions for our people in Italy."
221. Klarsfeld, *Calendrier,* 887.
222. Lublin archives, 5, Nice, "Report on border crossings and living conditions of our people in Italy."
223. Joint, SM 32, report on Saint-Martin, October 6, 1943. See also the Lublin archives, 5, Nice.
224. Joint, SM 32, "Report on the refugees in Italie," received by Marc Jarblum, December 5, 1943.
225. Susan Zucotti, *The Italians and the Holocaust: Persecution, Rescue, Survival* (New York: Basic Books, 1987), 92–93.
226. Joint, SM 47, Furmanski, Kastersztein and Dr. Léon(?) to Jarblum, Natan, and Raffal, Rome, February 10, 1944.
227. Zucotti, *The Italians and the Holocaust,* 95.
228. To borrow an expression from Marrus and Paxton, *Vichy France and the Jews,* 315.
229. AN, AJ 38, 243, Nice, July 23, 1943, message from the prefect of the Alpes-Maritimes to the head of the regional public security office; Centre de Documentation Juive Contemporaine, CCXIV-20, Nice, July 12, 1943, UGIF.

11. *Scattering Far and Wide in France (pages 394–437)*

1. AIU, CC-1b, Consistory session of February 28, 1943.
2. AIU, CC-17, meeting of the regional delegates of the Consistory, November 17, 1942.
3. AIU, CC-17, meeting of the regional secretaries of the Consistory, December 15, 1942.
4. YIVO, France during WWII, 2, 24, Lyon, October 25, 1943, Albert Lévy, "Reflections on the Chief Rabbi's appeal for funds." See also AIU, CC-38.
5. AIU, CC-17, Albert Lévy's trips from June 22 to July 3, 1943, to Nîmes, Toulouse, Pau, Montauban, Agen.
6. AN, AJ 38, 289, March 28, 1943, SEC in Marseilles.
7. AN, AJ 38, 289, Marseilles, August 12, 1943, General Commission on Jewish Affairs.
8. AIU, CC-17, Albert Lévy's trips to Avignon (May 3–5) and Montauban (August 4).
9. AN, AJ 38, 30, Marseilles, January 13, 1943.
10. AN, AJ 38, 262, March 25, 1943.
11. AN, AJ 38, 1,090, a letter intercepted on December 15, 1942, speaks of numerous cases known to the one writing the letter.
12. AIU, CC-17, Albert Lévy's trip to Périgueux, August 1 and 2, 1943.
13. AIU, CC-28, centers served by the general chaplain's office, June 1943, according to region.
14. AN, AJ 38, 1,142. The prefects' responses kept on coming in until the end of July 1943.
15. I thank Pierre Vidal-Naquet, who provided me with a copy of this tract.
16. For information on how the Garel network functioned, see Centre de Documentation Juive Contemporaine CCXVIII-104, testimony by Georges Carel on the underground work of the OSE. See also Centre de Documentation Juive Contemporaine, CCXVII-12a, short report on the Garel network, undated, unsigned. And also, "Oeuvre de secours aux enfants," in *L'Activité des organisations juives en france sous l'Occupation*, 156ff. and Lazare, report probably written by Ruven Grinberg, July 30, 1941, AIU, cc-4, and YIVO, Tcherikower collection, dossier 1650, 191ff.
17. Centre de Documentation Juive Contemporaine, CCXVII-12a, brief report on the Garel network, undated, unsigned.
18. In January 1943, six hundred children were thus placed with non-Jewish families. As of June 1943, there were 2,250 such children. At the same time, 1,000 children were placed with Jewish families in January 1943, and 1,200 in June 1943. AN, AJ43, 16, "Report on the activity of the OSE in France," June 1943.
19. Joint, 611, August 26, 1942, message from the Joint in Lisbonne to the Joint in New York, and Gurevitch (Geneva), August 13, 1942.
20. Joint, SM 35 A-2, monthly budget of the OSE in France, May 26, 1943, Geneva.
21. Joint, SM 35 A-2, Geneva, letters from the OSE in Chambéry, May 31, 1943, and report dated June 31, 1943. In addition to the cost of transporting children from one place to another, it was necessary to have seven hundred francs per month for every hidden child.
22. AIU-CC, 25, July 9, 1943, discussions between the general chaplain's office (in Marseilles) and the OSE.
23. YIVO, RG 494, 20, Geneva, November 23, 1943, report sent by the OSE Union in Geneva to the American Committee of the OSE in New York.
24. YIVO, RG 494, 20, Geneva, excerpt from the messages of December 20 and December 28, 1943.
25. Centre de Documentation Juive Contemporaine CCCLXVI-70, letters from J. Millner in Switzerland, November 5, 1943.
26. The raid occurred on April 6, 1944. Serge Klarsfeld, *Les Enfants d'Izieu, une tragédie juive* (Paris: FFDJF, 1984), and Antoine Spire, *Ces enfants qui nous manquent, Izieu, 6 avril 1944*, with a preface by Elie Wiesel (Paris: Maren Sell, 1990).
27. Centre de Documentation Juive Contemporaine, CCCLXVI-71, letters from J. Millner in Switzerland, summary of the letters dated March 17, 26, 29, and 30, 1944.

28. Examples of such cases can be found in Sabine Zeitoun, *Ces enfants qu'il fallait sauver*, passim.

29. Saul Friedlander, *When Memory Comes* (New York: Avon Books, 1980).

30. This concern was shared by the Scouts, Centre de Documentation Juive Contemporaine, CCXXVII-8, report on the activity of the Israelite Scouts of France from 1939 to 1945.

31. A list of these organizations can be found in *L'Activité des organisations juives en France sous l'Occupation*, 160.

32. Up until 1942, the Joint, which had distributed about three million dollars to the various Jewish organizations, maintained a strictly legalistic approach. Thanks to the intervention of Joseph Schwarz, the Joint's representative for Europe in Lisbon who had designated Jules (Dika) Jefroykin, a member of the Jewish Army, as his representative in France, the money increasingly began to be increasingly used to finance clandestine activity from 1943 on. See Yehuda Bauer, *American Jewry and the Holocaust: The American Jewish Joint Distribution Committee, 1939–1945* (Detroit: Wayne State University Press, 1981), 158–159, 168–177 and passim. See also the interview with Dika Jefroykin, Polonski archives.

33. About the EIF, see Alain Michel, *Les Eclaireurs israélites de France*, concerning all the rescue operations, one should refer to Lazare, *Rescue as Resistance*; much information can be found in Anny Latour, *La Résistance Juive en France* (Paris: Stock, 1970) and Frédéric Chimon Hammel, *Souviens-toi d'Amalek; témoignage sur la lutte des Juifs en France* (Paris: CLKH, 1982).

34. Alain Michel, *Les Eclaireurs israélites de France*, 125.

35. Isaac Pougatch, *Charry*, 178.

36. Centre de Documentation Juive Contemporaine, CCXV-21, the account given by Charles Hartanu.

37. Centre de Documentation Juive Contemporaine, CCXVII-11, Lyon, October 1, 1944, report on the activity of the Office of Social Services for Youth (the "sixth"), 1942–1944. See the personal testimony by Liliane Klein-Liber, "Témoignage sur les opérations de sauvetage," *Annales, ESC*, 48–3, 1993, pp. 673–678.

38. Centre de Documentation Juive Contemporaine DLVI-36, personal testimony from Henri Wahl.

39. YIVO, RG 210, XCII-97, Vichy, January 5, 1943, General Commission on Jewish Affairs to general director of the UGIF.

40. AIU, CC-46, report on the trip to Vichy on January 12 and 13, 1943, and Raymond-Raoul Lambert, *Carnet d'un témoin*, 216, February 13, 1943; Centre de Documentation Juive Contemporaine, XXVIIIa-337, General Commission on Jewish Affairs to director-general of the UGIF, January 18, 1943.

41. Centre de Documentation Juive Contemporaine, LVIII-4, January 31, 1943, Edmond Fleg to the marshal of France; see also AIU, CC-42.

42. Centre de Documentation Juive Contemporaine, LVIII-4, Vichy, April 23, 1943.

43. Centre de Documentation Juive Contemporaine, CDX-11, Moissac, January 28, 1943; see also AIU, CC-42.

44. Michel, *Les Eclaireurs israélites de France*, 130–132.

45. AIU, CC-42, Moissac, February 26, 1943, Marc Haguenau to André Weill, report on the Office of Social Services for Youth.

46. Centre de Documentation Juive Contemporaine, CCXVII-11, Lyon, October 1, 1944, report on the activity of the Office of Social Services for Young People, 1942–1944.

47. Michel, *Les Eclaireurs israélites de France*, p. 166–167.

48. Centre de Documentation Juive Contemporaine, CDXX-48, January 1943, "To the EIF and MJS leaders."

49. Centre de Documentation Juive Contemporaine, CCXIV-117, August 1944, provisional report from the Zionist Youth Movement.

50. CZA, KKL 5, 13 146, Lyon, December 29, 1943, Zionist movement in 1943. See also CZA, A-303/19 and YV, P 7/3.

51. AN, AJ 38, 1 090, Toulouse, report for the head of the General Commission on Jewish Affairs, January 1, 1943.

52. CC-24, press review dated October 9, 1942.
53. A good account of this evolution can be found in Lazare, *La Resistance Juive en France*, 184ff; see also English edition, Lucien Lazare, *Rescue as Resistance: How Jewish Organizations Fought the Holocaust in France* (New York: Columbia University Press, 1996.
54. Gamzon, *Les Eaux claires*, 80.
55. Ibid., 76.
56. Joint, 611, confidential report dated November 15, 1943.
57. Michael R. Marrus, *The Unwanted: European Refugees in the Twentieth Century* (New York: Oxford University Press, 1985), p. 252ff.
58. Georges Loinger, "Le passage clandestin de la frontière par les enfants persécutés," undated, and Claude Lubezanski's interview of Georges Loinger, February 2, 1984, archives of the OSE (AIU), 12–13.
59. Archives of the OSE (AIU), Box VIII, Geneva archives, Union OSE, Geneva, central file card office, November 20, 1944.
60. By virtue of an agreement between the two organizations signed on June 1, 1944, Avraham Polonski archives.
61. Haïm Avni, "The Zionist Underground in Holland and France, and the Escape to Spain," in *Rescue Attempts during the Holocaust*, ed. Israel Gutman and Ephraïm Zuroff (Jerusalem: Yad Vashem, 1977), 582–585.
62. Lazare, *La Résistance Juive en France*, 289.
63. Archives of the OSE (AIU), 12–13, February 2, 1984, Claude Lubezanski's interview of Georges Loinger.
64. Ralph Schor, *Un évêque dans le siècle: Msgr Paul Rémond (1873–1963)* (Nice: Editions Serre, 1984), 118ff.
65. Renée Poznanski, "La création du Centre de Documentation Juive en France (CDJC), avril 1943," *XXe Siècle. Revue d'Histoire* 63 (July–September 1999): 61–73, and Annette Wieviorka, *Déportation et génocide; entre la mémoire et l'oubli* (Paris: Plon, 1992), 415ff.
66. Latour, *La Résistance Juive en France*, 88ff.
67. Centre de Documentation Juive Contemporaine, DLXXVIII-11, personal testimony from Toto Giniewski.
68. AN, Z 6, 1 380, June 14, 1943, message from the prefect of La Haute-Savoie to the General Commission on Jewish Affairs.
69. YIVO, RG 210, C-1, Avpril 16, 1943, report on the activity of the UGIF office in Nice.
70. Archives of the OSE (AIU), "Living in assigned residence in La Haute-Savoie," report from a social worker.
71. Centre de Documentation Juive Contemporaine, Lubetzki collection, visit of Saint-Martin-de-Vésubie on May 20 and 21, 1943.
72. Joint, SM 32, letter to Marc Jarblum, August 1943.
73. Centre de Documentation Juive Contemporaine, CCXIV-18, July 3, 1943, letter about Saint-Gervais.
74. Archives of the OSE (AIU), "Living in assigned residence in La Haute-Savoie," report from a social worker.
75. The first had come on April 8, and the seder was held on the evening of the fourteenth; AIU, CC-36, Sin Avram to the Chief Rabbi of France on the subject of his mission in Mégève, April 1943.
76. Joint, SM 32, report on Saint-Martin-de-Vésubie. See also Lublin archives, 5, Nice, October 5, 1943.
77. Ibid.
78. Joint, SM 32, letter addressed to Marc Jarblum, August 1943.
79. AIU, CC-16, undated, unsigned report.
80. Geneviève Priacel-Pitet, "Passages de frontières," in *Les Clandestins de Dieu*, 116.
81. Patrick Cabanel, "Musée du Désert, dimanche 6 septembre 1942," in Cabanel *Cévennes: Terre de refuge, 1940–1944*, ed. Philippe Joutard, Jacques Poujol, Patrick (Montpellier: Presses du Languedoc, 1987), 250–253.

82. Joutard, afterword, in *Cévennes: Terre de refuge*, ed. Joutard et al., 331.
83. Pierre Bolle, "Les protestants et leurs Eglises," in *La France et la question juive*, 171–195.
84. Pierre Vidal-Naquet, *Mémoires. La brisure et l'attente*, 1930–1955 (Paris: Seuil-La Découverte, 1995).
85. Pierre Vidal-Naquet, "Protestants et Juifs pendant la Seconde Guerre mondiale en France. Souvenir d'un témoin" in *Les Juifs, la mémoire et le présent* (Paris: La Découverte), 2:185.
86. Jacques Poujol, "Filières, répartition, caractéristiques du refuge juif," in *Cévennes: Terre de refuge*, ed. Joutard et al., 137.
87. Anny Bloch-Raymond, "Séjour en Cévennes de familles juives originaires de Nîmes et de l'est de la France," in *Cévennes: terre de refuge*, ed. Joutard et al., 154–155.
88. Poujol, "Filières, répartition . . . ," 140.
89. Patrick Cabanel, "Saint-Germain-de-Calberte," in *Cévennes: terre de refuge*, ed. Joutard et al., 265–275.
90. *Carnets du Pasteur Boegner*, 231; Pierre Vidal-Naquet, "Si Dieu le fit . . . ," *Esprit* 134 (1988): 3–12.
91. Philippe Joutard, "Postface," *Cévennes: terre de refuge*, ed. Joutard et al., 331.
92. Clara Malraux, *Le Bruit de nos pas*, vol. 6, . . . *Et pourtant j'étais libre* (Paris: Grasset, 1979), 184–185.
93. On the subject of Le Chambon, see Philippe Boegner, *Ici, on a aimé les Juifs; Le Chambon-sur-Lignon* (Paris: Jean-Claude Lattès, 1982) and Philip P. Halllie, *Lest Innocent Blood Be Shed. The Story of Le Chambon and How Goodness Happened There* (New York: HarperCollins Books, 1979).
94. AIU, CC-58, Marcel Bokanowski, Le Chambon-sur-Lignon, undated, written between the summer and the fall of 1942.
95. Pastor Marc Donadille, "Le Coteau fleuri au Chambon-sur-Lignon," in *Les Clandestins de Dieu*, 112–115.
96. Centre de Documentation Juive Contemporaine, DLXXII-49, testimony from Pastor André Trocmé.
97. *Carnets du pasteur Boegner*, February 14 and 18, 1943, pp. 232–233.
98. And that stirred up a heated controversy after Pierre Sauvage, in his film *Weapons of the Spirit*, defended the idea that the commander of the German garrison, Major Schmähling had granted protection to plateau surrounding Le Chambon.
99. AIU, CC-17, Albert Lévy's trip to maintain relations and gather information: Saint-Etienne, Tence, Le Chambon, October 10–13, 1943.
100. Centre de Documentation Juive Contemporaine, CLXXII-49, testimony from Pastor André Trocmé.
101. AIU, CC-58, July 26, 1942, regional chaplain's office, message from the assistant to the rabbi of Lyon to Hirschler, report on the visit paid to the institutions in Le Chambon on July 20, 21, 22.
102. Singer, *Vichy, l'université et les Juifs*, 286–287.
103. *Les Juifs sous l'Occupation*, 56–57.
104. Singer, *Vichy, l'université et les Juifs*, 110–111.
105. AN, F 9, 5579, memorandum from Jérôme Carcopino to regional school superintendants, March 14, 1942. See also Marc-Olivier Baruch, "L'application des statuts des Juifs à la fonction publique," 1992, typewritten manuscript.
106. Iancu, "Les Juifs à Montpellier," 363ff.
107. Ibid., 377–378.
108. Lazare, *La Résistance juive en France*, 251, Robert Gamzon, *Les Eaux claires*, 66–75, and Hammel 153.
109. Annie Kriegel, *Ce que j'ai cru comprendre* 195.
110. BN, Rés G. 1470[711], *Notre Voix*, Unoccupied Zone, September 1942.
111. Gourfinkel, *L'Autre Patrie*, 260–261.

112. Diamant, *Les Juifs dans la Résistance française,* 154.

113. Rolande Trempé, "La 35e brigade Marcel Langer (Toulouse)," in *Les Étrangers dans la Résistance en France,* ed. Philippe Joutard and François Marot (Besançon: Musée de la Résistance et de la Déportation, 1992, 116–119.

114. Diamant, *Les Juifs dans la Résistance française,* 141 and 157. For a list of operations carried out in Lyon by Carmagnole from December 1942 to September 1944, see David Diamant, *Jeune combat, La jeunesse juive dans la Résistance* (Paris: L'Harmattan, 1992), 85–97.

115. Hubert Desvages, "Les communistes de l'Isère dans la Résistance," *Cahiers d'histoire* (1980): 311–312.

116. Claude Collin, "Carmagnole et Liberté. Les FTP-MOI à Lyon et Grenoble," in *Les Etrangers dans la Résistance en France,* 120–123.

117. Desvages, "Les communistes de l'Isère," 319.

118. Claude Lévy, *Les Parias de la Résistance* (Paris: Calmann-Lévy, 1970).

119. Jean-Yves Boursier, *La Guerre de partisans dans le sud-ouest de la France, 1942–1944, La 35e brigade FTP-MOI* (Paris: L'Harmattan, 1992), 67ff.

120. See Catherine Varlin's testimony, "Une ville engloutie: la résistance des femmes juives," in RHICOJ, *Les Juifs dans la Résistance et la Libération. Histoire, témoignages, débats* (Paris: Le scribe, 1985), 101–103.

121. Collin, "Carmagnole et Liberte," 122.

122. David Ben Gourion archives, Sde Boqer, David Ben Gourion's *Journal,* May 15, 1945. Jean Laloum speaks of 370 children; Laloum, "La création des maisons d'enfants: l'exemple de la Commission centrale de l'enfance auprès de l'UJRE," *Pardès* 16 (1992): p. 252.

123. Centre de Documentation Juive Contemporaine, CCXV-19, MNCR, Alpes Division, report signed Michel, "the leader during the time of illegality." The document seems to date from the end of 1944 or the beginning of 1945.

124. Fayvel Shrager, *Un militant juif* (Paris: Editions Polyglottes), p. 103.

125. "Although it is difficult, if not impossible, to support such conclusions with figures or percentages, we are probably nearest to the truth, or at least in the domain of plausibility, when we affirm that the rate of participation of Jews in the Resistance was, with respect to the proportion of people of Jewish religion or origin in French society, the highest among all the religious or ethnic components of the Resistance"; Henri Michel, *La Guerre de l'ombre* (Paris: Grasset, 1970), 191.

126. André Weill-Curiel, *Le Temps de la honte* (Paris: Editions du Myrte, 1945), 3 vols. André Weill-Curiel tells of a conversation between Lieutenant de Sèze and Georges Boris, in which the former was complaining about the large number of Jews in General de Gaulle's entourage; *Le Jour se lève à Londres,* 1:269–271.

127. Claude Singer, "Servir la France, le *Journal* de René Cassin à Londres," *Les Nouveaux Cahiers* 81(1985): 56–64.

128. Boris Vildé, *Journal et lettres de prison, 1941–1942,* intro. François Bédarida and Dominique Veillon, annotated by François Bédarida, *Cahiers de l'Institut d'histoire du temps présen* 7 (1988).

129. Knout, *La Résistance juive en France,* 84.

130. Philippe Viannay, *Du bon usage de la France* (Paris: Ramsay, 1988), 32 On the subject of *Défense de la France,* see Olivier Wieviorka, *Une certaine idée de la Résistance. Défense de la france, 1940–1949* (Paris: Seuil, 1995).

131. Roderick H. Kedward stresses this point in *Resistance in Vichy France: A Study of Ideas and Motivation in the Southern Zone, 1940–1942* (Oxford: Oxford University Press, 1978), 169.

132. *La France et la question juive,* 386. See also in RHICOJ, *Les Juifs dans la Résistance et la Libération,* 47–65, the various personal testimonies voicing the same view.

133. Léo Hamon, *Vivre ses choix,* 104, Poznanski, "Avant les premières grandes rafles."

134. Stéphane, *Chaque homme est lié au monde,* 101.

135. Raymond Aron, *Chronique de guerre: La France Libre, 1940–1945,* ed. Christian Bachelier (Paris: Gallimard, 1990).

136. Raymond Aron, *Le Spectateur engagé* (Paris: Presses-Pocket, 1983), 100–101.

137. In fact, he only spoke once on the air, on the occasion of Henri Bergson's death, on January 14, 1941.

138. Aron, *Mémoires*, 192. The very opposite example is provided by René Cassin, a close follower of de Gaulle who did not hesitate to speak out directly against Vichy's antisemitic laws on several occasions.

139. Daniel Mayer's comments at the meeting of Le Poale Sion, March 1, 1945, Avraham Polonski archives.

140. Léo Hamon's study has been published in Poznanski, "Avant les premières grandes rafles," 57–124. In the interview he granted me upon the publication of this *Cahier*, he said that he had received an allowance from Jarblum in support of the intellectuals who had been put out of work by the Jewish Statutes (22)

141. It should be added, however, that Léo Hamon belonged to the first generation of immigrants and was a naturalized French citizen, while Daniel Mayer owed his familiarity with the Jewish immigrant milieus to his wife Cletta, who had immigrated to France from Romania.

142. Michael Burns, *Dreyfus, a Family Affair: From the French Revolution to the Holocaust* (New York: Harper Collins, 1992), 474.

143. Ibid., 475.

144. Ibid., 483.

145. Raymond Aubrac's parents, Hélène and Albert Samuel, were arrested in early December 1943 and deported. Laurent Douzou, *Le Mouvement de résistance Libération-sud (1940–1944)*, diss. Université de Paris-I, Sorbonne, 1993, pp. 188–193. See the published version: Laurent Douzou, *La désobéissance. Histoire du mouvement Libération-sud* (Paris: Odile Jacob, 1995).

146. Burns, *Dreyfus, a Family Affair*, 470.

147. Simon, *Les Juifs à Nîmes*, 43.

148. Werth, *Déposition*, 532, October 13, 1943.

149. Ibid., February 4, 1944, p. 565.

150. Idem.

151. Peter Schöttler, *Lucie Varga; les autorités invisibles* (Paris: Cerf, 1991).

152. AIU, CC-17, report from regional delegations dated August 1942, as well as the subsequent reports and the report from Albert Lévy's trip.

153. AIU, CC-42, Marseilles, February 22, 1943, Rabbi Samuel Klein, report for the Central Consistory, "The Situation of Youth Groups."

154. AIU, CC-4, Périgueux, May 15, 1943, Rabbi E. Cyper, report on religious instruction in Périgueux and in the département of La Dordogne.

155. Kapel, *Un rabbin dans la tourmente*.

156. *L'Activité des organisatioins juives en France sous l'Occupation*, 26.

157. AIU, CC-13, October 29, 1942, letter to Chief Rabbi Isaïe Schwarz.

158. AIU, CC-4, Périgueux, October 23, 1942, "Avis à messieurs les bouchers" from the butchers' and pork butchers' trade association, and Brive, November 5, 1942, message from Gaston Cahen to Albert Manuel. AN, F 1a, 3,706, April 19, 1943, message from Chief Rabbi Isaïe Schwarz to the chief of staff for the regional prefect in Limoges.

159. AIU, CC-13, October 29, 1942, lettre from Rabbi Schönberg addressed to Chief Rabbi Isaïe Schwartz. And AIU, CC-1b, report given by Helbronner on the incident to the members of the Consistory.

160. AIU, CC-13, Nice, September 14, 1942, report from Théo Kahn.

161. AIU, CC-13, Saturday March 6, 1943, oratory on Rue des Convalescents in Marseille.

162. AIU, CC-7, September 2, 1943, Mosse's report on the incidents in the temple in Toulouse.

163. CC-5, Toulouse, October 18, 1943, message from the regional delegation to Albert Lévy, consistory delegate.

164. AIU, CC-4, Grenoble, December 5, 1943, letter to Helbronner from the president of the worship association.

165. Joint, SM 33, report on the incident having occurred in Lyon on December 10, 1943 (in a letter to Marc Jarblum, February 3, 1944).

166. Centre de Documentation Juive Contemporaine-CCXVII-45, "How Monsieur René Hirschler, Chief Rabbi of Strasbourg and General Chaplain, was arrested by the Gestapo on December 22, 1943 in Marseille."

167. Moch, *L'Etoile et la francisque*, 196–197.

168. AIU, CC-33, minutes of January 10 and 11, 1944 sessions of the meeting.

169. *L'Etoile et la francisque*.

170. Centre de Documentation Juive Contemporaine, XXVIIIa, 61. Vichy, April 16, 1942, Ministry of the Interior to Raymond-Raoul Lambert.

171. Centre de Documentation Juive Contemporaine DXLIV-66, May 5, 1943, General Commission on Jewish Affairs to Raymond-Raoul Lambert.

172. AN, AJ 38, 1 141.

173. Cohen, *The Burden of Conscience*, 137–138.

174. AJ 38, 1,141, June 21, 1943, report from the general auditor of the UGIF to the General Commission on Jewish Affairs.

175. AN, AJ 38, 147, letter dated March 4, 1944, referring to a memorandum sent to prefects by the General Commission on Jewish Affairs on August 27, 1942.

176. Centre de Documentation Juive Contemporaine, XXVIII-190, Raymond-Raoul Lambert to General Commission on Jewish Afffairs, July 31, 1943, reprinted in Billig, *Le Commissariat général aux questions juives*, 1:281–282.

177. AN, AJ 38, 1,153.

178. AIU, CC-47, Lyon, May 17, 1944, Raymond Geismann to the president of the Central Consistory.

179. Cohen, *The Burden of Conscience*, 166ff.

180. Ibid. See also Adler, *The Jews of Paris and the Final Solution*, 129ff.

181. Cohen, *The Burden of Conscience*, 127ff. The council of the southern branch of the UGIF met in Nice, in the Italian Zone, on February 15, 1943. Acting on Lambert's suggestion, it appointed the two last inspectors of the UGIF's social services. Centre de Documentation Juive Contemporaine, CDX-3, report on the information gathering trip by Gamzon, Jefroykin, and Brener from May 5 through May 15, 1943.

182. See for example the report on the activity of the fifth office of the UGIF (CAR) for May 1943; YIVO, RG 210, C-1, Marseilles, June 10, 1943. From March to May 1943, the number of beneficiaries increased from 12,000 to 15,000.

183. YIVO, RG 210, XCII-109, Lyon, May 10, 1943, report on the regional delegation from Lyon for the months of March and April 1943.

184. AIU, CC-46, UGIF, "First Office," monthly report for June 1943.

185. YIVO, France during WWII, 2, 24, Albert Lévy, October 25, 1943, "Reflexions on the Chief Rabbi's Fund Drive," and AIU, CC-17, reports on Albert Lévy's trips, passim.

186. Szajkowski, *Analytical Franco-Jewish Gazetteer*, 168. For his part, Serge Klarsfeld speaks of nine mothers and twenty-eight children, *Calendrier*, 897–898.

187. Cohen, *The Burden of Conscience*, p. 131–132.

188. YIVO, RG 210, XCII-96, Geissmann to Edinger, Lyon, May 30, 1944. See also Centre de Documentation Juive Contemporaine, CDX-59.

189. Cohen, *The Burden of Conscience*, 133–134.

190. May 27, 1943. See Jean-Pierre Azéma, "Des résistances à la Résistance," in *La France des années noires*, 2:241–270.

191. Stéphane Courtois, "Le front national," in *La France des années noires*, 2:91–104.

192. Renée Poznanski, "Que savait-on dans le monde?" in *Qui savait quoi?* 21–43, and Raymond-Raoul Lambert, *Carnet d'un témoin*, 202, December 18, 1942.

193. Jan Karski, *Story of a Secret State* (Boston, 1944).

194. *Les voix de la liberté*, 3:207–208.

195. Ibid., 4:114–115.

196. Centre de Documentation Juive Contemporaine, DLXXXVIII-10, personal testimony of Ignace Fink.

197. Werth, *Déposition*, 536, November 4, 1943.
198. See the UJRE's manifesto in *La Presse antiraciste*, 155–160, in a version dating from April 1944. See also Adler, *The Jews of Paris and the Final Solution*, 209ff.
199. AIU, CC-15, minutes of the September 23, 1943, meeting.
200. Various analyses and studies of the questions asked can be found in the Consistory archives, particularly in AIU, CC-62.
201. Moreshet archives, D 1.11 941, letter dated December 21, 1943, seemingly written by Victor Szulklaper, extremely distrustful of the Jewish Army.
202. Moreshet archives, D.1.195, Bâle, December 23, 1943, Heini Bornstein to Henry Pohorylès, and D.1.1198, same date, to Victor.
203. Knout, *La Résistance juive en France*, 150.
204. On the subject of this agreement, see Shmuel R. Kapel, *Maavak yehudi be-Tsorfat ha-kvusha* [A Jewish struggle in Occupied France] (Jerusalem, 1981), 107. The document can be found in the Polonski archives.
205. Abitbol, *Les Deux Terres promises*, 68ff.
206. Annie Kriegel, "Pouvoir politique et expression communautaire: Le CRIF," *Pardès* 3 (1986): 199–206.
207. Shrager, *Un militant juif*, 139.
208. Centre de Documentation Juive Contemporaine, CDLXXIII-93, December 1943, internal report from Adam Rayski (Marcel).
209. Reprinted in Adam Rutkowski, *La lutte des Juifs en France*, 193–194.
210. See the charter of the CADJJ, February 1944, Centre de Documentation Juive Contemporaine, CDLXIX-13. A Union Committee was also created in Paris in january 1944, modeled after the General Defense Committee: see Adler, *The Jews of Paris and the Final Solution*, 218.
211. YV, P/7, 37.
212. Archives of the Resistance Museum, Champigny, Diamant collection, October 4, 1944, meeting of the CUDFJ.
213. Léo Glaeser, *Unzer Qempf*, November 1943 (in Yiddish); trans. *Les Nouveaux Cahiers* 108 (1992): 59–60.
214. Archives of the Resistance Museum, Champigny, Diamant collection, undated.
215. On the establishment of the CRIF, see Adler, *The Jews of Paris and the Final Solution*, 230–233. See also the eyewitness account by Adam Rayski, "La Fondation du Conseil représentatif des Juifs de France," *Le Monde juif*, no. 24–51 (1968): 32–37.
216. Léon Meiss had been the vice president of the consistory since June 7, 1943: see the minutes of the meeting on that date, AIU, CC-2.
217. The idea of a Jewish Representative Council apparently came from the steering committee of the Zionist Organization in France. Fisher-Ariel, *Souvenirs*.
218. This part of the CRIF's charter included the immediate abolition of the white paper of 1939, liberty for Jews to immigrate to Palestine and settle there, and political status for Palestine. In order for this paragraph to receive the approval of all parties present, the final version stipulated: "In order to ensure the normal, friendly coexistence of all segments of the population, the CRIF will support efforts aimed at achieving the greatest understanding between the Jewish and Arab populations of Palestine, in the broadest spirit of democracy. It is agreed that the national status of the Jews in Palestine will in no way affect either the status of Jews in the other countries or the ties that attach them to their native land." Cited by Adler, *The Jews of Paris and the Final Solution*, 232–233.

See the various plans for the charter establishing the CRIF in the Resistance Museum in Champigny, David Diamant files.
219. Fisher-Ariel, *Souvenirs*.
220. CC-5, report on the arrests in Vals-les-Bains in the département of l'Ardèche on September 30, 1943.
221. AIU, CC-36, Jean Avram, report on Chambéry, December 8, 1943.
222. AIU, CC-3, March 1943 meeting of the rabbinical commission, and request from Chief Rabbi Liber in November 1943.

12. *Liberation: Before and After (pages 438–473)*

1. Paxton, *Vichy France*, 326ff.
2. Marrus and Paxton, *Vichy France and the Jews*, 336ff.
3. AN, AJ 38, 146, Dijon, June 9, 1944, regional director in Dijon to secretary-general of the General Commission on Jewish Affairs in Paris, and Antignac's reply, June 12, 1944.
4. AN, AJ 38, 1 075.
5. AN, AJ 38, 265, memorandum dated February 17, 1944, from Lathière to all inspectors.
6. AN, AJ 38, 243, August 1, 1944, report from the SEC in Montpellier.
7. Many examples can be found in AN, AJ 38, 262.
8. AN, AJ 38, 6.
9. AN, AJ 38, 292, memorandum dated April 20, 1944, sent by the SEC office in Paris to the heads of its operations in both zones and to the regional agents.
10. AN, AJ 38, 1 153, report listing the names of Jews convicted by the criminal court in Nice from January to June 1944.
11. AN, AJ 38, 1 142, secretary-general in charge of labor to the General Commission on Jewish Affairs, April 14, 1944.
12. The notice was published by newspapers on May 1, 1944; Marrus and Paxton, *Vichy France and the Jews*, 310.
13. AN, AJ 38, 1 143, April 5, 1944, SEC director for both zones to SEC regional delegates.
14. *Les Juifs sous l'Occupation*, 181.
15. Denis Peschanski and Jean-Pierre Azéma, "Vichy Etat policier," in *La France des années noires*, 2:371ff.
16. *Paris-Soir*, January 27, 1944.
17. Roger Martel, "En écoutant Philippe Henriot," *Paris-Soir*, January 21, 1944.
18. Jean-Louis Crémieux-Brilhac and Hélène Eck, "France," in *La Guerre des ondes*, ed. Eck, 86. See also Denis Peschanski, "La propagande de l'Etat français. Contrôler ou encadrer," in Peschanski *La Propagande sous Vichy, 1940–1944*, by Laurent Gervereau and Denis Peschanski (Paris: BDIC, 1990), 29ff.
19. Roderick H. Kedward, "The Vichy of the Other Philippe," in, *Politics and Culture during the Nazi Occupation, 1940–1944*, ed. Gerhard Hirschfeld and Patrick Marsh (Munich: Berg, 1989), 32–46.
20. Crémieux-Brilhac and Eck, "France," 125.
21. *Paris-Soir*, January 1, 1944.
22. Crémieux-Brilhac and Eck, "France," 137–138.
23. AN, Z6, 1 391. This is the last broadcast of which I found any written record.
24. Pierre Mouton, "L'Europe contre le matérialisme," *Paris-Soir*, January 7, 1944.
25. Roger Martel, "Les étrangers et le terrorisme," *Paris-Soir*, January 22, 1944.
26. On the subject of the capture of the FTP-MOI in Paris in November 1943 and the Trial of the twenty-three, see *Le Sang de l'étranger*, 335ff.
27. *Paris-Soir*, February 22, 1944.
28. Olga Blancic was not executed immediately, but instead dragged from one prison to another. She was once again condemned to death in Stuttgart and guillotined in the prison courtyard on May 10, 1944. *La Résistance organisée des Juifs en France*, 219.
29. Roger Martel, "Les 'libérateurs' de l'armée du crime," *Paris-Soir*, March 6, 1944.
30. Archives of the Paris police prefecture, "Situation in Paris," report dated February 21, 1944.
31. Archives of the Paris police prefecture, "Situation in Paris," report dated April 3, 1944.
32. Philippe Burrin, "La guerre franco-française: vers Sigmaringen," in *La France des années noires*, 2:37ff.
33. Klarsfeld, *Calendrier*, 954.
34. AN, AJ 38, 1 154, SEC-Paris, March–July 1944, inspectors' reports.
35. AN, AJ 38, 172.

36. Klarsfeld, *Calendrier*, 1120.
37. Ibid., 1124.
38. AIU, CC-28, chaplain's main office, Valence, January 18, 1945, report on the fourth trimester of 1944.
39. This was the center at Alboussière in the département of L'Ardèche, AIU, CC-28, May 5, 1944, report from the chaplain's main office, from February 1 to April 30, 1944.
40. Adam Rutkowski, "Le camp d'internement et d'échange pour Juifs de Vittel," *Le Monde juif* 102 (1981): 152ff.
41. Itzhak Katzenelson, *Le Chant du peuple juif massacré*, translated from the Yiddish by Myriam Novitch (Israel: Ghetto Fighters House, 1983), 25. Excerpt translated into English by N. Bracher.
42. AN, A 38, 1, 153, July 8, 1944, chief of staff in the main office of the National Police to the regional prefects in the Southern Zone.
43. Klarsfeld, *Calendrier*, 934ff.
44. Ibid., 947.
45. Ibid., 968.
46. Ibid., 1016, 1033, 1041.
47. CZA, S 26, 1 452, report on Toulouse from March 1 to March 10, 1944.
48. Moreshet archives, D 1, 1 058, report on the situation in Limoges, June 1, 1944.
49. AIU, CC-30, Aubenas, March 2, 1944, report from Chief Rabbi Maurice Liber for January and February 1944.
50. Burrin, "La guerre franco-française," 35.
51. Jacques Delperrie de Bayac, *Histoire de la Milice* (Paris: Fayard, 1969), 216.
52. Françoise Basch, "Victor Basch et la passion de justice," *Les Temps modernes* 572 (1994): 42ff. See also Delperrie de Bayac, 231ff.
53. AIU, CC-21, report on the mass grave near Miremont, in the département of La Haute-Garonne.
54. Delperrie de Bayac, *Histoire de la Milice*, 165.
55. Roger Berg, *La persécution raciale* (Paris: Office Français d'Edition, 1947), 253ff.
56. Ibid., 258ff.
57. Cited by Delperrie de Bayac, *Histoire de la Milice*, 280.
58. Ibid., 481.
59. The episode has been magnificently analyzed by Tzvetan Todorov, in *Une Tragédie Française* (Paris: Editions du Seuil, 1994), which has been translated by Mary Kelly as *A French Tragedy* (Hanover, N.H.: University Press of New England, 1996).
60. Martin du Gard, *La Chronique de Vichy*, 383.
61. AN, AJ 38, 1,075.
62. "I advise the hundreds of thousands of French citizens (for there are hundreds of thousands of them) who have acquired Jewish possessions, be they large or small, of considerable or minimal value, to form a solid group in order to defend their rights. If they do not, they run the risk being duped. Once associated, though, they would be a force to contend with. And there you would have a whole army of people to serve the new order of French society," wrote Déat in *L'Oeuvre* on September 9, 1943.
63. See the tables displaying, in order of importance, the preoccupations of the French population, as synthesized from mail opened in Montpellier and Toulouse in 1944; Laborie, *L'opinion française sous Vichy*, 317–319.
64. AN, F 7, 14,929, mail opened and read from April to July 1944 in Limoges, Brive, Châteauroux, Guéret, and Périgueux.
65. AN, F 7, 14,931, Division of Technical Inspections with the Regional Inspection office in Lyon, January 1944.
66. See for example the report of January 1944 for Saint-Amand-Montrond, AN, F 7, 14,929, or that of the Division of Technical Inspections in Marseilles, January 1944, or the report for Gap in April 1944 (AN, F7, 14, 932).
67. AN, F 7, 14,732, commission postal inspection in Perpignan, April 1944.

68. AN, F 7, 14, 930, Commission of Technical Inspections in Montluçon, May and June 1944.

69. AN, F 7, 14, 929.

70. Joint, SM 33, "Grenoble sous la terreur," February 15, 1944, forwarded by Marc Jarblum to Saly Mayer on February 15, 1944.

71. Idem, February 1, 1944.

72. Centre de Documentation Juive Contemporaine, XXII-12. See also AN, Aj 38, 1,097.

73. *La Presse antiraciste,* 157, "L'Union des Juifs pour la résistance et l'entraide, son action, ses buts," April 1944.

74. *La Presse antiraciste,* 237, "Aux Juifs de Marseille."

75. Ibid., 136.

76. Ibid., February 1944, "Juifs lyonnais."

77. Centre de Documentation Juive Contemporaine, XXII-12, "Français . . . En Dordogne, en Corrèze, dans l'Ain, les Allemands incendient des villages, fusillent des centaines de Juifs et déportent des milliers de Français."

78. AN, F 7, 14,731, in particular the Technical Inspection Commmission in Lyon.

79. Wieviorka, *Ils étaient juifs, résistants, communistes,* 244ff.

80. AIU, CC-46, Lyon, February 2, 1944.

81. On the subject of this betrayal, see Centre de Documentation Juive Contemporaine, CDLXIX-29, "L'affaire Anne-Marie," the testimony of Ernest after his liberation from Drancy.

82. Centre de Documentation Juive Contemporaine, DLXI-38, testimony from Annette Zyman; Centre de Documentation Juive Contemporaine, CCXIV-118, "Rapport concernant l'OJC et son activité durant la période de l'Occupation"; Polonski archives, testimony from Henry Pohorylès.

83. Centre de Documentation Juive Contemporaine, CDLXIX-38, July 4, 1944, report for the months of May and June 1944, sent by the FFI in the département of Les Alpes-Maritimes to the regional head of the FFI-R2.

84. "Planned agreement to be submitted to London." I thank Jacques Lazarus for providing me with this document.

85. Central depository for the Military Justice archives, Le Blanc, dossier of the investigation of the Rue de la Pompe affair. Charges were dismissed because it was judged that Karl Rehbein's activity was "normal for an enemy intelligence officer who later returns to his army and is covered by the statutes of limitations of The Hague Convention (article 31)." Ordinance dismissing charges and communicating the decision by the permanent Military Tribunal, Paris, December 29, 1952.

86. About this last deportation train to leave France, see Chaigneau, *Le Dernier Wagon,* On the entire episode, see the testimony given by Jacques Lazarus, *Juifs au combat: témoignage sur l'activité d'un mouvement de résistance* (Paris: CDJC, 1947), 115ff; and the testimony from Kapel, *Un rabbin dans la tourmente.* In the Polonski archives, see the testimony from Henry Pohorylès. The episode of the escape in which the Dutch did not take part, although a collective escape had been decided, created tensions between the survivors of this group and the Jewish Combat Organization escapees after the Liberation. "There was probably a break in the communication line somewhere," explained Henry Pohorylès, one of the escapees from the train, in an interview with the author in Paris in 1987.

87. Roderick H. Kedward, "STO et maquis," in *La France des années noires,* 2:282ff.

88. Ravine, *La Résistance* organisée, 206.

89. Centre de Documentation Juive Contemporaine, CCXV-1, report on the organization and functioning of the maquis of the Israelite Scouts of France (EIF), undated, but obviously written before the end of 1944. See also Alain Michel, *Les Eclaireurs israélites,* 183.

90. Lublin archives (now in the Centre de Documentation Juive Contemporaine), "Reports on the inn," unsigned, dated June 1944, and written by Jewish Army militants. See also Centre de Documentation Juive Contemporaine, CDLXIX-39.

91. Centre de Documentation Juive Contemporaine, CCXV-21, narrative account given by Charles Hartanu.

92. Michel, *Les Eclaireurs israélites,* 187ff.

93. Hubert Beuve-Méry, "La guerre des Juifs," *Temps présent,* November 1944; repr. Centre de Documentation Juive Contemporaine, CCXV-2. See also Centre de Documentation Juive Contemporaine CCXIV-120, report on the attack on the train in Mazamet.

94. Centre de Documentation Juive Contemporaine, CCXIV-118, report concerning the OJC and its activity during the Occupation period.

95. Lublin archives (now in the Centre de Documentation Juive Contemporaine), lieutenant RL to MF, for November–December 1943. See also Centre de Documentation Juive Contemporaine, CDLXIX-36.

96. Polonski archives, Avraham Polonski to David Knout, December 28, 1946.

97. Roger Montpezat, *Le Corps-franc de la Montagne noire, Journal de marche (avril–septembre 1944)* (Albi, 1963), 90–91, 123–125; and Centre de Documentation Juive Contemporaine, CCXIV-19, "The Jewish Trumpeldor platoon with the CFMN."

98. The Black Mountain Fighting Unit was the only "stumbling block" on the path toward unity, said Serge Ravanel, who since April 1944, had been charged with setting up the special fighting units for the Liberation in the Toulouse region; Ravanel-Asher, excerpt from the interview granted to Michel Goubet, September 19, 1969, IHTP. Michel Goubet, "La résistance toulousaine, structures, objectifs, printemps-été 1944," *Revue d'histoire de la Deuxième Guerre mondiale* 99 (1975): 25–44. See also the warning letter of June 4, 1944, from Ravanel to Le Floc, head of the Black Mountain Fighting Unit, IHTP, Haute-Garonne.

99. Centre de Documentation Juive Contemporaine, DLXXII-2, testimony from Joseph Bass.

100. On the military vicissitudes experienced by the CFMN's blue-white platoon, see Lazare, *Rescue as Resistance,* 291ff. Those of the Marc Haguenau unit can be found on page 295ff. of the same book.

101. Lazarus, *Juifs au combat,* 80–81.

102. Lublin archives (CDJC), report dated June 27, 1944, "Report on the recruitment of new members of the AJ," July 1, 1944, Daniel followed by Pierrot's (Pierre Loeb was a Jewish Army platoon commander) comments, July 11, 1944.

103. Haïm Avni, "The Zionist Underground in Holland and France and the Escape to Spain," in *Rescue Attempts during the Holocaust,* ed. Israel Gutman and Ephraïm Zuroff (Jerusalem: Yad Vashem, 1977), 555–590. See also Haïm Avni, *Spain, the Jews, and Franco* (Philadelphia: Jewish Publication Society of America, 1982).

104. Dominique Veillon, "Les réseaux de Résistance," in *La France des années noires,* 392.

105. Centre de Documentation Juive Contemporaine, DLXXII-40, testimony from Jacques Roïtman, and Centre de Documentation Juive Contemporaine, DLXXXVII-15, testimony from Joseph Linnewiel.

106. Michel, *Les Eclaireurs israélites,* 184–185.

107. Lazare, *Rescue as Resistance,* 286ff.

108. Ibid., p. 311.

109. Haïm Avni, "The Zionist Underground," 573.

110. Lublin archives, CDJC, the report signed "Alexandre" deals with the period between November 1 and December 10, 1943 and describes the risks and dangers experienced by one group before their departure.

111. Lazare, *Rescue as Resistance,* 289.

112. Text of the agreement, Polonski archives.

113. Haïm Avni, *Spain, the Jews, and Franco,* 127.

114. On the subject of all these efforts, see Adler, *The Jews of* Paris, 217ff. On the constitution of patriotic militia groups led exclusively by the Communist Party, see Philippe Buton, "La France atomisée," in *La France des années noires,* 2:387–388.

115. Centre de Documentation Juive Contemporaine, CDLXIX-37, AJ Paris, undated message written to Lucien (probably written in July 1944) and telling about two of these executions.

116. Centre de Documentation Juive Contemporaine, CDLXXI-39, Ernest to Lucien, June 27, 1944.

117. Centre de Documentation Juive Contemporaine, XXII-12, "Why the UJRE is not yet part of the CGD," August 10, 1944.

118. YV, Joseph Fisher, 5, Lyon, May 1, 1944, "Report on the Jewish Youth Steering Committee."

119. YIVO, RG 210, XCII-96, Châteauroux, June 5, 1944, Rabbi G. Apeloig to the director-general of the UGIF in Lyon.

120. Joint, SM 33, July 11, 1944, excerpt from a letter.

121. Centre de Documentation Juive Contemporaine, CCXVI-155, minutes of the meetings of the committee which included Meiss, Grinberg, Adamitz, and Geissmann, Lyon, July–August 1944.

122. YIVO, France during WWII, 12, UJRE, June 10, 1944.

123. Moreshet archives, D 1, 1,067, general and particular instructions. See also the Lublin archives (CDJC), and Centre de Documentation Juive Contemporaine, CDLXIX-25.

124. Archives of the Resistance Museum, Champigny, Diamant collection, minutes of the meeting of the CUDJF, September 16, 1944.

125. Adler, *The Jews of Paris*, 221.

126. Jeanine Auscher, "Les derniers jours de Drancy," *Revue de la pensée juive* (April 1950): 122–123.

127. Centre de Documentation Juive Contemporaine, CCXVII-26, "The Liberation of the Drancy camp," unsigned and undated, but written a few days after Drancy's liberation.

128. Centre de Documentation Juive Contemporaine, CDXXX-40, The Liberation of Drancy. See also Centre de Documentation Juive Contemporaine, CCVII-44.

129. Centre de Documentation Juive Contemporaine, DIII-61 eyewitness account from Tony Gryn (in Yiddish); Latour, *La Résistance juive en France*, 254–255.

130. Klarsfeld, *Calendrier*, 1090.

131. Archives of the Resistance Museum in Champigny, David Diamant collection, A. Alpérine, August 21, 1944; Adler, *The Jews of Paris*, 159. See also YV, Joseph Fisher collection, 2, Paris, September 21, 1944, Simon Lévitte to Joseph Fisher.

132. AIU, CC-47, Lyon, August 23, 1944, Raymond Geissmann, decision.

133. Centre de Documentation Juive Contemporaine, CCXV-21, report from Charles Hartanu.

134. CZA, Z 4/10 300, Marc Jarblum, Paris, December 1, 1944.

135. In addition to the Jews deported from the Northern and Southern Zones, there were 748 Jews who were deported from the départements of Le Nord and Le Pas-de-Calais, via the Malines camp in Belgium. Delmaire, ed., *1942, L'Année tragique des Juifs du Nord, Tsafon, Revue d'études juives du Nord* 9–10 (1992) (Lille).

136. On this subject, and on construction of the memory of deportation in the immediate postwar period, see Annette Wieviorka, *Déportation et génocide: entre la mémoire et l'oubli* (Paris: Plon, 1992). See the chapters "The Impact of the Genocide on the Community," and "The Children," esp. 390ff.

137. Gadala, *A travers la grande grille*, 285.

138. Wieviorka, *Déportation et génocide*, 86–89.

139. *Les voix de la liberté*, 5:113–114.

140. The questionnaires were sent out by the CUDJF in the fall of 1944. Archives of the Resistance Museum in Champigny, and several examples of responses received.

141. Centre de Documentation Juive Contemporaine, XXII-12, July 1944, message from the leaders of the Jewish Communists to the General Defense Committee (CGD). A jury of honor was nevertheless put together by the CRIF: its discussions centered on the arrests of children carried out by Brunner in late July 1944. In a two-part procedure, it concluded that no "actively committed fault of the kind that could blemish their honor" could be found against them. Léon Meiss succeeded in having the case reexamined after a preliminary judgment had found Edinger as well as Schendel and Colonel Kahn at fault; Adler, *The Jews of Paris*, 159–161. See also YV, P 7/16, copy of the jury of honor's two rulings, on January 14 and December 3, 1946.

142. Martin du Gard, *La Chronique de Vichy*, 348–349.

143. Gabriel Marcel, "Lendemain de persécution," *Témoignage chrétien*, October 21, 1944, first-page article cited by Henry Rousso, *The Vichy Syndrome; History and Memory in France Since 1944* (Cambridge, Mass.: Harvard University Press, 1991), 1120–1121.

144. André Weill-Curiel, *Règles de savoir-vivre à l'usage d'un jeune juif de mes amis* (Paris: Editions du Myrte, 1945).

145. YV, Joseph Fisher collection, 2, September 21, 1944, Simon Lévitte to Joseph Fisher.

146. Polonski archives (CDJC), October 30, 1944, director of *Renaissance* to the commissioner of information in Toulouse.

147. Polonski archives, letters dated January 15, 1945, and addressed to Daniel Mayer, Emmanuel d'Astier and others.

148. Archives of the Resistance Museum, Champigny, David Diamant Collection, Chavanis to the CGD, Paris, October 23, 1944.

149. Pierre Novick, *The Resistance versus Vichy: The Purge of Collaborators in Liberated France* (London: Chatto and Windus, 1968), 111–112, and Rousso, *The Vichy Syndrome*, 139.

150. Some of these organizations were disbanded in December 1944, but they immediately sprung back up under another name; Szajkowski, *Analytical Franco-Jewish Gazetteer*, 108. See also American Jewish Conference, *Jews in Liberated Europe, Survey of Conditions and Prospects of Rehabilitation* (New York, 1945).

151. CC, plundering dossier 1944–1945.

152. Centre de Documentation Juive Contemporaine, Lubetzki collection. See also CC, antisemitism dossier.

153. CC, antisemitism dossier.

154. The tracts denouncing these demonstrations can be found in the Archives of the Resistance Museum in Champigny, David Diamant collection, This wave of antisemitism is the main subject of the correspondence of that time between the Unity Committee in Paris and the local committees; idem. See also *La Terre retrouvée*, June 12 and 20, 1945.

155. Centre de Documentation Juive Contemporaine, CCXXI-10.

156. Resistance Museum, Champigny, David Diamant collection, December 22, 1944.

157. Joseph Lubetzki, study on the subject, Centre de Documentation Juive Contemporaine, Lubetzki source.

158. Danièle Voldman, "Crise du logement et intervention de l'État: l'ordonnance du 11 october 1945," *Les Cahiers du Groupement pour la recherche sur les mouvements familiaux*, 7 (1993): 28–29.

159. David Weinberg, "The French Jewish Community after World War II: the Struggle for Survival and Self Definition," *Forum* 45 (1982): 46.

160. Resistance Museum, Champigny, David Diamant collection, report from Toulouse on the occasion of the first convention of the UJRE, April 14 and 15, 1945.

161. Archives of the Resistance Museum, Champigny, David Diamant collection, September 11, 1944, letter to comrades of the UJJ in its various sections.

162. Joint, SM 33, "Report on the activity of the General Defense Committee," Paris, October 18, 1944, and, from the same date, "Statistics on those receiving aid": from the figure of 9,630 people at the eve of the Liberation, their numbers had increased to 29,786 for the month of September 1944.

163. The total had reached 32,938, according to a report from the Joint dated November 23, 1944. Joint, 596, "Note concerning the situation of Jews in Paris and all over France after the Liberation."

164. Archives of the Paris police prefecture, "Situation in Paris," Synopsis dated May 10, 1945, from the General Information Bureau. Seven Jews were arrested.

165. Joint, 596, Report for France for the last quarter of 1944.

166. Archives of the Resistance Museum, Champigny, David Diamant collection, charter establishing the COJASOR and moral and financial report for 1945.

167. Joint, SM 32, A-2, "OSE activities in France."

168. Joint, SM 35, A-2, Geneva, December 15, 1944, main office of the OSE-Union, "Explanatory notes for the Budget-Scheme of the French Section of OSE-Union."

169. Lublin archives (CDJC), "Report On the Situation of Jewish Children in France,"

Paris, May 4, 1945. See also CZA, S 26, 1,452. Archives David Ben Gourion, Sde Boqer, *Journal*, May 15, 1945, and YIVO, RG 343, 158, Paris, May 8, 1945, letter from Jacobowicz to the Federation.

170. Danan, "La guerre des enfants," *Libération*, December 30, 1945, and response from Jacquel (Jacques Lazarus), Polonski archives (CDJC).

171. YIVO, RG 343, 159, "Report on the investigation conducted at Le Petit-Bourg on November 6, 1946 subsequent to the report and request of Rabbi Bauer pertaining to Jewish children remaining in the custody of local inhabitants."

172. Other examples can be found in Wieviorka *Déportation et génocide*, 380ff.

173. See Jacob Kaplan, *L'Affair Finaly* (Paris: Cerf, 1993).

174. Wieviorka, *Déportation et génocide*, 384–385.

175. CZA, S 26/1 194, David Shaltiel to Eliahu Dobkin, March 19, 1945.

176. Archives of the Resistance Museum, Champigny, David Diamant collection, Plan for a Resolution on the Committee for Children, presented at the convention of the UJRE on April 14 and 15, 1945. See also Jean Laloum, "La création des maisons d'enfants: l'exemple de la Commission centrale de l'enfance auprès de l'UJRE," *Pardès* 16 (1992): 247–270.

177. YV, Joseph Fisher collection, January 28, 1946, "Oral report on the activity of the CRIF," presented before the Assembly of the Central Consistory by Joseph Fisher.

178. On the subject of such developments occurring within the Zionist movement, see Renée Poznanski, "L'héritage de la guerre: le sionisme en France dans les années 1944–1947," in Doris Bensimon and Benjamin Pincus (Editors), *Les Juifs de France, le sionisme et l'État d'Israël*, ed. Doris Bensimon and Benjamin Pincus, 248.

179. CZA, Z 4/10 300, Fisher to A. Granovsky, October 13, 1944.

180. See for example Joseph Fisher, "Déchéance," *La Terre retrouvée* 9 (May 1, 1945).

181. "Reports on name changes," report requested in April 1945 and presented to the general assembly of the Central Consistory by Gaston Hildenfinger in June 1947, Archives of the Resistance Museum in Champigny, David Diamant collection. See also Wieviorka, *Déportation et génocide*, 364ff.

182. Henry Rousso, "Cet obscur objet du désir," in *La Mémoire de Français; 40 ans de commémorations de la Seconde Guerre mondiale* (Paris: Editions du CNRS, 1986), 47–61.

183. See Philippe E. Landau, *Les Juifs et la Grande Guerre, 1914–1941; Patrie, République, Mémoire*, diss., University de Paris-VII (1992).

184. Annie Kriegel, "De la résistance juive," *Pardès* 2 (1985): 193.

185. The term is Raymond Aron's in his *Mémoires*, 191.

186. *Gloire éternelle aux héros juifs de la Résistance française* (Paris: Union des Juifs pour la résistance et l'entraide, 1963).

187. Ibid., 16.

188. *La Terre Retrouvée*, 16[167,] August 25, 1945. The article is signed "La Terre Retrouvée."

189. On the importance given to the persecution of the Jews in the purge trials, see Katy Hazan, *La Persécution des Juifs dans quelques procès d'épuration et de collaboration*, diss., Institut d'études politiques (Paris, 1993); and Henry Rousso, "Une justice impossible. L'épuration et la politique antijuive de Vichy," *Annales, ESC*, 48–3, 1993, pp. 745–770.

190. Henri Hertz, "Le procès Pétain. Les Juifs à la barre," *La Terre Retrouvée*, 16[167], August 25, 1945.

Conclusion (pages 474–491)

1. See Renée Poznanski, "Vichy et les Juifs. Des marges de l'histoire au coeur de son écriture," in *Vichy et les Français*, ed. Jean-Pierre Azéma and François Bédarida (Paris: Fayard, 1992), 57–68, for a more precise analysis of the historiography of "Vichy and the Jews."

2. Justin Godart, preface to Léon Poliakov, *La Condition des Juifs en France sous l'occupation italienne* (Paris: CDJC, 1946), p. 15.

3. Itzhak Schneersohn, *Le Monde juif* 9–10 (1947): 25.

4. See Rousso, *Le Syndrome de Vichy*.

5. The transition had been initiated in France by Joseph Billig in his seminal work *Le Commissariat général aux questions juives*, and by Henri Michel in *Vichy. Année 40* (Paris: Laffont, 1966).

6. Marrus and Paxton, *Vichy France and the Jews*, 356ff.

7. *La Résistance juive en France*.

8. *Vichy-Auschwitz*, 2:190–191; Klarsfeld repeatedly stresses this conclusion in each of his publications.

9. *Persécutions et sauvetages*.

10. On the stakes involved in the various definitions of the Jewish Resistance, see Renée Poznanski, "Reflections on Jewish Resistance and Jewish Resistants in France," *Jewish Social Studies* 2, no. 1 (1995): 122–158.

11. Klarsfeld, *Vichy-Auschwitz*, 2:179–181.

12. Pierre Laborie, "The Jewish Statutes in Vichy France and Public Opinion," *Yad Vashem Studies* 22 (1992): 81.

13. Renée Poznanski, "Avant les grandes rafles," 33 and 78.

14. "To put it clearly, this ecclesiastical language means that protesting on a spiritual level against a crime for which Marshal Pétain is responsible does not entail the refusal to obey Pétain on a temporal level," remarked Léon Werth, *Déposition*, 355, October 5, 1942, and note 1 by Jean-Pierre Azéma.

15. Pierre Laborie, "1942 et le sort des Juifs: Quel tournant dans l'opinion?" *Annales, ESC*, 48–3, 1993, pp. 662–663.

16. Roderick H. Kedward, *Resistance in Vichy France*. op. cit.

17. AN, AJ 38, 1,157.

18. Stéphane, *Chaque homme est lié au monde*, May 10, 1941, p. 62.

19. Gourfinkel, *L'Autre Patrie*, 315.

20. YIVO, France during WW II, 3–45, S. Majerowicz's *Journal*, Nice, from September 3 to September 12, 1943 (Yiddish).

21. Werner Rings, *Life with the Enemy: Collaboration and Resistance in Hitler's Europe, 1939–1945* (New York: 1982).

22. Werth, *Déposition*, August 22, 1944, pp. 721–722.

23. CC, Plunderings file, 1944–1945.

24. Henry Rousso, "Le souvenir de la Seconde Guerre mondiale et des persécutions antisémites. Contexte historique et repères chronologiques," *Annales, ESC*, 48–3, 1993, p. 809.

25. Annette Wieviorka, *Déportation et génocide*.

Bibliography

ARCHIVES

France

National Archives, Paris (AN).
Archives of the Ministry of Foreign Relations, Paris (MAE).
Archives of the Police Prefecture, Paris (PP).
Central Depository for the Archives of Military Courts, Le Blanc.
Historical Department of the French Army Ground Forces, Vincennes (SHAT).
Center for Contemporary Jewish Documentation, Paris (CDJC).
Archives of the Central Consistory during World War II, Maurice Moch Collection, Library of the Alliance Israélite Universelle (AIU), Paris (AIU, CC).
Archives of the Central Consistory during World War II, Rue Saint-Georges, Paris. (CC)
Archives of the OSE, Library of the AIU, Paris (OSE, AIU).
Archives of the Resistance Museum in Champigny.
Lucien Lublin Archives, Paris.
Claude Urman Archives, Paris.

Israel

Central Zionist Archives, Jerusalem (CZA).
Yad Vashem Archives, Jerusalem (YV).
Moreshet Archives, Guivat Haviva.
David Ben Gourion Archives, Sde Boqer.
Avraham Polonski Archives, Yad Tabenkin, Efal.

The United States

Archives of the YIVO Institute for Jewish Research, New York (YIVO).
Archives of the American Jewish Joint Distribution Committee, New York (Joint).

Russia

Russian Center for the Conservation and Study of Documents on Contemporary History, Moscow (CRCEDHC).

WAR-ERA NEWSPAPERS

Paris-Soir
Le Petit Marseillais

DIARIES, PERSONAL NOTES, CORRESPONDENCE

Auscher, Jeanine. "Les derniers jours de Drancy." *Revue de la pensée juive*. (April 1950): 118–123.
Baumann, Denise. *Une famille comme les autres*. 2d ed. Paris: Albin Michel, 1985.
Biélinky, Jacques. *Journal, juillet 1940–décember.* 1943 Text edited, annotated and with an introduction by Renée Poznanski. Paris: Cerf, 1992.
Bobkowski, Andrzej. *En guerre et en paix; Journal, 1940–1944*. Paris: Editions Noir sur Blanc, 1991.
Bohny-Reiter, Friedel. *Journal de Rivesaltes, 1941–1942*. Geneva: Editions Zoé, 1993.
Bood, Micheline. *Les Années doubles*. Paris: Robert Laffont, 1974.
Calef, Noël (Nissim). *Drancy 1941; Camp de représailles*. Edited and with an introduction by Serge Klarsfeld. Paris: Fils et Filles des Déportés Juifs de France, 1991.
Carnets du Pasteur Boegner, 1940–1945. Annotated and with an introduction by Philippe Boegner. Paris: Fayard, 1992.
De Monzie, Anatole. *Ci-devant*. Paris: Flammarion, 1941.
Gadala, Marie-Thérèse. *A travers la grande grille, mai 1940 à octobre 1941*. Paris: Editions du Grand Siècle, 1946.
———. *A travers la grande grille, octobre 1941 à juillet 1945*. Paris: La Plume d'Or, n.d.
Galtier-Boissiere, Jean. *Mon journal pendant l'Occupation*. Garas: La Jeune Parque, 1944.
Gamzon, Robert. *Les eaux claires: Journal, 1940–1944*. Paris: EIF, 1981.
Guéhenno, Jean. *Journal des années noires*. Paris: Gallimard, 1947.
Jacob, Henri. "Journal de Compiègne, 11 décembre 1941–11 avril 1942." Manuscript held by his daughter, Claude Bloch.
Jeanneney, Jules. *Journal politique, septembre 1939–juillet 1942*. Edited annotated, and with an introduction by Jean-Noël Jeanneney. Paris: Armand Colin, 1972.
Jünger, Ernst. *Premier journal parisien, Journal II, 1941–1943*. Paris: Christian Bourgeois, 1980.
———. *Premier journal parisien: Journal III, 1943–1945*. Paris: Christian Bourgeois, 1980.
Katzenelson, Itzhak. *Le Chant du peuple juif massacré*. Translated from Yiddish by Myriam Novitch. Israel: Editions Ghetto Fighters House, 1983.
Kohn, Georges. Excerpt of notes taken daily at Drancy from 1941 to 1944, AN F 9, 5579.
Lambert, Raymond-Raoul. *Carnet d'un témoin, 1940–1943*. Annotated and with an introduction by Richard Cohen. Paris: Fayard, 1985.
Langeron, Robert. *Paris, Juin 1940*. Paris: Flammarion, 1946.
Limagne, Pierre. *Éphémérides de quatre années tragiques*. 3 vols. Lavilledieu: Editions de Candide, 1987.
Martin du Gard, Maurice. *La Chronique de Vichy, 1940–1944*. Paris: Flammarion, 1948.
Montpezat, Roger. *Le Corps-franc de la Montagne noire (CFMN); journal de marche (avril–septembre 1944)*. Albi, 1963.
Stéphane, Roger. *Chaque homme est lié au monde, Carnets août 1939–août 1944*. Paris: Sagittaire, 1946.
Vidal-Naquet, Lucien. *Journal (15 septembre 1942––29 février 1944). Annales, ESC*, 48–3 (1993): 513–543.
Werth, Léon. *Déposition, Journal, 1940–1944*. Text edited by Lucien Fèvre. Annotated and with an introduction by Jean-Pierre Azéma. Paris: Viviane Hamy, 1992.

DOCUMENT COLLECTIONS

Aron, Raymond. *Chronique de guerre: La France libre, 1940–1945*. Edited by Christian Bachelier. Paris: Gallimard, 1990.

Berg, Roger. *La persécution raciale*. Paris: Office Français d'Edition, 1947.

Billig, Joseph. *Le Commissariat général aux questions juives*. 3 vols. Paris: Editions du Centre, 1960.

———. *L'Institut d'etude des questions juives*. Paris: Editions du Centre, 1974.

Bédarida, François, and Denis Peschanski, eds. "Marc Bloch à Étienne Bloch, Lettres de la 'drôle de guerre.'" *Cahiers de l'IHTP* 19 (December 1991).

Courtois, Stéphane, and Adam Rayski, eds. (with the collaboration of Philippe Burrin, Claude Lévy, Denis Peschanski, and Renée Poznanski). *Qui savait quoi?* Paris: La Découverte, 1987.

Crémieux-Brilhac, Jean-Louis ed. *Les voix de la liberté; Ici Londres, 1940–1944*. 5 vols. Paris: La Documentation Française, 1976.

Das vort fun viderstand und zig (The word of resistance and victory). In Yiddish. Paris: UJRE, 1949.

Diamant, David. *Par-delà les barbelés*. Paris: 1986.

Gronowski-Brunot, Louis. *L'Antisémitisme, le racisme et le problème juif*. Editions du Parti Communiste Français, SFIC, underground publication from November 1941. 79 pages. BN, Rés. 16° Lb58 676 (mistakenly attributed to Georges Politzer).

Halphen, Louis. "Le Judaïsme en France." Library of Contemporary International Documentation, Q pièce 195, rés. 1/2, typewritten manuscript.

Hoover Institute. *La Vie de la France sous l'Occupation, 1940–1944*. 3 vols. Paris: Plon, 1947.

Les Juifs sous l'Occupation. A collection of official French and German texts, 1940–1944. Paris: CDJC-FFDJF, 1982.

Klarsfeld, Serge. Additif au Mémorial. Paris, 1980.

———. *Calendrier de la persécution des Juifs de France*. Paris: FFDJF, 1993.

———. *Les Enfants d'Izieu; Une tragédie juive*. Paris: FFDJF, 1984.

———. *Le Livre des otages*. Paris: Les Editeurs Français Réunis, 1979.

———. *Mémorial de la déportation des juifs de France*. Paris, 1978.

———. *Le Statut des Juifs de Vichy*. Paris: FFDJF-CDJC, 1990.

———. *Vichy-Auschwitz*. 2 vols. Paris: Fayard, 1983 and 1985.

Lubetzki, Joseph. *La Condition des Juifs en France sous l'Occupation allemande*. Paris: CDJC, 1945.

Monneray, Henri. *La Persécution des Juifs en France et dans les autres pays de l'Ouest présentée par la France à Nuremberg*. Paris: Editions du Centre, 1947.

Perrault, Gilles. *Paris sous l'Occupation*. With commentary by Jean-Pierre Azéma. Paris: Belfond, 1987.

Pétain, Philippe. *Discours aux Français, 17 juin 1940–20 août 1944*. Text edited, annotated, and with an introduction by Jean-Claude Barbas. Paris: Albin Michel, 1989.

Poliakov, Léon. *La Condition des Juifs en France sous l'Occupation italienne*. Paris: Editions du Centre, 1946.

La Presse antiraciste sous l'Occupation hitlérienne. Paris: UJRE, 1950.

Procès de Xavier Vallat. With an introduction by his friends. Paris: Editions du Conquistador, 1948.

Rutkowski, Adam, ed. *La Lutte des Juifs en France à l'époque de l'Occupation*. With a preface by Georges Wellers. Paris: Editions du Centre, 1975.

Schumann, Maurice. *La Voix du couvre-feu; Cent allocutions de celui qui fut le porte-parole du général de Gaulle, 1940–1944*. With a preface by General Charles de Gaulle. Paris: Plon, 1964.

Steinberg, Lucien. *Les Autorités allemandes en France occupée*. Paris: CDJC, 1966.

Szajkowski, Zosa. *Analytical Franco-Jewish Gazetteer, 1939–1945*. New York, 1966.

MEMOIRS, REMEMBRANCES, TESTIMONIES

Amiel, Jo. *La Rafle; Un sana très ordinaire, 1942–1944*. With a preface by Annette Wieviorka. Paris: Cerf, 1993.

Aron, Raymond. *Mémoires, 50 ans de réflexion politique*. Paris: Julliard, 1983.

———. *Le Spectateur engagé*. Paris: Presses-Pocket, 1983.

Aron, Robert. *Fragments d'une vie*. Paris: Plon, 1981.

Aubrac, Raymond. *Où la mémoire s'attarde*. Paris: Odile Jacob, 1996.

Barthélémy, Joseph. *Ministre de la Justice, 1941–1943: Mémoires*. Paris: Pygmalion-G. Watelet, 1989.

Béalu, Marcel. *Dernier Visage de Max Jacob, 1937–1944*. Paris: Editions Pierre Fanlac, 1946.

Benda, Julien. *La Jeunesse d'un clerc; Un régulier dans le siècle, exercice d'un enterré vif*. Paris: Gallimard, 1968.

Bénédite, Daniel. *La Filière marseillaise; Un chemin vers la liberté sous l'Occupation*. Paris: Editions Clancier Guénaud, 1984.

Berl, Emmanuel. *Interrogatoire* (by Patrick Modiano). Paris: Gallimard, 1976.

Bernard, Jean-Jacques. *Le Camp de la mort lente*. Paris: Albin Michel, 1944.

Bloch, Marc. *L'Étrange défaite*. Paris: Franc-Tireur, 1946. Reprint, Gallimard, 1990.

Bulawko, Henry. *Les Jeux de la mort et de l'espoir*. Paris: Encres, 1980.

Carcopino, Jérôme. *Souvenirs de sept ans*. Paris: Flammarion, 1953.

Cassou, Jean. *La mémoire courte*. Paris: Editions de Minuit, 1953.

Corti, José. *Souvenirs désordonnés*. Paris, 1983.

Courouble, Alice. *Amie des Juifs*. Paris: Editions Bloud and Gay, 1946.

Crémieux-Dunand, Julie. *La Vie à Drancy, 1941–1944: Récit documentaire*. Paris: Librairie Gedalge, 1945.

Debré, Robert. *L'Honneur de vivre*. Paris: Stock, 1974.

De Lubac, Henri. *Résistance chrétienne à l'antisémitisme; Souvenirs, 1940–1944*. Paris: Fayard, 1988.

Du Moulin de Labarthète, Henri. *Le Temps des illusions; Souvenirs, juillet 1940–avril 1942*. Paris: Le Cheval Ailé, 1947.

Dunoyer de Segonzac, Pierre. *Le Vieux Chef; Mémoires et pages choisies*. Paris: Seuil, 1971.

Erlanger, Philippe. *La France sans étoile; Souvenirs de l'avant-guerre et du temps de l'Occupation*. Paris: Plon, 1974.

Fride, Bernard. *Une mauvaise histoire juive*. With a preface by Pierre Vidal-Naquet. Paris: Ramsay, 1991.

Fry, Varian. *Assignment: Rescue*. New York: Four Winds, 1968.

Gillouin, René. *J'étais l'ami du Maréchal*. Paris: Plon, 1966.

Gourfinkel, Nina. *L'Autre Patrie*. Paris: Seuil, 1953.

Grant, Alfred. *Paris, a shtot fun front* (Paris, a city on the front; in Yiddish). Paris: Oifsnoi Farlag, 1958.

Gronowski-Brunot, Louis. *Le Dernier Grand Soir*. Paris: Seuil, 1980.

Hammel, Frédéric Chimon. *Souviens-toi d'Amalek; Témoignage sur la lutte des Juifs en France (1938–1945)*. Paris: CLKH, 1982.

Hamon, Léo. *Vivre ses choix*. Paris: Robert Laffont, 1991.

Heftler, Nadine. *Si tu t'en sors; Auschwitz, 1944–1945*. With a preface by Pierre Vidal-Naquet. Paris: La Découverte, 1992.

Heilbronn, Max, and Jacques Varin. *Galeries Lafayette—Buchenwald—Galeries Lafayette*. Paris: Economica, 1989.

Holban, Boris. *Testament*. Paris: Calmann-Lévy, 1989.

Yakubowicz, Yehuda. *Ru Amelot, hilf und viderstand* (Rue Amelot, aid and resistance; in Yiddish). Paris: Editions Colonie Scolaire, 1948.

Jérôme, Jean. *Les Clandestins, 1940–1944*. Paris: Acropole, 1986.
———. *La Part des hommes; Souvenirs d'un témoin*. Paris: Acropole, 1983.
Kapel, René Shmuel. *Un rabbin dans la tourmente (1940–1944); Dans les camps d'internement et au sein de l'Organisation juive de combat*. Paris: CDJC, 1986.
Kaplan, Jacob. *L'Affaire Finaly*. Paris: Cerf, 1993.
Karski, Jan. *Story of a Secret State*. Boston, 1944.
Knabel, Serge. "De Saint-Mandé à Auschwitz; La déportation d'une famille juive française." Typewritten manuscript. Paris, 1992.
Kriegel, Annie. *Ce que j'ai cru comprendre*. Paris: Robert Laffont, 1991.
L'Entraide temporaire; Sauvetage d'enfants juifs sous l'Occupation. Booklet. CDJC.
L'Un des Trente-Six, David Rapoport. Paris: Kyoum, 1946.
Lazarus, Jacques. *Juifs au combat; Témoignage sur l'activité d'un mouvement de résistance*. Paris: CDJC, 1947.
Lindon, Raymond. "Hommage à André Baur." Typewritten manuscript, CDJC.
Lissner, Abraham. *Un Franc-tireur juif raconte . . .* With a preface by Henri Rol-Tanguy. Paris, 1969.
Lunel, Armand. *Par d'étranges chemins*. Monaco: L. Jaspard, 1946.
Malraux, Clara. *Le Bruit de nos pas*. vol. 1, *Apprendre à vivre* (1963); vol. 5, *La Fin et le commencement* (1976); vol. 6, . . . *Et pourtant j'étais libre* (1979). Paris: Grasset.
Merle d'Aubigné, Jeanne, Violette Mouchon, and Emile Fabre, eds. *Les Clandestins de Dieu; CIMADE, 1939–1944*. Paris: Fayard, 1968.
Mesnil-Amar, Jacqueline. *Ceux qui ne dormaient pas*. Paris: Editions de Minuit, 1957.
Morin, Edgar. *Autocritique*. Paris: Seuil, 1970. Reprint, 1975.
Muller, Annette. *La Petite fille du Vel'd'hiv'*. Paris: Denoël, 1991.
Nodot, René. *Les enfants ne partiront pas; Témoignages sur la déportation des Juifs, Lyon et sa région, 1942–1943*. Lyon: Imprimerie Nouvelle Lyonnaise, 1970.
———. "Résistance non–violente, 1940–1944; Mémoires." Typewritten manuscript, 1978.
Papanek, Ernst, with Edward Linn. *Out of Fire*. New York: Morrow, 1975.
Poliakov, Léon. *L'Auberge des musiciens*. Paris: Mazarine, 1981.
Pougatch, Isaac. *Charry*. Paris: Oreste Zeluck Editions, 1945.
Ratz, Joseph. *La France que je cherchais*. Limoges: Imprimerie A. Bontemps, 1945.
Ravannel, Serge. *L'esprit de résistance*. Paris: Seuil, 1995.
Rayski, Adam. *Nos Illusions perdues*. Paris: Balland, 1985.
Schramm, Hanna, and Barbara Vormeier. *Vivre à Gurs; Un camp de concentration français, 1940–1941*. Paris: Maspero, 1979.
Shrager, Fayvel. *Un militant juif*. Paris: Editions Polyglottes, 1979.
Spire, André. *Souvenirs à bâtons rompus*. Paris: Albin Michel, 1979.
Steindling, Dolly. *Vinah, Tsarfat, Vinah: Kortav shel palit ve-lohem-mahteret Yehudi*. Jerusalem: Rubin Mass and Hebrew University, 1989. Published in English as *No Past!—No Present!—No Future!: An Austrian Jew in the French Resistance*. Bethesda: University of Maryland, 2000.
Vallat, Xavier. *Le Nez de Cléopâtre; Souvenirs d'un homme de droite, 1919–1944*. Paris: Editions Les Quatre Fils Aymon, 1957.
Vidal-Naquet, Pierre. *Mémoires. La brisure et l'attente, 1930–1955*. Paris: Seuil-La Découverte, 1995.
Vigée, Claude. *La Lune d'hiver*. Paris: Flammarion, 1970.
Villon, Pierre. *Résistant de la première heure*. Interview by Claude Willard. Paris: Editions Sociales-Messidor, 1983.
Vogel, David. *Et ils partirent pour la guerre*. Translated from Hebrew by Rosie Pinhas-Delpuech. Paris: Denoël, 1993.
Weill, Joseph. "Déjà!. . . Essai autobiographique." Typewritten manuscript, n.d.
Weill-Curiel, André. Règles de savoir-vivre à l'usage d'un jeune Juif de mes amis. Paris: Editions du Myrte, 1945.

——. *Le Temps de la honte*. 3 vols. Paris: Editions du Myrte, 1945.
Wellers, Georges. *L'Étoile jaune à l'heure de Vichy*. Paris: Fayard, 1973. Reprinted as *Un Juif sous Vichy*. Paris: Editions Tirésias, 1991.

BOOKS AND THESES

Abitbol, Michel. *Les Deux Terres promises; Les Juifs de France et le sionisme*. Paris: Olivier Orban, 1989.
——. *Les Juifs d'Afrique du Nord sous Vichy*. Paris: Maisonneuve et Larose, 1983.
Activité des organisations juives en France sous l'occupation. Paris: Centre de documentation juive contemporaine, 1947, repr. 1983.
Adler, Jacques. *The Jews of Paris and the Final Solution: Communal Response and Internal Conflicts, 1940–1944*. New York: Oxford University Press, 1987.
Alexis-Monet, Laurette. *Les Miradors de Vichy*. With a preface by Pierre Vidal-Naquet. Paris: Editions de Paris, 1994.
Andrieu, Claire. *La Banque sous l'Occupation*. Paris: FNSP, 1990.
Appelbaum-Rosengart, Laurence. *Qui est Juif? L'oeuvre législative du régime de Vichy*. Diss., Institut d'Etudes Politiques, Paris, 1990.
Aron, Robert. *Histoire de Vichy*. Paris: Fayard, 1954.
Audiat, Pierre. *Paris pendant la guerre*. Paris: Hachette, 1966.
Avni, Haïm. *Spain, the Jews, and Franco*. Philadelphia: Jewish Publication Society of America, 1982.
Azéma, Jean-Pierre. *La Collaboration, 1940–1944*. Paris: PUF, 1975.
——. *From Munich to the Liberation, 1938–1944*. London: Cambridge University Press; Paris: Editions de la Maison des Sciences de l'Homme, 1984.
——. *1940, L'Année terrible*. Paris: Seuil, 1990.
Azéma, Jean-Pierre, and François Bédarida. *La France des années noires*. 2 vols. Paris: Seuil, 1993.
——. *Vichy et les Français*. Paris: Fayard, 1992.
Azéma, Jean-Pierre, Antoine Prost, and Jean-Pierre Rioux. eds. *Le Parti communiste des années sombres, 1938–1941*. Paris: Seuil, 1986.
Badia, Gilbert, et al. *Les Barbelés de l'exil*. Grenoble: Presses Universitaires de Grenoble, 1979.
Bartosek, Karel, René Gallissot, and Denis Peschanski, eds. *De l'exil à la Résistance*. Paris: Arcantère, 1989.
Baruch, Marc-Olivier. *Le régime de Vichy*. Paris: La Découverte, 1996.
Bauer, Yehuda. *American Jewry and the Holocaust: The American Jewish Joint Distribution Committee, 1939–1945*. Detroit: Wayne State University Press, 1981.
Bédarida, François, ed. *La Politique nazie d'extermination*. Paris: Albin Michel, 1989.
Bédarida, Renée. *Les Armes de l'esprit; Témoignage Chrétien, 1941–1944*. Paris: Editions Ouvrières, 1977.
——. *Pierre Chaillet*. Paris: Fayard, 1988.
Bensimon, Doris. *Les Grandes rafles*. Toulouse: Privat, 1987.
Berg, Roger. *La Persécution raciale*. Paris: Office Français d'Edition, 1947.
Berkovitz, Jay. *The Shaping of Jewish Identity in Nineteenth-Century France*. Detroit: Wayne State University Press, 1989.
Bertin-Maghit, Jean-Pierre. *Le Cinéma sous l'Occupation*. Paris: Olivier Orban, 1989.
Birnbaum, Pierre. *La France aux Français; Histoire des haines nationalistes*. Paris: Seuil, 1993.
——, ed. *La France de l'affaire Dreyfus*. Paris: Gallimard, 1994.
——, ed. *Histoire politique des Juifs de France*. Paris: Presses de la Fondation Nationale des Sciences Politiques, 1990.
——. *The Jews of the Republic: A Political History of State Jews from Gambetta to Vichy*. Stanford: Stanford University Press, 1996.

———. *Un mythe politique: La République juive*. Paris: Fayard, 1988.
Blumenkranz, Bernard, ed. *Histoire des Juifs de France*. Toulouse: Privat, 1972.
Boegner, Philippe. *"Ici, on a aimé les Juifs"; Le Chambon-sur-Lignon*. Paris: Jean-Claude Lattes, 1982.
Boursier, Jean-Yves. *La Guerre de partisans dans le sud-ouest de la France, 1942–1944; La 35ᵉ brigade FTP-MOI*. Paris: L'Harmattan, 1992.
Braibant, Charles. *La Guerre à Paris*. Paris: Corréa, 1945.
Burns, Michael. *Dreyfus, a Family Affair: From the French Revolution to the Holocaust*. New York: HarperCollins, 1992.
Burrin, Philippe. *La Dérive fasciste, Doriot, Déat, Bergery (1933–1945)*. Paris: Seuil, 1986.
———. *Hitler and the Jews: The Genesis of the Holocaust*. London: Arnold; New York: Routledge, Chapman and Hall, 1994.
Capelle, Christophe. "La Destruction des Juifs de Seine-Inférieure." 2 vols. Master's thesis, Rouen, 1991.
Caron, Vicki. *Between France and Germany: The Jews of Alsace-Lorraine, 1871–1918*. Stanford: Stanford University Press, 1988.
Carpi, Daniel. *Between Mussolini and Hitler: The Jews and the Italian Authorities in France and Tunisia*. Hanover, N.H.: Brandeis University Press / University Press of New England, 1994.
Chaigneau, Jean-François. *Le Dernier Wagon*. Paris: Julliard, 1981.
Cohen, Asher. *Persécutions et sauvetages; Juifs et Français sous l'Occupation et sous Vichy*. With a preface by René Rémond. Paris: Cerf, 1993.
Cohen, Monique-Lise, and Eric Malo, eds. *Les Camps du sud-ouest de la france, 1939–1944. Exclusion, internement, déportation*. Toulouse: Privat, 1994.
Cohen, Richard I. *The Burden of Conscience: French Leadership during the Holocaust*. Bloomington: Indiana University Press, 1987.
Cohen-Albert, Phyllis. *The Modernization of French Jewry: Consistory and Community in the Nineteenth Century*. Hanover, N.H.: University Press of New England, 1977.
Cointet, Jean-Paul. *Pierre Laval*. Paris: Fayard, 1993.
Cointet-Labrousse, Michèle. *Vichy et le fascisme*. Brussels: Complexe, 1987.
Comte, Bernard. *Une utopie combattante; L'école des cadres d'Uriage*. Paris: Fayard, 1992.
Conan, Eric. *Sans oublier les enfants; les camps de Pithiviers et de Beaune-la-Rolande, 19 juillet–16 septembre 1942*. Paris: Grasset, 1991.
Courtois, Stéphane. *Le PCF dans la guerre*. Paris: Ramsay, 1980.
Courtois, Stéphane, Denis Peschanski, and Adam Rayski, eds. *Le Sang de l'étranger*. Paris: Fayard, 1989.
Courtois, Stéphane, and Adam Rayski, eds. With the collaboration of Philippe Burrin, Claude Lévy, Denis Peschanski, and Renée Poznanski. *Qui savait quoi?* Paris: La Découverte, 1987.
De Montclos, Xavier, Monique Luirad, François Delpech, and Pierre Bolle, eds. *Églises et chrétiens dans la Seconde Guerre Mondiale, La France*. Acts of the colloquium held in January 1978 in Grenoble. Presses Universitaires de Lyon, 1982.
———. *Églises et chrétiens dans la Seconde Guerre Mondiale; La région Rhône-Alpes*. Acts of the colloquium held in October 1976 in Grenoble. Presses Universitaires de Lyon, 1978.
De Rochebrune, Renaud, and Jean-Claude Hazera. *Les patrons sous l'Occupation*. Paris: Odile Jacob, 1995.
Delpech, François. *Sur les Juifs; Études d'histoire contemporaine*. Presses Universitaires de Lyon, 1984.
Delperrie de Bayac, Jacques. *Histoire de la Milice*. Paris: Fayard, 1969.
Diamant, David. *Le Billet vert:* La vie et la Resistance à Pithiviers et Beaune-la-Rolande, camps pour Juifs, camps pour Chretiens, camps pour Patriotes. Paris: Editions du Renouveau, 1977.
———. *Héros juifs de la Résistance française*. Paris: Editions du Renouveau, 1962.
———. *Jeune Combat; La jeunesse juive dans la Résistance*. Paris: L'Harmattan, 1992.
———. *Les Juifs dans la Résistance française, 1940–1944* (avec armes ou sans armes), Roger Maria Éditeur, Paris: La pavillon, 1971.
Douzou, Laurent. "Le Mouvement de résistance Libération–sud (1940–1944)". Diss., Uni-

versity of Paris I–Sorbonne, 1993. Published as *La désobéissance. Histoire du mouvement Libération–sud*. Paris: Odile Jacob, 1995.
Le droit antisémite de Vichy, Le Genre humain. Paris: Seuil, 1996.
Duquesne, Jacques. *Les Catholiques français sous l'Occupation*. Paris: Grasset, 1966.
Durand, Yves. *La France dans la Deuxième Guerre mondiale*. Paris: Armand Colin, 1989.
Duroselle, Jean-Baptiste. *L'Abîme, 1939–1945*. Paris: Imprimeries Nationales, 1982.
Eck, Hélène, ed. *La Guerre des ondes*. With a preface by Jean-Noël Jeanneney. Paris: Armand Colin, 1985.
Epelbaum, Didier. *Aloïs Brunner*. With a preface by Serge Klarsfeld. Paris: Calmann-Lévy, 1990.
Epstein, Simon. *Les Institutions israélites françaises de 1929 à 1939. Solidarité juive et lutte contre l'antisémitisme*. Diss., University of Paris I–Sorbonne, 1990.
Études sur la France de 1939 à nos jours; L'histoire. Paris: Seuil, 1985.
Ferro, Marc. *Pétain*. Paris: Fayard, 1987.
Fink, Carole. *Marc Bloch: A Life in History*. New York: Cambridge University Press, 1989.
Font, Christian, and Henri Moizet. *Les Juifs et l'antisémitisme en Aveyron pendant la Deuxième Guerre mondiale*. CRDP de l'Aveyron, 1994.
Fontaine, André. *Le Camp d'étrangers des Milles, 1939–1943*. Aix-en-Provence: Edisud, 1989.
Fouché, Pascal. *L'Edition française sous l'Occupation*. 2 vols. Paris: Bibliothèque de Littérature Française Contemporaine de L'Université Paris 7, 1987.
Froment, Pascale. *René Bousquet*. Paris: Stock, 1994.
Gervereau, Laurent, and Densi Peschanski. *La Propagande sous Vichy, 1940–1944*. Paris: BDIC, 1990.
Girard, Patrick. *Les Juifs de France de 1789 à 1860*. Paris: Calmann-Lévy, 1976.
Gloire éternelle aux héros juifs de la Résistance française. Paris: Union des Juifs pour la Résistance et l'Entraide, 1963.
Graetz, Michael. *Les Juifs en France au XIX*[e] *siècle*. Paris: Seuil, 1982.
Grandjonc, Jacques, and Theresia Grundtner eds. *Zone d'ombres, 1933–1944*. Paris: Alinea, 1990.
Green, Nancy. *Les Travailleurs immigrés juifs à la Belle Époque*. Paris: Fayard, 1985.
Grynberg, Anne. *Les Camps de la honte*. Paris: La Découverte, 1991.
Haft, Cynthia. *The Bargain and the Bridle: The General Union of the Israelites of France, 1941–1944*. Chicago: Dialog Press, 1983.
Hallie, Philip P. *Lest Innocent Blood Be Shed. The Story of the Village of Le Chambon, and How Goodness Happened There*. New York: Harper & Row, 1979.
Halls, Wilfred Douglas. *Les Jeunes et la politique de Vichy*. With a preface by Jean-Pierre Rioux. Paris: Syros-Alternatives, 1988.
Haymann, Emmanuel. *Le Camp du bout du monde; 1942, des enfants juifs de France à la frontière suisse*. Lausanne: P-M Favre Editions, 1984.
Hazan, Katy. *La Persécution des Juifs dans quelques procès d'épuration et de collaboration* Diss., Institut d'Etudes Politiques, Paris, 1993.
Hilberg, Raul. *The Destruction of the European Jews*. Rev. ed. 3 vols. New York: Holmes and Meier, 1985.
Hoffmann, Stanley. *Essais sur la France: Déclin ou renouveau?*. Paris: Seuil, 1974.
Husson, Jocelyne. *La Déportation des Juifs de la Marne*. Diss., University of Reims, Champagne–Ardenne, 1993.
Hyman, Paula E. *The Emancipation of the Jews of Alsace*. New Haven: Yale University Press, 1991.
———. *From Dreyfus to Vichy: The Remaking of French Jewry, 1906–1939*. New York: Columbia University Press, 1979.
Israël, Gérard. *Heureux comme Dieu en France*. Paris: Robert Laffont, 1975.
Jäckel, Eberhard. *La France dans l'Europe de Hitler*. Paris: Fayard, 1966.
Job, Françoise. *Gustave Nordon, 1877–1944*. With a preface by André Kaspi. Nancy: Presses Universitaires de Nancy, 1992.
Joutard, Philippe. *Ces voix qui nous viennent du passé*. Paris: Hachette, 1983.

Joutard, Philippe, Jacques Poujoul, and Patrick Cabanel, eds. *Cévennes: Terre de refuge, 1940–1944*. Montpellier: Presses du Languedoc, 1987.
Joutard, Philippe, and François Marcot, eds. *Les Étrangers dans la Résistance en France*. Besançon: Musée de la Résistance et de la Déportation, 1992.
Kahn, Annette. *Le Fichier*. With a preface by Serge Klarsfeld. Paris: Robert Laffont, 1993.
Kaspi, André, and Antoine Marès, eds. *Le Paris des étrangers*. Paris: Imprimerie Nationale, 1990.
Kaspi, André. *Les Juifs pendant l'Occupation*. Paris: Seuil, 1991.
Kedward, Roderick H. *Resistance in Vichy France; A Study of Ideas and Motivation in the Southern Zone, 1940–1942*. Oxford: Oxford University Press, 1978.
Kedward, Roderick H., and Roger Austin, eds. *Vichy France and the Resistance, Culture and Ideology*. London: Croom Helm, 1985.
Kershaw, Ian. *Qu'est-ce que le nazisme? Problèmes et perspectives d'interprétation*. Paris: Gallimard, 1992.
Klarsfeld, Serge. *L'Etoile des Juifs*. Paris: L'Archipel, 1992.
———, ed. *Il y a cinquante ans: Le statut des Juifs*. Paris: CDJC, 1991.
Klatzmann, Joseph. *Le Travail à domicile dans l'industrie parisienne du vêtement*. Paris: Armand Colin, 1957.
Klein, Théo. *Oublier Vichy? A propos de l'arrêt Touvier*. Paris: Critérion, 1992.
Knout, David. *La Résistance juive en France*. Paris: Editions du Centre, 1947.
Kupferman, Fred. *Laval, 1883–1945*. Paris: Flammarion, 1988.
L'Allemagne nazie et le génocide juif. Colloquium at the École des Hautes Études en Sciences Sociales. Paris: Gallimard/Le Seuil, 1985.
La Mémoire des Français; 40 ans de commémorations de la Seconde Guerre mondiale. Paris: Editions du Centre National de Recherche Scientifique, 1986.
Laborie, Pierre. *L'opinion française sous Vichy*. Paris: Seuil, 1990.
Laharie, Claude. *Le Camp de Gurs, 1939–1945; Un aspect méconnu de l'histoire du Béarn*. Pau: Infocompo, 1985.
Laloum, Jean. *La France antisémite de Darquier de Pellepoix*. Paris: Syros, 1979.
Lambert, Annie. *Les Juifs dispersés de quatre départements bretons face à l'antisémitisme institutionnalisé: 1939–1945*. Diss., University of Haute-Bretagne, 1990.
Landau, Philippe E. *Les Juifs et la Grande Guerre; 1914–1941, Patrie, République, Mémoire* Diss., University of Paris, 1992.
Laroche, Gaston. *On les nommait des étrangers; Les immigrés dans la Résistance*. Paris: Les Editeurs Réunis, 1965.
Latour, Annie. *La Résistance juive en France*. Paris: Stock, 1970.
Lazare, Lucien. L'abbé Glasberg. Paris: Cerf, 1990.
———. *Le Livre des Justes*. Paris: Jean-Claude Lattès, 1993.
———. *Rescue as Resistance: How Jewish Organizations Fought the Holocaust in France*. New York: Columbia University Press, 1996.
Lefébure, Antoine. *Les Conversations secrètes des Français sous l'Occupation*. Paris: Plon, 1993.
Lemalet, Martine, ed. *Au secours des enfants du siècle, regards croisés sur l'OSE*. Paris: Nil Editions, 1993.
Lévy, Claude. *Les Parias de la Résistance*. Paris: Calmann-Lévy, 1970.
Lévy, Claude, and Paul Tillard. *Betrayal at the Vel d'hiv*. New York: Hill and Wang, 1967.
Marcou, Jean. *Le Conseil d'État sous Vichy* Diss., Grenoble, 1984.
Marrus, Michael R. *The Holocaust in History*. Hanover, N.H.: University Press of New England, 1987.
———. *The Politics of Assimilation, A Study of the French Jewish Community at the Time of the Dreyfus Affair*. New York: Oxford University Press, 1971.
———. *The Unwanted: European Refugees in the Twentieth Century*. New York: Oxford University Press, 1985.
Marrus, Michael R., and Robert O. Paxton. *Vichy France and the Jews*. New York: Basic Books, 1981. Reprint, Schocken Books, 1983.

Mayer, Daniel. *Les Socialistes dans la Résistance*. Paris: PUF, 1968.
Michaelis, Meir. *Mussolini and the Jews: German-Italian Relations and the Jewish Question in Italy, 1922–1945*. Oxford: Clarendon Press, 1978.
Michel, Alain. *Les Eclaireurs israélites de France pendant la Seconde Guerre mondiale*. Paris: Editions des EIF, 1984.
Michel, Henry. *Paris Allemand*. Paris: Albin Michel, 1982.
——. *Vichy—Année 40*. Paris: Laffont, 1966.
Millman, Richard. *La Question juive entre les deux guerres; ligues de droite et anti-sémitisme en France*. Paris: Armand, Colin, 1992.
Milza, Pierre. *Fascisme français, Passé et présent*. Paris: Flammarion, 1987.
Moch, Maurice in *L'Etoile et la francisque; Les institutions juives sous Vichy*, edited by Alain Michel, Paris: Cerf, 1990.
Nicault, Catherine. *La France et le sionisme, 1897–1948*. Paris: Calmann-Lévy, 1992.
Nicolaïdis, Dimitri, ed. *Oublier nos crimes; L'amnésie nationale, une spécificité française*. Paris: Editions Autrement, 1994.
Novick, Pierre. *The Resistance versus Vichy, The Purge of Collaborators in Liberated France*. London: Chatto and Windus, 1968.
Oppetit, Christian, ed. *Marseille, Vichy et les nazis: Le temps des rafles; la déportation des juifs*. With a preface by Pierre Vidal-Naquet. Marseille: Amicale des déportés d'Auschwitz et des camps de Haute-Silésie, 1993.
Ory, Pascal. *Les Collaborateurs, 1940–1945*. Paris: Seuil, 1976.
Paxton, Robert O. *Vichy France, Old Guard and New Order, 1940–1944*. New York: Columbia University Press, 1972.
Perrault, Gilles. *Paris sous l'Occupation*. With commentary by Jean-Pierre Azéma. Paris: Belfond, 1987.
Philippe, Béatrice. *Etre juif dans la société française*. Paris: Montalba, 1979.
Pierrard, Pierre. *Juifs et catholiques français; De Drumont à Jules Isaac (1886–1945)*. Paris: Fayard, 1970.
Poliakov, Léon. *L'Etoile jaune*. Paris: Editions du Centre, 1949.
Polonski, Jacques. *La Presse, la propagande et l'opinion publique*. Paris: Editions du Centre, 1946.
Pressac, Jean-Claude. *Les Crématoires d'Auschwitz; La machinerie du meurtre de masse*. Paris: CNRS Editions, 1993.
Ragache, Gilles, and Jean-Robert Ragache. *La Vie quotidienne des écrivains et des artistes sous l'Occupation, 1940–1944*. Paris: Hachette, 1988.
Rajsfus, Maurice. *L'An prochain la révolution; Les communistes juifs immigrés dans la tourmente stalinienne, 1930–1945*. Paris: Mazarine, 1985.
——. *Des Juifs dans la collaboration; l'Union générale des israélites de France*. With a preface by Pierre Vidal-Naquet. Paris: EDI, 1980.
——. *Drancy, un camp de concentration très ordinaire, 1941–1944*. Levallois-Perret: Manya, 1991.
——. *Jeudi noir, 50 ans après: La rafle du 16 juillet 1942*. Levallois-Perret: Manya, 1992.
——. *Une Terre Promise? Des Juifs dans la collaboration (II)*. Paris: L'Harmattan, 1989.
Ravine, Jacques. *La Résistance organisée des Juifs en France*. Paris: Julliard, 1973.
Rayski, Adam. *Le Choix des Juifs sous Vichy; Entre soumission et résistance*. With a preface by François Bédarida. Paris: La Découverte, 1992.
Regnier, Hélène. *La Déportation des Juifs en Haute-Garonne de 1942 à 1944*. Diss., University of Toulouse Le Mirail, 1990.
Rémond, René. *Le "Fichier juif"*(Report of the commission presided over by René Rémond). Paris: Plon, 1996.
——, ed. *Le Gouvernement de Vichy, 1970–1972*. Paris: Presses de la FNSP, 1972
Rémy, Dominique. *Les Lois de Vichy*. Paris: Romillat, 1992.
RHICOJ. *Les Juifs dans la Résistance et la Libération; Histoire, témoignages, débats*. Paris: Le Scribe, 1985.
Rings, Werner. *Life With the Enemy. Collaboration and Resistance in Hitler's Europe, 1939–1945*. New York: Doubleday, 1982.

Rioux, Jean-Pierre, ed. *La Vie culturelle sous Vichy*. Brussels: Complexe, 1990.
Roblin, Michel. *Les Juifs de Paris*. Paris: Editions A. et J. Picard, 1952.
Rossignol, Dominique. *Histoire de la propagande en France de 1940 à 1944*. Paris: PUF, 1991.
Rousso, Henry. *Les Années noires; Vivre sous l'Occupation*. Paris: Gallimard, 1992.
———. *Pétain et la fin de la collaboration*. Brussels: Complexe, 1984.
———. *The Vichy Syndrome; History and Memory in France Since 1944*. Cambridge, Mass.: Harvard University Press, 1991.
Sauvy, Alfred. *La Vie économique des Français*. Paris: Flammarion, 1978.
Schnapper, Dominique. *Jewish Identities in France: An Analysis of Contemporary French Jewry*. Chicago: University of Chicago Press, 1984.
Schor, Ralph. *L'Antisémitisme en France pendant les années trente*. Brussels: Complexe, 1992.
———. *Un évêque dans le siècle: Mgr Paul Rémond (1873–1963)*. Nice: Editions Serre, 1984.
———. *L'Opinion française et les étrangers*. Paris: Publications de la Sorbonne, 1985.
Schöttler, Peter. *Lucie Varga: Les autorités invisibles*. Paris: Cerf, 1991.
Schwarzfuchs, Simon. *Du juif à l'israélite*. Paris: Fayard, 1989.
Sémelin, Jacques. *Sans armes face à Hitler; La résistance civile en Europe, 1939–1943*. With a preface by Jean-Pierre Azéma. Paris: Payot, 1989.
Shapiro, Léon. *The History of ORT: A Jewish Movement for Social Change*. New York: Schocken Books, 1980.
Simon, Lucien. *Les Juifs à Nîmes et dans le Gard durant la Deuxième Guerre mondiale*. Nîmes: Lacour Librairie-Editeur, 1985.
Singer, Claude. "Le Cinéma en France pendant l'Occupation et les Juifs." Master's thesis, University of Paris I–Sorbonne, 1980.
———. *Vichy, l'université et les Juifs*. Paris: Les Belles Lettres, 1992.
Sirinelli, Jean-François , ed. *Histoire des droites en France*. 3 vols. Paris: Gallimard, 1992.
Spire, Antoine. *Ces enfants qui nous manquent, Izieu, 6 avril 1944*. With a preface by Elie Wiesel. Paris: Maren Sell, 1990.
Steinberg, Lucien. *La Révolte des justes; Les Juifs contre Hitler*. Paris: Fayard, 1970.
Steinberg, Maxime. *L'Étoile et le fusil*. 3 vols. Brussels: Editions Vie Ouvrière, 1983.
Sternhell, Zeev. *Ni droite, ni gauche; L'idéologie fasciste en France*. Paris: Seuil, 1987.
Sweets, John F. *Choices in Vichy France*. New York: Oxford University Press, 1996.
Szajkowski, Zosa. *Jews and the French Foreign Legion*. New York: Ktav, 1975.
Thalmann, Rita. *La Mise au pas; Idéologie et stratégie sécuritaire dans la France occupée*. Paris: Fayard, 1991.
Tocze, Claude. *L'Antisémitisme économique, aryanisation de l'économie et spoliation des Juifs en Bretagne de 1940 à 1944* Diss., University of Haute-Bretagne, Rennes II, 1990.
Todorov, Tzvetan. *A French Tragedy: Scenes of Civil War, Summer 1944*. Hanover, N.H. University Press of New England, 1996.
Vegh, Claudine. *Je ne lui ai pas dit au revoir; Des enfants de déportés parlent*. With a preface by Bruno Bettelheim. Paris: Gallimard, 1979.
Veillon, Dominique *La Collaboration*. Paris: Le Livre de Poche, 1984.
———. *Le Franc-Tireur, un journal clandestin, un mouvement de résistance, 1940–1944*. Paris: Flammarion, 1977.
———. *La Mode sous l'Occupation*. Paris: Payot, 1990.
Vidal-Naquet, Pierre. *Les Assassins de la mémoire*. Paris: La Découverte, 1987.
———. *Les Juifs, la mémoire et le présent*. 2 vols. Paris: La Découvert, 1981 and 1991.
Vormeier, Barbara. *La Déportation des Juifs allemands et autrichiens de France*. Paris: Editions La Solidarité, 1980.
Walter, Gérard. *La Vie à Paris sous l'Occupation*. Paris: Armand Colin, 1960.
Weill, Joseph. *Contribution à l'histoire des camps d'internement dans l'Anti-France*. Paris: Editions du Centre, 1946.
Weinberg, David. *A Community on Trial: The Jews of Paris in the 1930s*. Chicago: University of Chicago Press, 1977.
Weisberg, Richard H. *Vichy Law and the Holocaust in France*. New York: Harwood Academic Publishers and New York University Press, 1996.

Wellers, Georges, André Kaspi, and Serge Klarsfeld (editors). *La France et la question juive, 1940–1944*. Acts of the colloquium held at the CDJC, March 10–12, 1979. Paris: Editions Sylvie Messinger, 1981.
Wellers, Georges. *Un Juif sous Vichy*. Paris: Editions Tiresias, 1991.
Wieviorka, Annette. *Déportation et génocide; entre la mémoire et l'oubli*. Paris: Plon, 1992.
——. *Ils étaient juifs, résistants, communistes*. Paris: Denoël, 1986.
Wieviorka, Olivier. *Une certaine idée de la Résistance: Défense de la France, 1940–1949*. Paris: Seuil, 1995.
Winock, Michel. *Nationalisme, antisémitisme et fascisme en France*. Paris: Seuil, 1982.
Wormser, Georges. *Français israélites*. Paris: Editions de Minuit, 1963.
Wormser-Migot, Olga. *Le Retour des déportés*. Brussels: Complexe, 1985.
Yahil, Leni. *The Holocaust: The Fate of European Jewry, 1932–1945*. New York: Oxford University Press, 1990.
Zeitoun, Sabine. *Ces enfants qu'il fallait sauver*. Paris: Albin Michel, 1989.
——. *L'Oeuvre de secours aux enfants (OSE) sous l'Occupation en France*. Paris: L'Harmattan, 1990.
Zucotti, Susan. *The Holocaust, the French, and the Jews*. New York: Basic Books, 1993.
——. *The Italians and the Holocaust: Persecution, Rescue, Survival*. New York: Basic Books, 1987.

ESSAYS

Ariel, Joseph. "Jewish Self-defence and Resistance in France during World War II." *Yad Vashem Studies* 6 (1967): 221–250.
Avni, Haïm. "The Zionist Underground in Holland and France, and the Escape to Spain." In *Rescue Attempts during the Holocaust*,555–589. Jerusalem: Yad Vashem, 1977.
Baruch, Marc-Olivier, "L'application des statuts des Juifs à la fonction publique." Manuscript. 1992.
Basch, Françoise. "Victor Basch et la passion de justice." *Les Temps modernes* 572 (1994): 13–50.
Bauer, Yehuda. "When did they know?" *Midstream* 4 (1968): 54–58.
Bédarida, François. "L'histoire de la Résistance, lectures d'hier, chantiers de demain." *Vingtième siècle. Revue d'histoire* 11 (juillet–septembre 1986): 75–89.
Belot, Robert. "*Les décombres*, un best-seller sous l'Occupation." *L'Histoire* (special number, *L'Antisémitisme en France*). (October 1991).
Berg, Roger. "Les Juifs dans l'espace politique français." *Pardès* 14 (1991): 33–52.
——. "La question de la restitution des biens juifs." *Le Monde juif* 149 (1993): 120–160.
——. "Toulouse qui fut la capitale de la résistance juive." *Actualités* 7 (1980): 4–5.
Bertin-Maghit, Jean-Pierre. "Les Juifs dans l'économie du cinéma français." Paper delivered at the colloquium Les Juifs et l'économique: Miroirs et mirages. Toulouse, UTM-CIREJ, January 1989.
Caron, Vicki. "Jewish Refugees in France before Vichy." *Journal of Contemporary History* 20 (1985): 157–176.
——. "Loyalties in Conflict: French Jewry and the Refugee Crisis, 1933–1935." *Leo Baeck Institute Yearbook* 36 (1991): 305–338.
——. "The Politics of Frustration: French Jewry and the Refugee Crisis in the 30's." *Journal of Modern History* 65, no. 62 (1993): 311–356.
Cohen, Asher. "Le peuple aryen vu par le CGQJ." *Revue d'histoire moderne et contemporaine* 25 (1988): 482–494.
——. "La presse clandestine face à la question juive de 1940 à 1942." *Le Monde juif* 117 (1985): 1–17.
Cohen, Richard I. "French Jewry's Dilemma on the Orientation of its Leadership, 1942–1944." *Yad Vashem Studies* 14 (1981): 167–204.

———. "Jews and Christians in France during Word War II: a Methodological Essay." In *Judaism and Christianity under the Impact of National Socialism,* edited by O. D. Kulka, and P. R. Mendès-Flohr, 327–340. Jerusalem, 1987.

Cohen-Albert, Phyllis. "Ethnicité et solidarité chez les Juifs de France au XIXe siècle." *Pardès* 3 (1986): 29–53.

Courtois, Stéphane. "Luttes politiques et élaboration d'une histoire: le PCF historien du PCF dans la Deuxième Guerre mondiale." *Communisme* 4 (1983): 5–26.

Delmaire, Danielle, ed. 1942, *L'Année tragique des Juifs du Nord, Tsafon. Revue d'études juives du Nord* 9–10 (1992).

Desvages, Hubert. "Les communistes de l'Isère dans la Résistance." *Cahiers d'histoire* (1980): 299–327.

Eley, Geoff. "Labor History, Social History, *Alltagsgeschichte*: Experience, Culture, and the Politics of the Everyday—a New Direction for German Social History?." *Journal of Modern History* 61 (June 1989): 297–343.

Estèbe, Jean. "Les Juifs en Midi toulousain pendant la Seconde Guerre mondiale: état de la question." *Annales du Midi* 104, nos. 199–200 (1992): 461–475.

Felstiner, Mary, "Commandant de Drancy: Aloïs Brunner et les Juifs de France." *Le Monde juif* 128 (1987): 143–172.

Fink, Carole. "Marc Bloch: l'historien et la Résistance." In *Marc Bloch aujourd'hui, Histoire comparée et sciences sociales,* edited by Astma Hartmut and André Bruguière, 51–64. Paris: Editions de l'EHESS, 1990.

Friedländer, Saul. "Some Reflections on the Historicisation of National Socialism." *Tel Aviver Jahrbuch für deutsche Geschichte* 16 (1987): 310–324.

Gottlieb, Roger S. "The Concept of Resistance: Jewish Resistance during the Holocaust." *Social Theory and Practice,* 9–10 (1983): 31–49.

Goubet, Michel. "La résistance toulousaine, structures, objectifs (printemps–été 1944)." *Revue d'histoire de la Deuxième Guerre mondiale* 99 (1975): 25–44.

Greilsammer, Ilan. "The Democratization of a Community: French Jewry and the FSJU." *Jewish Journal of Sociology* 21 (1979): 109–124.

Grynberg, Anne. "Une découverte récente: le fonds d'archives de la Commission des camps (1941–1943)." *Le Monde juif* 131 (1988): 108–130.

———, "Le grand rabbin Hirschler, aumônier général des camps d'internement (1905–1945)." *Combat pour la Diaspora* 23–24 (1988): 35–47.

Hamon, Léo, and Renée Poznanski, *Cahiers de l'Institut l'histoire du temps présente* 22 (December 1992).

Hoffmann, Stanley. "Aspects du régime de Vichy." *Revue de la FNSP* (1956): 44–69.

Iancu, Carol. "Les Juifs à Montpellier pendant la Deuxième Guerre mondiale." In *Les Juifs à Montpellier et dans le Languedoc. Du Moyen Age à nos jours,* edited by Carol Iancu, 337–99. Montpellier: Centre de Recherches et d'etudes juives et hébraïques, 1988.

Judt, Tony. "'We Have Discovered History': Defeat, Resistance, and the Intellectuals in France." *Journal of Modern History* 64, supp. (1992): 147–172.

"Les Juifs de France et d'Algerie pendant la Seconde Guerre mondiale." *Yod* 15–16 (1982). Kaspi, André, "Le Juif et la France: Une exposition à Paris en 1941." *Le monde juif* 79 (1975): 8–20.

Kaspi, André, Annie Kriegel, and Annette Wieviorka, eds. *Les Juifs de France dans la Seconde Guerre mondiale. Pardès* (special issue) 16 (1992).

Kedward, Roderick H. "The Vichy of the Other Philippe." In *Politics and Culture during the Nazi Occupation, 1940–1944,* edited by Gerard Hirschfeld and Patrick Marsh, 32–46. Oxford and Munich: Berg, 1989.

Kieval, Hillel J. "Legality and Resistance in Vichy France: The Rescue of Jewish Children." *Proceedings of the Philosophical Society* 124, no. 5 (October 1980): 339–366.

Knobel, Marc. "Etude d'un registre d'inscription d'une école parisienne, Fanny, Béatrice, Esther, Rose et les autres." *Le Monde juif* 134 (1989): 60–65.

Kriegel, Annie. "De la résistance juive." *Pardès* 2 (1985): 191–209.

———. "Pouvoir politique et expression communautaire: le CRIF." *Pardès* 3 (1986), 199–206.

——. "Résistants communistes et Juifs persécutés." In *Réflexions sur les questions juives,* 29–58. Paris: Hachette, 1984.
Laborie, Pierre. "The Jewish Statutes in Vichy France and Public Opinion." *Yad Vashem Studies* 22 (1992): 89–114.
Laguerre, Bernard. "Les dénaturalisés de Vichy, 1940–1944." *Vingtième siècle, Revue d'histoire* (October–December 1988): 3–15.
Laloum, Jean. "L'UGIF et ses maisons d'enfants: le centre de Montreuil-sous-Bois." *Le Monde juif* 116 (1984): 153–172.
——. "L'UGIF et ses maisons d'enfants: l'enlèvement d'une enfant." *Le Monde juif* 124 (1976): 172–176.
——. "L'UGIF et ses maisons d'enfants: Témoignages." *Le Monde juif* 139 (1990): 121–145.
Landau, Philippe E. "Religion et patrie: les prières israélites pour la France." *Pardès* 14 (1991): 11–32.
Lavabre, Marie-Claire, and Denis Peschanski. "L'histoire pour boussole? Note sur l'historiographie communiste, 1977–1981." *Communisme* 4 (1983): 105–114.
Leveau, Rémi, and Dominique Schnapper. "Etre immigré en France." *Histoire de la vie privée, de la Première Guerre mondiale à nos jours edited by Antoine Prost and Gérard Vincent,* 491–525. Paris: Seuil, 1987.
Lévy, Claude. "La Résistance juive en France. De l'enjeu de mémoire à l'histoire critique." *Vingtième siècle. Revue d'histoire* 22 (1989): 117–128.
Lindenberg, Daniel. "Guerres de mémoire en France." *Vingtième siècle. Revue d'histoire* 42 (1994): 77–95.
Lochak, Danièle. "La doctrine sous Vichy ou les mésaventures du positivisme." In *Les Usages sociaux du droit,* 250–285. Paris: Presses Universitaires de France, 1989.
Luirard, Monique. "Les Juifs dans la Loire pendant la Seconde Guerre mondiale." *Cahiers d'histoire* 16, no. 2 (1971): 181–215.
Malo, Éric. "Le camp de Noé (Haute-Garonne) de 1941 à 1944." *Les Annales du Midi* 100, no. 183 (July–September 1983): 337–352.
Marcot, François. "La Résistance et la population; relations d'une avant-garde et des masses." *Guerres mondiales et conflits contemporains* 146 (1987): 3–22.
Marrus, Michael R. "French Churches and the Persecution of Jews in France, 1940–1944." In *Judaism and Christianity under the Impact of National Socialism,* edited by O. D. Kulka and P. R. Mendès-Flohr, 305–326. Jerusalem, 1987.
——. "Jewish Leadership and the Holocaust: The Case of France." In *Living with Antisemitism: Modern Jewish Responses,* edited by Jehuda Reinharz, 380–396. Hanover, N.H.: University Press of New England, 1987.
——. The Strange Story of Herschel Grynspan." *American Scholar* 57 no. 1 (1987–88): 69–79.
Mayeur, Jean-Marie. "Les Églises devant la persécution des Juifs en France pendant la Seconde Guerre mondiale." *Commentaire* (Summer 1981): 254–263.
Michel, Henri. "Jewish Resistance and the European Resistance Movement." *Yad Vashem Studies* 7 (1968): 7–16.
Panicacci, Jean-Louis. "Les Juifs et la question juive dans les Alpes-Maritimes de 1939 à 1945." *Recherches régionales, Côte d'Azur et contrées limitrophe* 3 (1983): 239–327.
Peschanski, Denis. "Le régime de Vichy a existé. Gouvernants et gouvernés dans la France de Vichy, juillet 1940–avril 1942" In *Vichy, 1940–1944: Archives de guerre d'Angelo Tasca,* edited by Denis Pechanski, 3–49. Paris and Milan: Editions du CNRS and Fondation Giangiacomo Feltrinelli, 1985.
——. "La répression anticommuniste dans le département de la Seine (1940–1942)." In *Vichy, 1940–1944, Archives de guerre d'Angelo Tasca,* edited by Denis Peschanski, 111–137. Paris and Milan: Editions du CNRS and Fondation Giangiacomo Feltrinelli, 1985.
——. "The Statutes on Jews—October 3, 1940 and June 2, 1941." *Yad Vashem Studies* 22 (1922): 65–88.
——. "Vichy au singulier, Vichy au pluriel. Une tentative avortée d'encadrement de la société (1941–1942)." *Annales, ESC* 3 (May–June 1988): 639–661.
Poliakov, Léon. "An Opinion Poll on Anti-Jewish Measures in Vichy France." *Jewish Social Studies* 15, no. 1 (1953): 135–150.

——. "Les différentes formes de la résistance juive en France." In *Jewish Resistance during the* Holocaust, edited by Moshe Kohn, 524–532. Jerusalem: Yad Vashem, 1971.
Poznanski, Renée. "Avant les premières grandes rafles. Les Juifs à Paris sous l'Occupation (juin 1940–avril 1941)." In Léo Hamon and Renée Poznanski, *Cahiers de l'Institut d'histoire du temps présent* 22 (December 1992): 25–56.
——. "La création du centre de documentation juive contemporaine en France (Avril 1943)." *Vingtième siècle, Revue d'histoire* 63 (July–Sept. 1999): 51–64.
——. "Des Juifs parlent aux Français: Le document vert de Henri Hertz (1942)." In *Transmission et passages en monde juif,* edited by Esther Benbassa, 201–225. Paris: Publisud, 1997.
——. "L'héritage de la guerre: le sionisme en France dans les années 1944–1947." In *Les Juifs de France, le sionisme et l'Etat d'Israël,* edited by Doris Bensimon and Benjamin Pincus, 237–273. Acts of the International Colloquium of 1987. Paris: Publications Langues Orientales, 1989.
——. "The Jews of France and the Statutes on Jews, 1940–1941." *Yad Vashem Studies* 22 (1992): 115–146.
——. "La résistance juive en France." *Revue d'histoire de la Deuxième Guerre mondiale* 137 (1985): 3–32.
——. "Résistance juive, résistants juifs: Retour à l'Histoire." Preface to the acts of the colloquium "La Résistance et les Français," 241–264. University of Toulouse–Le Mirail, December 1993.
——. "Le sionisme en France pendant la Deuxième Guerre Mondiale: développements institutionnels et impact idéologique" in *Les Juifs de France, le sionisme et l'Etat d'Israël,* edited by Doris Bensimon and Benjamin Pincus, 193–226. Acts of the International Colloquium of 1987. Paris: Publications Langues Orientales, 1989.
"Présence du passé, lenteur de l'histoire. Vichy, l'Occupation, les Juifs." *Annales, ESC* 48-3 (1993).
"Problemes de méthode en histoire orale." *Cahiers de l'Institut d'histoire du temps présent* (June 1980).
"Que faire de Vichy?" *Esprit* (May 1992).
"Questions à l'histoire orale." *Cahiers de l'Institut d'histoire du temps présent* (June 1980).
Rayski, Adam. "L'UGIF et le CRIF: les choix de la communauté, 1940–1944." *Pardès* 6 (1987): 159–801.
"La résistance juive en France, où en est son histoire?" *Le Monde juif* 118 (April–June 1985).
Rutkowski, Adam. "Le camp d'internement et d'échange pour Juifs de Vittel." *Le Monde juif* 102 (1981): 35–70.
——. "Le camp de Royallieu à Compiègne, 1941–1944." *Le Monde juif* 104 (1981): 121–50, and 105: 12–30.
——. "Le camp d'internement de Beaune-la-Rolande." *Le Monde juif* 106 (1982): 39—74.
Schnapper, Dominique. "Une mémoire de l'enracinement: les Juifs français avant 1940." *Revue des Sciences Humaines* 62, no. 191 (July–September 1983).
Schnapper, Dominique, and Rémi Leveau. "Etre immigré en France." In *Histoire de la vie privée, de la Première Guerre mondiale à nos jours,* edited by Antoine Prost and Gérard Vincent, 491–525. Paris: Seuil, 1987.
Schwarzfuchs, Simon. "L'UGIF et l'histoire." *Les Nouveaux Cahiers* 83 (1985–86): 48–55.
Simon-Nahum, Perrine. "Etre juif en France." In *Histoire de la vie privée, de la Première Guerre mondiale à nos jours,* edited by Antoine Prost and Gérard Vincent, 459–489. Paris: Seuil, 1987.
Singer, Claude. "Adrien Benveniste. Itinéraire, d'Alexandrie à Paris, 1913–1944." *Les Nouveaux Cahiers* 108 (1992): 61–69.
——. "Servir la France. Le *Journal* de René Cassin à Londres." *Les Nouveaux Cahiers* 81 (1985): 56–64.
Steinberg, Lucien. "Austerlitz, Lévitan, Bassano; trois camps annexes de Drancy." *Le Monde juif* 146 (1993): 34–37.
Steinberg, Madeleine. "Les camps de Besançon et Vittel." *Le Monde juif* 137 (1990): 6–23.
Szajkowski, Zosa. "The French Central Consistory during the Second World War." *Yad Vashem Studies* 3 (1959): 187–202.
——. "Di yidishe presse in Frankreich, 1940–1946." (The Yiddish Press in France, 1940–1946). *Yivo Bleter* 28 (1946): 388–99.

Vidal-Naquet, Pierre. "Si Dieu le fit . . ." *Esprit* 134 (1988): 3–12.
Voldman, Danièle, ed. "La bouche de la vériteé? La recherche historique et les sources orales." *Cahiers de l'Institut d'historique du temps present* 21 (1992).
Weber, Eugen. "About Marc Bloch." *American Scholar* 51 (1981–82): 73–82.
Weinberg, David. "The French Jewish Community after World War II: the Struggle for Survival and Self-Definition." *Forum* 45 (1982): 45–54.
Wieviorka, Annette. "La construction de la mémoire du génocide en France." *Le Monde juif* 149 (1993): 23–37.
———. "Une lieu de Mémoire et d'histoire: Le Mémorial du Martyr juif inconnu." *Revue de l'université de Bruxelles* 1–2 (1987): 107–132.
Yahil, Leni. "The Jewish Leadership of France." In *Patterns of Jewish Leadership in Nazi Europe, 1933–1945*, 317–333. Jerusalem: Yad Vashem, 1979.

INTERVIEWS

Amit Dan, Beer Sheva, 1994.
Bulawko, Henri, Paris, 1988.
Cohen, Francis, Paris, 1993.
Cohen, Marie-Elisa, Paris, 1993.
Furth, Rodolphe, Jerusalem, 1987.
Gorzyczanski (Gorans), Yehuda Leib, Paris, 1988.
Grinberg, Avraham, Paris 1987.
Hamon, Léo, Paris, 1992.
Hamon, Lucienne, Paris, 1992.
Insel, Fella, Paris, 1987.
Jakubowicz, Emile, Paris, 1988.
Jarreau, Catherine, Paris, 1987.
Jarreau, Jacques, Paris, 1987.
Klein, Théo, Paris, December 1992, 1993.
Krisher, Henri, Paris, 1988.
Lazarus, Jacques, Paris 1987.
Lévy, Claude, Paris 1987.
Lublin, Lucien, Paris, 1987.
Mayer, Daniel, Paris, 1988.
Minczeles, Henri, Paris, 1993.
Minczeles, Léa, Paris, 1993.
Mossé, Claude, Paris, 1993.
Pohorylès, Henry, Paris, 1987.
Poliakov, Léon, Paris, 1988.
Polonski, Avraham, Paris, 1987.
Rayski, Adam, Paris, 1987.
Rodgold, Eta, Paris, 1993.
Schwarz, Sophie, Grasse, 1988.
Siekierski, Denise (Colibri), Jerusalem, 1990.
Sigman, Aharon, Beer Sheva, 1990.
Slovès, Henri, Paris, 1988.
Urman, Claude, Paris, 1988.
Weintrob, Lea, Tel Aviv, 1989.
Welt, Paula, Jerusalem, 1987.

Index